OS/2
PROGRAMMER'S GUIDE

Ed Iacobucci

Osborne **McGraw-Hill**
Berkeley, California

Osborne **McGraw-Hill**
2600 Tenth Street
Berkeley, California 94710
U.S.A.

For information on translations and book distributors outside of the
U.S.A., please write to Osborne **McGraw-Hill** at the above address.

A complete list of trademarks appears on page 1085.

OS/2 Programmer's Guide

 234567890 DODO 898

ISBN 0-07-881300-X

OS/2
PROGRAMMER'S
GUIDE

To a most talented design team, without whose dedication, creativity, and vision OS/2 would not be a reality: Gordon, Mike, Mark, Ross, Ray, Anthony, Jerry, and Ann; and to my dear wife Susan, whose constant support and understanding has made it all worthwhile.

CONTENTS

FOREWORD

I believe OS/2 is destined to be the most important operating system, and possibly program, of all time. As the successor to DOS, which has over 10,000,000 systems in use, it creates incredible opportunities for everyone involved with PCs.

The goals for OS/2 were extremely ambitious. We wanted to create a system that would set the standard for desktop use for the next decade. Of course there were some challenging constraints like compatibility and the 286 architecture. In addition, our DOS users had a very long list of things they wanted to see in their next generation operating system. Finally, it was vital to put together a system that would ship in early 1988.

The IBM and Microsoft teams, which jointly developed this product, worked very closely together. The number of plane trips, conference calls, and downloaded source codes was impressive. Despite the distance between the two development sites we managed to get the best work out of both.

Putting together a system of this nature involved adopting a philosophy about the relationship between the operating system and the application.

To really understand how OS/2 works and to see how it should be put to best use, it is invaluable to have the insights of the architects. Ed Iacobucci was a key architect during the entire project and made very important contributions. I remember being in many late night meetings with Ed when he came up with simple solutions to complex demands. The design document for this project grew to almost 1000 pages by the end of the project. We frequently went through a simplification process to cut out any features we felt were unnecessary. Ed is one of the few individuals who can explain the foundation that OS/2 will provide for the industry in the years to come. Since he wrote this book immediately after the completion of OS/2, what you will read here represents the real ideas behind the operating system and what can be done with it.

Bill Gates
November 1987

ACKNOWLEDGMENTS

The OS/2 project was a team effort. Unfortunately, it would be impossible to name all the people who contributed to its creation. But as with any project, there are always certain individuals who deserve special recognition for their tireless efforts in making the project a reality.

I would like to thank Jay Martinson and Steve Balmer for getting the ball rolling, Bill Gates for his support and vision, and Bob Spaulding for giving me the lattitude and support I needed to get my job done.

Special thanks to Mel Hallerman, Ross Cook, and Mike Kogan for the time and effort they spent reviewing this book. Their valuable comments have helped make it a better book.

PREFACE

In the fall of 1985, the IBM and Microsoft Corporations announced a joint software development agreement. With this agreement came the charter to develop a new generation of system software for the personal computer. Over the next several years, a team of designers and programmers from both companies worked together in pursuit of a common goal—to build the programming base for the PC applications of tomorrow.

There were many goals for the product, some conflicting, some not. But one overriding factor was clear— the new system had to start with the best features of today's system software and build on them to arrive at a solid platform for future growth.

In many ways, this was a challenge. At the start, we did not realize just how hard it would be to make the right tradeoffs among function, usability, and performance. Because of their profound ramifications, the decisions were not easy. There is seldom a choice that satisfies all user requirements.

During this time there was much speculation about the new system. The speculation escalated over time until eventually the system took on mythic proportions — becoming all things to all people. Industry rumors abounded, at different times referring to the system as NEWDOS, ADOS, DOS 5.0, DOS/286 or CP/DOS.

On April 2, 1987, at the Miami Beach convention center, the long wait ended. IBM (and later that day, Microsoft) announced a new operating system called Operating System/2. OS/2 is the culmination of the efforts of a talented group of programmers in development labs around the world including Boca Raton, Florida (IBM); Redmond, Washington (Microsoft); Austin, Texas (IBM); and Hursley, England (IBM).

OPERATING SYSTEM/2

Actually, OS/2 is more than one system. The April announcement described two different versions of OS/2; the OS/2 Standard Edition and the OS/2 Extended Edition. The OS/2 Standard Edition is the work of the IBM/Microsoft joint development effort. It comes in two releases. OS/2 Standard Edition release 1.0 is the core set of services and functions that are the foundation for all OS/2 releases. It contains the kernel services (such as memory, task, and interrupt management); I/O subsystems (video, keyboard, mouse); utilities; and a basic text user interface. OS/2 Standard Edition release 1.1 adds a full-function graphics, windowing end-user interface to the base.

The OS/2 Extended Edition is the OS/2 Standard Edition with extensions in the areas of communications management and database management. Most of the design and development work for Extended Edition is being done by IBM. It, too, comes in two releases, OS/2 Extended Edition release 1.0 (based on OS/2 Standard Edition 1.0) and OS/2 Extended Edition release 1.1 (based on OS/2

Standard Edition 1.1).

Microsoft Corporation also markets versions of OS/2 (called MS OS/2). Like their IBM counterparts, these systems are based on the jointly developed OS/2 Standard Edition system.

This book is devoted to OS/2 Standard Edition Release 1.0, which defines the architectural framework used by all the other OS/2 versions. The lessons you learn here are directly applicable to the other versions of OS/2 and MS OS/2.

SYSTEM ARCHITECTURE

OS/2 is a new operating system built expressly for Intel 80286/80386 protected mode operation. This fact makes many of the OS/2 advanced features a practical reality. OS/2 is a dramatic departure from the familiar PC DOS system. By exploiting the protected mode features of the hardware, OS/2 resolves the classic limitations of the PC DOS system. Most notably, it is not bound by a 640K address space, nor is it limited to running only one program at a time.

OS/2 requires a machine that is based on the Intel 80286 (or 80386) microprocessor. This includes many popular systems, including the PC/AT, the XT/286, and of course, the PS/2 models 50, 60, and 80. Because they are based on the 8088 (and 8086) microprocessor, the PC, PC/XT, Portable PC, PC Convertible, and PS/2 models 25 and 30 cannot run OS/2.

But OS/2 is much more than an improved version of PC DOS. The system has a fundamentally different architecture that is designed for growth. Many system functions are replaceable and extendable. The OS/2 programming interfaces are based on a model that is optimized for high level languages (C, Pascal, COBOL, FORTRAN, and so forth). The total package is a system that we believe will meet the needs of the industry for many years to come.

ABOUT THIS BOOK

This book is a true programmer's guide. It discusses the important issues you will face when you start to use this new environment. The book is written by a programmer for programmers who want to dive in and start using OS/2.

The book is divided into three major parts:

Part 1 gives you the background material that you will need to understand the evolution of the system. It is not very long, but it covers many of the factors that influenced the design of OS/2. This information should help you put the rest of the book in perspective.

Part 2 teaches you about the overall structure and function of OS/2. In particular, you will see how the individual components implement each part of the system and how they interact with one another.

The material in this part is heavily influenced by the type of information you will need to build OS/2 programs. There are not many (if any) esoteric discussions of obscure functions or facilities.

Part 3 applies the concepts learned in Part 2, using practical programming examples. In general, the examples are small stand-alone programs that demonstrate the programming interfaces and perform useful tasks.

The examples are written in assembler so that the interfaces can be demonstrated without getting too involved in language-specific constructs. However, since you can call the OS/2 interfaces directly from high-level languages, you will be able to transcribe all of the samples to your favorite language.

To help keep the examples simple I have dispensed with much of the normal error checking code. You can add this later if you use the code in your own programs. Also, the samples make liberal use of assembler macros, often making them look as if they were written in a high-level language. All the macros and the samples themselves are listed in Appendix E.

Finally, to leave room for program examples and discussions, the exact mechanics of assembling and linking the programs are not covered in this book. You should refer to the documentation that comes with your language(s), or simply use the BUILD command file, which is also included in Appendix E.

Naturally, OS/2 is a very sophisticated system. To do justice to all its functions and capabilities in a single book is impossible. To narrow the scope of the material the book gives you an overview of the entire system, but focuses on those functions necessary to write an application program. In general, the programming portions of the book concentrate on two things; the basic functions you will need to use in almost all OS/2 programs, and the functions that are significantly different or new in OS/2 (such as memory management and multitasking).

The program listings contained in this book (both the sample programs and macro library) are available in diskette form. To order, clip the coupon and send $24.95 to:

System Software Associates
Suite 285
7154 North University Drive
Tamarac, Florida 33321

Check or Money Order only. Please allow 4-6 weeks for delivery. The sample programs are provided in both assembler (MASM) and C.

SSA

OS/2 Programmer's Guide
Program Source Disk

Name: _____

Street: _____

City: _____ ZIP: _____

Format: 360K _____ 720K _____

Language: MASM _____ C _____ Both _____

PART

1

INTRODUCTION

CHAPTER 1
WHY A NEW SYSTEM?

Without much fanfare, one autumn day in 1981, IBM announced its newest in a long line of computers. But this one was different. It did not reside in a large "glass house" with dozens of operators. It was a computer for the people—the IBM PC.

What followed was the most explosive period of growth any industry has ever seen. Overnight, entire business segments were created. From this climate sprung Microsoft (system software), Lotus (business applications), Compaq (IBM PC clones), Borland (languages), Hayes (communications), and many others too numerous to count.

Not long after, this young industry standardized two things: the PC architecture and the PC DOS (MS DOS) operating system. PC DOS became the software platform on which a vast array of applications were based. It was the software common denominator.

PC DOS gave applications a simple, yet powerful, programming environment. The basics were covered: a file system to manage the data stored on diskettes, a command prompt, a command (batch) language, and a number of utilities. Soon, the basic environment was extended with a host of add-on features that made it easier to use: full-screen editors, terminal emulators, and a family of new business applications.

In 1981, a basic PC system came with a 4.77-MHz 8088 microprocessor, 16K of memory and a single 160K disk drive. But within a year the standard shifted to 256K of memory and two 360K disk drives. In 1983 the PC XT brought Winchester hard-disk technology to the PC, and in 1984 came the PC AT with its 80286 microprocessor. Also in 1984 the PC received its first local area network (LAN) support, connecting many PCs into a single system.

As the PC hardware evolved, so did PC DOS. The first release supported the simplest PC configurations. As new technology found its way into the PC, PC DOS was there with a new release to exploit it. Table 1-1 maps the evolution of PC DOS.

As the technology pressed forward, the PC DOS application base grew in complexity. *Integrated solutions* became the byword. Integrated solutions are application programs that give the PC user a complete solution — decision support (spreadsheet), word processing, data base, and communications. However, this type of application carries its price in memory and disk cost. The PC DOS system, which worked so well in the first PC configurations, started to run out of steam.

At the same time, the users of the PC were becoming more sophisticated. They started demanding more out of their expensive hardware investment. Graphic interfaces, windowing systems, and multitasking started to creep up the priority lists of the users. With its roots entrenched in the early PC configurations, PC DOS did not have the basic capabilities to support these types of applications. In fact, when the PC AT was announced in 1984, PC DOS could only run its advanced 80286 microprocessor in real mode, making the PC AT the equivalent of a fast PC.

Table 1-1. PC DOS Versions

Version	Year	Major Functions
1.0	1981	Initial operating system
1.1	1982	Double-sided (360K) disk support
2.0	1983	PC XT support • 10MB Winchester • Boot from hard disk • Subdirectories and I/O redirection
2.1	1984	PCjr support
3.0	1984	PC AT support • 20MB Winchester • New keyboard • 80286 (real mode)
3.1	1985	PC Network (1.0) support
3.2	1986	PC Convertible and PC Network (1.1) support • 720K diskettes (3.5-inch)
3.3	1987	Personal System/2 support • Micro Channel • 1.44M diskettes • 80386/80387 (real mode)

But the industry did not stop. The applications continued to grow in complexity. Since PC DOS did not support multitasking, application developers created the support themselves. The "popup" application soon appeared. These applications are loaded in memory and sit passively waiting for a particular key combination to bring them alive—"passive" multitasking.

But the one PC DOS shortcoming that cannot be easily corrected with software is the 640K memory limitation. As the integrated applications and popup applications grew, so did their appetite for memory. Real multitasking and memory are inexorably intertwined.

On April 2, 1987, IBM and Microsoft announced OS/2, a new-generation operating system that picks up where PC DOS leaves off. OS/2 is to the new generation of 80286/80386 machines what PC DOS was to the 16K 8088 PC of 1981. This chapter discusses how OS/2 overcomes the current limitations of PC DOS, and how it paves the way for the next generation of PC application programs.

PC DOS LIMITATIONS

PC DOS is a basic operating system for personal computers based on the Intel microprocessor. PC DOS was designed around the 8088 microprocessor. It provides rudimentary file (hard disk, diskette), device (printer, keyboard), and memory-management services. With tens of millions of users, PC DOS is the most popular general-purpose operating system in the world today, but it is not without its problems.

Most PC DOS limitations stem from the way in which it runs the computer's microprocessor (CPU). Even when it runs in a system equipped with the more powerful 80286 and 80386 microprocessors, PC DOS runs the system in 8088 mode. In this chapter, references to the 8088 mean the 8088 as well as the 80286 and 80386 CPUs in real mode. Chapter 2 discusses how the various modes of these microprocessors work. However, for the time being, consider the environment from the perspective of an application program.

Memory Addressability

The single biggest challenge facing PC applications today is the limited memory addressability of the PC DOS system. Theoretically you can install enough memory in a PC AT (up to 16MB) and you can use it with certain special programs, such as a Virtual Disk (VDISK). However, the extended memory cannot be used to run a PC DOS application. PC DOS runs the CPU in a mode that does not allow programs to access memory above 1MB. So the operating system and all its applications live in a 1MB universe.

This 1MB addressing limitation minus approximately 360K of address space reserved for the hardware I/O routines (BIOS) yields the infamous PC DOS 640K barrier. Out of this 640K comes the memory used by PC DOS and its extensions (50K for a stripped-down DOS 3.3), leaving the application about 590K for its code and data. At first this does not seem too restrictive, but consider that the data alone from a 700×200 spreadsheet could easily exceed 590K.

The situation is further compounded when you load multiple "DOS extensions," such as a print spooler and a popup application. Each consumes its share of memory and it must all fit in 590K. If you already use a multitasking DOS shell (such as TopView or MS Windows), you are familiar with the practical limitations of 590K. While these shells claim to enable you to run more than one application in your system, running more than one useful application at a time is often impossible because of the memory the applications (and the environment manager) consume.

Static Memory Manager

But why are these programs so big? The root cause of the problem is the PC DOS memory manager. The 8088 is a simple CPU that provides no significant memory-management help to an operating system. In fact, 8088 programs directly address the PC physical memory. Thus, PC DOS can never "move" the memory of an application. Once started, an application program owns the physical memory in which it runs. This also holds true for *terminate-and-stay-resident* (TSR) system extensions such as popup applications and print spoolers. These programs are started before the main application is started. The TSR programs carve out all the memory they will ever need in one big "chunk" since they can never count on getting additional memory once another application is running. This situation tends to make TSR routines much fatter than they really need to be.

In some cases, the more-sophisticated TSR programs ask you through installation options to define the memory resources the programs will later need. For example, the perplexing array of parameters used to install the PC Network program exist because the PC Network is not able to dynamically allocate memory after it has been started. So, unless you plan to run the minimum configuration, you must tell the program how many resources (sessions, names, buffers, and so forth) you will use.

Memory Integrity

Under the 8088, the entire 640K address space is presented as a single, contiguous memory block with no distinction between operating system code and application code. Any program can examine and modify any portion of memory.

With no separation between programs, a simple programming error in one application can bring down the entire system. How many times have you had to power off your PC to recover a "hung" application? As you increase the number of applications running concurrently, you increase the probability of that situation occurring.

Errors caused by program side effects in an unprotected memory system are virtually impossible to diagnose. By the time the system fails, it is too late. The only recovery option is rebooting the system. Of course, this eliminates the information that could have been used to fix the bug causing the hang-up. A reliable multitasking system requires a minimum level of separation between application and system memory.

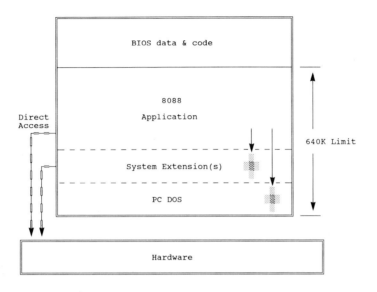

Figure 1-1. PC DOS system structure

Figure 1-1 illustrates the PC DOS structure. Notice how the 1MB address space is distributed among BIOS, PC DOS, the system extensions, and the application program. Note that the application program can accidentally modify PC DOS or its extensions.

I/O Control

When it comes to managing the system input/output (I/O), PC DOS is a "consultant" rather than a "controller." However, PC DOS is not entirely at fault. The 8088 mode in which it runs the system gives all programs full I/O privilege. This means that any application can directly modify the state of hardware devices without going through the system software.

Worse yet, in this CPU mode application programs can disable the system interrupts indefinitely. While interrupts are disabled, external events (such as the timer ticks or communications data) are lost. For example, the maximum speed of the communications ports is directly related to how often and how long interrupts are disabled. If you disable interrupts in a multitasking environment, you have effectively shut off the dispatcher, since it is tied to the clock interrupts. While interrupts are disabled, the system cannot run the other application programs.

The irony of this situation is that the lack of I/O control imposed by PC DOS is either a serious problem or an attractive feature, depending on your viewpoint. Many popular programs have been written for the PC because of its inherent openness and flexibility. In certain instances, a practical approach is to start I/O operations directly from your application. However, it is also true that most multitasking systems explicitly forbid applications from performing direct I/O. Instead, these systems impose more structure on their programs and isolate functions dealing with the hardware into special programs (such as device drivers). Such an authoritarian approach is not the obvious choice in this environment. After all, the PC is still a personal computer. If you wish to write a program that kills your machine, you should be allowed to do so.

As you may have noticed, Figure 1-1 also depicts how the PC DOS application and DOS extensions directly access the hardware, totally bypassing PC DOS.

Multitasking

PC DOS is a single-threaded operating system—as far as it is concerned, only one application is in the system. When it loads an application, PC DOS gives it free reign of the machine. In many cases, application programs have a legitimate need to multitask (such as the word processor that prints the document while you continue to edit it). Since PC DOS does not provide the required services, the application programs must assume the responsibility to multitask themselves.

On the surface, this is easy enough. The application can take over the hardware timer interrupts and "dispatch" its own pseudo-tasks. This built-in dispatcher can then distribute the CPU cycles to different program functions. This is precisely what the PC Network program does when it runs the server in the background while you run application programs in the foreground.

However, things become complicated if the pseudo-tasks use PC DOS services. PC DOS is not reentrant—it can only service one request at a time. If you try to request a PC DOS service (such as reading a file) while the system is processing a request from a different pseudo-task, it will get terribly confused and your system will likely hang. So, programs that implement their own multitasking functions usually concoct complex serialization mechanisms that guarantee PC DOS will only receive one service request at a time.

A "big plus" in a true multitasking system comes from *overlapped I/O*, where two or more I/O operations happen at the same time. For instance, the system might read data from the disk at the same time it writes other data to the disk. Because of the PC DOS reentrancy issues, even applications that perform their own multitasking cannot fully achieve overlapped I/O.

Consider one other point: Since many PC DOS applications have implemented a unique brand of multitasking, the probability is high that these applications will have serious conflicts if they are ever loaded in the same system. In fact, many such programs explicitly warn you that they cannot co-exist with other multitasking programs. For example, you cannot run the PC Network server program under TopView or MS Windows. You can find yourself in a situation where several of your favorite programs cannot co-exist.

Another obstacle to multitasking under PC DOS is the nature of the 8088 memory manager. In 8088 mode, the CPU does not virtualize memory (that is, the applications are actually manipulating physical memory pointers). Thus, PC DOS cannot move the memory without damaging the application program. Therefore, PC DOS cannot optimize (or "compact") memory, so holes develop over time as different-sized application segments are allocated and freed.

System Extendability

The PC DOS application programming interface (API) is based on *software interrupts*. A software interrupt is a CPU-assisted transfer of control between two programs.

Figure 1-2 illustrates how a software interrupt works, as follows:

1. The application issues an interrupt instruction directed to the PC DOS interrupt handler (INT21).

2. The CPU looks up in a memory-resident interrupt vector table the address of the routine that will handle INT21.

3. Using the resulting address, the CPU transfers control to the interrupt routine.

4. After PC DOS completes processing the application request, it issues an IRET (Interrupt RETurn) instruction to indicate that it has completed processing the software interrupt.

5. The CPU then returns control to the next instruction in the application program.

A software interrupt is a type of call/return interface between a program and some other arbitrary program in the system. However, the key is that the target program can be anything, since the CPU transfers control to whatever address is in the interrupt vector.

Since all PC DOS and BIOS interfaces are accessed with this mechanism, and since memory is unprotected, a

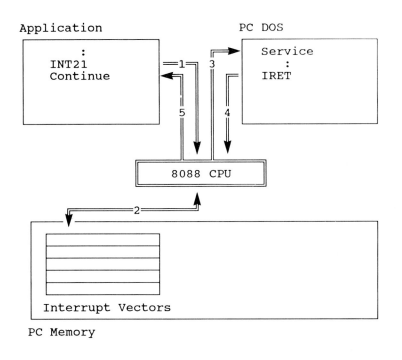

Figure 1-2. Software interrupt

program can change the contents of an interrupt vector to point to a routine within itself. This, in fact, is the basis for most existing PC DOS extensions. A program can replace PC DOS and BIOS interrupts to intercept, examine, or modify the system functions. Over the years, many useful PC DOS extensions have been built using this technique.

While flexible, this approach to extending the system has one major drawback. As you load more than one extension into your system, the interactions between the extensions are unpredictable. In fact, two or more programs can intercept the same interrupt vector. In cases where the extension modifies (or otherwise changes) the service request, "downstream" extensions are sure to fail.

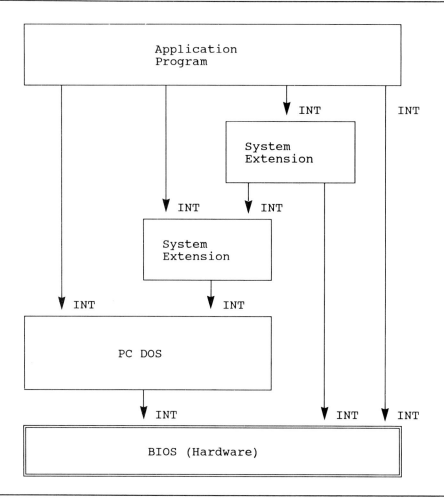

Figure 1-3.   Extending PC DOS

Figure 1-3 illustrates the myriad possible combinations. Notice that one of the system extensions has intercepted functions fed to a second extension.

This ad hoc, unstructured approach leads to unpredictable co-existence problems. The PC DOS user assumes the responsibility to sort out which extensions can be safely loaded together. Unfortunately, the user is often the least-qualified to do this job. Some programs include instructions to "load me last" or "load me first."

THE OS/2 ENVIRONMENT

PC DOS has been a major catalyst in the evolution of the PC industry. It provided the basic system services that were the foundation for an entire generation of new business application programs. PC DOS is a good programming environment that surpassed its predecessors in function and usability.

However, over the years the PC world has changed because the hardware technology has evolved, because the PC's role has changed from a stand-alone machine to an integrated office workstation, and because the user requirements are different. The demands of the application programs have stretched PC DOS beyond its capabilities. OS/2 was built to address the new requirements of a mature PC industry.

Architectural Relief

OS/2 runs the 80286 and 80386 CPUs in protected mode. In this mode, the processor helps the operating system run the hardware by giving it more control over what the application programs are allowed to do. Chapter 2 discusses how protected mode works.

Because of protected mode, OS/2 is able to give its application programs a significantly enhanced operating environment. Many of the PC DOS restrictions (such as the 640K memory limitation) are brought about because of how PC DOS runs the CPU. OS/2 exploits the capabilities of the CPU to eliminate these restrictions.

Large Real Memory

Perhaps the single greatest growth inhibitor for PC DOS applications is the system's limited memory support. Using the 80286/80386 capabilities, OS/2 enables you to use up to 16MB of real (physical) memory. Unlike their PC DOS counterparts, OS/2 application programs do not have to fit in 640K.

More significantly, this feature allows you to install more memory as your application requirements increase. This is especially relevant in a multitasking environment (such as OS/2) where you run multiple applications simultaneously.

Using the native processor support is a more natural way to break the 640K limit than bank-switching alternatives, since your programs do not have to be built using an "overlay" model. Any program routine can call any other routine in the application.

Virtual Memory

While 16MB is the limit on system physical memory, protected mode enables OS/2 to implement a larger *virtual address space*. Using the CPU facilities, OS/2 presents its application programs with individual virtual address spaces. This means that multiple programs can actually share the same physical memory. OS/2 takes on the responsibility of moving the application memory to and from secondary (disk) storage as necessary. Figure 1-4 demonstrates how the system maps multiple virtual address spaces into physical memory.

OS/2 application programs do not directly manipulate physical memory. Instead, these programs see virtual segments. OS/2 moves these segments in and out of memory when they are not being used by the application. This process, called *segment swapping*, enables you to run programs that consume more memory than is installed in your system. Chapter 4 discusses how this works.

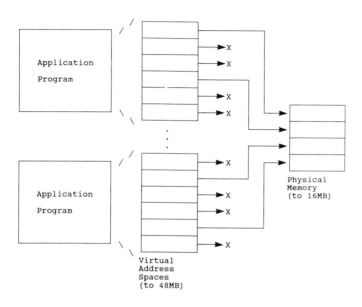

Figure 1-4. Virtual addressing

To the application programs, the OS/2 system has unlimited memory. The system hides how much physical memory is really installed by juggling programs between memory and disk. This entire process is transparent to the applications.

In effect, segment swapping accomplishes two goals. First, it gives applications a large "logical" address space. Applications actually use more memory than exists in the machine. Second, the virtual address spaces provide you with a more graceful end-of-memory condition. In PC DOS, a program dies when it exhausts memory. In OS/2, the program will continue to run, though more slowly. Thus, OS/2 raises the application memory barrier above 16MB and softens the impact of the out-of-memory case.

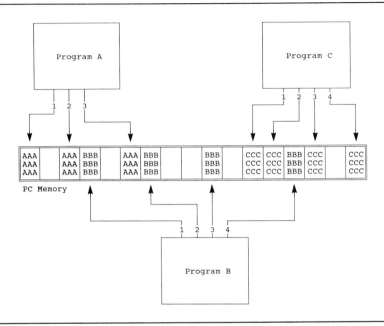

Figure 1-5. Memory isolation

Memory Isolation

The OS/2 memory model solves yet another PC DOS problem: the isolation of programs. All PC DOS programs run in a common memory "pool" with complete access to one another. This means that a programming error in one program may inadvertently modify another. Since OS/2 runs in 80286 protected mode, it isolates each application in its own address space.

The address spaces, then, are logical "subpools" of system memory. A program may only address that memory it has allocated. Thus, if you make an accidental (unauthorized) reference to memory outside your address space, OS/2 is able to detect the error and terminate the program.

Consider the following example. Figure 1-5 illustrates three programs (A, B, and C) that are coresident in memory. Each has direct access to one or more virtual segments. Although all three programs use the same memory, OS/2 prevents them from interfering with one another. For instance, suppose Program A is zeroing out its segment number 2, but it has miscalculated the length. When it attempts to modify the data one byte beyond its allocated segment, OS/2 detects the condition and terminates Program A. Contrast this to PC DOS, where the situation would go undetected until Program B failed some time later (depending on the severity of the damage inflicted by Program A).

Just as programs are separated from one another, so is the system isolated from the applications. If an application program attempts to modify the OS/2 code or data, the program is ended before it can damage the system. Thus, no OS/2 application program can inadvertently bring down the system.

In PC DOS, the typical error-recovery scenario is to reboot your machine, whereas in OS/2 the same error is recovered by restarting the application. Since the system does not end when an application fails, it can report failure information you can use to correct the problem in the application program. Figure 1-6 illustrates what you see when an application program fails.

Since you can determine what caused an application to end, the overall quality of OS/2 application programs will probably be higher. The application user can accurately describe the failure conditions to the application developers. Protected mode operation enhances the serviceability of the OS/2 system and its application programs.

```
Session Title: OS/2 Command Prompt

    SYS1943: A program caused a protection violation.

    TRAP 000D
    AX=0000 BX=00C8 CX=000A DX=0000 BP=0000 SI=0008
    DI=082A DS=002F ES=002F FLAGS=2246 MSW=FFFB
    CS:IP=003F:0076 SS:SP=001F:01F0 ERRCD=0000
    CSLIM=00DC SSLIM=01FF DSLIM=0009 ESLIM=0009
    CSACC=FB SSACC=F3 DSACC=F3 ESACC=F3


    > End the program
```

Figure 1-6. Abnormal program termination

I/O Protection

The OS/2 architecture enables you to control the way in which application programs interact with the hardware. In PC DOS, any program may perform direct I/O to hardware devices. This is not a problem in that environment because the system is normally running only one application at a time. In OS/2, you can run multiple applications concurrently, so the state of the hardware must be controlled more carefully.

The solution implemented by OS/2 is a compromise. You can still perform direct I/O from the application, but you must do it in a controlled environment. OS/2 uses features of protected mode to force applications to isolate direct I/O in special code segments. These segments must be properly identified or else the application will fail. In addition, you can tell OS/2 whether or not you wish to run "ill-behaved" programs by way of a configuration option. In this way, the level of I/O protection enforced by the system is determined by you.

Resource Management

Unlike PC DOS, OS/2 assumes a more active role in managing the machine's resources (disks, memory, peripheral devices, and so forth). To a large extent, this is out of necessity, since in a multitasking environment the resources must be shared between multiple programs. OS/2 is the traffic cop that determines when resources are available for use and when they are not.

Application programs that need to use resources do so through a set of OS/2 services. In all cases, OS/2 is aware of what program is using what resource. Most of the time, OS/2 manages the resource on behalf of the application. But even when a program directly manipulates the hardware, the program first requests permission from OS/2 through an I/O access request. Thus, OS/2 resolves all program conflicts.

The system provides applications with a wide variety of resource-access techniques, ranging from the tightly controlled (such as memory management) to the loosely controlled (such as direct I/O). Chapter 7 discusses resource management.

Multitasking Services

Since PC DOS does not have multitasking primitives, PC DOS application programs perform concurrent, multiple tasks on their own. OS/2 provides a well-defined set of multitasking primitives which you can use in your programs. These services essentially replace the dispatching functions that had heretofore been part of the PC DOS application programs.

These multitasking services allow you to build application programs with more than one task. For example, you can write a program that has a task devoted to reading data from a disk and a different task that writes the data to an output device (such as a printer). When you run this program, OS/2 runs the two tasks simultaneously. Note that with OS/2 you only write the tasks; OS/2 provides the dispatcher.

As a user, OS/2 also enables you to run more than one application (or more than one copy of the same application) at a time. Each application program runs in a virtual console, as if it had the machine to itself. You can switch between the active applications with a hot-key sequence.

Since all system tasks are run by the OS/2 dispatcher, the application programs can peacefully co-exist.

System Extendability

OS/2 greatly differs from PC DOS in structure. The system functions are organized in a well-architectured structure, as shown in Figure 1-7. The core system services needed by all programs are contained in the kernel;

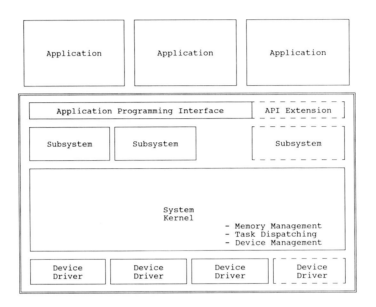

Figure 1-7. OS/2 system extendability

hardware-specific support is contained in device drivers; and high-level system services are contained in subsystems. All system functions are accessed through the API.

You may extend the system in the following ways:

- The API functions of the most critical subsystems (keyboard, video display, and mouse) may be replaced by your own subsystem functions. The replacement is done on an application-by-application basis. This is conceptually similar to taking over a PC DOS interrupt vector, except that OS/2 intervenes to ensure that only one extension at a time has control of the function.

- You may entirely replace a subsystem. This is a global replacement for all applications in the system.

- You may write your own device drivers to support new devices. As in PC DOS, device drivers are loaded at initialization through the system configuration file.

- You may create your own subsystem and add the function calls to the system API, thereby making your service calls a "logical" extension of the system.

OS/2 retains as much of the PC DOS flexibility as is practical in a multiprogramming environment.

SUMMARY

In many ways, PC DOS has played a critical role in the evolution of the PC industry. Its services have been used to create an entire generation of business application programs. As the industry has matured, the PC DOS functions have been stretched to their limits. Over the years, creative application developers have found ways to circumvent the PC DOS weaknesses, but in so doing have created myriad application incompatibilities.

OS/2 addresses this environment by starting where PC DOS left off and enhancing the system services to include large real-memory support, memory integrity, and multitasking—thus creating a platform for future PC development.

As you read through this book, you will be introduced to many of the capabilities of OS/2. When you finish, you may want to return to this chapter to relate what you learned back to the PC DOS environment.

Review the following topics before moving to the next chapter:

- Where PC DOS originated
- The source of the PC DOS 640K limitation
- Static versus dynamic memory management
- The significance of memory integrity
- How PC DOS programs perform multitasking
- Software interrupts
- Benefits of using 80286 protected mode
- Virtual memory through segment swapping
- Isolation of programs in memory
- Centralized resource management and I/O protection
- OS/2 multitasking services
- Extending OS/2

CHAPTER 2
THE INTEL ARCHITECTURE

OS/2 is a highly functional personal computer operating system designed to operate on the Intel 80286 microprocessor. This CPU is best known for its use in the IBM PC AT. The 80286 microprocessor is one of the important features that sets the IBM PC AT apart from its predecessor, the IBM PC (which uses the Intel 8088 microprocessor).

The 80286 is an advanced microprocessor upwardly compatible with the Intel 808X family. All machine instructions of the 808X processor family can also be executed on the 80286, thus ensuring that programs written for the IBM PC will also run on the IBM PC AT. Figure 2-1 illustrates the evolution of IBM personal computer systems and the Intel processors contained in each system.

The 80286 includes significant architectural extensions to the 808X in the areas of memory management, multitasking, and I/O protection. These extensions are specifically intended for advanced operating systems.

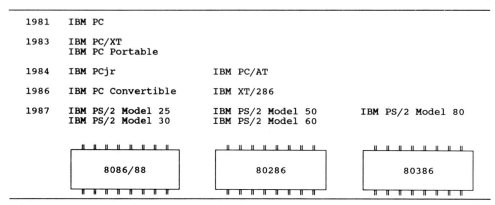

1981	IBM PC		
1983	IBM PC/XT IBM PC Portable		
1984	IBM PCjr	IBM PC/AT	
1986	IBM PC Convertible	IBM XT/286	
1987	IBM PS/2 Model 25 IBM PS/2 Model 30	IBM PS/2 Model 50 IBM PS/2 Model 60	IBM PS/2 Model 80
	8086/88	80286	80386

Figure 2-1. Intel microprocessors in IBM systems

To appreciate the functional capabilities of OS/2, you must understand the processor for which it was designed. This chapter contains a basic tutorial on the chip and sets the stage for the operating system discussions to follow. The emphasis is on the differences between the 80286 and its predecessors. If you need more information about the other aspects of the chip, read the *iAPX 80286 Programmer's Reference Manual*. (You can get this book directly from The Intel Corporation, Literature Department, 3065 Bowers Avenue, Santa Clara, CA 95051.)

Note: The 80386 microprocessor also incorporates the 80286 extensions. However, OS/2 runs the 80386 as an 80286, so the discussion of the Intel architecture is generally presented in the context of the 80286.

MODES OF OPERATION

The 80286 executes in one of two modes: real addressing mode (real mode) or virtual protected mode (protected mode). When in real mode, the 80286 operates similar to an 808X. On the other hand, protected mode is unique to the 80286 processor. The 80286 can be switched between the two modes by way of program control. By switching modes dynamically, an operating system can simultaneously run both real mode and protected mode programs.

Real Addressing Mode

Real mode makes the 80286 fully compatible with its 808X predecessors in terms of operating characteristics and functions. However, in this mode the 80286 does not assist operating systems in managing the machine resources. In fact, every program (including the operating system and the application) has equal access to all the system resources.

First consider the real mode memory model. The 80286 is a 16-bit processor, meaning that its internal registers are 16 bits long. In real mode the 80286 supports a physical memory size of up to 1MB. Each byte is identified by a physical address. However, 80286 programs only recognize 16-bit quantities (64K) so they cannot directly address the physical memory. Instead, a program identifies a physical memory location with two 16-bit values: a segment and an offset. The *segment* defines a starting location in memory. The *offset* is the number of bytes from the start of the segment. The processor then accesses memory in a relatively simple fashion by "adding" the segment and offset to arrive at a physical address.

Offsets may be contained in a register, a combination of registers, or they may be a constant. The segment value is loaded into a special register called a *segment register*. The actual memory address is computed by taking the contents of the segment register, shifting it by 4 bits, and adding it to the offset. The resulting physical address corresponds to a location in memory.

Figure 2-2 illustrates how the processor (CPU) computes physical addresses every time it accesses memory.

A common notation used for a segment and offset value is *seg:ofs*, where *seg* is the name of the segment register (or

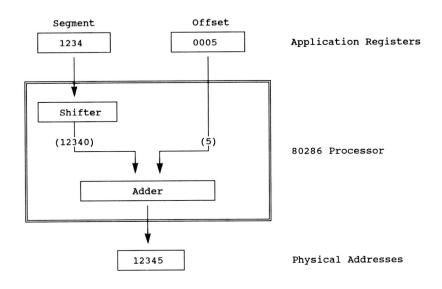

Figure 2-2.   Computing addresses in real mode

value) and *ofs* is the offset register (or value). The following are some common examples:

DS:BX   Segment in DS register; offset in BX register
ES:200   Segment in ES register; offset is 200 bytes
100:200   Segment is 100; offset is 200 bytes

Real mode physical addresses are 20 bits, so their largest possible value is 1MB. Thus, the real mode physical address space is 1MB. This architectural limitation is precisely the source of the infamous "PC DOS 640K barrier."

While in real mode, the processor computes memory addresses arithmetically. Hence, many different seg:ofs values point to the same physical memory location (see Figure 2-3). The value contained in the segment register

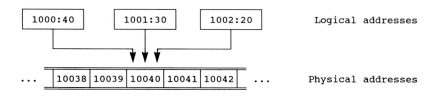

Figure 2-3.   Logical versus physical addressing

can also be arithmetically manipulated by an application program. For instance, you can skip through data areas 16 bytes at a time by simply incrementing the segment register. This technique is common in PC DOS programs that use large data structures.

The 80286 supports the following four types of segment registers:

CS   Code segment
DS   Data segment
SS   Stack segment
ES   Extra segment

Each segment register has a specific use. For example, the processor fetches the next instruction to be executed from the segment pointed to by the code segment register (CS) at the offset indicated by the instruction pointer register (CS:IP). The current top of the application stack is determined by the segment value contained in the stack segment register (SS) and the offset contained in the stack pointer (SS:SP). Data is accessed by using the data segment (DS) or the extra segment (ES). The DS and ES are used together in many string operations.

In real mode, the 80286 provides no hardware assists to

enable memory protection. Any program can destroy the data and code of other programs, or even the operating system itself.

Real mode operation does not provide the operating system with control over application I/O processing. Any program is free to issue instructions that interact with the hardware (such as IN, OUT) or disable interrupts (such as CLI, STI). Programs in PC DOS can (and often do) directly manipulate the computer hardware. This causes few problems in a single-user, single-tasking environment such as PC DOS. However, it becomes a real concern when multiple, uncooperative application programs run simultaneously, since each program thinks it "owns" all the machine resources.

The biggest challenge to writers of PC DOS environment managers such as TopView or Windows is to invent ways that allow multiple real mode applications to co-exist. Applications must be tricked into thinking that not all of the computer hardware is present. By tricking some applications and not others, the environment manager controls which application has access to the hardware. Unfortunately, this delicate balance is not always possible and results in application programs that cannot be loaded together.

Protected Mode

In protected mode, the 80286 provides hardware assists to help the operating system better manage the machine. The processor enables large real memory support, memory protection, I/O protection, multitasking, and hierarchical software privilege levels. These features significantly increase an operating system's functions and reliability. The remainder of this chapter provides an overview of the 80286 protected mode.

MEMORY MODEL

The memory model is expanded from real mode by "virtualizing" the contents of the segment registers. Rather than containing a physical segment value, protected mode segment registers contain a logical handle representing a location in memory. Figure 2-4 illustrates the level of indirection imposed by protected mode operation.

The memory handles are called *selectors*. The CPU associates a selector with a data structure, called a *segment*

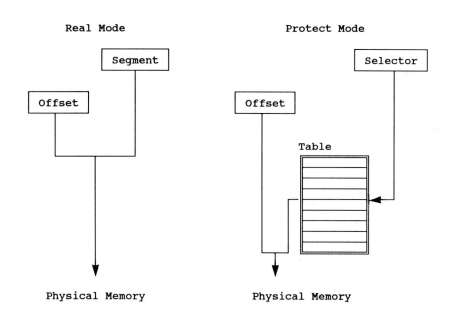

Figure 2-4. Memory indirection in protected mode

descriptor, that describes the characteristics of the memory segment. Descriptors are grouped together in a special table called a *descriptor table.* The selector is really an index to a descriptor table.

Selectors, segment descriptors, and descriptor tables are data structures that are allocated and maintained by the operating system. They are used by the processor to help manage the system memory.

Each segment descriptor defines the attributes of a part of physical memory. The operating system uses a set of access rules to tell the processor where the memory is, how big it is, what things can be done with it, and who can use it, all by updating the segment descriptors. If any program violates any of the segment access rules, the CPU generates a fault to notify the operating system. Thus, the operating system enlists the aid of the processor in its memory-management tasks.

Since the segment registers do not contain addresses, the system software has a greater degree of freedom to manage memory. A program has only a "handle" to its memory, so the operating system can move the segment in physical memory as required. Unlike real mode programs, protected mode applications do not really know the location of their memory.

While this freedom is absolutely necessary for the implementation of a robust memory-management system, it does create a significant compatibility problem. Most existing PC DOS applications were designed to run in real mode and, in many cases, actually manipulate the contents of their segment registers. This almost surely guarantees the application will fault in protected mode since the resulting (modified) selector is invalid. PC DOS application programs generally must be rewritten to operate in 80286 protected mode.

To provide the most compatibility for PC DOS applications, the CPU must run in real mode. In the 80286 environment, the mode of the processor can be changed by the operating system. The 80386 provides a more eloquent solution with a variation of protected mode that emulates the 808X environment. (OS/2 does not use this facility in its first release.) Later in this chapter you will see how OS/2 implements DOS compatibility support.

Segmentation

The entire Intel family of microprocessors is based on a segmented memory model. This model implies that memory is seen as a collection of segments, rather than as linear address space. Individual segments are identified by selectors that the application program is responsible for loading into the segment registers. The CPU always addresses segments through the segment registers.

The CPU requires that programs correctly load segment registers before referencing memory. For programs written in high-level languages, the segment registers are automatically maintained by the compiler. For assembly language programs, the programmer is responsible for maintaining the segment registers.

Protected mode memory segments are referenced using selectors. Similar to a segment value in real mode, a selector describes a memory location and is loaded in a segment register. However, selectors are an index into a segment descriptor table. Selectors tell the 80286 which segment descriptor is to be used to compute a memory location. Figure 2-5 illustrates how the processor uses these data structures to access memory. Note that if an invalid selector is loaded, the 80286 detects the condition and generates a protection fault for the operating system. Since selectors are indexes and not really pointers, they cannot be arithmetically manipulated by the application.

The Segment Descriptor

As defined previously, a segment is a portion of physical memory that is defined by a segment descriptor. A program

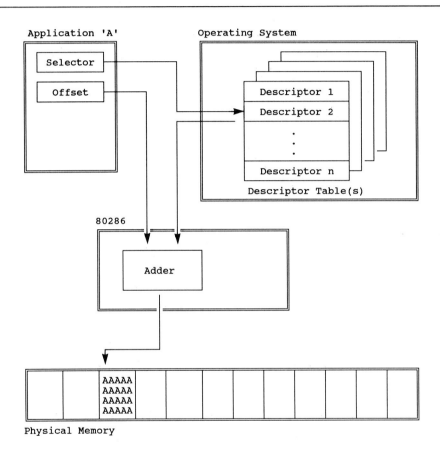

Figure 2-5.   80286 virtual memory addressing

references a segment by loading its selector into a segment register. Although the application can see the selectors, it is not aware of the segment descriptor. The operating system creates, modifies, and deletes segment descriptors on behalf of the application program. The CPU uses the selector to locate a segment descriptor in the descriptor

Table 2-1. 80286 Segment Descriptor Data

Segment Base Address	24 bits
Segment Size	16 bits
Access Rights	8 bits
Present	Present/not present indicator
DPL	Segment privilege level
Executable	Code/data indicator
Conform	Conformance/expand down indicator
Read/Write	Code readable or data writeable
Accessed	Segment descriptor accessed indicator

table. The segment descriptor contains all the information defining a memory segment. Table 2-1 lists the various attributes of 80286 memory segments.

The segment base address establishes the physical memory location where the segment begins. Note that this is a 24-bit value, allowing an operating system to directly support up to 16MB of real memory. The segment base address is equivalent to the segment value that is loaded into the segment register by real mode applications. Since the segment base address is contained in a data structure invisible to the application, it permits the operating system to slide segments around in physical memory.

As later chapters explain, the ability to load and execute multiple programs simultaneously requires the operating system to be able to juggle the contents of real memory to make room for new segments. Thus, the memory-management capabilities of the 80286 allow the operating system not only to protect the application memory segments from inadvertent modification, but also to easily arrange the contents of memory.

The *limit field* defines the size (END) of the segment.

If a program attempts to access data beyond the end of the segment, the CPU generates a general-protection fault. The 80286 is a 16-bit processor, hence the maximum segment size is 16 bits. This yields a maximum segment of 64K. While the 80286 can support up to 16MB of real memory, it must do so using multiple memory segments no larger than 64K each.

The segment access rights define how and by whom a segment may be used. The 80286 uses this data to enforce the access rules established by the operating system. By setting the access rules, an operating system can load a program and allow it to run. If the program attempts to use a segment that it is not authorized to use, or if the program attempts to use a segment in a manner incompatible with its access rights, the 80286 notifies the operating system with a general protection fault. The operating system can then terminate the program in a graceful fashion. The access-rights indicators have the following uses:

Present   Indicates whether or not a segment is physically present in memory. If a segment is marked as "not present" and a program attempts to use it, the CPU generates a segment-not-present fault. This indicator can be used to implement a storage overcommit function within an operating system and allow applications to allocate more virtual memory than the system has in physical storage

DPL   The 80286 supports multiple privilege levels. These levels are used by the operating system to define how "trusted" the programs are. The descriptor privilege level (DPL) is used in conjunction with the 80286 program authorization function to define which level of programs can access a segment. This can be used to protect the data and code in a trusted program (such as the kernel) from a less-trusted program (such as applications). If a program at a lower privilege level than the DPL attempts to access the segment, a general-protection fault is generated

Executable   This indicates whether the segment is code or data. If a program attempts to execute a data segment or modify a code segment, the CPU generates a general-protection fault

Conform   The 80286 introduces the notion of "conforming" code segments. A *conforming code segment* is one that can be called at the DPL or any higher privilege level. This indicator is used to mark a code segment as conforming

Read/Write   For executable code descriptors, this indicator is used to mark the segment as "execute only." This can be used to mark code so that it may not be examined. If the CPU reads this type of segment it generates a general-protection fault. For data descriptors, this indicator designates the segment as "read only." Writing a read-only data descriptor also causes a general-protection fault

Accessed   This bit is reset each time the selector is loaded. It can be used by an operating system to profile the use of selectors as input to a "least-recently used" (LRU) algorithm. Virtual memory systems such as OS/2 extensively use LRU algorithms. A later chapter shows how the OS/2 segment LRU algorithm is used to manage physical memory

As you have already seen, the segment descriptors can be used by the operating system to implement a memory-management model that overcommits physical memory.

Gates

In a segmented architecture, code is contained in different segments. To facilitate transfer of control between segments, the 80286 defines a special type of descriptor called a *gate*. All intersegment transfers (such as far calls) are done with gates. The 80286 defines the following four types of gates:

- Interrupt gates
- Trap gates
- Task gates
- Call gates

All gates are defined by a special data structure, as seen in Table 2-2. Although the gate descriptors are contained in descriptor tables, they differ from the other types of descriptors in that they represent an entry point rather than a memory location. In fact, if you load a gate

Table 2-2.   80286 Gate Descriptor Data

Validity Indicator	0 = Descriptor is valid
	1 = Descriptor is invalid
DPL	Descriptor privilege level
Gate Type	4 = Call gate
	5 = Task gate
	6 = Interrupt gate
	7 = Trap gate
Word Count	Number of words to copy from caller's stack
Destination Selector	Selector of the target code segment
Destination Offset	Entry point offset within target code segment

descriptor into any segment register other than CS, the 80286 generates a fault.

Interrupt gates and trap gates are used by the system to process system interrupts and exceptions. They may be included only in a special table called the interrupt descriptor table (IDT).

Task gates transfer control to a different code segment and also perform a hardware task switch. OS/2 performs software task switches and does not use the hardware task switching of the 80286. Task gates may be contained in any system descriptor table.

The most common type of gate is the call gate. All far calls require a call gate to transfer control between segments. As shown in Table 2-2, gates contain both the selector and the offset of the target routine. This means that although you provide both the selector and offset in a far call, only the call gate selector is needed to identify a routine. In effect, the selector defining a gate is a "callable handle" that defines an entry point outside your own segment. The operating system is responsible for creating call gates and placing them in a descriptor table when your program is loaded.

A gate is also used to change the privilege level of the code. A gate contains the privilege level of the target routine. Thus, call gates may be seen as restricted entry points into more trusted code. Programs normally pass data on the stack. The 80286 maintains a different stack for each privilege level; also the call gate identifies the number of words (parameters) to be copied between stacks.

An operating system can create a call gate for each of its service-routine entry points. The applications can, therefore, only get to the routines that the operating system exposes in the descriptor tables.

Figure 2-6 illustrates how a call gate is used to transfer control between segments. Notice that the offset value in the call instruction is ignored. Also, the call gate does

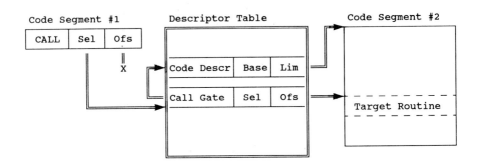

Figure 2-6.   Intersegment transfer of control

not contain the physical memory location of the code segment. Instead, the gate contains the selector corresponding to the descriptor of the target code segment.

Descriptor Tables

As mentioned, segment descriptors are grouped in descriptor tables. The 80286 processor has the following three types of descriptor tables:

- Global descriptor table (GDT)
- Local descriptor table (LDT)
- Interrupt descriptor table (IDT)

The global descriptor table (GDT) comprises all the segment descriptors available to all tasks in the system. It is the common portion in the address space of each task. Typically included in the GDT are the call gates to common system services and the kernel code and data

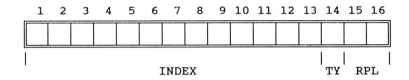

Where: INDEX   Offset into Descriptor Table
           TY   Table type (0=GDT, 1=LDT)
          RPL   Requested Privilege Level

Figure 2-7. Selector format

areas. A GDT selector is identified by a 0 in the fourteenth bit of the selector (see Figure 2-7). Since the GDT is always present, it also contains the Interrupt Service Routine (ISR) code and data descriptors.

A local descriptor table (LDT) contains all the segment descriptors common to a task. It is the private portion of the address space of each task. When the operating system selects a different task for execution (called a *task switch*), it saves the state of the task so that it may be restarted at a later time. This operation (called *context switching*) also switches the task's LDT. The LDT is considered to be part of the context maintained across task switches.

Selectors associated with the program executable (code, static, and dynamic data) and dynamically allocated memory segments are typically maintained in an LDT. Selectors in the LDT are identified by a 1 in the fourteenth bit of the selector. Since the LDT is part of a task's context, it is not used for interrupt routine code and data descriptors.

The interrupt descriptor table (IDT) contains the gates associated with each of the processor exceptions, as well as the hardware and software interrupts. When the 80286 services an interrupt, it uses the information in the appropriate gate in the IDT to locate the interrupt handler.

Processor Exceptions

The 80286 communicates with the operating system by way of reserved hardware interrupts (see Table 2-3). Most of the program errors described in this section (inappropriate privilege level, writing to a read-only segment, and so on) are reflected to the operating system as general-protection faults. Error information describing the specific failure mode (such as the cause of the general-protection fault) is passed on the stack. Other common faults include stack overruns and segment not present. Depending on the sophistication of the operating system, most processor exceptions are "restartable."

Table 2-3.   Processor Exceptions

IVECT	Cause
00	Divide error exception
01	Single step interrupt
02	NMI interrupt
03	Breakpoint interrupt
04	INTO detected overflow exception
05	BOUND range exceeded exception
06	Invalid opcode exception
07	Processor extension not available exception
08	Double exception detected
09	Processor extension segment overrun interrupt
0A	Invalid task state segment
0B	Segment not present
0C	Stack segment overrun or not present
0D	General protection

THE PROTECTION MODEL

An important feature of the 80286 protected mode is its ability to isolate programs and protect them from one another. The CPU also allows the operating system to manage access of the machine's resources by restricting the application code's use of I/O instructions. The protection provided by the 80286 can be summarized as follows:

- Execution privilege levels
- Address space protection
- Memory attributes
- I/O protection

Execution Privilege Levels

80286 protected mode provides a four-level privilege model. View the different privilege levels as a software hierarchy. Code can be defined to reside in any level, from most-trusted (Privilege 0) to least-trusted (Privilege 3). Data and code placed at Privilege 0 (PL0) can only be accessed by code executing at that level. Data and code residing in the other three levels can only be accessed by code executing at the same or a numerically lower level. For example,

- Code at PL0 can access data in rings 0, 1, 2, and 3
- Code at PL1 can access data in rings 1, 2, and 3
- Code at PL2 can access data in rings 2 and 3
- Code at PL3 can access data in ring 3

Any other combination generates a processor fault.

Figure 2-8 demonstrates a potential system implementation that utilizes the 80286 protection levels. The most-

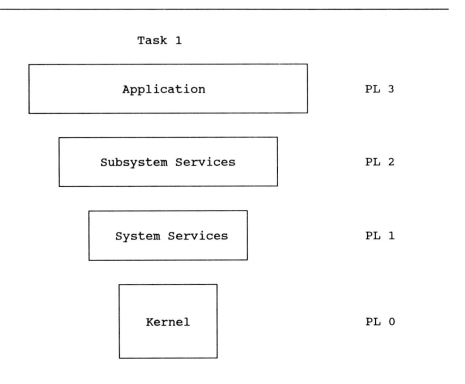

Figure 2-8.   80286 privilege levels

trusted code is the base kernel services (memory management, task scheduling, interrupt processing, and so forth). Since the kernel executes at PL0, it has access to all the data in the system. Ring 1 contains the system-services components (file system, interprocess communications, device drivers, and so forth). The base system services have access to all the client data areas, but not to the kernel. Ring 2 contains subsystems (video system, windowing/graphics, and so forth). Ring 3 contains the application code. Note that each successive level does not have access to the other, more primitive components on which it is built. This type of hierarchical system structure can be built using the 80286 segment privilege authorization functions.

Address Space Protection

Private-application memory can be isolated from other application programs by associating a different LDT with each task. In effect, each system task has its own private address space. Common system code (such as operating system service routines) can be addressed through the GDT, which is accessible to all tasks. Absolute separation of address spaces is the most effective way of isolating application programs.

Segment Descriptor Attributes

For descriptors contained in the LDT or in the GDT additional protection is available by way of the segment descriptor attributes. These attributes allow the operating system to control the conditions under which a program can access a segment.

The descriptor privilege level (DPL) defines at which privilege level a code must execute to access the memory defined by the descriptor. For example, if the operating system kernel executes at PL0 and applications at PL3, operating system data structures could be mapped in the GDT marked with DPL0. If an application (PL3) attempts to access the segment, the 80286 generates a fault. However, an operating system service routine (PL0) could access the segment.

Read/write access rights are also used to protect data. Segment descriptors marked as read-only data can be created in the LDT or GDT. If a program attempts to write into one of these segments, a processor fault is generated. Using this attribute, an operating system can map system data structures in such a way that an application can read but not write them.

Similarly, code descriptors can be marked as execute-only, resulting in code that can be executed but not examined. System routines can be protected using this type of descriptor.

I/O Protection

The 80286 architecture has instructions that allow programs to enable/disable interrupts (CLI, STI) and perform hardware I/O operations (IN, OUT). While very useful, these functions are dangerous in a multitasking environment. To help manage which programs are allowed to manipulate the hardware, the 80286 and 80386 processors implement the notion of I/O protection level (IOPL).

The IOPL defines the minimum protection ring at which a program must execute to perform I/O instructions (CLI, STI, IN, OUT). The operating system may set IOPL so that some or all of the least-trusted programs are not permitted to do I/O operations. For example, with IOPL set to ring 1, programs executing at PL2 and PL3 would generate a general-protection fault if they attempted to execute an I/O instruction. Programs executing at PL0 and PL1 would not be restricted. This feature allows an operating system to control the state of the hardware devices.

OS/2 IMPLEMENTATION

OS/2 exploits most features of the 80286 architecture. Programs that are written to the OS/2 application programming interfaces (API) are run in the 80286 protected mode. PC/DOS programs running in the compatibility environment are run with the processor in 80286 real mode.

The system switches between modes, as necessary, to run the different types of programs. All new functions relating to large real memory protection and multitasking require the use of 80286 protected mode. These are therefore available only to applications written to the OS/2 interfaces.

Large Real Memory

OS/2 exploits the memory-management assists provided by the 80286 processor to provide its application programs with a virtual memory environment. This means that OS/2 programs can dynamically allocate memory segments which (collectively) exceed the total system physical memory.

OS/2 uses an LRU algorithm to determine the least-used segments and swap them to disk when additional physical memory is used. Once swapped, the segment descriptors are marked "not present." When an application references a swapped segment, the CPU generates a segment-not-present fault, which causes OS/2 to read the segment back into memory. Thus, segments are demand-loaded.

Memory segments are periodically compacted to prevent memory fragmentation. Reducing memory fragmentation increases the largest available portion of physical memory, thus minimizing the need to swap segments in and out of memory. OS/2 is able to move the segments around in physical memory because, unlike PC DOS programs in real mode, applications in protected mode are not sensitive to the physical memory location of their segments.

Using segment attributes, OS/2 marks all application descriptors as either code or data segments. Code segment descriptors are created when program segments (marked CODE) are loaded from the executable disk program file. Although an application is not allowed to dynamically allocate a code segment, OS/2 does provide a system service to create an executable code alias for a data segment. OS/2 creates data segment descriptors when program segments (marked DATA) are loaded from the disk-executable file or when memory is dynamically allocated with the system memory allocation services.

OS/2 creates and maintains an LDT for each process in the machine. A program's segments are always addressed by way of the LDT. Services are provided for one program to make a segment addressable to another program by way of an alias entry in the second program's LDT.

Storage Protection

Since a different LDT is created for each system process, OS/2 programs are protected from inadvertent memory modification. If one program attempts to modify a segment not mapped to its own LDT, the CPU generates a general-protection fault, causing OS/2 to terminate the program.

The GDT contains all the segments that belong to the kernel and the device drivers. Application programs may not create or destroy GDT descriptors, nor are they permitted to modify the storage mapped by the descriptors.

I/O Protection

OS/2 sets IOPL to PL2 and runs application programs and system extensions at PL3. So, programs generally cannot interfere with the OS/2 resource-management functions. In certain cases where hardware access is mandatory (such as EGA high-resolution graphics), OS/2 lets programs define special I/O (PL2) code segments.

Multitasking

Two critical aspects of multitasking, memory protection and I/O protection, are supported by the 80286. OS/2 uses these features to create a multitasking model with fully isolated tasks. Each task has a set of resources, called its *context*, that is managed by OS/2. As the system switches from one task to another, it maintains the appropriate execution contexts. A context includes the address space (LDT), register values, CPU mode, and stack. OS/2 does not use the 80286 task-switching functions to maintain the task contexts. Instead it does software context switching.

DOS Compatibility Environment

The OS/2 compatibility environment allows you to run your PC DOS application programs. Since many existing PC DOS programs can only run in real mode, the OS/2 DOS compatibility environment runs with the CPU in real addressing mode.

The DOS environment includes mapping routines for PC DOS and BIOS functions (INT21, INT10, and so forth). These routines emulate the PC DOS services by intercepting the software interrupts and passing control to internal service routines. Since most of these routines reside in high memory (above 1M), OS/2 mode switches to service the DOS application program requests as necessary.

The memory required for the DOS environment is allocated as a contiguous area from the bottom of physical memory. OS/2 memory-management functions do not alter the contents of the DOS environment. Once allocated during system initialization, the DOS environment cannot be moved or deleted.

SUMMARY

You have now seen the most important features of the 80286 processor. As you progress through other parts of this book, you may wish to refer back to this chapter. The following are the most important concepts you should remember about the 80286:

- Compatibility with 808X processor family
- Differences between 80286 real and protected modes
- Segmented memory model
- Virtual memory capabilities
- Large real memory (16MB) support
- Memory isolation and protection
- Hierarchical privilege model
- I/O isolation and protection
- Processor exceptions

PART

2

HOW OS/2 WORKS

CHAPTER 3

THE OS/2 APPLICATION PROGRAMMING INTERFACE

Depending on how you look at OS/2, you may think that some of its features look "just like" this system or feel "just like" that system. If you have a heavy PC DOS background, the OS/2 command facilities will be quite familiar. If your background is UNIX, then certainly the OS/2 serial file I/O model needs no introduction. Those with large systems experience will find that the OS/2 virtual memory constructs and tasking model are familiar. Top-View or 3270PC programmers will recognize the system queuing services. The list of similarities goes on and on. OS/2 is many things to many people.

But the truth of the matter is that OS/2 is not *exactly* like any of those systems. It is a new operating system, built from the ground up to meet the requirements of a new generation of PC application programs. It is a blend of concepts, some old and some new, that together comprise a system. The chapters that follow discuss how the individual parts of OS/2 fit together to make this system.

The first stop is the OS/2 application programming interface (API). In OS/2, the API is more than a simple set of programming interfaces. It is the blueprint that defines the capabilities of the system, and an integral part of the overall OS/2 system structure.

API CHARACTERISTICS

The OS/2 API is quite different, yet quite familiar. As you read through this book and learn about the individual OS/2 functions, you may recognize some and not recognize others. However, in all cases you undoubtedly will notice that the style of the OS/2 API does not look like anything you are accustomed to using in PC DOS. The OS/2 interfaces differ in form as well as in content. This chapter discusses the mechanics of the interface, rather than the individual system calls.

Call Model

The OS/2 API is based on a different programming model than the one in PC DOS. OS/2 uses a *call model* (rather than the traditional software interrupt model) to invoke the system service routines. Each API is associated with a function name that, in turn, corresponds to a system entry point. You access the API much in the same way you might call a program subroutine—with a *far call instruction*.

Figure 3-1 illustrates the equivalent "system" calls that close an open file in OS/2 and PC DOS. The differences are immediately obvious. First, the parameters (in this

```
                    PC DOS

        mov     ax,1000h        ;function code
        mov     bx,fhand        ;file handle
        int     21h             ;call system
        or      ax,ax           ;error?
        jnz     error           ;yes


                    OS/2

        push    fhand           ;file handle
        call    DosClose        ;call system
        or      ax,ax           ;error?
        jnz     error           ;yes
```

Figure 3-1.   PC DOS versus OS/2 interface styles

case the file handle, FHAND) are passed by using different techniques. In PC DOS the parameters are passed in the CPU registers, while in OS/2, they are passed on the stack. Second, the transfer of control to the system routine is performed differently. In PC DOS, you load a register with a function number, and then jump to the function router (through interrupt vector 21H). In OS/2, you call the function directly. The only thing that the two have in common is that they both return the function error code in the AX register.

What does this mean? Is one model necessarily better than the other? A careful analysis of the benefits of each model would reveal that neither is clearly superior to the other. Except for one point: nearly all high-level languages (HLLs) use the call model for their native subprocedure linkage. When you "call" a subroutine, the HLL compiler generates code that is nearly identical to the OS/2 linkage. On the other hand, the PC DOS direct-vectoring approach is better suited for assembly language programs where the parameters can be loaded in registers as a "side effect" of other program functions.

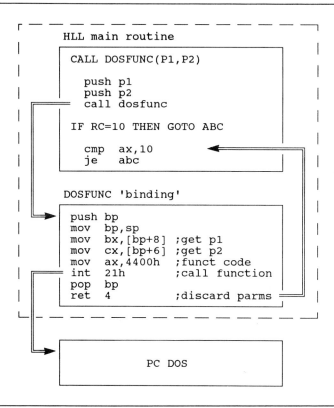

Figure 3-2.   Calling PC DOS from a high-level language

For example, consider what happens when an HLL program calls a "directly vectored" PC DOS service routine. Figure 3-2 illustrates a high-level language program that calls an arbitrary PC DOS function (DOSFUNC). The function expects two parameters (P1 and P2), so the program includes them in the function call. In response to this statement, the compiler generates logic (shown in lowercase letters) that pushes the parameters on the stack and calls DOSFUNC.

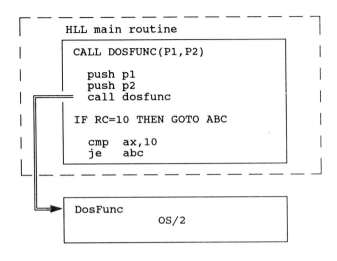

Figure 3-3.   Calling OS/2 from a high-level language

But this will not work well if DOS expects the parameters in registers (instead of in the stack). So, a special program called a *binding* removes the parameters from the stack, initializes the appropriate registers, and issues the software interrupt. This type of binding is needed to convert the compiler linkage to the DOS linkage.

Compare this to what the same program would do to call an OS/2 function (see Figure 3-3). Note that the program source code and the generated assembler are identical. But in this case, the code is already in the form expected by OS/2. Thus, the binding is not required.

This leads to the first observation about the OS/2 API. The API is optimized for direct HLL calls. If you program in a high-level language, you will find that you can call any OS/2 function directly, just as if you were calling an external subroutine. This chapter later discusses how to call an OS/2 API from C and Pascal programs.

Dynamic Linking and
the System API

The call interface is implemented by using an OS/2 feature called *dynamic linking*. (How dynamic linking works is discussed later in the book.) Consider how dynamic linking is used to implement the system interfaces.

The entire concept behind dynamic linking is that a program can call a subroutine not included in its executable file. The linkage between the calling program and the called routine is set up by OS/2 at the time it loads the program.

When applied to the OS/2 API, dynamic linking has the following significant advantages:

- An API can change between OS/2 releases, without affecting existing programs.

- Some operating system functions that are not "core" services can be implemented outside of the kernel in special dynamic-link libraries called *subsystems*.

- An application cannot distinguish between a call to "in-line" routine versus a dynamic-link library routine. Therefore, you can build programs that include an in-line version of the routine *and* a call to a dynamic-link version of the same routine. This is the basis for the DOS family API.

Now consider the consequences of these points. In PC DOS, every program (regardless of the PC DOS release for which it was written) calls the same operating system entry point. This is because the interrupt instruction resolves to the same address for every call. Figure 3-4 illustrates this point. Notice that all versions of the program ABC.EXE wind up calling the same entry point.

The implications of this scheme are subtle, but important. First, as the operating system changes from release to release (and most do), the software interrupt routines

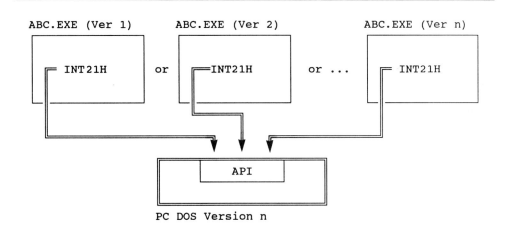

Figure 3-4. PC DOS interface migration

must be changed in an upwardly compatible fashion. The API that version 1.0 of ABC.EXE called must still be present in exactly the same form that ABC 1.0 expects it. The API must be extended by either adding new subfunction codes or by exploiting "side effects" (such as using previously undefined registers to pass "magic" values).

Over time, this leads to complex interfaces as one function is "pasted" on top of the other. To see a good example of this, look at the evolution of the BIOS INT15H function. From its humble beginnings as the interface for the (now defunct) cassette port, this API has grown and expanded in many different directions. The end result is an interface that is more difficult to understand with each release of the BIOS.

A dynamic-link interface, on the other hand, can evolve more cleanly. At the time it is loaded into memory, an application program is "linked" by OS/2 to the system service routine(s). OS/2 can therefore support different versions of the same interface in the same system. When it

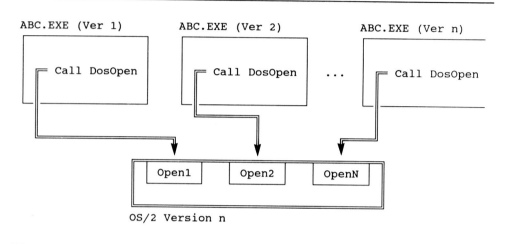

Figure 3-5.   OS/2 interface migration

performs the dynamic link, OS/2 can match the level of the program to the appropriate interface entry point. Figure 3-5 illustrates this concept.

Each version of ABC.EXE calls what it thinks is Dos-Open. In reality, they call different system APIs "under the covers." Functionally, this is similar to the interrupt case. However, one major difference is that the OS/2 API can evolve from release to release without (necessarily) dragging the constructs and syntax of the previous release. This degree of freedom is important in a dynamic environment such as the PC, where a change in hardware technology might necessitate corresponding changes to system programming interfaces.

Direct Function Access

Using direct calls in an API has another obvious benefit. The system software does not have to "route" application service requests to internal service routines. Instead, the applications call the routines directly. The "connection" between application and service routine is done once, at the time the application is started. From then on, when the application calls an API, the transfer of control is managed by the CPU without additional operating system intervention.

For example, consider the difference between the two approaches, as illustrated in Figure 3-6. In the PC DOS case, application ABC calls the service named "FOO" by loading AX with its function number and issuing an interrupt instruction. In response to the interrupt, the CPU transfers control to a PC DOS function router, which determines the destination of the request (by examining AX) and calls the FOO "worker" routine.

In the OS/2 case, the ABC application calls the system function FunFoo with a direct Call. Since the call contains the actual address of FunFoo, the CPU transfers control directly to the worker and eliminates the need for the routing layer.

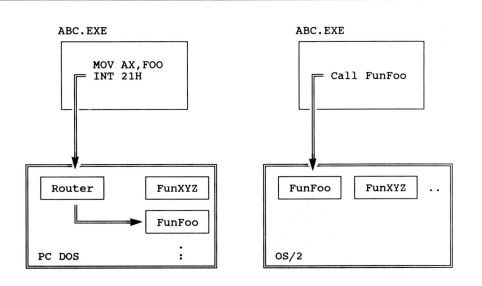

Figure 3-6. Direct function routing

80286 Synergy

To find the roots of the OS/2 API, you do not need to look any further than the Intel architecture for which OS/2 was designed. As discussed in Chapter 2, the 80286 gives to an operating system a number of building blocks. One of these building blocks is the 80286 *call gate*. A call gate enables one program to call another with a level of CPU-enforced "isolation." In this model, the calling program can be less trusted (or *privileged*) than the called program.

You can easily imagine how to adapt this structure to a client-server model, where the application program is the client and the operating system is the server. Since the entire OS/2 API is based on a call model, it fits nicely with the CPU-protection facilities.

Actually, not all OS/2 API calls are implemented with 80286 call gates. However, an application program cannot tell the difference. All interactions between program and system are performed through individual far calls. Some are real call gates (with a privilege-level transition) and others are not.

The most critical OS/2 functions (such as memory management and tasking) are implemented in the kernel. To maximally isolate this critical logic from application programs, the kernel runs at the highest 80286 privilege level (0). Yet, an application program can still call the kernel directly because the API goes through a call gate.

At the other end of the spectrum are OS/2 functions that are nothing more than common application subroutines. These services are also accessed through the API, but the code for these services runs at the same privilege level as the application program.

API Extendibility

Since the API is built by using a standard OS/2 programming technique (dynamic linking), nothing prevents you from extending the system with a new set of API functions. In fact, the OS/2 I/O subsystems are just this type of extension. From an application programmer's perspective, there is nothing different about a base kernel function, a base I/O subsystem, or an API extension (other than the function names). The mechanics of the API are identical in all cases.

If you plan to use this feature to create your own API extension(s), be sure to use a naming convention that is consistent with the one used in OS/2 (see Table 3-1). For instance, if you build a screen-management API, you might select the name prefix SCR. Thus, you could name the individual APIs as follows:

    ScrDefineInputField
    ScrGetUserInput
    ScrWritePanel
    ScrUpdateField

Do not use the API prefix values already used in OS/2 because you might discover a name conflict in a future OS/2 release.

Table 3-1. OS/2 API Naming Conventions

Prefix	API Class	Examples
DOS	Main System Services	DosOpen, DosFreeSeg
VIO	Video subsystem	VioWrtTTY, VioSetFont
KBD	Keyboard subsystem	KbdCharIn, KbdStringIn
MOU	Mouse subsystem	MouGetPtrPos, MouOpen

THE API IMPLEMENTATION

So far you have seen the justification and architecture of the system API. Now consider how the API functions are actually implemented.

Dynamic Linking

This chapter previously discussed how the OS/2 API is based on a call interface. But knowing that the services are accessed with a call instruction does not provide enough information about how the parameters are passed.

Many parameter-passing conventions are in use today. The one used in the OS/2 API is the PL/M convention (sometimes referred to as the Pascal convention). To be more precise, this convention has the following attributes:

- Parameter information is passed on the execution stack.

- The individual parameters are pushed in the order of occurrence.

- The called program is responsible for removing the parameter data from the stack before returning to the calling program.

- Variable-length parameter lists are not supported.

- Error codes are returned in the AX register.

These conventions work across a wide range of programming languages in all the memory-addressing models (huge, large, small, and so forth).

As you become familiar with the OS/2 API calls, you will see that each expects a unique set of parameters. These parameters comprise many different types of data objects, from a simple word value to a complex data structure. In OS/2, however, all the object types are passed on the stack in one of the following three ways:

WORD	A one-word value pushed directly on the stack
DWRD	A double-word value pushed directly on the stack (low word first, followed by the high word)
PTR	A far pointer to a memory area. Far pointers are passed as a double-word value, selector followed by offset

Single-word or double-word *input* parameters are always passed as WORD and DWRD, respectively. If the API returns information to the application in the parameter, then it is pushed as a PTR type—even if the object is a single-word or double-word value. Variable-length data objects (such as data structures or ASCIIZ strings) are always passed as PTR objects.

When the dynamic-link service routine gains control, the stack contains the application parameter data in a stack frame of the format shown in Figure 3-7. Note that the stack pointer points to the "bottom" of the stack frame. To extract the parameters, a dynamic-link routine must "skip" over the application return address and index into the individual entries.

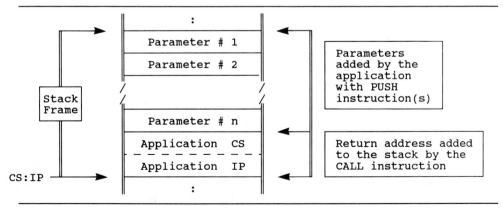

Figure 3-7. API stack frame format

```
                    extrn myapi:far

        Data Segment ...

        parm_data    dw        0                    ;parameter area

        Code Segment ...

                     push      10                   ;immediate value (parm1)
                     push      ds                   ;DATA_IN segment
                     mov       ax,offset data_in    ;get DATA_IN offset
                     push      ax                   ;push it on stack
                     call      myapi                ;call MYAPI
```

Figure 3-8.   Application program making API call

For example, if an application program makes the API
call shown in Figure 3-8, then the dynamic-link routine
(MYAPI) might work as shown in Figure 3-9. MYAPI
first saves the caller's BP register, then it copies the current SP to BP. At this point, the BP (and SP) registers
point to the first word below the stack frame, so MYAPI

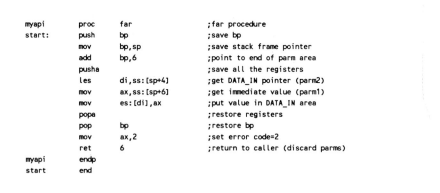

```
myapi       proc      far                ;far procedure
start:      push      bp                 ;save bp
            mov       bp,sp              ;save stack frame pointer
            add       bp,6               ;point to end of parm area
            pusha                        ;save all the registers
            les       di,ss:[sp+4]       ;get DATA_IN pointer (parm2)
            mov       ax,ss:[sp+6]       ;get immediate value (parm1)
            mov       es:[di],ax         ;put value in DATA_IN area
            popa                         ;restore registers
            pop       bp                 ;restore bp
            mov       ax,2               ;set error code=2
            ret       6                  ;return to caller (discard parms)
myapi       endp
start       end
```

Figure 3-9.   MYAPI routine

adds 6 (2 to get to the stack frame and 4 more to skip the caller's return address) to point to the bottom of the parameter list.

From here, the routine is simple. Since the second parameter is passed as a pointer (PTR), MYAPI loads ES:DI from the stack frame ([SP-4]) and addresses the DATA __ IN field in the caller's data segment. It then copies parameter #1 into the AX register. Since this parameter is passed as an immediate value, MYAPI extracts it directly from the stack ([SP-6]).

When it has both parameters, MYAPI copies the immediate value (AX) into DATA __ IN (ES:[DI]) and exits by restoring the registers, setting the error code to 2 (in AX), and executing a far return to the caller. Notice the far return also strips the six bytes of parameter data from the stack.

Therefore, when MYAPI returns to its caller, it has copied the data passed in the first parameter (10) into the data area pointed to by the second parameter (DATA __ IN), and the return code is set to "2." This function could be called by any program to perform the same operation.

High-Level Languages and the OS/2 API

Recall that the OS/2 API is especially well-suited to high-level language programs. From a high-level language, the OS/2 functions look like (far) subroutines. You call them as if you were calling your own code. For example, if you wanted to call the MYAPI routine from a C program, you could write the code shown in Figure 3-10.

Notice that the API is declared as a "Pascal" type entry point, so that the C compiler will generate the appropriate linkage. Other than that, the code looks exactly as you would expect. On return from MYAPI, the RETC variable will contain "2," corresponding to the return code set by MYAPI.

```
API Declaration ...

extern unsigned far pascal MYAPI (
        unsigned,                    /* input value      */
        unsigned far * );            /* destination  word */

Data Declaration ...

        unsigned data_in

C Code ...

        retc = MYAPI(10, &data_in)
```

Figure 3-10. Calling MYAPI from a C program

Similarly, to call MYAPI from a Pascal program, you would write the code shown in Figure 3-11.

The same holds true for any of the OS/2 languages. Naturally, the individual language constructs for the function calls will differ, but the concept is the same. Refer to your compiler documentation for specific details.

```
API Declaration ...

function  MYAPI (
                my_value :integer;    /* input value */
            vars data_in  :integer    /* destination  word */
            ): integer;

Data Declaration ...

        var  my_value,
             data_in  :integer;

Code ...

        retc := MYAPI(10, data_in);
```

Figure 3-11. Calling MYAPI from a Pascal program

Most of the examples in this book are in assembly language. However, an extensive use of API macros makes the examples look much like a high-level language. As an ongoing work exercise, try converting each program to your favorite high-level programming language. This will not be as difficult as you may think.

Before moving on to a different topic, you should be aware that some types of OS/2 programs require you to use reentrant run-time libraries. Run-time libraries are precompiled subroutine packages that are (typically) supplied with your language compiler (for example, the C language PRINTF routine). If these library routines do not take into account that there may be more than one concurrently executing instance of the application code (as in a multithreaded application), then it may fail unpredictably. Be sure to check the capabilities of your language run-time package before you intermix OS/2 function calls and run-time API calls in a single program.

The Family API

All OS/2 system functions are implemented as dynamic-link API calls. The total collection of system functions is called the *OS/2 system API*. An OS/2 protected mode program can use any of these system functions.

What if you want to write a program which will run under *both* OS/2 (protected) mode and PC DOS? The prospect of writing and maintaining two different versions of the program (one that makes OS/2-style calls and the other that makes PC DOS-style INT calls) is not appealing. Creating, maintaining, installing, and using two different sets of EXE files is also an unpleasant prospect — both for the application developer and the end user.

To address this area, OS/2 introduces a variation of the system API called the DOS *family API* (FAMAPI). The FAMAPI is a proper subset of the system API that roughly corresponds to the system functions provided by PC DOS and BIOS. These services are generally the basic,

High Level Functions

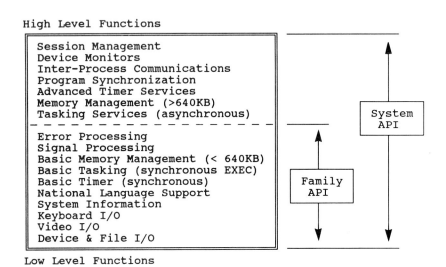

```
┌─────────────────────────────────────────┐
│ Session Management                       │
│ Device Monitors                          │
│ Inter-Process Communications             │
│ Program Synchronization                  │
│ Advanced Timer Services                  │
│ Memory Management (>640KB)               │
│ Tasking Services (asynchronous)          │
│ ─ ─ ─ ─ ─ ─ ─ ─ ─ ─ ─ ─ ─ ─ ─ ─ ─ ─ ─ ─ │
│ Error Processing                         │
│ Signal Processing                        │
│ Basic Memory Management (< 640KB)        │
│ Basic Tasking (synchronous EXEC)         │
│ Basic Timer (synchronous)                │
│ National Language Support                │
│ System Information                       │
│ Keyboard I/O                             │
│ Video I/O                                │
│ Device & File I/O                        │
└─────────────────────────────────────────┘
```

Low Level Functions

Figure 3-12.   The OS/2 system API

non-multitasking, system API functions. Consider the function list in Figure 3-12.

The system API includes OS/2 functions that range from the most basic video and file I/O services to the most sophisticated tasking functions. High-level functions such as interprocess communications, asynchronous tasking, event synchronization, and session-management services are the sole domain of OS/2.

On the other hand, low-level functions such as video I/O, keyboard I/O, file I/O, and device-management services are fully contained within FAMAPI. In fact, you can almost predict what OS/2 functions fall into this category by looking at the PC DOS INT21H, BIOS INT10H, and BIOS INT16H functions. If you take the sum total of these calls and compare it to the OS/2 system API, any functions on both lists will probably be part of the FAMAPI.

Some functions that you have traditionally implemented within application programs (such as a BEEP routine) are also part of FAMAPI.

In the "gray zone" you find system services that are part of FAMAPI, but carry functional restrictions. For instance, a FAMAPI program can issue the basic OS/2 memory-management calls, but it does not get the benefit of the OS/2 virtual-memory management facilities—it must live within 640K. Appendix B summarizes the FAMAPI functions and their associated restrictions.

Family API Operation

To understand exactly what the FAMAPI does, you must remember one of the points made previously in this chapter. The application program does not know (nor does it care) if an API call resolves to a "real" dynamic-link call or to a subroutine within the EXE file. Using this information, picture an executable file that contains both an in-line version of the FAMAPI routine and a dynamic-link call to the same API. Also imagine that the program includes a small OS/2 routine that is smart enough to detect the run-time environment (PC DOS or OS/2) and "adjust" the program API calls to go to the in-line subroutine or the native OS/2 dynamic-link entry point. This, in fact, is exactly how a FAMAPI program works.

Figure 3-13 shows a program named PROGF that has been converted to a FAMAPI executable file. The first thing you notice is that the OS/2 executable file header format is upwardly compatible with the PC DOS layout. Other than a single (previously reserved) bit that identifies the header as an OS/2 file, the first part of the OS/2 EXE header is identical to the PC DOS EXE header.

When you load an OS/2 EXE file under PC DOS, the loader recognizes it as a normal PC DOS program (PC DOS does not look at the reserved bit) and attempts to load the program. The PC DOS EXE header contains a field

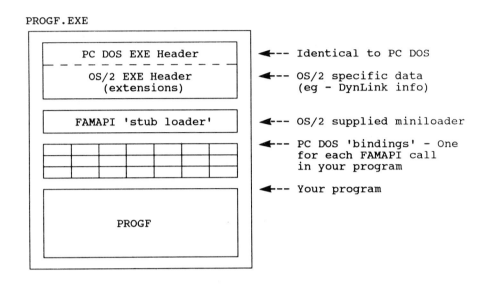

PROGF.EXE

Figure 3-13.   Family API EXE file structure

that identifies the starting point of the EXE program. In a FAMAPI program, this field points to a special routine called the *stub loader*.

The stub loader is an OS/2 routine that was added to the EXE file when PROGF was converted to FAMAPI format. When you start the program under PC DOS, the stub loader gets control. It "fixes up" the OS/2 API calls in the FAMAPI program so that they point to FAMAPI bindings, which were also added to the EXE file when you converted PROGF to FAMAPI format.

Remember, a binding is a program that converts a "CALL-style" function call to an "INT-style" function call. Each FAMAPI call in your program is tied to a binding that pops the parameters off the stack, loads the registers, and issues the appropriate PC DOS INTxxH (as in Figure 3-2). But what about the FAMAPI functions that have no PC DOS counterparts, such as DosBeep? In these cases, the binding includes the entire service routine. In effect, the FAMAPI binding is a PC DOS subroutine counterpart of the OS/2 dynamic-link service.

When you load PROGF under PC DOS, the individual FAMAPI calls are associated with bindings, the rest of the program is loaded, and it runs like any other PC DOS program. The stub loader also deletes itself right before it starts PROGF, so its memory is available to the application program.

On the other hand, when you load PROGF under OS/2, the system recognizes the EXE file as a "normal" executable file. The loader brings PROGF into memory, resolves the (FAMAPI) function calls to dynamic-link entry points, and starts the program. From the OS/2 perspective, PROGF is no different from any other protected mode OS/2 program. The stub loader and FAMAPI bindings are not even brought into memory.

Figure 3-14 demonstrates the differences between the two environments. Under PC DOS, the FAMAPI bindings actually become part of PROGF. Note that not all the bindings resolve to PC DOS INT functions. In this example, the DosBeep function is wholly contained within the binding. In the OS/2 environment, the picture is quite different. The bindings are not needed since the dynamic-link calls are resolved to OS/2 entry points.

Building a Family API Program

You should realize that a FAMAPI program *is* an OS/2 program. You write FAMAPI programs by using exactly the same tools, languages, and system facilities that you use to build OS/2 protected mode programs. In fact, you will probably want to develop and test the FAMAPI program in protected mode, then convert it to a family program. Generally, there is nothing special about FAMAPI programs, other than that they use a subset of the complete OS/2 API.

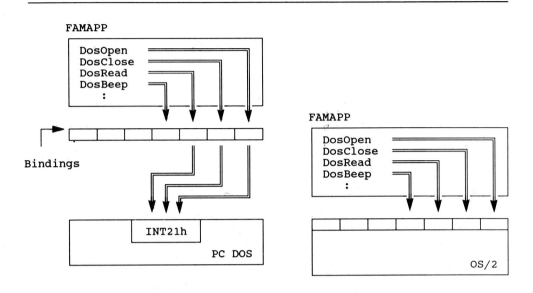

Figure 3-14.   Running a family API program

Consider how you build a FAMAPI program. In the example shown in Figure 3-15, you start the process with a C program named MYPROG. The compile step (1) converts MYPROG.C to an object file named MYPROG.OBJ.

Next, you use the LINK program (2) to link the object file with the compiler run-time routines (LLIBC.LIB) and the system API definitions library (DOSCALLS.LIB). Actually, the API definitions file is a special kind of library that is used by the LINK program to create dynamic-link records in the resulting EXE file. This library does not actually contain object code (subroutines) like the more traditional LIB files you may be accustomed to using.

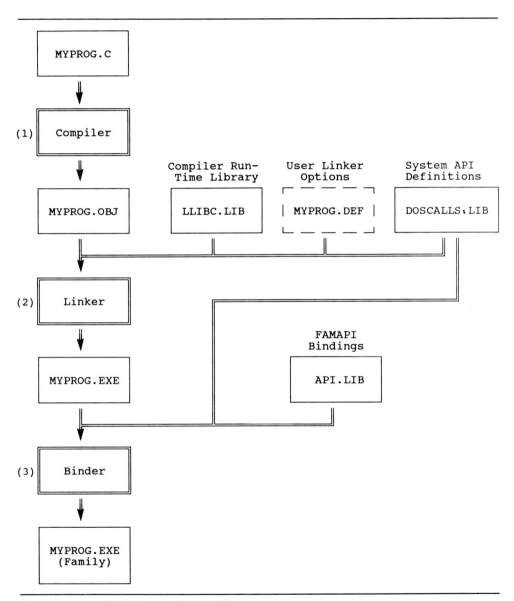

Figure 3-15. Building a FAMAPI program

The OS/2 LINK program also accepts an (optional) ASCII file, called a *link-definitions file,* that provides more detailed information about the program. Because OS/2 runs programs in 80286 protected mode, the LINK program supports a number of features with which you specify the exact characteristics of each program segment (read-only, code, and so forth). The link-definition file contains this type of information (see Appendix D). In most cases, you will not use this file and accept the default values assigned by the compiler.

You have now created an EXE file that will run in a protected mode OS/2 session. It has all the functional capabilities that the family version of MYPROG.EXE will ultimately have. Once MYPROG has been debugged, you can move to the final step (3) to build the FAMAPI version. In this step you use a new OS/2 tool, called BIND, that converts protected mode EXE files to FAMAPI format. Figure 3-16 illustrates how BIND works.

Note that every OS/2 executable file (even non-FAMAPI programs) contains the PC DOS EXE header. Furthermore, the PC DOS EXE header points to a small PC DOS routine that issues the "This program cannot run under DOS" message. Thus, if you try to run an OS/2 EXE file under PC DOS, you will see the error message. When you convert the EXE file to FAMAPI format, the BIND utility replaces the error routine with a stub loader (contained within BIND).

The BIND utility also scans the EXE file and determines which FAMAPI bindings need to be extracted from API.LIB for inclusion in the family executable file. The bindings are brought in in "groups" that correspond to the API functional categories. For instance, if the program uses a VIO (Video I/O) call, then the entire set of VIO bindings is added to the file.

The BIND output is an EXE file that can run on either PC DOS or OS/2. Depending on which FAMAPI functions you use (or how you use them) the FAMAPI program could

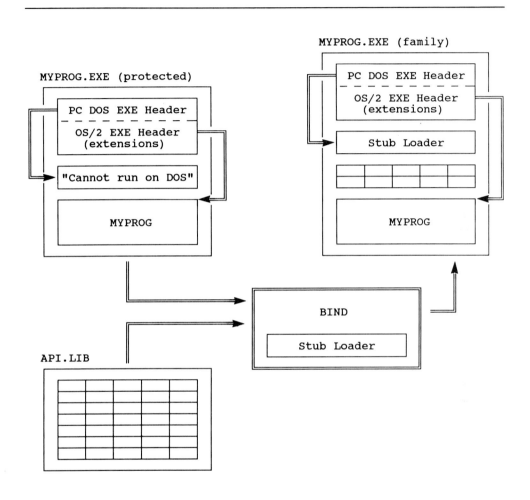

Figure 3-16.   The OS/2 BIND utility

be run on any version of PC DOS ranging from 2.1 to 3.3. Refer to Appendix B for a list of the FAMAPI PC DOS version prerequisites.

Special Considerations

The family API is a useful OS/2 concept. With it you can build programs that run in the OS/2 protected mode environment without forsaking PC DOS. But like anything else, you should know when to use this facility and when not to.

A good rule of thumb is to design programs so they only use the OS/2 services they really need. In other words, if your application does not need full OS/2 API, then by all means do not use it. A simple application (such as a file BROWSE program) may not need the power of the OS/2 multi-tasking facilities. You could build this program as a FAMAPI program and run it on PC DOS and OS/2. Never use an API "because it is there."

On the other hand, if you need an API function, then use it. Even if the particular API forces you to a protected mode environment, you should never try to "circumvent" the system by implementing the function yourself. In the long run, this will cause more trouble than you could ever possibly avoid. For example, if your application is fundamentally multithreaded, you should use OS/2 threads rather than building your own dispatcher. For the effort that you will expend building this "system-like" code, you could have used the OS/2 API and improved the overall function of the application.

SUMMARY

The API is one of the simplest, yet most powerful, architectural concepts in OS/2. It provides a standard, consistent, extendable mechanism that all programs use to request system services. Because it is based on the subroutine CALL model, the OS/2 API is especially well-suited to high-level languages. In fact, you can directly call all the system functions from any OS/2 language, just as if you were calling a program subroutine.

The DOS family API provides an added degree of flexibility. With it, you build OS/2 programs that run in either OS/2 or PC DOS. The family API turns many OS/2 functions into useful programming subroutines that you can call from PC DOS programs.

You are now ready for the remainder of this book. In the chapters that follow, you will explore the OS/2 functions in detail. You will first see how the API functions work, and then learn how to use them. As you read about the functions, remember the basic architectural concepts behind the API itself. The API is a part of every OS/2 function.

Before moving to the next chapter, you should review the following points:

- The differences between CALL-style and INT-style interfaces

- A binding

- How high-level languages pass parameters to subroutines

- The advantages of using dynamic-linking mechanisms in an API

- The OS/2 system API

- The DOS family API

- The FAMAPI file structure

- How the BIND utility works

CHAPTER 4
MEMORY MANAGEMENT

Perhaps the single greatest difference between OS/2 and its predecessors is its extensive set of memory-management capabilities. To a large extent, these capabilities result from the exploitation of the 80286 processor memory-management facilities.

As discussed previously, the OS/2 Kernel allocates and maintains descriptor tables that map the use of physical memory. From an application standpoint, OS/2 provides services to allocate multiple "chunks" of memory, with no regard to their real locations. An application may request (and get) more memory than what is installed in the system.

By using the 80286 memory-management unit, OS/2 can move the least-frequently used code and data segments to disk and make room for additional programs. Then segments are brought back into physical memory as they are needed. This process, called *segment swapping*, is transparent to application programs and is achieved through close interactions between OS/2 and the 80286 processor.

In the DOS compatibility environment, OS/2 emulates PC DOS memory-management services. In other words, an application running in this environment has the identical linear, contiguous address space it has in PC DOS. Since compatibility mode applications are run in 80286 real mode, the maximum application addressability is 1MB. The DOS environment occupies low system memory up to 640K. As in PC DOS, BIOS and adaptor storage occupy the memory between 640K and 1MB.

Look at Figure 4-1 and note the placement of the DOS environment and reserved BIOS areas in low memory. Also note that a portion of the system actually is contained within the DOS environment. In fact, the low kernel, device drivers, and some system data areas are allocated out of the DOS environment. The total memory available to your PC DOS application programs is the total DOS environment minus approximately 100K.

You can configure the system with a smaller DOS environment (or none at all) and free the lower 640K for 80286 protected mode application programs. OS/2 uses all the memory not allocated to the DOS environment (up to 16MB) to run the OS/2 applications. In effect you define how much of the memory is to run PC DOS application programs and how much of the memory is left for OS/2 applications. If you do not anticipate running PC DOS programs, you can use all the system memory for protected mode programs.

For instance, consider Figure 4-2. In the first case (RMSIZE = 640), the system is configured so that all available memory below 1MB (640K) is allocated to the DOS environment. The PC DOS applications have access to the entire real mode address space.

The second example (RMSIZE = 320) illustrates a configuration that splits low memory between protected mode

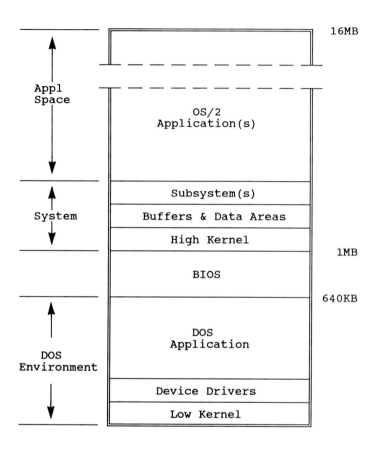

Figure 4-1.   OS/2 memory map

and real mode application programs. Note, however, that
in this configuration OS/2 application (protected mode)
segments reside in the lower 1MB of system memory. Such
segments are addressable by PC DOS applications running in the DOS environment and could be inadvertently
modified.

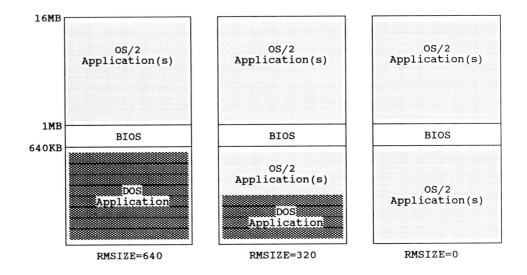

Figure 4-2. Memory configuration options

The final case (RMSIZE = 0) illustrates a system with no DOS compatibility environment. OS/2 uses all the system memory to run protected mode programs. This is the most secure configuration since all programs are protected from one another by the 80286 memory-protection facilities.

Memory that is allocated by (or on behalf of) OS/2 applications is always movable and capable of being swapped. This means that application code, data, and stack segments are subject to being swapped out to disk or moved around in memory, depending on their frequencies of use and the demands being imposed on real memory by other programs in the system.

One exception to this rule is that OS/2 device drivers are allowed to "lock" application segments in storage for short periods of time (typically only for the duration of an I/O operation). The application buffers must be locked, since the device driver may need to access the data when OS/2 is not able to swap the buffer back into memory (such as during device-interrupt processing).

To minimize long-term storage fragmentation, the memory manager migrates fixed segments to the bottom of memory. Figure 4-3 illustrates fixed segments with

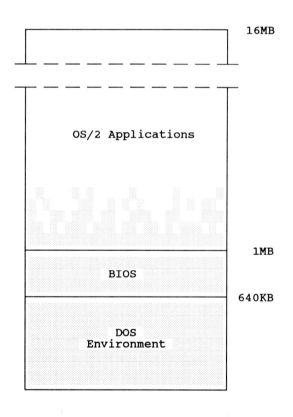

Figure 4-3. Fixed memory segments

darker shading. This fragmentation is caused by "holes" in memory, which come about when different sized program segments do not fit neatly into physical memory. Since the 80286 treats each segment as a separate entity, your programs may reside in separate, disjoint locations in memory. (See Figure 4-4.)

The DOS environment, the system device drivers, and critical portions of the kernel (such as the memory manager or dispatcher) are permanently fixed in memory and are not subject to being moved or swapped.

SYSTEM ADDRESS SPACE

OS/2 maintains a common address space for all of its programs. Mapped through the *global descriptor table* (GDT), this address space contains segments that must be accessible at all times, from all system processes (including the kernel code and data segments, the API entry points, and the device driver code and data segments).

Each program in the system has the same logical view of the memory segments mapped by the GDT (see Figure 4-5). The total number of GDT entries is fixed at system start-up. All applications have equal access to the memory mapped by this descriptor table.

Global Descriptor Table (GDT)

The GDT is a fixed region of memory containing the descriptors that define the system address space.

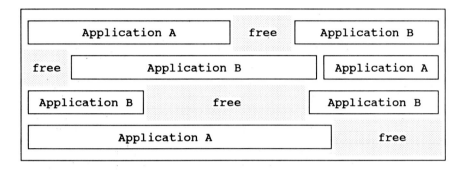

Figure 4-4. Program segments in physical memory

APPLICATION ADDRESS SPACES

OS/2 allots to each application program its own "local" address space. Each program's address space is mapped by its own Local Descriptor Table (LDT). The segments associated with a program's executable module are addressed by way of its LDT. In addition, segments brought into memory on behalf of the loaded program (such as dynamic-link service routines) are also mapped in its LDT. As the program dynamically allocates segments, OS/2 makes additional entries in its LDT. OS/2 shrinks or enlarges the size of the LDT as required. Figure 4-5 illustrates how each program in the system has its unique set of segments.

A natural side effect of this system structure is the absolute isolation of memory segments between application programs. For example, the memory and code seg-

Local Descriptor Table (LDT)

The LDT is a region of memory containing the descriptors that define the application's address space.

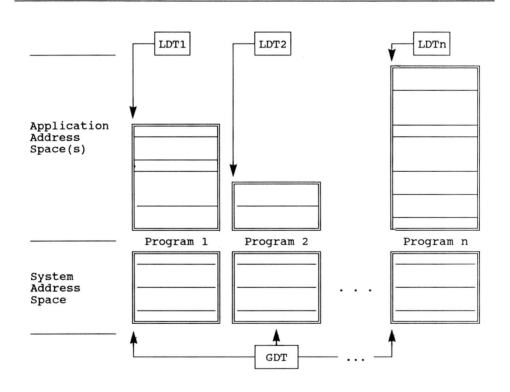

Figure 4-5.   System address spaces

ments belonging to Program 1 cannot be viewed, modified, or in any way affected by other programs in the system.

The concurrent execution of several programs requires increased operating system integrity. If one application program can accidentally access another program's memory, it could change the second program's memory and possibly cause erroneous results. OS/2 guards against this situation by using the 80286 memory-protection facilities to create a unique address space for each application. A special exception to this isolation is shared memory segments (discussed later in this chapter).

LOADING APPLICATIONS

OS/2 is responsible for managing memory for each application. Before starting a new application program, OS/2 allocates and initializes an LDT. As it loads the program, OS/2 makes LDT entries that correspond to each segment defined in the program. If the program contains references to dynamic-link libraries (DLL), the OS/2 loader reads the library into memory and creates LDT entries for each of its segments. If either the program or the DLL is already present in memory, the loader creates an LDT entry that points to the preexisting segment in physical memory. So, if you start a program more than one time (or if two different programs use the same dynamic-link routine) only one copy of the code is loaded into memory.

By the time the program is given control, all the segments needed to execute the program have been added to the LDT. Note that although an entry is made in the LDT, the actual memory segment need not be physically loaded. This concept, called *demand loading*, is discussed later in this chapter.

MEMORY ALLOCATION AND DEALLOCATION

OS/2 programs may allocate, deallocate, shrink, and enlarge data segments using OS/2 API calls. Table 4-1 lists these calls.

When a program uses the DosAllocSeg API call to allocate a segment, the OS/2 memory manager searches physical memory for a free area large enough to satisfy the request. If the memory manager finds one, it marks the area in use, adds the descriptor to the LDT, and passes the associated selector back to the program. The system may expand the LDT and make room for additional descriptors as necessary.

Table 4-1. Memory-Management API Calls

API Call	Description
DosAllocSeg	Allocate a memory segment
DosReallocSeg	Shrink or enlarge a memory segment
DosFreeSeg	Deallocate a memory segment
DosAllocShrSeg	Allocate a named shared-memory segment
DosGetShrSeg	Gain access to a named shared segment
DosGiveSeg	Give another process a shared segment
DosAllocHuge	Allocate multiple memory segments
DosGetHugeShift	Get selector increment (for huge segments)
DosReallocHuge	Shrink or enlarge huge memory segment(s)
DosCreateCSAlias	Create executable alias for data segment
DosMemAvail	Return size of largest block of free memory

You can use the DosFreeSeg API to deallocate a memory segment. When an application makes this call, OS/2 marks the LDT descriptor free and releases the physical memory. This function allows you to free any segment contained in your LDT. You may not use it to free GDT segments, since these segments do not belong to your application.

The initial size of a memory segment is defined by a parameter of the DosAllocSeg call. If an application program finds that it must change the size of an allocated segment, it may do so by using the DosReallocSeg function. You may shrink or enlarge a segment up to the maximum 64K segment size.

Since memory is allocated by using system services, OS/2 can clean up memory when a program terminates. OS/2 releases physical memory during program termination, decrements shared-memory use counts, and frees the LDT. Although the system performs these functions when a program is terminated, it is a good practice for application programs to free their own to segments during normal termination.

SHARED MEMORY

The system supports direct application interaction by using shared-memory segments. Shared memory is the simplest form of inter-process communications (IPC). You may allocate a segment and then make it available to other programs in the system. As additional programs share a memory segment, OS/2 increments a use count associated with the memory segment. When programs free a shared segment (or when programs terminate), OS/2 decrements the segment use count. The OS/2 memory manager does not actually free a shared-memory segment until its use count is 0. OS/2 implements two types of shared-memory segments: globally and locally shared segments.

Global Shared Memory

Global shared-memory segments are accessible to all programs in the system. This kind of shared memory is named with a null-terminated ASCII (ASCIIZ) string. Shared-memory names have the same format and structure as OS/2 file names, for example:

```
\SHAREMEM   \MYSEG
\SHAREMEM   \GLOBAL.DTA
```

When a program issues the DosAllocShrSeg API call, it passes to OS/2 the size of the memory area and a name. OS/2 allocates the segment and adds the name to the system shared-memory name table. Subsequently, other OS/2 programs that know the name can gain access to the memory by using the DosGetShrSeg API call. If the name provided to this API call matches an existing shared-memory segment name, OS/2 sets up addressability to the shared segment in the LDT of the requesting program.

This type of shared memory is useful for common system data areas, which must be accessible to any program. If you create such a segment, any program in the system that knows the name string can gain access to the segment.

Local Shared Memory

Local shared memory is a facility that two programs can use to privately share memory. Unlike global shared memory, you do not access local shared-memory segments by name, but rather by handle. For example, suppose you have two programs that are to share a common data area. The first program would

1. Allocate a segment to be shared.

2. Put data into the segment to be passed to the second program.

3. Use the DosGiveSeg API call to request a "handle" from the system that the second program will use to access the shared-memory segment. You identify the second program by its process ID (PID).

4. Pass the handle to the target program (perhaps through a global shared segment).

The *handle* is actually a selector that is only valid in the LDT of the second program. By using local shared memory, two programs can pass data by way of a data segment that has alias selectors in both programs' address spaces.

A distinct advantage to this type of shared memory is that only the two participating programs can access the memory segment. The shared-memory selector is valid only in the LDT of the program that was "given" the segment.

In both global and local shared memory, OS/2 employs a use-count algorithm. Each time a program accesses a shared-memory segment (using DosGetShrSeg) or "gives" a shared-memory segment (by using DosGiveSeg), the OS/2 memory manager increments the use count of the segment. When the programs free the shared-memory segments (by way of DosFreeSeg) the count is decremented.

SEGMENT MOTION

The 80286 segmented architecture allows for variably sized memory segments ranging from 164K bytes in length. OS/2 supports this architecture and allows program segments to be any size within these limits. This poses a unique physical memory-management program: Since the segments are variable in size, memory is easily fragmented. The probability is low that a particular "hole" in memory is precisely the same size as the next allocation

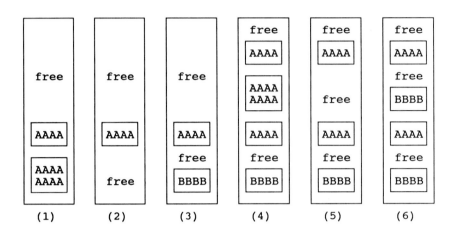

Figure 4-6.   Memory fragmentation

request. If nothing is done, continued dynamic allocation and deallocation of memory will result in numerous unused "slivers" of memory.

Consider the example shown in Figure 4-6.

1. Program A allocates two data segments—200 and 100 bytes in length.

2. Later it deallocates the 200-byte segment.

3. Program B, running at the same time as A, now allocates a 100-byte segment.

4. Assume program A allocates a second set of 100-byte and 200-byte segments. This time there is not sufficient room for the 200-byte segment, so the system allocates the segment out of the next available contiguous, free area.

5. Once again, A frees the larger of the two segments.

6. Program B (or another program) allocates a 100-byte segment.

As you see, over time the available memory tends to be dispersed among different-sized segments, creating thousands of small holes too small to satisfy the average memory-allocation request. This example was simple, with only two (not 65,536) segment sizes, yet the result was a 3/7 (or 43%) storage fragmentation ratio.

To prevent the storage fragmentation described in this example, OS/2 implements a solution called *segment motion*. Whenever OS/2 is presented with a storage request that cannot be satisfied with the available free memory, it reorganizes the segments and creates larger free areas.

In contrast to the previous case, consider the same example with segment motion (see Figure 4-7).

1. Program A allocates the same 100-byte and 200-byte segments.

2. As before, it deallocates a segment.

3. Again, program B allocates its 100-byte segment. So far all is the same as the first example.

4. Program A now allocates its set of segments. The system recognizes it has a large memory fragment and moves the segments around to create a large free area, which it then uses to satisfy A's request.

5. Once again, A frees the larger of the two segments.

6. Program B (or another program) allocates a 100-byte segment.

This example shows that OS/2 is now more intelligent about the use of its memory resources. This results in a better utilization of the system memory resources and leads to a more efficient, and predictable, operating environment.

The environment is more predictable because if storage compaction were not employed, the system would report out-of-storage conditions in differing situations, depending on the order of allocation or deallocation requests. The storage

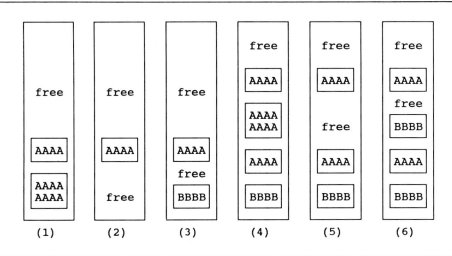

Figure 4-7.   Memory defragmentation with segment motion

fragmentation manifests itself as an "inefficient" system, where memory is wasted at some times, but not others.

SEGMENT SWAPPING

While segment motion increases the efficiency of the OS/2 memory-management services, it does not provide a complete solution. Programs running in the system are bound by the amount of physical memory installed in the machine. This is acceptable in a single-tasking system, but it is an inconvenience in a multitasking environment where most programs (and their associated memory segments) lie dormant when not actively interacting with the user.

By exploiting the capabilities of the 80286, OS/2 implements a more elegant memory management scheme.

As you saw in Chapter 2, memory segments are defined by a descriptor in one of the system descriptor tables. Each memory segment has characteristics that are defined in the attribute field of the descriptor. One of these attributes is the "segment-not-present" indicator. If set, this indicator causes the 80286 to generate a processor fault when any program references the segment.

OS/2 uses this particular segment attribute to implement virtual address spaces. As a program allocates segments, the OS/2 memory manager creates entries in the LDT. It also carves out a portion of physical memory and sets the LDT descriptor base address to point to the physical memory associated with the segment.

If enough free, contiguous memory does not exist to satisfy the request (and segment motion does not help), the memory manager "throws out" one of the other active segments to make room for the new request. To help decide which segment to swap, OS/2 maintains a table that contains reference counts for all the segments in the system. When more physical memory is needed, OS/2 selects the least-used segment and moves it to the system swap file.

At the same time, OS/2 updates the descriptor associated with the swapped segment to indicate the segment is no longer present. If another program then references the swapped segment, the 80286 generates a segment-not-present fault. This fault allows OS/2 to retrieve the segment from disk (throwing out other segments, if necessary), reset the descriptor, and allow the program to continue as if the segment had been present in memory.

Consider the following example:

1. Memory is fully allocated to programs A and B (Figure 4-8). The system now loads a new program, named C. Program C requires 100 bytes of memory. However, since all memory is used, OS/2 cannot immediately load C.

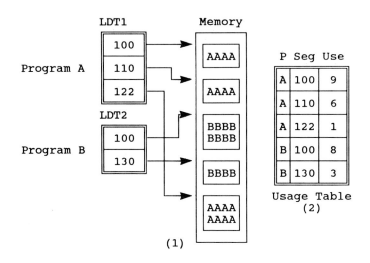

Figure 4-8. OS/2 segment swapping

2. The memory manager scans its internal table and determines that segment 122, belonging to program A, is the least-used segment in memory (referenced only one time). The memory manager also notes that segment 122 occupies an area large enough to satisfy the 100-byte memory requirement of program C.

3. OS/2 then swaps segment A.122 to disk, and marks the descriptor in A's LDT as "not present." If the segment is shared among multiple programs, OS/2 updates all the appropriate LDT (see Figure 4-9).

4. The memory allocation request can now be completed. OS/2 creates the LDT of C and sets the descriptor base address to point to the correct physical memory location.

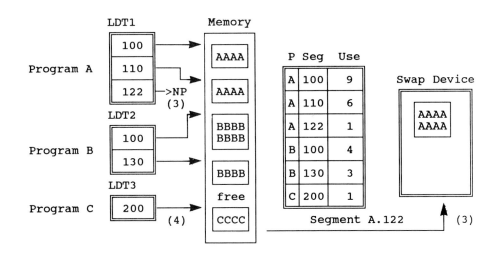

Figure 4-9. Loading program C

5. Later program A references the swapped segment. The 80286 processor inspects the descriptor and, on the basis of the attribute setting, generates a segment-not-present fault.

6. The OS/2 fault handler retrieves the segment from the swap device and returns it to memory. To do so, OS/2 repeats steps 2 and 3, this time swapping segment 100 from program B to make room in memory. (See Figure 4-10.)

While segment swapping provides a virtual address space, it differs from a similar concept, called *paging*, in several respects. Paging always involves identically sized memory "pages." Since each hole is the same, compaction algorithms are not necessary. In addition, the pages are

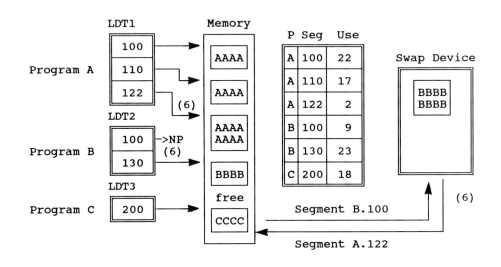

Figure 4-10.   Generating a processor segment-not-present fault

carved out by the system, so the programmer does not have to worry about the structure of the application program. Paging support is one of the important features of the 80386 processor. However, OS/2 1.0 does not exploit the 80386 paging-assist functions.

While segment swapping is useful, you should avoid running a heavily overcommitted system. With average seek times of 20ms-80ms, today's personal computer hard disks are too slow to implement a true virtual paging system. In reality, the OS/2 memory overcommit functions soften the physical memory barrier. Programs (or, more important, combinations of programs) whose memory requirements exceed the system memory can be run. How an over-committed system performs is totally dependent on the memory reference patterns of the programs. In general, the performance may be improved by adding more system memory (up to 16MB).

Swapping and compaction can be turned off using the OS/2 configuration options.

DEMAND LOADING

OS/2 programs comprise multiple segments, packaged together in an executable file. As OS/2 loads the program into memory, it builds an LDT descriptor for each program segment. In most cases the segments are brought into memory when the file is loaded. However, OS/2 also gives you a different option, called *load on demand*, that delays the loading of segments until they are referenced (if ever). A segment is marked "demand loadable" when the executable file is created. The system creates LDT entries for demand-loaded segments and marks the descriptor as "not present." When the program references the segment, a fault is generated and OS/2 reads the segment from disk—much in the same way the system handles segment-not-present faults for swapped segments.

By demand-loading infrequently used routines, an application often may consume less memory and initialize more quickly.

MEMORY SUBALLOCATION

OS/2 provides services to suballocate memory within segments. In many cases, applications request and free small portions of memory at a very frequent rate (such as internal control blocks). In these cases, incurring the overhead of a physical memory allocation request is not always sensible. Each time a segment is allocated and then freed, the OS/2 memory manager must build the LDT entry, update

Table 4-2.   Memory-Management Suballocation API Calls

API Call	Description
DosSubAlloc	Allocate a memory element
DosSubSet	Initialize a segment for suballocation
DosSubFree	Deallocate a memory element

the descriptor, locate the physical memory, more segments, swap segments, free the physical memory, and update the descriptor. This is clearly overhead you may not always need or want.

As an alternative, OS/2 has a special facility, called the *memory suballocation package* (MSP), that allows you to allocate and free portions of a (suballocated) memory segment. The MSP functions, shown in Table 4-2, are simple memory allocation and deallocation routines that carve up a previously allocated memory segment into smaller pieces.

From the perspective of the system, suballocation is invisible. The MSP subsystem never actually allocates or deallocates segments. Instead, the services keep track of which portions of the memory segment are in use and which are not. Since these portions are all contained within one memory segment, the suballocated elements are not subject to swapping or compaction.

Consider the following points when deciding whether to use memory suballocation in your application:

- How frequently do you allocate and deallocate memory? MSP requests are fast, since they do not enter the OS/2 Kernel.

- How much memory do you use? The maximum area to be suballocated is one segment (64K). Naturally, you can use a pool of suballocatable segments. However, the bookkeeping may be cumbersome.

- Do you need storage protection between memory elements? There is no storage protection between suballocated portions of the segment so they are alright to use within a single program, but they should not be used to pass data between programs.

Carefully weigh the advantages and disadvantages of suballocation before you build your application. In some cases, suballocated memory is best, while in other cases, the segments should be allocated by the system.

SUMMARY

Memory management is an important aspect of OS/2. To a large extent, effective multitasking is not possible without effective memory management. OS/2 exploits the capabilities of 80286/80386 protected mode operation to implement an application environment where the programs are truly isolated from one another. The memory manager allows you to run programs (or combinations of programs) whose memory requirements exceed the physical system memory. This is especially useful in the multiprogramming environment where multiple applications are run concurrently.

Consider the following points as you read other chapters:

- OS/2 memory layout
- DOS environment configuration options
- The system address space and the GDT
- The application address space and the LDT
- How OS/2 applications are loaded
- The OS/2 memory-management API
- Allocating and freeing memory

- Shared memory alternatives
- Segment motion and compaction
- Segment swapping
- Demand-loading program segments
- Memory suballocation

CHAPTER 5
MULTITASKING AND DYNAMIC LINKING

OS/2 is significantly different from PC DOS in the areas
of program management and task control. This chapter
discusses how OS/2 implements these functions and how
they are represented through the API.

TASK MANAGEMENT

At the heart of any multitasking operating system is its
ability to manage resources. The most critical of these
resources is the processor (CPU) itself. The CPU is a
shared resource, which OS/2 shares among multiple programs by giving each a short period of execution time
called a *time slice*.

This ability to manage multiple programs, distributing system resources and processor time among them, is called *task management*. OS/2 introduces a *tasking model* that defines the rules which govern how programs run concurrently. OS/2 implements the tasking model in its task-management component and makes the services available to all applications through a standard system API. The OS/2 tasking API functions are summarized in Table 5-1.

Before exploring these functions, consider what happens in the PC DOS environment. Because PC DOS has no multitasking capabilities, most of its applications are *single-threaded*. But this does not mean that PC DOS

Table 5-1. OS/2 Tasking APIs

**Process
Functions**

DosExecPgm	Execute program as a process
DosKillProcess	Terminate process or processes
DosCWait	Wait for termination of child process(es)

**Thread
Functions**

DosCreateThread	Create a new thread of execution
DosExit	Terminate the current thread
DosResumeThread	Continue execution of specific thread
DosSuspendThread	Stop execution of specific thread
DosEnterCritSec	Allow only one thread to run (in process)
DosExitCritSec	Permit all threads to run (in process)

**Priority
Manipulation**

DosGetPrty	Query execution priority
DosSetPrty	Set execution priority

applications cannot multitask. In fact, many PC DOS applications do. By taking over the system timer and sharing time slices between its own program functions, a PC DOS application can do more than one thing at a time. An example of this kind of programming is found in the DOS PRINT command (on the PC DOS distribution disk).

In contrast, OS/2 provides a standard set of multitasking facilities that are functionally equivalent, but more generic and far easier to use. OS/2 moves the time-slice management functions out of the application and into the system, making them available to all programs.

Figure 5-1 illustrates this fundamental difference between the OS/2 and PC DOS systems. Notice that by moving the dispatching services into the system, OS/2 becomes

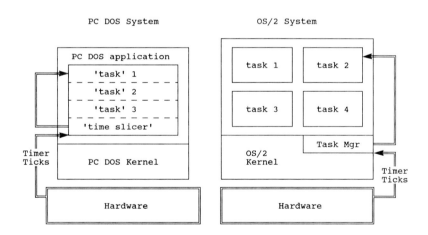

Figure 5-1. Multitasking on OS/2 versus PC DOS

aware of the dispatching. This enables OS/2 to tie other resource-management functions to CPU dispatching. For example, each task can have its own set of resources (such as open files or devices). As the OS/2 dispatcher switches tasks, it also changes the resource set associated with the task.

THE OS/2 TASKING MODEL

In a multitasking system, programs are associated with *dispatchable units*. Dispatchable units identify the programs the operating system may run concurrently. An operating system must also know which set of dispatchable units is associated with which system resources. The role of the OS/2 tasking model is to provide a framework by which programs can identify dispatchable units of work and their associated resources.

The OS/2 tasking model introduces several concepts which identify the characteristics of each program. A *thread* identifies a dispatchable unit of work (a program runs within a thread). A *process* is a collection of one or more threads and associated system resources (such as memory, open files, and devices). A *session* is a collection of one or more processes associated with a virtual console (keyboard, videodisplay, or mouse). You should understand the role of each element, since they affect the design of your application programs.

Threads

The basic unit of execution in OS/2 is the thread. Every process in the system has at least one thread. The thread provides program code with an execution environment that consists of the register values, stack, and the CPU mode. The execution environment is collectively referred to as the thread's *context*. OS/2 automatically maintains the correct context for each thread. For example, if a thread is preempted and later redispatched, it has precisely the same data in its registers and stack that it had before the preemption. In fact, a program does not know (nor should it care) when the preemptions occur.

A program, or rather the program's code, is a static element with no "life" of its own. The thread provides the code with an execution instance that differentiates it from all other threads in the system. In fact, the same code may run in multiple threads at the same time. Figure 5-2 illustrates the relationship of programs to threads. Notice that TEST-CODE is executing in two threads, each with its own context.

OS/2 programs are *reentrant* and must obey the following rules:

- Program code cannot modify itself.

- The program must allocate a "dynamic" data segment to keep the data areas and control blocks that it modifies on the fly. Alternatively, it may allocate dynamic data from the stack, which is unique to the thread.

- If the program "shares" a data area with programs running in other threads, it must serialize references to the data by using OS/2 synchronization facilities.

If you write your programs in a high-level language (C, COBOL, FORTRAN, Pascal, and so forth), the compiler ensures that the program is reentrant. On the other hand, if you program in assembler, you must make sure your code does not violate these rules.

An application may employ one or more threads. For example, consider Figure 5-3 where the application program reads from the diskette with one thread while it prints the data with a second thread. When you run this

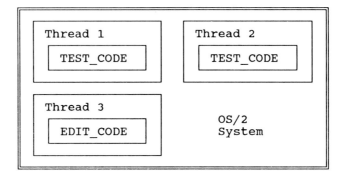

Figure 5-2. Relationship of programs to threads

program, the diskette and the printer appear to run at the same time. The advantage of this type of programming is that multiple events occur concurrently. In reality, OS/2 is allotting each thread a short period on the CPU and giving the appearance that the threads are running simultaneously.

Threads do not own system resources. Other than their own execution stacks, threads share the resources of the

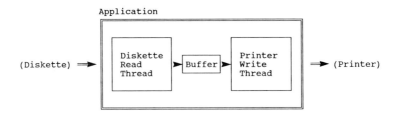

Figure 5-3. Multithreaded OS/2 application

process. A thread may create another thread by using the DosCreateThread API. The task manager creates the new thread in the process of the program that issued the API call. A thread may also suspend and resume other threads in the process with the DosSuspendThread and DosResumeThread calls. Note that OS/2 allows you to manipulate only those threads contained in your process.

The task manager does not have an explicit API call for one thread to terminate another (such as DosKillThread). However, a thread can terminate *itself* in one of the following two ways:

- By returning to the dispatcher (FAR RET)
- By issuing the DosExit API call

When all the threads of a process have ended, OS/2 terminates the process.

Within a process, all the threads are "cooperative" in that they are all part of the same program. View this as separate application subroutines all running concurrently. Since you cannot predict their order of execution, you must serialize access to common resources. In other words, if one thread is updating a field, it must first set a flag indicating that the data is being updated. Other threads needing access to the data must wait until the first thread is finished (and clears the flag) before they proceed. In reality, this is done with a special system facility called *semaphores*, which is discussed later in this chapter.

Threads are not hierarchically organized, meaning that no notion of parent-child relationships exists between threads. When your program starts a thread, it becomes a peer to all the other threads in the process.

Processes

Program resources in OS/2 are grouped into logical units called processes. More precisely, a process is a collection of system resources allocated to a particular program. For

Thread

A thread is the basic OS/2 unit of execution. A thread gives a program its context, including registers, stack, and CPU mode.

example, the threads, memory, files, and devices created by a program all become part of the process.

Whenever OS/2 starts a program, it first creates a process to "own" the resources. OS/2 then loads the program and starts a thread to run the code. As the program allocates (or acquires) additional resources, they become part of the process. For example, memory segments, files, queues, semaphores, and threads are all resources a program may dynamically allocate. Figure 5-4 illustrates a system with two processes. Notice that each process has its own unique collection of resources. In particular, each has at least one thread, a number of open files, devices, queues, and several memory segments.

As the OS/2 dispatcher switches the CPU context between threads, it reestablishes ownership of the correct resources on the basis of the thread's process. So, while Thread 1 in Process A is running, it has access to the resources of Process A. Similarly, when Thread 1, Thread 2, or Thread 3 from Process B is running, the thread has access to the resources of Process B. In this way, OS/2 allows you to concurrently run different programs without fear of resource conflicts.

As programs free their resources (that is, close files or free memory segments), OS/2 deletes the resources from their respective processes. If a program terminates abnormally, the OS/2 housekeeping services free the program's system resources. Processes are used by OS/2 to organize the system resources.

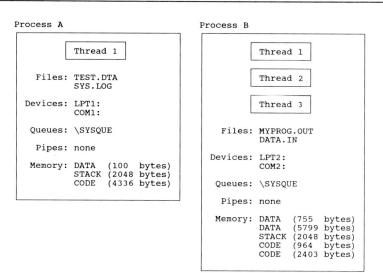

Figure 5-4.   OS/2 processes

Processes are created with the OS/2 DosExecPgm API. This API allows you to identify a program (EXE file) to be read in from disk and run as a process. If the program is already running, OS/2 creates a new process with a new execution instance of the code.

Processes are created in a hierarchical structure. A process that executes a second process is called the *parent*, while the executed process is called the *child*. Figure 5-5 illustrates the parent-child relationship of processes. Process A is the parent of B and C. Process B is the parent of D and E. Processes B and C are children of A; collectively, processes B, C, D, and E are called A's descendents.

The parent retains control of its children. The parent process may issue tasking API calls that affect all of its descendents. For instance, a parent may terminate itself and all its descendents with the DosKillProcess API. In Figure 5-5, B can terminate itself, D, and E with a single DosKillProcess call.

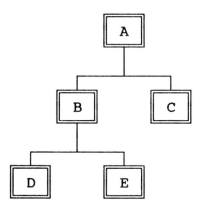

Figure 5-5. Hierarchical process structures

When a child is created, it inherits the resources of the parent, unless the resources were acquired with no inheritance options. For instance, open file handles corresponding to files opened with inheritance rights by the parent can be used by the child process. When it starts a program the parent can also specify the input parameters and environment the child is to receive.

The parent can choose to EXEC the child synchronously or asynchronously. A synchronous EXEC suspends the parent until the child terminates (identical to the PC DOS EXEC function). On the other hand, the asynchronous EXEC allows the parent to continue executing after the child is started, unaware of the child's termination. Optionally, the parent may request the system to hold the completion code of the child for later interrogation with the DosCWait API.

Consider the scenarios shown in Figure 5-6 and Figure 5-7. In Figure 5-6, Process A executes Process B to perform a single task. Process A is suspended until Process B completes. Once B completes, Process A resumes as if it

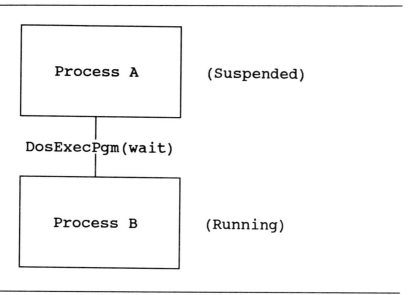

Figure 5-6.   *A suspended process waiting for completion*

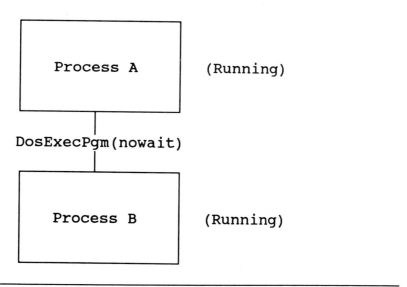

Figure 5-7.   *Processes running simultaneously*

Process

A process is a collection of system resources and includes threads, file devices, memory segments, pipes, and queues. These resources are brought together to run a program.

had never waited. An example of this scenario might be Process A spawning Process B to display a directory listing.

In Figure 5-7, Process A continues to execute concurrently with its child, Process B. In this case, Process A may have spawned Process B to print a file in the background while Process A continues to run.

Priorities

All the threads in the system compete for CPU time. However, all systems contain some tasks that should always take precedence over other tasks. For instance, a thread controlling a communications line should have priority over a thread running a printer.

OS/2 implements a multilevel priority scheme with dynamic variation and round-robin dispatching within a priority level. Simply put, this means that all the threads in the system have an associated priority. A higher-priority thread that is ready to run always gets the CPU before a lower-priority thread. Within the regular priority class, the thread priorities are modified by the system, depending on how often the thread performs I/O operations and how much CPU time the thread consumes. Finally, threads of equal priority are given CPU time in round-robin order (see Figure 5-8).

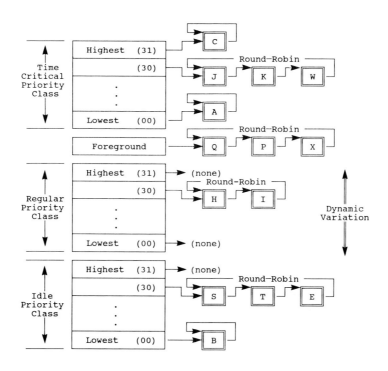

Figure 5-8. OS/2 dispatching priorities

OS/2 uses *priority classes* to separate threads with different operational characteristics. The four classes are

- Time critical
- Foreground
- Regular
- Idle

The time-critical class has 31 distinct priority levels. Threads requiring immediate attention (such as communications or real-time applications) can run in this class. For example, the OS/2 session manager runs in the lowest time-critical priority level.

Foreground class has a single priority level. The application program on the screen always runs in this class, and receives priority favor over threads executing in the regular and idle classes.

Regular class implements 31 priority levels with dynamic variation. The system automatically adjusts the priority levels of threads in this class, depending on the operational characteristics of the threads (such as I/O frequency and relative use of the CPU).

Idle class (the opposite of time critical) provides 31 priority levels for the lowest-priority threads in the system. The system idle task runs at the lowest idle priority.

Figure 5-8 illustrates a system with 14 threads. Note the round-robin sequence at priority levels that have more than one active thread.

A program may query or change the priority and level of its thread with the DosGetPrty and DosSetPrty APIs, respectively.

Time Slicing

OS/2 has a preemptive time-slicing dispatcher. This means that all threads in the system get a fixed period of time (a time slice) on the CPU. The threads are preempted when their time slice is finished. This can happen between any two instructions in the program.

An advantage of this type of dispatching technique is that OS/2 does not have to rely on programs to voluntarily yield the CPU. In fact, OS/2 actually "takes away" the CPU when the system needs to run another thread. In general, a preemptive dispatcher distributes CPU time fairly between threads.

However, this technique does have a major drawback. Since programs do not know exactly when they will be preempted, they must take special precautions when they reference or modify shared data structures. In fact, a thread may be preempted while it is updating a data structure.

You can configure the minimum and maximum time-slice values by using a CONFIG.SYS statement.

Serialization

Because OS/2 applications can be preempted, they must be especially careful when they access shared system resources (such as a shared memory area). To help application threads serialize the use of shared resources, OS/2 provides a special facility called semaphores. A semaphore is a data structure that OS/2 guarantees to give to only one thread at a time. For example, if two different threads (in the same or different processes) need to access a common data structure, the threads first ask for a semaphore. OS/2 allows one thread to get the semaphore and blocks the second thread until the first relinquishes control. In this way, all threads wishing to access the data structure are blocked until the thread writing the data structure completes its task.

Under PC DOS, resource serialization is seldom required because most programs are single-threaded. However, in cases where a PC DOS application does need to synchronize events (such as when waiting for video retrace), the application disables interrupts with the 80286 CLI instruction. The OS/2 semaphore functions are important because, unlike their PC DOS counterparts, OS/2 programs are not allowed to disable interrupts.

OS/2 implements two types of semaphores: *system semaphores* and *RAM semaphores* (see Figure 5-9). You should use a system semaphore when you serialize events between processes. The data structure representing a system semaphore is maintained in a kernel data area, so requests to get and free the data structure are processed by

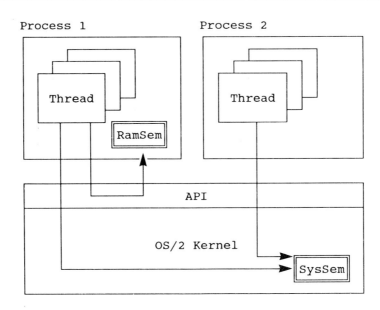

Figure 5-9. Resource serialization using semaphores

the kernel. If a process dies while holding a system semaphore, OS/2 resets the semaphore state as part of the process termination (cleanup) functions. Thus, OS/2 guarantees that a system semaphore will never be hung because
the process owning it died unexpectedly.

While system semaphores are safe, they are not optimal
if used within a single process. OS/2 provides a conceptually similar, but simpler, implementation with RAM semaphores. These semaphores are functionally equivalent to
system semaphores, except that the semaphore data structure is contained in the memory of the process. Since the
memory is not in the kernel, the service routines used to
claim and free the semaphore execute in the application
context (outside of the kernel) and give you better performance.

Table 5-2. Semaphore Functions

*Enqueuing on
a Resource*

DosSemClear	Clear a semaphore
DosSemRequest	Obtain a semaphore

Signaling

DosSemSet	Set a semaphore
DosSemSetWait	Set a semaphore and wait (atomic)
DosSemWait	Wait for a semaphore to be cleared
DosMuxSetWait	Wait on a semaphore list

Miscellaneous

DosSemOpen	Open named (system) semaphore
DosSemClose	Close named (system) semaphore
DosSemCreate	Create named (system) semaphore

However, you must be careful to use RAM semaphores only between threads in a single process. Using a RAM semaphore between processes will result in a deadlock if the process dies while it is holding the RAM semaphore. The system is not aware of the RAM semaphore state, so it cannot free the semaphore while it performs the process-termination functions.

The OS/2 semaphore functions are summarized in Table 5-2.

Display Sessions

OS/2 allows you to run multiple processes (or combinations of processes) that directly interact with the keyboard, video screen, and mouse. If all these processes were allowed to read from the keyboard or write to the screen simultaneously, the system usability would be questionable. OS/2 supports this type of concurrent processing through multiple logical sessions.

A session is roughly equivalent to a virtual console. Picture it as multiple copies of PC DOS running concurrently on the same machine. When you start a session, OS/2 creates an environment in which you can run an application. This environment includes a virtual keyboard, screen, and mouse.

You may start up to 12 concurrent sessions, with a different application program in each. This provides you with the equivalent function of 12 copies of PC DOS on a single machine. For example, concurrent execution of multiple application programs may allow you to edit a document in one session, print it in a second, and send it to a host processor in a third.

The application sessions draw heavily on the OS/2 tasking modem, and are very similar to processes. Within each session, OS/2 enables you to run one or more processes. However, these sessions are implemented at a higher logical level than processes. In fact, sessions are not implemented by the kernel, but rather by the session manager.

TIMER SERVICES

In a multitasking system, the timer becomes an important system resource. The timer is the basis for all the OS/2 timer-related functions (including dispatcher time-slicing, device timeouts, and the system clock). Because the timer plays such a crucial role in the system, OS/2 does not permit applications to directly access the timer interrupts. However, OS/2 does provide equivalent functions through an architected timer-services API (summarized in Table 5-3).

The OS/2 timer services allow an application thread to

Table 5-3.   Timer Services API

Interval Timers

DosSleep	Wait for time interval (synchronous)
DosTimerAsync	Wait for time interval (asynchronous)
DosTimerStart	Start asynchronous, periodic timer
DosTimerStop	Reset asynchronous timer

System Date/ Time

DosGetDateTime	Query system clock
DosSetDateTime	Set system clock

perform most timer-related activities (such as waking up for an alarm, becoming dormant for a period, or receiving periodic shoulder taps).

The granularity of these services is determined by the frequency of the system clock (approximately 32 ms). In general, this granularity is adequate for most applications. However, the accuracy of the OS/2 timer function is affected by several factors, including the system load and relative priority of the timing thread.

Asynchronous Interval Notification

PC DOS programs often use countdown timers as a basis for generating alarms. In OS/2, you can do this with an asynchronous timer. OS/2 signals the expiration of the timer interval by clearing a semaphore (provided by the thread when the timer is started).

You set an asynchronous interval with the (DosStart-Async) API. If you want to disable the timer before it expires, you use the DosTimerStop function.

Periodic Notification

A periodic notification timer is identical to an asynchronous interval timer, except that the thread's semaphore is cleared at a regular, cyclical interval. These timers are conceptually similar to direct hardware timer interrupts, except that you can set the interval of interruption.

You set a periodic interval timer with a DosTimerStart function and stop it with a DosTimerStop function.

Sleeping

You can stop an application thread for a period of time with the OS/2 DosSleep function. This is a synchronous version of the asynchronous interval timer. The thread that issues DosSleep is suspended until the expiration of the timer interval. You would, for instance, use this function from within a thread that is polling an external device.

Date and Time

OS/2 allows you to query the date and time with the (Dos-GetDateTime) function, and set the date and time with DosSetDateTime function. These functions are equivalent to the PC DOS DATE/TIME INT21 service routines. However, you should note that OS/2 maintains only one system clock. If you change the setting of the clock, you are changing the value for all processes in the system.

INTERPROCESS COMMUNICATIONS

Once a system has concurrent processes, a need arises for ways in which these processes can coordinate their actions. Since not all programs are written by the same person, interprocess communications (or IPC) must be provided in a well-defined, standard form. IPC is a consistent set of interfaces for sending data between programs. These programs may have been written independently but are expected to operate together.

OS/2 provides a rich set of IPC mechanisms, each with strengths and applicability in different situations. This section examines each facility and explores the operational characteristics of each.

Table 5-4 lists the IPC API calls.

Flags

OS/2 uses *flags* as a basic form of notification to signal a process that a particular event has taken place. To receive a flag event, the process must register a signal handler in Thread 1 with the DosSetSigHandler function call. If this registration is not done, the system handles the flag for the process and takes appropriate default actions.

One process triggers a flag event in another process by calling the DosFlagProcess API function. A flag is similar to a software interrupt. Using flags, processes can interrupt one another asynchronously.

Table 5-4. Interprocess Communications API

Flags

DosSetSigHandler	Register a signal handler
DosFlagProcess	Send a flag

Pipes

Dos MKPIPE	Create a pipe
DosRead	Read from a pipe
DosWrite	Write into a pipe
DosClose	Close a pipe

Queuing

DosCloseQueue	Close a queue (finish using)
DosCreateQueue	Create a new queue
DosOpenQueue	Open a queue (start using)
DosPeekQueue	Look at a queue element
DosPurgeQueue	Delete all elements from a queue
DosQueryQueue	Determine element count of a queue
DosReadQueue	Read an element from a queue
DosWriteQueue	Write an element into a queue

Shared Memory and Semaphores

Shared memory and semaphores are the two fundamental elements on which all forms of IPC are constructed. In the most basic form, all IPC consists of

- Passing data between processes

- Event synchronization

As discussed previously, shared memory is a data-passing mechanism. It can be used to allocate, format, and pass along a memory segment. The OS/2 semaphore mechanisms are the most rudimentary form of synchronization services.

Two programs can create their own IPC by establishing a data convention (format) for a shared piece of memory. The programs pass information by writing and reading specific fields. Synchronization can be performed by "peeking" in a control area in a tight loop. However, "polling" techniques are strongly discouraged in multitasking systems because of the amount of system overhead these techniques generate. A far preferable solution uses semaphores for synchronization.

Consider the example illustrated in Figure 5-10. Process A and Process B communicate through a shared segment named \SHARESEG\IPC. The data in the segment

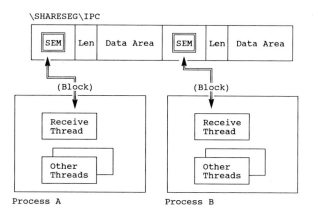

Figure 5-10. IPC with shared memory and semaphores

is formatted into two areas, one for communications from A to B, and the other for communications from B to A. Each area contains a semaphore (SEM), a length field (Len), and a data area. Both processes create a dedicated thread to receive data. The receive thread for Process A is blocked on the semaphore in the B-to-A area. The receive thread for Process B is blocked on the other semaphore. If one process wants to send data to the other, it puts the data in the buffer and clears the receive semaphore for the thread of the other process. This wakes up the other process to handle the data.

Pipes

OS/2 provides *pipes* as a form of standard IPC protocol. The model for a pipe is a serial character stream, identical to a file-system character stream. In other words, a program reads/writes data to a pipe in the same way it does to a file (with DosRead, DosWrite, and DosClose requests).

The obvious advantage of this model is that the output of programs writing data in a standard fashion can be "redirected" to a pipe. Similarly, programs receiving input in a standard fashion can receive input from a pipe.

View a pipe as a fixed-length character stream. Figure 5-11 illustrates how a pipe works. Output from Program A is serially moved into the pipe memory segment. Program B is reading the serial character stream. Program A is filling the pipe while B is draining it. If one program gets ahead of the other, OS/2 will eventually block it. For instance, if Program A is writing data at a faster rate than Program B is reading, the pipe will fill up and A will be blocked. Conversely, if Program B reads faster than Program A writes, the pipe will drain and B will be blocked while waiting for the next character.

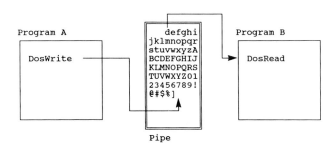

Figure 5-11.   Pipes

Another possible use for a pipe is as a fixed-length, first-in-first-out (FIFO) circular queue. In this scheme, multiple client processes can write data to a single-server process. As the server drains the pipe, more data can be written by the clients. If the pipe is filled, the client processes are blocked. Thus, the system automatically provides data-flow control for the server.

Queues

Pipes do not provide an optimal structure for all situations. In some cases data should be considered as a collection of discrete items, rather than as a continuous data stream. A program may wish to be selective about the requests it processes and accept some but not others. Alternatively, a program may wish to establish a multi-tiered priority scheme for individual requests. These IPC characteristics are not easily accommodated with stream-oriented protocols like pipes.

For this reason, OS/2 provides a second, conceptually different IPC model called *queuing*. In this model, data is

Pipe

A pipe is a form of IPC where programs send data as continuous data streams. The receiver processes the data in the same order it was sent (serially).

---

not viewed as a single serial data stream, but rather as a collection of finite-length queue elements. The individual elements are chained together to form a queue. Each element in the queue is separately addressable. A server may remove any element without having to disturb the remainder of the queue.

An important aspect of queues is that the elements may be accessed in different ways including FIFO, LIFO, and by priority. The priority of an OS/2 queue element is determined by the data in the element, not by the execution priority of the sending thread. Multiple processes may add elements to a queue, but only the process that created the element may read (dequeue) it.

The example in Figure 5-12 illustrates how a queue passes requests to a server process. Using the DosCreate-Queue service, the server (Program C) creates a queue named \QUEUE\IN. Using the DosOpenQueue API, the clients (Program A and Program B) open the queue by identifying it by its ASCIIZ name (\QUEUE\IN). OS/2 returns a one-word handle, which the clients then use with the DosWriteQueue API to add elements to the queue. Each client program can format data blocks and send them to the queue of Program C. As the elements are added to the queue, they retain the identity of the sender and the element priority assigned by the sender.

Each element is dequeued by using the algorithm specified by Program C when it created the queue (FIFO,

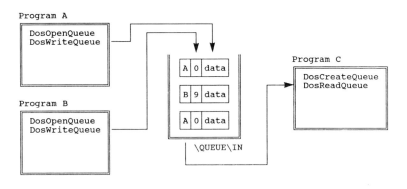

Figure 5-12.   Queues

LIFO, or by priority). Individual elements may be "peeked" without being taken out of the queue. The queue continues to exist until it is closed by Program C, at which time the queue handles being used by Program A and Program B are invalidated.

PROGRAM MANAGEMENT

All disk-based operating systems have a component responsible for reading programs from disk and loading them into memory. In OS/2 this component is a part of the system kernel and is called the *loader*.

OS/2 uses the loader to start all programs (including applications, subsystems, system shell, and device drivers). In fact, the loader is the single interface for all program start functions. This chapter has discussed the DosExec-Pgm function, an API processed by the loader.

Queue

> A queue is a form of IPC where programs send discrete data packets. The queue owner may dequeue the elements in any order.

OS/2 programs are stored on disk in an executable (EXE) format which is an evolutionary outgrowth of the PC DOS EXE format. An EXE file is really nothing more than the compressed image of a program. It includes each of the program segments (code, data, and stack), plus control records that tell the loader how to tie them all together.

When the loader receives an EXEC function call, it interacts with other portions of the kernel to create a process and build the basic memory-management structures (such as the LDT). The loader then reads the EXE file and allocates a memory segment for each program segment described by the EXE records. Since programs can have multiple code and data segments, the loader also resolves intersegment references (such as a CALL to a FAR subroutine).

This section discusses the two techniques the OS/2 linker uses to resolve the intersegment references: static linking and dynamic linking.

Static Linking

In many systems (such as PC DOS), executable file intersegment references are only valid between segments contained in the program file. In other words, the target of each call or data segment reference made by a program must be contained in one of the other segments linked to form the EXE file.

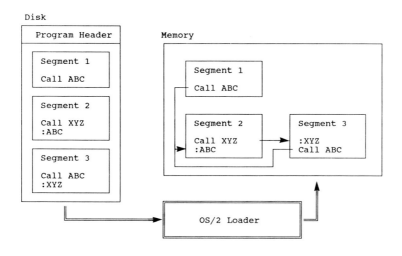

Figure 5-13.   External references in executable programs

Consider Figure 5-13. Notice that references in all segments are resolved to other segments within the program. This type of binding is called *static linking* because it is done before the program is loaded into the system, and all references are resolved to fixed offsets within the load module. The linker has already packaged all the required segments into the EXE file. From the perspective of the loader, most of the work is already done. The pieces required to run this program are together in a neat little package. The loader's only remaining chore is to bring the segments into memory and fix up the code so the intersegment references are valid.

Dynamic Linking

OS/2 significantly extends the loader function by allowing programs to reference segments not included in the EXE file. This notion, called *dynamic linking*, differs from static linking in that the loader may resolve the EXE references to segments included in special program libraries called *dynamic-link libraries* (DLL).

A far reference to a DLL segment causes the loader to bring the DLL into memory, as if it were part of the program's EXE file. In fact, a DLL file has the same format and structure as an EXE file, so it may have far references to other DLLs. When a program is loaded that references a DLL already in the system (brought in by another program), the loader resolves the intersegment references to the DLL segment already present in memory. In fact, DLL routines are common subroutines that can be called by any OS/2 program. OS/2 makes extensive use of the dynamic-link facility. In fact, the entire OS/2 API is based on dynamic linking.

Consider an example illustrating how dynamic linking works. Figure 5-14 shows a program named TEST.ASM that uses a subroutine named RUNIT. However, the subroutine is not in the program, but rather it is a dynamic-link service contained in a DLL file. To use a dynamic link, you write the TEST.ASM program as if you were going to include the routine in a different code segment. That is, the entry point (RUNIT) is coded as a normal far routine. TEST.ASM branches to the subroutine with a standard far call.

You then assemble the program to create an object file. Since the RUNIT routine is not included in the program, the assembler generates an *external-reference* (EXTERN) record as part of the object file. An EXTERN record tells the linker program about a reference that has not yet been matched with a target. These records are common in programs that make calls to run-time routines (such as those calls that the C language makes to the C run-time). Up to this point, nothing unusual has happened. TEST.ASM looks like a normal program with a normal unresolved external reference to a routine named RUNIT.

The next step is to create an EXE file by running the TEST.OBJ program through the linker. The linker's job is to accept various forms of binary program files, such as

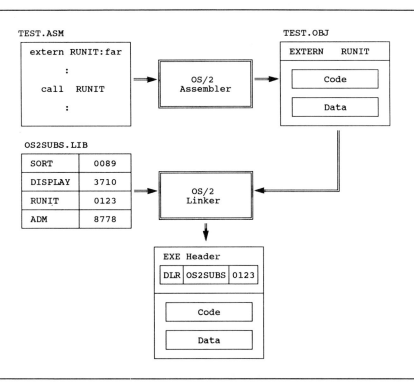

Figure 5-14. Creating a program which calls a dynamic link routine

object (OBJ) files and library (LIB) files, and to create a single EXE file that the operating system understands. When statically linking programs, all external references must be found in either one of the LIB or one of the OBJ files. However, in this example, the RUNIT routine is in neither.

With dynamic linking, OS/2 introduces a third option: a new type of LIB file called a *dynamic-link definition library*. This type of LIB file resolves the reference to RUNIT—not by including the RUNIT code, but rather by building a dynamic-link reference record in the EXE file. This record tells the OS/2 loader where to "find" RUNIT when you start TEST.

Note the distinction between the dynamic-link definition library (LIB) and the dynamic-link library (DLL). A
LIB contains the data needed to build a program EXE file
(in this case, TEST.EXE) and does not contain the dynamic-
link programs themselves. The DLL, on the other hand, is
the run-time component of the dynamic-link program. It is
a special EXE file that contains the actual dynamic-link
run-time code.

When starting TEST (see Figure 5-15), the OS/2
loader examines the EXE file for dynamic-link reference
records. In this case, it finds RUNIT. The dynamic-link
reference record indicates that RUNIT is found in the file
named OS2SUBS.DLL at an offset of 123h. If OS2SUBS

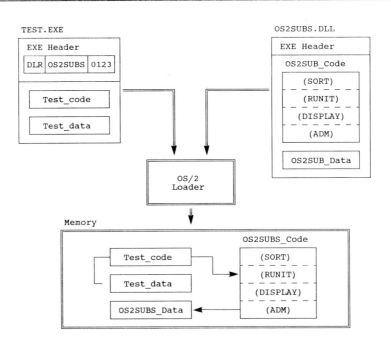

Figure 5-15.   Running a dynamic-link program

has already been loaded (by another program), the loader updates the call instruction to point to RUNIT. If it is not present, the loader first loads OS2SUBS.DLL and then resolves the call.

Since a DLL is a form of an EXE file, it might contain references to other DLLs. In this example, should OS2SUBS.DLL call routines in another DLL, the whole process would be repeated (bringing the second DLL into memory) and would fix up the OS2SUBS.DLL calls.

The dynamic-link references were resolved at load time; this type of dynamic linking is called *load-time dynamic linking*. The function is especially useful if you plan to implement a shared-service routine (such as an API). Since this is the same mechanism OS/2 uses for its API, you can build extensions that have the same "look and feel" as the basic system services.

Run-Time Dynamic Linking

OS/2 implements a second type of dynamic linking called *run-time dynamic linking*. A disadvantage with load-time dynamic linking is that the references must be known at the time the program is written. The names of the DLL fixes are hard-coded into the EXE files. This is not desirable in all cases.

Run-time dynamic linking allows you to access a DLL by name. You may use this form of dynamic linking after

---

Dynamic Linking

Dynamic linking enables programs to have external references to segments that are not included in the program (EXE) file. It is a form of delayed binding.

Table 5-5.   Run-Time Dynamic Linking API

API	Description
DosFreeModule	Free a DLL
DosGetProcAddr	Get the DLL entry point(s)
DosGetModHandle	Get the handle of a previously loaded DLL
DosGetModName	Get the name of a previously loaded DLL
DosLoadModule	Load a DLL and return its handle

your program has been loaded by using the DOS load module API. Using this API, you can load a DLL and retrieve the entry points of the individual routines, which you can later call as if they were contained in your program. Table 5-5 summarizes the OS/2 run-time dynamic linking functions.

Consider the following example. You want to write a program to process transactions received from a network connection. You want to implement each transaction processor as a separate dynamic-link routine. However, if you use load-time dynamic linking, all possible transaction processors must be loaded when your program is started. This means that only those transactions you had the foresight to include in your transaction processor can be sent by the remote clients. Adding more dynamic-link references would involve rebuilding and reloading your program.

Run-time dynamic linking solves this dilemma by allowing any OS/2 program to perform the dynamic link some time after it has been loaded. Using the OS/2 run-time dynamic-link API, you can load a DLL by name and retrieve the addresses of its internal routines.

In this example, you can establish a convention whereby each transaction name corresponds to a DLL name.

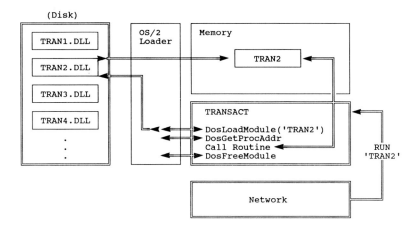

Figure 5-16.   Using run-time dynamic linking

Each transaction would have an associated DLL file on the disk.

Figure 5-16 illustrates this design. The program (TRANSACT) receives a request from a network workstation to run the transaction named TRAN2. TRANSACT then uses the transaction name to locate the transaction processor. It does this by passing the transaction name, TRAN2, to the OS/2 DosLoadModule function. Once loaded, TRANSACT gains addressability to the routine with the DosGetProcAddr API. It then uses this routine address to call the transaction program. When the transaction is finished, the DLL module is deleted with the DosFreeModule API.

Run-time dynamic linking enables you to load dynamic-link modules on the fly, while retaining the best attributes of dynamic linking.

Demand-Loading and Dynamic Linking

OS/2 implements a form of delayed-segment loading called *demand-loading.* You use this facility by setting an indicator in the EXE program-segment definitions, instructing the loader to create the LDT descriptor and to mark the segment "not present." Since a DLL is a form of an EXE file, its individual segments can be marked demand-loadable.

Using the dynamic linking facilities, you can write a library that provides common dynamic-link service routines to other programs. If you then put each subroutine in a different segment and mark each demand-loadable, the code associated with the service routines is not brought into memory until they are called. Note that the loader will still resolve the calls when an application that uses your services is loaded, but the actual memory segments of each service routine are not read into memory until needed.

Demand-loading and dynamic linking are complementary tools you can use to build flexible programs.

Program I/O Privilege

The OS/2 loader enables another different, yet equally important, program function — *I/O privilege authorization.*

OS/2 uses the hardware support provided by the 80286 processor to limit the programs in the system with direct I/O privilege. In a single-threaded environment like PC DOS, it makes little difference which program controls the hardware, as long as the hardware is not left in an unpredictable state.

With PC DOS multitasking environment managers (such as TopView, MS Windows, DESQ, and so forth), one significant item of concern is the degree of "well-behavedness" of applications. The better "behaved" the applications are, the more reliable the system becomes. Since all programs are not built by the same people, substantial amounts of time must be invested in coexistence testing to ensure that the side effects of one application do not kill another application (or the system). Unfortunately, the burden of this testing often belongs to the least-qualified person—the PC user. Running the 80286 processor in its native protected mode helps ensure that one application does not affect another.

Chapter 2 defined a program having I/O privilege as one that is allowed to issue 80286 instructions to disable interrupts (CLI/STI) and directly manipulate hardware (IN/OUT). This permission is enabled by the system's setting of IOPL. OS/2 runs applications at PL3, and sets IOPL at PL2. An application (or subsystem) can perform I/O only in specially designated I/O segments (IOPS). You identify a segment as an IOPS at the time the program is linked, by using a linker control statement. Segments marked as IOPS cannot contain dynamic-link references. Figure 5-17 illustrates such a structure.

When the OS/2 loader detects an IOPS, it builds a PL2 call gate for the segment's entry points. This means that when normal PL3 application code calls the segment, a privilege level transition occurs and the IOPS actually executes at PL2.

If the segment is not marked as an IOPS, the level transition does not occur and the program causes a protection fault when it attempts to do I/O from PL3. In effect, the identification of segments that perform I/O operations is enforced by the hardware. All OS/2 program segments requiring use of trusted I/O instructions must be properly identified by using indicators in the EXE header, or else they will not execute.

Since programs that perform I/O must properly identify themselves before they can run, the information is used to restrict their operation. Users who do not want to run these types of programs can set a system configuration (CONFIG.SYS) option that tells the OS/2 loader not to honor IOPS requests. Running with IOPL off ensures that applications will not interfere with one another.

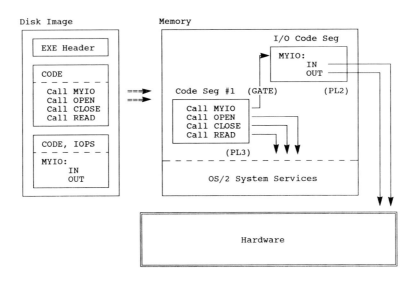

Figure 5-17. I/O privilege application/subsystem structure

SUMMARY

The material in this chapter will be directly applicable to your first OS/2 programs. Some of the information should help you understand what other programs are doing (perhaps on behalf of your program). In any event, the topics covered in this chapter will be referenced time and again as you proceed through this book and as you become more familiar with the OS/2 system.

The OS/2 tasking model defines the "rules of the road" for multitasking programs. This model is the underlying architecture on which the entire OS/2 system is built. From this model comes threads, processes, and sessions, each with a specific role in the overall system. OS/2 runs a preemptive dispatcher, so event synchronization becomes an important application issue. Semaphores give you a robust set of synchronization primitives that you use in almost any multithreaded application.

Timer services and interprocess communications are advanced functions that make your complex applications easier to write. The OS/2 dynamic-linking facility will be in every program you see or write, since it is the basis for all system APIs.

The following list summarizes the most important points covered in this chapter. Spend a few minutes reviewing these concepts until you feel comfortable with the information.

- The OS/2 tasking model

- Threads and processes

- Thread dispatching priorities

- Serializing resources in a multithreaded environment

- Timer services

- Interprocess communications principles

- Differences between pipes and queues (when each is appropriate)

- Program management in OS/2

- Dynamic linking (how it works)

- Run-time dynamic linking

- Dynamic linking and demand-loading

- How programs receive I/O privilege

CHAPTER 6
THE FILE SYSTEM

The OS/2 kernel contains the *file system*, a component that organizes and maintains application program data on external devices. In an ideal sense the file system is the part of the operating system that "hides" characteristics of devices by providing applications with a "logical" view of the storage media (such as diskettes).

System devices such as disks (or diskettes) hold data in 512-byte blocks called *sectors*. The sectors are organized in concentric circles (called *tracks*) around the disk. A fixed disk drive (or hard disk) has one or more *platters*, with two heads on each. The combination of all the heads aligned on the same track is called a *cylinder*.

Figure 6-1 depicts this structure. The number of sectors on a track, tracks on a platter, and heads in a cylinder are all fundamental characteristics of a drive that are collectively referred to as the *disk geometry*. Removable disks

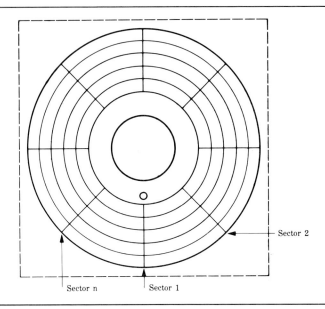

Figure 6-1a. Components of diskettes (a, b) and hard disks (c, d)

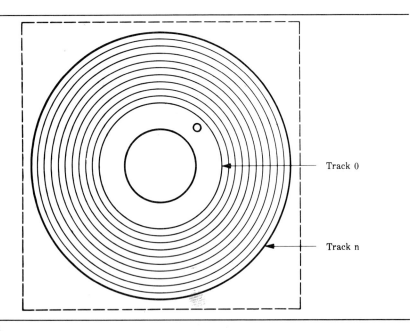

Figure 6-1b.

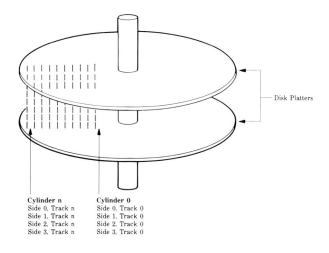

Figure 6-1c.

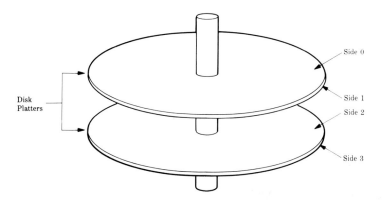

Figure 6-1d.

(diskettes) follow the same rules as fixed disks, except that removable disks have a maximum of two heads.

If an application program was required to understand these geometries for every possible disk on which it ran, it would be a very complex program indeed. The file system relieves the applications of this responsibility.

The file system ties together disk sectors in a "logical" fashion. For example, sectors 1, 2, and 3 might make up the payroll file, while sectors 7 and 9 make up a ledger file. The file system performs the resource management functions that ensure the resources (in this case, disk sectors) are properly allocated to programs, and that no two programs ever think they "own" the same sector at the same time.

Under most operating systems, application programs view disks as a collection of files, with each file containing a collection of data. The low-level structure of the disks (sectors, tracks, heads, and so forth) is never seen by application programs. This fundamental concept allows programs to be fully independent of the storage media. An application program does not care about the disk geometries. It works equally well with a 10MB or 30MB disk, with 2 or 4 heads, with 300 or 600 cylinders. This is an important concept because without this independence, constructing an application that would run on different machines would be virtually impossible.

Technically speaking, a file system is not really part of the system kernel. The functions it provides are higher-level logical operations that are independent of the kernel implementation. In OS/2 the file system is contained in the kernel.

The OS/2 file system is externally compatible with PC DOS, allowing full interchangeability of disks and diskettes between the two systems. The file system is sometimes referred to as the FAT system because of the primary data structures this system uses to keep track of available, used, and corrupted disk space—the *file allocation table* (FAT).

FILE SYSTEM MODEL

The OS/2 file system employs a hierarchical model, similar to that found in PC DOS and UNIX. Take a moment to review the characteristics of this type of file system.

The most basic user element is a *file*. Files are a logical view of a collection of sectors on a disk and are represented as a serial stream of characters. Files have ASCII names, structured as an eight-character name followed by a three-character extension. The *extension* is used to designate the type of data contained in the file (see Figure 6-2). For example, OS/2 uses the following extension types:

EXE	An executable file
CMD	A command file
OBJ	An object file (output of an assembler or compiler)

When displaying file names, separate the name and extension with a period. OS/2 provides services to create, read, write, and delete files.

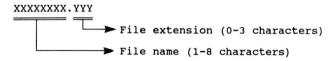

```
Name Format:

          XXXXXXXX.YYY

                          ──► File extension (0-3 characters)

                          ──► File name (1-8 characters)

      Examples:

          MYPROG.ASM
          ADMS.EXE
          TEST
```

Figure 6-2. File names

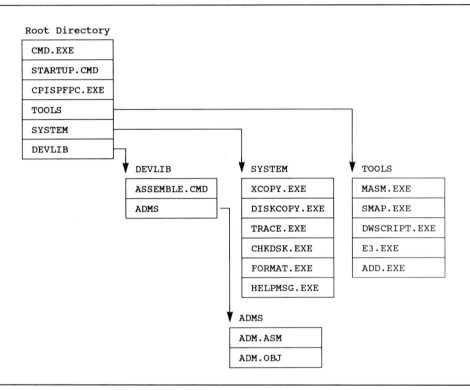

Figure 6-3.   Hierarchical directory structure

A collection of files is represented by a *directory*. Each disk contains at least one directory, called the *root directory*. A directory is nothing more than a special file, so directories may contain other directories. Looking at the hypothetical directory structure in Figure 6-3 you can see how directories are used to organize data.

The root directory in this example contains several programs and three subdirectories: one for development projects (DEVLIB), one for the system utilities (SYSTEM), and a third for development tools (TOOLS). Each subdirectory contains a group of files, and in the case of DEVLIB, contains lower-level subdirectories (ADMS).

Using these mechanisms, you may organize the contents of a disk into logical "groups" of files.

A file name is "path qualified" if the name includes its directory path. A backslash (\ ) is used to designate a directory name. For instance, the following are valid (path qualified) file names from the previous directory structure example:

```
CMD.EXE
STARTUP.CMD
DEVLIB\ADMS\ADM.OBJ
SYSTEM\FORMAT.EXE
TOOLS\E3.EXE
```

FILE MANIPULATION FUNCTIONS

OS/2 provides a number of API functions that allow programs to create, read, write, and destroy files, and to create and delete subdirectories. Table 6-1 lists the OS/2 file system API calls.

Creating and Deleting Files

A program gains access to a file by using the file system DosOpen function. The DosOpen request is the mechanism programs use to request permission to access files. Since files are named with an ASCII Z string, OS/2 programs must provide a file name when they perform a DosOpen operation. The name can be a simple file name or a fully qualified (by subdirectory) name.

The DosOpen request also contains an *option indicator*, which tells the system how to process the open request. Using this indicator, a program can tell what type

Table 6-1. File System Functions

File System API	Description
DosBufReset	Flush the OS/2 buffers
DosChDir	Change the current directory
DosChgFilePtr	Move the logical file pointer
DosClose	Close a file
DosDelete	Delete a file
DosDupHandle	Duplicate a file handle
DosFileLocks	Lock or unlock a range of bytes
DosFindClose	Close a directory search
DosFindFirst	Locate the first matching file
DosFindNext	Find the next matching file
DosMkDir	Create a new directory
DosMove	Move a file between directories
DosNewSize	Change the file size
DosOpen	Open or create a file
DosQCurDir	Query the current directory name
DosQCurDisk	Query the current disk
DosQFHandState	Query the file handle state
DosQFileInfo	Query file information
DosQFileMode	Query the file mode
DosQFsInfo	Query file system data
DosQVerify	Query the verify variable
DosRead	Read data from a file/device
DosReadAsync	Read data from a file/device asynchronously
DosRmDir	Remove a directory
DosSelectDisk	Select a disk
DosSetFileInfo	Change the file information
DosSetFileMode	Set the file mode
DosSetFsInfo	Set file system information
DosSetFHandState	Change the file state
DosSetMaxFH	Change the active file handle count
DosSetVerify	Set the verify setting
DosWrite	Write data to a file/device
DosWriteAsync	Write data to a file/device asynchronously

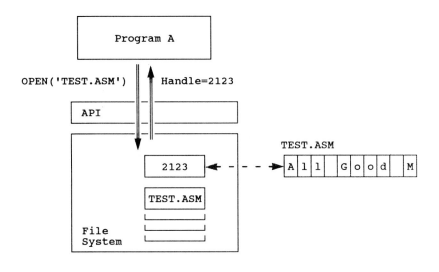

Figure 6-4. Opening a file

of access rights (ReadOnly, ReadWrite, and so forth) the program wishes to receive.

In Figure 6-4 Program A has requested the use of a file named TEST.ASM. The file system uses the name to locate and validate the file name in its internal data structures.

Since the file already exists, the file system creates a file identifier (2123) and passes it back to the application program. This identifier is called a *file handle* and is the basis for all future references to the file. If the file did not exist, the DosOpen request would be rejected or the file would be created (depending on the DosOpen options).

Once a file has been opened, a program must use the file handle for each I/O request. As you might expect, programs may open many files at the same time, so the file handles are used to associate an application request (read, write, delete, and so forth) with the appropriate open file.

Reading and Writing Data

Files are represented as a serial character stream. The next location in the stream to be read or written is determined by a special pointer called the *logical file pointer.* The logical file pointer is implicitly moved on each Dos-Read and DosWrite request, or can be unconditionally set with the file system DosChgFilePtr function. When a program first opens a file, OS/2 sets the file pointer to the first character in the file (see Figure 6-5).

Continuing the example with Program A, assume the program wants to read data from TEST.ASM. It does this by issuing a DosRead request to the file system. DosRead requests require the following three pieces of information:

- A file handle to identify the file being read

- An application buffer to be used to receive the data

- The number of bytes to be transferred

Program A issues a DosRead request for five bytes into a buffer named BUF1, using file handle 2123. The system uses the file handle to locate TEST.ASM and transfers the first five bytes of the file into the buffer. Note that the transfer started at the beginning of the file because the logical file pointer is initially set to the start of the file.

Suppose the program wishes to read data from the end of the file (for example, from bytes 7-9). Program A can do this by first calling the DosChgFilePtr to set the file pointer to byte 7 and then calling DOS read to read three bytes. Note that the DosChgFilePtr function also requires the file handle to identify which logical file pointer is to be changed.

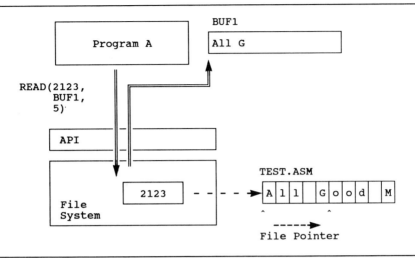

Figure 6-5.   Reading data from a file

This process is illustrated in Figure 6-6. As before, the DosRead operation transfers data from the file to the buffer. However, this time the application changed the starting point of the transfer before reading the data.

To write data to an open file, you use the DosWrite function. As with DosRead, the DosWrite calls require the following information:

- A file handle to identify the file being written

- An application buffer containing the data

- The number of bytes to be transferred

Suppose Program A now wishes to add several bytes to the file. The file pointer is still at the end of the file (from the last read operation in the previous example). So you can issue a DosWrite request using a file handle (2123), a length (5), and a pointer to the data buffer (BUF2). As with the DosRead, the system uses the file handle to locate TEST.ASM. It then transfers the first five bytes of BUF2

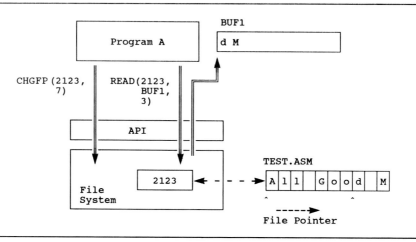

Figure 6-6.   Reading random data from a file

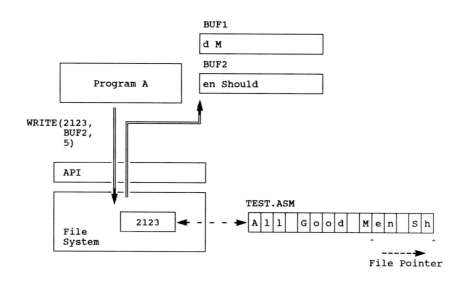

Figure 6-7.   Writing data to a file

into the file, starting at the current file pointer. Since the file pointer was at the end of the file, the data is actually appended to the existing file (see Figure 6-7).

By using the DosChgFilePtr function, programs may write data to random of files.

Creating and Deleting Directories

Just as a program is able to create files, it may also create subdirectories. Remember that a subdirectory is nothing more than a special type of file containing links to other files. OS/2 provides the Dos MK Dir and Dos RM Dir function calls to create and destroy subdirectories.

IMPLEMENTATION

Now consider how the system works to make these functions possible.

At the highest level, application programs manipulate disk data in a logical fashion by using files and subdirectories. Programs use DosOpen to open files, and then DosRead or DosWrite to read or write data as required. Each file is associated with data on the disk. The file system maintains a table, called a file allocation table (FAT), that links the sectors comprising a file together to form a chain. Each sector on the chain contains a small portion of the file. As programs read or write data, the file system uses the FAT to determine which sector contains the data to be read or written.

Like applications, the file system is also independent of the specific file geometries (see Figure 6-8). The file system does this by dealing with the disk as a series of logical sectors, numbered 1 to n, where n is determined by the disk geometry, as follows:

$$\text{Total sectors }(n) = \text{(sectors/track)}*\text{(total tracks)}*\text{(number of heads)}$$

The file system requests logical sector numbers from the disk device driver. Remember that the device drivers are responsible for shielding the kernel from device specifics. In this case, the disk device driver converts logical sector numbers to head/track/sector requests understood

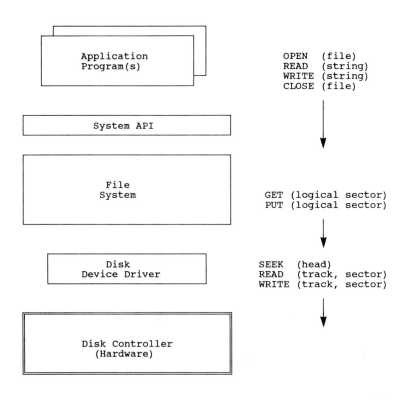

Figure 6-8. File system management of disk space

by the hardware. Thus, the file system is not required to understand just how the disk is organized, but only that it contains a certain storage capacity.

PC DOS disks are restricted to 32MB because the logical sector count is kept in a word (2 bytes). This means the maximum disk size is

(65536 sectors)*(512 bytes/sector) = 32767KB (or 32MB)

The OS/2 1.0 file system also has this limitation.

FILE SHARING

OS/2 is a multitasking operating system where multiple programs execute concurrently. Since any program can issue file system calls, it is possible that two programs may try to access the same file at the same time. In some cases this is tolerable (such as when printing a file), while in other cases this is disastrous (such as when updating a data base). OS/2 provides a full range of facilities that programs can use to control the access of files.

File Access Control

OS/2 requires that programs open files before the file can be accessed. The DosOpen function carries information about how the program intends to use the file (access mode) and how other programs are allowed to use the file (sharing mode). Table 6-2 lists the access and sharing modes supported by OS/2.

The first process to open the file defines how subsequent processes can use the file. In this way, a process can block out activity that might cause problems, but allow other activities to continue.

Table 6-2.   Access and Sharing Modes

Access Modes

READ_ONLY	Only Read requests are permitted
WRITE_ONLY	Only Write requests will be permitted
READ_WRITE	All Requests are permitted (Default)

Sharing Modes

DENY_ALL	All Subsequent OPEN requests are rejected
DENY_READ	Read requests rejected
DENY_WRITE	Write requests rejected
DENY_NONE	All Subsequent OPEN requests are honored

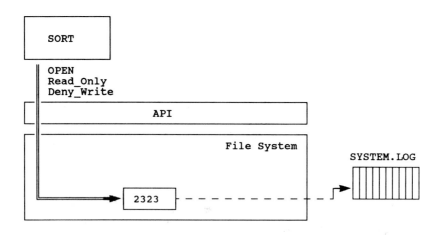

Figure 6-9.   File sharing (SORT)

Consider an example demonstrating the use of sharing modes. A file named SYSTEM.LOG is shared among multiple programs in the system. A program named SORT is started to sort the output of the file by date, and copy it to another file. Since SORT does not intend to update the file, it specifies a READ—ONLY access mode. SORT is not concerned about other programs reading the data, but does care that no other program modify the file. Thus, SORT specifies a DENY—WRITE sharing mode (see Figure 6-9).

While SORT is executing, a second program named PRINTIT is started (see Figure 6-10). It also opens SYSTEM.LOG with a READ—ONLY access code. PRINTIT is not concerned about other programs changing the file, so it specifies a DENY—NONE sharing mode. Since PRINTIT declared it would only read the file, the file system honors the access request and grants access to the file. At this point, two programs have read-only handles to the file SYSTEM.LOG.

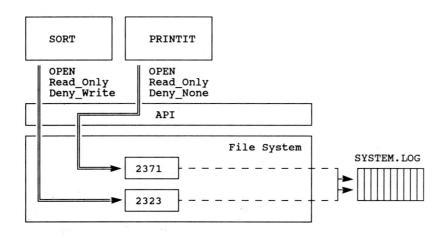

Figure 6-10. File sharing between SORT and PRINTIT

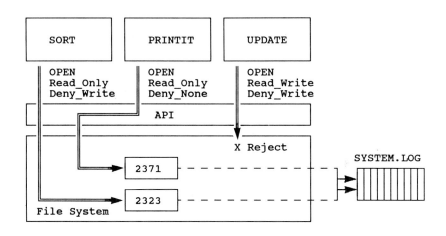

Figure 6-11.   File sharing between SORT, PRINTIT, and UPDATE

A third program named UPDATE is started (see Figure 6-11). Since UPDATE will change the contents of SYSTEM.LOG, it requests the file with READ—WRITE access. UPDATE also wants to be sure that no other program will interfere, so it requests DENY—ALL sharing mode. Unfortunately, SORT is already running and has indicated that no programs with write access be allowed to run. The file system detects this condition and rejects the DosOpen request from UPDATE.

These mechanisms give OS/2 programs control over file access rights. However, this is not sufficient in certain situations. Suppose a database management program has a large file that contains data. Using the file access mechanisms described here would mean that the data file would be opened and closed each time the data file were referenced. File access techniques *serialize* all file operations.

Serializing access to a large file requires programs to break up large accesses into small requests to avoid "locking out" the file for extended periods of time. Large numbers of small requests inevitably result in serious performance problems, since each request carries the system overhead of an DosOpen-DosWrite-DosClose (or DosOpen-DosRead-DosClose) sequence. Sharing large files with frequent access characteristics requires a fundamentally different access mechanism.

File Locking

File locking solves this dilemma by allowing processes to protect small portions of a file, while leaving the rest of the file accessible to other processes. An OS/2 file system call is provided to lock byte ranges of an open file. Remember that a file is represented as a serial character stream, so a byte range can be defined with an OFFSET and a LENGTH. While a process holds a file lock, other processes attempting to access the range are blocked until the first process releases the lock. This is done without having to close and open the file.

Consider an example in which processes A and B have opened a file named SYSTEM.LOG with READ—WRITE access mode. Both A and B want to read and write different portions of the file. To perform these tasks, SYSTEM.-LOG is broken up into multiple 80-byte records. The 80-byte value is arbitrary; any record length (fixed or variable) could be defined by A and B. In fact, OS/2 sees these records as simple byte ranges in the file.

File protection is implemented with a simple update strategy. Each process can get any record (for writing) by first locking the corresponding byte range, reading the data into memory, writing the data out, and then unlocking the range. If both processes collide on a record, the second simply waits until the first releases the record.

In this example, Process A wishes to update Record #2, so it starts by issuing a DosFileLocks call to lock the byte range 81-160. When the DosFileLocks request completes,

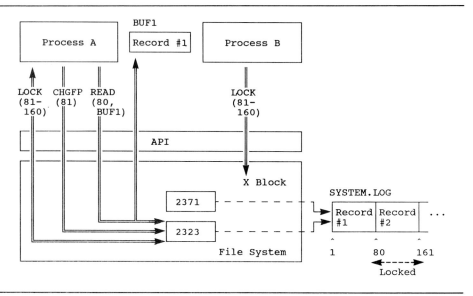

Figure 6-12.   Locking a record

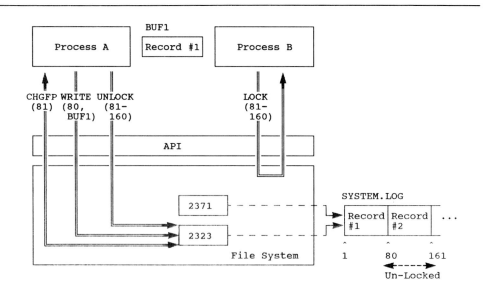

Figure 6-13.   Unlocking a record

Process A has exclusive ownership of the bytes associated with Record #2. Process A then positions the logical file pointer at the start of Record #2 (byte 81) using the file system Dos CHG FILE PTR function. Eighty bytes are then copied into BUF1 using the DosRead function. Process A now begins updating the data in the buffer. (See Figure 6-12.)

In the meantime, Process B wishes to update Record #2, so it starts by locking the byte range 81-160. This time the file system recognizes that the bytes are already locked by a different process (A), so the request is blocked. Process B is effectively suspended until bytes 81-160 are unlocked. Process A then finishes the update, repositions the logical file pointer to the start of Record #2 (byte 81), and writes the data back to the file.

When Process A unlocks the record, the byte range is once again available for other processes. Process B is no longer suspended and continues execution with sole ownership of Record #2. (See Figure 6-13.)

Notice that the order of these requests is critical. Byte ranges must be locked before the data is read because any process may be preempted by the OS/2 dispatcher. If a program is preempted after it reads the data (but before it locks it), another process may sneak in and update the record, thus invalidating the data in the buffer of the first program. Writing programs in a preemptive environment requires special care.

These OS/2 file-locking facilities allow programs to share large files in an organized, well-structured method.

VOLUME MANAGEMENT

In any multitasking system, special considerations must be made for removable disk media. Since the user can change diskettes at any time, two different programs could have opened the same file on two different diskettes.

Consider the following example. You have a data file named MYDATA that you wish to edit from disk (see Fig-

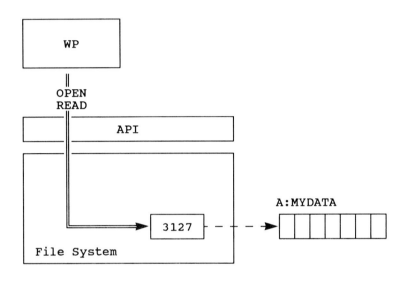

Figure 6-14. Removable media conflicts

ure 6-14). To do this you start a word processor (named WP) and give it the name of a data file. WP opens the file, reads your data, and displays it for modification. So far, this is no different than the previous examples. The fact that MYDATA is on a diskette is hidden from WP by the file system. At this point the file could be modified and written back to the diskette and the example would be complete.

However, assume that you had some question about the data in the file. To validate some information, you want to look at an older version of MYDATA stored on an older copy of the diskette.

Since OS/2 is a multitasking system, all you must do is start a second copy of WP, change diskettes, and edit the older version of MYDATA. Then you can switch the screen between the two copies of WP and see the differences in the files. This process may be simple, but it has a serious pitfall. What happens when you try to save your version of MYDATA? The file names are the same, but the contents

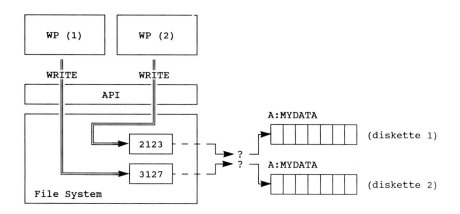

Figure 6-15. Removable media conflict between two files with same name

are different. What is contained in bytes 100-200 of one MYDATA is different from what is contained in bytes 100-200 of the second MYDATA. Yet, they are indistinguishable. They are both named MYDATA and were both loaded from drive A. If the wrong data is saved on the wrong diskette, the file could be destroyed. (See Figure 6-15.) Clearly there must be some mechanism to keep track of this information.

OS/2 provides the solution to this problem by introducing volume serial numbers. A *volume serial number* (or VOLSER) is a unique one-word value that is contained in the first sector of each diskette. This sector (called the *boot sector*) contains system information describing the diskette characteristics. All PC DOS and OS/2 diskettes have system data in this sector, even if the diskette is not usable as a boot disk.

OS/2 reads the VOLSER the first time you insert a diskette in the drive and every time the diskette is changed. OS/2 uses the VOLSER information to further qualify the names of the file. To OS/2, the file named

MYDATA from diskette 1234 is different from the file named MYDATA from diskette 4567. All open files are associated with their respective diskettes. Whenever the file system reads or writes data to a diskette, it verifies that the correct diskette is inserted in the drive. If the wrong diskette is inserted, OS/2 prompts the user to change diskettes. This is done automatically and with no intervention by the application program.

A VOLSER is always created when a diskette is formatted with the OS/2 FORMAT utility. The VOLSER value is generated by using the system clock. To prevent the inadvertent creation of multiple diskettes with the same VOLSER, the system DISKCOPY utility does not copy the VOLSER field from one disk to another. Likewise, the OS/2 DISKCOMP utility disregards the VOLSER field. (**Note:** If you use DISKCOPY to duplicate an OS/2 diskette under OS/2, and DISKCOMP to compare the two diskettes under PC DOS 3.2 or below, you will get a compare error at track 0, head 0.)

To help the user keep diskettes straight, OS/2 supports volume labeling. A *volume label* is an ASCII name for a disk or diskette. It is provided by the user at the time the disk or diskette is formatted, or later using the OS/2 LABEL utility. If a volume label is present, OS/2 remembers the name and uses it when prompting for the "correct diskette." You should label all OS/2 removable media (diskettes) at the time they are formatted.

Figure 6-16 illustrates the previous example with volume serial control. Each file is uniquely identified to the system by name and diskette. Each version of WP writes data to the appropriate version of MYDATA. If the wrong diskette is inserted, the system prompts the user to insert the correct diskette.

If a diskette does not have a VOLSER (such as a PC DOS diskette), OS/2 computes a value by running a checksum on the diskette's FAT. This value is then used as the diskette VOLSER. Thus, even old diskettes can participate in the file system volume-control mechanism.

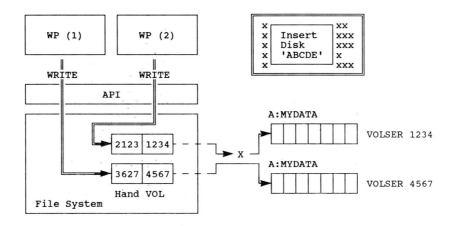

Figure 6-16.   Volume serial numbers

SECTOR BUFFERING

A critical aspect of any file system is how well it performs. All application file I/O is done through the file system, so small performance enhancements are magnified many times. Relative to the speed of a computer, file operations are slow. Reading a sector from a disk is 100-200 times slower than copying the same amount of data from memory. A typical disk access on a PC is in the range of 40-80 milliseconds, depending on the location of the sector on the disk, the location of the read/write heads, and the speed of the disk. A memory-to-memory move of 512 bytes takes approximately 0.4 milliseconds on an 8-MHz machine.

A common performance strategy is to replace slow disk accesses with fast memory-to-memory copies. By keeping a memory pool of disk sectors, a file system can "remember" the contents of the file. As sectors are written out to disk,

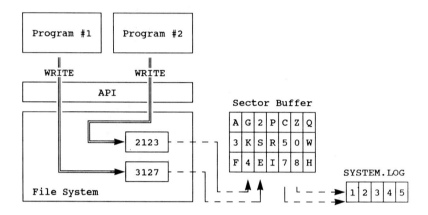

Figure 6-17.   Sector buffering

the memory copy is modified first. When a program requests the file system to read data, the memory pool is first examined. Read requests for sectors in the pool are satisfied without actually going back to the disk. The data is simply copied from the system memory to the application buffer. This technique, called *sector buffering,* is illustrated in Figure 6-17.

On each file operation, the file system first looks in the sector buffer pool to determine if it can directly service the request. Consider the previous example with SORT and PRINTIT. Both programs are reading the file SYSTEM.LOG. The file is comprised of six disk sectors, five of which are in the sector buffer pool (2-6). When either of the programs reads the part of the file associated with the sectors in the buffer pool, the file system simply copies the data and does not perform disk operations.

The total size of the memory buffer pool is usually much smaller than the total size of the disk device, so sectors are periodically "thrown out." Usage counts are maintained for each sector and an LRU algorithm determines which buffers should be re-used. In general, the most frequently used data tends to stay in memory, while randomly accessed segments are directly read in from the disk.

The OS/2 file system provides this sector buffering mechanism for all application I/O operations. The size of the buffer pool is defined by the user with the BUFFERS= configuration command. You can set aside up to 49.5K (99 sectors) of the system memory for this use.

DISK PARTITIONS

The OS/2 1.0 file system supports a maximum of 65,536 logical disk sectors, resulting in a 32MB hard-disk file limitation. Large hard files (greater than 32MB) are supported as multiple "logical" devices. The technique used in OS/2, called *disk partitioning*, is the same as that used in PC DOS 3.3.

Disk partitioning is a very simple concept. It is implemented primarily in the disk device driver.

Each physical disk is broken into one or more areas. These areas, called *partitions*, are defined by using the system FDISK utility. The various disk partitions are treated as separate volumes. The file system refers to each partition with a different drive identifier as if it were a different disk. As might be expected, each partition is limited to 32MB.

Figure 6-18 illustrates a system with a partitioned hard disk. An application program has requested the file system to read data from a file on drive E. The file system processes the request and, by looking in an internal device table, determines that drive E corresponds to device 2

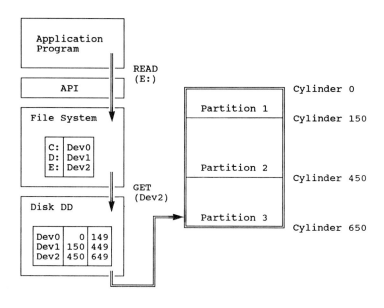

Figure 6-18. Disk partitioning

(DEV2). At this point, the device could be either a separate disk or a partition, and the file system does not know which. The request to read data from DEV2 is sent to the disk device driver (DISK DD). This DISK DD understands that DEV2 is located in cylinders 450-649 on the real device. The file system's request is adjusted by the start of the disk partition and it is then sent to the hardware.

This type of disk partitioning scheme allows OS/2 to support hard disks up to 768MB in size, or 24 drive designations (letters C thru Z) with 32MB per partition. This assumes no other drive letters were used for pseudo-devices (such as VDISK, Network, and so forth).

DEVICE I/O SERVICES

A computer's I/O devices are not limited to disks. In fact, today's personal computers allow a variety of attachment devices, from the most common (such as printers and modems) to the more exotic (such as digital-to-analog converters, voice synthesis, voice recognition, and so forth). Since OS/2 applications cannot directly access the hardware, how are these devices supported? The answer lies in the file I/O model discussed in the previous section. As with other existing operating systems (such as PC DOS or UNIX), OS/2 uses the file model to manage application device access.

OS/2 supports system devices with a stream-oriented I/O model. In most cases, devices look just like files. OS/2 devices are uniquely identified with ASCII names. The following is a list of the names of the devices that are part of every OS/2 system:

COM1-COM3	Serial ports
CLOCK$	System clock
CON	Console
SCREEN$	Screen driver
KBD$	Keyboard
LPT1-LPT3	Parallel (printer) ports
NUL	Null device
POINTER$	Pointer draw (Mouse) device

(**Note:** Devices whose names end with "$" are not directly accessible by application programs.)

Using the device name, an application program may issue to the system a DosOpen request to gain access to the device (see Figure 6-19). DosOpen requests for devices are conceptually similar to DosOpen requests for files. When an application passes a DosOpen request to the system, the system compares it to the list of system device names.

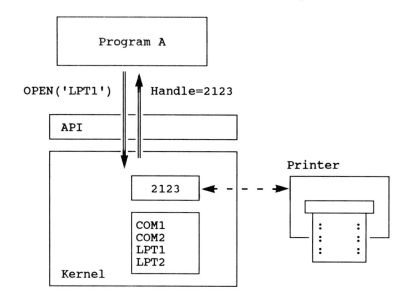

Figure 6-19. Opening a device

If a match is found, the device is opened. Otherwise the request is treated as a file open. In either case, an identifier is generated and returned to the application, which is then used for subsequent I/O operations. In the case of devices, this identifier is called a *device handle*.

Device handles are used with DosRead and DosWrite requests to pass data to and receive data from devices. The major difference between files and devices is that all device output and input must be processed in a serial fashion. That is, the DosChgFilePtr function cannot be used to write or read data randomly from a device as it is from a file. As with file handles, a child process may inherit device handles that were obtained by its parent.

Aside from the basic devices supported by OS/2, you may add additional devices with installable device drivers. Chapter 8 examines how device drivers work.

INPUT/OUTPUT REDIRECTION

When each OS/2 process is started, the system provides it with a special set of device handles. These handles are already in an open state. They can be used directly with the DosRead and DosWrite system calls. They are specially designated for the following tasks:

0000   Standard input (STDIN)   Reading from this handle gives you the input character stream. It is typically set as a console (CON) device handle, with the input coming from the keyboard

0001   Standard Output (STDOUT)   Output to be presented to the user should be written to this handle. It is typically set as a console (CON) device handle, with the output directed to the screen

0002   Standard Error (STDERR)   Error information to be presented to the user should be written to this handle. It is typically set as a console (CON) device handle, with the output directed to the screen

Programs that exclusively use these handles for their device I/O operations are called *standard I/O* programs. Standard I/O programs have a significant advantage over other programs in that their input and output is fully redirectable. Since these programs read from STDIN and write to STDOUT, their input could be received from a different source and their output could be sent to a different target. By simply replacing the STDOUT handle with an open file handle, the output of a program normally destined for a screen could be fed into a disk file. Similarly, the input which would normally come from the keyboard could also come from a file. This redirection is transparent to the program because the device and file I/O models are identical—a file handle is indistinguishable to an application from a device handle.

Consider the example in Figure 6-20. COMPUTE is a program that reads data from STDIN and writes it out to STDOUT. It normally takes input from an operator at the

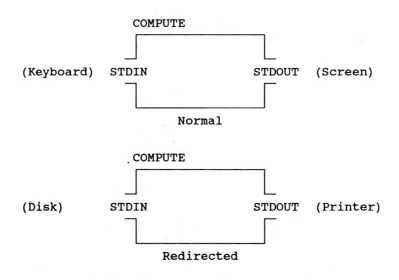

Figure 6-20.   Redirection to files and devices

computer, performs a series of computations, and writes the results to the screen. With redirection, however, the program might operate in a totally different way.

If you replace the STDIN handle with a file handle and the STDOUT with an open printer handle, COMPUTE takes its input from a file and prints the results on the printer attached to the LPT1 port. Any other combination of devices and files could also be substituted.

Perhaps the greatest strength of redirection, however, is when you substitute a pipe handle for STDIN or STDOUT. Remember that the OS/2 pipes also utilize the file I/O (character stream) model (see Figure 6-21). By redirecting output to a pipe, you can send the output of one program to the input stream of the next program. In this example, the output of COMPUTE is piped into a second program (SORT) that sorts the data before writing it to STDOUT.

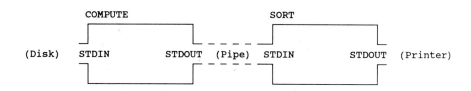

Figure 6-21. Redirection between programs

All OS/2 utilities receive their input from STDIN and write their output to STDOUT and STDERR. A common way to use the file redirection facilities is with the system command interpreter.

SUMMARY

The serial file model is an important notion on which the OS/2 I/O model is based. The file system gives you a set of interfaces you can use to build application programs that write to files and I/O devices in a device-independent way. You will be using the concepts discussed in this chapter in most OS/2 programs you write. Review this chapter when you begin writing OS/2 programs. Some of the more important points include the following:

- Disk geometries (sectors, tracks, and cylinders)
- The file model (file naming conventions and sub-directories)
- The file system API calls
- Creating and deleting files

- Reading and writing data
- File sharing and locking
- Volume management functions
- Sector buffering
- Disk partitions
- Device I/O services
- I/O redirection

CHAPTER 7
RESOURCE MANAGEMENT

A primary responsibility of all operating systems is the management of the machine's *resources*. The term "resources" collectively describes the hardware system. System I/O devices such as printers, keyboards, display monitors, disks, the system memory, numeric coprocessors, and the main processor (CPU) are examples of resources.

CONTROL VERSUS RESPONSIVENESS

To what extent resources are centrally controlled has wide-ranging implications. Control generally implies structure. Too much structure leads to rigidity and high system overhead. Not enough structure results in low system overhead with less overall reliability.

How much control is needed depends on the environment. A *multiple virtual system* (MVS) is a multi-user operating system that runs on IBM 370 series machines. In a large MVS system with thousands of users, control is a must because this type of system must be reliable and predictable.

The MVS disk files might be shared among tens of thousands of programs at a time. No single program may have exclusive control of any file. The same can be said about all other devices, including the CPU. MVS ensures that each program has a fair shot at each resource. To make this feasible, programs request all their services from MVS and never access a 370 resource directly. In most large systems, the operating system is the only means by which programs can access the machine resources.

At the other end of the spectrum are small, single-user, single-tasking systems, such as PC DOS. In this world, programs can do anything they wish, including directly manipulating the system hardware. Since at any time only one program is in the system, the state of the devices can be changed without the knowlege of the operating system. In fact, PC DOS can be viewed as an optional interface that gives programs the most crucial resource-management facilities (such as file management). A program may use all, some, or none of the PC DOS services. In this environment, control must be carefully weighed against overall system responsiveness.

OS/2 is somewhere in between. It is a single user environment with multitasking facilities. OS/2 differs from PC DOS in that it concurrently runs many programs. When more than one program is in a system some control function must decide how resources are to be shared. However, the machine is still a personal computer and system responsiveness is critical. In fact, responsiveness is what differentiates a personal computer from large multi-user systems (such as MVS).

To achieve this goal, OS/2 employs a variety of resource-management techniques. In some cases, these techniques are stringent; in others they are not. This chapter examines the various aspects of resource management implemented by OS/2.

RESOURCE MANAGEMENT AND THE API

OS/2 employs several simple resource-management strategies that:

- Provide a functionally rich API and provide the user with the ability to trade off between function and responsiveness by choosing the "right" API.

- Provide high-performance system services for functions traditionally implemented by direct hardware manipulation (such as the video and keyboard).

- If system services are not adequate, allow applications to request direct hardware access. Identify these "Direct-I/O" programs and give the end-user the option not to run them (through the use of a CONFIG.SYS option).

The 80286 protected mode allows OS/2 to enforce these strategies. In general, the system handles all functions that involve the PC resources. In special cases, an application program may directly manipulate I/O devices, but only after OS/2 grants permission to do so.

The amount of control imposed by OS/2 varies greatly from device to device. Visualize this concept in terms of layers (see Figure 7-1). The layers represent how much function the operating system provides in managing each resource. A thick layer implies a lot of operating system

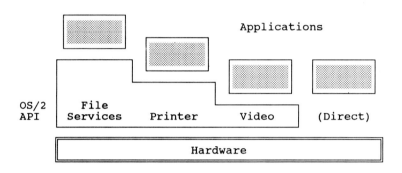

Figure 7-1. System APIs

function; a thin layer implies little or no function. In OS/2, some functions such as the video subsystem are thin, while others such as the file system are not. In the case of I/O privileged applications, no layer exists, so in controlled circumstances the application programs are able to directly interact with the noninterrupt-driven devices.

DEVICE MANAGEMENT

OS/2 uses the file model for supporting devices. Each device installed in the system is accessed through a device driver. In fact, from a software standpoint, a device is not "installed" in the system until a device driver has been added to the system configuration. Device drivers provide the software interface for I/O devices.

Each I/O device has unique sharing characteristics and rules governing the use of the device. The device driver is responsible for understanding these sharing rules and enforcing them. The device driver screens the device OPEN requests and tells the OS/2 kernel which to honor and which to reject. Criteria used for this decision include the number of programs that have opened the device and the specific characteristics of that particular device. By rejecting OPEN requests, device drivers limit the number of users of the device.

For example, consider two devices: a printer (LPT1:) and a serial port (COM1:). In the case of printer I/O, two different programs may have access to the printer. Since print data streams can be lengthy, serializing all accesses to the printer does not make sense. As illustrated in Figure 7-2, the printer device driver accepts multiple OPEN requests from different processes by using the PID provided in the requests to separate the output into different data streams. Note that although the kernel generates the device handles for Programs A and B, the device driver decides whether the OPEN requests are to be accepted.

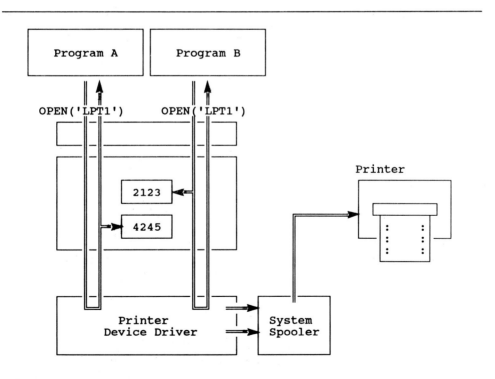

Figure 7-2. Shared access device

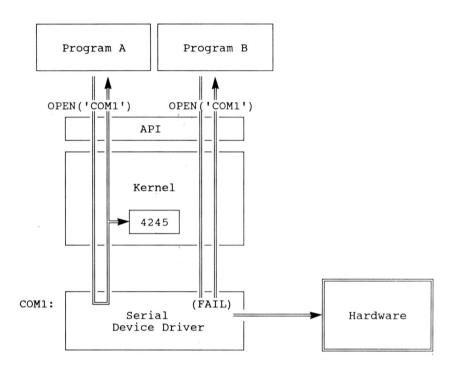

Figure 7-3. Exclusive access device

In the case of the COM1: device, the application program may be engaged in a conversation (over an asynchronous communications line) with another program running on a different machine. Allowing other applications to open (and use) the communications port while this conversation is in progress does not make sense. Thus, the COM1: device is logically dedicated to the first program that opened it. The COM1: device remains allocated to that program until the connection is terminated and the device is closed. Therefore, multiple OPEN requests to the COM1: device cannot be honored.

The COM1: device driver remembers which PID opened the device and rejects subsequent OPEN requests from other processes until the first process sends a CLOSE request. Therefore, the serial device driver implements exclusive-use access authorization (see Figure 7-3). When one application is accessing the device driver, all others are excluded from it.

In general, the OS/2 kernel delegates device access authorization to the individual device drivers.

FILE SYSTEM

The file system is another system component that participates in system resource management. The file system implements the following two levels of resource management:

- General name and access management
- Block device (disk, diskette) allocation and control

The general name and access controls are provided for all devices and files. For block devices, the file system performs the logical suballocation of media. Figure 7-4 illustrates the relationship between the file system, device drivers, and application programs.

Name Space Management

All OS/2 devices and files have ASCII names. File directories are logical tables which are maintained by the file system. No two files in the same directory can have the same name. The file system processes OPEN requests and ensures that duplicate entries are never created. Similarly, all system devices have unique names. The file system does

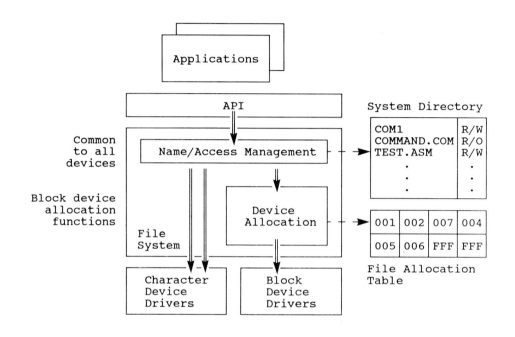

Figure 7-4.   File system resource management

not permit application programs to create files with a name currently assigned to a device.

Access Authorization

Managing the names themselves is a small part of file management. The file system also controls how different programs are allowed to access devices and files. OS/2 file-access authorization functions are implemented in the file system.

Two levels of file-access control are provided in OS/2: file attributes and sharing modes. Each file can be given a set of attributes (such as READ_WRITE or

READ—ONLY). Any program request to OPEN the file in a manner inconsistent with these attributes, is rejected. This mechanism allows the user to mark files so the files are less susceptible to accidental erasure.

The file system also permits programs to OPEN files in restricted modes. When a program opens a file, the program tells the file system which types of requests coming from other programs are to be honored. More selective, record-level access is also achievable by using the LOCK and UNLOCK functions of the file system.

Block Device Management

Applications are shielded from the disk characteristics (geometries) by the file system and the disk device driver. The file system creates a logical view of the media and presents applications with the concept of files and directories. Using these concepts, programs do not have to deal with the disks themselves.

The file system is responsible for mapping the files and directory structures to logical disk sectors (see Figure 7-5), as well as managing the logical devices. No two files may contain the same disk sector at the same time. The OS/2 file system accomplishes this by using a file allocation table (FAT). The FAT is nothing more than a large array with an entry for each allocation unit on the disk. *Allocation units* are a group of sectors (usually four) that are manipulated by the file system. Allocation units are used instead of logical sectors to minimize the size of the FAT. A four-sector allocation unit implies that all files on the disk occupy multiples of 2048 (4*512) bytes.

Each position in the FAT array corresponds to a disk location. An array element contains the index of the next element in the file. The last allocation unit in the file is designated by a special value (65535). You can locate the start of a file by looking in the directory entry for the file (where the starting FAT element is kept).

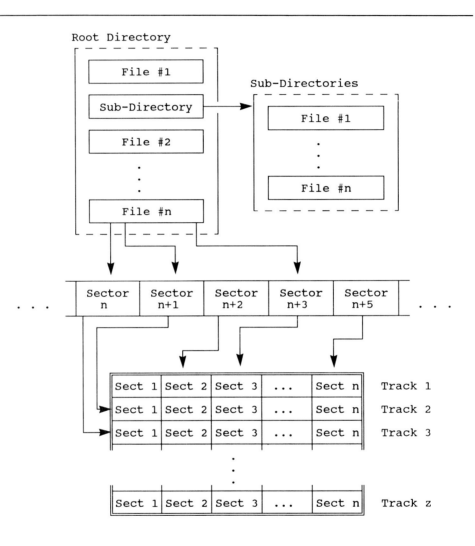

Figure 7-5.   DOS logical file model

Consider the example in Figure 7-6. A file named TEST.ASM is in the file directory. To locate all the data associated with this file, start with the first FAT element

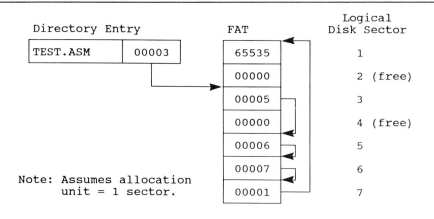

Figure 7-6. File allocation

indicated in the directory entry (00003). Find the next entry (00005) by looking at offset 3 in the FAT. Repeat this process until you reach the end of file marker (65535). This file is comprised of five allocation units: 3, 5, 6, 7, and 1 (in that order). Since, (in this example) an allocation unit is equal to one sector, the file can be read in from disk by requesting logical sectors 3-5-6-7-1 from the disk device driver. Also note that "free" segments are marked by null (0) entries in the FAT.

The OS/2 file system manages the content of the disk by ensuring that FAT elements are in only one file chain at a time.

PROCESSOR MANAGEMENT

An important resource often overlooked is the system processor (CPU). Unlike PC DOS, OS/2 is a multitasking operating system, which implies that it runs many differ-

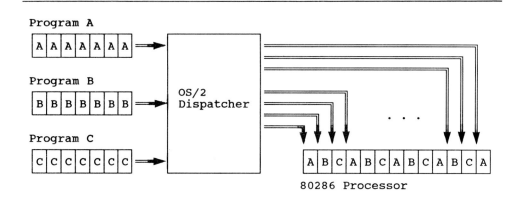

Figure 7-7. Sharing the 80286 time with time-slicing

ent programs at the same time. However, this is clearly impossible since there is only one CPU, and it is able to do only one thing at a time. The programs running in OS/2 must therefore share the processor (see Figure 7-7).

Time Slicing

OS/2 shares the processor time by running a *time-slicing dispatcher*. This dispatcher breaks up the total processor time into many small periods of time, giving each thread a "slice" of time in which to execute.

By rapidly time-slicing, OS/2 makes it appear as if threads are running concurrently when, in fact, they are executing serially (sequentially—one after the other). Time-slicing is a common technique employed by many operating systems to distribute the processor time fairly among many clients.

Each thread in the system has an execution priority. This priority is used by OS/2 to determine the next thread to receive the processor. Priorities are established by the application programs, depending on the urgency of their work. Programs that monitor external devices (such as a communications line or a robot) generally run at the higher priorities, while those programs performing "background" activities (such as a compiler) run at the lower priorities.

Preemptive Dispatching

If a single thread were to monopolize the machine, no other threads could execute. This can have disastrous effects if the thread that is denied the processor manages an external device (such as a communications line). So how does OS/2 ensure that threads do not run away with the processor?

The dispatcher actually "takes away" the processor at specified intervals, without intervention by an application program. In fact, from the program's perspective, it owns the processor. The program is not aware of the numerous interruptions received in the course of doing its work.

These periodic "preemptions" are triggered by the system clock. On each timer tick, the OS/2 dispatcher runs through the list of current threads and dispatches a different thread if the one currently using the processor has run for a complete time slice.

The timer interrupts cannot be disrupted in any way, since they are the triggering event for dispatch cycles. For this reason, OS/2 does not permit applications to disable interrupts. Normal application programs execute at a privilege level not authorized to disable interrupts (CLI instruction).

Programs can be constructed to directly manipulate the hardware using *I/O privileged segments* (IOPS). Since code executing in one of these segments is capable of disabling interrupts, the user is provided with a configuration option that tells OS/2 not to load applications containing IOPS. In certain scenarios when dispatcher integrity is critical (such as high-speed communications), the IOPL configuration option allows the user to run OS/2 in this restrictive mode.

MEMORY MANAGEMENT

The 80286 processor provides operating systems with a number of useful memory-management assists. OS/2 exploits these features to create a segmented *virtual memory* model. Physical memory is not directly manipulated by applications. Instead, the system gives applications access to virtual segments. OS/2 memory segments are "virtual" because the applications are never aware of the real physical location of the segments. This notion enables OS/2 to manage the physical memory space.

As application programs request memory, OS/2 creates descriptor entries representing the segments. While they are free to use the selectors provided to them, programs do not have direct access to the system descriptor tables (GDT or LDT). The system data structures are accessible only by the kernel code running at PL0. The kernel manipulates the descriptor tables, as required to satisfy the application memory-management requests. OS/2 is responsible for ensuring that physical memory belongs to only one descriptor at a time, unless the application has indicated that a segment was to be shared.

OS/2 imposes stringent control over the system memory resources. Applications are isolated from one another and from the system through the use of the 80286 protected mode facilities.

INTERRUPT MANAGEMENT

A major difference between OS/2 and PC DOS is the latitude that applications are given in the area of interrupt processing. Under PC DOS, application programs may directly trap hardware interrupts. OS/2, on the other hand, allows only device-driver interrupt-service routines to receive interrupts. In a multitasking system, the processing of interrupts becomes a responsibility of the operating system and not of a user application (see Figure 7-8).

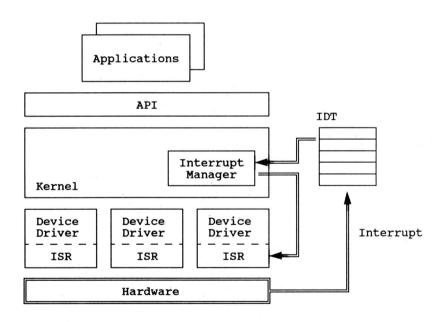

Figure 7-8. OS/2 interrupt management

Interrupts are processed by the kernel *first-level inter-rupt handler* (FLIH). Certain interrupts (such as timer ticks and processor faults) are directly handled by the kernel. Other interrupts belonging to I/O devices are first fielded by the kernel and then passed on to the appropiate device driver ISR.

Application programs do not have access to (nor are they provided with) system services to edit the Interrupt Descriptor Table (IDT). The IDT defines the code segments that are to be given control to process an interrupt. You will see how device drivers manage interrupts in Chapter 8.

SUMMARY

Resource management is an important function of all multitasking operating systems. Since multitasking systems run more than one program concurrently, the hardware must be shared in an effective and efficient manner.

OS/2 makes it possible for application programs to share the screen, keyboard, mouse, disks, printers, serial ports, and CPU in an organized way. The system grants access to the devices in either shared mode or exclusive-use mode, depending on the hardware characteristics. Special I/O code segments are also permitted to directly access the hardware in cases where no system overhead can be tolerated (such as graphics).

You should remember the following concepts relating to OS/2 resource management:

- The relationship of control and responsiveness

- The OS/2 resource-management strategy

- How device drivers implement device management

- Exclusive versus shared device access

- How the file system manages block devices
- Sharing the CPU through preemptive dispatching
- How the kernel manages memory
- Managing hardware interrupts

CHAPTER 8
DEVICE DRIVERS

Device drivers are OS/2 components that are responsible for isolating the kernel, subsystems, and applications from the system hardware. Each hardware device (such as a disk, keyboard, printer, and so forth) is associated with a device driver.

This "insulating" role is critical, for without it the OS/2 kernel would have to be customized for each new piece of hardware. This customization is not practical in the PC environment because the hardware usually is not developed in conjunction with the system software. In fact, the open architecture of many of today's computers dictates that the system software must be independent of the hardware on which it operates.

I/O operations originating from the kernel or from other programs are performed by device drivers. The device driver, therefore, is the single point of interface for the device it supports. An exception to this rule is non-interrupt-driven devices (such as some display adapters) that can be directly accessed by programs with I/O privilege.

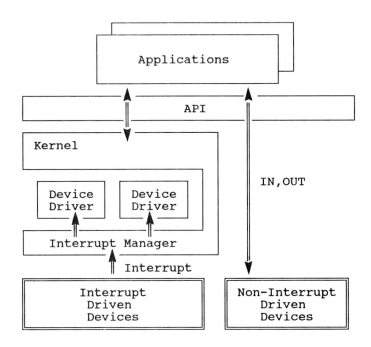

Figure 8-1.   OS/2 I/O flows

All devices that generate interrupts must be supported by a device driver. As shown in Figure 8-1, the OS/2 kernel receives hardware interrupts and passes them to the appropriate device drivers. Aside from the kernel, device drivers are the only code in the system that OS/2 authorizes to handle interrupts.

View device drivers as logical representations of I/O devices. The device drivers give the hardware device names (for example, LPT1: or COM1:) that are used by programs to request I/O operations.

A device driver is an authorized OS/2 program. It runs at the same execution privilege level as the kernel (PL0), with I/O privilege always enabled. It actually executes in the kernel context, so it cannot access the OS/2 API. Instead, it receives services through a special set of kernel interfaces called *device helper routines* (DevHlp). In general, a device driver is more like the kernel than an application program.

This chapter discusses the role that device drivers play in an OS/2 system. The chapter examines the basic architecture of these programs and how the programs interact with the kernel and the hardware to do their jobs.

DEVICE TYPES

The OS/2 device driver architecture defines two types of devices: character devices and block devices. Both are accommodated by the OS/2 device driver model.

From the standpoint of the application, the two device types are very different. Application programs directly interact with the character devices by reading and writing data as if the device were a file. A block device, on the other hand, is typically "hidden" from the application. A logical device manager (such as the OS/2 file system) normally issues the block I/O requests on behalf of the application.

Character Device Drivers

Character device drivers support *stream-oriented devices*. A stream-oriented device expects data in a particular sequence. The printer (LPT), serial port (COM), and keyboard (KBD) are examples of stream-oriented devices.

The information passed between a character device and a program is sometimes referred to as a *data stream*. The data stream is understood by the program and the device. OS/2 routes data streams between programs and devices.

A fundamental attribute of character devices is that I/O is performed in a serial fashion. This means that the application program must read all the bytes in the order they were sent by the device. No random I/O is permitted, as it is with disks and diskettes.

The OS/2 API permits applications to issue multiple-character I/O requests to character devices. For instance, an application may write a 100-byte block to the printer device by issuing a single DOSWRITE call. Since most character devices accept only one character at a time, the device driver is responsible for queuing the characters and passing them to the device as the device becomes ready to accept more data.

Character stream I/O is performed directly by the device driver one character at a time. Block moves are not typically supported by these types of devices. Character device drivers often use OUT instructions to move the data directly into the device while running under the control of the main processor. This type of I/O is referred to as *program I/O* (PIO).

Character device drivers assign ASCII names (up to eight characters in length) to the devices. During system initialization, the OS/2 file system adds the device names to its internal directory and makes them available to the OS/2 applications. When an application wishes to access a device, it requests permission from the file system by way of the DosOpen function, using the device name to identify the appropriate device driver. The file system then establishes a path between the program and the device driver. As the application reads data (using DosRead) or writes data (using DosWrite), the file system passes the requests to the device driver.

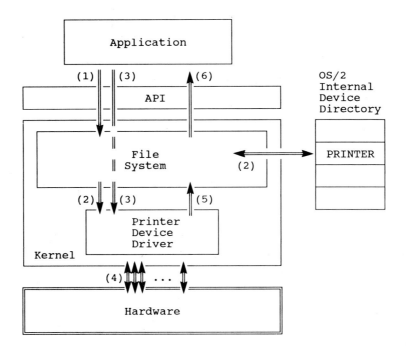

Figure 8-2. Character device operation

Consider an example of how a typical OS/2 character device driver works. Figure 8-2 illustrates a system with a single character device driver. The device driver (PRINTER) manages a printer adapter. At the time the system is initialized, OS/2 loads the device driver and places an entry containing the device name (PRINTER) in the name space of the file system. Some time later, an application program is started that uses the printer device. It uses the following sequence to write output to the device.

1. The application requests access to the device named PRINTER by using a DosOpen call.

2. The file system verifies the device name in its name table and asks the device driver for access authorization.

3. The application issues a multiple-byte DosWrite request to the device.

4. The character device driver accepts the request and begins transferring the information to the device. The device driver handshakes with the device numerous times until the entire data stream is transferred.

5. The device driver notifies the file system that the DosWrite request for the application is successfully completed.

6. The file system returns a successful completion code to the application program.

The most important aspect of character devices is that their input and output character data streams are processed serially. Because of this, the order of the characters in the data stream is critical. OS/2 presents the data stream to the device driver in the same order it was sent by the application. Conversely, it is presented to the application in the same order it was received from the device. Because of the serial nature of these devices, the character device model does not support random-access I/O.

Block Device Drivers

Block devices (such as disks, diskettes, virtual disks, and CD ROMs) are very different from character devices. A block device normally holds a large volume of data that is accessed in a random order. In contrast to character device data streams, block devices pass data in blocks. In most cases, the data blocks are hidden from the application by another system component, which in the case of

OS/2 is the file system. An application program reading or writing data to a disk, therefore, is not aware of the blocks being transferred to complete the program's file I/O request.

To OS/2 applications, block I/O operations are represented as serial device I/O. That is, an application sees a file as a serial data stream, similar to the way it sees a device. This simplification facilitates the redirection of file and device I/O. However, if the application understands that it is really dealing with a file and not a device, the application can perform random operations by using the DOSCHGFILEPTR function to move the logical file pointer. In any case, the file system maps the serial I/O requests to random block device requests.

Block device data is represented as discrete packets that may be retrieved in any order. Thus, block device drivers are free to service the I/O requests in an arbitrary order.

For example, consider a disk driver that examines the requests in its work queue and optimizes the work in terms of the disk geometries. If the device queue looks like Figure 8-3, the disk driver could avoid jumping from one

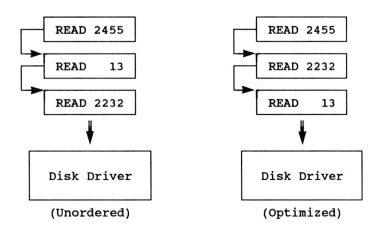

Figure 8-3. Ordering request packets

end of the disk to the other by simply reorganizing the requests as shown. It is the responsibility of the requesting program to keep the data ordered. In this case, the OS/2 file system maintains the order of the data for its applications.

The OS/2 block devices are named by a *unit drive identifier*. The first block device is named A:, the second B:, and so on. Block device drivers cannot assign ASCII names to their devices.

Applications do not directly open block devices. Instead they deal with the logical representation of the device (files, directories, and so forth) created by the file system.

Since block devices generally move a considerable amount of data, they often use the hardware to move the data directly into the application's buffer. This hardware is a special device called a *dynamic memory access (DMA) controller*. A DMA controller is a dedicated CPU that moves data between devices and memory. A DMA controller does this work on behalf of the main CPU (80286/80386). Unlike the PIO normally used with character devices, DMA transfers are much more efficient because they leave the main processor for more important tasks (such as running other application programs).

Consider the example in Figure 8-4. A disk device driver is installed in the system. At the time it is loaded, OS/2 assigns this device logical device identifier F:. An application can now read data from the disk, as follows:

1. The application requests access to the file F:TEST.ASM is accessed with the file system DosOpen request. The file system validates the name and returns a file handle.

2. The program issues a DosRead for the first 512 bytes of TEST.ASM.

3. The file system processes the request and, on the basis of its internal information, determines that the requested data is in a logical sector on device F:. The file system builds a request for the sector and passes the request to the specific block device driver.

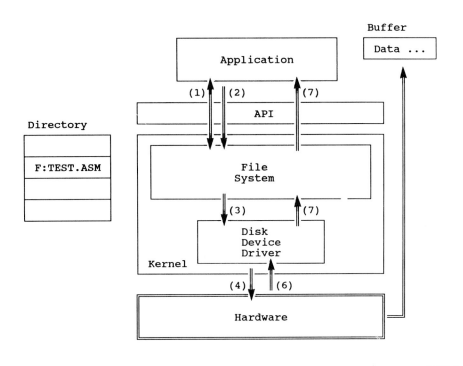

Figure 8-4.　Block device operation

4. The block driver determines the precise location of the logical sector (track, head, and so forth) and sends the request to the hardware.

5. The hardware moves the requested sector directly into the application data buffer. (**Note:** Had the request been for something less than a complete sector of 512 bytes, OS/2 would have instructed the hardware to move the data into a system buffer and subsequently to copy a portion of the sector into the application buffer.)

6. The hardware "wakes up" the device driver by generating a device interrupt.

7. The disk driver notifies the file system, which in turn notifies the application that the I/O request is complete and the data is in the buffer.

THE DEVICE DRIVER MODEL

OS/2 device drivers have the specific role of providing the kernel with a standard interface to the system I/O devices. Unlike application programs, OS/2 device drivers have a mandatory structure with well-defined subcomponents and interfaces. The set of rules defining how a device driver is constructed is called the *device driver model*. Device drivers must adhere to this model to ensure the proper operation of OS/2.

Overlapped I/O

The OS/2 device driver model is different from the PC DOS model because OS/2 device drivers run in a multitasking environment. Multitasking implies that system events are occurring concurrently. Multitasking systems start I/O operations and run other programs while the (relatively slow) device is performing its operations. This concept, called *overlapped I/O*, is implemented in OS/2 with the cooperation of the device drivers.

Figure 8-5 illustrates how overlapped I/O works. It all starts when a program asks OS/2 for data from a file. The file system processes the DosRead call and sends a sector READ request to the disk device driver. The disk driver then starts the hardware operation. At this point, however, nothing remains for the device driver to do. Disk operations are slow, especially compared to the speed of the CPU. In order to make the best use of this time, the disk driver requests that the dispatcher block the application thread waiting for the I/O to complete. Simply put, the

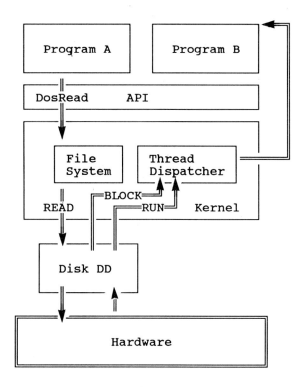

Figure 8-5. Overlapped I/O

thread is put to sleep until the disk work is completed.

In the meantime, OS/2 can run other programs. In fact, the dispatcher can relinquish control to any other program in the system that is ready to be run. Later when the disk operation completes, the hardware issues an interrupt. The interrupt is routed to the disk driver, which then runs the application thread. The disk I/O operation is thus overlapped with the execution of other programs.

Note that from the perspective of the application, the I/O is synchronous. The application does not realize that the device driver yields the CPU for other programs to execute while the hardware retrieves the data.

This notion of blocked application threads is introduced because of the multitasking nature of OS/2. Most PC DOS device drivers "hang around" while waiting for the I/O operation to complete. This may be acceptable in a single-tasking environment, but it is disastrous in a multitasking environment. If a device driver were to do this in OS/2, the overall performance of the system would be adversely affected.

OS/2 provides device drivers with DEVHLP routines to block and run threads.

Device Driver Components

A device driver has three major components: an initialization routine, a strategy routine, and an interrupt routine. All device drivers share this basic structure, which is illustrated in Figure 8-6.

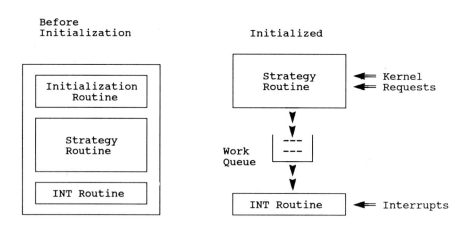

Figure 8-6. OS/2 device driver components

Initialization Routine

The device driver initialization routine is run when the device driver is first loaded. This routine initializes the device and establishes any data structures needed by the device driver when the system is running. This routine runs only once. When it finishes, it may delete itself and any initialization data it used during initialization.

The device driver initialization routine runs as a system thread in protected mode with I/O privilege. Compared to the other parts of the device driver, the initialization routine is more like an application. It is the only device driver component that can issue OS/2 API calls, even though they are a limited set of calls. (See Table 8-1)

At initialization time, the device driver has access to multiple data segments. These extra segments come in the executable file and may hold data used only at initialization (such as user messages). However, all but one code and one data segment are freed by OS/2 when the initialization routine completes.

This routine is a mandatory part of each device driver. When it finishes initializing the device, it returns a status code to the kernel that indicates whether or not the device was successfully initialized. OS/2 allows application programs to access only those devices successfully initialized.

Table 8-1. *OS/2 API Calls Available at Initialization Time*

OS/2 Services		
DosBeep	DosFindNext	DosFindNext
DosCaseMap	DosGetCtryInfo	DosQCurDir
DosChgFilePtr	DosGetDBCSEv	DosQFileInfo
DosDelete	DosGetEnv	DosQFileMode
DosDevConfig	DosGetMessage	DosRead
DosFindClose	DosOpen	DosWrite
DosFindFirst	DosPutMessage	

Strategy Routine

The strategy routine is the part of the device driver that receives I/O requests from the kernel. The strategy routine roughly corresponds to the "top half" of the device driver. The kernel always passes I/O requests in request packets. Later, this chapter discusses the types of packets the strategy routine can expect to receive.

The strategy routine interprets the kernel request packets and starts the I/O operation. In the case of queued I/O devices, the strategy routine may sometimes add the request packet to the device work queue if the device is already servicing a previous I/O request.

A strategy routine always runs in the context of the thread that initiated the I/O, acting as an "I/O subroutine." This means that these routines always have access to the address space of the thread (LDT). The application data buffers are addressed through an LDT descriptor. Visualize this as though each thread that is using the device driver actually gets a "logical" copy of the strategy routine. This copy runs under the thread to start the

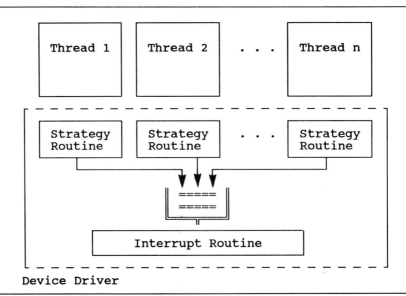

Figure 8-7. Strategy routine contexts

requested I/O activities. Figure 8-7 illustrates how multiple instances of the strategy routine run under the threads and add the request packets to a single device driver work queue.

In some cases, the strategy routine is responsible for converting the request packet's logical addresses (buffer pointers) to physical addresses that can later be used by the interrupt routine. This is an important concept because the interrupt routine may have to access the buffers later while the dispatcher is running a different thread (for example, when a device interrupt is received). This logical-to-physical address conversion is accomplished with a special DevHlp service routine.

READ/WRITE request packets already contain the buffer physical address. The OS/2 file system automatically performs the conversion on behalf of the device driver.

Strategy routines run at PL0 in kernel mode, and thus are not preemptable by an OS/2 task switch. However, they usually run with interrupts enabled, so they can be interrupted by any external (device) interrupt.

Interrupt Service Routine (ISR)

The device driver Interrupt Service Routine (ISR) is the only type of OS/2 program authorized to receive hardware interrupts. Each device driver can have an ISR to process the device interrupts.

One aspect that distinguishes this component is the environment in which it executes. Hardware interrupts are asynchronous events—they may come in at any time while the kernel is running any thread. This is significant for two reasons. First, the context of the system at the time of the interrupt is indeterminate. Second, the time spent executing in an ISR detracts from some other activity in the system. The ISR literally preempts all other programs (including the kernel itself).

When the interrupt routine is given control, it cannot make assumptions about memory addressability. It has access to the system address space (GDT), but not to any specific application address space (LDT). Interrupt routines must rely on kernel DevHlp routines to access application buffers. These services let the ISR convert the physical address of the application buffer to a GDT selection, which the ISR can then use to access the buffer. The device driver's own data segment is mapped through the GDT, so it is always present.

In a multitasking environment, code for interrupt processing logic is carefully written. In most cases, the ISR does only what is required to satisfy the device, deferring the bulk of the work until after the interrupt is dismissed.

Most systems have a special hardware device called an *interrupt controller*. This controller associates device interrupts with interrupt request levels (IRQ). Interrupts at a higher IRQ have priority over those at a lower IRQ. Until it is notified that an interrupt has been serviced, the controller does not allow lower-level interrupts to be processed. The ISR must operate in an expeditious manner while processing on the interrupt level. The longer it takes to dismiss the interrupt, the higher the probability that a lower-level interrupt will be lost.

In an Edge-Triggered interrupt environment (such as the PC/AT), the ISR's are entered with interrupts disabled. While in this state, all interrupts (from all levels) are masked. The ISR must quickly get the device to a state where it can re-enable interrupts. Spending too much time with all interrupts masked might cause other devices to fail.

The ISR receives its work from a device work queue (see Figure 8-7). The queue is anchored off the device driver data segment. Strategy routines chain request packets to the queue by using kernel DevHlp services. When the device is ready for more work, the interrupt routine retrieves the next request packet from the device queue.

Interrupt routines run at PL0 in kernel mode, and thus are not preemptable by OS/2 task switches. When interrupts are enabled, an ISR can be interrupted by another interrupt. OS/2 supports nested interrupts.

Device Driver

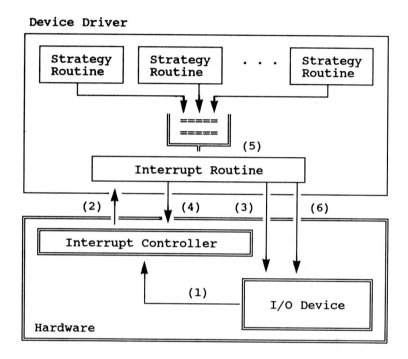

Figure 8-8. Device driver interrupt processing

Figure 8-8 illustrates a device driver that supports a queued, interrupt-driven device. Several threads in the system have outstanding I/O requests. In each case, the device driver strategy routine (running in the thread context) has added a request packet to the device work queue. Also notice that the device is currently busy servicing one of the I/O requests. The following process then takes place:

1. The device finishes the I/O operation and generates an interrupt, indicating to the interrupt controller that the device is ready for more work.

2. The interrupt controller makes note of the IRQ that generated the interrupt and notifies the operating system.

3. OS/2 now routes the interrupt to the device driver ISR. Recognizing that the I/O operation is complete, the interrupt handler handshakes with the device, retrieving the error status, and resetting the interrupting condition. If the device does not use the DMA controller to move data (such as the hard file controller on the IBM PC/AT), the interrupt handler retrieves the data and moves it to the application buffer. If the device uses DMA, the information already is in the buffer, and the interrupt simply serves as a "shoulder tap."

4. Once the information is retrieved from the device, the interrupt processor communicates with the interrupt controller and re-arms the interrupt level. Until now, the interrupt controller has prevented other interrupts at the same or lower level from being sent to the kernel. Once the level is re-armed, all interrupts are free to enter. After the IRQ is re-armed, the device driver interrupt handler may be preempted by another interrupt.

5. Since the first request has been completed, the interrupt handler now takes the next request packet from its work queue.

6. The I/O request is sent to the device and the process starts over.

In PC DOS, no rules govern hardware access by applications. This is generally not a problem because the application handling the interrupts is usually the only program in the system. However, when trying to run multiple PC DOS applications under an environment manager, conflicts are inevitable. OS/2 addresses this problem by isolating the interrupt management functions to device driver interrupt routines.

Timer Interrupt Handler

In some cases, device drivers must time I/O operations. For instance, a diskette driver has to recognize when a user has opened the drive door so that it may fail the I/O operation. If the driver simply waited for the device interrupt, the application thread would hang up forever. Instead, the device driver should wait for some time period and then tail the request.

To handle this, OS/2 allows device drivers to have a second (optional) interrupt processor for timer interrupts. The device driver can set a counter when it starts an I/O operation and decrement it on each timer tick. If the counter reaches zero before the I/O is complete, the device driver can abort the application request with an error.

Timer interrupt handlers are subject to the same constraints as other interrupt routines. However, because of their frequencies of interruption, timer interrupt routines must be written carefully and efficiently. OS/2 timer interrupts are received every 32 milliseconds.

DEVICE DRIVER FILE STRUCTURE

A device driver disk file has exactly the same structure as a Dynamic Link Library routine (DLL). A DLL is basically an EXE file with no stack segment. Since they execute in kernel mode, device drivers use the kernel stack.

A device driver is built with the OS/2 LINK utility using a module definition (DEF) file. The DEF file must include a LIBRARY control statement.

Device drivers must be written using the small programming model. They can have only one code segment and one data segment, each limited to 64K. Additional data segments may be included during initialization, but they cannot be used after the device driver is running. The EXE file must have the segments ordered as follows: the data segment must be first, followed by the code segment, and lastly the extra segment(s) (see Figure 8-9).

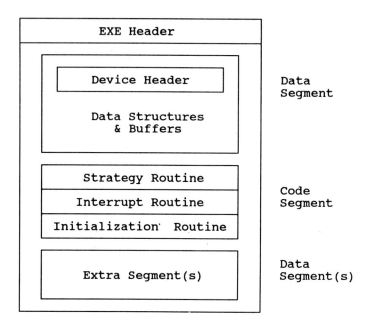

Figure 8-9.   Device driver segment layout

Code Segment

The code segment contains the device driver interrupt handler, the strategy routine, and the initialization routine. The initialization routine should be the last thing in the code segment, so you can discard it at the end of the initialization process (by "shrinking" the code segment).

The entry point of the strategy routine is specified in the device header. The initialization routine is really the part of the strategy routine which processes the type OO (INIT) request packet. Finally, the interrupt routine is dynamically registered by the initialization routine using a kernel DevHlp routine.

Data Segment

The data segment must start with a device header. The *device header* is a data structure that defines the charac-

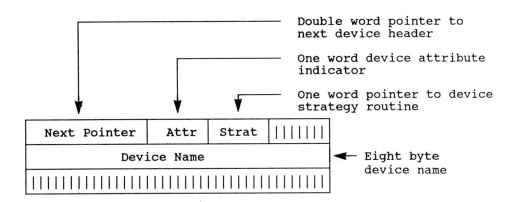

Figure 8-10. Device header

teristics of the device driver (see Figure 8-10). The device header fields are used in the following ways.

Next device A single device driver file may support multiple devices. Each device is identified with a device header. If more than one header is contained in the file, the headers must be chained by using this field. The last device in the chain must have a null (zero) pointer. Although this is a double-word pointer, all device headers must be contained in the device driver data segment.

Device attributes A device attribute describes the characteristics of the device driver, including the device type (block or character), an indicator defining whether the device is to receive OPEN and CLOSE packets, and the system level indicator (0 for OS/2 1.0).

Strategy routine This is the address of the strategy routine that will process request packets for the device. It is a single-word offset from the start of the device driver code segment.

Device Name   The device name is a 1-8-character ASCII name for character devices, or a unit count (number) for block devices.
The remainder of the data segment is available for device
driver data structures and buffers. A device driver can
use a kernel DevHlp routine to allocate additional physical memory for its use, so the minimum set of structures
should be packaged in the data segment.

For instance, if a device driver can support 1-6 devices,
root pointers for six device data blocks can be included in
the data area. As each device is initialized, a block of
memory can be allocated and chained to the root pointer.
If the user indicates that less than six devices are to be
supported, the initialization routine can "shrink" the data
structure.

The initialization routine has the option of packaging
its data structures as extra data segments. Only the initialization routine can access these extra segments. The system frees these segments when initialization is complete.

For example, Figure 8-11 illustrates how a device
driver file might be structured. In this example, the
device driver supports two character devices: MYLPT1
and MYLPT2. Note that each device requires a different
device header, but not necessarily a different strategy routine or interrupt handler.

KERNEL REQUEST PACKETS

All device drivers receive I/O requests in request packets.
A request packet is a data structure created by the kernel
and passed to the device driver strategy routine. The kernel calls strategy routines with ES:BX pointing to the
request packet. The request packet has a general (architected) header with device-specific extensions (see Figure
8-12).

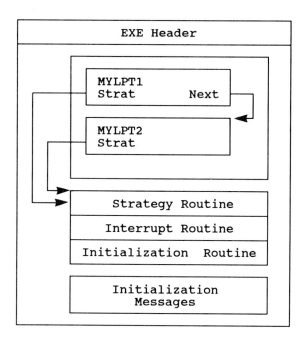

Figure 8-11. Sample device driver

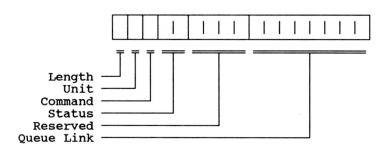

Figure 8-12. OS/2 request packet format

Request packet fields have the following meanings:

Length   The total length of the request packet includes
                the header, the length field, and other command-
                specific data following the header

Unit   The block device unit number (reserved in char-
                acter device driver packets)

Command   This is the specific command code

Status   This is device status code that is used by the
                device driver to return error and status infor-
                mation to the kernel when the request is complete

Queue Link   This is an 8-byte area used by the device driver
                to chain request packets in the device work
                queue. The queue link is a double-word value
                because request packets may be in different
                segments. A segment register and offset must
                be saved

Command Codes

The request packet command field describes the action(s)
the device driver is being asked to perform. OS/2 generates a variety of commands that are listed in Table 8-2.
Some of these commands are generated on behalf of applications to complete I/O requests (for example, DosOpen,
DosClose, DosRead, and DosWrite). Others are generated
to perform specific functions for the kernel (such as
INSTALIZATION, DEINSTALL, and MEDIA CHECK).

Error Codes

When a strategy routine completes the I/O operation, it
notes the completion status in the request packet status

Table 8-2. Device Request Packets

Code	Function	Block Device?	Character Device?
00	Initialization	Yes	Yes
01	Media check	Yes	
02	Build BPB	Yes	
04	Read (input)	Yes	Yes
05	Nondestructive read (no wait)		Yes
06	Input status		Yes
07	Input flush		Yes
08	Write	Yes	Yes
09	Write with verify	Yes	Yes
10	Output status		Yes
11	Output flush		Yes
13	Device open	Yes	Yes
14	Device close	Yes	Yes
15	Removeable media check	Yes	
16	Generic IOCtl	Yes	Yes
17	Reset media	Yes	
18	Get logical drive map	Yes	
19	Set logical drive map	Yes	
20	Deinstall		Yes

field. The status field contains a one-word error code. OS/2 recognizes numerous error codes (see Table 8-3). The device driver must use one of these codes when signaling a device error. The kernel uses the information to generate a hard error to reflect the error to the application program.

Table 8-3. Device Error Codes

Code	Meaning
00	Write-protect violation
01	Unknown unit
02	Device not ready
03	Unknown command
04	CRC error
05	Bad drive request structure length
06	Seek error
07	Unknown media
08	Sector not found
09	Printer out of paper
10	Write fault
11	Read fault
12	General failure
13	Change disk (logical switch)
16	Uncertain media
17	Character I/O call interrupted

DEVICE HELPER SERVICES (DEVHLP)

Device drivers provide a device independent layer which insulates the kernel from the hardware. To do this job the device drivers need access to system services (such as memory allocation, queueing services, and so forth). But device drivers often need to call the services at times when the normal OS/2 API is not available (such as during an external interrupt). For this reason, OS/2 provides its device drivers with a special set of functions called *Device Helper (DevHlp) services*.

The DevHlp interface uses a register parameter passing convention, instead of the stack convention used by the

Table 8-4. Device Helper (DevHlp) Routines

Name	CD	Description	Use		
DevDone	01	Indicate an I/O operation is complete	S	I	
Yield	02	Yield CPU to higher priority thread(s)	S		
TCYield	03	Yield CPU to Time Critical thread(s)	S		
Block	04	Block the application thread	S		
Run	05	Resume the application thread	S	I	
SemRequest	06	Claim a semaphore	S		
SemClear	07	Release a semaphore	S	I	
SemHandle	08	Obtain a semaphore handle	S	I	
PushReqPacket	09	Add I/O request packet to work queue	S		
PullReqPacket	0A	Get next I/O request packet from queue	S	I	
PullParticular	0B	Get specific I/O request packet	S	I	
SortReqPacket	0C	Sort I/O request packets in queue	S		
AllocReqPacket	0D	Create a new request packet	S		
FreeReqPacket	0E	Release a request packet	S		
QueueInit	0F	Initialize a character queue	S	I	N
QueueFlush	10	Clear a character queue	S	I	
QueueWrite	11	Write a character to a character Q	S	I	
QueueRead	12	Read a character from a character Q	S	I	
Lock	13	Fix a memory segment	S		
Unlock	14	Release a memory segment	S	I	N
PhysToVirt	15	Convert Logical @ to 32bit Physical @	S		N
VirtToPhy	16	Convert Physical @ to Logical @	S		N
PhysToUVirt	17	Convert Physical @ to Logical @ (LDT)	S		
AllocPhys	18	Allocate memory segment	S		N
FreePhys	19	Free memory segment	S		N
SetROMVector	1A	Set software interrupt vector	S		N
SetIRQ	1B	Request hardware interrupt vector	S		N
UnSetIRQ	1C	Release hardware interrupt vector	S	I	N
SetTimer	1D	Set timer handler	S		N
ResetTimer	1E	Release timer handler	S	I	N
MonitorCreate	1F	Create a monitor chain	S		N
Register	20	Add a monitor to a chain	S		
DeRegister	21	Remove a monitor from a chain	S		
MonWrite	22	Pass data to monitor chain	S	I	
MonFlush	23	Flush monitor chain	S		
GetDOSVar	24	Get system information segment	S		N

Table 8-4. Device Helper (DevHlp) Routines (continued)

Name	CD	Description	Use
SendEvent	25	Send a system unit	S I
ROMCritSection	26	Enter/exit ROM critical section	S
VerifyAccess	29	Verify validity of a memory segment	S
EOI	31	Issue end-of-interrupt	I N
UnPhysToVirt	32	Mark completion of virtual address use	S I N
TickCount	33	Modify timer tick frequency	S I N
GetLIDEntry	34	Obtain a logical ID (ABIOS)	S N
FreeLIDEntry	35	Release logical ID (ABIOS)	S N
ABIOSCall	36	Call an ABIOS routine (OS convention)	S I N
ABIOSCommonEntry	37	Call an ABIOS routine (common conv.)	S I N

Legend: S=Strategy Routine, I=Interrupt Handler, N=Initialization

system API. To call a service, a device driver loads the appropriate registers (depending on the function), loads a function code in the DL register, and calls the kernel Device Help function router. OS/2 passes the address of the Device Help function router to the device driver in the initialization request packet. The initialization routine must save this address in the device driver data segment, for later use by other device driver components.

Table 8-4 lists the individual DevHlp functions. Note that not all services are available in all the device driver contexts (interrupt, task, and initialization). This section examines the level of support provided by the DevHlp interface.

Queue Management Services

OS/2 provides two types of services for managing device queues.

Request Queue Services provide the device driver with the ability to chain request packets in a single threaded linked list. The PUSHREQPACKET and PULL REQPACKET functions add and remove packets from the request queue. The ALLOCREQPACKET and FREER EQPACKET functions let you allocate and free new (internal) request packets. A device driver can allocate a new packet and add it to its work queue. This is especially useful for multi-stage I/O, such as disk operations where a single kernel request packet may result in a seek followed by a read. The SORTREQPACKET function sorts the request packets in the device queue. For instance, you can use this function to sort disk I/O requests by track and sector, thus minimizing the motion of the disk arm(s).

Character Queue Services give a device driver a simple set of routines to manage a circular character buffer. The QUEUEINIT function initializes a character queue and the QUEUEREAD and QUEUEWRITE functions add and extract characters from the buffer. Most character devices use circular buffer schemes to manage serial data streams.

Synchronization Services

In certain cases, a device driver must synchronize its activity with an OS/2 thread. The SEMREQUEST function will request a semaphore and the SEMCLEAR function will release it. The semaphores may be used to synchronize a thread on device events, much in the same way they are used to synchronize threads.

Memory Management Services

I/O request packets sometimes include application supplied pointers to data buffers. Before using these pointers, however, the device driver must validate that it is not an invalid memory location (that is, the selector maps to a valid descriptor in the application's LDT). This is done with the VERIFY ACCESS DevHlp routine. **Note**: Buffer pointers in the read and write request packets are automatically validated by the kernel.

In cases where data will be transferred directly into the user buffer at interrupt time (either by the interrupt routine or the DMA controller), the OS/2 memory manager must be told not to move (or swap) the segment containing the buffer. The LOCK function fixes a segment in memory and the UNLOCK function releases it. Normally, a device driver will LOCK the segment when it starts the I/O and UNLOCK it when the data has been transferred. **Note**: Buffer pointers contained in the READ and WRITE I/O packets are automatically locked by the file system before the request is sent to the device driver.

Because the thread context might change, OS/2 cannot guarantee that a buffer will still be addressable by the active LDT when the device interrupt is received. Consequently, device drivers convert (and save) logical buffer pointers to 32-bit physical addresses. The VIRTTOPHYS DevHlp function converts a logical address (selector:offset or segment:offset) to an absolute physical address. The PHYSTOUVIRT and PHYSTOVIRT services convert a physical address back to a logical address (in the local or system address spaces). **Note**: Buffer pointers contained in the READ and WRITE I/O packets are automatically converted to 32-bit form by the file system before the request is sent to the device driver.

Finally, a device driver may allocate and free additional physical memory. The ALLOCPHYS function allocates a memory block and the FREEPHYS function releases it.

Process Management Services

To enable overlapped I/O, an OS/2 device driver is responsible for telling the OS/2 dispatcher when a thread is to be suspended. The BLOCK DevHlp routine freezes an application thread and the RUN DevHlp thaws it. Normally, the BLOCK function is called by the device driver strategy routine when it starts an I/O operation and the RUN function is called by the interrupt handler when the I/O is complete.

When an I/O request is complete, the device driver notifies the kernel by "passing back" the original request packet. The device driver can (optionally) set an error code in the request packet I/O status field. The DEVDONE service routine signals the end of an I/O operation.

Device drivers run in kernel mode. While in this mode, the system is not preemptable (that is, the dispatcher does not switch between tasks). Since certain device driver operations may be very lengthy (such as moving a large block of memory in a VDISK driver), device drivers can "break up" the processing time by periodically calling the YIELD service routine. The TCYIELD service is similar to YIELD, except that it only relinquishes control to time critical threads. In general, device drivers should not execute for more than 3 milliseconds without yielding the CPU.

Interrupt Management Services

Device drivers are interrupt driven components. The SETIRQ function ties the device driver interrupt service routine to a particular IRQ. The UNSETIRQ function releases the IRQ. When associated with an IRQ, the device driver is passed the individual device interrupts. **Note:** OS/2 only supports interrupt sharing in a level-triggered interrupt environment (such as the PS/2 MicroChannel). In an edge-triggered environment (such as the PC/AT), OS/2 allows only one device driver interrupt handler per interrupt level.

OS/2 also provides device drivers with a service to emulate Real mode functions by "trapping" the software interrupt vectors. The SETROMVECTOR DevHlp service routine associates a device driver routine with one of the software interrupt vectors. Since only real mode (PC DOS) applications may issue software interrupts, this function is used for compatibility support only.

Timer Services

A device driver may register a routine to handle timer ticks with the SETTIMER service. Timer processing may be discontinued with the RESETTIMER function. While registered, the device driver will see each clock tick. To modify the frequency of the timer ticks, a device driver may use the TICKCOUNT DevHlp function. **Note**: This function changes the frequency of timer ticks seen by the device driver, but it does not affect the real timer frequency. This is analogous to chaining to the PC DOS interrupt 1C. A device driver may use this facility to implement a device time-out.

Monitor Services

OS/2 allows application program threads to *monitor* character device data streams. The OS/2 device monitoring functions require the cooperation of the character device drivers. A special set of DevHlp services is used to build character device drivers which support application device monitors. The MONITORCREATE function initializes a monitor chain. The REGISTER and DEREGISTER functions add a new application thread to the device monitor chain. To write data into an active monitor chain, the device driver uses the MONWRITE function.

COMPATIBILITY ENVIRONMENT SUPPORT

OS/2 device drivers receive request packets that were generated by both OS/2 protected mode application programs and DOS environment (compatibility) programs. The system maps the PC DOS-style interfaces into the same request packets it generates for new programs. For the most part, the device driver processes the two types of packets in the same way. However, some special considerations must be taken into account when writing device drivers that will support the compatibility environment.

Bimodal Device Model

OS/2 runs the DOS compatibility environment in 80286 real addressing mode. When running on an 80386, OS/2 1.0 does not use the virtual 8086 capabilities of the CPU. The memory addressing scheme is quite different in real and protected modes. Real mode memory is identified with a segment address, while protected mode segments are referenced with a selector. This incompatibility in addressing modes causes a unique problem for device drivers.

OS/2 device drivers receive request packets from both DOS compatibility programs and protected mode programs. If the program requesting the I/O is a PC DOS (INT 21H) program, the device driver receives the request packet with the CPU in real mode. If the program requesting the I/O is a protected mode application, the device driver is run in protected mode.

On the surface, this is not a serious problem since the application buffers may be accessed using whatever style of pointers returned by the PhysToVirt DevHlp. But if the device is already busy and the request has to be queued, the actual I/O is not started until the current device operation is completed. The I/O is actually started when the device interrupt (signifying the completion of the previous operation) is received.

Since the device driver has no control over when an interrupt is received, the interrupt may come in when the CPU is in a different processor mode. If this happens, the data pointers are useless and the device driver has no way of getting to the application buffers.

In an earlier example (Figure 8-5), you saw how OS/2 overlaps I/O operations with program execution. Consider what would happen if the program which started the I/O operation (Program A) was a PC DOS program. As in the previous example, OS/2 would start the I/O operation and block Program A. The dispatcher could then run program B. However, since B is a protected mode program, the CPU mode is changed to protected mode.

Now the device interrupt comes in. The device driver attempts to write the second sector and it discovers that it cannot. The data it needs to write to the device is in a buffer that is no longer addressable because the CPU is running in a protected mode.

The solution to this problem is physical addressing of data buffers. Remember that every OS/2 device driver is responsible for converting the 32-bit physical addresses contained in the request blocks to logical form (selector: offset or segment:offset) before using it to access the application buffer. The device drivers call the OS/2 DevHlp service PhysToVirt to perform this transition. It is this service routine which masks the CPU mode from the device driver. When the CPU is running in protected mode, the logical address returned by PhysToVirt is a valid GDT selector. When the CPU is in real mode, Phys-ToVirt returns a temporary segment value. Thus, the device driver is impervious to the processor mode. The OS/2 device driver model is called a *bimodal programming model*.

In this case, the buffer addresses in the request packets are always 32-bit physical addresses. When the interrupt routine is called to service the device interrupt in protected mode, it calls PhysToVirt to convert the address to logical form. In so doing, OS/2 automatically creates a GDT descriptor and passes the device driver a valid selector it uses to access the buffer.

BIOS Emulation

PC DOS applications often bypass the file system and access the hardware directly by using the *basic I/O services* (BIOS). BIOS is a set of ROM-resident routines that provide access to the hardware devices.

An OS/2 device driver managing a device that is also accessible by the BIOS (such as a printer, disk, diskette, keyboard, and so forth) synchronizes these requests with those coming from OS/2 programs. A special DevHlp service called SetROMVector allows device drivers to "hook" software interrupt vectors. In this way, a compatibility application directly calling the BIOS actually is asking the device driver for the I/O. You will see how this works in more detail in Chapter 11.

OS/2 DEVICES

The OS/2 system includes device drivers for the most common personal computer I/O devices. These device drivers process request packets from the kernel, emulate BIOS services, and support both new OS/2 applications and DOS compatibility programs. The OS/2 device drivers also provide extended capabilities through generic IOCTL request packets. IOCTL request packets are used to request specific I/O services not accommodated by the device model.

These IOCTL packets are normally only used by the system. They are published so that you can write replacement device drivers which provide the services expected by the system.

Application progams should minimize their dependence on these functions, since they are not part of the system API. However, in some cases the IOCTL commands must be used because no equivalent API functions exist (for example, COMPORT control).

CHARACTER DEVICE MONITORS

OS/2 application programs cannot directly intercept hardware interrupts. As discussed in this chapter, hardware interrupts are special events closely managed by the kernel and the device driver interrupt handler routines. Yet, there are situations where applications rely on processing the raw device input (such as keyboard translation routines or printer device data-stream translation programs).

If you needed to view the device data stream, you could always write a replacement device driver. But in most cases this is much more work than is required since the replacement driver would have to support all the functions of the original driver to ensure the proper operation of the system. In addition, device driver interrupt handler code has a restricted number of system functions available for its use. If you needed access to normal system services (such as the file system API), the device driver would have to enlist the help of a thread. This obviously complicates the design of the application.

The OS/2 system provides a special facility (called *character device monitors*) for writing this type of application program. Character monitors are application threads that register themselves to "watch" device data streams. As data flows through the device driver, each character is passed through the kernel to the application monitor threads. The monitors may then inspect, modify, delete, or augment information in the data stream. Since the monitor threads run in the application context, they have access to all the system APIs.

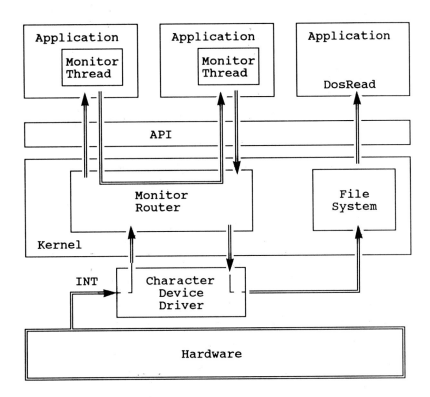

Figure 8-13. Character device driver monitors

Structure

Figure 8-13 shows the relationship between the device drivers, the kernel, and the monitor applications. Normally data flows from the hardware to the device driver, file system, and application program. Monitors introduce a new flow. Before delivering a character to the file system, the device driver copies the character into a data structure called a *monitor packet* and passes it to a special OS/2 component called the *monitor router.* The router is

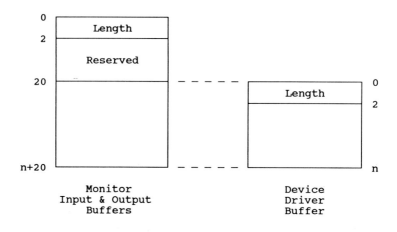

Figure 8-14. Monitor buffer format

responsible for sending monitor packets to applications that are monitoring the device.

To monitor a device, an application program must first create a dedicated monitor thread. The thread identifies itself to the monitor router with a DOSMONOPEN API call. Like the DosOpen system call, the MONOPEN function accepts a device name and returns a device handle. This handle must be used by the thread when making other monitor function calls.

When it is ready to start processing the device data stream, the thread allocates an input data buffer and an output data buffer and issues a DosMonReg API call to add itself to the device monitor chain. The input buffer is used to receive monitor packets destined for the monitor. The output buffer is used to hold packets destined for the next monitor (or the device driver).

The input and output buffers must be at least 20 bytes larger than the buffer contained in the device driver being monitored (see Figure 8-14). The length of the entire buffer (including the length field) must be contained in a one-word field at the start of each buffer. The monitor

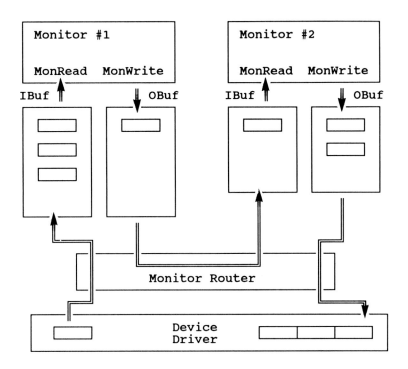

Figure 8-15.   Monitor data flows

router permits multiple applications to monitor the same device, so the input and output buffers from the registered monitors make up a buffer chain. Figure 8-15 illustrates how data is passed between monitor thread buffers.

When the device interrupt is serviced, the monitor router moves the packets from the device driver to the first monitor's input buffer. Subsequently, the monitor router moves the packets at task time in the monitor thread contexts. Each thread in the chain is responsible for retrieving the packets from the thread's input buffer (with a DosMonRead call) and putting them in its output buffer (with a DosMonWrite call).

Note that the monitors are not required to write back the same packet into the output buffer. In fact, a monitor could write back the same packet, write a different packet, write more than one packet, or write none at all. The monitor router is responsible for moving the packets from the output buffer of one monitor to the input buffer of the next. From the final monitor output buffer, the packet is returned to the device driver.

The buffers are required because most of the time the packets are moved at task time rather than when the interrupt is processed. The monitors are therefore subject to normal task dispatch latency. If no buffers were in the monitor chain, data might be lost, especially in frequently interrupting devices such as the mouse or the keyboard (in keymatic mode).

Monitors are special programs whose design must be carefully considered. A faulty monitor could affect the overall performance of the system. Some of the things you should consider when building a monitor are the thread priority, the size of the input and output buffers, and the path length of the code that directly processes the packets. Table 8-5 lists the monitor API function calls.

Since a monitor executes as a system thread, it is permitted to use the full OS/2 API. This is especially useful if the monitor must refer to disk-resident tables when processing the monitor packets. A monitor is functionally equivalent to a PC DOS program that directly hooks a hardware interrupt, except that the processing happens long after the system has dismissed the interrupt.

Table 8-5. Monitor Function Calls

Monitor API	Description
DosMonOpen	Open device for monitoring
DosMonReg	Register I/O buffers to device chain
DosMonRead	Read monitor packet
DosMonWrite	Write monitor packet
DosMonClose	Close device monitor (and deregister)

Supported Devices

If an application is to monitor a particular device, the device driver must support the monitor functions. Not all OS/2 device drivers include this support. In OS/2 version 1.0, the mouse, keyboard, and printer device drivers allow application programs to register device monitors.

SUMMARY

OS/2 isolates applications from the PC hardware. Its high-level programming interface enables you to write application programs that are not dependent on the idiosyncracies of specific hardware devices. The kernel implements the system APIs in a device-independent way by processing I/O requests through device drivers. The device drivers receive generic I/O request packets from the kernel and translate them to low-level hardware interactions. A device driver is a logical interface to a device.

Applications do not handle device interrupts. However, an application may intercept low-level input and output by using the character device monitor facility. This facility allows application threads to monitor (and change) the raw device input and output.

Device drivers play an important role in OS/2. Whether or not you intend to write your own device driver, you should remember the following important points:

- The relationship of OS/2 device drivers to the system
- Character device driver characteristics
- Block device driver characteristics
- How overlapped I/O works
- The device driver components
- Interrupt service routine considerations
- The device driver file structure
- Device header layout
- Kernel request packet layout
- The device helper (DevHlp) functions

- DOS compatibility environment considerations
- Character device monitor structure and function
- Monitor data flows
- The monitor API functions

CHAPTER 9
I/O SUBSYSTEMS

To this point, the discussion of the OS/2 I/O services has been in the context of the serial file model. These particular services are actually a subset of the overall system I/O capabilities. OS/2 includes a larger set of I/O services for those devices that are critical in the implementation of an OS/2 user interface (specifically the keyboard, video display, and mouse).

For these devices, the low-level system I/O is performed by special OS/2 components called *I/O subsystems*. An I/O subsystem performs basic I/O operations on behalf of OS/2 programs. View these subsystems as the protected mode counterparts of the PC DOS-environment BIOS services. OS/2 implements I/O subsystems for the keyboard, video display, and mouse. All input from, or output to, these devices (whether from an application or the system itself), is eventually resolved to an I/O subsystem primitive.

WHY SUBSYSTEMS ARE NECESSARY

You may wonder why these services exist. Does the file model not provide all the functions required to access these devices? The answer lies in a simple function-versus-responsiveness trade-off. For example, consider how these trade-offs are made with video services.

The file I/O model can be used for handle-based console I/O. This model is more than adequate for "standard" I/O functions, such as writing to the console in teletype (TTY) mode. In fact, TTY I/O precisely matches the serial-character data-stream model and is, therefore, compatible with OS/2 file I/O services. The system utilities write to the console as if the console were a TTY device. This has obvious advantages in that OS/2 may pipe or redirect the output to other programs, devices, or files.

However, in the personal computer environment, simple TTY I/O is not always adequate. Advanced user interfaces demand that the screen be dealt with as a presentation space with random access to various screen coordinates. This is clearly demonstrated by observing how "full screen" applications such as spreadsheets update the display. A spreadsheet program moves a view port (the screen) over a much larger presentation space (the spreadsheet workspace). Random portions of the screen are updated as the user moves from one area to another. Writing the entire screen each time the user moves the cell pointer is not practical.

In addition, I/O redirection makes no sense in this environment since the interface is visual. The meaning of a particular keystroke or character is determined purely by the relative location of the cursor within the spreadsheet workspace.

Most full-screen applications require optimal video performance, since the responsiveness of the interface is critical to the usability of the application. In the PC DOS

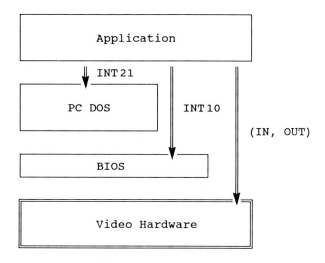

Figure 9-1.   Video I/O in PC DOS applications

environment full-screen application programs are seldom written directly to the INT21 READ/WRITE interface.
Instead, application writers opt for BIOS services or direct
hardware access (memory-mapped I/O).

As you venture farther down the functional hierarchy
you gain performance, but lose function. Figure 9-1 shows
how this concept applies in the case of PC DOS video I/O.
At the highest level, application programs access the console through the PC DOS file system. In this case, the
application gets redirection services, ANSI support, and a
high-level representation of the screen as if the console
were a dumb terminal. *Dumb terminal* is a term used to
describe display devices with no local intelligence. This
type of device is often designed to support a particular
data stream (such as ANSI, 3270, and so forth) typically
sent from a host computer.

If file I/O redirection is not important, the application can directly access the BIOS services to randomly write characters and character attributes. This technique provides better performance while retaining independence from the hardware. This technique shields the type of display adaptor, the screen mode (graphics or text), and unique characteristics of the display from the application.

At the other end of the spectrum, the highest video performance is achieved by directly writing to the video display buffer. However, in this case the application must understand all the characteristics of the device because it assumes all the responsibilities of the system video drivers. Developers who have written directly to the hardware are familiar with all the idiosyncracies of individual display adapters (such as CGA video retrace synchronization to prevent "snow" while writing characters).

OS/2 I/O subsystems provide a facility for application programs that are willing to trade off the "generic" attributes of standard I/O for enhanced performance. Numerous levels of subsystem services provide a wide range of interface levels (from TTY-like output with full ANSI support to direct hardware manipulation).

OS/2 I/O STRUCTURE

Before examining the individual subsystems, consider the common implementation architecture of the subsystems. The I/O subsystems are implemented using the OS/2 subsystem model. Each subsystem provides a set of dynamic-link APIs through which an application can access its services. Each subsystem has a corresponding DLL run-time file and a device driver. Subsystem service routines execute on behalf of the requesting program as a subroutine at PL3 in the caller's context (LDT).

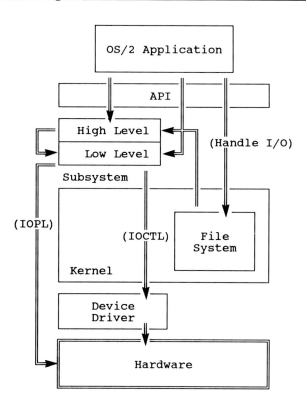

Figure 9-2. OS/2 I/O flows

Figure 9-2 shows the overall system I/O flow. At the highest level, an application program may perform direct calls to the file system or the I/O subsystem. In the case of handle-device I/O, the call first goes to the file system router to determine if redirection is in effect. If the device is redirected, the output is sent to the appropriate device or file. If the device is not redirected, the request is passed to an I/O subsystem for completion. In all cases, the request is eventually serviced by the subsystem. The OS/2 I/O subsystems are the only point of interface to the keyboard, video display, and mouse devices.

If an application program does not need redirection services (or if it wants to access the device in a random manner), the I/O subsystem can be called directly. The I/O subsystem APIs are another part of the total OS/2 API. When using these APIs directly, the application program forefeits the serial data stream model and the model's redirection capabilities, but the program gains more control over the device.

The I/O subsystem API calls are structured in levels, ranging from the more primitive functions to higher functions. In the case of video I/O, a high-level WriteTTY interface implements the basic TTY capabilities without I/O redirection. Calls to the WriteTTY service are decomposed into a number of character-write and cursor-positioning calls. Note that in OS/2 the TTY services actually are implemented as part of the I/O subsystem, rather than in the file system.

Replacing I/O Subsystem Functions

Since all OS/2 I/O is funneled through the I/O subsystems, this area is a convenient place to "hook" the functions. In other words, the OS/2 I/O subsystems are fully replaceable by application programs or system extensions. The structure of each I/O subsystem (see Figure 9-3) contains a router component and a set of service routines. When any program (application or system) writes to or reads from one of the I/O subsystems, the request is processed by the router and, in most cases, passed to the system-supplied I/O service routine. A standard service routine is provided by OS/2 for each subsystem API.

A system extension (either part of the application or a different process) can register itself to handle any or all of the I/O subsystem APIs. The router simply sends the individual API calls to the system service routine or the sys-

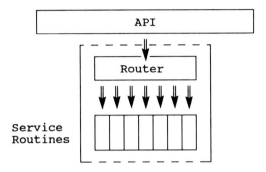

Figure 9-3. I/O subsystem structure

tem extension registered to process the service. In the default case, all I/O subsystem calls go to the service routines provided with OS/2. When the system extension receives the API call, it may do one of the following:

- Process the I/O request

- Examine the request and pass it to the OS/2 service routine (with or without modification of the application data)

- Do nothing and return control to the application (thereby "swallowing" the function request)

Figure 9-4 illustrates how a system extension can register itself to handle some of the I/O subsystem services. Notice that only one system extension at a time can be registered to provide alternate subsystem services. OS/2 does not permit chaining of system extensions.

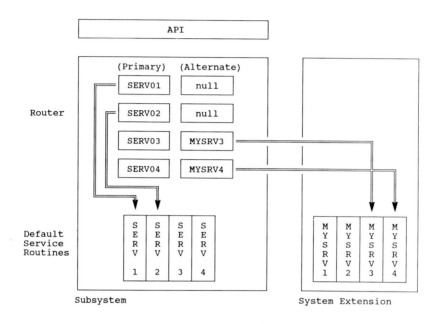

Figure 9-4. Replacing OS/2 I/O subsystem functions

Sessions

OS/2 implements multiple user sessions. A *session* is one or more processes running together that all share the keyboard, video display, and mouse. In most cases, a session corresponds to an application program. The OS/2 user may start up to 12 concurrent sessions.

In terms of the I/O subsystems, the notion of sessions is important because it defines a "logical instance" of the subsystem. Although only one version of the subsystem is loaded in the system at a time, each session has a different context. In other words, each session has its own set of data areas that define the state of the keyboard, video display, and mouse. As the user switches from session to session, the context of the devices is restored.

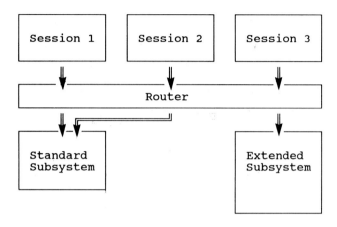

Figure 9-5.   OS/2 sessions

In the case of the video services, the system maintains a *logical video buffer* (LVB) for each session. The LVB is a shadow of the screen contents. OS/2 programmers access the LVB using the video subsystem function calls. These function calls are available at all times, so an application can update the screen even when it is in a background session.

In the case of keyboard and mouse, OS/2 subsystems maintain unique input queues for each session. As the user switches sessions, OS/2 switches the input focus between the input queues.

Figure 9-5 illustrates how OS/2 supports multiple sessions. The replaceability of subsystem functions (described previously) is performed on a session-by-session basis. For instance, different system extensions in different sessions can take over the I/O subsystem services. A system extension can only register itself to manage I/O requests for its session. However, since the base services are contained in a system dynamic-link module, they can be replaced (for all sessions) by simply replacing the DLL file.

Family API Implications

Most OS/2 subsystem services are included in the family API. In fact, the family API bindings associated with subsystem I/O calls actually bind the subsystem routines with the application program. To provide the same level of performance in the PC DOS environment, these bindings do not utilize the system BIOS.

In effect, the I/O subsystem API is a set of standard I/O subroutines. When a family application runs under PC DOS, the code included in the binding performs the I/O services. When the same application is run under OS/2 (in protected mode), the binding is discarded and the base subsystem services are used.

VIDEO I/O SUBSYSTEM SERVICES

The video I/O services (collectively referred to as the *VIO API*) are a set of functions equivalent to BIOS video (INT10) routines. However, the VIO services go beyond the BIOS facilities by including extensions for manipulating character strings, attributes, and cells in a more functional way than the BIOS services it replaces. A *character cell* is the combination of a character and its display attribute.

One notable exception is the graphics (pixel-oriented) functions that are not supported through the VIO APIs. Thus, the VIO subsystem supports the display in text modes. Although VIO does not contain graphics primitives, it does allow an application to set graphics display modes. When an application sets the display in a graphics mode, it assumes the responsibility for managing the display. But this is not as serious a restriction as it may seem. Applications in the PC DOS environment virtually never use the BIOS services to write individual pixels to the screen. In PC DOS, graphics services are usually provided by higher-level graphics interfaces, such as the *virtual device interface* (VDI) or *graphics device interface* (GDI).

VIO provides numerous levels of display access. Which technique should be used greatly depends on the specific characteristics of the application program.

Virtual TTY Output

The VIO virtual TTY service gives applications a high-level interface to the screen. The VIO virtual TTY is functionally similar to the handle-based I/O provided by the file system. However, if an application program uses this function, the screen output is not redirectable. The file system uses the VIO TTY function to write the characters on the screen.

In TTY mode, the character data is always written at the current cursor position. After writing the character, the cursor moves forward one position. If the character is written at the last position of a line, the cursor wraps to the next line. The following special characters in the output stream are treated as commands rather than data:

Carriage return (13)	Causes the output to continue on the next line. If the output is on the last display line, the contents of screen scroll up one line
Line feed (10)	Has the same effect as a carriage return. If it follows a carriage return, the line feed is ignored
Backspace (08)	The cursor moves back one space (non-destructively)
Tab (09)	The cursor moves to the next tab stop. Tab stops occur every 8 bytes
Bell (07)	A short tone is sounded

An application can use the VIO TTY function at any time. If the application is not the current foreground session, the session's LVB is updated. When the user returns the session to the foreground, the data will be presented correctly.

Table 9-1. ANSI Escape Sequences

Sequence	Description
ESC[#;#H	Move cursor to specified coordinates (ROW;COL)
ESC[#;#f	Move cursor to specified coordinates (COL;ROW)
ESC[#A	Move cursor up one or more lines
ESC[#B	Move cursor down one or more lines
ESC[#C	Move cursor forward one or more columns
ESC[#D	Move cursor back one or more columns
ESC[#;#R	Report cursor position
ESC[6n	Report device status
ESC[s	Save cursor position
ESC[u	Restore cursor position
ESC[2J	Erase display
ESC[K	Erase to end of line
ESC[#;...;#m	Set character attributes
ESC[=#h	Set display mode
ESC[=#1	Reset display mode
ESC[#;...;#p	Reassign keyboard input

The VIO TTY function also implements the standard ANSI escape sequences for cursor positioning, enhanced attribute control, and screen mode control (see Table 9-1). The ANSI mode may be turned on or off by using a VIO API or the ANSI utility program.

Character String Operations

At the next lower functional level, the OS/2 VIO subsystem includes a complete set of low-level character I/O services. These services closely approximate the type of functions provided by BIOS INT10 in the PC DOS environment with some extensions. Table 9-2 contrasts BIOS with the

Table 9-2. BIOS INT10 Versus VIO Text Functions

BIOS	VIO API	Description	Notes
00	VioSetMode	Set display mode	
01	VioSetCurType	Set cursor type	
—	VioGetCurType	Get cursor type	
02	VioSetCurPos	Set cursor position	
03	VioGetCurPos	Read cursor position	
04	n/a	Read light pen position	Light pen not supported
05	n/a	Select active page	Multiple pages not supported
06	VioScrollUp	Scroll page up	
07	VioScrollDn	Scroll page down	
—	VioScrollLf	Scroll page left	
—	VioScrollRt	Scroll page right	
08	VioReadCellStr	Read cell	VIO will read string
—	VioReadCellStr	Read character	VIO will read string
09	VioWrtCharStr	Write cell at cursor	
—	VioWrtNCell	Replicate cell	
10	VioWrtCellStr	Write character at cursor	
—	VioWrtNChar	Replicate character	
—	VioWrtNAttr	Replicate attribute	
11	VioSetPal	Set color palette	
12	n/a	Write dot (graphics)	Graphics not supported
13	n/a	Read dot (graphics)	Graphics not supported
14	VioWtrTTY	TTY write	VIO includes ANSI
15	VioGetMode	Query video state	
1900	VioWrtCharStrAtt	Write char string	Same attribute
1901	VioWrtCharStrAtt	Write char string+cursor	Same attribute
—	VioWrtCharStr	Write char string	Characters only (no attribute)
1902	VioWrtCellStr	Write cell string	
1903	VioWrtCellStr	Write cell string+cursor	

VIO character support. Significant differences include the ability to write multiple-byte character strings (with or without attributes); the ability to read character, attribute, and cell strings; and vertical scrolling.

As with the virtual TTY support, applications may use the character functions at any time. If the session is in the background, the changes are made in the session's LVB.

In almost all cases, you can implement text-based applications strictly using the VIO character functions. The performance of these functions is significantly better than the corresponding BIOS services. The VIO routines are optimized to the display adaptor in the system. For instance, when operating with the CGA display adaptor, the VIO functions utilize both horizontal and vertical retrace synchronization algorithms to maximize video throughput.

An application program is fully independent of the hardware when using character VIO functions. The VIO subsystem masks the differences and optimizes performance between the various display adaptors supported by OS/2 (CGA, EGA, VGA, and so forth).

Logical Video Buffer

Applications also can directly access the LVB. The OS/2 VIO subsystem includes an API that gives a program direct addressability to its LVB. With this address, programs can directly update any portion of the logical screen. Once the updates have been made, the real screen buffer can be updated with a single "show" operation. This form of video I/O is useful for applications that update large portions of the screen. When the screen is updated in large blocks, the video performance is further optimized. Figure 9-6 uses the following example to show how you would use this technique to update the screen:

1. The application requests access to the LVB from the VIO subsystem. A selector is created in the applications LDT and the selector is returned to the program.

2. Using the selector, the application directly updates the LVB, as if it were the "real" video buffer. At this point, however, the changes are not reflected on the screen.

3. When all the updates are completed, the application requests that the changes be made on the "real" screen. The VIO subsystem then uses the data contained in the LVB to change the physical screen buffer.

Direct LVB access is the lowest-level video I/O function that still maintains device independence. Specific device characteristics are hidden from the application. This LVB access is equivalent to the INT10 subfunctions FE and FF that are provided by TopView in the PC DOS environment.

Since the application is dealing with a logical representation of the display, LVB updates can be made at any time (with the session in the foreground or background). When in the foreground, the SHOW operation directly updates

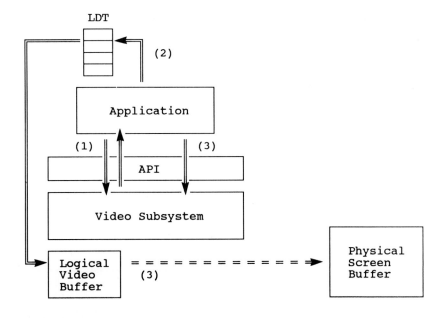

Figure 9-6. Accessing the logical video buffer

the screen. While in the background, the information is simply saved until the session returns to the foreground.

The decision to use the LVB directly rather than the VIO character functions depends on the characteristics of the application. An application that updates small portions of the screen is best suited to the character I/O functions. Conversely, large block updates can best be performed by using LVB manipulations. VIO character functions and LVB updates are not mutually exclusive—an application can use both interchangeably in different situations.

Physical Display Access

At the lowest level, the OS/2 VIO subsystem grants applications direct access to the physical display buffer. Since OS/2 is a multitasking system, special provisions must be made to ensure that the screen resource is shared in a well-behaved manner. The VIO subsystem includes several mechanisms that must be used when an application program performs direct screen I/O.

Note that writing an application program that performs direct screen I/O is not necessary (nor desirable) in most cases. The performance of the OS/2 character VIO functions is adequate for almost any application. If this performance is not sufficient, the screen I/O can be optimized by directly using the VIO LVB. Using the display directly should be considered only as a last resort. However, in certain cases such as graphics applications, physical device access is mandatory.

If an application writes directly to the display, it assumes the responsibility of understanding the physical characteristics of the screen. Thus, physical screen I/O is said to be a *device-dependent* application function.

Sharing the Display Buffer

Much in the same way you request the LVB, you use a special OS/2 API to request direct addressability to the physical screen buffer. The VIO subsystem creates an LDT descriptor that maps the display buffer and gives your application a selector to access the memory segment. However, since only one real screen buffer is in the system, the selector can only be used while the application is in the foreground. When the user switches the session to the background, the LDT descriptor is invalidated. If the program attempts to use it in this state, the CPU generates a general-protection fault and OS/2 terminates the application program. Figure 9-7 illustrates how multiple sessions share the display buffer.

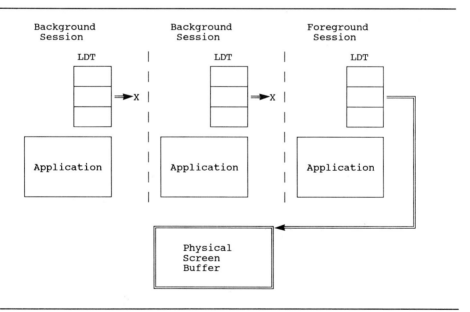

Figure 9-7. Direct video I/O

Synchronization of Screen Updates

It is very important a program access only the physical display device while it is in the foreground session. To help determine when it is safe to write to the screen, OS/2 provides a display-synchronization service.

Whenever a program wishes to perform physical screen I/O, the program requests exclusive use of the display by using a VioSer Lock call. If the session is in the background, the program is suspended until the user switches back to foreground, at which time the screen LOCK function successfully completes. While the display is in a locked state, OS/2 does not allow the user to switch to another screen session. The program indicates when it is finished writing to the screen by issuing VioSer UNLOCK function. Thus, the screen can be updated only while it is in a locked state.

The application is responsible for breaking up large screen updates into smaller elements to ensure that the session manager is not locked out for long periods of time.

Saving and Restoring the Video State

OS/2 automatically saves and restores the screen context for all application programs running in text modes. However, whenever the display device is placed in a graphics display mode, saving the display context becomes the responsibility of the application program.

A special function called VIOSAVEREDRAWWAIT performs this task. The application program creates a special execution thread whose only job is to save and restore the display context. This thread (called the SAVE-REDRAW thread) identifies itself to the VIO subsystem by issuing the SAVEREDRAW function call. Once the call is issued, the system suspends the thread. The SAVERE-DRAW thread is "awakened" right before the state of the session changes from foreground to background or vice versa. When the thread is awakened, it examines an indicator that tells the thread if the state of the screen is to be saved or restored. The thread then performs the save or restore function and reissues the VIOSAVEREDRAW-WAIT call.

In effect, the SAVEREDRAW thread is a special function provided by the application that understands the state of the screen and can be called by the VIO subsystem to save and restore the screen content on behalf of the application.

Video POPUPs

Background programs sometimes urgently need to communicate with the user. For instance, a print spooler may wish to signal an out-of-paper condition, or an alarm program may need to present a message. These messages obviously should not wait until the user switches to the right session.

For these kinds of situations, background programs may call a special VIO function called VIOPOPUP to place a message on the screen. However, an OS/2 POPUP is not a general-purpose function, since only one POPUP may be active at a time. If multiple programs issue a POPUP, one will be serviced and the others are blocked. Applications should restrict the use of this facility to critical situations demanding user action.

Video Mode Control

The VIOSETMODE function call sets the display video modes. Although the VIO subsystem supports only text operations, applications may use the call to set all video modes supported by the display adaptor. This includes 40- and 80-column text (with or without color burst), monochrome text, and all graphics modes.

If two displays are attached to the machine, the VIO subsystem switches to the device that best approximates the selected mode. For instance, if a monochrome and a CGA adaptor are installed, setting MONO mode activates the monochrome display and setting 80-line color text activates the CGA display.

The VIOGETMODE function is used to query the current display mode. Table 9-3 summarizes the remaining VIO functions.

KEYBOARD I/O SUBSYSTEM SERVICES

The keyboard I/O services, collectively referred to as the KBD API, are a set of functions equivalent to BIOS keyboard (INT16) routines. In addition, KBD incorporates a number of extensions for receiving character strings and determining shift states. As with VIO services, the KBD functions are implemented in two logical levels.

High-Level KBD (String) Input Services

As with the VIO subsystem, the KBD subsystem also contains a high-level interface to the keyboard. In fact, the KBDSTRINGIN function is the input analog of the VIO TTY services. This function is similar to the handle-based I/O provided by the file system. However, if an application program uses this function, the input is not redirectable. The file system uses the KBDSTRINGIN function to read characters from the keyboard.

An application may use the call KBDSTRINGIN function at anytime. If the program is not currently in the

Table 9-3.   VIO Functions

VIO API	*Description*
VioRegister	Define alternate VIO routine(s)
VioDeRegister	Undefine alternate routine(s)
VioGetBuf	Get logical video buffer (LVB)
VioShowBuf	Refresh physical display from LVB
VioGetPhysBuf	Get physical display buffer
VioScrLock	Lock physical screen for I/O
VioScrUnlock	Unlock physical screen
VioSavRedrawWait	Identify screen Save/Restore thread
VioSavRedrawUndo	Undo previous SavRedrawWait call
VioPopUp	Put up POPUP screen
VioEndPopUp	End POPUP
VioGetANSI	Get ANSI state
VioSetANSI	Set ANSI state (on or off)
VioPrtSc	Print screen (equivalent to BIOS INT5)
VioPrtScToggle	SHIFT-PRTSC state query
VioGetConfig	Query machine configuration
VioGetFont	Query current display font (EGA, VGA)
VioSetFont	Change display font
VioGetCP	Query current code page
VioSetCP	Change code page

foreground, the thread is blocked waiting for the session to be returned to the foreground.

The KBDSTRINGIN function also implements the standard ANSI escape sequences for input filtering (see Table 9-1). The ANSI mode is set by using a VIO API or the ANSI utility program. In the default case, ANSI mode is on. Note that the ANSI sequences are interpreted only when the input is read using this function (or file-system handle input).

Low-Level KBD (Character) Input Services

The KBD subsystem also supports low-level character I/O functions. Programs can use these calls to examine the keyboard scan codes, shift states, to flush the input buffer, and to peek the input queue. These functions are directly analogous to the BIOS INT16 interface in the PC DOS environment. Table 9-4 illustrates the differences between BIOS services and the low-level KBD functions.

Table 9-4. BIOS INT16 Versus OS/2 KBD Functions

BIOS	VIO API	Description	Notes
00	KbdCharIn	Read next ASCII char	Wait indicator on
01	KbdCharIn KbdPeek	Test if char is ready	Wait indicator off
02	KbdGetStatus KbdCharIn KbdPeek	Return shift state	
—	KbdPeek	Peek character	Remains in input queue
—	KbdFlushBuffer	Clear input buffer	
—	KbdSetStatus	Set keyboard state	
	KbdStringIn	String input	ANSI sequences supported

Other Functions

	KbdRegister	Define alternate KBD routine(s)
	KbdDeRegister	Undefine alternate routine(s)

MOUSE I/O SUBSYSTEM SERVICES

Unlike the keyboard and video services, the OS/2 mouse subsystem (called the MOU API) has no direct BIOS equivalent. This subsystem provides applications with a full range of services needed to manage the pointing device. Mouse I/O is not redirectable, nor does mouse I/O contain any form of ANSI support. Table 9-5 summarizes the functions provided by the MOU subsystem.

Table 9-5.   OS/2 Mouse Subsystem Functions

MOU API	*Description*
MouRegister	Define alternate MOU routine(s)
MouDeRegister	Undefine alternate routine(s)
MouOpen	Open MOU subsystem for session
Mouclose	Close MOU subsystem
MouFlushQue	Flush event queue
MouGetDevStatus	Query pointer status flags
MouGetEventMask	Query event mask
MouGetHotKey	Query system hot key
MouGetNumButtons	Query number of buttons
MouGetNumMickeys	Query mickeys-per-centimeter
MouGetNumQueEl	Query pointing device event queue
MouGetPtrPos	Query current pointer position
MouGetPtrShape	Query pointer shape/size
MouGetScaleFact	Query scale factors
MouReadEventQue	Read pointer event queue
MouSetEventMask	Set event mask
MouSetHotKey	Set system hot key
MouSetPtrPos	Set current pointer position
MouSetPtrShape	Set pointer shape/size
MouSetScaleFact	Set scale factors

SUMMARY

The OS/2 subsystems provide significant extensions to the PC DOS I/O model. Conceptually, these components provide the high-performance primitives required to build the OS/2 user interface. Important points to remember are

- The subsystem model
- How OS/2 subsystems relate to the PC DOS I/O model
- I/O subsystem structure and components
- Replacing subsystem functions
- OS/2 sessions
- Video I/O (VIO) functions
- Keyboard I/O (KBD) functions
- Mouse I/O (MOU) functions

CHAPTER 10
SESSION MANAGEMENT

Chapter 9 introduced the concept of sessions. A session is a collection of resources defining the user-interface context. You might compare an OS/2 session with a PC DOS system. Every application program that is started under PC DOS has access to the screen and keyboard. The PC DOS applications are sole owners of the user interface. Since PC DOS runs only one program at a time, the application always understands the state of the I/O devices. In fact, most applications assume that they are the sole users of the keyboard, video display, and mouse. To concurrently run more than one PC DOS application, you need special programs called *environment managers* (such as TopView, Microsoft Windows, and so forth) to provide each program with virtual resources.

OS/2 is a multitasking system that allows you to run more than one application at a time. To manage which application is visible on the screen and which is receiving input from the keyboard or mouse, OS/2 uses a special component called the *session manager*. The session manager runs individual application programs in virtual I/O groups (sessions). However, sessions are not a kernel concept; they are implemented by the I/O subsystems. The session manager is responsible for coordinating the subsystems so that the I/O flows to the correct applications. In effect, sessions are a logical grouping of system resources that provide the user with multiple virtual consoles.

This chapter begins with a discussion of how the session manager interacts with the I/O subsystems and the user to manage the sessions.

SESSION MANAGER STRUCTURE

Figure 10-1 shows the relationship of the session manager to the rest of the system. Each application program is run in a different session. The user selects which program to display by way of a session-manager user interface called the *session manager shell*. The shell actually is an application program running in its own session to interact with the user and pass session start, switch, and stop commands to the session manager component. The shell is the user-visible portion of the session manager.

From the application standpoint, it sees a dedicated keyboard, video display, and mouse. The session manager assumes the responsibility of associating the right subsystem context with the foreground application. From the subsystem standpoint, each session is a video buffer (LVB), keyboard queue (KBQ), and mouse event queue (MEQ). As

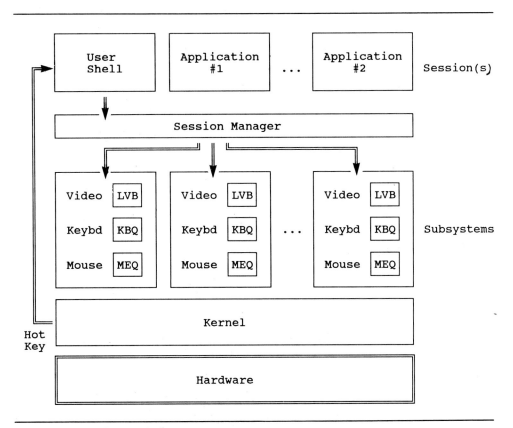

Figure 10-1. OS/2 session management components

the user switches from session to session, the session manager switches the subsystem *focus* to the appropriate application.

A session is a logical concept that transcends the kernel tasking model. Each session contains at least one process. Descendants of this process are automatically asso-

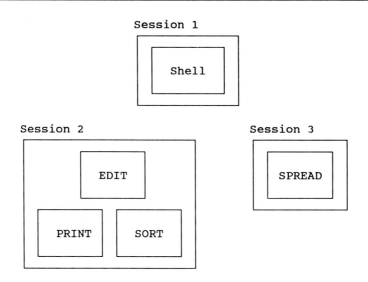

Figure 10-2.   Sample sessions

ciated with the same session. For example, Figure 10-2
shows a system with three sessions. The first is the session
manager shell that has created two user sessions, EDIT
and SPREAD. Note that the EDIT process has started
child processes PRINT and SORT. If EDIT, PRINT, or
SORT use VIO services, their outputs appear on the same
logical screen. If, on the other hand, SPREAD writes to

Table 10-1.   Session Manager Functions

API	Description
DosStartSession	Start a new session (and program)
DosSelectSession	Switch to parent or child session(s)
DosSetSession	Set session characteristics
DosStopSession	Stop child session

the screen, its output does not appear on the EDIT session screen. Similarly, the keyboard and mouse input from the user are sent to whichever current session is in the foreground. Within the session, any process that issues the MOU or KBD input calls is given the data. Since EDIT has three processes, any (or all) could read from the same logical keyboard and mouse. Normally, only one process in a session should read data from the input devices.

Session Hierarchy

The hierarchical relationship of sessions is similar to the process hierarchy implemented by the kernel. A process in one session may start a new session using the session manager API (see Table 10-1).

The DosStartSession function requests the session manager to EXEC a process into a new session. Therefore, DosStartSession is the only exception to the session inheritance rule described previously in this chapter.

Once the session is established, all subsequent DOSEXEC calls create processes in the new session. Figure 10-3 illustrates the relationship of sessions to the OS/2 tasking model.

Note the similarity between the hierarchical structure of sessions and processes, as well as the independence of the two models. Each hierarchy has its own set of parent-child relationships which match in some cases and not in others. Note Session 3, where the parent process and one of its children are in the same session, but a second child (Process 5) is in a different session.

Starting, Stopping, and Switching Sessions

Any process can start a new session with the session manager DosStartSession API function. This is precisely what the session-manager shell process uses to start the sessions on behalf of the user. A DosStartSession request creates

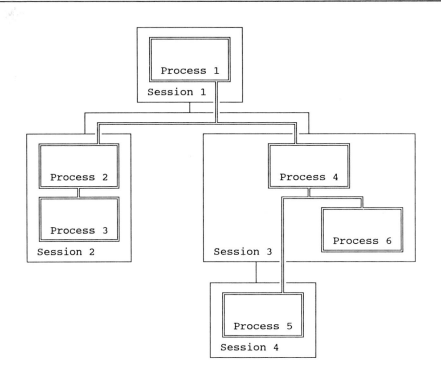

Figure 10-3. Session and process hierarchies

the session and EXECS the requested program. The session manager creates a unique Session identification (SESSID) and returns it to the caller. The parent uses the SESSID to identify the session in all subsequent calls to the session manager.

As in the OS/2 tasking model, a parent session may optionally be notified of the termination of child sessions. This is done asynchronously by using a termination queue. A parent session can start a child and have one thread wait on the termination queue. When any child session terminates, the session manager posts the parent's termination queue.

DosStartSession provides a number of options that define how the child session is to be treated. One option allows the parent to indicate if the child session is to be added to the session-manager shell-session switch list, thus enabling the user to switch to it by using the shell. Another option "binds" the parent to the child and causes the child to be brought to the foreground when the user selects the parent, or vice versa.

The OS/2 DosSelectSession API can be used by a parent session to bring any of its child sessions to the foreground. However, this can only be done when the parent or one of its other children is currently in the foreground. Since the session manager shell is the parent of all the system sessions, the session manager is the only process in the system that can select any session to run in the foreground.

A parent can stop any child session it created with the DosStopSession function. Only child sessions can be stopped with this API. The parent cannot explicitly stop itself, nor descendants of its child sessions (grandchildren). However, if a child is stopped, the session manager automatically stops all descendant sessions.

The DOS compatibility environment, if it exists, is started as a system session. From the user's perspective, this environment is just another session that can be selected from the session manager shell. The session manager APIs may not be used to dynamically create, destroy, or select the DOS compatibility session.

THE SYSTEM SHELL

When the system is started, OS/2 creates a special session called the *user shell*. The user shell is an application program that interacts with the user and the session manager to start, stop, and switch application sessions. The OS/2 system always has a session that is designated to act as the user shell.

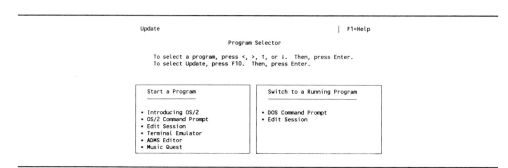

```
    Update                                    |  F1=Help
                         Program Selector
         To select a program, press <, >, ↑, or ↓.  Then, press Enter.
         To select Update, press F10.  Then, press Enter.


    ┌─────────────────────────────┐    ┌─────────────────────────────┐
    │  Start a Program            │    │  Switch to a Running Program│
    │  ─────────────────          │    │  ─────────────────────────  │
    │                             │    │                             │
    │  • Introducing OS/2         │    │  • DOS Command Prompt       │
    │  • OS/2 Command Prompt      │    │  • Edit Session             │
    │  • Edit Session             │    │                             │
    │  • Terminal Emulator        │    │                             │
    │  • ADMS Editor              │    │                             │
    │  • Music Quest              │    │                             │
    └─────────────────────────────┘    └─────────────────────────────┘
```

Figure 10-4.   The OS/2 program selector

OS/2 1.0 includes a user shell program called the Application Selector. However, you may replace the Application Selector with a different shell by using the PROTSHELL system configuration (CONFIG.SYS) option.

Starting and Switching Sessions

After OS/2 is booted, the main shell menu immediately appears. Unlike the traditional PC DOS C: >command line, the OS/2 user shell is a full-screen application that can be operated with the keyboard or the mouse. Figure 10-4 depicts the OS/2 user shell.

Using the shell, you may select an application program from the *installed program list* that appears on the left-hand side of the screen. You add applications to this list with the shell UPDATE function. Normally, you would add your most commonly used application programs to this list, such as a program editor or a terminal emulator.

When you select a program, the shell instructs the session manager to start a new (foreground) session and load the application into the system. Thus, you may start applications without using the command-line interface.

The shell displays the currently loaded applications in the right-hand portion of the screen in an area called the *application switch list*. Switching to an existing application session is similar to starting a new session, except that you select the application from the switch list instead of the installed program list. When you select a program from the switch list, the shell instructs the session manager to switch the desired session to the foreground. Again, this is accomplished without the use of the OS/2 command-line interface.

Shell Hot Keys

While in an application session, OS/2 reserves two key sequences (CTRL-ESC and ALT-ESC) for use as shell *hot keys* (see Figure 10-5). The CTRL-ESC sequence always returns the shell program to the foreground. While in an application, you may use CTRL-ESC to return to the shell to start a new session, or to switch to another session in the switch list. The ALT-ESC sequence is used to toggle between the active sessions (except the shell). To switch to another session, you can either press CTRL-ESC to go to the shell and select from the switch list, or you can press ALT-ESC until the desired session is displayed.

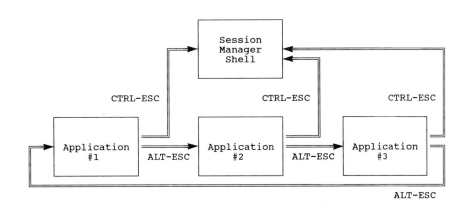

Figure 10-5. Hot keys

The OS/2 Command Line

A traditional PC DOS-style command line is available as a "system" application. The OS/2 program selection list always contains the command line as a selection option. OS/2 starts the command line as an application program that runs in its own session. Application programs and command (CMD) files (the OS/2 equivalent of PC DOS batch files) can be run from an OS/2 command line. Therefore, you can run frequently used applications (such as an editor or terminal emulator) from the program selection list and less frequently used programs from a command line. OS/2 allows you to start multiple copies of the OS/2 command line.

The OS/2 command interpreter provides commands that you can use to asynchronously start an application from within the current session (DETACH command) or in a new session (START command). Command files may use these commands to "spin-off" other programs that run concurrently. For instance,

```
START SPOOL "System Spooler"
DETACH MASM MYPROG; >LPT1:
```

starts the system spooler in a new session and adds the name string "System Spooler" to the shell switch list. A copy of the MASM program is then started in the current session with the output redirected to the printer. Since DETACH and START both operate asynchronously, the CMD file finishes and returns the screen to the command line. MASM and SPOOLER continue to run.

Automatic Startup

In the event that the system is to start without user interaction (unattended operation), or that certain sessions are always to be started, OS/2 has an automatic start-up facility. When the system is booted, OS/2 searches the root directory for a file named STARTUP.CMD. If it finds this file, a command interpreter session is started and is passed the STARTUP command file. STARTUP.CMD is run as a normal OS/2 command file with access to all the command interpreter functions. You can use this file to start other OS/2 sessions or to initialize system resources (such as communications lines).

For example, consider the following file:

```
MODE COM1: 2400,8,n,1
START PE3  "My Editor"
START TERM "Terminal Emulator"
EXIT
```

The MODE command initializes the communications port (COM1:) for all sessions. The START commands create two sessions and add the session names to the shell switch list. Finally, the EXIT statement terminates the command interpreter (and the session) that is running the STARTUP.CMD file. You are presented with the session manager shell. Note that if the EXIT statement were left off, OS/2 would leave the command session on the screen. By omitting the EXIT statement from your STARTUP.CMD file, you can make OS/2 look like PC DOS. In the second scenario, you never see the shell program.

THE COMMAND INTERPRETER

The *command interpreter* is a special component that provides you with a command-line interface to OS/2. Unlike PC DOS, where the command line is the only user interface, the OS/2 command line is not required to run application programs. You can start applications directly by selecting them from the shell application list. However, it is impractical to add all the programs that are installed in the system to the shell. For instance, if you have a directory full of small tools, it would be too time-consuming to add each program as an individual entity on the shell application selection list. In this situation, it is easier to start the utility programs by using their names.

In general, the command interpreter has three primary functions:

- It provides you a user interface for starting programs by name (command line).

- It implements a number of commonly used system functions (commands).

- It has the ability to interpret and execute special files that contain combinations of OS/2 commands (CMD files).

Command Line

The familiar PC DOS command line (C>) is implemented in OS/2. A command line is a less-sophisticated user interface that has the appearance of a TTY device. This type of user interface is common in large multi-user systems where end users interact with the system by using dumb terminals. This interface causes the output from the application programs to be scrolled. The OS/2 utilities are examples of progams that use the console in TTY mode. For instance, if you enter a directory list command (DIR), the output is presented as a series of lines. As each line is written, the previous lines are scrolled up in the screen image.

The OS/2 command interpreter presents a prompt when the system is ready for command input. In OS/2, the default user prompt is "[x: \]" for protected mode command lines and "*x*>" for DOS-compatibility environment command lines (where *x* is the current drive). The prompts are one way you can distinguish a protected mode command line from the DOS command line. However, you can always change the prompt by using the PROMPT command.

You enter commands at the prompt. The ENTER key signals the end of the command input. The command interpreter then parses the input buffer, locates the desired program, and issues the kernel EXEC call to create the process and run your program.

Current Drive

The commands you enter at the command line are really programs on one of your disks. The command interpreter uses the command to locate a program or command file with the same name on one of your disk drives. Since it would be very inefficient to search all the disks every time you enter a command, the command interpreter has the notion of *current drive*. The current drive is the device OS/2 always searches for the program.

When the interpreter is started, the current drive is set to the boot volume (C:). As you enter commands, the file directory on the current drive is searched for an EXE file with the same name as the command. If no EXE match is found, the interpreter searches for a command (CMD) file with the same name.

Note that the OS/2 protected mode environment requires all programs to have an extended EXE header, so the command interpreter search sequence does not include COM files (this type of program only runs in the OS/2 DOS-compatibility environment).

You can reset the current drive by entering a drive identifier at the command line. For instance, to execute a program from your diskette drive, enter the following sequence of commands:

```
[C:\]A:
[A:\]MYPROG
... program output ...
... program output ...
... program output ...
[A:\]
```

Notice that the change in current drive is reflected in the system prompt ([A:\]), and that it remains set after MYPROG ends. All subsequent commands execute from drive A.

You may override the current drive by including the drive identifier in the command string. In the previous example, the following sequence also runs MYPROG:

```
[C:\]A:MYPROG
... program output ...
... program output ...
... program output ...
[C:\]
```

In this case, however, the current drive value (C:) is not changed after the program ends.

Current Directory

The command interpreter also has the notion of *current directory*. Like the current drive, the current directory tells the system which directory should be searched for commands. You may change the current directory with the Change Directory (CD) command. OS/2 maintains a current directory for each drive. For example, consider the following series of commands:

```
[C:\]cd c:tools
[C:\TOOLS]cd d:programs
[C:\TOOLS]MYPROG1
... program output ...
[C:\TOOLS]D:MYPROG2
... program output ...
[C:\TOOLS]
```

The first CD command sets the current directory for drive C to the subdirectory named TOOLS. Likewise, the second CD sets the current directory for drive D to the subdirectory named PROGRAMS. When you then execute MYPROG1 from the current drive, the OS/2 command interpreter searches the directory C:\TOOLS for the program. On the other hand, when you run MYPROG2 from drive D, the command interpreter searches the subdirectory named D:\PROGRAMS. As with the current drive, the change in current directory is reflected in the system prompt and remains set after the programs are run.

You may explicitly name the directory to be searched for your command by adding the subdirectory information to the command. Command names with prepended subdirectory names are said to be *fully qualified commands*. For example,

```
[C:\]tools\myprog1
... program output ...
[C:\]d:programs\myprog2
... program output ...
[C:\]
```

has the same effect as the previous example, except that the current directories for drive C and drive D are not changed.

Command Search Path

The command interpreter always searches the current drive and directory to resolve command names. However, you can extend the search order with other drives and directories that differ from the current drive and directory by providing an *execution path*. A path is nothing more than a list of drive-qualified subdirectory names. Suppose that you have a system that has a file with three subdirectories named DOS, PROGRAM, and TOOLS. When you entered the command,

[C: \]path c: \dos;c: \tools;c: \program;a: \

the command interpreter search path would become the current directory, followed by DOS, TOOLS, and PROGRAM subdirectories on the drive C, and the root directory on the drive A. OS/2 would then use this search path every time it processes a command. Naturally, the search always ends when the first match is found. Generally the subdirectories containing the most frequently used commands (such as DOS utilities) should be placed early in the search path.

The search path can be used to augment the current directory and current subdirectory functions to create an environment that suits your needs. However, remember that long search paths cause additional overhead for the command interpreter and should be avoided.

Environment

The command interpreter creates a special area that contains information to be shared among programs. This area, called the *environment*, is a series of named variables and associated values. Every program started under the command interpreter is given a copy of the environment. As descendants are created, each is given a copy of its parent's environment.

You create environment values with the SET command. A new environment variable is created (or an existing one

Table 10-2. System Environment Variables

Name	Set By	Usage
COMSPEC	Command interpreter	Command interpreter name
PATH	PATH command	Command search path
APPEND	APPEND utility	File append path
PROMPT	PROMPT command	Command prompt
DPATH	DPATH command	Data search path

is updated) with the following command:

    SET variablename=value

OS/2 stores the variable name and its associated value in the environment area. The value is a string composed of valid ASCII characters (including blanks). To delete an environment variable, enter the SET command with a null-value string, as follows:

    SET variablename=

The SET command with no parameters lists the contents of your environment. As you will see in Chapter 13, environment variables are useful as input data for OS/2 command (CMD) files.

Several system functions use environment variables to hold information. (See Table 10-2.) Avoid using environment variable names that conflict with these reserved system names.

The current directory, current drive, and environment are unique to each instance of the command interpreter. If you start multiple command lines, each will retain its settings as you switch from one session to another.

Special Operators

The OS/2 command interpreter includes a number of special operators that you can use to construct complex command sequences. The operators (listed by precedence in

Table 10-3. Special Operators

Operator	Description
^	Lexical escape character
( )	Execution grouping
< > > >	I/O redirection
¦	Piping output between programs
&&	AND command execution
¦¦	OR command execution
&	Command separator

Table 10-3) allow you to tap advanced features of the command interpreter (including standard I/O redirection, program execution control, and output piping). You invoke these functions by including the special characters within your command sequence. These characters are treated as commands by the command interpreter, so if you intend to use one as part of your input (rather than as a command interpreter function), the character must be preceded by the lexical escape character (^). For example, the command sequence

ECHO Enter your name ^& address ==^>

will print the string,

Enter your name & address ==>

Because of the lexical escape sequence, the command interpreter treats "&" and ">" as normal characters rather than command operators.

Standard I/O redirection   You can redirect the standard output of a command to a file or device by using the > operator. For instance, consider the following commands:

```
DIR *.* >LPT1:
DIR *.* >DIR.OUT
```

In the first case, the output of the directory listing is sent to the device named LPT1: Any valid OS/2 output device can be sent the redirected command output. Output directed to the NUL: device is discarded, so this technique is often used to run programs without echoing information to the screen. The second example sends the output to a file named DIR.OUT. If the file already exists, it is replaced.

You can append the output to an existing file by using the >> operator. For example,

```
DIR *.* >>DIR.OUT
```

appends the output of the DIR command to the contents of the DIR.OUT file. If the file does not exist, the command interpreter creates it.

Input that a command normally would receive from the default input device (the keyboard) can be retrieved from any file or device. This is accomplished by using the < operator, as follows:

```
FORMAT <COM1:
FORMAT <FORMAT.IN
```

In the first example, the input to the FORMAT command is taken from the COM1: device. You can use any valid OS/2 input device to redirect input to a command. In the second example, the input for the FORMAT command is read from the file named FORMAT.IN. The file must contain all the input expected by FORMAT, including carriage returns.

As you will recall, the OS/2 file system supports several forms of standard input and output. Different handles are used for STDIN, STDOUT, and STDERR. The command interpreter supports redirection of up to nine STDIO handles from the command line. You redirect a particular handle by specifying the handle number with the redirection character. For example, since STDOUT is handle 1 and STDERR is handle 2, you may enter the following command:

CHKDSK *.* 1>CHKDSK.OUT 2>CHKDSK.ERR

The normal output (handle 1) of the command CHKDSK is sent to a file named CHKDSK.OUT. The error output (handle 2) is sent to CHKDSK.ERR. *Handle redirection* is a generalized function that may be used with all STDIO handles (including handles 3-9).

The command interpreter allows you to duplicate the output (or input) from one handle to another with the duplicate handle operator (&). For example:

CHKDSK *.* 1>CHKDSK.OUT 2>&1
MYPROG 2>&1 3>&1 4>&1

In the first case, STDERR (handle 2) is duplicated into STDOUT (handle 1), causing the error output to be merged with the normal output. Furthermore, all the output is sent to the file CHKDSK.OUT. This is conceptually similar to redirecting the output of both STDOUT and STDERR to CHKDSK.OUT. In the second example, all output generated by MYPROG from handles 2, 3, and 4 is sent to handle 1.

Only one redirection is permissible per handle. If more than one redirection operator is used, the last one entered is honored and the rest are ignored.

Command execution operators

The OS/2 command interpreter allows you to enter more than one command at the command line. Three types of operators are used as command separators: one for unconditional and two for conditional execution.

The & operator delimits multiple commands for unconditional execution. This means each command is executed regardless of the command termination codes. For example, the command

COPY C:MYPROG.ASM D: & ERASE C:MYPROG.ASM

copies the file MYPROG.ASM from drive C to drive D and then erases it from the drive C. In effect, this command moves the file from one drive to another.

But what happens if drive D is full? The copy fails and the file is erased from the drive C—clearly an undesirable effect. The AND (&&) operator solves this dilemma by conditionally executing a series of commands. Each command in the list is executed if the previous command completed successfully. So if you enter

COPY C:MYPROG.ASM D: && ERASE C:MYPROG.ASM

the ERASE command is not executed unless the COPY command completes without an error. If the COPY command succeeds, the file is erased. The AND operator may be used with any valid OS/2 commands. For example, if you enter

MASM MYPROG; && LINK MYPROG;

MYPROG is assembled and linked. The LINK is run if the program was assembled without error.

The inverse of the AND operator is the OR (¦¦) execution delimiter. This delimiter is also a conditional execution operator, but in this case the commands in the list are executed until one succeeds. For example, the command line

COPY C:MYPROG.ASM A: ¦¦ COPY C:MYPROG.ASM B:

attempts to copy MYPROG.ASM to drive A and drive B.

If the first COPY succeeds, the second is not attempted. If the disk in drive A is full, the first COPY fails and the second command is executed, copying the file to the disk in drive B.

You can change the command execution precedence by using the command grouping operators ( ). These operators override the normal precedence of the other operators. For example, the command line

(MASM MYPROG; >MP.OUT) && (LINK MYPROG; <LINK.IN)

demonstrates the use of the command grouping operators in conjunction with I/O redirection and conditional execution operators. First, MYPROG is assembled and the screen output is redirected to a file named MP.OUT. If the assembly is successful, the program is linked with the input coming from a file named LINK.IN. Note that command grouping operators clarify which redirection operation is associated with which command.

You may use command interpreter operators from the command line or within OS/2 command (CMD) files. When you use command interpreter operators in a CMD file, the error code returned by the last command is retained in the ERRORLEVEL variable.

Piping

The command interpreter pipe operator (|) allows you to "hook" the standard output of one program to the standard input of another. Conceptually, the following commands are equivalent:

(DIR *.* >$TEMP) & (MORE <$TEMP) & ERASE $TEMP
DIR *.* | MORE

However, there is a big difference in the two examples. In the first case the programs are executed serially, with the output passed in a temporary disk file named $TEMP.

In the second case, the programs are run concurrently and the output is passed by using a pipe.

The pipe operator (|) instructs the command interpreter to start the commands asynchronously, connecting the standard output of one command to a pipe and the standard input of the other to the other end of the same pipe. The OS/2 command interpreter uses kernel EXEC and IPC functions to implement command-line pipes. Each program in the pipe is running concurrently. As one generates output, it is immediately passed to the next.

OS/2 has a set of special utilities called *filters* that always receive input from STDIN and send output to STDOUT. These filters can be chained together with the pipe operator. For example, in the command line

DIR *.* | SORT | MORE

the DIR command lists the contents of the current directory. Normally this would be scrolled on the screen with the programs appearing in directory sequence. However, in this case, the data is sent to the SORT filter to sort in alphabetical sequence and then to the MORE filter to be presented in individual pages.

As with all operators, pipes may be used from the command line or within CMD files.

Built-in Commands

In OS/2, the most commonly used system commands are not implemented as separate programs, but rather are a part of the command interpreter. By incorporating these functions, the command interpreter does not have to read the programs from the disk, thus improving performance and useability.

Whenever you enter a command at the command line, the command interpreter first checks the command name against its internal command table. If found in the table,

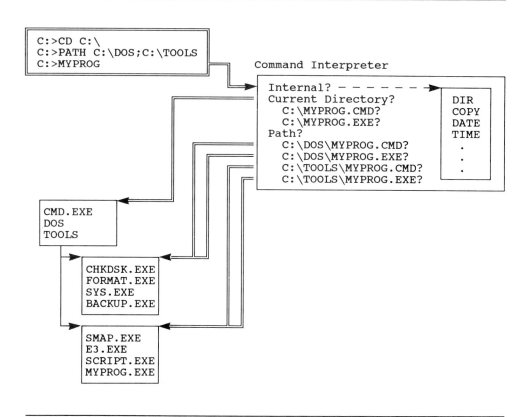

Figure 10-6.   Command search order

the command is immediately executed. If not found, the command name is assumed to be an external program and the current directory (or path) is searched for the appropriate CMD or EXE file. Figure 10-6 summarizes the OS/2 command-search algorithm.

In effect, the internal command names are a set of "reserved" program names. Avoid naming your programs with one of these names, since using one of these names means the program could never be run from the OS/2 command line. Note, however, that even if a program has a name conflict with an internal command (such as DIR.EXE), it can still be run by using the OS/2 EXEC API.

Command (CMD) Language

While the command line provides a flexible and powerful mechanism for starting programs, entering a repetitive series of commands sometimes becomes tedious. To assist you in these situations, the OS/2 command interpreter allows you to group a set of commands in a special file called a *command (CMD) file*. As discussed previously, CMD file names can be entered at the command line. When the command interpreter recognizes the command as a CMD file, it reads its contents into memory and executes each statement as if you entered it as a separate command. Thus, you can automate a repetitive series of commands with a single command file.

OS/2 command files generally are upwardly compatible with PC DOS batch files. You can run existing BAT files in OS/2 by converting the file extension from BAT to CMD. Of course, this assumes that the BAT file does not depend on programs that will not execute in OS/2 protected mode. The DOS compatibility environment runs PC DOS BAT files unchanged.

CMD files contain a series of ASCII statements, each separated by a carriage return. The statements contain a command and its operands, as if you had entered the statements at the command line. For example, consider the following CMD file:

```
CD PROGRAMS
MASM MYPROG,,MYPROG;
LINK MYPROG;
ERASE MYPROG.OBJ
PRINT MYPROG.LST
ERASE MYPROG.LST
CD \
```

When you enter the command BUILD at the command line, the command interpreter recognizes the file as a CMD file and processes its contents as a series of commands. First, the CD (internal) command changes the current directory to a subdirectory named PROGRAMS. The CMD file then invokes MASM and LINK to assemble and link a program named MYPROG. Since it is no longer needed, the ERASE command erases the MYPROG.OBJ file created by MASM. The program listing (MYPROG.LST) is printed with the PRINT command and the file is erased. Unlike PC DOS, the OS/2 print spooler makes a copy of the print output to a spool file, so the listing can be erased once the spooler receives the data. Finally, the current directory is reset to the root directory.

In this example, the CMD file allows you to enter a single command to do what would otherwise have required seven different commands. More significantly, you can start the CMD file and switch to another session, thus enabling you to do other work while your program is being assembled and linked.

Substitution Variables

The CMD facility is useful for creating command lists for frequently performed functions. A CMD file has a specific set of commands that perform a particular task. However, if you look at the typical tasks which you perform every day, you realize that you seldom do exactly the same thing every time. In fact, you often perform related sets of functions with a small variation here or there. A CMD file that does one (and only one) thing is limited in its usefulness. The OS/2 command interpreter includes a function, called *variable substitution*, that allows you to build general-purpose CMD files.

When a CMD file is started, the command interpreter

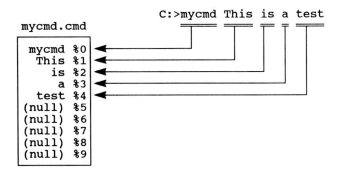

Figure 10-7. CMD input variables

parses into tokens the data entered at the command line (following the CMD name). Each token is then placed into variables that can be used within the CMD file. For instance, if the CMD file contains the string %1 in one of its statements, the command interpreter substitutes the first parameter entered at the command line for the %1 before the command is executed.

Figure 10-7 illustrates how four words following the command name are placed in CMD variables. Note that %0 is a special variable that always contains the name of the CMD file. Depending on what you enter at the command line, the CMD file can do different things.

In the previous example, the CMD file built a program named MYPROG.EXE. The *only* program the CMD file could build was MYPROG. However, the steps used to assemble and link a program are the same regardless of the program being built. So, using substitution variables, the CMD file could be changed, as follows:

```
CD PROGRAMS
MASM %1,,%1;
LINK %1;
ERASE %1.OBJ
PRINT %1.LST
ERASE %1.LST
CD \
```

In each instance, the command interpreter replaces the %1 with the first parameter entered after the BUILD command. So the command

[C:\]BUILD MYPROG

has the same effect as before. However, since it is now parameter-driven, the BUILD.CMD file is more flexible and can be used to assemble and link any program.

In most cases, you can use input variable substitution to generalize CMD files so that they perform a series of commands based on operator input.

Conditional Execution

If something goes wrong, or if the processing has to differ depending on the user input, the CMD file must be a bit more intelligent about how it processes the commands. The CMD file cannot "blindly" execute the command list. The OS/2 command interpreter allows you to *conditionally execute* command sequences.

The CMD language IF and GOTO commands enable you to write a CMD file that can test conditions and exe-

```
IF [NOT] condition command
```

Where:

    condition = ERRORLEVEL value
         string1 = = string2
         EXIST filename

    command = Any OS/2 command

GOTO label

Where:

    label = :string (somewhere in CMD file)

Figure 10-8. CMD file conditional execution commands

cute different command sequences. Figure 10-8 shows the syntax of the CMD conditional functions.

Note that the IF statement supports three types of conditions: the equality of strings (including variables), the existence of files, or the error code returned by the previous command. Be careful when using the ERRORLEVEL condition—it is not an equality test. An ERRORLEVEL IF condition is TRUE when the error code is greater-than-or-equal-to the value specified. The inverse of all the conditions can be tested by adding the NOT operator before the condition.

The GOTO command is a handy mechanism for branching to a different portion of the CMD file. The target of the GOTO command is a label and can be located anywhere in the file. In the CMD file, the label is represented by the same ASCII string used in the GOTO statement, preceded by a colon to distinguish it from other commands.

Using these facilities, the BUILD.CMD file could be updated as follows:

```
CD PROGRAMS
IF NOT EXIST %1.ASM GOTO END3
MASM %1,,%1;
IF ERRORLEVEL 1 GOTO END2
LINK %1;
IF ERRORLEVEL 1 GOTO END1
PRINT %1.LST
:END1
ERASE %1.LST
:END2
ERASE %1.OBJ
:END3
CD \
```

Notice that three conditionals (IF statements) have been added to the CMD file. The first tests if the user input is valid. If the file name does not correspond to an ASM file in the PROGRAMS subdirectory, the CMD file branches to the label END3, resets the current directory, and exits. The second test verifies that the assembly completed successfuly (error level greater than 0). If an error occurs, the CMD file erases the OBJ file, resets the current directory, and exits. The final test verifies that the LINK command worked. If the LINK error code is nonzero, then all the files are erased, the current directory is reset, and the CMD file ends.

Suppressing Screen Output

A CMD file is nothing more than a collection of commands. As each command is executed, the command interpreter echoes the command and its resulting output to the screen. If you run the BUILD file created in the previous section, the output looks like Figure 10-9.

Each CMD statement, the external utilities (MASM

```
[C:\]build test
[C:\]CD PROGRAMS
[C:\]IF NOT EXIST test.ASM GOTO END3
[C:\]MASM test,,test;

IBM MACRO Assembler/2
Version 1.00
(C)Copyright IBM Corp 1981, 1987
(C)Copyright Microsoft Corp 1981-1987. All rights reserved.

50096 Bytes free

Warning Severe
Errors  Errors
0       0

[C:\]IF ERRORLEVEL 1 GOTO END2
[C:\]LINK test;

IBM Linker/2  Version 1.00
Copyright (C) IBM Corporation 1987
Copyright (C) Microsoft Corp 1983-1987.  All rights reserved.

[C:\]IF ERRORLEVEL 1 GOTO END1
[C:\]PRINT test.LST
```

Figure 10-9.   BUILD.CMD screen output

and LINK), and their outputs are displayed on the console. This output is useful when you debug the CMD file, but is not always desirable. The command interpreter provides several techniques that enable you to control what you see while the CMD file is running.

The ECHO statement turns the screen echo ON and OFF from within the CMD file. The "@" operator suppresses output for a particular command. The quiet switch (/q) allows you to start a CMD file with no screen echo (see Figure 10-10).

The command interpreter maintains an internal screen echo state. When screen echo is ON, it echoes each of the commands to the screen as it executes them. When a CMD file is started, the screen echo state is ON. If the quiet flag is included in the command line

[C:\]BUILD /q test

```
ECHO ON|OFF|string

    Where:

          ON =  Enables command echo
         OFF =  Disables command echo
      string =  Writes string to screen

@command            Suppresses command screen echo

cmdfile /q          Runs CMD file with ECHO OFF
```

Figure 10-10. Suppressing CMD file screen output

the CMD file is started with screen echo OFF. The ECHO command can also be used within the CMD file to turn screen echo ON or OFF. Any combination of ECHO ON and ECHO OFF commands is permitted in the file. Executing an ECHO ON command while screen echo is ON, or an ECHO OFF command while the screen echo is OFF, has no effect. The screen echo for a single command can be bypassed by prepending the command with the special character "@". For example,

    @GOTO END

executes the GOTO command without echoing on the screen. Output can always be displayed (regardless of the echo state) with the ECHO string statement. For instance,

    ECHO This is a CMD file

prints the string "This is a CMD file" on the console.

These functions can be incorporated in the BUILD.CMD file, as follows.

```
@ECHO OFF
CD PROGRAMS
IF NOT EXIST %1.ASM GOTO END3
ECHO **** Program %1 being assembled
MASM %1,,%1;
IF ERRORLEVEL 1 GOTO END2
ECHO **** Program %1 being linked
LINK %1;
IF ERRORLEVEL 1 GOTO END1
PRINT %1.LST
:END1
ERASE %1.LST
ERASE %1.OBJ
ECHO **** Link Failed
GOTO ENDIT
:END2
ERASE %1.OBJ
ECHO **** Assembly Failed
GOTO ENDIT
:END3
ECHO **** Invalid Program Name
:ENDIT
CD \
```

The @ECHO OFF statement disables the command echo. The leading @ operator causes the "ECHO OFF" string to not be echoed to the screen. With a little restructuring, the error paths are enhanced with error messages describing the three failure conditions. Finally, two informational messages are displayed while the input file is being assembled and linked. The screen output of the modified BUILD file is illustrated in Figure 10-11.

Notice that while the output from the command interpreter has been suppressed, the utility (MASM, LINK, PRINT) output has not. This is because the ECHO OFF statement directs the command interpreter, but not the programs it runs, to suppress screen output.

The output of programs written to the OS/2 standard I/O facilities (such as all the OS/2 utility programs) can be

```
[C:\]build test
**** Program test being assembled
IBM MACRO Assembler/2
Version 1.00
(C)Copyright IBM Corp 1981, 1987
(C)Copyright Microsoft Corp 1981-1987. All rights reserved.

50096 Bytes free

Warning Severe
Errors  Errors
0       0

**** Program test being linked
IBM Linker/2  Version 1.00
Copyright (C) IBM Corporation 1987
Copyright (C) Microsoft Corp 1983-1987.  All rights reserved.

[C:\]
```

Figure 10-11.   BUILD.CMD with ECHO OFF

suppressed by redirecting the output to another device. The BUILD file can be further refined, as follows:

```
@ECHO OFF
CD PROGRAMS
IF NOT EXIST %1.ASM GOTO END3
ECHO **** Program %1 being assembled
MASM %1,,%1; >%1.ERR
IF ERRORLEVEL 1 GOTO END2
ECHO **** Program %1 being linked
LINK %1;        >%1.ERR
IF ERRORLEVEL 1 GOTO END1
PRINT %1.LST >NUL:
ERASE %1.ERR >NUL:
:END1
ERASE %1.LST >NUL:
ERASE %1.OBJ >NUL:
ECHO **** Link Failed
TYPE %1.ERR | MORE
GOTO ENDIT
:END2
ERASE %1.OBJ >NUL:
ECHO **** Assembly Failed
TYPE %1.ERR | MORE
GOTO ENDIT
:END3
ECHO **** Invalid Program Name
:ENDIT
CD \
```

Note that output redirection is used for two purposes: suppression of output and retention of program data. Wherever the command output is discardable, the output is redirected to the NUL: device. For instance, the screen output of the ERASE command can be discarded in this way. However, the information returned by MASM and LINK is important if either step fails. So this output is saved in a special file whose file specification is the program name (%1) with the .ERR extension. If MASM and LINK complete successfully, the ERR file is erased. If not, the ERR file is retained for future reference.

Since the error data is in a file, it could be passed to your program editor or displayed on the screen by using the TYPE command. However, since TYPE output can be scrolled, it should be piped into the MORE filter to stop the data from scrolling off the screen. This is important if the CMD file is run in a background session.

Figure 10-12 shows the output of the modified BUILD.CMD. file.

Environment Variables

The command interpreter environment space takes on a special meaning when running a CMD file. If a CMD statement includes the name of one of the environment variables delimited by percentage signs (%), the corresponding environment variable value is substituted into the command.

For instance, suppose you enter

SET PRINTER=LPT1:

sometime during the session and you then run a CMD file that contains

COPY DATA %printer%

the following command then executes

COPY DATA LPT1:

You can set environment variables at the time the session is started for subsequent use in CMD files. Using this technique, you can write CMD files that do not have "hard-coded" values for things that are subject to change (such as your current printer). A CMD file can change the value of the environment variables.

If you wish to temporarily change an environment value, you can make a "local" copy of the environment space, the current directory, and the current drive with the SETLOCAL command. The original values can be restored with the ENDLOCAL command. Using SETLOCAL/ENDLOCAL enables you to change the values for the duration of the CMD file, returning them to their original state when the CMD file ends.

```
Normal:

    [C:\]build test
    **** Program test being assembled
    **** Program test being linked
    [C:\]


Error:

    [C:\]build test
    **** Program test being assembled
    **** Assembly Error
    [C:\]
```

Figure 10-12. BUILD.CMD output with redirection

These concepts can be incorporated in the BUILD.CMD file, as follows:

```
@ECHO %ECHO%
SETLOCAL
CD PROGRAMS
IF NOT EXIST %1.ASM GOTO END3
ECHO **** Program %1 being assembled
MASM %1,,%1; >%1.ERR
IF ERRORLEVEL 1 GOTO END2
ECHO **** Program %1 being linked
LINK %1;      >%1.ERR
IF ERRORLEVEL 1 GOTO END1
IF %PRINT%. == ON. PRINT %1.LST >NUL:
ERASE %1.ERR >NUL:
:END1
ERASE %1.LST >NUL:
ERASE %1.OBJ >NUL:
ECHO **** Link Failed
TYPE %1.ERR | MORE
GOTO ENDIT
:END2
ERASE %1.OBJ >NUL:
ECHO **** Assembly Failed
TYPE %1.ERR | MORE
GOTO ENDIT
:END3
ECHO **** Invalid Program Name
:ENDIT
ENDLOCAL
```

BUILD now uses two environment variables (%print% and %echo%) in its processing logic. The %echo% variable determines if the CMD file echoes characters to the screen. If you issue

SET ECHO=ON

from the command line before running BUILD, then %echo% is set to ON. If you then run BUILD (or any other CMD file which interrogates %echo%), the %echo% string is substituted with ON and the output is echoed to the screen.

Similarly, the %print% environment variable is used by the CMD file to decide whether to print the file. Rather than directly printing the listing, BUILD first compares the string "%print%." to the constant "ON." Note the use of the period to guard against the situation where the %print% environment variable does not exist. If the strings match, the print command executes; if not, the print command is bypassed. If all your CMD files are written to use environment variables in a consistent way, you can control their actions with the SET command.

The SETLOCAL command saves the initial setting of the current directory. At the end of the CMD file, the ENDLOCAL command restores the directory value. Thus, BUILD can be run from any subdirectory on the disk.

SUMMARY

This chapter has discussed the primary components of the OS/2 user interface. As you become more familiar with the OS/2 system, you can review some of the concepts described here. The following items are important points to remember:

- OS/2 sessions as virtual consoles
- Relationship of sessions to processes
- The session manager
- The session manager API

- The user shell
- Command interpreter
- Command-line functions
- Current disk and current directory
- Input/output redirection
- Command (CMD) files

CHAPTER 11
SYSTEM TOPICS

OS/2 is a very new operating system. However, this system is more than a simple collection of memory-management and multi-tasking services. It is a complete, full-function operating system with many of the functions and facilities that you would normally find only in a "mature" operating system. This chapter discusses some of the OS/2 functions sometimes overlooked, and yet critically important to the overall system. Compatibility, error-processing, National Language Support, and system-serviceability aids are all important pieces of the OS/2 puzzle.

THE DOS COMPATIBILITY ENVIRONMENT

In today's personal computing environment, most people have made significant investments in PC DOS application software. A user who buys a new operating system (such as OS/2) expects his software investment to be protected. No new operating system can ever succeed if it ignores application migration and compatibility issues.

OS/2 is no exception. In this system, existing applications are supported by way of a special user session called the DOS compatibility session. From the user's perspective, the DOS session is nothing more than another display session dedicated to PC DOS-style application programs. It appears on the Session Manager session switch list and you select it either directly from the session switch list or with the round-robin session switch key (ALT-ESC).

But inside the DOS session, things are quite different. To a program, this session looks just like a PC DOS environment, rather than the OS/2 environment you have seen thus far. In fact, the OS/2 APIs and facilities you have learned about are not available to programs running in the DOS session. Instead, OS/2 emulates the PC DOS API and facilities. This environment is a good rendition of PC DOS. With few restrictions, a PC DOS application can do anything in the DOS environment that it does in a real PC DOS system.

DOS Environment Characteristics

When OS/2 runs a program in the DOS environment, it switches the CPU to real addressing mode. As discussed in Chapter 2, this is the native 8088 operating mode. While in real mode, an 80286 processor does not exhibit the advanced characteristics that make many of the OS/2 functions possible. Most significantly, the application address space is bounded by the 640K limitation.

But this mode does offer one important advantage — application compatibility. In real mode, application programs can manipulate segment registers as they do in PC DOS. This is critical because without this capability, many existing PC applications would not run.

When you select the DOS session as the foreground session, OS/2 automatically switches the CPU to real mode. While you work with a compatibility program, the OS/2 dispatcher continues to run and gives CPU time slices to background (protected mode) programs. As OS/2 multitasks the foreground real mode program and the background protected mode program(s), it switches CPU modes on the fly, making the CPU mode part of the thread context. Remember, the thread context is the system "state" information automatically maintained for each thread of execution (register values, stack, and so forth).

When you select a protected mode session to run in the foreground, the DOS session does not continue to run. While it is in the background (not visible on the screen), the DOS session is frozen. If you want to run a PC DOS program, you must place the DOS session in the foreground. Therefore, CPU mode switching *only* happens when the DOS session is in the foreground. While a protected mode session is in the foreground, the DOS session is frozen and all the context switches are between protected mode threads.

OS/2 imposes this restriction on the DOS session to protect the integrity of the system hardware resources. For example, many PC DOS applications assume that they "own" the PC, so they write directly to the video hardware. If you were to run these programs in the background, they would inadvertently modify the screen image of a different session. The 80286 real mode provides no way to intercept this type of "ill-behaved" program, so OS/2 runs them only when it can supply a dedicated (foreground) screen.

Because it runs in real mode, the DOS environment must reside in dedicated memory below the 1MB "line." This is because of the addressing limitations of real mode programs dictates that an application (plus all the service routines it calls) must be within the first 1MB of the system memory. In practical terms, this means that the DOS environment is still limited to 640K.

The entry points of all the emulated system "services" reside in the lower 640K. But this does not mean that the system service routines must reside entirely within the 640K area. In fact, the routines could reside above the 1MB line, so long as the CPU mode is reset before the (protected mode) routine starts running.

This is exactly how OS/2 works. To minimize the size of the system code in the lower 640K, many DOS emulation services call protected mode functions that reside outside of the 640K area. Figure 11-1 illustrates a PC DOS application program that requests a system service by issuing an INT 21H. The OS/2 INT 21H router traps the request and

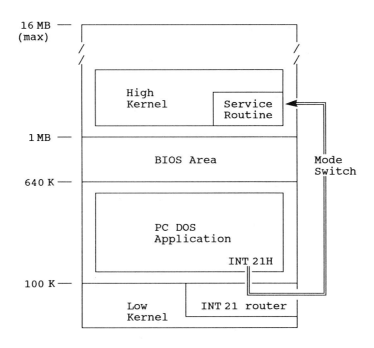

Figure 11-1. DOS environment services

passes it to a service routine in the "main" kernel. However, since it is above the 1MB line, the router switches the CPU mode to protected mode before branching to the high kernel service.

But not all the system services reside in the high kernel. If they did, OS/2 would have to mode switch every time an application requested any service—clearly resulting in an unacceptable performance impact. So the DOS service routines are split between the high and low kernel. Services that are called infrequently, or that generate (relatively slow) I/O, generally are in the high kernel. Those services that are called frequently or must perform quickly are kept in the low kernel.

Because of this structure, you will find that the DOS environment causes OS/2 to switch CPU modes even when no protected mode threads are dispatchable. However the mode switching happens only while the DOS session is in the foreground.

Device Driver Considerations

The low-level OS/2 device support is implemented in device drivers. Device drivers perform device I/O on behalf of the application programs. OS/2 supports only one device driver per device, so the device drivers will receive I/O requests from both protected mode (OS/2) and real mode (PC DOS) application programs.

When an application program requests I/O, it passes the address of a data buffer. Since the applications run in either real mode or protected mode, the device driver must address the buffer in a mode-independent way. Chapter 8 discussed how the CPU addressing modes were masked by the bimodal OS/2 device driver model.

If you plan to write your own OS/2 device drivers, be sure to follow the OS/2 device driver model, even if you intend to support only protected mode applications. So long as a DOS environment is in the system, device interrupts could possibly arrive when the CPU is "in the wrong mode." Thus, the device drivers must always convert user buffer address(es) to the "correct" form.

Many PC DOS applications bypass the operating system altogether and directly call the BIOS services by using software interrupts. For example, an application can directly access the disk device with INT 13H, the printer with INT 17H, or the keyboard with INT 16H. In a multi-threaded environment, all I/O requests (especially multi-stage I/O, such as with a disk) must be carefully orchestrated. For example, if a DOS environment program were to randomly start a disk I/O operation (INT 13H) while the disk device driver was between the SEEK and the WRITE operations of a protected-mode disk I/O request, the results would be disastrous.

Therefore, OS/2 device drivers trap BIOS software interrupts to insert the (real mode) I/O requests in their internal work queues. They can then process the BIOS requests in an orderly fashion without disrupting other (active) device I/O operations.

For example, consider Figure 11-2. Notice in this diagram how the OS/2 disk device driver receives a software INT 13H from the DOS environment application and a disk I/O request from the file system (in the high kernel). Since the same device driver handles both requests, it can complete the first operation before it starts the next. Note that in this example the device driver supports the INT 13H function without ever calling the "real" BIOS routine.

Alternatively, a device driver can call the ROM BIOS routine instead of processing the software interrupt itself. However, it must take some special precautions even in this situation. As far as OS/2 is concerned, a device driver BIOS software interrupt handler (and the BIOS) is part of the application program because it runs in the application context. Thus, if the user were to switch to a protected mode session in the midst of the I/O request, the BIOS code would be frozen and the hardware might be left in an unpredictable state.

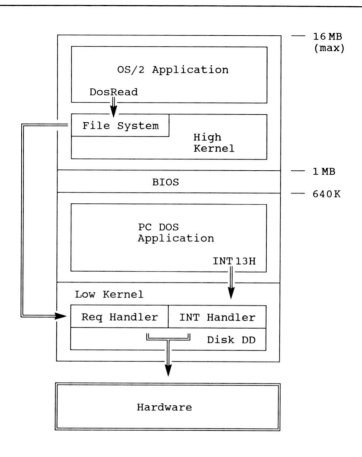

Figure 11-2. BIOS interrupt emulation

To prevent this problem, a device driver must put the system in a "nonpreemptable" state before it calls the BIOS. This does not actually affect background thread dispatching, but rather only stops the user from switching the screen session to a protected mode session. Device drivers set this state by calling a special kernel DevHlp routine called EnterROMCritSec.

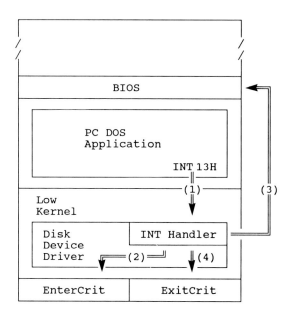

Figure 11-3. BIOS critical section

Figure 11-3 illustrates how a disk device driver could
use the ROM BIOS (directly). The process starts when a
PC DOS application running in the DOS environment
issues a BIOS INT 13H (1). Instead of going directly to the
BIOS, the interrupt goes to the disk device driver. Assuming that it has no other requests in its work queue, the disk
driver enters a critical section (2), and calls the real BIOS
routine to process the request (3). From this point on, OS/2
blocks the session switch function. When the BIOS finishes, the device driver once again calls the kernel to mark
the end of the I/O and re-enable the session switch function (4). Thus, the BIOS becomes a system critical section.
While the BIOS code is executing, OS/2 does not allow

the user to "suspend" the DOS session. In practice, this is a relatively rare occurrence because most OS/2 requests do not use the system BIOS. You will only see its effect when a foreground PC DOS program issues a direct BIOS interrupt at the same time you are trying to switch screens. The visible result is a small delay in screen switching. However, this has no effect on (background) thread-switching operations.

If you plan to write a device driver to support a device that has a corresponding BIOS interface, you must implement a similar structure. Your device driver must trap the appropriate BIOS software interrupt and either handle the request itself or pass it to the BIOS, bracketing the BIOS call with a critical section.

PC DOS API Support

Together, the OS/2 Kernel and the system device drivers support most of the PC DOS and BIOS interfaces. From the perspective of the application program, the interfaces are identical to what it "sees" in a stand-alone PC DOS system. Table 11-1 summarizes the software interrupt functions included in the DOS environment.

Table 11-1. DOS Environment Software Interrupt Support

BIOS Services

05H	Print Screen	Ignored
10H	Video	Fully supported
11H	Equipment Check	Fully supported
12H	Memory Size	Only the DOS environment size is reported
13H	Diskette	Fully supported
	Disk	Funct 01H, 02H, 0AH, and 15H are supported

Table 11-1. DOS Environment Software Interrupt Support (continued)

BIOS Services

14H	Serial	Not supported if COM device driver is installed **Note**: SETCOM40 utility will re-enable
15H	Miscellaneous	Funct 87H, 88H, 89H, 90H, 91H not supported Funct 83H/86H limited to 32ms timer granularity
16H	Keyboard	Fully supported
17H	Printer	Fully supported
19H	Reboot	Works as if CTRL-ALT-DEL were pressed
1AH	Time of Day	Functions 02H-07H are not supported
1BH	Break	Fully supported
1CH	Periodic Timer	Fully supported
1DH	Video Parameters	Fully supported
1EH	Diskette Parameters	Only used during system initialization
1FH	Graphics Fonts	Fully supported

PC DOS Services

20H	Program Terminate	Fully supported
21H	Function Request	Fully supported
22H	Terminate Address	Fully supported
23H	CTRL-BREAK	Fully supported
24H	Hard Error	Fully supported
25H	Direct Read	Fully supported
26H	Direct Write	Only works for removable media
27H	Terminate and Stay Resident	Fully supported

These restrictions are primarily because of unresolvable system resource conflicts.

Almost every significant PC DOS and BIOS function is supported without restrictions. However, the native OS/2 support is in conflict with the DOS environment in the following three areas:

- Direct I/O writes are not permitted to the system hard file(s). In a multitasking environment, the disk data structures (such as FAT or directories) may be dynamically updated by a background program. Existing PC DOS programs are not designed to compensate for this type of overlapped activity. If such a program changes a disk data structure while a background program is also updating the disk, then the disk integrity would be at risk. **Note:** Protected mode programs still can do direct sector I/O, but they must first lock the entire disk (or partition).

- The mode-switching and block-memory move functions (INT 15H) are not permitted because OS/2 uses high memory to run protected mode programs. This memory is no longer accessible to PC DOS applications.

- The real-time clock may not be updated or reset by PC DOS application programs. OS/2 uses this clock to drive the system dispatching functions.

PC DOS Device Driver Support

As discussed in Chapter 8, OS/2 device drivers are not at all like their PC DOS counterparts. In OS/2, device drivers are written to conform to a stringent device driver model that supports bimodal, multithreaded I/O operations. Device drivers are specialized, performance-sensitive, low-level device I/O programs.

PC DOS device drivers are different from their OS/2 counterparts in this respect. Many times these device drivers are simply "application program extensions" that are in device driver format only because this is a convenient way to load the code into the system. This distinction is important because it characterizes the level of support for PC DOS device drivers in the DOS environment.

To be supported in OS/2, a PC DOS device driver must abide by the following limitations:

- It cannot support an interrupt-driven device (such as a disk). Only true OS/2 device drivers can handle hardware interrupts. However, a PC DOS device driver can support noninterrupt-driven devices (such as a display) if it does not violate the other restrictions.

- It must be a "character" device driver (see Chapter 8). Block devices are only supported with OS/2 device drivers.

- It must not communicate with the application by using READ/WRITE packets. The only supported packet types are OPEN, CLOSE, and IOCTL. However, it can use a software interrupt to receive application requests.

The implication of these restrictions is that "true" I/O device support requires an OS/2 device driver. However, PC DOS application "extensions" or video drivers (such as VDI) can still be used in the DOS environment.

Print Spooling

The DOS environment printer output is spooled with the OS/2 SPOOL program. Since OS/2 print spooling is done from the device driver (with output monitors), it will work regardless of how the application writes to the printer (INT 21H WRITE function to the "LPTx" device or with the BIOS INT 17H).

The printer output is spooled until the application closes the print file or terminates. This means that in some situations you will not see the print output as the application program writes it, but some time later. If the application never "closes" the printer (or if it uses INT 17H), then the output will not start until you end the application program.

You can always force OS/2 to "flush" the print output by pressing the CTRL-ALT-PRTSC key combination. This flush function does not affect the application, but rather it instructs OS/2 to print whatever has been spooled.

Timing Sensitivity

You will find that almost all your PC DOS applications will run in the DOS compatibility session with no problems. The OS/2 DOS interface emulation is robust enough to support almost anything that a PC DOS application program might attempt.

But there are some exceptions. You have already seen that if an application uses high memory, performs direct hard disk (sector) I/O, or modifies the CMOS clock, it will not run as expected. But these are obvious restrictions that are traced to fundamental differences in the PC DOS and OS/2 operating environments.

A more subtle issue is the way an application deals with the interrupt controller (8259). DOS environment programs are not allowed to reprogram this device. This is because OS/2 "re-vectors" the hardware interrupts to a different interrupt range so that it can handle the "real" device interrupts before the application does. If an application reprograms the 8259, you get unpredictable results. For example, a device interrupt might be lost if it comes in while the 8259 is vectored to an application-defined interrupt range. To make matters worse, OS/2 periodically resets the 8259, so these effects may be transient.

PC DOS applications that "hook" the hardware interrupt vectors (00H-0FH) work correctly because OS/2 "simulates" the hardware interrupt once it has been handled by the device driver. However, if the application tries to hook the "re-vectored" interrupt, OS/2 terminates the program.

The other area to look out for is PC DOS programs that are excessively time-dependent. Since other (protected mode) threads are always running in the background, the DOS environment never receives 100% of the CPU. In most cases, this is not a problem, but it can get you in trouble if an application assumes that it will never be preempted. For example, a program that depends on seeing every timer tick (INT 1CH) to update a clock on the screen will "lose" time because it does not see timer ticks while a background thread is dispatched.

Also, PC DOS applications that have tight interrupt latency requirements could lose interrupts. The PC DOS application code must run in real mode, so if an interrupt arrives while the CPU is running a protected mode thread, OS/2 must switch thread context, CPU mode, and then dispatch the DOS environment. This will naturally take longer than in a "native" PC DOS system, where the interrupt is handled directly by the application (with no system intervention). Consequently, PC DOS application programs that receive external interrupts at a fast rate may not operate as expected. Note that OS/2 device drivers do not share this problem because their interrupt handlers do not run in task mode, nor do they require a CPU mode switch.

Finally, the user can switch the DOS session to the background, thus effectively "freezing" the PC DOS application. While in this state, OS/2 cannot route the hardware interrupts to the application interrupt handler. Therefore, all hardware interrupts destined for a PC DOS application are lost while the DOS session is in the background. This may or may not be a problem, depending on the characteristics of the device and the application.

You should generally stay away from "timing-dependent" PC DOS application programs. You may find that some of these applications work under certain system loads, but not under others. For example, an ASYNC terminal emulator might work at 2400 baud if the system is relatively free, but fail in a loaded system (that is, one with heavy background activity). In the OS/2 announcement materials, IBM has recommended that you not run timing-dependent PC DOS applications in the OS/2 DOS compatibility environment.

Command Environment

The DOS compatibility session always comes up with the familiar "C:>" prompt. The command processor used in this session (COMMAND.COM) is compatible with DOS 3.3. Some of the command-line enhancements (such as &, &&, and ‖ operators) introduced by OS/2 are only supported in the protected mode command interpreter(s).

COMMAND.COM supports all the PC DOS BAT file functions, so you will be able to move existing BAT files to the DOS environment with no changes (assuming, of course, that the BAT file is not dependent on programs not compatible with OS/2).

The native OS/2 command (CMD) files are a functional superset of PC DOS BAT files, so they will not necessarily run in the DOS environment.

Configuring the DOS Environment

The PROTECTONLY= statement in the CONFIG.SYS file configures the DOS session. If you specify PROTECTONLY=NO, OS/2 creates a DOS session and adds it to the active session switch list. If you code PROTECTONLY=YES, the system runs in protected mode only, and the DOS session does not appear on the session list.

You tell OS/2 how much memory to set aside for the DOS environment with the RMSIZE statement in the CONFIG.SYS file. The maximum DOS environment size is 640K, or the amount of memory installed below 1MB, whichever is smaller. The minimum size for this environment depends on what else you load in the system (such as device drivers). A 256K DOS environment generally will leave you with about 156K for your PC DOS application(s).

Note that if you configure a DOS environment that is smaller than the total memory below 1MB, the remaining memory is used by OS/2 for protected mode programs. However, in this situation the protected mode programs and data are not "protected" from inadvertent modification by a PC DOS application. If you can afford the memory, the "safest" configuration is when you set RMSIZE to the total memory below 1MB.

ERROR PROCESSING

In any system, things sometimes do not proceed as planned. The application programs and (in extreme cases) the end user may have to take "recovery" actions to correct a system failure. Error processing is an important (but sometimes neglected) part of an application program. In OS/2, the application programs define how much of the error recovery is to be done by the system, by the application, and by the user.

Hard Errors

Causes of program errors range from user mistakes to application programming errors and hardware failures. When a program error is caused by something external to

Table 11-2. Common OS/2 Hard Errors

Hard Error	Possible Cause
Device not ready	Diskette drive door open
Sector not found	Invalid disk/diskette format
General failure	Invalid disk/diskette media
Sharing violation	File in use by another process
General-protection fault	Addressing violation (unrecoverable)

the software (application and system), the error is called a *hard error*. Table 11-2 illustrates some of the most common OS/2 hard errors. In PC DOS, you would recognize hard errors by the familiar "Abort, Retry or Ignore?" prompt.

In OS/2, hard errors are handled by a special system thread (called the *hard-error handler*) that the system starts during initialization. This thread is responsible for receiving catastrophic system errors and prompting the user for recovery actions.

For example, consider Figure 11-4. In this scenario, an application program has issued a DosWrite call to start an I/O operation. As usual, OS/2 routes the call to the file system, which then sends a request packet to the device driver. So far, this is no different than what you have seen in previous chapters. But, suppose that the low-level I/O operation fails. OS/2 detects this failure and routes the information to the hard-error processor. The thread then interrupts the user and requests a recovery action.

The common recovery actions include the following:

End   End the program that caused the error. If you select this option, OS/2 sends a termination signal (SIG_TERM) to the process starting the I/O operation that caused the error

Retry	Retry the failing operation. If you select this option, OS/2 repeats the failing I/O operation without notifying the application program. This is especially useful in situations where you forget to change diskettes or forget to close the diskette drive door before you run the application
Ignore	Do not retry the I/O operation. Continue running the application as if the operation had succeeded. **Note:** This can be a dangerous option because the application program is not notified about the I/O failure
Fail	Fail the operation and pass the error to the application program. If you select this option, the recovery action(s) are left to the application program. Depending on how it is written, the application could terminate, retry the operation, ignore the failure, or prompt you for recovery actions

Depending on the hard error, you could be presented with one or more of these options.

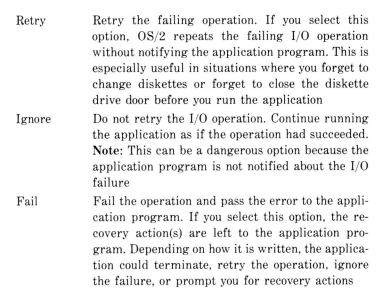
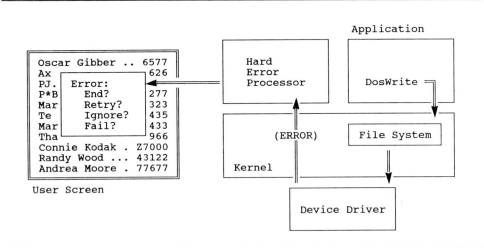

Figure 11-4. System hard-error flows

In contrast to PC DOS (which writes the hard-error prompt directly on the application screen), OS/2 presents hard errors as a popup window. Since the popup is a separate display session, it does not corrupt the application presentation space. So when you clear the error condition, the application screen is restored to its original state.

If you prefer to handle the error conditions within your application (without user intervention), then you can disable the error popup function with the DosError API. This API notifies OS/2 that all hard errors are to be treated as if the user had selected "fail" from the hard error popup. When an application sets hard-error prompting off, it then assumes the responsibility for error recovery. This type of application program must check error codes after every I/O call.

DosError also enables you to disable the popup message that results from 80286 CPU faults (such as a general-protection fault). However, even though the popup is suppressed, the application is still terminated. OS/2 does not attempt to recover programs after these types of failures.

Should a process disable hard-error processing with DosError, it does so for all forms of I/O errors. Alternatively, a process can disable hard-error processing for a specific device or file by appropriately coding the options flag in the DosOpen call. When opened in this way, all I/O performed with the device handle or file handle is not subjected to system hard-error prompting. Other I/O operations within the same process will still generate hard-error popups.

Error Mapping

Every OS/2 API function can either succeed or fail. When a call fails, it returns an error code in the AX register (see Appendix C). Naturally, you do not want to write a program that ignores these error conditions, or else it might behave unpredictably.

```
call      DosOpen
cmp       ax,0              ;all OK?
je        openOK            ;yes - continue processing
cmp       ax,2              ;invalid name?
je        error1            ;yes - go issue message
cmp       ax,32             ;sharing violation?
je        error2            ;yes - go issue message
cmp       ax,21             ;drive open?
je        error3            ;yes - go issue message
jmp       error_term        ;terminate (miscellaneous error)
          .
          .
          .
```

Figure 11-5. **Program to test AX for error codes and generate messages**

Suppose you write a program that opens arbitrary files. This program reads an input string from the keyboard and uses the string as the file name parameter for a DosOpen call. This works if the user enters a valid file name. But what if the file name is not valid? Or if the file is not shareable? Or if the file is on a diskette but the drive door is open? Each of these conditions generates a unique error code. Of course, your program could test AX for each error code and put out different messages (see Figure 11-5).

This approach works if any of the specific hard-coded errors is generated by DosOpen. In general, you enumerate all the error conditions you want to recover from and end the program for the rest (ERROR—TERM). In this way, any error condition is handled appropriately.

However, if you enumerate the error conditions, then your program works as expected for all the error codes you know about today. But what about the next release of OS/2? What if it introduces a "new" DosOpen error code that has almost the same meaning as a previous code (such as "the file name has invalid characters"). If a user ran your program on this new level of OS/2, the program would end in what should be a recoverable situation — simply because it did not understand the new error code.

Good programming practice dictates that you never

hard-code constants, especially when they represent values that are likely to change over time. This is exactly the problem with this example. However, it begs the obvious question: How does a program "generically" differentiate between recoverable and nonrecoverable error conditions?

The answer is the OS/2 DosErrClass function. It "categorizes" a specific error code into an error class, recommended recovery action, and error locus. These values are listed in Table 11-3.

With DosErrClass, a program can deal with error codes in an abstract sense. Rather than hard-coding the error numbers and recovery actions, you use DosErrClass to first classify the error number, then decide your course of action (and message text, if any) on the basis of the returned values. If your programs use this function to deal with errors, they will continue to work in future OS/2 releases. As new error codes are added to the system, they will be mapped by the DosErrClass function.

Table 11-3. Error Classification Categories

Class Definitions

1	OUTRES	Out of resources
2	TEMPSIT	Temporary situation
3	AUTH	Not authorized
4	INTRN	Internal error
5	HRDFAIL	Device hardware failure
6	SYSFAIL	System failure
7	APPERR	Application error (probable)
8	NOTFND	Not found
9	BADFMT	Bad parameter format
10	LOCKED	Resource or data is locked
11	MEDIA	Incorrect media or CRC error
12	ALREADY	Resource or action already taken/done/exists
13	UNK	Unclassified error
14	CANT	Cannot perform the requested action
15	TIME	Time-out

Table 11-3.   Error Classification Categories (continued)

Recommended Actions

1	RETRY	Retry the operation
2	DLYRET	Wait awhile then retry
3	USER	Bad user input—new data
4	ABORT	Terminate in an orderly manner
5	PANIC	Terminate immediately
6	IGNORE	Ignore the error
7	INTRET	Retry after user intervention

Error Locus

1	UNK	Unknown
2	DISK	Disk error (block device)
3	NET	Network error
4	SERDEV	Serial device error
5	MEM	Memory error

SYSTEM SERVICEABILITY

OS/2 is a sophisticated, full-function operating system. Unfortunately, with the many functions and capabilities of OS/2, things are bound to go wrong. This is based on the simple fact that the more capabilities a system has, the more code it contains. The more code that is in the system, the greater the probability of an error.

In an environment not constrained by a 640K address space where more than one application runs concurrently, the probability of errors is enhanced even more. OS/2 introduces a class of inter-program interactions that are simply not possible in the PC DOS system.

But this is not unique to the OS/2 environment. Historically, one of the biggest inhibitors to complex PC DOS software is the inherent difficulty of diagnosing and isolating problems. In the PC environment, error recovery is often rebooting the machine. By the time a software problem manifests itself, it is often too late for anything other than restarting the machine. Even IBM does not generally make PC DOS software part of its comprehensive service offerings.

But there is something fundamentally different about OS/2—it runs the 80286/80386 CPU in protected mode. The ramifications of this are subtle, but important. Because the CPU traps programs that accidentally modify or access memory outside of their address space(s), the operating system has an opportunity to report the situation to the user. You caught a glimpse of this in Chapter 1 during the discussion of the factors that led to the development of OS/2.

In OS/2, one program can cause a fault and not affect the other programs in the system. This means that certain OS/2 components will continue to run even when the system is partially disabled. A special class of components, called *serviceability aids*, can be used by trained technicians to gather failure information at a customer site. With this data, a software developer (operating system, subsystem, or application) can see the events that led to a failure and fix the problem. Largely because of these new capabilities, IBM has included full software support as a part of OS/2.

Trace Facilities

OS/2 contains a full complement of system trace facilities. To trace events, you first configure a trace buffer with the TRACEBUF= statement of the CONFIG.SYS file. This buffer holds trace "entries" that are generated by different portions of the OS/2 system. Once the system is started, you use the TRACE command to activate or deactivate selected traces (ranging from the API function calls to internal system events).

A typical scenario in which you would use the system trace facility is an intermittent (random) error. Complex system errors are frequently not directly caused by an obvious program error. Instead they are the side effect of several (seemingly) unrelated events. To diagnose this type of problem, you start one or more traces and try to re-create the error condition.

When the error once again surfaces, you shut off the trace and run the TRACEFMT utility to display a formatted version of the trace buffer. This trace information helps pin down the system activity leading to the failure condition, and may provide the clue needed to isolate the system problem.

These facilities are primarily intended for trained service personnel. However, they are included in the system distribution disk, so you can experiment with them when you debug OS/2 programs. TRACE and TRACEFMT are described in greater detail in Chapter 12.

System Dumps

For situations where the error causes the system to hang, OS/2 allows you to dump the contents of memory to disk. You start a system memory dump by pressing the CTRL-ALT-NUMLOCK key combination twice (successively).

In response to this request, OS/2 resets the system to a known state (without erasing memory) and copies the contents of physical memory to one or more dump disk(s).

Before you start a dump, you must have a disk that was prepared with the CREATEDD (create dump disk) utility. You should have one of these disks available at all times, since you will probably not be able to run CREATEDD when you need to take the dump. For a multidisk dump, only the first disk is prepared with CREATEDD. The rest are cleanly formatted OS/2 disks.

Like the trace facilities, system dumps are intended for use by qualified service personnel. You will probably not use this function unless requested to by an OS/2 service representative. The CREATEDD utility is described in Chapter 12.

Note: The level of OS/2 service is determined by the manufacturer of your computer. The preceding discussions were based on the IBM support services announced with OS/2. To determine what level of support is available to you, check with the dealer who sold you OS/2.

NATIONAL LANGUAGE SUPPORT

OS/2 is fully enabled for multi-language operation. This means that the system is adaptable to the data conventions, keyboard layouts, code pages, and language translations used in different countries. You will probably purchase an OS/2 version that has already been customized for your native national language. However, many of these facilities are also available to application programs so they too can be built to adapt to these different environments.

In OS/2, National Language Support (NLS) is provided as a series of general-purpose API functions. An NLS-enabled application does not assume any country-specific and language-specific information. Instead, it is table-driven and uses OS/2 NLS services to interpret input, to format data (such as DATE and TIME), and to generate output.

Table 11-4 summarizes the OS/2 NLS API functions. The remainder of this chapter examines each function in greater detail.

Table 11-4. National Language Support API Functions

General Country Information

DosGetCtryInfo	Get country information table
DosCaseMap	Case map a binary string
DosGetCollate	Get collating sequence table (for sorting)
DosGetDBCSEv	Get DBCS environment vector

Code Page Switching

DosGetCP	Get the process (default) code page
DosSetCP	Set the process (default) code page
VioGetCP	Get the session video code page
VioSetCP	Set the session video code page
KbdGetCP	Get the session keyboard code page
KbdSetCP	Set the session keyboard code page

External Message Processing

DosGetMessage	Get message text (with variable insertion)
DosInsMessage	Insert variable text into existing message
DosPutMessage	Put message (with wrap processing)

Country and Language Information

The OS/2 country information table is a collection of data elements that characterize the data conventions of the country for which the OS/2 system has been configured. An application program retrieves this table with the DosGetCtryInfo API. The table contents are illustrated in Figure 11-6.

The country information table contains all the information that varies between countries (such as the currency symbol, the DATE and TIME format, and the decimal/thousands separators). If you write a program that presents this type of data to the user, you should retrieve the country information table and use its formatting "rules" to generate the user output.

```
    DW   Country code
    DW   Reserved (0)
    DW   Date Format: 0=mmddyy 1=ddmmyy 2=yymmdd
5   DB   Currency indicator    (ASCIIZ)
2   DB   Thousands separator   (ASCIIZ)
2   DB   Decimal separator     (ASCIIZ)
2   DB   Date separator        (ASCIIZ)
2   DB   Time separator        (ASCIIZ)
    DB   Currency format:

         RRRRRISC
         =====||L
              ||L__ Currency Indicator (1=Trailing 0=Leading)
              |L___ Spaces between CI and value (1=1 0=0)
              L____ CI Replaces Decimal Indicator (ignore other bits)
         L_____ Reserved (0)

    DB   Decimal places in currency
    DB   Time format:

         RRRRRRRC
         =====|L
              |L__ Format: (1=24HR 0=12HR)
         L_____ Reserved (0)

    DD   Reserved (0)
2   DB   Data list separator (ASCIIZ)
5   DW   Reserved (0)
```

Figure 11-6. Country information table format

If your applications run in a Double Byte Character Set (DBCS) environment (such as Kanji), you can retrieve the DBCS environment vector with the DosGetDBCSEv API. This vector defines the valid character range(s) for the DBCS lead bytes. Since this information varies between DBCS languages, you must use this data to differentiate between double-byte and single-byte characters in program data streams. The format of the DBCS environment vector is illustrated in Figure 11-7.

In many NLS languages, the collating (sort) sequence of characters does not necessarily correspond to the character ASCII values. Consequently, a simple sort using the ASCII codes will not always yield the expected results. To help you deal with this situation, OS/2 has a collating

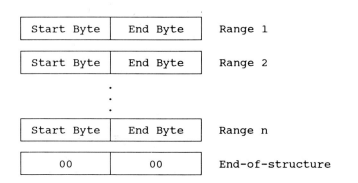

Figure 11-7.   DBCS environmental vector

sequence table that corresponds to the current country setting. You retrieve this table with the DosGetCollate API.
The table format is illustrated in Figure 11-8.

To sort information, you should use the weight values
associated with the characters in the table rather than the

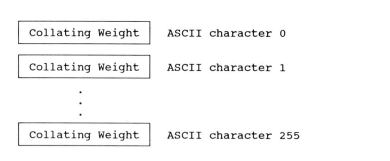

Figure 11-8.   Collating weight table format

ASCII values themselves. In other words, use the ASCII byte as an index into the weight table. The resulting weight value is what determines the collating sequence of the original ASCII byte.

The country information table, DBCS environmental vector, and collating sequence table are determined by the setting of the COUNTRY statement in the CONFIG.SYS file. Table 11-5 lists the supported OS/2 country codes.

Table 11-5. Country Codes

Code	Country	Code Page	Keyboard Layout
001	United States	437	US
002	Canada	863	CF
003	Latin America	437	LA
031	Netherlands	437	NL
032	Belgium	437	BE
033	France	437	FR
034	Spain	437	SP
039	Italy	437	IT
041	Switzerland	437	SG, SG
044	United Kingdom	437	UK
045	Denmark	865	DK
046	Sweden	437	SV
047	Norway	865	NO
049	Germany	437	GR
061	Australia	437	--
099	Asia	437	--
351	Portugal	860	PO
358	Finland	437	SU
785	Arabic*	864	--
972	Hebrew*	862	--

*Country code is supported, but video and printer code pages are not.

Code Pages

A *code page* is a table that associates ASCII code points to individual characters. In two different code pages, the same ASCII value could generate different "characters."

OS/2 supports a primary and a secondary code page, defined by the CODEPAGE command in the CONFIG.SYS file. Every OS/2 process is associated with one of the two system code pages. OS/2 uses the default process code page to establish the display, keyboard, and printer code pages. You query or switch the process code page with the DosGetCP/DosSetCP API calls.

In OS/2, you can also query and set the video and keyboard code pages with the VioGetCP/VioSetCP and KbdGetCP/KbdSetCP APIs. Since you set the keyboard and video code pages independently, an application could conceivably display data in one code page and process user input in another. If you change the video or keyboard code pages, the process code page is unaffected.

When you print information, the printer data stream is tagged with the process code page. Therefore, once the print data has been spooled, you can reset the process code and not affect the spooled output. Notice that you must install the OS/2 print spooler if you want to print data in more than one code page.

In some situations, you may need to map a binary character string to its associated character values (using a particular code page). To do this, OS/2 provides the DosCaseMap API. DosCaseMap converts an arbitrary character string to its translated ASCII equivalent.

To support display code pages, OS/2 requires a display adapter that allows downloaded character fonts (EGA, VGA, and so forth). Likewise, for printer code pages you must have a printer that supports downloaded character fonts.

Message Facility

Perhaps the most difficult part of converting a program to another language is the actual translation of the program text and messages. This is especially difficult if the message text is hard-coded in the application binary (EXE) file. OS/2 has a set of facilities that make this translation process easier.

In an OS/2 program, you can place the program text and messages in a special file called a *message file*. When the program needs to issue a message, it requests the message text (by message number) with the OS/2 DosGetMessage API. Since the actual text is separated from the program, a third party can change the messages without modifying the program executable file(s). This is precisely how the OS/2 command and utility programs work. For instance, the OSO001.MSG and OSO001H.MSG files contain all the OS/2 messages and associated help "text" for all the OS/2 utilities and commands.

In cases where it is not practical to keep the messages in an external file (for performance reasons), the messages can be bound to the executable file with the MSGBIND utility. Even though the message text is physically attached to the EXE file, it is still "external" in the sense that it can be augmented or replaced without changing the code. In fact, a program that retrieves its messages with DosGetMessage does not know if the text is really in its own external file or bound to the EXE file.

Whenever possible, you should build programs using DosGetMessage. If you do, it will make them easier to translate into different languages.

SUMMARY

OS/2 includes a variety of functions that make it a complete system. With its compatibility support, OS/2 enables you to run most PC DOS application programs. The DOS environment is an optional user session that is selected from the Session Manager. In this session, you interact with the system by using the familiar PC DOS "C>" prompt.

With OS/2 error-processing services, an application program can either handle its own critical errors or let the system hard-error handler interact with the user to recover error conditions. Finally, the National Language Support functions enable you to build application programs that will automatically adapt to different national versions of OS/2.

You should review the following points before moving to the next chapter:

- The relationship of the DOS environment to the rest of the system

- Emulated DOS and BIOS services

- DOS environment mode switching implications

- Device driver implications of DOS environment

- How hard-error processing works

- How to classify error codes

- The OS/2 serviceability aids

- System NLS functions and why you should use them

- Code-page switching support

CHAPTER 12
OS/2 COMMANDS AND UTILITIES

The OS/2 system provides a number of utilities. These utilities and the command-interpreter internal functions make up the OS/2 command environment. This chapter introduces these programs with a series of "hands-on" examples. However, this is not a replacement for a command reference guide.

The OS/2 commands are generally compatible with their PC DOS counterparts. However, the functions are not identical in all cases. This is inevitable because of the inherent differences between the OS/2 and PC DOS system environments (multitasking, large real memory, and so forth). Whenever possible, the syntax and semantics of the individual commands are the same.

Some commands entail unique OS/2 functions, and thus have no PC DOS counterparts. In these cases the command semantics are equivalent to those of the other OS/2 commands.

You may run most OS/2 commands and utilities from the protected-mode command line or the OS/2 DOS-compatibility command line. Most OS/2 utility programs are implemented as DOS family API applications.

The system has different command interpreters for protected mode (CMD.EXE) and real mode (COMMAND.COM). COMMAND.COM is compatible with PC DOS 3.3, but it does not have all the extensions included in CMD.EXE. The primary goal of the DOS environment is to run existing programs (and batch files) without modification. Therefore, functional enhancements are only implemented in the protected-mode command interpreter.

INTERNAL COMMANDS

Both the OS/2 real-mode and protected-mode command interpreters have built-in commands. A function is implemented as a built-in command if it is either frequently used (such as COPY) or so small that it does not justify a separate disk utility program (such as DATE and TIME). Table 12-1 lists the OS/2 built-in commands. Note that some are available only in the DOS environment (RM) while others can only be used from the protected-mode command line (PM). However, in most cases, the same commands are supplied by both command interpreters.

BREAK

The keystroke combination CTRL-BREAK terminates a running application. PC DOS normally checks for the CTRL-BREAK combination only when the application reads from the keyboard. The BREAK command instructs PC DOS to check for CTRL-BREAK more frequently. However, CTRL-BREAK checking in OS/2 is active at all times, so this

Table 12-1. OS/2 Internal Commands

Command	Mode(s)	Description
BREAK	RM	Turn BREAK checking on or off
CD	RM PM	Change the current directory
CHCP	RM PM	Change the system code page
COPY	RM PM	Copy files
DATE	RM PM	Set or display the system date
DIR	RM PM	List the entries in an OS/2 file directory
DETACH	PM	Run program (asynchronously)
ERASE	RM PM	Erase a file
EXIT	RM PM	Ends command interpreter
LABEL	RM PM	Change a disk volume label
MD	RM PM	Make a new directory
PROMPT	RM PM	Change the command-line prompt
RD	RM PM	Remove a directory
RENAME	RM PM	Rename a file
SET	RM PM	Set environment variable
START	PM	Start new session
TIME	RM PM	Set or display the system time
VER	RM	Display the OS/2 version number
VERIFY	RM PM	Turn write-verification on or off
VOL	RM PM	Display a disk volume label
d:	RM PM	Change current drive to d: (A,B,C,...)

command is not needed. It is included as a real-mode command to provide compatibility with existing PC DOS batch files.

CHDIR (CD)

The change directory (CHDIR or CD) command changes the current directory to some other directory in the system. You may enter a fully qualified directory or a relative directory name. For instance, the following commands,

```
[C:\DOS]CD C:\DOS\UTILITY
[C:\DOS]CD UTILITY
```

have the same effect of changing the current directory to the subdirectory named C:\DOS\UTILITY (assuming it exists). If you enter CD with no parameters, the current directory of the default drive is displayed. Using CD with just a drive identifier displays the current directory of the target drive. For example,

```
[C:\DOS]CD
C:\DOS
[C:\DOS]CD D:
D:\PROGRAMS
[C:\DOS]
```

CHCP

The change code page (CHCP) command resets the current code page. OS/2 supports two code pages (specified in the CONFIG.SYS file). The CHCP command switches you from the primary to the backup, or vice versa. Only the current session is affected. For example,

```
[C:\]CHCP 863
```

changes the active code page to 863 (Canadian frequency). To display the code pages that are loaded in your system, enter CHCP with no parameters, as follows:

```
[C:\]CHCP
Active code page: 437
Prepared system code pages: 437 850
[C:\]
```

Note that you must include a CODEPAGE= command in

your CONFIG.SYS file to load the system code pages before you use the CHCP utility.

CLS

The CLS command clears the screen. Only the current session is affected.

COPY

The COPY command copies one or more files between directories or devices. The command accepts two names corresponding to the source file and the target file. If you specify no target name, the source is copied to the current directory of the current drive. If you supply a second name, COPY gives the copied file a new name. For example, consider the following commands:

```
COPY A:AUTOEXEC.BAT
COPY AUTOEXEC.BAT D:
COPY AUTOEXEC.BAT D:\PROGRAMS\MYAUTO.BAT
```

The first example copies the file named AUTOEXEC.BAT from drive A to your current drive and directory. In the second case AUTOEXEC.BAT is copied to the current directory of drive D. The third COPY example copies AUTOEXEC.BAT to the directory named PROGRAMS on drive D and gives it the name MYAUTO.BAT.

All OS/2 commands that accept a file name as a parameter also accept "wild-card" characters. Wild cards allow you to specify a pattern of characters. All files that match the pattern are selected by the command. This allows you to select a group of files without having to enter each name separately.

The two types of wild cards are arbitrary match (*) and specific match (?). With the arbitrary match character, you specify how a file name or extension must start. Any character combinations after the wild card are acceptable. For instance,

```
COPY C:*.ASM D:
COPY C:MY*.* D:
COPY *.* A:
```

The first COPY copies all files on the currrent directory of drive C with an extension of ASM to the current directory of drive D. The second example copies all files, with any extension, whose names start with "MY" to drive D. The length of the file name does not matter, so long as the file names start with "MY." In the last example, all files (any name and any extension) on the current directory of drive C are copied to the drive A.

The second type of wild card (specific match) allows you to specify file names of determined length. By using a "?" you are saying you do not care what character is in that position of the name, but all others must match. For example,

```
COPY C:MY??NAM.ASM D:
COPY C:????.INC D:
```

In the first example, all files whose names are exactly seven characters long, with "MY" in positions 1-2, "NAM" in positions 5-7, and with an extension of ASM, are copied to the current directory of drive D. The second example simply copies all files whose names are four characters long with an extension of INC to drive D.

As you would expect, both types of wild-card characters can be used in one file specification. For instance,

```
COPY C:M?A*.* D:
```

copies all files with an "M" in the first position of the name, "A" in the third position, followed by any number of characters and any extension to drive D.

The COPY command also allows you to copy more than one source file into the target file. For example,

```
COPY HEADER.ASM+BODY.ASM+TRAILER.ASM
    PROGRAM.ASM
```

combines files named HEADER.ASM, BODY.ASM, and TRAILER.ASM into a new file named PROGRAM.ASM.

Finally, you can copy to or from character devices by using the COPY command. OS/2 files often take on the appearance of character devices. Both the files and the devices can be accessed by using the serial-character I/O model. The COPY command simply reads a serial character stream from the source file and writes a serial character stream to the target file. By replacing the source or target file name with a device name, the COPY command transfers the data to or from the device. For example,

```
COPY PROGRAM.ASM LPT1:
```

reads the file named PROGRAM.ASM and sends it to a device named LPT1: (a printer). When it finishes writing the data, COPY closes the target and source files. When the printer is closed the output file is sent to the print spooler and added to the print queue.

Device names also can be used as both the source and target of the COPY command. For instance, the following command sends a message to the printer:

```
[C:\]COPY CON: LPT1:
This is a printed message!^Z
1 file(s) copied
[C:\]
```

The COPY command redirects all console input to the printer. When you type the string "This is a printed message!" COPY passes the data to LPT1:. However, the string is not actually printed until you tell COPY that the "file" is finished. You signify the end of a file in OS/2 with a logical end-of-file (EOF) character (026).

You can generate special characters (such as EOF) from the keyboard with CTRL key combinations. In this case, the EOF character is generated when you press CTRL-Z. Note that CTRL-Z is echoed to the screen as ^Z. When you then press ENTER, COPY recognizes the EOF as the signal to end the copy operation. COPY then closes the file and sends the string "This is a printed message!" to the printer device.

By substituting a file name for the printer device name, you can use the same technique to create a file from the keyboard input. For example,

```
[C:\]COPY CON: DATA.FIL
This is line one ...
This is line two ...^Z
1 file(s) copied
[C:\]
```

creates a disk file named DATA.FIL that contains two lines. Note that you create a new line each time you press RETURN (CR). As before, the COPY ends when you send a logical EOF character followed by a CR.

DATE

You may reset the system date by using the DATE command. The date is used by OS/2 in a number of internal functions, including file-access time-stamps, prompt displays, and in system APIs.

If you enter DATE with no parameters, you see the following prompt:

```
The current date is: Thu 6-20-1987
Enter the new date: (mm-dd-yy)
```

You may press ENTER to leave the date unchanged, or enter a different value. The input must be in the format

mm-dd-yy

where the following is true:

mm is the month (1-12)
dd is the day (1-31)
yy is the year (80-99 or 1980-2079)

The month, day, and year values can be separated by hyphens (−), slashes (/), or periods (.). The order in which the information is entered is typically *mm-dd-yy*, although this differs in the various national-language versions of OS/2 (English, Japanese, French, and so on).

If you enter DATE with a date value, OS/2 does not prompt you. For example,

[C:\]DATE 9/26/87
[C:\]

resets the date to 9/26/87.

Unlike PC DOS, the OS/2 DATE command automatically resets the hardware (CMOS) clock.

The date display format (AM/PM or 24 HR) and the date order (MM-DD-YY or YY-MM-DD) are determined by the country information in your CONFIG.SYS file.

DIR

The DIR command allows you to display the contents of a directory. If you enter DIR with no parameters, it displays the contents of the current directory of the current drive. For instance, Figure 12-1 shows how OS/2 displays the contents of the drive D root directory. As with other OS/2

```
[D:\]DIR

The volume label in drive D is OS2_SYSTEM.

        .              <DIR>        9-26-87    2:11p
        ..             <DIR>        9-26-87    2:11p
        SAMPLES        <DIR>        9-26-87    2:26p
        MASMDIR  @@@     2381       9-26-87    2:29p
        MASM     EXE   111435       8-24-87   12:00p
        SALUT    EXE    31514       8-24-87   12:00p
        LINK     EXE    90280       8-24-87   12:00p
        CREF     EXE    24809       8-24-87   12:00p
        MASM     PIF      369       8-24-87   12:00p
        SALUT    PIF      369       8-24-87   12:00p
        LINK     PIF      369       8-24-87   12:00p
        CREF     PIF      369       8-24-87   12:00p
        CV       HLP    35663       8-24-87   12:00p
        LIB      EXE    44934       8-24-87   12:00p
        LIB      PIF      369       8-24-87   12:00p
        CV       EXE   197260       8-24-87   12:00p
        EXEMOD   EXE    20770       8-24-87   12:00p
        EXEMOD   PIF      369       8-24-87   12:00p
         19 Files     15937536 bytes free
```

Figure 12-1.   Display of contents of root directory on drive D

commands, you can use wild-card characters to narrow the directory listing to only those files meeting certain display criteria. For example,

```
[D:\]DIR CV.*

The volume label in drive D is OS2_SYSTEM.

CV       HLP    35663   8-24-87  12:00p
CV       EXE   197260   8-24-87  12:00p
         2 Files     15937536 bytes free
```

displays only the files named CV.

As with other commands, DIR accepts fully qualified file names. But if you only enter the name of a directory, then DIR lists only those files contained in the directory. For instance,

DIR D:\PROGRAMS

lists the contents of the subdirectory named PROGRAMS in the root directory of drive D. Of course, you may also use both directory names with wild cards. So, the command

    DIR D:\PROGRAMS*.EXE

displays all the files with an extension of EXE in the PROGRAMS subdirectory.

Hidden files (such as IBMBIO.COM), are not displayed by the DIR command.

In protected mode, the DIR command also accepts multiple file specifications. For example,

    DIR A: B:*.ASM

lists all the files on drive A and the .ASM files on drive B.

DETACH (DET)

The DETACH command allows you to start a program in your current session and, while it is still running, return to the command line. The program is run asynchronously. To start a program in this way, you prefix the program name and parameters with the DETACH command string. For instance,

    DETACH XCOPY A: B:

runs the program named XCOPY as a detached program in your session. XCOPY then runs concurrently with any other programs you subsequently start from the command line.

The OS/2 DETACH function is equivalent to the PC DOS terminate-and-stay-resident (TSR) function. However, since the detached program is started as an OS/2 process, it participates in system time-slicing. PC DOS TSR programs, on the other hand, are forced to do their own dispatching if they are to continue running concurrently with the command line.

You may detach any program that you could otherwise run from the OS/2 command line. However, if the program expects input from the keyboard it may not operate correctly. The DETACH command starts the program in a null (non-selectable) display session, so the program cannot write to the screen or read from the keyboard. If you run a standard I/O program (such as an OS/2 utility) by using DETACH, you can use the I/O redirection facilities of the command interpreter to "feed" the program input and "catch" the screen output. For example,

        DETACH XCOPY A: B: >COM1:

runs the same XCOPY program (as in the previous example), except that the screen output is sent to the COM1: device rather than the real screen.

Using input redirection also enables you to run a program that expects keystrokes. Thus,

        DETACH FORMAT A: <FORMAT.IN >FORMAT.OUT

runs FORMAT as a detached process. All its input is satisfied from the file named FORMAT.IN. The screen output is sent to the file named FORMAT.OUT.

DETACH is only supported by the OS/2 protected-mode command interpreter.

DPATH

The DPATH (Data Path) command defines the search path OS/2 uses when opening files. The DPATH command is similar to the PATH internal command that defines the search path OS/2 uses to locate programs for the EXEC function. For example, after you issue

        [C:\]DPATH C:\TOOLS
        [C:\]

OS/2 searches the current drive and directory, then the directory C:\TOOLS each time it receives a DosOpen request. You can specify more than one directory to be searched by separating them with a semicolon, as follows:

```
[C:\]DPATH C:\TOOLS;D:\SOURCE\ADMS
[C:\]
```

Note that you can include directories on different drives in a single DPATH string. If you enter DPATH with no parameters, OS/2 displays the current DPATH string. For example,

```
[C:\]DPATH
C:\TOOLS;D:\SOURCE\ADMS
[C:\]
```

To cancel the function, enter a null path (designated as a single semicolon), as follows:

```
[C:\]DPATH ;
[C:\]
```

DPATH is an internal command in the protected-mode command interpreter, so it can only be used in protected mode. However, the external command APPEND provides essentially the same function in the DOS-compatibility environment. The DPATH string is kept in an environment variable of the same name.

ERASE (DEL, DELETE)

The ERASE command erases one or more files from a file directory. For example,

```
ERASE A:AUTOEXEC.BAT
```

erases the file named AUTOEXEC.BAT from the root directory drive A.

You can use wild-card characters with the ERASE

command to erase a series of files. For instance, consider the following commands:

```
ERASE *.CMD
ERASE C:\SOURCE\M*.ASM
ERASE D:\????.*
```

The first example erases all CMD files from the current directory of the current drive. The second example erases all ASM files whose names start with "M" from the subdirectory named SOURCE in drive C. The third example erases all files whose names are exactly four characters long in the root directory of drive D.

You can erase all the files in a particular subdirectory by using the ERASE command with a directory name instead of a file name. For example, the following are equivalent commands:

```
ERASE C:\SOURCE
ERASE C:\SOURCE\*.*
```

Both commands erase all the files in the subdirectory named SOURCE in drive C. This powerful function could be disastrous if you mistype the directory name. To protect you from this type of error, OS/2 prompts you to make sure that you really want to erase all the files, as follows:

```
[C:\]ERASE SOURCE
Are you sure (Y/N)? Y
[C:\]
```

Use the ERASE command carefully. An erased file is not easily recovered. When a file is erased, the file system updates the FAT so that all the disk sectors that contained the data can be reused in other files.

A file whose attributes are set to read-only cannot be deleted with the OS/2 ERASE command.

In the protected-mode command interpreter, the ERASE command accepts multiple file specifications. For example,

ERASE *.OBJ *.LST D:\PROGRAMS*.ASM

erases all files with OBJ or LST extensions from the current drive and directory, and all files with an ASM extension in the D:\PROGRAMS directory. You can erase files in different drives and directories with a single ERASE command.

EXIT

You can nest multiple copies of the real-mode or protected-mode command interpreters by entering the names of the interpreters (CMD or COMMAND) at the prompt (see the section "Command Interpreters" later in this chapter). You use the EXIT command to terminate a command interpreter and return to its parent process.

Entering EXIT from the last command processor in a protected mode session instructs OS/2 to terminate the session and return to the session manager shell.

On the other hand, the DOS session command interpreter allows you to use the EXIT command to end nested command interpreters, but is ignored if only one copy of the command interpreter remains in the session. Remember that in OS/2 the DOS session cannot be dynamically added or deleted.

LABEL

You can change the volume label of any hard disk or diskette with the OS/2 LABEL command. For example,

[C:\]LABEL A: MYVOL

assigns the label "MYVOL" to the diskette in drive A. You can use any valid file-name character in the volume label.

If you do not enter the volume label, LABEL prompts you, as follows:

```
[D:\]LABEL A:
Volume in drive A has no label.
Enter a volume label of up to 11 characters
or press Enter for no volume label update. MYVOL
[D:\]
```

You typically label a disk when you format it. However, the LABEL command enables you to change the disk name. OS/2 uses the volume label to prompt you for removable media, so always try to label your diskettes with unique names.

MKDIR (MD)

You can use the Make Directory (MKDIR or MD) command to create a new subdirectory on a disk or diskette. Directory names follow established file-naming conventions. A directory name may contain a one- to eight-character name and an optional one- to three-character extension. Consider the following examples:

```
MD PROGRAMS
MD PROGRAMS.ASM
```

The MD command allows you to enter path-qualified directory names. However, all the higher-level directories must exist before the new directory is created. Consider the following example:

```
MD PROGRAMS\USER\SOURCE
```

The total length of the qualified name for any directory

cannot exceed 63 characters.

Directories are actually special types of files that the file system uses to hold links to other files (or directories). Therefore, a subdirectory cannot have the same name as another file in the directory. The MD command fails if you attempt to create a duplicate directory or file name.

In the protected-mode command interpreter, the MD command accepts multiple subdirectory names. So, the following command,

    MD PROGRAMS BIN SOURCE

creates three subdirectories named PROGRAMS, BIN, and SOURCE.

PROMPT

The PROMPT command enables you to change the command-interpreter input prompt. The prompt is a simple ASCII character string. To make more meaningful prompts, the string can contain special variables. These variables represent different types of system information that is substituted into the string by the command interpreter (see Table 12-2).

Consider the following sequence:

```
[C:\]PROMPT Command:

Command:PROMPT ==$g

==>PROMPT Date$c$d$f Time$c$t$f

Date(10/27/1987) Time(12:10:02)PROMPT

[C:\]
```

In each case, notice how the command changed the value of the system prompt. Also note that a PROMPT command with no ASCII string resets the prompt to its default value.

Table 12-2. OS/2 Prompt Variables

Variable	Use
$$	The '$' character
$t	The system time
$d	The system date
$p	The current directory of the default drive
$v	The OS/2 version number
$n	The default drive
$g	The ">" character
$l	The "<" character
$b	The "¦" character
$-	A carriage return/line feed
$s	A leading space
$e	An ACSII escape code (X'1B')
$c	The "(" character
$f	The ")" character
$a	The "&" character

The prompt string can also contain ANSI escape sequences. If ANSI is ON (protected mode), or the ANSI.SYS device driver is installed (DOS environment), then these sequences are interpreted every time the prompt is displayed. For example,

PROMPT $e[s$e[1;70H$E[7m$t$e[0m$e{ung

saves the cursor position, moves the cursor to the upper-right corner of the screen, writes the system time (in reverse video), returns to the prompt location, and displays the current drive followed by the ">" character. The ANSI functions greatly enhance the capabilities of the PROMPT command.

RMDIR (RD)

The RD (or RMDIR) command removes an OS/2 subdirectory. You can specify any valid subdirectory for deletion, so long as

- It does not contain other subdirectories (they must be deleted first).

- It does not contain any files.

- It is not the current directory for any active process.

For example,

RD C:\PROGRAMS

deletes the subdirectory named PROGRAMS from the root directory of drive C.

In protected mode, the RD command accepts multiple subdirectory names. So, the command

RD PROGRAMS BIN SOURCE

deletes three subdirectories named PROGRAMS, BIN, and SOURCE.

RENAME

The RENAME command changes the name of a file. The command requires two parameters: a *target file name* and the *new name* the target file is to be given. You may include a drive letter and subdirectory name with the first name, but not with the second. In fact, the file always remains on the same drive and in the same subdirectory after it has been renamed. Consider these examples:

```
RENAME STARTUP.CMD STAR.CMD
RENAME C: \PROGRAMS \TEST.ASM TEST2.ASM
```

Wild-card characters take on special meaning in the RENAME command. In the target file-name field, the wild cards provide a string-match selection capability, similar to other commands. In the new-name field, the wild cards indicate which characters are not to change. Consider the following examples:

```
RENAME *.ASM *.E
RENAME ????.ASM *.AS4
RENAME *.E MYPRO?.ASM
```

In the first case, the file extension of all ASM files is changed to "E." The second example renames all files whose names are exactly four characters long and whose extensions are "ASM" to files with the same names and extensions of "AS4." Note that in both cases the second parameter (the "*" wild card) indicates that the same file name is to be used. The third example renames all files whose extensions are "E" to files whose names are comprised of the characters "MYPRO" followed by the sixth character of the original name and the file extension "ASM."

SET

Each command interpreter creates and maintains an environment. An *environment* is a collection of variables that you create and set for later use by application programs or command files. The SET command is used to create environment variables or to modify the contents of an existing environment variable. It has the following form:

    SET *varname=value*

The *varname* is an ASCII string to be associated with the variable. The *varname* and *value* are separated by an equal sign (=). No spaces can separate the *varname* from the equal sign. The variable names are established by usage convention. For example, in Chapter 10 you saw how to use the environment variables PRINT and ECHO in a command file.

If the environment variable you enter does not already exist, SET creates it and stores the ASCII value string. If the variable already exists, SET replaces its value with the ASCII string. For example, consider the following commands:

    SET MYVAR=test
    SET PATH=a:\;b:\;c:\DOS

The first example creates a new variable named MYVAR and copies the string "test" into the environment. If MYVAR existed before you issued the SET command, its previous contents are replaced with "test." The second case changes the value of the PATH environment variable. Some OS/2 commands keep data in environment variables (such as PATH, APPEND, and so forth).

If you enter a SET command with no value, you delete the variable from the environment. For instance,

    SET MYVAR=

removes the variable named MYVAR from the environment.

If you enter the SET command with no parameters, the environment variables are listed as follows:

```
[C:\]SET
COMSPEC=C:\CMD.EXE
PATH=E:\;D:\OS2;D:\DEVLIB;D:\TOOLS
TOOLDIR=tools
LIST=off
MASM=masm
LINK=link
ECHO=off
PROMPT=$e[s$e[1;70H$e[7m$t$e[0m$e[u$n$g
[C:\]
```

Environment variables are a general-system facility for storing global program information. How you use them depends on the types of programs you run from the command line(s).

START

The START command is similar to DETACH except that the program is started in a user selectable session. To use this command you must enter the name of the program you want to run, plus any command-line parameters it requires. For example,

```
START MASM myprog,,myprog;
```

starts a copy of the macro assembler in a different session. You may start any program that can be entered from the command line, including OS/2 command (CMD) files. Starting a CMD file has a significant advantage in that the file can SET environment variables before it runs the EXE program and can EXIT the command interpreter when it finishes.

Consider the example in Figure 12-2. In this example, the START command creates a separate (background) session that runs the CMD file named MASMC. Since the

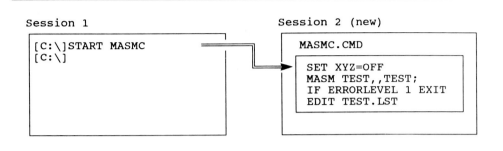

Figure 12-2. Starting a session from the command line

second session runs asynchronously, the command line is immediately available for your use. Meanwhile, in Session 2 the CMD file sets the environment variable named XYZ and starts the MASM program. When MASM completes, the CMD file checks the error level and either invokes an editor to examine the listing (error case) or issues an EXIT command to terminate the session (no errors).

START is only supported by the OS/2 protected-mode command interpreter. When you use the START command, the resulting session is user selectable. This means that the session will appear on the session manager switch list.

TIME

You can reset the system clock by using the TIME command. OS/2 uses the system clock in a number of internal functions, including file-access time-stamps, prompt displays, and system APIs. The clock is internally maintained in a 24-hour format. However, the method of display (AM/PM or 24 HR) is determined by country-specific information.

If you enter the command with no parameters, you are presented with the following prompt:

The current time is: 0:06:12.81
Enter the new time:

At this point you may press ENTER to leave the time unchanged, or enter a different value. The input must be in the format

hh:mm:ss.cc

where the following is true:

hh is hours (0-24)
mm is minutes (0-59)
ss is seconds (0-59)
cc is hundredths of a second (0-99)

The hours and minutes fields are mandatory. The seconds and hundredths of a second are optional and default to 0 if not entered.

The hours, minutes, and seconds are typically separated by a colon (:) and the hundredths by a period (.). Note that both separators are part of the country-specific information and may differ in various national-language translations of OS/2 (French, Japanese, and so forth).

If you enter TIME with a time value, OS/2 does not prompt you. For example:

```
[C:\]TIME 12:12:10
[C:\]
```

Unlike PC DOS, the OS/2 TIME command automatically resets the hardware (CMOS) clock.

TYPE

The TYPE command enables you to display a file on the screen. For example,

```
[C:\]TYPE STARTUP.CMD
```

reads the file STARTUP.CMD from the current directory of the current drive and writes its contents to the screen. The file data is written in TTY mode, so the screen may scroll. Since reading large files as they scroll by on the screen may be difficult, you can use the CTRL-NUMLOCK or CTRL-S key combinations to stop the scrolling temporarily. Unlike PC DOS, these functions only suspend the foreground session and allow background programs to continue executing.

The output of the TYPE command is written to the standard output (STDOUT) handle, so it is redirectable from the command line. This enables you to pass the contents of a file to one or more filters. For instance,

[C:\]TYPE DAILY.LOG ¦ SORT ¦ MORE

passes the contents of the file named DAILY.LOG to the sort filter where the records are sorted in ascending sequence. The sorted data is then piped to the MORE filter, which presents it as single-page images.

As with other file-oriented OS/2 commands, TYPE accepts file specifications containing wild card characters. For example,

[C:\]TYPE *.ASM

displays the contents of all the files in the current drive and directory that have an ASM file extension.

In protected mode, TYPE allows you to enter multiple file names. The command

[C:\]TYPE *.ASM BUILD.CMD

types all the ASM files in the current directory, followed by the file named BUILD.CMD.

One caution about the TYPE command: The output is sent to the screen in binary form. Whatever characters are contained in the file are sent to the screen without testing their validity as displayable ASCII. So, if you type a non-ASCII file (such as a program file) the results are unpredictable. The data could be interpreted as carriage returns, line feeds, bells, and so forth.

VERSION (VER)

The VER command displays the OS/2 version number. Its output is written to STDOUT, so it can be redirected to another device or file.

```
[C:\]VER
The Operating System/2 version is 1.0
[C:\]
```

VERIFY

The VERIFY command turns disk write-verification ON or OFF. When verification is on, all disk-write operations are verified by reading the data back and comparing it against the original. You may use this command to make sure that important data is copied correctly.

```
[C:\]VERIFY ON
[C:\]COPY IMPORTAN.DTA A:
[C:\]VERIFY OFF
```

If you run VERIFY with no parameters, it displays the current VERIFY mode.

```
[C:\]VERIFY VERIFY is OFF.
[C:\]
```

Today's disks are reliable, so you probably do not need to run your system with verification ON. The default VERIFY state is OFF when OS/2 is started.

VOLUME (VOL)

The VOL command displays a disk's volume label. The volume label is created when the media is formatted (or later) by using the LABEL command. You enter a drive letter to tell VOL which volume is to be displayed.

[C:\]VOL A:
The volume label in drive A is OS2__SYSTEM.
[C:\]

In the protected-mode command environment, VOL accepts multiple drive letters. So,

[C:\]VOL A: B: C:

displays volume labels of the media in drives A, B, and C.

d:

You change the current drive by entering a new drive value followed by a colon (:). This drive becomes the new current drive, and it remains so until you either change it again or a program changes it through the OS/2 API.

[C:\]A:
[A:\]

COMMAND INTERPRETERS

OS/2 has a different command interpreter for the DOS-compatibility environment (COMMAND.COM) and for the protected-mode environment (CMD.EXE). Both interpreters are similar in appearance and function. Both present you with the identical command-line interface, with the same command-edit functions, and the same system-prompt function. You can use most of the internal commands from either prompt. Table 12-1 identifies which commands are valid in each environment.

However, some small differences do exist between these command interpreters.

DOS Environment (COMMAND.COM)

This command interpreter is identical to DOS 3.3. Like PC DOS, (and unlike CMD.EXE), this program runs in real mode. You can run real mode (PC DOS) and family application programs from COMMAND.COM.

PC DOS batch files (with BAT extension) are supported, so you can run batch files developed under PC DOS in the compatibility environment. However, a BAT file cannot call an OS/2 CMD file.

Since DOS environment is single-threaded, command-interpreter functions requiring multitasking services are not supported. For example, if you pipe output between programs, the data is passed through a temporary disk file, as it is in PC DOS. Also, COMMAND.COM does not provide you with the DETACH and START commands to asynchronously execute other programs.

You can start secondary copies of the command interpreter with the COMMAND command. As in PC DOS, a second copy of COMMAND is loaded into memory. You cannot start the protected-mode command interpreter (CMD.EXE) from COMMAND.COM.

The DOS environment is totally isolated from the OS/2 protected-mode functions.

Protected Mode (CMD.EXE)

The protected-mode command interpreter builds on the function of COMMAND.COM by exploiting more of the capabilities of OS/2. The program CMD.EXE is a true protected-mode application. If you start multiple copies with the CMD command, only one copy of the program is loaded into memory. The CMD.EXE piping functions use real OS/2 pipes, causing the programs in the pipe to run concurrently.

The CMD language is very similar to the BAT language, so moving a command procedure from real mode to protected mode involves little more than changing the file extension from BAT to CMD. However, an OS/2 CMD file cannot call a BAT file, nor real-mode-only programs.

SYSTEM UTILITIES

OS/2 offers numerous utilities to manipulate the system and its attached devices (see Table 12-3). Unlike the command-interpreter built-in commands, OS/2 utilities are loaded from disk. The remainder of this chapter provides a brief introduction to these programs. Refer to your OS/2 command reference for a complete explanation of all the utility parameters and functions.

ANSI

The ANSI utility is used to enable or disable ANSI escape-sequence processing in VIO. For example, you may enter:

    ANSI ON
    ANSI OFF

If you enter ANSI with no parameters, the utility displays the current VIO ANSI state:

```
[C:\]ANSI
Ansi is ON
[C:\]
```

Note that this utility only affects the ANSI state for protected-mode display sessions. The DOS-compatibility environment ANSI state is set by installing the ANSI.SYS console driver, as it is in PC DOS. For protected mode, the default ANSI state is ON. For the DOS compatibility environment, ANSI is OFF unless the ANSI.SYS driver has been installed.

Table 12-3.   OS/2 System Utilities

Command	Mode(s)	Description
ANSI	PM	Turn VIO ANSI processing ON or OFF
APPEND	RM PM	Define data search path
ASSIGN	RM	Associate one disk with another
ATTRIB	RM PM	Change file attributes
BACKUP	RM PM	Back up data on diskette
CHKDSK	RM PM	Check the status of a disk
CREATEDD	PM	Prepare an OS/2 memory-dump diskette
DISKCOMP	RM PM	Compare diskettes
DISKCOPY	RM PM	Copy diskettes
EDLIN	RM	Line editor
COMP	RM PM	Compare files
FDISK	PM	Update/Display hard-disk partition(s)
FIND	RM PM	Search for string (filter)
FORMAT	RM PM	Format a disk/diskette
GRAFTABL	RM	Define graphics character set
HELP	RM PM	Display help text for message identification
JOIN	RM	Attach disk to directory
KEYB	PM	Define alternate keyboard layout
LABEL	RM PM	Add/change volume label on disk
MODE	RM PM	Change mode of system devices
MORE	RM PM	Prompted display of data (filter)
PATCH	RM PM	Patch program
PRINT	RM PM	Print a file or manipulate the spooler
RECOVER	RM PM	Recover damaged files/disk
REPLACE	RM PM	Replace like-named files on disk
RESTORE	RM PM	Restore backed up files
SETCOM40	RM	Modifies BIOS area to hide/restore COM port

Table 12-3.   OS/2 System Utilities (continued)

Command	Mode(s)	Description
SORT	RM PM	Sort data (filter)
SPOOL	RM PM	Start system spooler
SUBST	RM	Create a virtual drive
SYS	RM PM	Copy the system files to a disk
TRACE	PM	Enable/disable OS/2 traces
TRACEFMT	PM	Format OS/2 trace buffer
TREE	RM PM	Display the directory tree
XCOPY	RM PM	Copy subdirectories

APPEND

The APPEND utility provides the same function in real mode that the DPATH command provides in protected mode. These are identical except that APPEND is a disk utility and DPATH is an internal command. Also, APPEND will not add its path information to the environment unless you use the /e switch. For example,

```
[C:\]APPEND C:\TOOLS /e
[C:\]
```

creates an APPEND environment variable, while

```
[C:\]APPEND C:\TOOLS
[C:\]
```

does not. APPEND is included in OS/2 to ensure compatibility with PC DOS 3.3. It is only supported in the DOS environment.

ASSIGN

The ASSIGN utility tells OS/2 to redirect I/O requests (destined for a particular drive) to a different drive. For example,

    ASSIGN A=C

causes all I/O intended for drive A to be sent to drive C. If you enter ASSIGN with no parameters, OS/2 cancels the current assignment (if any is in effect). ASSIGN is included in OS/2 as a migration tool for existing PC DOS BAT files. It is only supported in the DOS environment.

ATTRIB

The ATTRIB utility enables you to display or modify the read-only and archive file attributes for a specific file or group of files. For example,

    [C:\]ATTRIB STARTUP.CMD +r +a
    [C:\]

sets the read-only and archive attributes for the file named STARTUP.CMD. Similarly, you can reset the attributes with the *-a* and *-r* parameters. ATTRIB accepts wild-card characters, so you can change the attributes of a group of files. For example,

    [C:\]ATTRIB D:*.ASM -a
    [C:\]

resets the archive attribute for all files with an extension of ASM in the current directory of drive D. You can also direct ATTRIB to process all nested subdirectories by adding the */s* switch. For example,

    [C:\]ATTRIB D:*.* -a /s
    [C:\]

resets the archive bit for all files in all directories on drive

D. File attributes are handy tools you can use to manage your files. Refer to Chapter 6 for a more complete description of file attributes.

BACKUP

The BACKUP utility archives files. Using this program, you can back up files from a hard disk or diskette to another hard disk or diskette. You generally use BACKUP to save data from your hard disk on diskette, but the opposite is also possible. BACKUP accepts two parameters: *source* and *target*. All files matching the source file specification are backed up to the target device. For example,

    [C:\]BACKUP D:*.ASM A:

backs up all files with an extension of ASM on the current directory of the disk in drive D to the diskette in drive A. The output is written in a format that can only be read by the RESTORE utility.

BACKUP supports the following options:

/a	Add the backed up files to an existing back-up disk. This also works with back-up disks created by PC DOS version 3.3
/d	Back up files modified *after* a specific date
/f	Format the target diskette (does not work if the target is a hard disk)
/l	Create a back-up log
/m	Only the files that have changed (archive attribute is ON) since the last backup are processed
/s	Indicates that all nested subdirectories are also to be processed
/t	Back up files modified *after* a specific time

You can use any or all of these options to define specific back-up criteria. For example,

    [C:\]BACKUP C:\A: /s /d:09-03-87 /t:12:00:00 /l:back0926.log backs up all files in all subdirectories of drive C that have been changed since 12:00 on 9/3/87. The resulting output is sent to drive A, and a log of the backup is written in a file named BACK0926.LOG.

Back-up disks created by the OS/2 BACKUP utility can be restored by PC DOS (version 3.3).

CHKDSK

The CHKDSK utility reads a disk drive and checks it for errors. In certain situations (such as during a power outage while updating the FAT), the OS/2 file system may leave a disk drive in an invalid state. You can use the CHKDSK utility to identify this type of problem and (optionally) take corrective action. When it runs successfully, CHKDSK produces the following reports:

```
(DOS compatibility environment)

Volume OS2_SYSTEM created -- Aug 9, 1987  11:17am

31977472 bytes total disk space.
       0 bytes in 1 hidden files.
   26624 bytes in 11 directories.
14131200 bytes in 261 user files.
17819648 bytes available on disk.

[DOS mode storage report]
  524256 bytes total storage
  324144 bytes free



(OS/2 Protected mode)

Volume OS2_SYSTEM created -- Aug 9, 1987  11:17am

31977472 bytes total disk space.
       0 bytes in 1 hidden files.
   26624 bytes in 11 directories.
14129152 bytes in 259 user files.
17821696 bytes available on disk.
```

Notice that the memory report only appears when CHKDSK is run in the DOS-compatibility environment.

If a disk has errors, you must rerun CHKDSK with the

/*f* (fix) option. Depending on what is wrong with your disk, CHKDSK takes the most reasonable recovery action. The most common disk error is when the FAT and the directory are out of synchronization. In this case CHKDSK creates "dummy" files for each FAT chain that has no associated directory entry. You must inspect these files and rename (or delete) them as appropriate.

Note that while CHKDSK is actively fixing a disk, it must lock the drive to prevent other (background) programs from modifying the disk contents. Therefore, if another program is already using a disk, CHKDSK cannot fix it. In particular, the boot volume is *always* in use by the OS/2 kernel. Therefore, you *cannot* use CHKDSK to fix errors in the boot disk partition.

The /*v* option allows you to view the progress CHKDSK is making while processing your request.

If you give CHKDSK a file specification instead of a drive letter, it displays how many noncontiguous parts of the disk the file occupies. You may use wild cards in the file specification to analyze a number of files. For example,

    [C:\]CHKDSK D:\OS2*.CMD

produces the standard disk report for the disk in drive D, plus,

    D:\OS2\STARTUP.CMD
            contains 3 non-contiguous blocks
    D:\OS2\CP.CMD
            contains 2 non-contiguous blocks

You can use CHKDSK in this way to determine how fragmented your disk data is.

COMP

The COMP utility compares the contents of two or more files. Unlike DISKCOMP (which compares exact disk images), COMP compares the contents of the files, regardless of where they are located on the disk. Furthermore, the files may be located on different disks, on the same disk, and in the same or in different directories.

The COMP utility accepts two parameters: the *source* and *target* files. For example,

[C:\]COMP C:\STARTUP.CMD A:\STARTUP.CMD

compares the file named STARTUP.CMD in the root directory of drive A to a file with the same name in the root directory of drive C. COMP reads the files and compares their contents. For each discrepancy it encounters, COMP issues a message telling you the offset and the contents of each file. If COMP finds ten or more mismatches, it stops comparing the files.

If you enter only a drive letter as the target, COMP assumes that the second file has the same file name and extension as the first. For example,

[C:\]COMP C:\STARTUP.CMD A:

tells COMP to compare the same files as in the previous example.

You may include wild-card characters in the target and source file specifications. For instance, if you enter

[C:\]COMP C:*.WKS D:*.WKS

COMP tries to match all the files with the WKS extension in drive C with their counterparts in drive D. Wherever the file names match, COMP compares the contents of the files.

On the other hand, if you enter a directory name, then COMP searches the entire directory for matching file names to compare. For example,

[C:\]COMP C:\TOOLS D:\OLDTOOLS

causes COMP to compare all files in the subdirectory

C:\TOOLS whose names match files in the subdirectory D:\OLDTOOLS. Of course, you can use subdirectory names and wild cards in the source and target file specifications. So,

[C:\]COMP C:\TOOLS*.EXE D:\OLDTOOLS

causes COMP to compare all files with an EXE extension in the C:\TOOLS subdirectory to any files with the same name and extension in the D:\OLDTOOLS subdirectory.

CREATEDD

You use the CREATEDD utility to prepare a diskette for an OS/2 memory dump. If a dump requires more than one diskette, the first must be prepared with CREATEDD while the rest can be formatted diskettes. When you run CREATEDD, you must specify which drive contains the diskette. For example,

[C:\]CREATEDD A:

converts the diskette in drive A to dump format.

DISKCOMP

The DISKCOMP utility compares the contents of two diskettes. The utility accepts two parameters: *source* and *target* drive letters. If the source and target drives are the same, DISKCOMP performs a single drive comparison and prompts you to alternatively insert the source and target diskettes. Consider the following examples:

[C:\]DISKCOMP A: B:
[C:\]DISKCOMP A: A:

In the first case, DISKCOMP compares the diskettes in drives A and B. In the second example, DISKCOMP compares two diskettes but uses only drive A. In both cases, if any discrepancies are found, DISKCOMP displays a message telling you the track and side number that do not match.

DISKCOMP will only work when the source and target diskettes are formatted in the same way. If you try to compare dissimilar diskettes, DISKCOMP issues an error message and ends.

Note that all OS/2 diskettes are not exactly equal, since each has a unique volume serial number in track 0, head 0. DISKCOMP skips over this serial number.

DISKCOPY

The DISKCOPY utility creates an exact (sector-by-sector) copy of a diskette. Like DISKCOMP, DISKCOPY accepts two parameters: the *source* and *target* drives. If you enter the same value for both, DISKCOPY performs a single-drive copy. For example,

    [C:\]DISKCOPY A: B:

copies the contents of the diskette in drive A to the diskette in drive B. If the diskette in the target drive is unformatted, DISKCOPY formats it as it copies the data, using the same format as the source diskette.

If the source diskette was originally formatted by OS/2, DISKCOPY copies all but the serial number of the source diskette. In its place, DISKCOPY generates a new, unique number. Note that if you create a diskette in this way and then compare it to the source under PC DOS 3.2 or earlier, the diskette images will not compare in track 0 head 0.

EDLIN

The EDLIN utility creates and updates text files. EDLIN is a real-mode-only utility and thus can only be used from the DOS environment. OS/2 provides essentially the same

EDLIN program included in PC DOS. Refer to the PC DOS 3.3 command reference guide for a complete description of the EDLIN features.

FDISK

The FDISK utility creates, inspects, modifies or deletes partitions on an OS/2 hard disk. It also creates OS/2 extended partitions and logical drives to subdivide hard files larger than 32MB.

FDISK is a menu-driven utility. Figure 12-3 summarizes the FDISK menu functions.

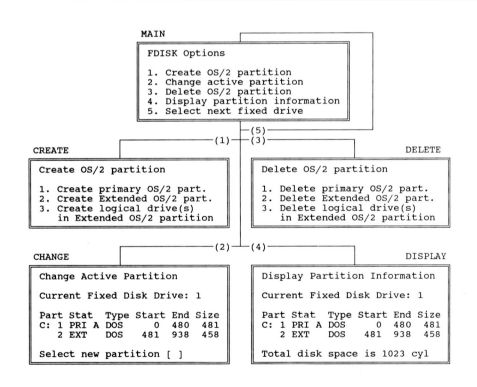

Figure 12-3. FDISK utility menus

MAIN

The main FDISK menu provides five options. If you select 1-4, you move to the CREATE, CHANGE, DELETE, and DISPLAY menus, respectively. If you select option 5, FDISK switches to your second hard disk (if you have one). The ESC key returns you to the command interpreter.

CREATE

If you select option 1 from the main menu, FDISK displays this menu. From here you can create a primary OS/2 partition, an extended OS/2 partition, or a logical drive for an extended partition. Before you can create an extended partition, the disk must have a primary OS/2 partition. Likewise, the logical drives can be created only after the extended partition exists. The ESC key returns you to the main FDISK menu.

CHANGE

If you select option 2 from the main menu, FDISK displays this menu. From here you may change the active (bootable) partition. This option is used when you have more than one operating system installed in different primary partitions (such as Xenix). If you only have OS/2 (or PC DOS) installed in your system, then this menu indicates

Only bootable partition on Drive is already marked active

The ESC key returns you to the main FDISK menu.

DELETE

If you select option 3 from the main menu, FDISK displays this menu. FDISK provides three options: delete the primary partition, delete an extended partition, or delete a logical drive. If you select an extended partition or logical drive, you are presented with a list and asked to choose one to delete. To delete an extended partition, you must first delete its logical drive. To delete the primary partition, you must first delete the extended partition(s).

Note: If you delete a partition, you lose all the data on that logical disk. Be sure you really want to do this before you select these options.

The ESC key will return you to the main FDISK menu.

DISPLAY

If you select option 4 from the main menu, FDISK displays this menu. The DISPLAY menu lists the partition information for the current disk. If the disk contains extended partitions and logical drives, the following message appears on the screen:

The Extended OS/2 partition contains logical OS/2 drives. Do you want to display logical drive information? [Y]

If you reply "yes," the logical drives are displayed. The ESC key returns you to the main FDISK menu.

If you use FDISK to add a new partition or delete an existing partition, the system resets (reboots) when you exit FDISK.

FIND

The FIND utility is a special type of OS/2 program called a *filter*. Filters take their input from the standard input device (STDIN), perform some kind of operation on the data, and then send their output to the standard output device (STDOUT). In this case, the FIND filter searches the input data stream for a particular ASCII string, and writes only those records containing the string. Since FIND expects its input from the STDIN device, you may use it in conjunction with a pipe command. For example,

[C: \ ]DIR C: ¦ FIND "9-26-87"

searches the directory listing for the records containing the string "9-26-87" and writes the output to the console.

Thus, you only see the files in the current directory of the disk in drive C that were last updated on 9-26-87.

The /c switch causes FIND to write the count of records that match the search string, rather than the records themselves. For instance,

    [C: \ ]DIR C: ¦ FIND /c "9-26-87"

displays the number of files on the current directory of drive C that were last updated on 9-26-87.

The /v switch tells FIND to select all records in the input stream that do not contain the ASCII string. The command

    [C: \ ]DIR C: ¦ FIND /v "-87"

displays all the files that were not last updated in 1987.

Finally, you can also use the FIND utility to search for occurrences of strings in ASCII files. To use FIND in this way (rather than as a filter), you simply add one or more file names following the search string. For example,

    [C: \ ]FIND "ECHO ON" STARTUP.CMD TEST.CMD

locates all the records in the files STARTUP.CMD and TEST.CMD that contain the string "ECHO ON." Notice that the FIND utility does not accept wild-card characters, so you must explicitly list the files you want it to search.

Since ASCII files can sometimes be lengthy, the FIND utility can list the relative line numbers of each record that matches the search string. To do this, you must include the /n switch.

    [C: \ ]FIND /n "ECHO ON" STARTUP.CMD TEST.CMD

Notice that a switch (/n, /c, or /v) must precede the search string. Otherwise, FIND tries to open the switch as if it were a file name.

FORMAT

The FORMAT utility prepares a disk or diskette for the OS/2 file system. FORMAT initializes the disk data structures (FAT, root directory, and so forth) and checks the disk for bad sectors. FORMAT accepts only one parameter: the *drive identifier.* If you do not tell FORMAT which drive to process, it formats the current drive. For instance, both of these commands

```
[C:\]FORMAT C:
[C:\]FORMAT
```

format drive C.

Note: If you format a fixed disk, be sure you do not need the data already on the disk. The FORMAT utility clears the disk.

If you format a diskette, FORMAT uses the highest density format supported by the drive. However, you can tell FORMAT to format a diskette as low-capacity (360K) in a high-capacity drive (1.2MB) by adding the /4 switch. For example,

```
[C:\]FORMAT A: /4
```

formats the diskette in drive A in low-capacity format.

If you are formatting a 3.5-inch diskette, the /t and /n switches specify the number of tracks per side and sectors per track, respectively. So, the statement

```
[C:\]FORMAT B: /T:80 /N:18
```

formats a high-capacity 3.5-inch diskette with 80 tracks per side and 18 sectors per track.

If you want to create a bootable disk, you use the /s switch to add the system files to the newly formatted disk. For instance,

```
[C:\]FORMAT A: /s
```

creates a bootable system diskette. However, this option only works if the target disk/diskette has a capacity of at least 1.2MB. Note that this option only works if all the system files are on the root directory of the boot volume. If you have moved these files to a different directory, you can still create a system disk manually by first using SYS to transfer the hidden files and copying the remainder with the OS/2 COPY command. The files that are required to be on a boot disk are listed in the file named FORMATS. TBL.

Unlike PC DOS, the OS/2 FORMAT utility always prompts you for a volume label. This is because OS/2 uses the volume label to prompt you when it detects the wrong diskette in a drive. If you want to avoid the prompt, provide the volume label by using the /v switch.

[C:\]FORMAT A: /V:123_WKS_A

Wherever possible, use significant names to label your diskettes.

GRAFTABL

The GRAFTABL utility loads a graphics-mode character set for the ASCII characters 128-255. Since OS/2 1.0 does not support protected-mode text operations in graphics display modes, this utility may only be used from the DOS compatibility environment. GRAFTABL is included in OS/2 for compatibility with PC DOS.GRAFTABL and expects no parameters.

HELPMSG (HELP)

HELP accepts a message number and gives you its extended error information. Unlike PC DOS, OS/2 assigns an error number to all error messages. For example, consider the following scenario:

[D: \ ]mode jjjj
SYS2092: The MODE parameter jjjj is incorrect.
[D: \ ]help 2092
SYS2092: The MODE parameter *** is incorrect.
EXPLANATION: The MODE command accepts the following
    parameters:
To set parallel printer modes:
    MODE LPT# chars,lines,P
To set display modes:
    MODE display,rows
To set asynchronous modes in DOS mode:
    MODE COMn:baud,parity,databits,stopbits
To set asynchronous modes in IBM Operating System/2 mode:
    MODE COMn:baud,parity,databits,stopbits,
    TO=ON¦OFF,XON=ON¦OFF,IDSR=ON¦OFF,ODSR=ON¦OFF,
    OCTS=ON¦OFF,DTR=ON¦OFF¦HS,RTS=ON¦OFF¦HS¦TOG
ACTION: Check the MODE parameters and retry the command.
[D: \ ]

When you mistype the MODE command parameters
(jjjj), OS/2 generates error message SYS2092. If you do not
understand the message text, you can retrieve additional
information by using HELP. Note that HELP accepts the
entire message number (SYS2092), or the numeric portion
of the message number (2092).

For compatibility with PC DOS, OS/2 only generates
message numbers in the protected-mode command sessions. However, you may run HELP from either the real-
mode or protected-mode command interpreters.

The HELP utility is actually a command file (HELP.CMD)
that calls the utility named HELPMSG.EXE. You can also
use HELP to turn a constant help prompt ON or OFF. For
example,

   [C: \ ]HELP ON

causes OS/2 to display the information in Figure 12-4 at

```
(DOS environment)
 ┌─────────────────────────────────────────────────────────────────────┐
 │  DOS       │    Ctrl+Esc=program selector    │   Type HELP=help      │
 └─────────────────────────────────────────────────────────────────────┘

(Protected mode)
 ┌─────────────────────────────────────────────────────────────────────┐
 │  OS/2      │    Ctrl+Esc=program selector    │   Type HELP=help      │
 └─────────────────────────────────────────────────────────────────────┘
```

Figure 12-4.   HELP screen display

the top of your screen.

Note, that if you use HELP in this way, it changes the value of your prompt. If you have a special prompt and still wish to use this function, edit the HELP.CMD and HELP.BAT files to include your prompt statement.

JOIN

The JOIN utility allows you to logically attach a drive (such as drive A) to a second disk and make it appear like a disk subdirectory. For example,

```
[C:\]JOIN A: C:\ADISK
[C:\]
```

makes your disk in drive A a logical extension of your disk in drive C. To access files on drive A, you change the current directory on drive C to the subdirectory named ADISK. In fact, as far as your programs are concerned, drive A no longer exists. If the specified directory does not exist, then JOIN will create it.

You may only JOIN a disk to a root subdirectory. For example,

[C:\]JOIN A: C:\TOOLS\ADISK

will fail. To display the disks currently JOINed, you run JOIN with no parameters. For example,

```
[C:\]JOIN
    A: is joined to C:\ADISK
[C:\]
```

To delete a previously joined disk, use the /d switch, as follows:

[C:\]JOIN A: /d

A disk may be joined only if it is not being used by another process. For example, if you boot OS/2 from diskette and then try to join the boot drive, the operation fails, since OS/2 continues to use data from the diskette.

JOIN is included in OS/2 as a migration tool for existing PC DOS BAT files and is only supported in the DOS environment.

KEYB

The KEYB replaces the OS/2 default (US English) keyboard layout with a different national layout. KEYB accepts one of the character codes shown in Table 12-4. For example,

[C:\]KEYB SP

changes the primary keyboard layout to Spanish. This change is global, so all sessions (including the DOS session) are affected. However, you can only start the KEYB utility from a protected-mode command interpreter.

Once you have loaded an alternate keyboard, you may

Table 12-4.   OS/2 Country Codes

Code	Country
BE	Belgium
CF	Canadian-French
DK	Denmark
FR	France
SU	Finland
GR	Germany
IT	Italy
LA	Latin-American Spanish
NL	Netherlands
NO	Norway
PO	Portugal
SP	Spain
SV	Sweden
SF	Swiss-French
SG	Swiss-German
UK	United Kingdom English
US	United States English

switch between it and the standard US keyboard with the CTRL-ALT-F1 and CTRL-ALT-F2 key combinations.

LABEL

The LABEL utility adds or changes a disk volume label. LABEL accepts two optional parameters: the *drive identifier* and the *volume label*. If you do not specify which drive, LABEL assumes the default drive. If you do not enter a volume label, LABEL prompts you. For example,

    [C: \ ]LABEL C:SYSRES

applies the label "SYSRES" to the disk in drive C. The label may be 1-11 characters in length and may contain any characters allowed in file names.

Disk labels are more important in OS/2 than in PC DOS because the OS/2 volume manager uses the string to prompt you for the correct diskette when you have open files on more than one diskette.

MODE

The MODE utility changes the characteristics of the OS/2 devices. You can use this utility to change the printer, asynchronous ports, and the display.

When using MODE to change a printer (PRN, PRT1, PRT2, and so forth), you can set the following values:

CPL	The number of characters to a line (80 or 132)
LPI	The lines-per-inch (6 or 8)
Retry	The retry mode (P)

For example,

[C:\]MODE LPT1: 132,8,P

resets the printer to 132 characters per line, 8 lines per inch with continuous retry mode on printer time-outs.

If you use MODE to change an asynchronous port (COM1, COM2, or COM3), you can set the following values:

Baud	The baud rate may be 110, 150, 300, 600, 1200, 2400, 4800, 9600, or 19200. You can enter just the first two characters of the baud rate. This parameter is required
Parity	The parity is specfied as (E)ven, (O)dd, (N)one, (M)ark, or (S)pace. Mark indicates that the parity is always one; Space indicates the parity is always zero. Even and Odd are self-explanatory. If you do not specify the parity, OS/2 assumes Even

Databits   The data bits may be 5, 6, 7, or 8. The default is 7

Stopbits   The stop bits may be 1, 1.5, or 2. The default is 2 for 110 baud; otherwise 1

In addition, you may use the following options when you run MODE from protected mode:

TO=   Infinite write time-out (ON or OFF). The default is OFF

XON=   Automatic transmit flow control (ON or OFF). Initialized as OFF

IDSR=   Data-set-ready (DSR) input handshaking (ON or OFF). Initialized as ON

ODSR=   Data-set-ready (DSR) output handshaking (ON or OFF). Initialized as ON

OCTS=   Clear-to-send (CTS) output handshaking (ON or OFF). Initialized as ON

DTR=   Data-terminal-ready (DTR) control (ON, OFF, or HS). HS enables handshaking. Initial value is DTR=ON

RTS=   Request-to-send (RTS) control (ON, OFF, TOG, or HS). HS enables handshaking. TOG enables RTS toggling. Initial value is RTS=ON

For example,

```
[C:\]MODE COM1: 96,N,8,1,XON=ON,RTS=HS
Asynchronous Communications mode has been set.
[C:\]
```

resets the COM1 port to 9600 baud, no parity, 1 stop bit, enables XON/XOFF flow control, and request-to-send (RTS) handshaking. In protected mode you enter the name of an asynchronous port to display its current status. For example:

```
[C:\]MODE COM1:
COM1:9600,N,8,1,TO=OFF,XON=ON,IDSR=ON,ODSR=ON,
[C:\]OCTS=ON,DTR=ON,RTS=HS
```

Table 12-5. OS/2 Display Modes

Code	Description
CO80	Color 80 column
CO40	Color 40 column
CO80	Black and white (color burst disabled) 80 column
CO40	Black and white (color burst disabled) 40 column

Finally, you can use the MODE command to change a session's display mode. The supported video modes are listed in Table 12-5.

[C:\]MODE CO40

switches your display to 40-column mode. With certain display adaptors (such as an EGA or VGA), you can also change the number of rows to 43 or 50. For instance,

[C:\]MODE CO80,43

changes the display mode to 80 columns by 43 rows.

MORE

MORE is an OS/2 filter that accepts an input data stream from the standard input device and writes it to the standard output device one screen at a time. You can use MORE to view large files without having information scroll off the screen. For example,

[C:\]MORE < LARGE.FIL

presents the data in the file named LARGE.FIL one screen at a time. MORE waits for you to press a key before it writes the next screenful of data. Since MORE reads data from STDIN, you can also use it as part of a pipe. For instance,

[C:\]DIR C: | MORE

shows you the files in the current directory of the drive C one screen at a time.

PATCH

The PATCH utility applies patches to program files. PATCH runs either in automatic or manual mode, depending on the input it receives.

To run PATCH in manual mode, you give it the name of a file to patch. The file can be any valid OS/2 file, including binary program files and ASCII data files. PATCH then interactively prompts you for changes to the file. For instance, consider the dialog shown in Figure 12-5.

```
[C:\]PATCH MYPROG.EXE
Patching MYPROG.EXE

End of file is at D022
Enter the hexadecimal offset of patch: 128
00000128    10 10 10 10 10 10 10 10 64 20 65 6E 76 69 72 6F    2 comm

Do you want to continue patching MYPROG.EXE? (Y/N)

Patches entered for MYPROG.EXE

00000128    10 10 10 10 10 10 10 10 64 20 65 6E 76 69 72 6F    ......

Do you want these patches applied to MYPROG.EXE? (Y/N)
Patches applied to MYPROG.EXE

[C:\]
```

Figure 12-5. Sample dialog from PATCH

PATCH reads the file and prompts you for the location you wish to patch. When you enter an address, PATCH displays the contents of the next 16 bytes. You can then change as many bytes as you desire. When you press the ENTER key, PATCH asks you if you want to continue patching (in a different part of the file). If you enter "No," PATCH displays the changes you made and asks you if they should be applied to the file. When you answer "Yes," the data is written to the disk and the file is updated.

To run PATCH in automatic mode, you give it the name of an automatic patch file and add the /a switch.

    [C: \ ]PATCH /a CHANGES.PAT

The file named CHANGES.PAT contains patch instructions that the PATCH utility executes to update one or more program files.

If you intend to use PATCH, be careful, since it could destroy your files.

PRINT

As its name suggests, the OS/2 PRINT utility prints files. For example,

    [C: \ ]PRINT MYDATA.FIL

sends the file named MYDATA.FIL to the printer. Unlike PC DOS, the OS/2 PRINT utility does not spool the output itself. Instead, it sends the data to the OS/2 print spooler, which is a different program. When PRINT ends, you may erase, move, or rename the file (even if it has not yet printed).

If you do not tell it otherwise, PRINT will send the file to the first available printer (LPT1: in most cases). If your system has more than one printer, you can select the printer with the /d switch. Thus,

    [C: \ ]PRINT MYDATA.FIL /D:LPT2

prints the file on the device named LPT2:. As in PC DOS, the /t switch cancels all the files in the print queue and the /c switch cancels the file currently printing.

    [C:\]PRINT /c
    [C:\]PRINT /t

RECOVER

The RECOVER utility re-creates files and directories that develop bad sectors (minus the bad data, of course). To recover a file, you give RECOVER a file specification. To recover a root directory, you give RECOVER a drive letter. For example,

    [C:\]RECOVER C:\DEVLIB\MYPROG.ASM

recovers the file named MYPROG.ASM in the directory C:\DEVLIB. Similarly,

    [C:\]RECOVER C:

recovers the root directory on drive C. RECOVER marks the defective sectors so that the OS/2 file system will not use them again to hold other data.

REPLACE

The REPLACE utility copies files on a selective basis. REPLACE accepts two parameters: the *source* and *target* file specifications. The source file specification replaces the target file specification (if it exists). For instance,

    [C:\]REPLACE C:MYPROG.ASM D:MYPROG.ASM

replaces the file named MYPROG.ASM on the disk in drive D with a similarly named file from the disk in drive

C. You can use wild cards and subdirectory names to replace groups of files. So,

[C:\]REPLACE C:\DEVLIB*.ASM C:\BACKUP

replaces all the files in the directory named C:\BACKUP with an ASM extension with the like-named files from the subdirectory named C:\DEVLIB. The /p switch causes REPLACE to prompt you before a file is overwritten (allowing you to selectively replace files). For example,

[C:\]REPLACE C:\MASM*.PIF D:\MASM2 /P

might generate the dialog shown in Figure 12-6.

Notice that the files named LINK.PIF and EXEMOD. PIF were not replaced because you responded "N" to the REPLACE prompt. REPLACE stops replacing files when it finds no more files to match the replacement criteria or when it encounters a file that is marked read-only. However, you can force REPLACE to overlay read-only files by using the /r switch. So, if you enter

```
Do you want to replace D:\MASM2\MASM.PIF (Y/N)? y
Replacing file D:\MASM2\MASM.PIF.
Do you want to replace D:\MASM2\SALUT.PIF (Y/N)? y
Replacing file D:\MASM2\SALUT.PIF.
Do you want to replace D:\MASM2\LINK.PIF (Y/N)? n
Do you want to replace D:\MASM2\CREF.PIF (Y/N)? y
Replacing file D:\MASM2\CREF.PIF.
Do you want to replace D:\MASM2\LIB.PIF (Y/N)? y
Replacing file D:\MASM2\LIB.PIF.
Do you want to replace D:\MASM2\EXEMOD.PIF (Y/N)? n
Do you want to replace D:\MASM2\MAKE.PIF (Y/N)? y
Replacing file D:\MASM2\MAKE.PIF.
5 files were replaced.
```

Figure 12-6. Sample dialog from REPLACE

[C:\]REPLACE C:\DEVLIB*.ASM C:\BACKUP /R

all files that match the replacement criteria are overlayed, including any marked read-only. After replacement, the target files remain read-only.

The /a switch tells REPLACE to add any files in the source file specification that are not in the target. Thus, the following commands

[C:\]REPLACE C:\DEVLIB*.* C:\BACKUP
[C:\]REPLACE C:\DEVLIB*.* C:\BACKUP /A

copy all the files in the subdirectory C:\DEVLIB into C:\BACKUP. The first command copies the common files and the second copies those that are in C:\DEVLIB, but not in C:\BACKUP.

The /s switch copies the target file specification into all matching file specifications in the target directory, plus all nested subdirectories. If you wanted to update all instances of MASM.EXE in drive D, you would enter the following command:

[C:\]REPLACE C:MASM.EXE D:\/S

The /s and /a switches are mutually exclusive.

RESTORE

The RESTORE utility restores files that you had previously saved using the BACKUP command. The data can be restored from diskette to hard disk, or vice versa. RE-STORE accepts two parameters: a *source device* and *target* file specification. RESTORE locates the BACKUP data on the source device and restores it in the target.

To restore a specific file or combination of files (by using wild cards), you enter the source drive and a file specification. For example,

[C:\]RESTORE A: C:STARTUP.CMD

restores the file named STARTUP.CMD from the back-up diskette in drive A.

To restore an entire disk, you enter two drive letters. You must also include the /s switch if you want to restore all subdirectories. So, the command

[C:\]RESTORE A: C: /s

restores the back-up data on the diskette in drive A to the disk in drive C, including the nested subdirectories. If the subdirectories do not exist on the disk in drive C, RE-STORE creates them, as needed, to hold the restored files. If the back-up data spans multiple diskettes, RESTORE prompts you between diskettes.

RESTORE supports the following options:

/p   Causes RESTORE to prompt you before it overlays a file marked read-only or that has been modified since it was backed up

/b   Restores the target files modified *on* or *before* a given date

/a   Restores the target files modified *on* or *after* a given date

/e   Restores the target files modified *on* or *earlier* than a given time

/l   Restores the target files modified *on* or *later* than a given time

/m   Restores the target files modified since the last backup (the archive attribute is set)

/n   Only restores those files no longer existing in the target drive

You may use any or all of these options to define specific restoration criteria. For example,

[C:\]RESTORE A: C:\/S /A:09-03-87 /L:12:00:00 /P

restores all files in all subdirectories of drive C that have been changed since 12:00 on 9/3/87. If any file about to be restored is marked read-only, RESTORE prompts you.

Back-up disks created by PC DOS (version 3.3) may be restored by the OS/2 RESTORE utility.

SETCOM40

The SETCOM40 utility enables and disables DOS-compatibility environment application access to the system COM ports by resetting the BIOS data area. When you load the OS/2 COM device driver (COM.SYS), it updates the BIOS data area to indicate that the system has no serial (COM) ports. It does this because some PC DOS applications write directly to the COM hardware. This may adversely affect protected-mode applications in the background that are using the same COM device(s).

However, real-mode applications that access the COM devices through the OS/2 file system (using OPEN, READ, WRITE, and CLOSE) will continue to run, irrespective of the BIOS data area status. If you want to use an application that directly manipulates the hardware, and you are sure that no protected-mode application is using the ports, you may use SETCOM40 to modify the BIOS area and "unhide" the COM port(s).

To use SETCOM40 you enter the COM port and its desired state. For example:

```
[C:\]SETCOM40 COM1=ON
[C:\]SETCOM40 COM2=ON
[C:\]SETCOM40 COM3=OFF
```

As a precaution, always turn off DOS-compatibility environment access to the COM ports as soon as you end the application that used the ports. SETCOM40 may only be used from the real-mode command interpreter.

SORT

The SORT utility is an OS/2 filter program that reads data from STDIN, sorts the data, and writes the resulting data stream to STDOUT. For example,

    [C:\]DIR A: ¦ SORT

produces an alphabetical listing of the contents of the disk
in drive A. Normally, SORT will sort the data records in
ascending order (collating sequence). The /r switch causes
SORT to sort the records in descending order. For example,

    [C:\]DIR A: ¦ SORT /R

produces a reverse-alphabetical listing of the files on the
disk in drive A. You can also sort the information starting
at a particular column by using the /+ switch. For instance,

    [C:\]DIR A: ¦ FIND "-87" ¦ SORT /+15 /R

generates a listing of the files updated in 1987 on the disk
in drive A in reverse-size order (largest first). The DIR
size field starts in column 15.

SPOOL

The SPOOL utility starts the system print spooler. When
active, SPOOL separates the print data generated by different application programs (processes) into separate print
files. SPOOL copies the data into the system spool directory and sends it to the printer when the printer becomes
available.

Print data coming from the DOS-compatibility environment is also spooled. In some cases you may have to
press CTRL-ALT-PRTSCR to send the data to the spooler.
This is because most PC DOS applications do not close the
printer when they finish printing. The key sequence tells
OS/2 that the print stream is complete and the data should
be printed.

You can give SPOOL the name of a disk subdirectory to
hold the temporary spool print files. This directory must

exist before you start SPOOL. If you specify none, SPOOL uses \SPOOL on the current disk. For example,

    [C:\]SPOOL C:\SPOOLDTA

starts the spooler and establishes C:\SPOOLDTA as the SPOOL subdirectory.

SPOOL uses OS/2 character-device monitors to intercept the print data streams. Therefore, it can manage output directed to any device that supports monitors (for example, LPT1: or LPT2:). You use the /d switch to define the device to be spooled. Similarly, the SPOOL output can be sent to any output device that supports monitors or any COM port (the OS/2 1.0 COM device driver does not support device monitors). The /o switch defines the output device. For example,

    [C:\]SPOOL /D:LPT2 /O:COM3

instructs the utility to spool all output going to the device named LPT2:, and send it to COM3:. If you do not specify /o or /d, SPOOL will spool the LPT1: print data and send it to the LPT1: device.

You can start more than one copy of SPOOL to manage print data streams destined for several different devices. For example, the commands

    [C:\]SPOOL /D:LPT1 /O:LPT1
    [C:\]SPOOL /D:LPT2 /O:LPT2

cause SPOOL to manage the print data for LPT1: and LPT2:. However, you cannot use spool to merge output of two printers. For example, the commands

    [C:\]SPOOL /D:LPT1 /O:LPT1
    [C:\]SPOOL /D:LPT2 /O:LPT1

produce unpredictable results.

If you start SPOOL from the command line, it takes over your display session. To avoid wasting a session, you can DETACH SPOOL so it will run as a background process. Alternatively, you can start SPOOL from your system configuration (CONFIG.SYS) file. For example, the statement

    RUN=SPOOL.EXE

starts the spooler each time you boot the system. The spooler is automatically added to your CONFIG.SYS by the OS/2 installation aid.

SUBST

The SUBST utility creates virtual drives out of system subdirectories. To your programs, these drives look like a real disk or diskette. You create a virtual drive by giving SUBST a directory name and the drive letter with which it is to be associated. For example,

    [C:\]SUBST Q: C:\TOOLS

makes the subdirectory C:\TOOLS look like drive Q:. When programs read or write data to drive Q, the data is actually being written into C:\TOOLS. SUBST is the opposite of JOIN (discussed previously in this chapter).

To display the subdirectories currently aliased as virtual drives, run SUBST with no parameters. For example,

```
[C:\]SUBST
Q: is substituted for C:\DOSTOOL
[C:\]
```

To delete a virtual drive, use the /d switch, as follows:

    [C:\]SUBST A: /d

SYS

The SYS utility copies the OS/2 system files to another disk. To use SYS, you must use a newly formatted disk that contains no other data. SYS transfers the hidden system files IBMBIO.COM and IBMDOS.COM to the target disk. For example,

    [C:\]SYS A:

copies the system files to the diskette in drive A. Note that unlike PC DOS, the OS/2 SYS command does not transfer all the files necessary to boot and run the system to the target disk. After running SYS, you must copy CMD.EXE, COMMAND.COM, and the files listed in the file named FORMATS.TBL onto the root directory of the new boot disk. To build a system diskette you must use either 1.2MB or 1.44MB media, since the files required to run OS/2 total more than 720K.

TRACE

The TRACE utility dynamically activates or deactivates the OS/2 system traces. It accepts a trace state (ON or OFF), followed by an optional list of numeric trace codes. Every OS/2 trace point is in one of 255 major trace codes (shown in Table 12-6).

Traces are activated or deactivated by major trace code. When you enter one or more codes following the trace state, the traces associated with the codes assume the state. For example,

    [C:\]TRACE ON 1,2,22,37

activates major trace codes 1, 2, 22, and 37, and leaves the state of all other traces unchanged. Similarly,

    [C:\]TRACE OFF 4,17

Table 12-6.   OS/2 Major Trace Points

Major Code	Traces
10	Tasking services
14	Program-execution services
18	Inter process communication services
1C	Other miscellaneous services
24	Memory-management services
30	File-system services
38	Timer services
60	Device-management services
61	Device management —interface to device drivers
62	DevHelp services
64	Keyboard device driver
6A	Mouse device driver
6C	VIO services
70-7F	External interrupts
80	Session-manager services
83	Message-retriever services
88	Queuing services

turns off the trace for major codes 4 and 17, again leaving all other traces intact. If you do not specify any major trace codes, all system traces are turned on or off. For example,

    [C:\]TRACE ON

activates all OS/2 trace points.

Since it is a protected-mode utility, TRACE can only be used from a protected-mode OS/2 command interpreter. TRACE only activates the traces if you allocate a trace buffer when you start the system by using the TRACE-BUF statement in the CONFIG.SYS file.

TRACEFMT

The TRACEFMT utility formats the current contents of the system trace buffer and writes the output to the standard output (STDOUT) device. The records are formatted and written in reverse chronological order (most recent first). So,

[C:\]TRACEFMT > TRACE.DTA

generates a trace report and writes it to the file named TRACE.DTA.

The output of TRACEFMT identifies each trace event, when it occurred (pre-invocation or post-invocation), the process identification of the caller, the type of call (kernel or dynalink), the mode of the caller (protect or real), and a time stamp. Figure 12-7 illustrates a typical trace display.

If you do not allocate a trace buffer when you start the system, then TRACEFMT displays an error message. As

```
DosExecPgm Pre-Invocation
   Issuing Process ID=000B  Protect Mode   Kernel Call  Time Stamp=...
   Program Name=D:\OS2\370\TRACEFMT.EXE   Async Indicator=0002

DosEnterCritSec Post-Invocation
   Issuing Process ID=0004  Protect Mode   Kernel Call  Time Stamp=...

DosEnterCritSec Pre-Invocation
   Issuing Process ID=0004  Protect Mode   Kernel Call  Time Stamp=...

DosMonRead Pre-Invocation
   Issuing Process ID=0004  Protect Mode  Dynlink Call  Time Stamp=...
   Input Buffer=032F:0C7A  Wait Flag=1060
   Data Buffer=0001:037F  Byte Count=037F:0830

DosSemSetWait Post-Invocation
   Issuing Process ID=0004  Protect Mode   Kernel Call  Time Stamp=44.
   Return Code=0079
```

Figure 12-7. Sample OS/2 trace data

with the TRACE utility, TRACEFMT may only be run from a protected-mode command interpreter.

TREE

The TREE command displays the subdirectory structure of an OS/2 disk. For example,

    [D:\]TREE D:

produces the following output:

    Directory path listing
    Path: \OS2
    Subdirectories: BIN
    Path: \OS2\BIN
    Subdirectories: None
    Path: \SPOOL
    Subdirectories: None

If you add the /f switch, then TREE also lists the files contained in each directory. For example,

    [C:\]TREE D: /F

lists the same information as in the previous example with the addition of the files contained in the root directory and in the subdirectories OS2, OS2\BIN, and SPOOL.

XCOPY

The XCOPY command copies entire subdirectories. You run XCOPY with *source* and *target* file specifications. The source file specification is copied to the target file specification. XCOPY file specifications can be a single drive letter, a file name, or a subdirectory name. The file names may include wild cards. For example,

    [C:\]XCOPY \MASM \BACKUP

copies all the files from subdirectory MASM to subdirectory BACKUP. If BACKUP does not exist, XCOPY asks you if you want it to be created. The command,

    [C:\]XCOPY \MASM*.PIF \BACKUP

copies all the files in the MASM subdirectory with a PIF extension to the subdirectory BACKUP.

So far, XCOPY is not too different from COPY. However, the /s switch causes XCOPY to copy (and create, if necessary) the source directory and all its nested subdirectories. So,

    [C:\]XCOPY A: B: /S

copies all files and subdirectories from the diskette in drive A to the diskette in drive B. As before, XCOPY prompts you if it needs to create subdirectories in the target drive.

XCOPY allows you to further qualify what files are to be copied through a number of additional switches:

/e   When used with the /s switch, this creates directories in the target disk, even though they contain no files in the source.

/p   Prompts you before each file is copied.

/a   Copies only those files that have the archive attribute bit set, but does not reset the archive attribute.

/m Copies only those files that have the archive attribute set, and resets the archive attribute.

/d   Copies files that were modified after a particular date.

So, the command

[C:\]XCOPY A: B: /S /M /D:10-10-87

copies all files (in all subdirectories) on the diskette in drive A that were last updated after 10/10/87 and have the archive attribute set. The archive bit is reset after the files are copied.

SUMMARY

You have now seen all the functions provided by the OS/2 commands and utilities. You undoubtedly will become familiar with these functions as you begin working with OS/2. In most cases, the commands and utilities are based on PC DOS, so they should seem familiar to you. Nonetheless, you may wish to refer to this chapter if you have questions about their capabilities.

PART

3

USING OS/2

CHAPTER 13

FILE I/O SERVICES

This chapter begins with a discussion of the OS/2 functions you use to access the system file I/O services. *File I/O* is a term that collectively refers to the I/O you perform with the file-system interfaces (DosRead and DosWrite) regardless of whether the I/O is destined for a file, a device (such as a printer), or a pipe.

Most OS/2 file I/O functions have identical counterparts in PC DOS. In fact, nearly all of these APIs are part of the proper subset of system services that comprise the family API. If you write a program that exclusively uses only these APIs, you will be able to bind the program to run under PC DOS.

DEVICE I/O

OS/2 file I/O calls are used to read or write character streams to devices. When you call the OS/2 DosWrite function, you are sending a character stream to a device driver that will, in turn, send the data to an output device. Similarly, when you call the DosRead function, you are requesting a character stream from a device.

When you use either call, you must supply a handle to identify the device you are writing to or reading from. You get these handles when you request access to the devices by using the DosOpen call. In most cases, you cannot use the file I/O APIs until the system has authorized your access and given you a valid handle.

However, a notable exception to this rule is standard I/O. When OS/2 starts your program, it provides the program with access to several special devices, STDIN, STDOUT, and STDERR. These devices are associated with the handles 0-2, respectively. You do not have to use DosOpen to gain access to these devices because handles 0, 1, and 2 are always valid.

Using Standard I/O

Standard I/O is the simplest form of system I/O. A standard I/O program does not care about the source or destination of the data. Thus, a standard I/O program has the structure shown in Figure 13-1. It reads data from a "standard" source, manipulates it in some way, writes it out to a "standard" target, treating the data like a continuous character stream. This I/O model is intentionally simple so that the data streams can be retrieved from or passed to many different types of devices.

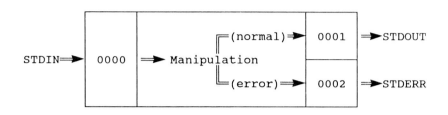

Figure 13-1. Structure of standard I/O program

Suppose you want to write a program that takes an arbitary data stream and converts all lowercase characters to uppercase. This easily fits the standard I/O model, and could be implemented as a standard I0/O program with the structure shown in Figure 13-2.

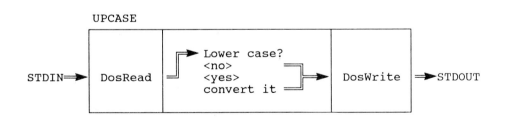

Figure 13-2. Sample I/O program model

You read from standard input in OS/2 by calling Dos-Read with handle 0. So, to read a character, you code the following sequence:

```
mov     ax,0              ;STDIO handle
push    ax                ;push it on stack      (1)
mov     ax,SEG in_buffer  ;get buffer selector
push    ax                ;push it on stack      (2a)
lea     ax,in_buffer      ;get buffer displacement
push    ax                ;push it on stack      (2b)
mov     ax,1              ;get buffer length
push    ax                ;push it on stack      (3)
mov     ax,SEG bytesxfer  ;get data area selector
push    ax                ;push it on stack      (4a)
lea     ax,bytesxfer      ;get data area displacement
push    ax                ;push it on stack      (4b)
call    DosRead           ;call system function
```

DosRead expects four parameters, so you must push them on the stack before you call the routine. Two of the parameters are passed as values—the handle (1) and the output buffer length (3). The other two are passed as addresses. In OS/2, addresses are passed as far pointers, so you must push two words for each address—the selector (2a, 4a) and the displacement (2b, 4b).

Parameters are passed as addresses because they are either potentially large (such as a buffer) or they are updated by OS/2 (such as bytes transferred). The parameters for DosRead are as follows:

WORD	An open device/file handle
PTR	Address of a user input buffer
WORD	Length of user buffer
PTR	Address of a word field that OS/2 updates with the number of bytes it transferred

The parameters for DosWrite are as follows:

WORD	An open device/file handle
PTR	Address of a user output buffer
WORD	Length of the user buffer
PTR	Address of a word field that OS/2 updates with the number of bytes it transferred

Each OS/2 API has a different predefined set of parameters you must pass in a specific way. You must always pass exactly the right number of parameters, in exactly the right order, in exactly the right form. If you make a mistake, OS/2 terminates your program.

If you had to remember the sequence and type of each parameter for all the OS/2 function calls, you would have difficulty writing programs. To make this task easier, you can use macros to generate the API linkages. For example, the following macro,

```
@DosRead     MACRO     HAND,BUFFER,BLEN,XFER
             .ERRB     <HAND>
             .ERRB     <BUFFER>
             .ERRB     <BLEN>
             .ERRB     <XFER>
             mov       ax,HAND
             push      ax
             mov       ax,SEG BUFFER
             push      ax
             lea       ax,BUFFER
             push      ax
             mov       ax,BLEN
             push      ax
             mov       ax,SEG XFER
             push      ax
             lea       ax,XFER
             push      ax
             call      DosRead
             ENDM
```

allows you to code

```
@DosRead  0,in_buffer,1,bytesxfer
```

to generate the same code you saw previously. Macros have several important advantages, including the following.

- They generate an error if you omit a parameter. The ".ERRB <HAND>" statement in the @DosRead macro instructs the assembler to generate an error if you forget to code the handle parameter.

- Macros always generate the right form for each parameter. In the @DosRead macro, the first and third parameters are passed as values on the stack, while the second and fourth are passed as addresses.

- The parameters are always pushed in the right sequence.

If you intend to write family API programs, make sure your macros do not generate instructions that only work on an 80286 CPU. In the DosRead macro it would be tempting to code

```
push    HAND
```

to push the value HAND on the stack. However, the PUSH IMMEDIATE instruction is only valid on the 80286 and 80386 CPUs, and fails on the 8086 and 8088. So instead you would use the instructions

```
mov     ax,HAND
push    ax
```

which are valid on any 808x or 80x86 CPU.

From this point forward, the programming examples use macros to illustrate the system calls. All the OS/2 system call macros are included in the file named OS2MAC, INC, listed in Appendix E. You can use this library to enter the sample programs listed in this book. Note that if you use this library to make OS/2 function calls, it can help you debug the programs through an option function call trace. If you add the following statement in front of your program,

```
bugflag       equ     1
```

then each system will print an execution trace to the standard error device. The system trace looks something like this:

```
        include os2mac.inc                 ;OS/2 macro library
        dgroup  group   UPC_data           ;defines automatic data segment
        ;
        UPC_stack       segment para stack       ;stack segment
                        dw      256 dup('s')
        UPC_stack       ends
        ;
        UPC_data        segment para public 'auto'
        in_char         db      0                ;input data buffer
        bytesxfer       dw      0                ;bytes transfered
        stdin           dw      0                ;STDIN handle
        stdout          dw      1                ;STDOUT handle
        UPC_data        ends
        ;
        UPC_code        segment para public 'code'
        main            proc
                        pusha                    ;Save registers
        ;
        ; Read character
        ;
        upc010:         @DosRead stdin,in_char,1,bytesxfer ;read byte
                        cmp       bytesxfer,0    ;no more input?
                        je        upc999         ;yes - leave
        ;
        ; Translate to upper case
        ;
                        cmp       in_buffer,'a'  ;less than a ?
                        jb        UPC020         ;yes - go write to STDOUT
                        cmp       in_buffer,'z'  ;greater than z ?
                        ja        UPC020         ;yes - go write to STDOUT
                        sub       in_buffer,'a'-'A' ;make upper case
        ;
        ; Write character
        ;
        upc020:         @DosWrite stdout,in_char,1,bytesxfer
                        jmp       upc010         ;go read next character
        ;
        upc999:         popa                     ;Restore saved registers
                        @DosExit 0,1             ;leave proc
        main            endp
```

Figure 13-3. UPCASE program

```
        Call --> DOSSCANENV
      Return --> DOSSCANENV     AX=   203
        Call --> DOSREAD
      Return --> DOSREAD        AX=    0
        Call --> DOSWRITE
      Return --> DOSWRITE       AX=    0
        Call --> DOSEXIT
```

You can use this trace facility until your program is debugged, then you can delete the statement to generate the "final" program. If you are curious about how this all works, take a look at OS2MAC.INC.

Getting back to the standard I/O example, UPCASE can use DosRead (handle = 0) to read a character from STDIN, convert the byte to uppercase, and finally write it to STDOUT by using DosWrite (handle = 1). The complete program (UPCASE) appears in Figure 13-3.

The @DosRead and @DosWrite macros are used to alternatively read, modify, then write each character in the data stream. The UPCASE program processes each character in this way until it detects that the input is finished when DosRead returns 0 bytes transferred. This signals the end of the data stream, so UPCASE ends by calling the DosExit function. You use DosExit to end OS/2 threads. The parameters for DosExit are as follows:

WORD	A one-word action code that tells OS/2 how much of your program it should terminate:
	0000h = Terminate the current thread (only)
	0001h = Terminate all the threads
WORD	A one-word termination code that OS/2 passes to your parent process (if the parent requests it)

DosRead and DosWrite are *synchronous functions*, meaning that each request completes after the data has been moved to or from the device. In this example, UPCASE regains control when each I/O operation is complete. So if UPCASE issues DosRead and a character is not yet ready (the user has not yet typed it), then DosRead *blocks* on the I/O operation.

If the input device is the keyboard (the normal STDIO device), then "bursts" of data are sent each time you press the ENTER key. In its default mode, the keyboard device sends a data stream on receipt of the 0Dh (CR) character. You can demonstrate this behavior by running UPCASE:

```
[C:\]UPCASE
dddddddddddddddd<CR>        <--- you enter
DDDDDDDDDDDDDDDD            <--- UPCASE output
aaa123ABC()!#<CR>          <--- you enter
AAA123ABC()!#              <--- UPCASE output
^Z<CR>                     <--- you enter
[C:\]
```

Each time you press ENTER (CR), OS/2 sends the data to UPCASE, which then echoes it back to the STDIO device (the console) in uppercase. Note that UPCASE does not actually end until you send an end-of-file (EOF) indicator (1AH). The OS/2 EOF is generated when you press CTRL-Z.

If the DosRead buffer is not large enough to receive the entire data stream, OS/2 buffers the information and passes along as much data as will fit. In this example, UPCASE has a 1-byte buffer, so it must issue 15 DosRead/DosWrite pairs to process the first line of data (ddddddddddddddd).

Since UPCASE reads from STDIN and writes to STDOUT, it can be used as an OS/2 filter. If you enter the command

[C:\]type upcase.asm ¦ upcase

the TYPE command reads the file named UPCASE.ASM and writes it to its STDOUT device, which happens to be the UPCASE standard input. UPCASE converts the data stream to uppercase and writes it to its STDOUT device (the screen). The file named UPCASE.ASM is converted to uppercase and listed on the screen.

It could just as easily be sent to a file as follows:

[C:\]type upcase.asm ¦ upcase > dir.dta
[C:\]

If you ran these examples, you probably noticed how slowly output was generated. The reason it is so slow is not because of the TYPE command, which is normally fast. The cause is probably not the pipe operation either, because other OS/2 pipes do not operate so slowly. So something must be wrong with UPCASE.

The previous display had more than 2800 characters. For each character, UPCASE issued two file I/O calls and the system switched context three times (kernel-UPCASE-kernel). With that much overhead, it is a wonder the output was a fast as it was.

```
;
; Read character
;
upc010:         @DosRead stdin,in_buffer,in_leng,bytesxfer
                cmp         bytesxfer,0           ;done?
                je          upc999                ;yes - leave
                mov         cx,bytesxfer          ;set loop count
;
; Translate to upper case
;
                mov         di,offset(in_buffer)  ;set pointer to buffer
upc020:         cmp         byte ptr [di],'a'     ;less than a ?
                jb          upc030                ;yes - skip byte
                cmp         byte ptr [di],'z'     ;greater than z ?
                ja          upc030                ;yes - skip byte
                sub         byte ptr [di],'a'-'A' ;make upper case
upc030:         inc         di                    ;point to next byte
                loop        upc020                ;continue processing
;
; Write character
;
upc040:         @DosWrite stdout,in_buffer,bytesxfer,bytesxfer
                jmp         upc010                ;go read next character
```

Figure 13-4. UPCASE program with buffering

The solution to this problem is simple. The OS/2 file I/O functions allow you to read and write more than 1 byte at a time, so UPCASE could buffer data. If you use a 4-byte buffer, then two function calls (DosRead and DosWrite) would transfer 4 bytes, a 400% improvement. So you can incorporate this in the UPCASE program (see Figure 13-4).

UPCASE is now able to read and write multiple bytes per function call. The uppercase translation routine was modified to loop through the buffer. Other than that, the changes are minor.

If you now rebuild UPCASE and use a reasonable buffer size (16-128 bytes), its performance is greatly enhanced, so much so that if you run the pipe example, it runs just as quickly without the uppercase conversion.

Before proceeding, consider the structure of this program. Note that it has the basic form shown in Figure 13-5.

The first item included in the program is a *macro library* that contains the system call macros and a number

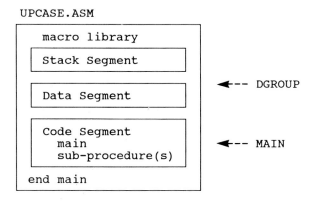

Figure 13-5.   Structure of UPCASE program

of data-structure definitions used in conjunction with the
system calls.

Following the macro library are three segments: Stack,
Data, and Code. Every OS/2 program is required to have a
stack. Note that the OS/2 kernel maintains its own stack,
but the dynamic link subsystems use the application stack.
The application stack requirements will therefore depend
on which OS/2 service it uses. A good starting point for
the stack size is double the internal application stack
requirement. However, this may not be adequate in all
situations, so you may have to experiment with different
values.

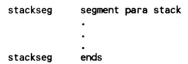

OS/2 programs are reentrant, so they must have a
dynamic data segment. OS/2 allocates a unique copy of this
data segment for each instance of your program. If you
start two copies of UPCASE (in different sessions), each
will share the same code segment but each will have a
unique dynamic data segment. In this way, each instance
can modify the data segment without affecting the other.

You can define more than one logical data segment in your program, but only those in the "dgroup" segment group are dynamic. For example,

```
dgroup      group data2

data1       segment para public 'auto'
              .
              .
              .
data1       ends
data2       segment para public 'auto'
              .
              .
              .
data2       ends
```

defines two data segments: data1 and data2. The segment data2 is dynamic, so OS/2 allocates a new copy for each instance of the program.

Finally, a program can have one or more *code segments*. The following defines a code segment named codeseg1:

```
codeseg1    segment para public 'code'
              .
              .
              .
codeseg1    ends
```

You can transfer control between code segments with a far call. The starting point in your program is defined by the MASM end statement. For example,

```
codeseg1    segment para public 'code'
main        proc
              .
              .
              .
main        endp
sub1        proc
              .
              .
              .
sub1        endp
codeseg1    ends
            end     main
```

creates a code segment (codeseg1) with two procedures (main and sub1). When OS/2 starts the program, it gives control to main. You may specify only one entry point per program.

DosOpen	
PTR	The address of an ASCIIZ name string
PTR	Address of a word field in which OS/2 will place the device/file handle
PTR	Address of a one word field in which OS/2 returns an action code: 0001H = Device/file existed 0002H = File was created 0003H = File was replaced
DWRD	Address of a word field which OS/2 uses to establish the initial file size (only valid when file is OPENED or CREATED)
WORD	A one word file attribute
WORD	An open flag, used by OS/2 to process your request: If file does not exist, 0000 xxxx Fail 0001 xxxx Create it If the file exists, xxxx 0000 Fail xxxx 0001 Open it xxxx 0010 Create it
WORD	The open mode, used by OS/2 to process your request: DWFRRRRRISSSRAAA Access Mode Reserved Sharing Mode Inheritance characteristics Reserved Fail Errors Unbuffered I/O flag DASD open

Figure 13-6.   The DosOpen Function

If you program in a high-level language (such as C, BASIC, COBOL, and so on) then the compiler takes care of these details for you.

Device OPEN

Although standard I/O is a powerful function, it has its limitations. You may use it to read or write to only those devices predefined by your parent process. In many situations you will want to write or read data from a specific device of your own choosing (such as a printer or communications port).

To do this you must first request (and receive) access to the device with a DosOpen call. DosOpen accepts a device name and returns a handle that you can then use with DosRead and DosWrite to perform I/O. Figure 13-6 shows the parameters of DosOpen.

To demonstrate how this works, consider a program (SPLIT) that receives its input from the STDIO device and writes it to the standard output and a second arbitrary device. SPLIT receives the name of the output device as a command line parameter. SPLIT works as shown in Figure 13-7.

Reading the standard input and writing the standard output is easy enough, but how does SPLIT determine the name of the output device? To answer this question, con-

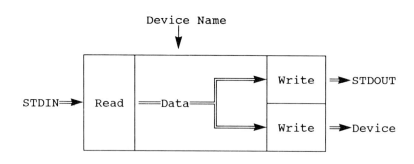

Figure 13-7. Operation of SPLIT

Table 13-1.   OS/2 Program Startup Conventions

Convention	Description
CS:IP	Program entry point
SS:SP	Top of program application stack
DX	Stack size
DS	Automatic data segment
CX	Length of data segment in DS
AX	Environment segment
BX	Command-line offset in environment

sider the OS/2 program startup information shown in Table 13-1.

Some of the values are intuitively obvious. For example, the DS segment contains the LDT selector associated with the program's automatic data segment; CS:IP points to the routine identified in the END statement; and SS:SP points to the top of the application stack. The size of the stack and the data segment are passed in DX and CX, respectively. Finally, AX contains a selector that maps the program's environment segment, and BX contains the offset within that segment where the command-line parameters are located. The environment segment layout is shown in Figure 13-8. Program—name is the fully qualified name of your program.

Figure 13-8.   Information contained in AX and BX segments

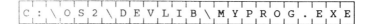

Figure 13-9.   Contents of program_name field

This means that even if OS/2 finds the program through the PATH, program_name still includes the exact location of the program. For example, if you enter

    [C:\]PATH OS2\DEVLIB
    [C:\]MYPROG

the program_name field in the environment contains the information shown in Figure 13-9 followed by a null termination character.

OS/2 enables you to create environment variables with the SET command. Any such data is contained in the null terminated environment_variables field. You may either parse this data yourself or use the DosScanEnv API to retrieve the data associated with a named variable. The parameters of DosScanEnv function are as follows:

PTR	Pointer to an ASCIIZ environment variable name that is to be located in the environment
PTR	Pointer to a double-word address field in which OS/2 returns a pointer to the data area of the requested environment variable

Finally, the environment also contains the data the user entered on the command line following the program name.

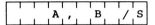

Figure 13-10.   Contents of Command__Line Field

For example, if you enter

    [C:\]MYPROG   A, B /S

then MYPROG will find the data shown in Figure 13-10 in the command__line field of the environment segment.

Notice that all the characters, including the leading blanks, are contained in this field. As with the other environment segment data areas, command__line is terminated with a null character.

The BX register contains the offset into the environment segment where you can find the start of the command-line parameters. This information is now used in the input parsing routing of the SPLIT program shown in Figure 13-11. This routine starts with the location of the command line (AX:BX), skips leading blanks (using the SCASB instruction), and moves the resulting name string into an internal buffer named DEV__NAME. In the process of moving the characters, SPLIT checks for either a colon (:) or a 0 to mark the end of the device name.

If the user did not enter a device name (first byte of DEV__NAME is 0), then SPLIT moves NULLDEV (NUL) to DEV__NAME using the @movs macro (included in OS2MAC.INC). In this way, SPLIT continues to work even when it does not find a device name. The user does not enter a device name.

```
            mov     es,ax                       ;environment selector
            mov     di,bx                       ;command line offset
            mov     cx,8                        ;maximum name length
            push    cx                          ;save count
    ;
            mov     ax,0                        ;end of command name delimiter
            repne   scasb                       ;search for end of command name
            mov     ax,' '                      ;blank
            repe    scasb                       ;skip leading blanks
            dec     di                          ;back up to first character
    ;
            push    es                          ;switch
            push    ds                          ;        ES
            pop     es                          ;              &
            pop     ds                          ;                DI (for MOVSB)
            mov     si,di                       ;set string source
            mov     di,offset dev_name          ;point to dev_name field (target)
            pop     cx                          ;restore count
    ;
    spl010: cmp     byte ptr [si],':'           ;end of device name?
            je      spl020                      ;yes - exit
            cmp     byte ptr [si],0             ;end of parameters?
            je      spl020                      ;yes - exit
            movsb                               ;copy byte
            loop    spl010                      ;continue copying
    ;
    spl020: push    es                          ;copy TEE DS ...
            pop     ds                          ;             ... to DS reg
            cmp     byte ptr dev_name,0         ;device name entered?
            jne     spl025                      ;yes - go process
            amoves  dev_name,nulldev,4          ;move NUL device name to dev_name
```

Figure 13-11. Parsing the device name in SPLIT program

Now that it has a device name, SPLIT can use DosOpen to gain access to the actual device (see Figure 13-12). As you see, SPLIT uses a number of fields that were defined

```
spl025:     mov      dev_flag,00000001b        ;open if it exists
                          ;eeeennnn
            mov      dev_mode,0000000010010001b ;open mode
                          ;dwfrrrrrisssraaa
      @DosOpen dev_name,dev_hand,dev_act,dev_size,dev_attr,dev_flag,dev_mode,dev_rsv
      @jaxz    spl030                   ;opened OK, continue
      @DosWrite stderr,msg0,msg0l,bytesout  ;Write error message
      jmp      spl999                   ;exit
```

Figure 13-12.   Opening the device

in its data segment to correspond to the DosOpen parameters:

```
;
; Open parameters
;
dev_name    db      64 dup(0)               ;device/file name
dev_hand    dw      0
dev_act     dw      0
dev_size    dd      0
dev_attr    dw      0
dev_flag    dw      0                       ;open flags
dev_mode    dw      0                       ;open mode
dev_rsv     dd      0                       ;reserved
```

The DEV—NAME field contains the device name entered by the user (or NUL if none was found). The DOS OPEN call includes the DEV—HAND, DEV—ACT, and DEV—SIZE parameters so that OS/2 can return information to SPLIT. Note that even if you do not need the information, the call must include the parameters so that the DosOpen stack frame contains the right number of elements.

Note that SPLIT initializes DEV—FLAG and DEV—MODE before it calls OS/2. Since these parameters tell the file system how to process the DosOpen function, they must be set correctly. The DEV—FLAG parameter is a byte that tells OS/2 what to do, based on the existence of the device. It is broken up into two parts. (See Figure 13-6.) The first four bits define what happens if the device named in DEV—NAME does not exist:

1. (0000) Fail the DosOpen call, or

2. (0001) Create a file

You cannot dynamically create devices, so if you use the second option and the named device does not exist, OS/2 creates a file with the same name. The second four bits define what happens when the device exists:

1. (0000) Fail the DosOpen call

2. (0001) Open the device/file, or

3. (0010) Create a new file

Naturally, you may only use the first two options when dealing with a device. If you code option 3 and DEV—NAME is a device name, then DosOpen fails. By setting DEV—FLAG to 01h, SPLIT has instructed OS/2 to open the device only if it exists.

The DEV—MODE parameter defines how your program intends to use the device. Table 13-2 lists its possible values. In this example, SPLIT has set the following:

- Inheritance off (I=1), meaning that the handle cannot be passed to a child process (it is private to SPLIT).

- Sharing mode to "deny all" (S=001); no other process in the system can access the device until SPLIT closes the handle.

Table 13-2. *Open Modes*

```
DWFRRRRISSSRAA
```

D	DASD open bit 0 = Normal Open 1 = Open disk drive for direct access
W	File Write-through 0 = File I/O can be buffered 1 = Do not complete request until data is written
F	Fail errors 0 = Use the system hard error handler 1 = Report errors directly with error codes
I	Inheritance indicator 0 = Handle can be inherited by child process(es) 1 = Handle is private to this process
S	Sharing mode 001 = Deny all (read/write) requests 010 = Deny write access requests 011 = Deny read access requests 100 = Deny none
A	Access mode 000 = READ_ONLY access 001 = WRITE_ONLY access 010 = READ_WRITE access

- Access mode to WRITE—ONLY (A=001), meaning that it can issue DosWrite(s) using the handle, but fails if it calls DosRead.

If the DosOpen succeeds, SPLIT is guaranteed exclusive write-access to the device name entered by the user. It will have this access until it either closes the device (with DosClose) or terminates. The DosClose parameter list is as follows:

WORD	File/device handle to be closed

All OS/2 API calls return their error codes in the AX register. If AX is 0, then the DosOpen has succeeded. The @jaxz macro simply branches to the label (spl030) if AX is 0. If AX is not 0, something has gone wrong, so SPLIT writes "Invalid device" to the STDERR handle and terminates.

Device I/O

Now that you have successfully opened a device, consider how you write data to it. Writing data to a device is equivalent to the standard I/O already discussed, except that you use the handle returned by DosOpen instead of the fixed STDIO handles. So the remainder of SPLIT is trivial (see Figure 13-13).

Note that SPLIT uses the number of bytes read (returned by DosRead in BYTESIN) as the number of bytes to be written by DosWrite. As before, 0 input bytes signifies the end of the data stream, causing SPLIT to close the device and terminate. Since the OS/2 process-termination code automatically closes any devices or files a process may have opened, SPLIT could end without explicitly closing the output device. However, you should get into the

```
spl030:     @DosRead   stdin,in_buffer,in_leng,bytesin ;read string
            cmp        bytesin,0            ;done?
            jne        spl040               ;no - continue
            jmp        spl999               ;yes - leave
;
spl040:     @DosWrite  dev_hand,in_buffer,bytesin,bytesout ;to device
            @DosWrite  stdout,in_buffer,bytesin,bytesout   ;to stdout
            jmp        spl030               ;go read next character(s)
;
spl999:     @DosClose  dev_hand             ;Close the device
            popa                            ;Restore saved registers
            @DosExit 0,1                     ;leave proc
```

Figure 13-13. SPLIT main routine

habit of closing the devices you open. In some cases, other processes may be waiting to use these devices, so you should release them as soon as possible.

IOCTL Interfaces

You can communicate directly with an OS/2 device driver by using the DosDevIOCtl function. This API bypasses the data-stream oriented (DosRead or DosWrite) I/O functions to deliver control information to a device driver. Use DosDevIOCTL if you must give a device driver data that you do not want passed to the device it supports. Most OS/2 device drivers have numerous device-specific functions they support with IOCTL *packets*. The parameters for DosDevIOCtl are as follows:

PTR	Pointer to IOCTL data area
PTR	Pointer to IOCTL parameter area
WORD	Device subfunction code
WORD	Device category
WORD	Open device handle

Suppose you are writing an application that uses the serial device COM1: to send data to a printer. Furthermore, your printer only operates at a transmission speed of 9600 baud. You have already seen how to open a device and send it data. This example could certainly use the same technique. However, how do you make sure that the device is set to transmit at the correct speed? You cannot send this control information to the COM1: device driver with the DosWrite function, because the device driver assumes all the Write data is intended for the printer. You certainly do not want to print the control requests. This is precisely where you would use the DosDevIOCtl API.

Consider an example. Changing the line speed of a communications port turns out to be trivial. One of the IOCTL packets (subfunction 041H) sets the line speed of a port—precisely what you need.

```
main          proc
;
; Open COM1:  & set line speed
;
              pusha                              ;save registers
;
              mov      s96_flag,00000001b        ;open if it exists
              mov      s96_mode,0000000010010010b ;open mode
              @dosopen s96_name,s96_hand,s96_act,s96_size,s96_attr,s96_flag,s96_mode,s96_rsv
              @jaxnz   s96999
;
              mov      s96_speed,9600
              @DosDevIOCTL NULL,s96_speed,041h,01h,s96_hand ;set line speed
;
              @DosClose s96_hand                 ;close device handle
s96999:       popa                               ;restore registers
              @DosExit 0,1                        ;end program
main          endp
```

Figure 13-14.   Program to reset COM1:

However, before you can send an IOCTL packet to a device, you must first get access to it. As before, you do this with the DosOpen function. Consider the program (SET 9600) shown in Figure 13-14. As with the previous example, SET 9600 begins by opening the device with exclusive access in WRITE—ONLY mode. The device name COM1 is pre-initialized in the data segment in the S96—SPEED field. If the open fails, SET9600 skips to the end and does not issue the DosDevIOCtl.

Note that this particular IOCTL request (category 1, subfunction 41) requires a null data pointer (first parameter). The @DosDevIOCtl macro pushes a double-word of 0's on the stack when it encounters the string 'NULL' as the data pointer parameter. The line speed is passed as a single-word parameter (S96—SPEED).

You can use DosDevIOCtl to send IOCTL packets to most OS/2 device drivers. However, before doing this, you should study the IOCTL parameters carefully because they differ greatly from device to device.

FILE SYSTEM I/O

The OS/2 file system gives you access to disk files through the same basic set of API functions. So far, you have seen how to use the file I/O API to write and read data from devices. Now you will see how to use the same functions to perform file I/O.

Creating and Deleting Files

The biggest difference between files and devices is that a disk is basically a random-access device, while character devices are serial-access devices. Standard I/O programs are written to the lowest common denominator (that is, they treat random-access files as a large serial character stream).

Clearly this is not desirable in all cases. For instance, it would be very strange if, to update a small portion of a file, your editor rewrote the entire file every time; or, worse yet, if your data base program rewrote the entire data base each time you changed a data record.

The OS/2 file system enables you to write random portions of a file by repositioning the logical file pointer. You do this with the DosChgFilePtr API. The parameters for DosChgFilePtr are as follows:

WORD	Open file handle
DWRD	A double-word value indicating the distance the file pointer will be moved
WORD	A one-word value indicating the method OS/2 must use to move the file pointer:
	0 = Relative to the start of the file
	1 = Relative to current location in the file
	0 = Relative to the end of the file
PTR	The address of a double-word field in which OS/2 will place the new file pointer value.

To illustrate the use of the file system functions, consider a program (FILEIO) that writes multiple, fixed-

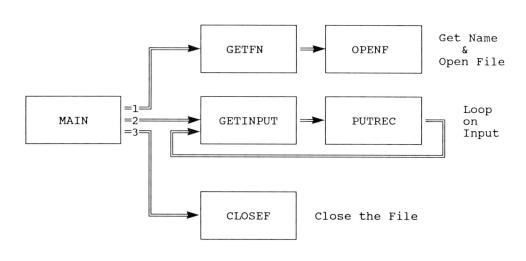

Figure 13-15.   Logical structure of FILEIO

length data records. FILEIO is logically structured as shown in Figure 13-15.

The main routine calls a series of subroutines to get the data file name, open the file for input, prompt the user for data records, write the data records to the file, and close the file. All I/O is done with the OS/2 file I/O services. For example, the main routine (shown in Figure 13-16) writes the initial message and calls the GETFN subroutine to get the input file name from the user. It then calls OPENF to open the data file. If successful (AX=0), MAIN enters a loop, alternatively calling GETINPUT then PUTREC to create the file. The end of data is signaled when the user enters a null data record.

This causes MAIN to call CLOSEF to close the file and exit. With the exception of the @DosWrite and @DosExit macros, this could be mistaken for a PC DOS program. The low-level file I/O is done in the individual subroutines.

```
main        proc
            pusha                               ;Save registers
            push    ds                          ;put data segment selector
            pop     es                          ;in ES
;
            @DosWrite stdout,msg0,MSG0L,bytesout ;program banner
;
            call    getfn                       ;get filename
            call    openf                       ;open the file
            @jaxnz  fio999                      ;open error, exit
;
fio010:     call    getinput                    ;get record from user
            @jaxnz  fio030                      ;done, go exit
            call    putrec                      ;put data record in file
            jmp     fio010                      ;go get next record
;
fio030:     call    closef                      ;close the file
;
fio999:     popa                                ;Restore saved registers
            @DosExit 0,1                         ;leave proc
main        endp
```

Figure 13-16. Main routine in FILEIO

GETFN (shown in Figure 13-17) is very similar to what was presented previously in this chapter. It writes to STDOUT to prompt the user for a file name, then reads from STDIN, waiting for the data. Notice that the input

```
getfn       proc
            @DosWrite stdout,msg1,msg1l,bytesout ;Prompt for file name
            @DosRead  stdin,dev_name,63,bytesin  ;Read device name
            mov     si,offset dev_name          ;get address of input buffer
            add     si,bytesin                  ;point to last byte
            sub     si,2                        ;back up before CR & LF
            mov     byte ptr [si],0             ;zero terminate the string
            ret
getfn       endp
```

Figure 13-17. GETFN subroutine

```
openf      proc
           mov        dev_flag,00000010b              ;open flags
                              ;nnnneeee
           mov        dev_mode,0000000010010010b      ;open mode
                              ;dwfrrrrrisssraaa
           @DosOpen   dev_name,dev_hand,dev_act,dev_size,dev_attr,dev_flag,dev_mode,dev_rsv
           @jaxz      ope010                ;opened OK - continue
;
           @DosWrite  stderr,msg3,msg3l,bytesout  ;Write error message
           mov        ax,0ffh               ;set error code
           jmp        ope999
;
ope010:    @DosWrite  stdout,msg2,msg2l,bytesout  ;Write file OPEN message
           xor        ax,ax                 ;clear error code
ope999:    ret
```

Figure 13-18.   OPENF subroutine

buffer (DEV—NAME) is the file name buffer that will later be used to open the file. For this reason, GETFN backs up 2 characters to eliminate the carriage return (CR) and line feed (LF) that OS/2 inserts after the user input and adds a null byte to delimit the name for DosOpen.

On return from GETFN, MAIN calls OPENF (see Figure 13-18) to open the data file. OPENF should also look familiar. It opens the file and either writes an error message (if AX<>0) or an informational message (if the DosOpen succeeded). The major difference between this routine and the others you have already seen is the mode and flag values OPENF uses with DosOpen. The open flag indicates that OS/2 should create the file if it does not already exist, and create it again (rewrite it) if it does. This has the effect of always creating a new file, since the old one would be overwritten if it existed. By using this combination of open options, you can ensure that FILEIO fails if the user enters a device instead of a file name. The replace option is invalid for devices.

The open mode used by FILEIO gives it exclusive

```
getinput    proc
            mov       di,offset msg4rec      ;data area
            mov       cx,5                   ;data area length
            mov       ax,recno               ;record number
            call      bta                    ;convert to ASCII
            @DosWrite stdout,msg4,msg4l,bytesout  ;Write prompt
;
            @DosRead  stdin,in_buffer,in_leng,bytesin ;Read data
            mov       bx,bytesin             ;get byte count
            add       bx,offset in_buffer - 2 ;address last two bytes
            mov       word ptr [bx],' '      ;strip CR & LF
;
            xor       ax,ax                  ;set return code
            cmp       bytesin,2              ;done?
            jne       gti999                 ;no - continue
            mov       ax,0ffh                ;set return code
gti999:     ret
```

Figure 13-19. GETINPUT subroutine

READ—WRITE access to the file, meaning that no other process in the system may open the file while FILEIO has it open.

The GETINPUT subroutine shown in Figure 13-19 first prompts the user for a new data record and then reads the STDIN device.

Like GETFN, GETINPUT must also strip the carriage return and line feed from the user input. The resulting data record is in the field named IN—BUFFER. In this program, the input buffer (and the data records written to the file) are 62 bytes long. GETINPUT does one other thing: It tests the input byte count (bytesin) to see if the user has entered a null record. Since DosRead will always return a CR/LF combination, a null record is 2 bytes long. So, if GETINPUT detects that only 2 bytes were entered, it sets an error code in AX, telling the main routine that the user input is complete.

Note that this routine also displays the record number in the prompt. In order to display the counter, GETINPUT must first convert the binary number to ASCII. A special routine called Binary-to-ASCII (BTA) does this

work for GETINPUT. This service is included in the
OS2PROC library listed in Appendix E.

The final two procedures are trivial, containing little
more than a single OS/2 function call in each. PUTREC
simply writes the user record in IN—BUFFER to the
data file and increments the record count for the GETIN-
PUT prompt:

```
putrec        proc
              @DosWrite dev_hand,in_buffer,in_leng,bytesout ;write data record
              inc       recno                 ;bump record number
              ret
putrec        endp
```

The CLOSEF procedure is called just before FILEIO
terminates. It closes the data file, thus making it available
to other OS/2 processes:

```
closef        proc
              @DosClose dev_hand                 ;close data file
              ret
closef        endp
```

If you run FILEIO, you will see the information shown
in Figure 13-20.

```
[C:\]fileio
OS/2 File I/O program

Enter File Name: names.dta

File is now OPEN, enter data or null record to End
Record  1 ==> Joe C. Legs, Coral Springs NY, 755-1212
Record  2 ==> B. G. Martineau, Washington DC
Record  3 ==> Coral Springs Cubs, 753-1234
Record  4 ==> Robert Johnson, Kansas City MO
Record  5 ==>

[C:\]
```

Figure 13-20. FILEIO output

As you enter data records, FILEIO writes the data and prompts you for the next.

What happens if another program tries to use the same file while you are entering data? If you switch to a different session, you can run a second copy of FILEIO. When you do, you will see the following:

```
[C:\]fileio
OS/2 File I/O program

Enter File Name: names.dta
File Open Error

[C:\]
```

If you switch to the first session and end the first FILEIO, then the second will be able to open the file. If you rerun FILEIO with the same file name, the original copy of names.dta will be replaced by the new version.

Reading and Writing File Data

To this point you have seen a program that creates a data file. But what if you want to update the data in an existing file? You can use the DosChgFilePtr API in conjunction with DosRead and DosWrite functions to read random portions of an existing file.

The FILEIO program created a data file that contains 62-byte records. A different program (UPDATE) updates the individual records.

UPDATE has the structure shown in Figure 13-21. UPDATE is structurally similar to FILEIO. It has a main routine that calls subroutines to read records from a file, prompts the user for updates, and then writes the updated record back to the file. In this program, GETFN and CLOSEF are virtually identical to their counterparts in FILEIO. However, the other subroutines are different. The main procedure looks like Figure 13-22.

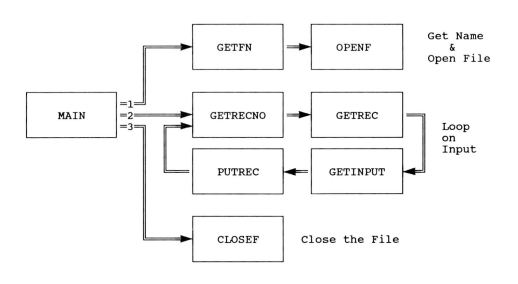

Figure 13-21. Structure of UPDATE

```
                call    getfn           ;get filename
                call    openf           ;open the file
                @jaxnz  upd999          ;open error
;
upd010:         call    getrecno        ;get record # from user
                cmp     recno,0         ;done?
                je      upd030          ;yes
                call    getrec          ;get record from file
                @jaxnz  upd010          ;error - go re-prompt
                call    getinput        ;get record data from user
                @jaxnz  upd010          ;no update - go re-prompt
                call    putrec          ;put data record in file
                jmp     upd010          ;go get next record
;
upd030:         call    closef          ;close the file
```

Figure 13-22. Main procedure of UPDATE

The OPENF routine uses a slightly different variation of the open flag:

```
mov     dev_flag,00000001b              ;open flags
                ;eeeennnn
mov     dev_mode,0000000011000010b      ;open mode
                ;dwfrrrrrisssraaa
@DosOpen dev_name,dev_hand,dev_act,dev_size,dev_attr,dev_flag,dev_mode,dev_rsv
```

This causes OS/2 to fail the DosOpen if the file does not exist, or simply open it (not replace it) if it does.

UPDATE is intended to randomly update records from a FILEIO data file, so the main processing loop starts by calling a subroutine named GETRECNO to prompt the user for a record number. As you can see in Figure 13-23, GETRECNO writes a prompt to STDOUT and reads the response from STDIN. After adjusting the input length to compensate for the CR/LF, it uses the macro @ATB to convert the input ASCII string to a record number.

The macro @ATB is another common function included in the OS/2 macro library. It converts an ASCII string to a

```
getrecno    proc
gtn010:     @DosWrite stdout,msg6,msg61,bytesout   ;Write prompt
            @DosRead  stdin,in_buffer,in_leng,bytesin ;Read data
            sub       bytesin,2                   ;less CR & LF
            @atb      in_buffer,bytesin           ;convert to binary
            @jaxz     gtn999                       ;valid number - go exit
            @DosWrite stderr,msg7,msg71,bytesout  ;Write error message
            jmp       gtn010                       ;go prompt again
gtn999:     mov       recno,bx                     ;record number
            ret
getrecno    endp
```

Figure 13-23. GETRECNO subroutine

binary value and returns it in the BX register. If the user enters an invalid number (that is, non-numeric), ATB fails (causing GETRECNO to write an error message to STDERR and reprompt).

Once it has a valid number, the main procedure calls the GETREC subroutine to read the data into memory. GETREC performs several functions, as shown in Figure 13-24. It starts by determining the size of the data file. Your first instinct might be to ask why this is necessary. Was the file size not returned in the DEV—SIZE field after the open? Unfortunately, the answer to this question is "not in this case." The DosOpen file size parameter tells OS/2 how big to make the file when you create or replace it, but it does not return the size of an existing file.

GETREC uses a slightly obscure technique to determine the size of the file—it changes the file pointer to a location 0 bytes past the end of the file (using DosChgFilePtr move option 2). DosChgFilePtr returns the new file pointer, which is actually the file length.

Next, GETREC computes the offset of the input record number by multiplying the number by the record length. If the resulting offset is past the end of the file, GETREC writes an error message to the STDERR device, sets an error code, and returns to the main procedure to retrieve a new record number. If the offset is valid, GETREC changes the file pointer by using DosChgFilePtr move option 0 (offset relative to start of file) and calls DosRead to read the record into IN—BUFFER.

Up to this point, UPDATE has opened the user's file and read in the requested record. Now the GETINPUT routine gets involved, as shown in Figure 13-25. GETINPUT displays the data record (in IN—BUFFER), writes a user prompt, and then reads the new data record from the STDIN device. When the user enters a carriage return (CR), OS/2 transfers the data to the GETREC input buffer (IN—BUFFER), overlaying the previous record. GETREC then clears out the remainder of the buffer to eliminate any remnants of the previous record. If the user

```
getrec          proc
;
; Determine file size
;
                mov         word ptr dev_ofs,0   ;no bytes past end-of-file
                @DosChgFilePtr dev_hand,dev_ofs,2,new_ofs ;move file ptr to eof
;
; Compute file offset
;
                mov         bx,recno             ;get record number
                dec         bx                   ;adjust (record zero base)
                mov         ax,in_leng           ;get buffer length
                mul         bx                   ;compute file offset
                cmp         ax,word ptr new_ofs  ;past end-of-file?
                jl          gtr010               ;no - go set file pointer
                @DosWrite stderr,msg4,msg4l,bytesout ;write error message
                mov         al,0ffh              ;set error code
                jmp         gtr999               ;exit with error
;
; Move file pointer
;
gtr010:         mov         word ptr dev_ofs,ax  ;set offset (low order word)
                @DosChgFilePtr dev_hand,dev_ofs,0,new_ofs ;move file pointer
                jmp         gtr999               ;exit with error
;
; Read record
;
gtr020:         @DosRead dev_hand,in_buffer,in_leng,bytesin ;read data record
;
gtr999:         ret
```

Figure 13-24. GETREC subroutine

did not enter data (only a CR or LF was in the input buffer), then GETREC sets an error code, indicating that the data should not be rewritten.

```
getinput        proc
;
; put out prompt
;
                @DosWrite stdout,msg8,msg8l,bytesout          ;Write prompt (1)
                @DosWrite stdout,in_buffer,bytesin,bytesout ;Write record
                @DosWrite stdout,nl,2,bytesout                ;New Line
                @DosWrite stdout,msg9,msg9l,bytesout          ;Write prompt (2)
;
; get user input
;
                @DosRead   stdin,in_buffer,in_leng,bytesin ;Read data
;
; blank out remainder of data buffer
;
                mov     cx,in_leng            ;get buffer size
                sub     cx,bytesin            ;less what was entered
                add     cx,2                  ;compensate for CR & LF
                mov     di,bytesin            ;get byte count
                add     di,offset in_buffer-2 ;address end of data (skip CR & LF)
                mov     al,' '                ;fill character
                rep     stosb                 ;blank remainder of buffer
;
                xor     ax,ax                 ;set return code
                cmp     bytesin,2             ;done? (only CR & LF)
                jne     gti999                ;no - continue
                mov     ax,0ffh               ;set return code
gti999:         ret
getinput        endp
```

Figure 13-25. GETINPUT subroutine

The final subroutine, PUTREC, is similar to the one found in FILEIO. It does, however, have one major change:

```
putrec      proc
            @DosChgFilePtr dev_hand,dev_ofs,0,new_ofs ;reset file pointer
            @DosWrite dev_hand,in_buffer,in_leng,bytesout ;write data record
            ret
putrec      endp
```

PUTREC must reset the file pointer to the correct location before it writes the data record. This is because the previous DosRead moved the file pointer past the record that was being updated. This DosChgFilePtr call simply moves it back, so the DosWrite will update the correct portion of the file.

If you build this program and run it from the console, you will see something similar to the information shown in Figure 13-26.

Because of the file-size range checking in GETREC, UPDATE only allows you to update records that already existed in the input file. When you enter a record number that was not created by FILEIO (6), UPDATE gives you an error message and allows you to continue.

```
[C:\]update
OS/2 File update program

Enter File Name: names.dta

File is now Open, enter record # or NULL to end

Record Number: 2
            ==> B. G. Martineau, Washington DC
    Update ==> C. B. O'Brien, Seattle WA

Record Number: 6
Can't go past end of file

Record Number: 3
            ==> Coral Springs Cubs, 753-1234
    Update ==> Jack 723-3434

Record Number:

[C:\]
```

Figure 13-26.   UPDATE output

Locking Byte Ranges

UPDATE opens the data file with exclusive access rights. This means that no other process can use the file until UPDATE closes it. This type of behavior forces you to serialize all file operations to the data file. For instance, you could not update the data from one program while viewing it from a second. In certain applications, this would be a severe limitation.

OS/2 provides facilities to write programs that share files cooperatively. The DosFileLocks function allows you to "lock" ranges of a file. While locked, OS/2 prevents other programs from reading or updating the range. However, the remainder of the file can be read (or updated) by other programs. Thus, a program can open the file in a less-restrictive mode. The parameters of DosFileLocks are as follows:

WORD	An open file handle
PTR	A pointer to a pair of double-word values. The first double-word contains the starting offset in the file where the data is to be unlocked. The second double-word is the length of the unlocked area.
	A null pointer signifies that no data is to be unlocked.
PTR	A pointer to a pair of double-word values. The first double-word contains the starting offset in the file where the data is to be locked. The second double-word is the length of the locked area.
	A null pointer signifies that no data is to be locked.

Adapting range-locking to the UPDATE program is a simple task since it already deals with records that are a form of byte ranges. First, you must change the DosOpen mode used by OPENF. Thus,

```
mov     dev_mode,0000000011000010b     ;open mode
                ;dwfrrrrrisssraaa
@DosOpen dev_name,dev_hand,dev_act,dev_size,dev_attr,dev_flag,dev_mode,dev_rsv
```

causes OS/2 to open the file in READ_WRITE mode with nonexclusive access (S=100). While open in this mode, the

```
;
; Lock record
;
gtr020:      push        word ptr dev_ofs         ;put record start offset
             pop         word ptr dev_lock_ptr    ;in record lock field
             push        in_leng                  ;put record length
             pop         word ptr dev_lock_len    ;in length field
             @DosFileLocks dev_hand,NULL,dev_lock_ptr ;request lock
             @jaxz       gtr030                   ;worked - continue
             @DosWrite stdout,msg10,msg101,bytesout ;Write error message
             jmp         gtr800                   ;exit with error
```

Figure 13-27. GETREC record locking logic

file may be used by any other program in the system.

But how does UPDATE protect the integrity of the data? If it reads a data record and another program updates it before UPDATE rewrites it, then the other program's changes will be lost when UPDATE writes its version. This is where the OS/2 DosFileLocks function can be put to good use. You can change UPDATE to lock a data record before it reads it, and unlock a data record after it rewrites it. This ensures that only one program modifies the data at a time. So, you augment GETREC with the statements shown in Figure 13-27 (after moving the file pointer, but *before* reading the record) and likewise PUTREC (*after* successfully writing the record) as shown in Figure 13-28.

```
;
; Unlock record
;
             push        word ptr dev_ofs         ;put record start offset
             pop         word ptr dev_unlock_ptr  ;in record lock field
             push        in_leng                  ;put record length
             pop         word ptr dev_unlock_len  ;in length field
             @DosFileLocks dev_hand,dev_unlock_ptr,NULL ;unlock record
```

Figure 13-28. PUTREC record unlocking logic

The order of the lock and unlock functions is important. You must lock the record before you read it and unlock it after you write it. If you do not follow this order, another program could "sneak in" and grab the record when you are between calls, thus totally invalidating the lock and unlock functions. If the lock fails, GETREC returns with an error code causing UPDATE to issue an error message.

You can now run two versions of UPDATE in different sessions that update the same data file. If you run UPDATE as shown in Figure 13-29, then switch to a different session to try to update the same record, you will see the information shown in Figure 13-30.

Note that even though you cannot update record number 1, you can access other parts of the file. If you switch back to the first session, enter record number 1, then return to the second session, you will then be able to read number 1.

Range-locking allows you to write OS/2 programs that access data files cooperatively.

```
[C:\]update
OS/2 File update program

Enter File Name: names.dta

File is now Open, enter record # or NULL to end

Record Number: 1
          ==> Joe C. Legs, Coral Springs NY, 755-1212
      Update ==>
```

Figure 13-29. UPDATE output in first session

```
[C:\]update
OS/2 File update program

Enter File Name: names.dta

File is now Open, enter record # or NULL to end

Record Number: 1
Sorry, that record is already in use - try again later

Record Number: 2
          ==> B. G. Martineau, Washington DC  55-1212
    Update ==>
```

Figure 13-30. UPDATE output in second session

Renaming and Moving Files

Not all OS/2 file I/O functions require a file handle. Some calls work on the basis of ASCIIZ file names. For example, the OS/2 DosMove function moves a file from one directory to another on the same disk. The input is two name strings—the source and target names. You also use DosMove to rename a file. The parameters of DosMove are as follows:

PTR	Pointer to an ASCIIZ string that contains the old path/file name
PTR	Pointer to an ASCIIZ string that contains the new path/file name
WORD	Reserved (must be 0)

Consider a simple example. The program MOVE shown in Figure 13-31 prompts you for two file/directory names and issues the DosMove function to move the source file to the target directory.

```
;
; Read source file name
;
        @DosWrite stdout,msg0,MSG0L,bytesout    ;prompt
        @DosRead  stdin,source_file,63,bytesin ;Read device name
        mov       si,offset source_file ;get address of input buffer
        add       si,bytesin              ;point to last byte
        sub       si,2                    ;back up before CR & LF
        mov       byte ptr [si],0         ;zero terminate the string
;
; Read target file name
;
        @DosWrite stdout,msg1,MSG1L,bytesout    ;prompt
        @DosRead  stdin,target_file,63,bytesin ;Read device name
        mov       si,offset target_file ;get address of input buffer
        add       si,bytesin              ;point to last byte
        sub       si,2                    ;back up before CR & LF
        mov       byte ptr [si],0         ;zero terminate the string
;
; Move it
;
        @DosMove  source_file,target_file,rsv ;Move file
        @jaxz     mov999                       ;finished
        @DosWrite stderr,msg2,MSG2L,bytesout  ;error message
```

Figure 13-31. MOVE program

As with previous examples, MOVE strips the input CR/LF and replaces it with a null termination byte. If the DosMove function fails, MOVE writes an error message to the STDERR device. The source and target file names may be fully qualified names, but they must both reside on the same device. If you simply enter two file names, OS/2 renames the source file to the target name.

Reading Directories

You can process the OS/2 file directories with the DosFindFirst and DosFindNext API calls. DosFindFirst locates the first file (in the current directory) that matches a particular pattern (including wild card characters). Then DosFindNext enables you to loop through all the directory entries that match the DosFindFirst criteria.

The parameters for DosFindFirst are as follows:

PTR	Pointer to an ASCIIZ string that defines the search criteria
PTR	Pointer to a one-word value where OS/2 will place the directory handle. If this field contains 0FFFFH, then OS/2 creates a new handle. If not, the value in this field is used as the handle. 0001h is always available as a directory handle
WORD	An attribute byte that tells OS/2 what type of files should be included in the search: 00h = Only search for normal files 02h = Include hidden files 04h = Include system files 10h = Include subdirectory entries
PTR	Pointer to the result buffer. The buffer may be large enough to receive more then one directory entry
WORD	The length of the result buffer
PTR	Pointer to a one-word result count. On entry, this word contains the number of entries that you want OS/2 to put in the result buffer. On return, this field is updated by OS/2 to indicate how many entries were found (valid). The result buffer must be big enough to accept the data
DWRD	Reserved (must be 0)

The parameters of DosFindNext are as follows:

WORD	A valid directory search handle
PTR	Pointer to the result buffer. The buffer may be large enough to receive more than one directory entry
WORD	The length of the result buffer
PTR	Pointer to a one-word result count. On entry, this word contains the number of entries that you want OS/2 to put in the result buffer. On return, this field is updated by OS/2 to indicate how many entries were found (valid). The result buffer must be large enough to accept the data

Figure 13-32. Structure of LISTDIR

DosFindFirst and DosFindNext are handle-based calls.
You can have more than one active search going, alternat-
ing between handles to read from one directory or another.

Consider a program that uses this feature to list the
subdirectories on a disk. Processing nested subdirectories
sounds like a job for a *recursive program* (one that calls
itself to process each subdirectory level). Figure 13-32
shows exactly how LISTDIR works.

The LISTDIR main procedure kicks off DISPDIR to
process the current directory. As DISPDIR encounters
other directories, it displays the subdirectory name with
the PRINTIT routine, changes the current directory to the
new subdirectory, and recurses on itself. When DISPDIR
reaches the end of a directory, it returns to the previous
directory and continues processing where it left off. Eventually, DISPDIR will have walked through all the subdirectories and displayed all their names.

The main routine is simple:

```
main      proc
          pusha                    ;Save registers
          push    ds               ;copy data segment selector
          pop     es               ;to ES
;
          xor     cx,cx            ;set nesting level (0)
          call    dispdir          ;display current directory
;
          popa                     ;Restore saved registers
          @DosExit 0,1             ;leave proc
main      endp
```

Note that before calling DISPDIR, the main routine sets the initial directory level in CX (0). The DISPDIR procedure (shown in Figure 13-33) is somewhat more complicated.

```
;
; Read first directory entry
;
            mov       dirhand,0ffffh          ;set dir initial handle
            @DosFindFirst dirall,dirhand,dirattrs,dirdata,dirdatal,dirnum,rsv
            @jaxnz    dcd999                  ;exit if none
;
; Process valid directory entries (loop)
;
dcd010:     cmp       dirdata.dirattr,10h     ;directory entry?
            je        dcd015                  ;yes - continue
            inc       bx                      ;bump file count
            jmp       dcd020                  ;read next file
;
dcd015:     cmp       byte ptr dirdata.dirname,'.' ;system directory?
            je        dcd020                  ;yes - skip it
;
            call      printit                 ;print data
;
            @DosChDir dirdata.dirname,rsv     ;go down one directory level
            inc       cx                      ;increment level
            push      dirhand                 ;save directory handle
            call      dispdir                 ;call self for next level
            pop       dirhand                 ;restore directory handle
            dec       cx                      ;retore level
            @DosChDir dirprev,rsv             ;return to prev (..) dir level
;
dcd020:     @DosFindNext dirhand,dirdata,dirdatal,dirnum
            @jaxnz    dcd999                  ;exit if end of directory
            jmp       dcd010                  ;else continue processing files
;
; Termination
;
dcd999:     mov       dirnum,1                ;reset 1 record (reset by EOD)
```

Figure 13-33. DISPDIR procedure

DISPDIR starts by setting the handle field to 0ffffh. This instructs OS/2 to allocate a new handle to this process. This is important because this routine relies on the fact that it will get a new handle on each recursion level. DISPDIR then issues a DosFindFirst call to locate the first file that matches the string in DIRALL (*.*). The attribute field (DIRATTR) contains 010h, meaning that the directory search should retrieve subdirectory names.

DISPDIR then starts a loop where it locates nonsystem (that is, ".", "..") subdirectories. When it finds one, it calls PRINTIT to display the subdirectory name and nesting level.

After the data is printed, DISPDIR uses the DosChgDir to change the current directory to the new subdirectory, increments the nesting level (in CX), saves the current directory handle on the stack (PUSH DIRHAND), and calls itself to process the subdirectory.

DISPDIR continues to process the entries in the subdirectories in this way until eventually one of the searches ends (no more files). The procedure then resets the number of data records field (DIRNUM), which OS/2 set to 0 when the search was exhausted. DISPDIR now returns to its caller, which could have been itself or MAIN.

If DISPDIR returns to itself, it restores the search handle (POP DIRHAND), decrements the nesting level, and returns to the previous directory level by calling DosChgDir with a directory value of ".." (parent directory). It then continues the directory search by using the previous directory handle. When DISPDIR restored the search handle from the stack, it restored the search context. The parameters of DosChgDir are as follows:

PTR	Pointer to an ASCIIZ directory name
DWRD	Reserved (must be 0)

If you run DISPDIR from the command line, it will list the directory structure of your current drive, starting at the current directory (see Figure 13-34).

```
[C:\]listdir

(0)  HP              Created: 20:50:06 07/02/88
(0)  OS2             Created: 13:40:14 07/03/88
(1)  .OBJ            Created: 13:41:03 07/03/88
(1)  .TOOLS          Created: 13:41:11 07/03/88
(1)  .DEVLIB         Created: 13:41:17 07/03/88
(2)  ..ASM           Created: 13:42:01 07/03/88
(3)  ...OBJLIB       Created: 13:42:17 07/03/88
(2)  ..EDIT          Created: 13:42:20 07/03/88
(2)  ..SOURCE        Created: 13:42:22 07/03/88
(0)  ARCHIVE         Created: 14:43:06 07/03/88
(0)  SCRIPTPC        Created: 18:38:24 07/06/88
(0)  DRAW            Created: 22:38:00 07/06/88

[C:\]
```

Figure 13-34.   Output from DISPDIR

Getting File Information

Using OS/2 API calls, you can retrieve information about directories, files, open handles, the disk media, or the file system itself. Table 13-3 lists these function calls. Your programs can find out just about anything about the file

Table 13-3.   File I/O Query Functions

API	Function
DosQCurDir	Determine current directory
DosQCurDisk	Determine current disk
DosQFHandState	Determine the state of a handle
DosQFileInfo	Get file information
DosQFSInfo	Get file system information
DosQHandType	Determine the handle type (device, file, pipe)
DosQVerify	Determine value of verify state

system without having to actually "peek" at the media. In fact, avoid writing programs that are dependent on disk layout because this data could change over time. A good example of such a situation is what happened to some programs when PC DOS 3.0 introduced the 16-bit FAT. Since they were dependent on the 12-bit FAT these programs ceased to operate on PC DOS systems with large hard files (greater than 10MB).

If you must determine information about the file system, use the API functions provided by OS/2. They will shield you from system changes.

```
;
; Parse input data & open file (if entered)
;
            @getparms  fname,63                   ;get command parameters
            @jaxz      inf050                      ;jump if no data entered
;
            mov        cx,ax                       ;get data length
            mov        di,offset fname             ;address buffer
            mov        al,' '                      ;blank
            repne      scasb                       ;scan for blank
            jcxz       inf010                      ;skip adjustment if end of string
            dec        di                          ;point to blank
inf010:     mov        byte ptr [di],0             ;make name zero terminated
            sub        di,offset fname             ;compute name length
            mov        fnlen,di                    ;save it
;
            call       getdrive                    ;get drive number in input
            mov        drive,ax                    ;save drive value
;
            @DosOpen   fname,fhand,fact,fsize,fattr,fflag,fmode,rsv
            @jaxz      inf030                      ;go print data if file opened OK
            @DosWrite  stderr,msg0,msg0l,bytesout  ;Write invalid file name msg
            jmp        inf050                      ;go print data
```

Figure 13-35. INFO initialization program

For example, consider the program named INFO in Figure 13-35. INFO uses DosQFileInfo and DosQFSInfo API calls to retrieve and display information about a file and the file system. The parameters of DosQFileInfo are as follows:

WORD	An open file handle
WORD	The file information level that you want OS/2 to return to you (level 1 is the only valid level for OS/2 1.0)
PTR	Pointer to a buffer into which OS/2 will place the file information data
WORD	The length of the data buffer

The parameters of DosQFSInfo are as follows:

WORD	A one-word value containing the drive number about which the data is to be presented (0=current drive) and the file-system information level: 1 = File system statistics (always exists) 2 = Volume label information (may not exist)
PTR	The address of a data buffer that will receive the information
WORD	The data buffer length

You pass the name of a file as a command-line parameter to INFO. INFO starts by retrieving the command buffer (using the @GETPARMS macro). @GETPARMS is the command-line parsing routine taken from SPLIT, repackaged as a common function in the macro library.

The code that follows the macro skips the file processing if the user did not enter a file name on the command line. If something was entered, INFO scans the command line to find the file name and null terminates the name. It then calls a subroutine to parse the drive letter (if entered) and convert it to a numeric value. INFO will use this later to identify the drive whose media characteristics are to be displayed. Finally, INFO uses the file name to open the

```
;
; Print file data
;
inf030:         @DosQFileInfo fhand,filvl,fidata,fisize   ;get file information
                @movs     fname,msg4fn,fnlen            ;file name
                @date     fidata.ficd,msg4dc            ;creation date
                @time     fidata.fict,msg4tc            ;creation time
                @date     fidata.fiad,msg4da            ;last access date
                @time     fidata.fiat,msg4ta            ;last access time
                @date     fidata.fiwd,msg4dw            ;last write date
                @time     fidata.fiwt,msg4tw            ;last write time
                @bth      fidata.fieh,msg4eh            ;file end to hex
                @bth      fidata.fiel,msg4el            ;file end to hex
                @bth      fidata.fiah,msg4ah            ;file end to hex
                @bth      fidata.fial,msg4al            ;file end to hex
                @DosWrite stdout,msg4,msg4l,bytesout    ;write file data
```

Figure 13-36.   INFO file data retrieval and display

file. It writes an error message to STDERR if the Dos-
Open function fails.

Now that the file is open, INFO uses DosQFileInfo to
retrieve an information block about the file (see Figure
13-36).

INFO maps the block with a data structure and converts each of the fields to printable ASCII, using the
@DATE, @TIME and @BTH macros. The @DATE and
@TIME macros convert the file system binary date and
time values to "MM/DD/YY" and "HH:MM:SS" format,
respectively. The @BTH macro converts a single binary
word to hexadecimal. INFO then writes the converted
data with a DosWrite call to the STDOUT device.

The entire process is then repeated with the
DosQFSInfo to retrieve the file system information (see
Figure 13-37).

```
;
; Print file system info
;
inf050:         @DosQFsInfo drive,fslvl2,fsdata2,fssiz2 ;get file system data 2
                @jaxnz    inf060                  ;no volume data - skip display
                xor       dx,dx                   ;clear ax
                mov       dl,fsdata2.vlen          ;move length to AX
                @movs     fsdata2.volid,msg6vid,dx ;file sys ID (char)
                @date     fsdata2.vdate,msg6vda   ;Volume date
                @time     fsdata2.vtime,msg6vti   ;Volume time
                @DosWrite stdout,msg6,msg6l,bytesout ;write file system data
;
inf060:         @DosQFsInfo drive,fslvl1,fsdata1,fssiz1 ;get file system data 1
                @bths     fsdata1.fsid,msg5fsid,4 ;file system ID
                @bth      fsdata1.spa+2,msg5spa   ;sectors per alloc unit (high)
                @bth      fsdata1.spa,msg5spa+4   ;sectors per alloc unit (low)
                @bth      fsdata1.nal+2,msg5nal   ;number of alloc units  (high)
                @bth      fsdata1.nal,msg5nal+4   ;number of alloc units  (low)
                @bth      fsdata1.aal+2,msg5aal   ;available alloc units  (high)
                @bth      fsdata1.aal,msg5aal+4   ;available alloc units  (low)
                @bth      fsdata1.bps,msg5bps     ;bytes per sector
                @DosWrite stdout,msg5,msg5l,bytesout ;write file system data
```

Figure 13-37. INFO file system data retrieval and display

Note that OS/2 provides two types of FS data—volume label information and file-system statistics. INFO uses the drive number to request, convert, and print the volume label data (if it exists), and then repeats the operation with the file-system statistics. The data structures that map these two information blocks (as well as the @DATE, @TIME and @BTH macros) are included in OS2MAC.INC

If you run INFO from the command line, you will see the report shown in Figure 13-38.

Note that although you ran INFO from the disk in drive C, it displayed the information pertaining to drive D,

```
[C:\]info d:\test.dta

                       File Name: d:\test.dta

                         Created: 00/00/80   00:00:00
                     Last Update: 08/20/87   23:26:16
                        Last Use: 00/00/80   00:00:00
                       File Size: 00000136
                          In Use: 00000800

                       Volume ID: OS2_SYSTEM
                         Created: 08/09/87   11:17:16

                 File System ID: 00000000
       Sectors per Allocation unit: 00000004
       Number of allocation units: 00003CFE
       Available Allocation units: 00001FA6
              Bytes per sector: 0200

[C:\]
```

Figure 13-38.   Report generated by INFO

where the file test.dta resides. This is because GETDRIVE set the drive number from the input file specifications. If you rerun INFO without a file specification, it skips the file information and displays the file system data for the current drive (see Figure 13-39). If the disk does not have a label, INFO skips the volume-label display.

```
[C:\]info

                 File System ID: 00000000
       Sectors per Allocation unit: 00000004
       Number of allocation units: 00003FB5
       Available Allocation units: 000012CC
              Bytes per sector: 0200

[C:\]
```

Figure 13-39.   Report generated by INFO if no file is specified

FAMILY API CONSIDERATIONS

Note that with the exception of some device-specific IOCTL packets, the OS/2 file I/O services are all included in the family API. This means that if you write programs that only write to these interfaces and are not dependent on other more-advanced OS/2 functions (such as multitasking), you can BIND the resulting EXE file to run on PC DOS.

Programs that read data from a disk, manipulate the information, and write it back to a file are excellent candidates to become "family applications." In fact, most OS/2 language compilers (MASM, C, and so forth) are family application programs that will run on either PC DOS or OS/2.

The program examples in this chapter all fit the family API criteria.

SUMMARY

File I/O services are an important part of the overall OS/2 system services. In this chapter you have learned to use DosOpen, DosRead, and DosWrite to perform I/O to OS/2 devices and files. This simple file I/O model is the basis for the I/O redirection facilities discussed in previous chapters.

To leave time for other important OS/2 functions, some of the other file I/O system calls have been omitted. However, they are all listed in Appendix A.

The following are some important points to remember:

- How to access standard input, output, and error

- What the file access modes are

- Sending control information to device drivers

- Opening files
- Writing randomly (changing the file pointer)
- Locking byte ranges
- Accessing the directory information
- Retrieving file information

CHAPTER 14
I/O SUBSYSTEMS

You should now understand how the OS/2 file I/O services are used to write information to system devices. The discussion in Chapter 13 used DosRead and DosWrite calls exclusively to read or write the console device. However, OS/2 has a different I/O mechanism for the primary "interactive" devices. This I/O mechanism, called subsystem I/O, allows you to build application programs with higher bandwith and more responsive user interfaces. This chapter explores the OS/2 I/O subsystem functions.

Often in the PC DOS environment, the only way to make a highly interactive application interface is to bypass altogether the operating system video services. Applications frequently forego the PC DOS interfaces in favor of the BIOS functions (or, more commonly, direct hardware access). Since OS/2 runs the CPU in protected mode, these techniques are more difficult to implement. Hence, OS/2 provides the I/O subsystems.

You can view subsystems as protected mode versions of the video, keyboard, and mouse BIOS. However, unlike the PC BIOS (which resides in ROM), I/O subsystems are standard operating system interfaces. They are also more functional and much faster than the equivalent real mode BIOS.

Because of the large number of subsystem functions, this chapter is structured differently than Chapter 13 with more emphasis on the actual APIs and less emphasis on sample programs. However, the remaining chapters in this part all contain sample programs that use subsystem I/O functions to interact with the screen and the keyboard. In fact, from this point forward, subsystem I/O is the preferred console I/O mechanism.

VIDEO I/O

The display is one of the most complex devices in a system. Because personal computer applications are highly interactive, how you use the display is a critical application design point. In fact, the user interface is often *the* most important feature of PC applications.

The *video subsystem* (*VIO*) is OS/2's most functionally rich (and flexible) I/O subsystem. It is also the most complex subsystem, with a full range of I/O services that enable you to access the display device in whatever manner best suits your program. At one end of the spectrum, VIO has high-level glass teletype (TTY) functions, with built-in ANSI support. At the other end is low-level direct hardware access. In between you will find BIOS-like (INT 10H) character-processing functions that enable you to read and write characters, attributes, or character cells from or to the display. VIO also has display-mode controls, cursor-manipulation services, font-management functions, and data-scrolling primitives. You can even augment or replace portions of the subsystem with your own low-level routines.

However, you should note that while the VIO services are functionally similar to the PC video BIOS, they are not identical. In most cases, the VIO services go well beyond the BIOS capabilities. However, in some cases, the BIOS has functions not supported by VIO.

The most notable omission comes in graphics-support facilities. The VIO subsystem is designed to support text applications. Its graphics support is limited to an API that you use to switch the display into graphics modes. Once in graphics, your application is on its own. Specifically, VIO does not include the read/write graphics text and read/write pel functions that are part of the video BIOS. Full graphics-text support is forthcoming in OS/2 release 1.1. In the meantime, you can use a graphics support system (such as BASIC/2) to write graphics output.

Naturally, the VIO subsystem does have services that enable you to port existing graphics applications that write to the display directly. But direct display access is somewhat trickier to use than what you may have been accustomed to in a single-tasking system.

Display Modes

The VIO subsystem has API calls that allow you to query and modify the states of the display adapter. Most PC adapters can run in either text or graphics modes.

In text modes, the display hardware is responsible for generating the actual character cells. To write data on the screen, a program places the individual ASCII character(s) and their display attribute(s) into a special hardware memory area called the *display buffer*. The video hardware reads the display buffer, converts each character to a collection of graphics pels, and then writes them to the screen.

Figure 14-1 illustrates this process. A program has written the character "A" with a display attribute 70h (black character on white background) into a location in the display buffer. The video hardware extracts this

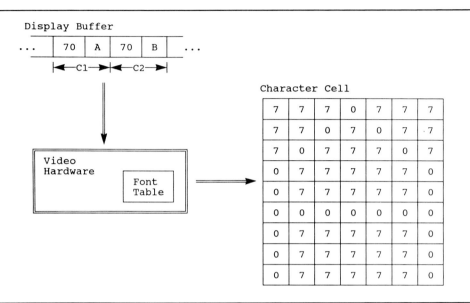

Figure 14-1.   *Text display mode operation*

information, and by using an internal font table, determines the pel pattern that corresponds to the letter "A." Then, by using the attribute information, the video hardware writes the actual character in the screen position that corresponds to the display buffer location.

In OS/2, the display buffer is normally hidden from the applications by other VIO functions that manipulate its contents on their behalf.

When set in a graphics mode, the display becomes a randomly addressable array of points, called *pels*. OS/2 release 1.1 includes services you can use to logically manipulate graphics images, much in the same way release 1.0 VIO services allow you to manipulate text. If you intend to use the graphics mode in OS/2 release 1.0, you must either manage the display yourself by directly accessing the display hardware, or use a commercially available graphics package (such as VDI or the BASIC/2 compiler).

PTR	A pointer to a video mode data structure (see VioGet Mode).
	Note: You can specify a partial video mode buffer. Minimum buffer length is 3 bytes and maximum buffer length is 12 bytes (fields cannot be split). The remaining fields are set to default values
WORD	A one-word VIO handle (0)

Which modes you can set depends on the capabilities of your display adapter. Table 14-1 summarizes the standard VIO mode support. If you have a unique display device,

You can switch the display adapter between text mode and graphics mode with the VioSetMode API. The parameters for VioSetMode are as follows:

Table 14-1. Supported VIO Display Modes

BIOS Mode	Type	Colors	Cols	Text Rows	Cell	Res	Adaptor(s)
0	Text (BW)	16	40	25	8x8	320x200	CGA,PGA,EGA,VGA,8514A
0*	Text (BW)	16	40	25/43	8x14	320x350	EGA,VGA,8514A
0+	Text (BW)	16	40	25/43/50	9x16	360x400	VGA,8514A
1	Text	16	40	25	8x8	320x200	CGA,PGA,EGA,VGA,8514A
1*	Text	16	40	25/43	8x14	320x350	EGA,VGA,8514A
1+	Text	16	40	25/43/50	9x16	360x400	VGA,8514A
2	Text (BW)	16	80	25	8x8	640x200	CGA,PGA,EGA,VGA,8514A
2*	Text (BW)	16	80	25/43	8x14	640x350	EGA,VGA,8514A
2+	Text (BW)	16	80	25/43/50	9x16	720x400	VGA,8514A
3	Text	16	80	25	8x8	640x200	CGA,PGA,EGA,VGA,8514A
3*	Text	16	80	25/43	8x16	640x350	PGA,EGA,VGA,8514A
3+	Text	16	80	25/43/50	9x16	720x400	VGA,8514A
4	Graphics	4	N/A	N/A	N/A	320x200	CGA,PGA,EGA,VGA,8514A
5	Graphics	2	N/A	N/A	N/A	320x200	CGA,PGA,EGA,VGA,8514A
6	Graphics	2	N/A	N/A	N/A	640x200	CGA,PGA,EGA,VGA,8514A
7	Mono Text	0	80	25	9x14	720x350	EGA,VGA,8514A
7+	Mono Text	0	80	25	9x16	720x400	VGA,8514A
D	Graphics	16	N/A	N/A	N/A	320x200	EGA,VGA,8514A
E	Graphics	4	N/A	N/A	N/A	640x200	EGA,VGA,8514A
F	Graphics	2	N/A	N/A	N/A	640x350	EGA,VGA,8514A
10	Graphics	16	N/A	N/A	N/A	640x350	EGA,VGA,8514A
11	Graphics	2	N/A	N/A	N/A	640x480	VGA,8514A
12	Graphics	16	N/A	N/A	N/A	640x480	VGA,8514A
13	Graphics	256	N/A	N/A	N/A	320x200	VGA,8514A

```
Data Segment ...

text80        modedata <12,00000001B,4,80,43,640,350> ;video mode (text)

Code Segment ...

              @VioSetMode text80,0       ;set the display mode
```

Figure 14-2. *Code to set color, high resolution 43 line text mode*

you can either extend VioSetMode yourself, or use a commercially available VIO package that includes support for your device.

When you call VioSetMode, you pass it the address of a data structure that defines in generic terms the desired mode. This departure from the traditional BIOS "mode numbers" allows OS/2 applications to deal with the screen geometries without being sensitive to the adapter implementations. A MASM structure named MODEDATA is included in OS2MAC.INC that maps this parameter area.

To reset the video mode, you simply initialize the data structure and call VioSetMode. For example, Figure 14-2 sets the display mode to 16-color, 80-column × 43-row text at a display resolution of 640×350 (EGA BIOS mode 3).

```
Data Segment ...

text40        modedata <12,00000101B,4,40,25,640,200> ;video mode (text)

Code Segment ...

              @VioSetMode text40,0       ;set the display mode
```

Figure 14-3. *Code to set black and white, 40 column text mode*

On the other hand, if you code as shown in Figure 14-3, you set the display mode to black-and-white (color burst disabled), 40-column $\times$ 25-row text, at a screen resolution of 640×200 (CGA BIOS mode 1). If you attempt to set a display mode not supported by your display device, then the function call fails (with error code 355).

You can also query the current display mode with the VioGetMode API. The parameters for VioGetMode are as follows:

PTR	A pointer to a video mode data structure:
	DW Structure length (including this field)
	DB Mode characteristics
	-------0 Monochrome/printer adapter
	-------1 Other adapter
	------0- Text mode
	------1- Graphics mode
	-----0-- Enable color burst
	-----1-- Disable color burst (B/W)
	DB Number of colors supported by display
	1 = 2 colors
	2 = 4 colors
	4 = 16 colors
	DW Number of text columns
	DW Number of text rows
	DW Horizontal resolution (pels)
	DW Vertical resolution (pels)
	DD Reserved
	Note: OS/2 returns only the data that will fit in the buffer. Minimum buffer length is 3 bytes and maximum buffer length is 12 bytes (fields cannot be split)
WORD	A one-word VIO handle (0)

Like VioSetMode, VioGetMode requires a pointer to a mode data structure. However, in this case OS/2 returns the current settings in the data area. Note that if you set or query the video mode, you are doing so only for the current session. The VIO subsystem saves and restores video modes as part of the session context.

Display adapters usually have other advanced capabilities that don't directly relate to the display mode, yet affect the screen appearance (border color, display attribute definition options, and so forth). To modify access to these options, OS/2 provides the VioSetState API. The parameters for VioSetState are as follows:

PTR	Pointer to a video state data structure, in one of several formats:
	  Type 0: Values of palette registers (EGA, VGA)
	  Type 1: Border color (CGA, VGA)
	  Type 2: Blink/background intensity state (CGA, EGA, VGA)

WORD	A one-word VIO handle (0)

Like VioSetMode, you pass VioSetState a data structure identifying what parameter(s) you want to change and to what you want to change them. Table 14-2 lists the three types of status request blocks supported by OS/2 1.0. A data structure for each request is included in OS2-MAC.INC.

Request block 0 is used to set the graphics palette registers. It is better to use this function to set these registers (rather than doing direct OUT instructions) because OS/2 can then save and restore the state automatically when it switches display sessions. If (for performance) your application directly manipulates the registers, then you must take on the responsibility of restoring them on screen switches.

The type 1 request block is used to set the display border color. Note that this is only valid with CGA and VGA displays. Finally, the type 2 request block enables you to change the operation of the display adapter so that the "I" bit in the background color attribute works as an intensity bit, rather than as a blink bit.

As you would expect, the VioGetState API is used to

Table 14-2. Video State Parameter Blocks

Type 0: Palette Registers

00	DW	Structure Length (including this field)
02	DW	Request Type = 0
04	DW	First Palette Register to be included (0-15)
06	DW	Palette register #n color value (first)
/ / /		/
xx	DW	Palette register #n + x color value (last)

Note: The total number of palette registers is determined by the structure length field.

Type 1: Border Color

00	DW	Structure Length = 6
02	DW	Request Type = 1
04	DW	The Border Color Value

Type 2: Blink/Background Intensity Mode

00	DW	Structure Length = 6
02	DW	Request Type = 2
04	DW	BBI Mode (0=Blink, 1=Intensity)

query the setting of the display states. The parameters for VioGetState are as follows:

PTR	Pointer to a video state data structure, in one of several formats: Type 0: Values of palette registers (EGA, VGA) Type 1: Border color (CGA, VGA) Type 2: Blink/background intensity state (CGA, EGA, VGA)
WORD	A one-word VIO handle (0)

VioGetState returns information in the same data structures that you use to set the parameters.

Clearly, the video modes and states are device-specific. That is to say, certain modes and options are valid on some displays but not others. Before you actually set them, you might wish to know what kind of display is attached to the system. The VioGetConfig API solves this dilemma. The parameters for VioGetConfig are as follows:

PTR	Pointer to a configuration data area:
	DW Structure length (includes length field)
	DW Adapter type
	0 = Monochrome/printer
	1 = CGA
	2 = EGA
	3 = VGA
	7 = 8514A
	DW Display type
	0 = Monochrome
	1 = Color
	2 = Enhanced color
	3 = IBM PS/2 8503 (monochrome)
	4 = IBM PS/2 8513 (color)
	9 = IBM PS/2 8514 (color)
	DD Adapter memory size
WORD	A one-word VIO handle (0).

With this API, you can determine the specific adapter and display type that comprise the system primary display device.

By definition, the *primary display device* is the display that the BIOS uses to boot the system. Note that while your system may have more than one physical display attached to it, the VIO subsystem only supports the primary display.

By using VioGetConfig, you could query the display type and use the information to "tailor" the display routines so that they make optimum use of the display device. For example, if an application is running on a system with a CGA or VGA adapter, you could prompt the user for a display border color.

Writing Data in TTY Mode

The highest-level text video service in VIO is the glass-teletype (TTY) output function, VioWrtTTY. The parameters for VioWrtTTY are as follows:

PTR	A pointer to a character string that OS/2 will write on the screen.
WORD	A one-word value containing the string length.
WORD	The VIO handle (must be 0).

In many ways, VioWrtTTY provides the same capabilities as the character-stream console I/O (DosWrite) you saw in Chapter 13. In fact, the DosWrite API winds up calling the VioWrtTTY function to physically write the characters on the screen.

The difference between the two services is that when you use DosWrite, the I/O is first processed by the file system and is thus redirectable. Direct VioWrtTTY output, on the other hand, bypasses the file system and cannot be redirected.

When deciding which service to use, you must make a trade-off of performance (VioWrtTTY is somewhat faster) versus redirection capabilities. In some cases, redirection is worthwhile (such as in a command-line utility program). In others (such as screen I/O generated in a full-screen application "window") you do not need the redirection capabilities, so you might use VioWrtTTY.

For example, the code shown in Figure 14-4 writes the data contained in the field "MSG1" to the screen in TTY mode. Notice that if the data declaration includes a Carriage Return (CR) and Line Feed (LF), this will cause VIO to advance to the next line after it writes the message. As discussed in Chapter 8, TTY data streams can contain characters (TAB, CARRIAGE RETURN, BELL, and so forth) that have special meanings. This is equally true when you write a character stream with VioWrtTTY or DosWrite.

```
Data Segment ...

msg1         db          'Hello World!',CR,LF
MSG1L        equ         $ - offset msg1

Code Segment ...

             @VioWrtTTY msg1,MSG1L,0         ;Write hello to the screen
```

Figure 14-4. *Code to write data to screen in TTY mode*

TTY output can also contain special ANSI escape sequences (see Chapter 8) that manipulate the display attributes and the cursor position. This ANSI processing is actually implemented in VioWrtTTY. The API functions VioGetANSI and VioSetANSI enable you to query and modify the ANSI processing state, respectively. The parameters for VioGetANSI are as follows:

PTR	Pointer to a one-word field in which OS/2 will return the current ANSI state: 0 = Off 1 = On
WORD	A one-word VIO handle (0)

The parameters for VioSetANSI are as follows:

PTR	A one-word value indicating how ANSI processing is to be set: 0 = Off 1 = On
WORD	A one-word VIO handle (0)

For instance, the code in Figure 14-5 returns the current ANSI setting in the field named ANSIQ, and the following code

```
@VioSetANSI 0,0                    ;reset ANSI
```

Figure 14-5. Code to return current ANSI setting

unconditionally turns ANSI processing off (0). Note that since DosWrite uses VioWrtTTY "under the covers," the VIO ANSI state also affects the DosWrite output. If (as in the last example) you turn ANSI processing off, then it will be off for all forms of OS/2 TTY output (including DosWrite).

Writing Character Cells

The most useful functions provided by the VIO subsystem are its character and string writing services. In a sense, these functions are similar to the familiar BIOS INT 10H character I/O services, except that they are much more flexible. Before discussing the specifics, review several concepts about display text modes.

Each character that appears on the screen is represented to the display adapter as a 2-byte pair, called a *character cell*. A character cell is composed of a 1-byte ASCII character and a 1-byte display attribute. A character is a code point that the display hardware uses to look up a particular pel pattern. When the hardware displays this pel pattern on the screen, you see the character.

The attribute byte tells the display adapter how to display the pel pattern (background color, foreground color, blink, intensity, and so forth). Figure 14-6 illustrates the format of a display attribute byte. Notice how the background intensity/blink state setting redefines the meaning

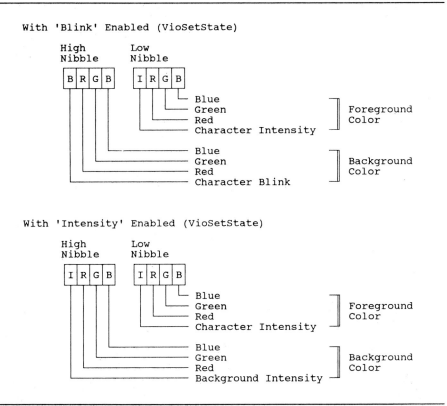

Figure 14-6. Display attribute byte format

of the background intensity bit. The different character (and background) colors are made up by combining the different primary colors (red, green, blue) and intensity. For example, consider the following attribute combinations:

1001   0010 = 92h = High-intensity blue on green background
0100   0111 = 47h = Red on white background
1111   0000 = f0h = High-intensity white on black background

Together, the character and the attribute bytes define

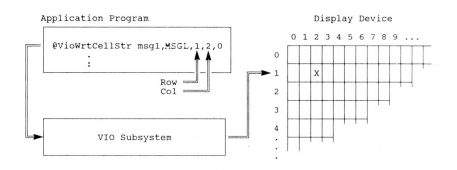

Figure 14-7. Character positions in text display

exactly what is to be displayed in a character cell.

By using the OS/2 VIO subsystem, you can randomly write combinations of characters, attributes, or cells to arbitrary portions of the screen. The screen itself is defined as a character cell matrix n rows by m columns. To write to a particular screen location, you identify the (row,col) coordinates. For example, in Figure 14-7 the application program wrote a character at the display location row 1, column 2.

Note that this is significantly different than TTY-style I/O where the output is always relative to the current cursor position. With VIO character services, you can randomly update different portions of the screen.

All the character-oriented VIO calls are really string operations. This means that you write more than one character (or cell) with a single API call. Each call, therefore, contains a length parameter that defines the length of the output string. If the string extends beyond one line, it will wrap to the next. However, if the string extends beyond the end of the screen, the extra characters are ignored.

To write an individual character cell, you use the

VioWrtCellStr API. The parameters of VioWrtCellStr are as follows:

PTR	A pointer to the cell (attr,char) string that OS/2 will write on the screen
WORD	A one-word value containing the character string length
WORD	A one-word value defining the row where the string is to be written
WORD	A one-word value defining the column where the string is to be written
WORD	The VIO handle (must be 0)

With this function, you specify a screen coordinate and a cell string of some arbitrary length that is to be written at the coordinates. For example, the code in Figure 14-8 writes the character string "Volume:" at line 10, column 10. Notice that with VioWrtCellStr you must include two bytes for each screen position. In other words, the character string has a unique attribute associated with each character. In this example, the first letter of the string is yellow with a blue background and the remaining charac-

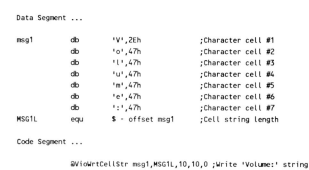

```
Data Segment ...

msg1      db      'V',2Eh         ;Character cell #1
          db      'o',47h         ;Character cell #2
          db      'l',47h         ;Character cell #3
          db      'u',47h         ;Character cell #4
          db      'm',47h         ;Character cell #5
          db      'e',47h         ;Character cell #6
          db      ':',47h         ;Character cell #7
MSG1L     equ     $ - offset msg1 ;Cell string length

Code Segment ...

          @VioWrtCellStr msg1,MSG1L,10,10,0 ;Write 'Volume:' string
```

Figure 14-8.   Code to write a cell string

ters are white with a red background. You can use this API whenever you need to exercise control over the individual character attributes.

The VioWrtNCell API is a variation of VioWrtCellStr with which you replicate a single character cell into several (contiguous) screen locations. The parameters for VioWrtNCell are as follows:

PTR	A pointer to a cell (attr,char) that OS/2 replicates on the screen
WORD	A one-word value containing the replication count
WORD	A one-word value defining the row where the cell(s) are to be written
WORD	A one-word value defining the column where the cell(s) are to be written
WORD	The VIO handle (must be 0)

For example, the code in Figure 14-9 replicates the cell defined by FILL in a screen area that starts in row 10, column 10 and extends for seven character positions. VioWrtNCell is a useful function if you need to blank out a portion of the screen. In this example, you overwrite the "Volume:" string with blanks and reset the attribute bytes to white characters with black background (07H).

```
Data Segment ...

fill        db       ' ',07h           ;Blank character cell

Code Segment ...

           @VioWrtNCell fill,7,10,10,0   ;blank out field
```

Figure 14-9. Code to replicate cell defined by FILL

If you simply want to write a character string and use the same attribute for each character, then you can use the VioWrtCharStrAtt API. The parameters for VioWrtCharStrAtt are as follows:

PTR	A pointer to the character string that OS/2 writes on the screen
WORD	A one-word value containing the character string length
WORD	A one-word value defining the row where the string is to be written
WORD	A one-word value defining the column where the string is to be written
PTR	A pointer to a 1-byte display attribute that OS/2 associates with each character in the string
WORD	The VIO handle (must be 0)

This API is similar to VioWrtCellStr in that it writes a cell string. However, in this case the attribute is included only once (as an API parameter), rather than with each character cell. Thus, the code in Figure 14-10 once again writes the string "Volume:" at line 10, column 10 of the screen, but this time all the characters are highlighted with the display attribute 27H (white characters on green background). Also note that the message declaration does not include the display attributes.

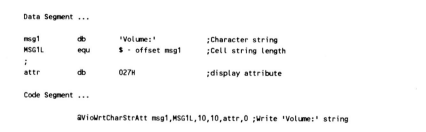

```
Data Segment ...

msg1      db      'Volume:'        ;Character string
MSG1L     equ     $ - offset msg1  ;Cell string length
;
attr      db      027H             ;display attribute

Code Segment ...

          @VioWrtCharStrAtt msg1,MSG1L,10,10,attr,0 ;Write 'Volume:' string
```

Figure 14-10. Code to write a character string

When you use this API, take special note that the attribute value is not passed as an immediate value, but as a pointer to a 1-byte attribute field. Thus, in this example the attribute byte is contained in the field named ATTR.

To write a character string without modifying the display attributes (at all), you can use the VioWrtCharStr API. The parameters for VioWrtCharStr are as follows:

PTR	A pointer to the character string that OS/2 writes on the screen
WORD	A one-word value containing the character string length
WORD	A one-word value defining the row where the string is to be written
WORD	A one-word value defining the column where the string is to be written
WORD	The VIO handle (must be 0)

This function is essentially the same as VioWrtCellStr, except that you only specify the character portion of the display cells. For instance, the code in Figure 14-11 also writes the string "Volume:" at line 10, column 10. However, this time the display attributes that are in the overwritten display locations are unchanged. Thus, you can change the data displayed on the screen and retain the previous highlighting.

```
Data Segment ...

fill        db        ' '              ;Blank character

Code Segment ...

            aVioWrtNChar fill,7,10,10,0   ;blank out field
```

Figure 14-11. Code to write string without changing the highlighting

These "character" APIs also have a replicate character counterpart called VioWrtNChar. The parameters for VioWrtNChar are as follows:

PTR	A pointer to a character that OS/2 replicates on the screen
WORD	A one-word value containing the replication count
WORD	A one-word value defining the row where the character(s) are to be written
WORD	A one-word value defining the column where the character(s) are to be written
WORD	The VIO handle (must be 0)

This function simply replicates a single character in a portion of the screen without changing the individual cell attributes. With VioWrtNCell you can blank out a portion of the screen without changing the highlighting. For instance, the code in Figure 14-12 blanks the field, but leaves the attributes unchanged. Note that the FILL field contains the character with no attribute.

```
Data Segment ...

msg1        db      'Volume:'          ;Character string
MSG1L       equ     $ - offset msg1    ;Cell string length

Code Segment ...

            @VioWrtCharStr msg1,MSG1L,10,10,0 ;Write 'Volume:' string
```

Figure 14-12. Code to blank a field, but leave attributes unchanged

Finally, with VioWrtNAttr you write a replicated string of display attributes without changing the characters. The parameters of VioWrtNAttr are as follows:

PTR	A pointer to a display attribute that OS/2 replicates on the screen
WORD	A one-word value containing the replication count
WORD	A one-word value defining the row where the attribute(s) are to be written
WORD	A one-word value defining the column where the attribute(s) are to be written
WORD	The VIO handle (must be 0)

For example, the code in Figure 14-13 changes the highlighting of screen row 10, column 10 for a length of seven characters to display attribute 47H (white on red background), without changing the characters currently displayed on the screen. In the previous example(s), this call would have the effect of turning the "Volume:" string into white letters on a red field.

```
Data Segment ...

fill        db        47h              ;Blank character cell

Code Segment ...

            aVioWrtNAttr fill,7,10,10,0  ;blank out field
```

Figure 14-13. Code to change highlighting

Reading Data from Screen

In some situations, your application might have to read information from the screen image. (Note that this is different from reading from the keyboard, as discussed later in this chapter.) If you actually "peeked" into the display buffer, you would effectively be eliminating the device independence of the VIO interfaces. Therefore, OS/2 provides two additional VIO functions: VioReadCharStr and VioReadCell. The parameters for VioReadCharStr are as follows:

PTR	Pointer to a buffer into which OS/2 will place the character string
PTR	Pointer to a one-word field which, on entry, tells OS/2 how many characters are to be read, and, on return, contains the number of characters actually read
WORD	A one-word value indicating the row where the read is to start
WORD	A one-word value indicating the column where the read is to start
WORD	A one-word VIO handle (0)

The parameters for VioReadCellStr are as follows:

PTR	Pointer to a buffer into which OS/2 will place the cell string
PTR	Pointer to a one-word field which, on entry, tells OS/2 the length of the cell buffer (in bytes), and, on return, contains the number of bytes actually read. **Note**: Each cell is 2 bytes, so the number of cells read is equal to half of this buffer length
WORD	A one-word value indicating the row where the read is to start
WORD	A one-word value indicating the column where the read is to start
WORD	A one-word VIO handle (0)

```
Data Segment ...

videobuf     db       7 dup (' ')          ;Input buffer
blen         dw       $ - offset videobuf  ;buffer length

Code Segment ...

             @VioReadCharStr videobuf,blen,10,10,0 ;read the field
```

Figure 14-14. Code to read characters from display

As its name implies, VioReadCharStr returns a character string corresponding to the actual ASCII characters contained in a range of display cells. The code in Figure 14-14 reads the characters displayed at row 10, columns 10-16, into a buffer named VIDEOBUF. If the screen was unchanged from the previous example, VIDEOBUF would contain the string "Volume:".

On input, the buffer length tells OS/2 how many characters it should read. On output, the field is set to the number of characters actually read. If the read request extends beyond the end of the line, it continues at the first column (0) of the next line. If you attempt to read beyond the end of the screen, then the read operation ends and the length field is set to the actual number of characters read.

Because OS/2 might update the length field, you pass it as a pointer to a data area rather than as an immediate value (as in the other VIO calls). Do not forget that OS/2 may reset the length. If you use VioReadCharStr repeatedly to read different parts of the screen into a buffer, you should always re-initialize the length field before each call, in the event that one of the calls causes the buffer length to be truncated.

If, on the other hand, you want to retrieve all the display cells (including attribute bytes), you can use VioReadCellStr as shown in Figure 14-15. This time, the

```
Data Segment ...

videobuf      db        14 dup (' ')          ;Input buffer
blen          dw        $ - offset videobuf   ;buffer length

Code Segment ...

              @VioReadCellStr videobuf,blen,10,10,0 ;read the field
```

Figure 14-15. Code to read character cells from display

entire contents of the display cells in positions 10-16 of row 10 are copied into VIDEOBUF. Note that in this case, the read length and the buffer size are equal to twice the number of cells read (14 versus 7). This is because each cell is really 2 bytes long (character, attribute). If you use this function, make sure that you take this fact into account when you allocate the input buffer.

Scrolling Screen Data

Up to this point, you have seen how to write information on the display on an individual character (or string) basis. If you write a small program using these functions, you will notice that it performs significantly faster than a similar program that uses DosWrite to write data. You gain this performance without sacrificing the benefits of application/ hardware isolation.

Suppose that you have written a screenful of information and want to move all the data up one line. By using the VIO cell read/write routines, you could read each individual line and write it in the previous line. For instance, consider the program shown in Figure 14-16.

As you see, the example starts with line 1 (the second line) and loops through line 24 (the bottom line). For each line, it reads the contents of the line with VioReadCellStr and then writes it to the previous line with VioWrtCellStr. Although this technique will work, it does not operate as quickly as would a direct (block) memory move within the video buffer. However, if you access the video buffer di-

```
Data Segment ...

linebuf     db      80*2 dup (' ')          ;Input buffer
blen        dw        $ - offset linebuf    ;buffer length


Code Segment ...

            mov     cx,25                   ;line count
            mov     dx,1                    ;initial line number
;
scrup:      @VioReadCellStr linebuf,blen,dx,0,0 ;read line in row n
            mov     bx,dx                   ;get current line number
            dec     bx                      ;previous line
            @VioWrtCellStr  linebuf,blen,bx,0,0 ;write the line to n-1
            inc     dx                      ;next line number
            loop    scrup                   ;go get next line
```

Figure 14-16. Code to loop and to move data up one line

rectly, your application forfeits screen independence.

Since it is a common application function, VIO includes a series of API functions that scroll the screen data with a single function call. The APIs VioScrollUp, VioScrollDn, VioScrollLe, and VioScrollRi scroll the screen up, down, left, and right, respectively. The parameters for VioScrollUp are as follows:

WORD	A one-word value defining the top row of the scroll area
WORD	A one-word value defining the left column of the scroll area
WORD	A one-word value defining the bottom row of the scroll area
WORD	A one-word value defining the right column of the scroll area
WORD	A one-word value defining the number of rows that OS/2 is to scroll. **Note:** A −1 causes OS/2 to "clear" the area
PTR	A pointer to a 2-byte cell (attr,char) that OS/2 uses to fill the scrolled area
WORD	The VIO handle (must be 0)

The parameters for VioScrollDn are as follows:

WORD	A one-word value defining the top row of the scroll area
WORD	A one-word value defining the left column of the scroll area
WORD	A one-word value defining the bottom row of the scroll area
WORD	A one-word value defining the right column of the scroll area
WORD	A one-word value defining the number of rows that OS/2 is to scroll. **Note**: A −1 causes OS/2 to "clear" the area
PTR	A pointer to a 2-byte cell (attr,char) that OS/2 uses to fill the scrolled area
WORD	The VIO handle (must be 0)

The parameters for VioScrollRi are as follows:

WORD	A one-word value defining the top row of the scroll area
WORD	A one-word value defining the left column of the scroll area
WORD	A one-word value defining the bottom row of the scroll area
WORD	A one-word value defining the right column of the scroll area
WORD	A one-word value defining the number of columns that OS/2 is to scroll. **Note**: A −1 causes OS/2 to "clear" the area
PTR	A pointer to a 2-byte cell (attr,char) that OS/2 uses to fill the scrolled area
WORD	The VIO handle (must be 0)

The parameters for VioScrollRi are as follows:

WORD	A one-word value defining the top row of the scroll area
WORD	A one-word value defining the left column of the scroll area
WORD	A one-word value defining the bottom row of the scroll area
WORD	A one-word value defining the right column of the scroll area
WORD	A one-word value defining the number of columns that OS/2 is to scroll. **Note**: A −1 causes OS/2 to "clear" the area
PTR	A pointer to a 2-byte cell (attr,char) that OS/2 uses to fill the scrolled area
WORD	The VIO handle (must be 0)

For example, the code in Figure 14-17 scrolls the screen up one line and fills the bottom line with blanks. With a single function call, you have implemented precisely the same function you saw in the previous example. Also, since it is a single atomic operation, the VIO subsys-

```
Data Segment ...

fill        db          ' ',07h              ;Blank character cell

Code Segment ...

            @VioScrollUp 0,0,24,80,1,fill,0
```

Figure 14-17. Code to scroll screen up one line and fill bottom with blanks

```
Data Segment ...

fill        db          ' ',07h              ;Blank character cell

Code Segment ...

            @VioScrollLe 3,5,7,15,3,fill,0
```

Figure 14-18.   Code to move screen data to left

tem can optimize the video memory accesses, and you wind up with a rapid data scroll.

But that is not all. As you see in its API definition, VioScrollUp also enables you to define the scroll coordinates and the number of lines to be scrolled. Thus, if you define coordinates other than the four corners of the screen, then you can use the scroll API calls to scroll a small window in the display an arbitrary number of lines. For instance, the code in Figure 14-18 scrolls the data within an area defined by the screen coordinates (3,5) and (7,15) left three columns. As you see in Figure 14-19, this results in moving a small portion of the screen to the left without disturbing the remainder of the screen.

```
                1           2                             1           2
        012345678901234567890123 4//            012345678901234567890123 4//
      ╔═══════════════════════════//          ╔═══════════════════════════//
  0   ║ Name List:                     0       ║ Name List:
  1   ║                                1       ║
  2   ║                                2       ║
  3   ║    123. Dave Hocker            3       ║    12Dave Hoc    ker
  4   ║    124. Eddie Hoyal            4       ║    12Eddie Ho    yal
  5   ║    125. Xylocane Co.           5       ║    12Xylocane    Co.
  6   ║    126. Bill Wellberry         6       ║    12Bill Wel    lberry
  7   ║    127. FWIJ Is.               7       ║    12FWIJ Is.
  8   ║    128. Ken Tucker             8       ║    128. Ken Tucker
  9   ║                                9       ║
      ║                                        ║
      ╱                                        ╱
      ╱                                        ╱
```

Figure 14-19.   Scrolling screen data

The other powerful side effect of the VIO scrolling APIs is that if you specify a scroll count of FFFFh (−1), then they will fill the window with the fill character, totally discarding the previous window contents. Thus, if you use a fill cell that corresponds to a blank, then the window is actually cleared. If you make the window the entire screen, then you clear the screen with a single API call.

Popups

In a multitasking system such as OS/2, a program may urgently need to communicate with the user, yet it is not currently the foreground program. For example, if a program is monitoring the state of an external device, such as a communications line, it might have to interrupt the user when the communications session is lost. Or, if the program is a print spooler, it might need to tell the user that the printer has just run out of paper.

If such a program uses VIO services to write data to the screen while it is in the background, the screen updates will be made to the session's logical video buffer (LVB), but they will not appear on the physical screen until the user switches the session to the foreground. Furthermore, certain OS/2 programs are associated with display sessions that can never be selected as the foreground session. For example, programs started with the RUN statement in the CONFIG.SYS file or DETACH (from the command line) are put into "null" display sessions that never appear in the application selection list.

The communications line monitor and the print spooler certainly qualify as programs that do not normally need their own display sessions. You might start them in null sessions. However, they do need to have the ability to force themselves to the foreground when they encounter a catastrophic situation requiring user intervention.

This is precisely why OS/2 has the VioPopUp function.

VioPopUp enables a program to "grab" the input focus (keyboard, mouse, video) by preempting the current foreground session. The parameters for VioPopUp are as follows:

PTR	Pointer to a one-word option flags field:
	RRRRRRRR RRRRRRXW
	R = Reserved
	X = Transparency indicator
	0 − Nontransparent
	1 − Transparent (text modes only)
	W = Wait flag
	0 − return with error if popup is not available
	1 − wait for popup
WORD	The VIO handle (must be 0)

When a program issues this API, it becomes the foreground session. This means that until it ends the popup operation (with VioEndPopUp), it can read from the keyboard and mouse, and write data to the screen.

For example, consider the program shown in Figure 14-20. When the program encounters a particular event, it jumps to an error routine. This routine places itself into the foreground, writes a message to the user, then waits for keyboard input. When the user enters a keystroke, the routine performs some type of recovery actions. Later when the recovery actions are complete, the routine issues VioEndPopUp to return to the background and reinstate the preempted foreground session. The parameter for VioEndPopUp is as follows:

WORD	The VIO handle (must be 0)

Notice that the VioPopUp function accepts an options word that contains several option flags. The first flag tells OS/2 whether you want it to clear the screen before the program is given the input focus. If you indicate that you want the screen cleared (nontransparent popup), then the

```
            cmp     ax,0                 ;error?
            jne     error                ;yes - go pop up
                      .
                      .
                      .

error:      @VioPopUp popopt,0                ;put myself in foreground
            @VioWrtCharStrAtt msg,MSGL,10,10,red,0 ;Write Panic! message
;
            @KbdCharIn kbdbuf,0,0             ;get character from user

                      .
                      .
                      .

            @VioEndPopUp 0                   ;return to background
```

Figure 14-20.   An error popup

popup always works, regardless of the foreground session video mode. With nontransparent popups, OS/2 always resets the video mode to a text display mode and clears the screen buffer before it gives your program the foreground session. This kind of popup request works even when the foreground session is running the display in a graphics display mode.

If you request a transparent popup, then it only succeeds if the foreground session (which you are interrupting) is running in a text mode. If it is in a graphics mode, VioPopUp returns an error code. This restriction exists because when you switch a display from graphics mode to text mode, the meaning of the data in the video buffer also changes. Thus, whatever graphics information is in the portions of the screen you do not overwrite is meaningless and would be displayed as random garbage.

Thus, if you want to put up a small popup window over the existing session, you should write your program so that it first tries to put up a transparent popup, and if that fails, then put up a nontransparent popup. For example, consider the code in Figure 14-21.

```
error:      mov       popopt,3              ;transparent pop-up
            aVioPopUp popopt,0              ;put myself in foreground
            ajaxz     doit                  ;continue if OK
            mov       popopt,1              ;non-transparent pop-up
            aVioPopUp popopt,0              ;put myself in foreground
;
doit:       aVioWrtCharStrAtt msg,MSGL,10,10,red,0 ;Write Panic! message


                      .
                      .
                      .


            aVioEndPopUp 0                  ;return to background
```

Figure 14-21. Code to attempt transparent popup

You should be aware of several other things about
VioPopUp. First (and probably most significantly), OS/2
only allows a single popup at a time. Thus, if you ask for a
popup while another program has an active popup, your
request fails. The VioPopUp API also includes a WAIT/
NOWAIT option that tells OS/2 whether you want it to
block until the popup is available. If you specify NOWAIT,
then VioPopUp fails with an error code if the system cannot give you the foreground session. Thus, if you have an
urgent condition of which the user must be aware, you
could implement the type of algorithm shown in Figure
14-22.

Notice that the first VioPopUp request is the NOWAIT
variety, so if OS/2 refuses the popup, the program receives
an error code. In this error situation, the program generates a short beep to warn the user, then re-issues
VioPopUp with the WAIT option. While this may not guarantee that the user will clear the existing popup (or that
the user even *can* clear the popup), it does warn the user
that something else is awaiting attention.

While a popup is on the screen, the system does not
allow the user to change display sessions. In fact, even the
session hotkeys are not active. Before you can do anything

```
error:          mov       popopt,0              ;NOWAIT pop-up
                @VioPopUp popopt,0              ;put myself in foreground
                @jaxz     doit                  ;continue if OK
                @DosBeep  1000,100              ;sound user alarm
                mov       popopt,1              ;WAIT pop-up
                @VioPopUp popopt,0              ;wait for pop-up
;
doit:           @VioWrtCharStrAtt msg,MSGL,10,10,red,0 ;Write Panic! message


                        .
                        .
                        .


                @VioEndPopUp 0                 ;return to background
```

Figure 14-22.   A conditional popup with a warning beep

else with the display, you must clear the popup. Note that this does not imply that the dispatcher stops running other threads. Even while a popup is active, the application threads continue to get timeslices. The popup only blocks the OS/2 session-management functions. However, if a background program attempts to write to the screen with a VIO function, it too blocks until the popup is dismissed.

When an application program requests (and receives) the foreground session by using the VioPopUp function, it can access the screen with the normal VIO API calls. However, certain things are not permitted from a popup. These restrictions are summarized in Table 14-3.

On the basis of what you already know about VIO, the most notable restrictions on this list are that you cannot nest VioPopUp calls nor can you change the display mode. The remaining restrictions deal with other, more primitive forms of video I/O that are discussed later in this chapter.

By now you have probably surmised that the VioPopUp function is not intended for "normal" application popups (such as a menu-selection list). If anything, the VioPopUp name is somewhat misleading. It might better be called VioTakeOverScreen. You should use this function most

Table 14-3.   Disallowed API Functions During VioPopUp

Subsystem Control	*Physical Screen I/O*
VioRegister	VioGetPhysBuf
VioDeRegister	VioScrLock
	VioScrUnLock
	VioSaveRedrawWait
Logical Screen I/O	VioSaveRedrawUndo
VioGetBuf	VioModeWait
VioShowBuf	VioModeUndo
Video Mode Control	*Popups*
VioSetMode	VioPopUp

judiciously. If too many programs were to arbitrarily issue popups, the user would not be able to effectively run the system.

Most application programs do not need the VioPopUp function. You should only seriously consider using it if you intend to write a "detached" program, in which case you have no other way to communicate with the user.

Using the System LVB

Thus far, you have seen how to use VIO API functions to indirectly manipulate the display buffer. In fact, the VIO character I/O APIs actually hide the video buffer from your application. Other than having a basic understanding of the screen geometry (number of rows and columns), VIO programs do not deal with the display as a "buffer."

Since character VIO calls continue to work even when the session is in the background, the system must maintain a "logical" representation of each session's display buffer. As discussed in Chapter 9, this logical buffer does indeed exist and is called the logical video buffer (LVB). OS/2 maintains an LVB per display session. The VIO calls shield you from your LVB. For instance, when you use VioWrtCharStr to write a character string, the routine actually writes the data to the LVB, on your behalf.

If for some reason the character VIO API functions are not well-suited to your application program, you can directly access the session LVB. In this way, a program can use its own video routines to read or write data from the "logical" display, while still maintaining a level of hardware independence.

The VioGetBuf API returns a selector that maps the LVB. The parameters of VioGetBuf are as follows:

PTR	Pointer to a double-word area into which OS/2 places a far pointer to the LVB
PTR	Pointer to a one-word field into which OS/2 places the LVB size (in bytes)
WORD	A one-word VIO handle (0)

After loading the selector in a segment register, you can directly manipulate the contents of the LVB. For example, the code in Figure 14-23 replaces the display cells at locations 810-816 with the cell contained in the field FILL. Notice that this is exactly equivalent to one of the previous examples, which cleared line 10, columns 10-16 by using VioWrtNCell. This is because (assuming the display is in 80-column mode) offset 810 into the display buffer is equivalent to line 10 (10*80), column 10. Also note that the sample deals with the buffer as a word array. Each word contains a character byte and an attribute byte.

```
Data Segment ...

fill      dw      2007              ;Blank character cell
lvbp      dd      0                 ;LVB pointer
lvbl      dd      0                 ;LVB length


Code Segment ...

          @VioGetBuf lvbp,lvbl,0    ;get LVB
          les     di,lvbp           ;address LVB
          mov     cx,7              ;replicate count
          add     di,810            ;Row 10, Col 10 offset
          mov     ax,fill           ;fill cell
          rep     movsb             ;initialize field
```

Figure 14-23. Code to replace display cells with cell contained in FILL

But this example does not actually update the physical display. All the program has done is to update an internal VIO work buffer. To make the changes appear on the screen, the program must issue a VioShowBuf call. VioShowBuf updates a portion of the screen by using the data contained in LVB. The parameters of VioShowBuf are as follows:

WORD	Offset into the LVB where OS/2 is to begin refreshing the physical screen
WORD	Length of the refreshed area
WORD	A one-word VIO handle (0)

Your program tells VioShowBuf what part of the screen should be refreshed. Thus,

```
@VioShowBuf 810,7,0              :display LVB
```

refreshes the physical screen in the screen locations 810—816, which happens to be where you just modified the LVB. Note that you are not required to immediately issue

VioShowBuf after modifying the LVB. In fact, you could modify numerous areas in the screen, then refresh the entire screen.

How much and how frequently you "show" the LVB really depends on how your application updates the screen. The more you can show in one shot, the "cheaper" the per-character display cost. Conversely, the less frequently you show the LVB, the "jerkier" the display becomes. The only way to pick the best algorithm for your application is to experiment with the APIs until you find something that works for you.

Note that even though you are manipulating an LVB, the actual hardware access is still being done by OS/2. Thus, you do not have to worry about device-specific quirks (such as synchronizing the video buffer access on a CGA adapter). OS/2 takes care of those details for you when it writes the data to the physical buffer.

You should also note that the LVB is only valid when the display is in text mode. If you write a graphics application (or subsystem), you must directly manipulate the video hardware. You may question why this is so, but there really is a method behind the madness. In most of today's graphics adapters (EGA, VGA, and so forth), a program that writes graphics to the display must also manipulate hardware I/O ports as it writes the data (such as to select color "planes"). Since VioShowBuf has no notion of when to do OUT instructions, it really cannot process graphics displays.

VioGetBuf and VioShowBuf are similar to the Top-View INT 10H FE/FF function calls. If you are porting an existing application written to be "TopView-aware," you should consider using these functions to access the display device. However, if you are writing a new application, you should first consider the character VIO functions, since their performance characteristics in most cases are more than adequate for building a highly interactive PC application program.

Direct Screen Manipulation

The final form of OS/2 video I/O is direct hardware manipulation. This is the least desirable form of OS/2 video I/O. In PC DOS, direct manipulation of the display is the preferred video-interface technique, partially because it is not too hard to do and partially because the alternatives are not good (BIOS and DOS services are just too slow).

In OS/2, multiple application programs share the video hardware, so direct hardware access is much trickier. Also, the alternative video interfaces perform reasonably well, so the incentive to run directly on the hardware is minimized. However, if your application is a graphics program, and you intend to write the graphics interface routines yourself, then you must use the techniques described in this section.

The first thing you must do to access the video hardware directly is to gain addressability to the physical display buffer. To do this, you call the VioGetPhysBuf API. The parameters for VioGetPhysBuf are as follows:

PTR	Pointer to a physical display buffer data structure
	Note: You must allocate enough space in this structure to hold n selectors, where n=(display memory/64K)+1
WORD	A one-word VIO handle (0)

VioGetPhysBuf expects a physical buffer parameter list with the following format:

DD	Buffer address (32-bit)
DD	Total buffer length
DW	Selector #1
DW	Selector #2
.	
.	
.	
DW	Selector #*n*

You initialize the first double-word to contain the physical address (in 32-bit form) of the buffer you want to access. For example, the EGA buffer address would be represented as A0000H. The next double-word contains the total buffer length you want to access. If you do not correctly initialize fields before calling VioGetPhysBuf, the request fails.

On return from VioGetPhysBuf, the selector array contains one or more selectors that your program can load to address each 64K portion of the total display buffer. Note that the number of selectors corresponds to the total buffer length/64K.

Thus, a 128K EGA buffer would have two selectors — one to address the first 64K and the other to address the last 64K. You are responsible for allocating a data structure large enough to contain all the selectors needed to map the display. To determine this you can divide the total display memory size (from VioGetConfig) by 64K. If you do not allocate a buffer large enough to hold the entire parameter area, VioGetPhysBuf will fail.

To get access to the physical buffer, you would write a program like the one shown in Figure 14-24. You must load the selector(s) into a segment register (in this case, ES) to access the display buffer. But the display selectors are valid only while the program is in the foreground session. If the user switches the program to the background,

```
Data Segment ...

physbuf     label    far
phystart    dd       0A0000h                  ;Physical buffer offset (32-bit)
phyleng     dd       2000h                    ;Physical buffer length (32-bit)
physel1     dw       0                        ;Physical buffer selector #1
physel2     dw       0                        ;Physical buffer selector #2
physel3     dw       0                        ;Physical buffer selector #3
physel4     dw       0                        ;Physical buffer selector #4

Code Segment ...

            @VioGetPhysBuf physbuf,0          ;get pd selectors
            push     physel1                  ;copy first selector
            pop      es                       ;to ES
```

Figure 14-24. Code to gain access to physical buffer

OS/2 temporarily invalidates the selectors to protect the integrity of the display. The program must only access the buffer while it is in the foreground. Otherwise, it will cause a general-protection fault.

To make sure it has exclusive control of the screen, a physical screen I/O program must "lock" the screen by using the VioScrLock API before it references the video buffer and "unlock" the screen using VioScrUnlock when it finishes. The parameters for VioScrLock are as follows:

WORD	A one-word wait flag: 0 = Return if screen is not available (NOWAIT) 1 = Wait until screen is available
PTR	Pointer to a one-word field in which OS/2 places the lock success code (if NOWAIT option is used): 0 = Lock successful 1 = Lock unsuccessful
WORD	A one-word VIO handle (0)

The parameter for VioScrUnLock is as follows:

WORD	A one-word VIO handle (0)

While it holds the screen lock the direct video I/O program has exclusive use of the screen. This means that, for the duration of the screen lock, the session manager will not honor any requests to switch to the foreground session (originating from the user or from another program). For example, the following program fragment

```
@VioScrLock    1,rc,0          ;lock the screen
call       write_dot           ;write pel
@VioScrUnLock  0               ;unlock the screen
```

locks the screen, calls a subroutine to write a graphics pel, then frees the screen. Because of the dire consequences of locking the display, you must avoid doing so for extended periods of time.

On the other hand, if you lock and unlock the display too frequently, the visible performance of your application program may be adversely impacted. Like other aspects of the video interface, the optimal lock granularity is dependent on your program's characteristics. The "right" value undoubtedly will differ from application to application.

When you call VioScrLock, you indicate whether it should block your program until the screen is available (WAIT), or return immediately (NOWAIT). The NOWAIT option allows a program to continue processing while it is in the background (without updating the screen, of course). When the user eventually switches the program back to the foreground, the lock succeeds and the program can refresh the physical screen image.

Figure 14-25 illustrates this technique. Notice that in this example, the program calls VioScrLock with the NOWAIT option (0). If the lock succeeds (RC=0), it updates the screen (as before). If the lock does not succeed, the screen is not available, so the program drops to a different logic loop that continues to compute data points and saves them in an internal structure (with SAVE—DOT). During this cycle, the program still attempts to get the screen by continuing to call VioScrLock (NOWAIT).

```
grf010:    call      compute_dot        ;compute next data point
           @VioScrLock 0,rc,0           ;lock the screen
           cmp       rc,0               ;lock successful?
           jne       grf050             ;no - go save data
           call      write_dot          ;write the data point
           @VioScrUnLock  0             ;unlock the screen
           jmp       grf010             ;continue processing dots
;
grf050:    call      save_dot           ;save display point
           call      compute_dot        ;compute next data point
           @VioScrLock 0,rc,0           ;lock the screen
           cmp       rc,0               ;lock successful?
           jne       grf050             ;no - go save it
           call      restore_dots       ;restore the saved points
           @VioScrUnLock  0             ;unlock the screen
           jmp       grf010             ;continue processing dots
```

Figure 14-25. Program to refresh physical screen image

When the user switches the program back to the foreground, the lock succeeds, and the program calls RESTORE—DOTS to refresh the saved data. It then unlocks the screen and returns to the primary (foreground) display loop. With this type of structure, the graphics program continues to run while it is in the background but it does not update the display.

You should consider one other important point when you write this type of application program. OS/2 does not save and restore the entire video buffer when the user switches sessions. OS/2 only saves the portion of the display buffer that is used in the video adapter text mode(s). Since this is normally only 4K, the majority of the graphics display buffer is unprotected.

If your program runs the display in a graphics mode, it is responsible for saving and restoring its own display buffer. To do this, the program must be notified when it is being moved from the foreground to the background (and vice versa). OS/2 introduces the notion of a SaveRedrawWait thread.

A SaveRedrawWait thread is a special application thread of execution that waits for notification the session state is about to change and takes the appropriate action(s). If a session is about to be moved to the background, the SaveRedrawWait thread saves the screen buffer contents (to private memory). If a session is about to be moved back to the foreground, the thread restores the buffer.

To use this function, an application program creates a dedicated thread. This thread then registers itself as the SaveRedrawWait thread by issuing the VioSaveRedrawWait API call. The parameters of VioSaveRedrawWait are:

WORD	A one-word request type: 0 = Notify on save or redraw 1 = Notify on redraw only
PTR	Pointer to a one-word field in which OS/2 places a notification type code: 0 = save the screen image 1 = restore the screen image
WORD	A one-word VIO handle (0)

OS/2 blocks the thread at the call. Right before the application session state is about to change, OS/2 unblocks the thread by returning from the call. The thread examines the SAVE/REDRAW indicator and either saves or restores the video buffer contents. When it finishes, the thread once again calls the VioSaveRedrawWait API to wait for the next session change. Thus, the thread is a dedicated "exit routine" that the OS/2 session manager runs when the session state changes.

Consider the SaveRedrawWait routine shown in Figure 14-26. It starts by allocating a single (64K) private buffer in which it can save the display buffer. Then it issues the VioSaveRedrawWait call to wait for the session change notification. When it returns from the call, it checks the field SRTYPE to determine if it must save or restore the screen. If it is a save request, it copies the contents of the

```
redraw    proc
;
          @DosAllocSeg  0,savsel1,0
;
loopdraw: @VioSavRedrawWait 0,srtype,0
          cmp       srtype,0
          je        save
          jmp       restore
;
save:     push      ds
          push      savsel1          ;target segment
          pop       es
          push      physel1          ;source segment
          pop       ds
          xor       di,di
          xor       si,si
          mov       cx,8000h
          rep       movsw
          pop       ds
          jmp       loopdraw
;
restore:  push      ds
          push      physel1          ;target segment
          pop       es
          push      savsel1          ;source segment
          pop       ds
          xor       di,di
          xor       si,si
          mov       cx,8000h
          rep       movsw
          pop       ds
          jmp       loopdraw
;
redraw    endp
```

Figure 14-26.   SaveRedrawWait routine

physical buffer into the save buffer. If it is a restore call, it does the opposite. Note that, at most, only one thread per session can issue the VioSaveRedrawWait call. If a second thread attempts to register itself, the API call fails.

To cancel an active SaveRedrawWait thread, a different thread can use the VioSaveRedrawUndo API. The parameters of VioSaveRedrawUndo are as follows:

WORD	A one-word ownership indicator:
	0 = Process should reserve ownership of SaveRedrawWait
	1 = Process can give up ownership
WORD	A one word "kill" indicator:
	0 = Do not kill SaveRedrawWait thread
	1 = Kill SaveRedrawWait thread
WORD	A one-word VIO handle (0)

This call can only be made by another thread in the same process that contains the current SaveRedrawWait thread. When you cancel the thread, you request that OS/2 either terminate (kill) the SaveRedrawWait thread, or that it terminate the VioSaveRedrawWait call with an error code. In either case, the thread no longer waits for the SaveRedraw event.

Similarly, you use VioModeWait and VioModeUndo to create and cancel another (dedicated) thread that is called whenever the video mode needs to be restored. The parameters of VioModeWait are as follows:

WORD	A one-word request type. Must be set to 0.
PTR	Pointer to a one-word field in which OS/2 places a type code. The only code supported in OS/2 1.0 is 0 (restore mode).
WORD	A one-word VIO handle (0)

The parameters for VioModeUndo are as follows:

WORD	A one-word ownership indicator:
	0 = Process should reserve ownership of ModeWait
	1 = Process can give up ownership
WORD	A one-word "kill" indicator:
	0 = Do not kill ModeWait thread
	1 = Kill ModeWait thread
WORD	A one-word VIO handle (0)

In particular, OS/2 calls this thread after a popup operation. Since popups can only operate in text modes, OS/2 automatically saves and restores the first 4K of the display buffer. Thus, the SaveRedrawWait thread does not have to be called. However, the ModeWait thread is called to restore the application video mode, which was reset to a text mode for the popup.

Directly accessing the OS/2 video buffer requires somewhat more work than in PC DOS. But this should not be a surprise. In OS/2, the physical screen is shared between multiple application programs, so all the direct accesses must be serialized.

You should generally avoid writing direct video access programs. Not only are they harder to write, they are also less portable (such as to future OS/2 versions). If you are writing a text-mode program, stick with the character VIO functions. If your program displays graphics, you can either use the functions described in this section or use a graphics package (such as the BASIC/2 compiler or VDI).

Manipulating the Cursor

Unlike the equivalent BIOS INT 10H functions, OS/2 VIO calls (other than VioWrtTTY) update the screen without moving the cursor. At first glance, this may seem like an oversight, but it is not. Moving the cursor is a relatively expensive operation. If you move it each time you write a character, you significantly slow down the performance of the screen operations. By "decoupling" the cursor movement from the screen-update functions, the VIO subsystem is able to significantly improve the speed of the screen operations.

In fact, this separation is not a serious problem because most interactive application programs update the screen and move the cursor independently. For instance, if you take a close look at a typical spreadsheet, you find that most of the time it updates the screen it does not move the cursor. In fact, the only time the cursor moves is when you type data into a cell. If you had to position the cursor each time you wrote to a random portion of the screen, you would be constantly moving it about needlessly.

The VIO character functions do not affect the position of the cursor. To move it, you use the VioSetCursorPos API. The parameters for VioSetCursorPos are as follows:

WORD	Cursor row number
PTR	Cursor column number
WORD	A one-word VIO handle (0)

For example, the code in Figure 14-27 writes a character (CHR1) in row 10, column 10, increments the column number, and then moves the cursor one position (row 10, column 11).

If you need to find out where the cursor is located, you can use the VioGetCursorPos API. The parameters for VioGetCursorPos are as follows:

PTR	Pointer to a one-word field in which OS/2 returns the current cursor row number.
PTR	Pointer to a one-word field in which OS/2 returns the current cursor row.
WORD	A one-word VIO handle (0).

```
mov      bx,10               ;row number
mov      dx,10               ;column number
@VioWrtCellStr chr1,1,bx,dx,0  ;Write character
inc      dx                  ;next column
@VioSetCursorPos bx,dx,0      ;move the cursor
```

Figure 14-27. Code to write a character and move the cursor

```
Data Segment ...

crow        dw        0                    ;cursor row
ccol        dw        0                    ;cursor column

Code Segment ...

            @VioGetCursorPos crow,ccol,0   ;get cursor position
```

Figure 14-28. Code to request current cursor row and column

For instance, the code in Figure 14-28 requests the current cursor row and column. On return from the call, the field CROW contains the current cursor row number, and CCOL contains the column number.

In some situations, you may want to change the "thickness" of the cursor. For instance, many application programs use a normal cursor while in text overlay mode and a large cursor when in "insert" mode. The cursor size is determined by the number of scan lines it comprises. The default size of the OS/2 cursor depends on the display adapter character cell size, but is normally the two lowest scan lines in the character cell.

To change the cursor size, you use the VioSetCurType API. The parameters for VioSetCurType are as follows:

PTR	Pointer to a cursor type data area:
	DW Cursor start line
	DW Cursor end line
	DW Cursor width
	DW Cursor attribute (-1=hidden)
WORD	The VIO handle (must be 0)

To use this API, you pass it a pointer to a data structure that contains the desired cursor size and attribute. Note that although this structure includes the cursor width, it is effectively ignored in OS/2 release 1.0. This field will be used to define the number of pels in the cursor when VIO supports text graphics (in a future release).

```
Data Segment ...

cursline    dw      1               ;cursor start line
cureline    dw      7               ;cursor end line
curwidth    dw      1               ;cursor width
curattr     dw      0               ;cursor attribute


Code Segment ...

            @VioSetCurType cursline,0      ;Set cursor size
```

Figure 14-29.　Code to change cursor to seven-scan-line cursor

In the initial release of OS/2, the field must be set to 0 (default width) or 1 (one character width). Similarly, the cursor attribute field can only be set to 0 (visible) or −1 (invisible).

Thus, the code shown in Figure 14-29 changes the cursor to a seven-scan-line cursor that starts at line 1 and goes to scan line 7. Since the API enables you to define the start and end scan lines, you can not only define the size, but also the position of the cursor (top, middle, or bottom of the cell). Figure 14-30 illustrates the relationship of the cursor to the cell size.

Note that if you intend to change the cursor size, your program must be aware of the number of scan lines per character cell. Since this will vary between display adapters and video modes, you should first query the adapter type with VioGetConfig and the display mode with VioGetMode. In order to retrieve the current cursor size you can use the VioGetCurType API. The parameters for VioGetCurType are

PTR	Pointer to a cursor type data area:
	DW　Cursor start line
	DW　Cursor end line
	DW　Cursor width
	DW　Cursor attribute (−1=hidden)
WORD	The VIO handle (must be 0)

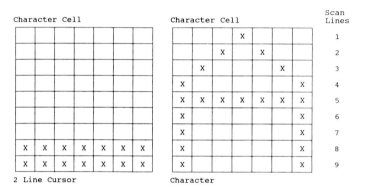

Figure 14-30.   Cursor size versus character cell

VioGetCurType uses the same data structure as VioSetCurType to return the cursor information. The code in Figure 14-31 returns the cursor information in the structure named CURDATA. The data structure named CUR (in OS2MAC.INC) maps the cursor structure.

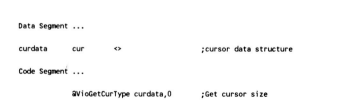

```
Data Segment ...

curdata      cur      <>                  ;cursor data structure

Code Segment ...

         @VioGetCurType curdata,0    ;Get cursor size
```

Figure 14-31.   Code to return cursor information to CURDATA

In some applications, you might want to hide the cursor altogether. This can be accomplished by setting the cursor display attribute to −1. However, you should always try to leave the cursor size unchanged when you reset the attribute, rather than re-initializing it to some arbitrary shape. The following code will do the trick:

```
@VioGetCurType curdata,0      ;Get cursor size
mov        curdata.curattr,-1 ;set 'hidden' attribute
@VioSetCurType curdata,0      ;Set cursor size
```

This code first queries the current cursor size, changes the cursor attribute, and finally calls VioSetCurType to hide it. When you restore the cursor, you reverse the procedure, as follows:

```
@VioGetCurType curdata,0      ;Get cursor size
mov        curdata.curattr,0  ;set 'default' attribute
@VioSetCurType curdata,0      ;Set cursor size
```

Two macros (@HideCursor and @ShowCursor) are included in the OS2MAC library to hide and restore the cursor using this technique.

Other VIO Functions

The VIO subsystem also enables you to change the display font and code page. Because of their similarities, fonts and code pages are often confused for one another. In reality, they are quite independent concepts.

A *font* defines the pel representation of a group of character cells. In fact, it is the shape of the characters. For example, one font might represent the letter "a" as an upright character, while another might represent it as an italic character. When you change the font, you do not change what character is displayed for each ASCII number. You just change the style of the character. Figure 14-32 illustrates this concept.

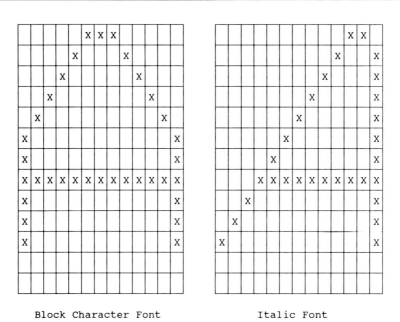

Block Character Font   Italic Font

Figure 14-32. Display fonts

A *code page*, on the other hand, is the mapping that associates ASCII code points to character numbers. Simply put, this means that the code page is what defines that the ASCII byte 41H corresponds to the letter "A," 42H to "B," and so forth. A code page does not define how the characters look, but only what they are.

If you live in the United States, you are probably accustomed to code page 437. However, OS/2 supports a number of different code pages for use in conjunction with different national languages. Code-page support becomes important if your application will run in a multilanguage environment. For example, a word processor could have a command that enables the user to switch between English and Portuguese displays to edit documents produced in

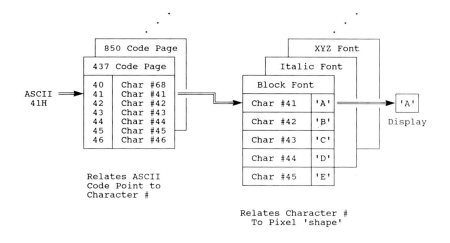

Figure 14-33. Code pages versus fonts

either code page. Figure 14-33 demonstrates the relationship of ASCII characters to display code points and fonts.

Changing the display font

You can use the VioSetFont API to change the active display font. The parameters for VioSetFont are as follows:

PTR	Pointer to a request block containing the information OS/2 needs to set the display font
WORD	A one-word VIO handle (0)

VioSetFont loads an arbitrary font definition into the display adapter. You must be sure that your adapter supports downloaded (RAM) fonts. Otherwise, the VioSetFont call will fail.

VioSetFont accepts a pointer to a font parameter request block (see Table 14-4). You may only use request type 0 (load RAM font) with the VioSetFont call.

Table 14-4. VIO Font Parameter Blocks

Type 0: GET/SET RAM Font

00	DW	Structure Length = 14
02	DW	Request Type = 0
04	DW	Pel columns in character cell
06	DW	Pel rows in character cell
08	DD	Far pointer to Font Definition Table
0A	DW	Font Definition Table length

Note: Only valid with EGA, VGA or 8514A adaptors

Type 1: GET ROM Font

00	DW	Structure Length = 14
02	DW	Request Type = 1
04	DW	Pel columns in character cell
06	DW	Pel rows in character cell
08	DD	Far pointer to ROM Font Definition Table
0A	DW	Font Definition Table length

Note: If pointer is set to 0, then OS/2 returns address of
      ROM area.

When you set a font with this API, OS/2 disables the active code page for the display session. If you call VioSetFont and then attempt to retrieve the code page (with VioGetCP), the function fails because OS/2 uses the display fonts to hold the video code pages. If you overwrite one of the fonts with a "private" font, you invalidate the active code page.

You can retrieve a font from the display adapter with theVioGetFont API. The parameters for VioGetFont are:

PTR	Pointer to a request block, in one of two formats:
	Type 0 Return RAM font (EGA, VGA)
	Type 1 Return ROM font (CGA, EGA, VGA)
WORD	A one-word VIO handle (0)

Depending on the data structure request code, VioGetFont either returns a pointer to the (default) ROM font, or the currently active (downloaded) RAM font. If you request a RAM font, you can either provide a buffer or request a system segment by setting the pointer value to 0. Likewise, if you request a ROM font, you can either provide a buffer or request a pointer to the actual ROM area by setting the buffer pointer to 0. The layout of the font itself is defined by the display adapter(s). Refer to the adapter technical reference manuals for more details.

If you are retrieving an internal (ROM) adapter font from a device that contains more than one font, you identify the desired one by setting the character cell width and height fields. Table 14-5 summarizes the ROM font sizes in the standard VIO display adapters.

Table 14-5. Display Adapter ROM Font Sizes

Adapter	*ROM Font(s)*				
CGA	8×8				
EGA	8×8,	8×14,	9×14		
VGA	8×8,	8×14,	9×14,	8×16,	9×16
8514A	8×8,	8×14,	9×14,	8×16,	9×16

Changing display code pages

In OS/2, the code-page support is implemented with down-loaded display fonts. During initialization, OS/2 loads the code-page font(s) into the display adapter on the basis of the CODEPAGE parameter in the CONFIG.SYS file. Naturally, this is only valid when the system has a display adapter that supports downloaded hardware fonts (such as an EGA or VGA).

A program may switch between the primary and back-up code pages with the VioSetCP API. The parameters of VioSetCP are as follows:

WORD	Reserved (must be 0)
WORD	A one-word code page number that OS/2 sets as the active video code page:
	000 Resident code page
	437 IBM PC US
	850 Multilingual
	860 Portuguese
	863 French-Canadian
	865 Nordic
	Note: The selected value must have been configured using the CODEPAGE= statement in the CONFIG.SYS file
WORD	A one-word VIO handle (must be 0)

VioSetCP tells OS/2 the code-page number (such as 437, 850, and so forth) you want the display to use. You must specify one of the two values that were loaded at initialization or VioSetCP will fail. When you change the display code page, you only affect the current display session. As the user switches from session to session, OS/2 automatically switches to the appropriate code pages.

Finally, the VioGetCP API enables you to determine the current (active) code-page number. The value will always be one of the two code page numbers set at system initialization. The parameters for VioGetCP are as follows:

WORD	Reserved (must be 0)
PTR	Pointer to a one-word field in which OS/2 returns the active video code page (see VioSet-CP)
WORD	A one-word VIO handle (must be 0)

Replacing Video Subsystem Functions

Now that you understand the capabilities of the OS/2 video I/O subsystem, consider how you can replace them with your own routines. As discussed in Chapter 9, the OS/2 subsystems are a set of modular subroutines that can be individually replaced. This enables you to write a program that extends or augments the VIO functions for all the other applications running in the session.

When you call the VioRegister API, you identify an alternate dynamic-link package that OS/2 uses to resolve the individual VIO calls. The parameters for VioRegister are as follows:

PTR	Pointer to an ASCIIZ module name that contains the dynamic-link replacement routine(s)
PTR	Pointer to an ASCIIZ entry point name within the dynamic-link module that is to gain control when the VIO function(s) are called by an application program
DWRD	A double-word function mask indicating which VIO functions are being replaced by this VioRegister call (1 of 2)
DWRD	A double-word function mask indicating which VIO functions are being replaced by this VioRegister call (2 of 2)

You tell OS/2 which VIO calls you want to process by setting one or more bits in a function-call bit map (see Figure 14-34).

Word0	Word1	Word2	Word3	API
------- -------	------- -------1	------- -------	------- -------	VioGetCurPos
------- -------	------- ------1-	------- -------	------- -------	VioGetCurType
------- -------	------- -----1--	------- -------	------- -------	VioGetMode
------- -------	------- ----1---	------- -------	------- -------	VioGetBuf
------- -------	------- ---1----	------- -------	------- -------	VioGetPhysBuf
------- -------	------- --1-----	------- -------	------- -------	VioSetCurPos
------- -------	------- -1------	------- -------	------- -------	VioSetCurType
------- -------	------- 1-------	------- -------	------- -------	VioSetMode
------- -------	------1 -------	------- -------	------- -------	VioShowBuf
------- -------	-----1- -------	------- -------	------- -------	VioReadCharStr
------- -------	----1-- -------	------- -------	------- -------	VioReadCellStr
------- -------	---1--- -------	------- -------	------- -------	VioWrtNChar
------- -------	--1---- -------	------- -------	------- -------	VioWrtNAttr
------- -------	-1----- -------	------- -------	------- -------	VioWrtNCell
------- -------	-1----- -------	------- -------	------- -------	VioWrtTTY
------- -------	1------- -------	------- -------	------- -------	VioWrtCharStr
------- ------1	------- -------	------- -------	------- -------	VioWrtCharStrAtt
------- -----1-	------- -------	------- -------	------- -------	VioWrtCellStr
------- ----1--	------- -------	------- -------	------- -------	VioScrollUp
------- ---1---	------- -------	------- -------	------- -------	VioScrollDn
------- --1----	------- -------	------- -------	------- -------	VioScrollLf
------- -1-----	------- -------	------- -------	------- -------	VioScrollRt
------- -1-----	------- -------	------- -------	------- -------	VioSetANSI
------- 1------	------- -------	------- -------	------- -------	VioGetANSI
------1 -------	------- -------	------- -------	------- -------	VioPrtSc
-----1- -------	------- -------	------- -------	------- -------	VioScrLock
----1-- -------	------- -------	------- -------	------- -------	VioScrUnLock
----1--- -------	------- -------	------- -------	------- -------	VioSavRedrawWait
---1---- -------	------- -------	------- -------	------- -------	VioSavRedrawUndo
--1----- -------	------- -------	------- -------	------- -------	VioPopUp
-1------ -------	------- -------	------- -------	------- -------	VioEndPopUp
1------- -------	------- -------	------- -------	------- -------	VioPrtScToggle
------- -------	------- -------	------- -------	------- ------1	VioModeWait
------- -------	------- -------	------- -------	------- -----1-	VioModeUndo
------- -------	------- -------	------- -------	------- ----1--	VioGetFont
------- -------	------- -------	------- -------	------- ---1---	VioGetConfig
------- -------	------- -------	------- -------	------- --1----	VioSetCP
------- -------	------- -------	------- -------	------- -1-----	VioGetCP
------- -------	------- -------	------- -------	------- -1-----	VioSetFont
------- -------	------- -------	------- -------	------- 1------	VioGetState
------- -------	------- -------	------- -------	------1 -------	VioSetState

Figure 14-34. VIO function-call register mask

When it receives each application VIO call, OS/2 first checks the VioRegister bit map. If it is a "registered" VIO function, it calls the replacement dynamic-link module. On entry, the dynamic-link module receives a stack frame that contains the following information:

```
(1-nn)   Normal function call parameters
  DD     Normal VIO far call
  DW     Function number
  DW     Near entry point                      ⎤  This information is
  DW     Caller's data segment (DS)            ⎦  inserted by OS/2
  DD     OS/2 (far) return address
```

The replacement dynamic-link routine can access the calling application's parameter information by backing up to the parameter information on the stack. The function number identifies which API you are processing (see Table 14-6); you can use this data to determine the number and type of user parameters.

Table 14-6. VIO Function Numbers

Function Number	*API*
0	VioGetPhysBuf
1	VioGetBuf
2	VioShowBuf
3	VioGetCurPos
4	VioGetCurType
5	VioGetMode

Table 14-6. *VIO Function Numbers (continued)*

Function Number	API
6	VioSetCurPos
7	VioSetCurType
8	VioSetMode
9	VioReadCharStr
10	VioReadCellStr
11	VioWrtNChar
12	VioWrtNAttr
13	VioWrtNCell
14	VioWrtCharStr
15	VioWrtCharStrAtt
16	VioWrtCellStr
17	VioWrtTTY
18	VioScrollUp
19	VioScrollDn
20	VioScrollLf
21	VioScrollRt
22	VioSetANSI
23	VioGetANSI
24	VioPrtSc
25	VioScrLock
26	VioScrUnLock
27	VioSavRedrawWait
28	VioSavRedrawUndo
29	VioPopUp
30	VioEndPopUp
31	VioPrtScToggle
32	VioModeWait
33	VioModeUndo
34	VioGetFont
35	VioGetConfig
36	VioSetCP
37	VioGetCP
38	VioSetFont
39	VioGetState
40	VioSetState

You may have noted that the function list includes a couple of VIO function calls not discussed in this chapter — VioPrtSc and VioPrtScToggle. The parameter for VioPrtScToggle is as follows:

| WORD | A one-word VIO handle (0) |

These functions are internal VIO interfaces called to print the current screen or to toggle the continuous print-screen function. While they cannot be called by an application program, they can be replaced. This is to allow you to process the screen-print functions in a manner consistent with your VIO extension. For example, if your VIO extension runs the display in a graphics mode, then it can interpret the screen contents and send the appropriate data to the printer.

The last double-word on the stack contains the return entry point into the VIO subsystem. When the dynamic-link module finishes processing the VIO call, it returns to OS/2 by calling this address. When you return, you set the AX register to tell OS/2 what you expect it to do with the request, as follows:

$AX = -1$ Pass the VIO call to the default VIO routine

$AX = $ other   Ignore this VIO call, pass AX to the application

Thus, a replacement VIO function can "change its mind" and instruct the VIO subsystem to process the function call by appropriately setting the AX register before it returns.

The registration remains in effect for the duration of the display session or until the process that issued VioRegister issues the VioDeRegister call. This function "detaches" the VIO extension and causes all subsequent VIO calls to again be processed by the base VIO services.

You should understand several "fine points" about VIO replacement. First, OS/2 allows only one process to register the VIO subsystem per session. If OS/2 receives a second VioRegister call while the first registration is still in effect, it fails the request. If the first process deregisters itself, then a second request is honored.

Secondly, a registered VIO extension sees the VIO requests made by all the processes running in the session. Thus, if the session contains more than one program that issues VIO calls, the registered program sees them all. The exception to this rule is if the extension processes VioPopUp calls and the application program issues VioPopUp while it is in the background. In this case, VIO uses the default VioPopUp routine.

Finally, VioRegister registers the extension in the session in which it is running. If you issue this function from a program that is in a "NULL" session, you may not get the results you expected. Most notably, the OS/2 DETACH command starts a program in a session different from the command-processor session. Thus, if you try to start a VIO extension in this way, it will not see the VIO calls issued by the other command-line programs.

Family API Considerations

Most of what has just been discussed is included as part of the OS/2 family API. This means that you can write PC DOS programs that take advantage of the VIO functions and performance. You can view the VIO subsystem as a set of "standard" video subroutines, with the added attraction that they happen to be the OS/2 system's native video interface. The only negative consequence is that the EXE file of a PC DOS application that uses these services will grow by approximately 22K. But this is a small price to pay considering the functional capabilities of the subsystem.

KEYBOARD I/O

In OS/2, keyboard I/O is also accomplished through a subsystem (KBD). Like video I/O, keyboard I/O has its file-system counterpart, DosRead. DosRead uses the keyboard subsystem to get input from the keyboard device. In fact, the VIO subsystem and the KBD subsystem have many parallels. Both are high-performance, high-function, low-level I/O facilities that are the basic building blocks for the OS/2 console I/O services.

If you are interested in I/O redirection, you should stick with DosRead. Otherwise, you can call the keyboard subsystem directly with the KBDXXXXX function calls. However, in the case of this subsystem, performance is not as much of a justification as it is function. Purely from a performance standpoint, the KBD functions and DosRead do not differ greatly.

However, the KBD I/O services get you somewhat "closer" to the keyboard hardware than the traditional character-stream I/O model. For instance, if your application needs to understand the key scan codes or shift states, then KBD is the way to go. If your application only uses "straight" ASCII character input, then DosRead will suffice. As always, you should carefully map out your application requirements before settling on which OS/2 APIs to use.

As discussed in Chapter 9, the KBD subsystem is a functional superset of the PC keyboard BIOS (INT 16H). You can view the KBD subsystem as a protected mode keyboard BIOS with numerous functional extensions. Like the VIO subsystem, KBD allows you to take over some or all of its API calls. Thus, you can replace or augment the subsystem functions with your own routines.

Getting Keyboard Input

With the KBD subsystem, you can read keyboard input in one of two ways: by character string or character-by-character. To read a character string, you use the KbdStringIn API. The parameters for KbdStringIn are as follows:

PTR	Pointer to an input character buffer. **Note:** This buffer must be large enough to hold the string whose length is in the buffer-length parameter
PTR	Pointer to a two-word buffer-length data structure: DW Input buffer length DW Returned data length
WORD	A one-word WAIT/NOWAIT indicator: 0 = Wait until the buffer is full (or CR pressed) 1 = Return immediately with whatever is in buffer
WORD	A one-word KBD handle (0 for default keyboard)

This API is similar to the DosRead function, except it doesn't require an open device handle, nor does it participate in I/O redirection. This is the low-level API that DosRead eventually calls to read information from the keyboard device.

KbdStringIn operates differently, depending on the current keyboard input mode. The keyboard modes are defined as follows:

ASCII	This is the default mode. In this mode, the keyboard is sensitive to the Carriage Return (CR) character. When the user enters a carriage return, the data is returned to the program (even if the buffer is not full). While in this mode, you must read the keyboard synchronously, so the KbdStringIn NOWAIT option is not supported. The "returned data length" field is used by OS/2 to determine how much of the

input buffer is to participate in the line-editing functions (such as F3 = retrieve last string, F1 = retrieve character, and so on). If you set this field to 0, then input editing is disabled. In this mode, two-byte (DBCS) character codes are returned in complete form

BINARY   Binary mode is equivalent to "raw" input mode. While in this mode, the buffer only is returned when filled, and the carriage return has no special meaning

ECHO   While ECHO mode is active, OS/2 automatically writes the characters on the screen as the user enters them. ECHO mode cannot be set in conjunction with BINARY input mode

You will see how to query and set keyboard modes later in this chapter.

To read a character string, you would write a program similar to the one shown in Figure 14-35. On input, the buffer-length data structure contains two values, each initialized to 10. This means that the user input (up to 10 bytes) is returned in the buffer named INBUF. Also, since the "returned data length" field is initialized to 10, OS/2 activates the line-editing keys. Thus, if the user presses the F3 key, then OS/2 places up to 10 bytes from the *previous* KbdStringIn request into the buffer.

```
Data Segment ...

inbuf      db      10 dup(' ')       ;Input buffer
iblen      dw      10                ;Input buffer length
rdlen      dw      10                ;returned data length

Code Degment ...

           @KbdStringIn inbuf,iblen,0,0   ;read from keyboard
```

Figure 14-35. Code to read character string

Note that you must allocate a buffer large enough to hold the number of ASCII characters specified in the buffer length. For example, if INBUF were not at least 10 bytes long, you would receive unpredictable results (possibly a general-protection fault).

As you probably noticed, KbdStringIn does not allow you to see the individual keyboard scan codes nor the shift state that was active when each key was pressed. In fact, this API returns an ASCII string much in the same way DosRead does.

If you need to see the detail keystroke information, you must use a different KBD API function called KbdCharIn. The parameters for KbdCharIn are as follows:

PTR	A pointer to a character input data structure: DB ASCII character code DB Scan code DB Character status DB NLS shift status DW Shift state DD Time stamp
WORD	A one-word value that tells OS/2 if it is to wait for the character: 0 = Wait for character 1 = Do not wait
WORD	A one-word KBD handle

KbdCharIn allows you to retrieve a single character from the keyboard. Unlike KbdStringIn, it also retrieves the keyboard state information that was in effect at the time the key was pressed.

To use this API, you pass it a pointer to an input character data structure (CHARBUF in OS2MAC.INC) in which OS/2 will return the specific character information. The CHARBUF data structure contains the following fields:

ASCII Code   The one-byte (translated) ASCII code that corresponds to the key. This is the output of the keyboard device driver translation routine. Certain keys, which have no ASCII counterparts, are passed as extended ASCII codes. If this is an extended ASCII code packet, then this field is set to 00h or E0h

Scan Code — Normally, this field contains the code generated by the keyboard to identify the key. However, if this is an extended ASCII data packet, then this field contains the extended ASCII code

Status — The status field contains information that describes the status of the input character. This is a bit-encoded byte where the individual bits have the meaning shown in Figure 14-36. Pay particular attention to bits 7 and 6. They define which byte of a multicharacter is included in this packet. So, 10 is first (or interim), 01 is last, and 11 is the only byte in character. To retrieve a multi-byte character (such as a DBCS character), you must call KbdCharIn once for each byte in the character

NLS Shift Status — Used in shift operations with National Language Support keyboards (reserved)

Shift State — A one-word field that describes the actual shift condition(s) in effect when the character was generated. See Figure 14-37 for the actual bit definitions

Time Stamp — A double-word (millisecond) time stamp corresponding to the time the key was generated

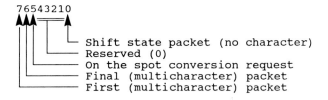

Figure 14-36. Bit-coded byte with meanings of bits

```
1------- --------   SysReq Key down
-1------ --------   Caps Lock Key down
--1----- --------   Num Lock Key down
---1---- --------   Scroll Lock Key down
----1--- --------   Right Alt Key down
-----1-- --------   Right Ctrl Key down
------1- --------   Left Alt Key down
-------1 --------   Left Ctrl Key down
-------- 1-------   Insert state on
-------- -1------   Caps lock state on
-------- --1-----   Num lock state on
-------- ---1----   Scroll lock state on
-------- ----1---   Either Alt key down
-------- -----1--   Either Ctrl key down
-------- ------1-   Left Shift key down
-------- -------1   Right Shift key down
```

Figure 14-37. Keyboard character data structure shift states

The IOWAIT option tells OS/2 whether you want to wait for a character to arrive. If you specify WAIT, your thread will block at the KbdCharIn call until a keystroke is available. If you specify NOWAIT, your thread continues to run, regardless of whether a character is available.

For example, you could use KbdCharIn as shown in Figure 14-38. Here you request a synchronous (WAIT), so the function call does not complete until the user enters a keystroke. When the user presses a key, the CHARIN buffer is filled with the key information. When it returns from the KbdCharIn call, the program checks if the keystroke is an extended ASCII character by comparing the ASCII field to 0 and EOH. If it is, it compares the scan-code field with 5Dh to determine if it was the F10 key. Finally, it tests the shift-state word with the 0200h mask to determine if the left ALT key was depressed when the user pressed F10. If it meets all these conditions, then the program calls a worker routine (DOIT). Otherwise, it reads the next character.

This is a program that reads characters from the keyboard until the user presses (left) ALT-F10. If your applica-

```
Data Segment ...

inkey         charbuf   <>                        ;Character data structure

Code Degment ...

readchar:     @KbdCharIn  inkey,0,0               ;read char from keyboard
              cmp         inkey.charascii,0        ;extended ASCII?
              jne         readchar                 ;no - go read another key
              cmp         inkey.charascii,0eh      ;extended ASCII?
              jne         readchar                 ;no - go read another key
              cmp         inkey.charscan,5dh       ;F10 key?
              jne         readchar                 ;no - go read another key
              test        inkey.charshift,0200h    ;Left-ALT down?
              jz          readchar                 ;no - go read another key
              call        doit                     ;got the key sequence
              jmp         readchar                 ;go read another key
```

Figure 14-38.   Code to use KbdCharIn API

tion program requires this level of keystroke sensitivity, you must use the KbdCharIn function to read the keyboard. The other forms of keyboard I/O (DosRead and KbdStringIn) do not provide enough information about the keystrokes to drive the program in this way.

If you need to look at the next character in the keyboard buffer without actually removing it, you can use the KbdPeek API. The parameters for KbdPeek are as follows:

PTR	A pointer to a character input data structure (see KbdCharIn)
WORD	A one-word KBD handle

This API is functionally equivalent to KbdCharIn, except that the character is not actually read in. In fact, KbdPeek uses the same input character data structure to hold the keystroke information.

For example, the code in Figure 14-39 does the same thing as the previous example, except that the key remains in the input buffer. Notice that since KbdPeek does not support the NOWAIT option, the program always gets control immediately after the call. To test whether a charac-

```
readchar:    @DosSleep    sleepct                  ;wait a little while
             @KbdPeek     inkey,1,0                ;read char from keyboard
             test         inkey.charstat,40h       ;character present?
             jz           readchar                 ;no - go read another key
             cmp          inkey.charascii,0        ;extended ASCII?
             jne          readchar                 ;no - go read another key
             cmp          inkey.charascii,0eh      ;extended ASCII?
             jne          readchar                 ;no - go read another key
             cmp          inkey.charscan,5dh       ;F10 key?
             jne          readchar                 ;no - go read another key
             test         inkey.charshift,0200h    ;Left-ALT down?
             jz           readchar                 ;no - go read another key
             call         doit                     ;got the key sequence
             jmp          readchar                 ;go read another key
```

Figure 14-39.   Code to use KbdCharIn, but with key remaining in buffer

ter was actually returned, the program tests bit 6 in the character status byte. Also, to prevent against using too many CPU cycles, the thread relinquishes the processor with a DosSleep call each time it reads the keyboard.

Naturally, if you do this, some other thread in the process must be reading the keystrokes. Otherwise, the keys would never be dequeued and the keyboard device driver buffer would eventually overflow.

Finally, you can purge the entire contents of the keyboard buffer with the KbdFlushBuffer API. The parameter for KbdFlushBuffer is as follows:

WORD	A one-word KBD handle

For example,

```
@KbdFlushBuffer 0              ;clear the input buffer
```

clears all the queued keystrokes in the keyboard device driver output buffer. This function is especially useful if you want to prevent application *skating*. Skating is what happens when keys are generated faster than your application program can process them. The result is that the program continues to act on the keys long after you stop pressing them.

You can avoid this annoying problem by using

KbdFlushBuffer immediately before you read from the keyboard. However, you should think about this carefully because whenever you flush the buffer you effectively clear the type-ahead buffer. In some situations you may want the type-ahead (such as a spreadsheet-command interface), and in others you may not.

Getting/Setting Status

The OS/2 keyboard subsystem operates in various modes. To set these modes, you use the KbdSetStatus API. The parameters of KbdSetStatus are as follows:

PTR	Pointer to a keyboard status data structure that OS/2 uses to set the keyboard status
WORD	A one-word KBD handle

The KbdSetStatus data structure defines how you want to set the keyboard states (see Figure 14-40). The individual options are:

ASCII mode	Set or reset the ASCII input mode, as discussed previously in this chapter
BINARY mode	Set or reset the BINARY input mode, as discussed previously in this chapter
ECHO mode	Set or reset the ECHO character mode, as discussed previously in this chapter
Shift Report	KbdCharIn normally only generates key packets when a data key is pressed, with the shift-state information included as part of the data packet (shift flags). However, if you enable the shift-report state, KBD generates data packets for each shift-status change regardless of whether a data key was pressed. This is useful if your application displays the shift status on the screen. With shift reporting enabled, you get key packets on shift-state changes without having to "poll" the keyboard. You identify a shift-state change packet by examining bit 0 in the CHARBUF status field

SET Keyboard Status

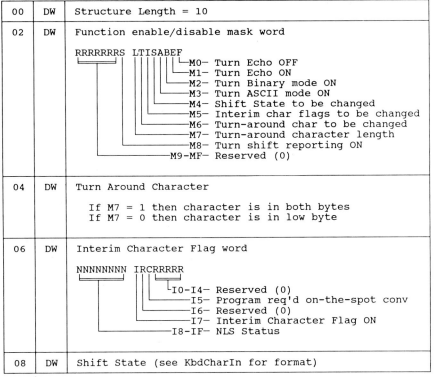

00	DW	Structure Length = 10
02	DW	Function enable/disable mask word
04	DW	Turn Around Character
06	DW	Interim Character Flag word
08	DW	Shift State (see KbdCharIn for format)

Note: If M0=0 and M1=0 then ECHO mode is unchanged
      If M0=1 and M1=1 then error is returned
      If M2=0 and M3=0 then input mode is unchanged (BINARY/ASCII)
      If M2=1 and M3=1 then error is returned
      If M2=1 then   M0 and M1 are ignored

GET Keyboard Status (the remainder of the structure as above)

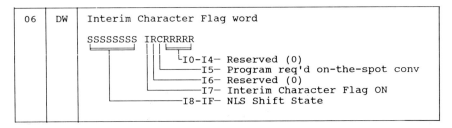

Figure 14-40. KBD status data structure

Turnaround Character	The keyboard turnaround character is the character that causes KBD to return a partially filled KbdStringIn buffer. Thus far, the carriage return (CR) has been used as the turnaround character. However, you can change this to any single or double-byte (NLS) character with the KbdSetStatus function. The default turnaround character is CR (0Dh)
Shift State	With KbdSetState, a program can force a shift condition, even when the user did not press the shift keys. You can select any combination of shift keys, as defined in the CHARBUF data structure
Interim Character Flag	Enables you to set or reset the interim character flag from a program. The interim character flag is used to process multibyte (NLS) characters

To use this API, you might code the program shown in Figure 14-41 to reset the keyboard status and then read from the keyboard. This example shows the bit-oriented fields in binary format to make them more readable. In

```
Data Segment ....

inbuf        db      10 dup(' ')          ;Input buffer
iblen        dw      10                   ;Input buffer length
rdlen        dw      10                   ;returned data length
;
kbdstat      dw      10                   ;data structure length
kbdmask      db      0000000001001010b    ;function mask
kbdtachr     dw      '+'                  ;turn around character
kbdicf       dw      0000000000000000b    ;Interim Character Flag
kbdshift     dw      0000000000000000b    ;Shift state

Code Segment ....

             @KbdSetStatus kbdstat,0         ;set new keyboard status
             @KbdStringIn inbuf,iblen,0,0    ;read from keyboard
```

Figure 14-41. Code to reset keyboard status and read from keyboard

this example, the keyboard status function mask sets the following options:

Input ECHO OFF	(bit 1 on)
ASCII input mode ON	(bit 3 on)
Change TAC	(bit 6 on)
TAC length = 1	(bit 7 off)
New TAC '+'	(in word 3)

This program sets the keyboard to ASCII input mode (unconditionally), changes the turnaround character to "+," and turns off input ECHO. If you enter the program and run it on your system, you will find that you can enter keystrokes (up to 10), but they will not be displayed on the screen. Also, the carriage return is treated as a data character. Instead, the "+" key acts as the "enter" function.

The DosRead function uses the KBD subsystem to read from the keyboard. When you set the keyboard status with KbdSetStatus, you set it for both the direct KBD calls and for the file I/O keyboard services (DosRead).

If you need to determine the current keyboard status, you can use the KbdGetStatus API. The parameters for KbdGetStatus are as follows:

PTR	Pointer to a keyboard status data structure in which OS/2 returns the current status
WORD	A one-word KBD handle

This function returns the information as described in the keyboard status data structure (with a very small exception noted in Figure 14-40). For example,

```
@KbdGetStatus kbdstat,0        ;get new keyboard status
```

returns the current keyboard status in the data area named KBDSTAT. Note that you can use this option to determine the keyboard shift state at any arbitrary time. However, if you need to constantly monitor the shift states, set the shift-report mode on. In this way, you will be notified (by a key packet) whenever the shift states change and you do not waste CPU cycles by "polling" the keyboard.

Code-Page Support

As with the video subsystem, KBD also supports multiple code-page translation tables. The keyboard operates in one of the two code pages specified in the CODEPAGE parameter of the CONFIG.SYS file. You can switch between these code pages by using the KbdSetCP API. The parameters for KbdSetCP are as follows:

WORD	Reserved (must be 0)
WORD	A one-word code page number that OS/2 will set as the active keyboard code page:
	000 Resident code page
	437 IBM PC US
	850 Multilingual
	860 Portuguese
	863 French-Canadian
	865 Nordic
	Note: The selected value must have been configured by using the CODEPAGE statement in the CONFIG.SYS file
WORD	A one-word KBD handle

For example,

```
aKbdSetCP 865,0               ;Switch code page
```

switches the keyboard to code page 865 (Nordic). You must specify one of the two code pages with which you initialized the system. If you use a different value, then KbdSetCP will fail. Also, when you switch code pages, OS/2 automatically flushes any characters present in the keyboard queue. If you set the code page value to 0, then the keyboard device driver resets to the default (internal) code page.

```
Data Segment ...

actcp        dw        0                    ;active code page

Code Segment ...

             @KbdSetCP actcp,0              ;Switch code page
```

Figure 14-42. Code to return active code-page value

To query the current (active) keyboard code page, use the KbdGetCP API. The parameters of KbdGetCP are as follows:

DWRD	Reserved (must be 0)
PTR	Pointer to a one-word field in which OS/2 returns the active keyboard code page (see KbdSetCP).
WORD	A one-word KBD handle

This function always returns one of the two system code-page values (or 0 if the keyboard is operating in its default code page). For example, the code in Figure 14-42 returns the active code-page value in the field ACTCP. Note that since you set the keyboard and video independently, you could conceivably display the video output in one code page and process the keyboard input in another.

Translate Table Support

The keyboard device does not actually generate ASCII characters. Instead, PC keyboards generate character-independent values called *scan codes*. A scan code is really an arbitrary number that uniquely identifies a key. The association of the key "number" to the actual character code is done by the keyboard device driver using a keyboard-specific translate table.

In OS/2, the keyboard device driver includes internal translate tables for several "standard" keyboard layouts, including the original AT-style keyboard and the enhanced keyboard. If you have a unique keyboard, or if you want to change the translation algorithm in some way, you can use the KbdSetCustXT API to load a custom translate table. Once loaded, this translate table is used by the keyboard device driver to convert all the keys generated within your session. The parameters of KbdSetCustXT are as follows:

PTR	Pointer to a translate table
WORD	A one-word KBD handle

The general translate table format is illustrated in Figure 14-43. Refer to the OS/2 technical reference manual for detailed table definitions.

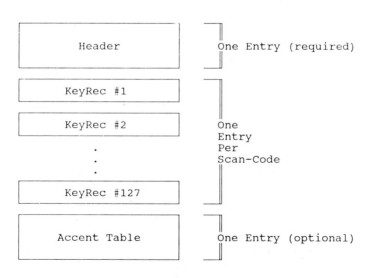

Figure 14-43. KBD translate table format

For example, assuming that you have a translate table named XTAB in your program's data segment,

```
@KbdSetCustXT xtab,0          ;set my translate table
```

instructs the keyboard device driver to use the table for all subsequent scan-code translations. The table is not actually copied, so your program must keep it around after it makes the KbdSetCustXT call. If you free the segment in which it is kept, then the scan-code translation(s) may fail. The new translate table is in effect until the session ends, or until you issue the KbdSetCP call to reset the keyboard code page (and translate table).

If you want to translate an individual scan code to the final-form ASCII character, you can use the KbdXlate API. The parameters for KbdXlate are as follows:

PTR	Pointer to a translate data record
WORD	A one-word KBD handle

KbdXlate actually passes the data record to the low-level translation routine as if it had been entered by the user. However, unlike a normal keystroke, the character is returned to your program. Figure 14-44 illustrates the format of the translate character data record.

Note that in some cases (as in multibyte characters), you may have to call KbdXlate more than once to complete the translation. In this situation, be sure to leave the translation state fields intact since they are used by KBD to keep interim translation status information.

Replacing Keyboard Subsystem Functions

You have now seen the main functions of the OS/2 keyboard I/O subsystem. However, since KBD is implemented as a subsystem, one more area remains to be explored — function replaceability. Like any OS/2 subsystem, KBD allows you to replace any or all of its function calls with your own routines.

The replacement mechanism is nearly identical to the one you saw in VIO. You can use the KbdRegister API to identify an alternate dynamic-link package that OS/2 uses to resolve the individual KBD calls. The parameters for KbdRegister are as follows:

PTR	Pointer to an ASCIIZ module name that contains the dynamic-link replacement routine(s)
PTR	Pointer to an ASCIIZ entry point name within the dynamic-link module that is to gain control when the KBD function(s) are called by an application program
DWRD	A double-word function mask indicating which KBD functions are being replaced by this KbdRegister call

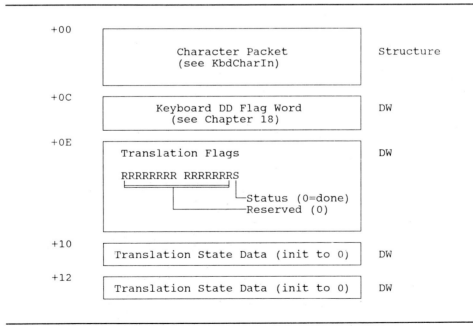

Figure 14-44. Translate scan-code packet

Word0	Word1	API
-------- --------	-------- -------1	KbdCharIn
-------- --------	-------- ------1-	KbdPeek
-------- --------	-------- -----1--	KbdFlushBuffer
-------- --------	-------- ----1---	KbdGetStatus
-------- --------	-------- ---1----	KbdSetStatus
-------- --------	-------- --1-----	KbdStringIn
-------- --------	-------- -1------	KbdOpen
-------- --------	-------- 1-------	KbdClose
-------- --------	-------1 --------	KbdGetFocus
-------- --------	------1- --------	KbdFreeFocus
-------- --------	-----1-- --------	KbdGetCP
-------- --------	----1--- --------	KbdSetCP
-------- --------	---1---- --------	KbdXlate
-------- --------	--1----- --------	KbdSetCustXT

Figure 14-45.   KBD function-call register mask

As with VIO, you tell OS/2 which KBD calls you want to process by setting one or more bits in a function-call bit map (see Figure 14-45).

As it receives each application KBD call, OS/2 first checks the KbdRegister bit map. If it is a "registered" KBD function, it calls the replacement dynamic-link module instead of its internal "worker" routine.

On entry, the KBD dynamic-link module receives a stack frame that is identical in format to what you saw earlier in this chapter in the video subsystem. Thus, the replacement KBD routine can extract the calling application's parameters directly from the stack. The API function number identifies which KBD API you are processing (see Table 14-7).

The last double-word on the stack frame contains the return entry point into the KBD subsystem. When the dynamic-link module completes its processing of the KBD

Table 14-7. KBD Function Numbers

Function Number	API
0	KbdCharIn
1	KbdPeek
2	KbdFlushBuffer
3	KbdGetStatus
4	KbdSetStatus
5	KbdStringIn
6	KbdOpen
7	KbdClose
8	KbdGetFocus
9	KbdFreeFocus
10	KbdGetCP
11	KbdSetCP
12	KbdXlate
13	KbdSetCustXT

call, it returns to OS/2 by calling this address. When you return, you set the AX register to tell OS/2 what you expect it to do with the request:

$AX = -1$	Pass the KBD call to the default KBD routine
$AX = $ other	Ignore this KBD call and pass AX to the application

Like their VIO counterparts, replacement KBD routines can dynamically determine which function calls they want to trap, and which should be passed to the default subsystem service.

The registration remains in effect for the duration of the display session or until the process that issued KbdRegister issues the KbdDeRegister call. This function detaches the KBD extension and causes all subsequent KBD calls to once again be processed by the base KBD services.

You should also remember that only one replacement subsystem can be active at any given time (per session). If a second program issues a KbdRegister call while the first registration is still in effect, the request fails. However, when the first program deregisters itself, then the second request is honored.

As you would expect, a registered KBD extension will see the KBD requests made by all the processes that run in the session. Thus, if the session contains more than one program that reads from the keyboard, then the KBD replacement program gets all the KBD calls.

Finally, you should not confuse KbdRegister with keyboard monitors. Since KbdRegister registers an extension program only in the session in which it is running, it can only see the keyboard I/O requests that originate from the session. Perhaps more importantly, the level of the requests it sees is exactly the same as the KBD API. Thus, a KBD extension can "trap" character I/O, string I/O, or any of the miscellaneous KBD functions. A keyboard monitor, on the other hand, is a low-level I/O trap. This type of program sees the data flows, not the API calls. It can process data destined for any session, not just the one in which it was started.

Family API Considerations

Like the VIO functions, most KBD API calls are included as part of the family API. View the KBD subsystem as a standard set of I/O subroutines that you use to access the keyboard (in either PC DOS or OS/2). This means that if you write your PC DOS application to write to the screen with VIO and read from the keyboard with KBD, it will be fully compatible with OS/2. Wherever possible, you should use these calls in place of BIOS INT 9h when writing PC DOS programs.

SUMMARY

Video and keyboard I/O are probably the most important aspects of PC programming. In personal computers, the user interface is a critical component that must be carefully thought through and implemented. In PC DOS, programs often bypass the system services because they are slow or functionally inadequate. Instead, they write "directly" to the hardware. Since doing this in a multiprogramming environment is tricky business, it becomes all the more important that the system services provide exactly what the applications need—speed and function.

The OS/2 I/O subsystems fill this gap. They give you a high-performance alternative to the serial I/O functions that nearly approximates direct hardware manipulation. Since most of these services are included in the family API, you can write subsystem I/O programs that will also run on PC DOS.

This completes the discussion of the OS/2 I/O subsystems. Of course, you have not yet seen many subsystem functions. In order to leave time for other aspects of OS/2 programming, the I/O discussions will be curtailed here. The functions you have seen in this chapter, in conjunction with the file I/O services from Chapter 13, will meet 99% of your application I/O requirements. As always, you may refer to Appendix A for a complete list of all the OS/2 API calls.

Before you move on to the next chapter, you should be sure that you have a good grasp of the material you have just read. Here are a few important points to remember:

- The differences between file I/O and subsystem I/O

- Supported video modes

- Setting and querying the video modes

- How text mode operation works

- VIO character primitives

- Scrolling screen data with VIO
- Accessing the LVB
- Accessing the video hardware (directly)
- The difference between code pages and fonts
- How to set the active code page
- How to change display fonts
- Reading character strings
- Reading character packets
- The keyboard states
- When to use string versus character keyboard functions
- Changing the keyboard code page

CHAPTER 15
MEMORY MANAGEMENT

Memory is one of the most critical system resources managed by OS/2. The memory-management API functions allow you to allocate, deallocate, shrink, and grow memory segments from your programs. This chapter discusses more about this aspect of OS/2, and explains how to apply the concepts in a number of sample programs.

ALLOCATION AND DEALLOCATION

A big difference between OS/2 and PC DOS programs is in how each deals with the computer's memory. In PC DOS, memory management is informal. If a PC DOS program needs memory, it simply "grabs" physical memory by manipulating the segment registers.

By running the CPU in protected mode, OS/2 introduces more structure into this environment. Other than the segments that were defined in the EXE header, OS/2 programs explicitly request memory segments from the OS/2 memory manager by using the DosAllocSeg API.

The parameters for DosAllocSeg are as follows:

WORD	One word containing the number of bytes to be allocated (maximum 65,536)
PTR	Pointer to a one-word value that, on return, will contain the selector of the allocated segment
WORD	A one-word sharing indicator, as follows: 0 = segment will not be shared 1 = segment will be shared

For each DosAllocSeg call, OS/2 builds an LDT entry, allocates physical memory, and returns a selector that your program can use to reference the memory. View these selectors as handles to logical memory segments. To use the memory, your program must load the selector into one of the CPU segment registers. For example, the following code

```
@DosAllocSeg 200,segp,0    ;allocate segment
push        segp           ;copy selector
pop         ds             ;to data segment register
```

calls OS/2 to allocate a 200-byte memory segment, and then places its selector in the DS register. All subsequent instructions that reference memory addressed by DS manipulate the data in this new segment. If you attempt to access data beyond offset 200, the CPU generates a fault and your program ends. This is a significant difference between OS/2 and PC DOS.

If you no longer need a memory segment, you may return it to the system with the DosFreeSeg call.

The DosFreeSeg parameter list is as follows:

WORD	The one-word selector of the memory segment that is to be released

For example,

```
@DosFreeSeg segp        ;free segment
```

releases the memory segment whose selector is contained in the field SEGP. In a multitasking environment, programs should always strive to relinquish resources they no longer need in order to minimize system-resource contention. This is especially true in the case of memory, since system memory requirements are dynamic.

You should generally design OS/2 programs so that the EXE file contains as little predefined data as possible. The "run-time" memory should be allocated dynamically by using the DosAllocSeg function. For instance, consider the example shown in Figure 15-1.

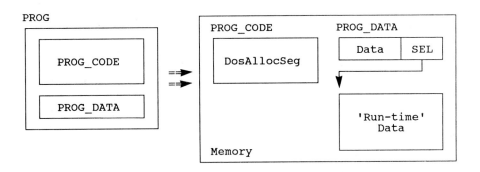

Figure 15-1. Allocating dynamic data structures

The program named PROG comprises a code segment and a small data segment. In reality, the data segment is nothing more than a common data area and a 2-byte field that contains a pointer (selector) to another memory segment. When PROG initializes, it uses the DosAllocSeg call to allocate a data segment large enough for its current needs and stores its selector in the data segment. If the needs of PROG change over time, the program can free the data segment and allocate a different one (smaller or larger). Contrast this with PC DOS where system extensions must reserve the most memory they will ever need in any situation.

```
            mov     cx,4                        ;outer loop
alo010:     push    cx                          ;save outer loop count
;
            mov     cx,COUNT                    ;inner loop count
            @movs   alloc,msg1type,12           ;type of operation (allocate)
alo020:     @DosAllocSeg segsz,segp,0           ;allocate segment
            push    segp                        ;save value
            push    segsz                       ;save size
            inc     dx                          ;increment segment count
            call    displaymsg                  ;display message
            add     segsz,80h                   ;increase segment size
            loop    alo020                      ;continue
;
            mov     cx,dx                       ;set sgment count (for loop)
            @movs   dealloc,msg1type,12         ;type of operation (deallocate)
alo030:     pop     segsz                       ;restore segment size
            pop     segp                        ;restore segment pointer
            @DosFreeSeg segp                    ;de-allocate segment
            call    displaymsg                  ;display message
            dec     dx                          ;decrement segment count
            loop    alo030                      ;continue
;
            pop     cx                          ;restore outer loop
            dec     cx                          ;decrement loop count
            jcxz    alo999                      ;done
            jmp     alo010                      ;loop
```

Figure 15-2. ALLOCMEM main routine

Now consider a real program that uses the memory-management APIs. The program (ALLOCMEM) allocates a number of data segments, then deallocates them. It repeats this allocation/deallocation sequence four times, as shown in Figure 15-2.

As it allocates each segment, ALLOCMEM pushes the selector and the segment size onto the stack. When they are all allocated, ALLOCMEM drops to a deallocation loop in which it retrieves each selector from the stack and issues a DosFreeSeg call to release its associated memory segment. For each allocation/deallocation, ALLOCMEM calls the subroutine DISPLAYMSG to display status information on the screen. The @MOVS macro moves a string into the message that tells the user if the program is "Allocating" or "Deallocating."

The DISPLAYMSG subroutine shown in Figure 15-3 converts the segment size, segment number (iteration), and selector value to printable form, and then displays the information in the center of the screen. DISPLAYMSG uses the DosSleep function to "slow down" the display so you can read the information as it is displayed. DosSleep is a useful service that suspends the execution of the issuing thread for a specified period of time. In this example, DISPLAYMSG waits for 200 ms (the value is in SLEEP-COUNT) each time it displays the allocation/deallocation message.

```
displaymsg   proc
             @bta        segsz,msg1sz,5      ;convert segment size
             @bta        dx,msg1no,2         ;convert segment number
             @bth        segp,msg1sel        ;convert selector value
             @VioWrtCharStrAtt msg1,MSG1L,10,4,green,0 ;write message
             @DosSleep sleepcount            ;pause for a while
             ret
displaymsg   endp
```

Figure 15-3. DISPLAYMSG subroutine

The parameters for DosSleep are as follows:

DWRD	A double-word value containing the number of milliseconds OS/2 is to suspend the calling thread.

Depending on the amount of memory installed on your system, and the number of other programs that are executing in parallel, ALLOCMEM could allocate more memory than you have available. The allocated segments start at 16K and increase by 256 bytes. So, with COUNT set to 64, ALLOCMEM requests 64 memory segments of an average size of approximately 24K — 1.5MB of real memory. If you have less than 2.5MB of physical memory installed in your system, ALLOCMEM causes OS/2 to overcommit memory. However, it does not really matter how much memory is in the system, since ALLOCMEM will work in any case (by allocating virtual memory space), albeit more slowly the more "memory-constrained" the system becomes.

In programs such as text editors, you can assume that memory is limitless. You simply bring the entire file into memory and let OS/2 manage the memory. However, in other programs such as a COPY utility, you should not overcommit memory, since it would add an unnecessary trip to the disk before the data is written to its destination.

In these situations, you might want to check the system memory availability with the DosMemAvail API. This function returns the size of the single largest unallocated memory area in the system. While not absolute (the memory condition may change the instant after your program gets the results), it does give you a good "sniff-test" of the current memory state. For instance, you could assume that if the available memory is less than 64K, the system is heading for trouble. Or, if the available area is less than 4K, the system is surely in an overcommitted state. Depending on the memory state, your COPY program could then allocate a larger or smaller work buffer. A smaller work buffer might cause the COPY program to

```
              @DosMemAvail availsizel        ;get available memory
              @bth      availsizeh,msg2as    ;available memory (high)
              @bth      availsizel,msg2as+4  ;available memory (low)
              cmp       availsizeh,0         ;less than 64KB?
              jbe       dis010               ;yes - warning
              jmp       dis030               ;go display
      dis010: cmp       availsizel,4096      ;less than 4KB?
              jbe       dis020               ;yes - warning
              mov       attrib,YELLOW        ;attribute
              jmp       dis030               ;go display
      dis020: mov       attrib,RED           ;attribute
      dis030: @VioWrtCharStrAtt msg2,MSG2L,12,20,attrib,0 ;write number
```

Figure 15-4. Memory available test in the DISPLAYMSG subroutine

go to the disk a bit more frequently but it would save the expense of segment swapping.

The parameters for DosMemAvail are as follows:

PTR   The address of a double-word field in which OS/2 will return the size of the largest (unallocated) memory segment in the system.

This function can be put to use in ALLOCMEM. First, the DISPLAYMSG subroutine could be enhanced with the code shown in Figure 15-4.

The DosMemAvail function returns the largest free memory block size in a double-word with two-word fields named AVAILSIZEL (low) and AVAILSIZEH (high). After converting the value to displayable form, DISPLAYMSG tests the memory condition, sets either a green, yellow, or red display attribute, and then displays the information on line 12. In addition, you can change the main procedure as shown in Figure 15-5.

Now if ALLOCMEM detects a red memory condition (less than 4K free), it stops allocating segments and starts deallocating them. Note that this is a far superior solution than tuning the program to your system configuration (changing COUNT), since it automatically compensates for situations where other programs in the system are stressing physical memory.

```
alo020:    aDosAllocSeg  segsz,segp,0    ;allocate segment
           push      segp                ;save value
           push      segsz               ;save size
           inc       dx                  ;increment segment count
           call      displaymsg          ;display message
           cmp       attrib,RED          ;over commited?
           je        alo025              ;yes - skip remaining allocations
           add       segsz,100h          ;increase segment size
           loop      alo020              ;continue
```

Figure 15-5.   Available memory test in ALLOCMEM

If you run ALLOCMEM on your system, you will see the display illustrated in Figure 15-6, with the segment count, allocation type, segment size, selector, and free

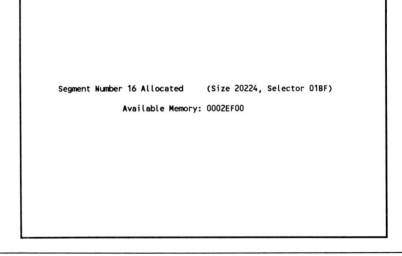

```
      Segment Number 16 Allocated      (Size 20224, Selector 01BF)
                    Available Memory: 0002EF00
```

Figure 15-6.   ALLOCMEM display

memory being constantly updated. If you start more than one copy of ALLOCMEM, each compensates for the other and does not allocate as many segments as it otherwise would have.

HUGE MEMORY

Many situations occur in which a program needs more than 64K of memory to hold its data. For example, text editors, compilers, and spreadsheets often manipulate data objects much larger than 64K. These programs must allocate multiple memory segments to hold a single data structure. The DosAllocSeg function certainly allows you to do this, as evidenced by the previous example. But it has one major drawback: You must maintain an array of selectors corresponding to each segment in the data structure. For example,

```
@DosAllocSeg  Offffh,segp1,0 ;allocate 64KB segment 1
@DosAllocSeg  Offffh,segp2,0 ;allocate 64KB segment 2
@DosAllocSeg  Offffh,segp3,0 ;allocate 64KB segment 3
@DosAllocSeg  Offffh,segp4,0 ;allocate 64KB segment 4
```

As the program allocates each segment, it saves the selector in a unique memory location. Then, while the program processes the data, it must look up the value of the next selector each time it crosses a segment boundary. For instance,

```
add     di,16           ;next element
cmp     di,0            ;passed sector boundary?
jne     continue        ;no - continue
mov     ax,[segp]+2     ;get next segment
mov     ds,ax           ;address it
```

This is an inconvenience for the program because if it does not have a predetermined data object size, it must manage a variable-length selector array. This process is also more complex than in PC DOS, where programs can simply assume that adding a constant (1000H) to the segment register will address the next 64K segment. But the real problem surfaces when one program must pass one of these large data structures to another program. What do you pass? A variable-length selector array is certainly a potential solution, but it is very cumbersome and unnecessarily complex.

For this type of situation, OS/2 introduces the concept of *huge data objects*. A huge data object is a collection of memory segments with a predefined relationship that together make up a large "logical" segment. In PC DOS, segments that comprise a large data object are contiguous, and thus programs can play the segment-manipulation tricks. However, these tricks do not work in protected mode because programs address memory indirectly through a descriptor table.

OS/2 solves this problem with a small observation. While segments cannot be assumed to be related, their selectors can. The DosAllocHuge API allows you to allocate a large data structure comprised of multiple segments whose selectors are arithmetically related.

The parameters for DosAllocHuge are as follows:

WORD	A one-word value indicating the number of 65,535-byte (whole) segments that OS/2 is to allocate
WORD	The length of the last segment
PTR	The address of a one-word data area that is to receive the initial segment selector
WORD	The maximum number of 65,535-byte segments to which OS/2 will allow you to grow this huge segment group (with the DosReallocSeg call)
WORD	A one-word sharing indicator, as follows: 0 = segment will not be shared 1 = segment will be shared

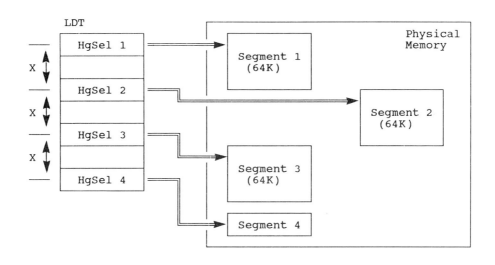

Figure 15-7. Huge memory object

For example, consider the structure depicted in Figure 15-7. The data is contained in segments that are dispersed throughout physical memory, but the selectors are separated by a constant value (X). When a program uses a huge data structure, it can address the next segment by adding X to the current selector. Note that this is conceptually identical to what you do in PC DOS except that in this case, the increment is exactly a 64K segment multiple (in other words, you cannot add X/2 to get an address halfway into the next segment).

To determine the selector index (X), you must use the OS/2 DosGetHugeShift API. This value is constant for all programs in the system, so you can allocate a huge structure in one program and pass it to another. The second program can request the shift value from OS/2 and process the first program's data. Note that the programs need only pass a single selector, corresponding to the first segment in the structure. The DosGetHugeShift parameter list is as follows:

DWRD	The address of a one-word area that is to receive the huge shift count

A very important benefit to this type of data manipulation is that it works equally well in PC DOS and OS/2. In fact, the DosHugeAlloc function is supported as part of the family API, so your program can allocate data structures larger than 64K in either environment (subject to PC DOS memory availability, of course).

When it runs under PC DOS, the DosGetHugeShift API returns a shift value that addresses the next contiguous memory segment. Thus, the OS/2 huge memory functions are a compatible addressing subset that masks the difference between the protected mode and real mode memory models. This is the only case where arithmetic-segment register manipulation is permitted in OS/2.

You deallocate huge memory structures by passing DosFreeSeg the selector of the first segment in the structure. The system recognizes the selector as part of the huge data structure and it frees all its associated segments.

The DosReallocHuge API allows you to shrink or grow a previously allocated huge structure. The parameters for DosReallocHuge are as follows:

WORD	The number of 65,535 segments that will exist after the reallocation
WORD	The size of the last (non-65,535) byte segment after the reallocation

Consider how to use these functions in a practical example. HEXDISP is a program that reads a file from disk and displays its contents in hexadecimal. It has the structure shown in Figure 15-8.

The whole principle behind HEXDISP is to read the data file into a huge data structure and then allow the user to interactively scroll through the information. The details

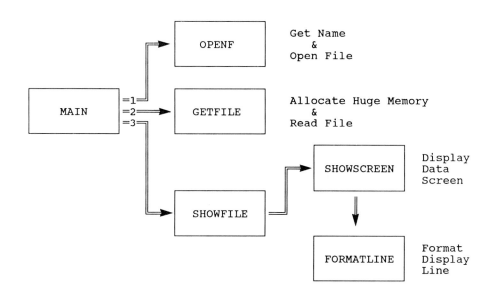

Figure 15-8. Structure of HEXDISP program

pertaining to opening the file and formatting the data are not discussed here. Instead, consider the logic that relates to huge memory allocation. (The complete HEXDISP listing is in Appendix E).

The GETFILE procedure is called to read the file into memory. It starts by determining the size of the data file, as shown in Figure 15-9.

```
;
; Determine file size
;
        mov     fofsl,0                 ;no bytes past end-of-file
        @DosChgFilePtr fhand,fofsl,2,fofsl ;move file ptr to end of file
        mov     word ptr nofs,0         ;file offset
        @DosChgFilePtr fhand,nofs,0,nofs ;move file ptr to start of file
```

Figure 15-9. GETFILE file size determination

You can determine the size of a file by moving the logical file pointer 0 bytes past the end of the file. OS/2 returns the size in a double-word area named FOFSL. Actually this is two separately addressed words: FOFSL (which contains the low word of the file size) and FOFSH (which contains the high word). Thus, FOFSH contains the number of whole 64K segments in the file and FOFSL contains the number of bytes in the last segment. You can use this data in a huge memory allocation, as shown in Figure 15-10.

FOFSH tells DosAllocHuge how many whole segments are needed and DX (FOFSL + 16) contains the number of bytes in the last segment. OS/2 returns the selector of the first segment in HEXSEGP. The final two parameters tell OS/2 that you do not intend to grow this huge data structure beyond its initial size (0) and that you do not intend to share it with other processes (0).

If the memory was allocated successfully, GETFILE continues by placing the initial selector in DS and retriev-

```
;
; Allocate buffer
;
get010:    mov      dx,fofsl             ;get low file size word
           add      dx,16               ;add pad bytes
           mov      hexsegsz,dx         ;save segment (file) size
           @DosAllocHuge fofsh,dx,hexsegp,0,0  ;allocate segment
           @jaxz    get015              ;continue if OK
           @DosWrite stderr,msg3,msg3l,bytesout ;Write not enough memory msg
           mov      ax,0ffh             ;set error code
           jmp      get999              ;exit
;
get015:    push     hexsegp             ;put new selector
           pop      ds                  ;in DS
           @DosGetHugeShift shift       ;get shift count
           mov      di,1                ;set increment base
           mov      cx,shift            ;get huge shift value
           shl      di,cl               ;compute segment shift count
           mov      shift,di            ;save it for later use
```

Figure 15-10. GETFILE memory allocation

ing the huge memory shift count with the DosGetHugeShift API. Note that the returned value is not the selector increment; instead it is a shift count. To arrive at the selector increment you load a register with 1 and shift it to the left by this count. The routine loads 1 into the DI register, shifts the value by the number returned in SHIFT, and stores the result back into SHIFT. The selector increment is now ready to be used by other parts of the program.

Next, GETFILE reads the contents of the file into the allocated memory, as shown in Figure 15-11. The routine first checks how many whole (65,536-byte) segments are contained in the data file. If none exist, GETFILE skips the first DosRead and proceeds to read the odd segment. If the file is larger than 64K, it loops through a number of DosRead calls, each reading a complete segment of data from the file. Note that after each segment is read, GET-FILE points to the next segment by adding the selector increment (SHIFT) to the current data selector. In this way, the entire file is read into the huge memory object.

```
;
; Read it into memory
;
                push    ds                      ;save initial selector
                xor     si,si                   ;set data area offset
                mov     cx,fofsh                ;get segment count
                jcxz    get030                  ;jump if no additional segments
;
get020:         @DosRead fhand,DS:SI,-1,bytesin ;read complete segment(s)
                mov     ax,ds                   ;get selector
                add     ax,shift                ;compute next segment
                mov     ds,ax                   ;set segment register
                loop    get020                  ;get all complete segments
;
get030:         @DosRead fhand,DS:SI,hexsegsz,bytesin ;read remainder of file
                @DosClose fhand                 ;close data file
                xor     ax,ax                   ;clear return code
                pop     ds
;
get999:         ret
```

Figure 15-11. Subroutine for GETFILE to read file contents into memory

The MAIN program now calls the subroutine SHOW-FILE to display the contents of memory in hexadecimal. The details pertaining to the display and keyboard processing are not important at this time. However, each time SHOWFILE crosses a segment boundary (forward), it executes the code

```
mov     ax,ds              ;get selector
add     ax,shift           ;compute next selector value
mov     ds,ax              ;set segment register
```

to address the next memory segment. When it crosses the memory segment boundary backwards, it executes the code

```
mov     ax,ds              ;get data segment selector
sub     ax,shift           ;compute previous selector value
mov     ds,ax              ;set segment register
```

to address the previous memory segment. Figure 15-12 depicts the HEXDISP screen you would see if you display the file HEXDISP.EXE with the following command:

[C:\]HEXDISP HEXDISP.EXE

With this simple example, you have a program that allows you to browse large files (theoretically up to 32MB). Yet, the program does not have to manage the system memory. It simply reads the file into a huge data structure and lets the operating system make sure that the correct segments are brought into memory as required. This is a program that is well-suited to the OS/2 LRU memory algorithm because it has a good locality of reference. At most, two data segments (128K) will ever be needed to display a screenful of hex data. The remainder of the data can be swapped out to disk.

```
HEXDISP: hexdisp.exe                    <PgUp> <PgDn> <ESC>   Page    0 of   9
   00000000    4D5A4700 07000000    04000000 FFFF0000    *MZG      ♦         *
   00000010    B8000000 00000000    40000000 00000000    *⌐         @        *
   00000020    00000000 00000000    00000000 00000000    *                   *
   00000030    00000000 80000000    00000000 80000000    *          ç        *
   00000040    0E1FBA0E 00B400CD    21B8014C CD215468    * ▼|  ┤ ─!⌐ºL─!Th*
   00000050    69732070 726F6772    61602063 616E6E6F    *is program canno*
   00000060    74206265 2072756E    20696E20 444F5320    *t be run in DOS *
   00000070    6D6F6465 2E202024    00000000 00000000    *mode.  $           *
   00000080    4E450500 BA000200    B400F06C 02000200    *NE♣  | ● ┤ ≡l● ● *
   00000090    00000000 00000300    00020100 03000300    *          ♥  ●○ ♥ ♥ *
   000000A0    0F004000 58005800    63006900 3C010000    *  @ X X c i <○ *
   000000B0    00000100 00000000    00000000 00000000    *  ☺                *
   000000C0    0100FF01 010C0002    02004E01 010C5B01    *○  ○○  ●● N○○ [○*
   000000D0    0300C505 0020C505    07484558 44495350    *♥ ¦♣  ¦♣ HEXDISP*
   000000E0    00000001 0000001D    00000844 4F534341    *   ○       DOSCA*
   000000F0    4C4C5308 4B424443    414C4C53 094B4244    *LLS KBDCALLS KBD*
   00000100    43484152 494E0856    494F4341 4C4C530B    *CHARIN VIOCALLS *
   00000110    56494F53 43524F4C    4C555000 56494F57    *VIOSCROLLUP VIOW*
   00000120    52544348 41525354    52105649 4F575254    *RTCHARSTR VIOWRT*
   00000130    43484152 53545241    54540000 0B484558    *CHARSTRATT   HEX*
   00000140    44495350 2E455845    00000000 00000000    *DISP.EXE          *
   00000150    00000000 00000000    00000000 00000000    *                   *
   00000160    00000000 00000000    00000000 00000000    *                   *
   00000170    00000000 00000000    00000000 00000000    *                   *
```

Figure 15-12.   HEXDISP screen display

SHARING MEMORY WITH OTHER PROCESSES

Thus far, you have seen how to allocate memory segments within your own LDT. As you recall, the LDT defines a logical address space for the process in which your program is executing. This allocated memory is private to the local process and is inaccessible by other programs in the system. But what happens when you want to share a segment with a program running in a different process? OS/2 allows you to do this in two ways: globally or privately.

Global shared memory is really a form of "named" memory. You allocate the segment and give it an ASCII name with the DosAllocShrSeg API. Other programs in the system can then gain access to the segment by passing the ASCII name to DosGetShrSeg.

The parameters for DosAllocShrSeg are as follows:

WORD	A one-word value that tells OS/2 the size of the new segment
PTR	A pointer to an ASCIIZ string that OS/2 will use to locate the "named" memory segment
PTR	A pointer to a one-word memory area in which OS/2 will place the segment selector

Thus, if you know the name of the segment, you can get access to it. Figure 15-13 illustrates this sequence. PROG1 creates a shared segment called \SHAREMEM\PROGD with the DosAllocShrSeg function. Subsequently, PROG2 uses DosGetShrSeg with the same name to gain access to the memory.

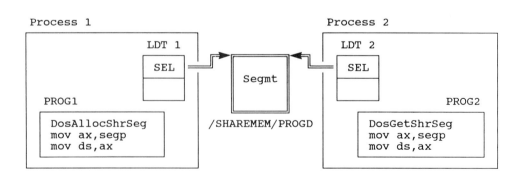

Figure 15-13.   Shared memory (global)

The parameters for DosGetShrSeg are as follows:

PTR	A pointer to an ASCIIZ string that OS/2 will use to locate the "named" memory segment
PTR	A pointer to a one-word memory area in which OS/2 will place the segment selector

You can also share memory with a specific OS/2 process, if you know its Process ID (PID). To share memory in this way, you must first allocate the memory using DosAllocSeg with the share indicator set to 1.

Then you use the DosGiveSeg API call to "give" the second process access to the segment. In reality, DosGiveSeg creates an alias descriptor in the LDT of the target process, giving it access to the memory.

The parameters for DosGiveSeg are as follows:

WORD	The selector of the segment that is to be "given" to another process
WORD	The Process ID (PID) of the process that is to be given access to the segment
PTR	A pointer to a one-word area that, on return, will contain a selector the "target" process can use to access the memory segment

For example, consider Figure 15-14. The first program allocates a memory segment with the shared indicator, then gives it to Process 2. OS/2 creates an entry in the Process 2 LDT, which maps the same segment. When PROG1 frees the memory, PROG2 becomes the only owner of the segment. PROG2 can load the selector and use the memory as if it had allocated it itself. Therefore, PROG1 can place information in the shared segment that can then be read by PROG2. This mechanism is the basis for interprocess communications (discussed in Chapter 16).

Notice that you must use a different mechanism (global shared memory, perhaps) to pass PROG1 the PID of Process 2 and likewise for PROG1 to pass PROG2 the memory selector.

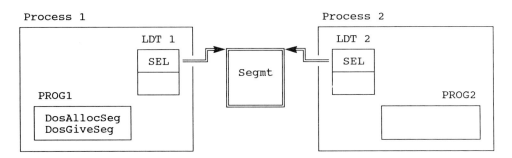

Allocating a Shared Segment

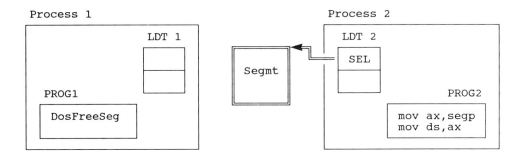

Figure 15-14.   Shared memory (private)

Now consider a practical example using shared memory. Two programs, GIVE and TAKE, use named shared memory to pass data between themselves. The GIVE program reads from standard input and writes the data to a shared segment. TAKE reads the data from the memory segment and writes it to the standard output device. The shared-memory segment used by these programs has the format shown in Figure 15-15. LEN is length of the data (0-124), IND is a data state indicator (0=empty, 1=full), and DATA is a 124-byte data area.

Figure 15-15. *Format of GIVE/TAKE shared-memory segment*

The GIVE program is shown in Figure 15-16. It allocates the named shared segment and immediately drops into a processing loop where it clears the buffer, reads from STDIN (directly into the buffer), copies the length (BYTESIN) into LEN, sets the buffer indicator to full (1), and waits for TAKE to empty the buffer.

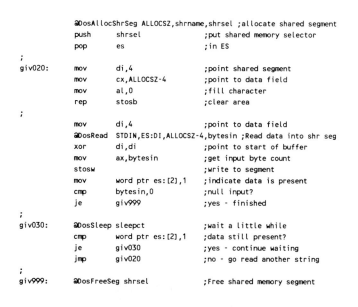

```
        @DosAllocShrSeg ALLOCSZ,shrname,shrsel ;allocate shared segment
        push    shrsel                  ;put shared memory selector
        pop     es                      ;in ES
;
giv020: mov     di,4                    ;point shared segment
        mov     cx,ALLOCSZ-4            ;point to data field
        mov     al,0                    ;fill character
        rep     stosb                   ;clear area
;
        mov     di,4                    ;point to data field
        @DosRead STDIN,ES:DI,ALLOCSZ-4,bytesin ;Read data into shr seg
        xor     di,di                   ;point to start of buffer
        mov     ax,bytesin              ;get input byte count
        stosw                           ;write to segment
        mov     word ptr es:[2],1       ;indicate data is present
        cmp     bytesin,0               ;null input?
        je      giv999                  ;yes - finished
;
giv030: @DosSleep sleepct              ;wait a little while
        cmp     word ptr es:[2],1       ;data still present?
        je      giv030                  ;yes - continue waiting
        jmp     giv020                  ;no - go read another string
;
giv999: @DosFreeSeg shrsel             ;Free shared memory segment
```

Figure 15-16. *Simple GIVE program*

```
          @DosGetShrSeg shrname,shrsel    ;get shared segment
          &jaxz      tak010               ;Segment acquired OK - continue
          @DosWrite stderr,msg1,msg1l,bytesout ;Write error message
          jmp        tak999               ;exit
;
tak010:   push       shrsel               ;put shared memory selector
          pop        es                   ;in ES
          mov        di,4                 ;point to data field
          jmp        tak030               ;go check for string
;
tak020:   @DosSleep sleepct               ;wait a little while
tak030:   cmp        word ptr es:[2],1    ;data exists?
          jne        tak020               ;no - continue waiting
          cmp        word ptr es:[0],0    ;null record?
          je         tak999               ;yes - exit
          @DosWrite stdout,ES:DI,es:[0],bytesout ;Write data
          mov        word ptr es:[2],0    ;indicate data has been read
          jmp        tak030               ;go check for another string
;
tak999:   @DosFreeSeg shrsel              ;Free shared memory segment
```

Figure 15-17. Simple TAKE program

Notice that instead of looping on the indicator, GIVE uses DosSleep to relinquish control of the CPU. Thus, it checks to see if TAKE has moved the data out of the buffer once every 500 ms (SLEEPCT=500). If the input data stream is null (BYTESIN=0), GIVE frees the buffer and ends.

The TAKE program is shown in Figure 15-17. It first tries to gain access to the shared-memory segment. If the segment does not exist, TAKE ends with an error message. If it does exist, TAKE also drops into a processing loop where it checks to see if the data is ready to be read. If the data is ready, TAKE writes it to STDOUT (directly from the memory segment). If it is not ready, TAKE sleeps for 500 ms and checks again. When it finds the data indicator set and the data length 0, it frees the memory segment and exits.

Thus, GIVE and TAKE pass data from the STDIN of one to the STDOUT of the other by way of a synchronized data flow through a shared-memory segment. These programs use a form of private IPC protocol to pass data between themselves.

To demonstrate how these programs work, use GIVE and TAKE to pass data *between* two display sessions. In the first session you would enter:

[C:\]DIR/GIVE

This command redirects the output of the DIR command to the standard input of the GIVE program. If you switch to a second session and then enter

[C:\]TAKE

the directory listing generated in the first session is displayed in the second session through the GIVE/TAKE shared-memory segment.

The display is a little jerky because GIVE and TAKE are looking for data only once every 1/2 second. You could reduce SLEEPCT to a smaller value and smooth out this jerkiness, but in the process you will waste a significant number of CPU cycles by doing useless work (looping). Chapter 16 discusses how to use semaphores to synchronize events more efficiently (without polling).

SUBALLOCATING MEMORY

Memory allocation is an important aspect of OS/2. It gives your programs the ability to dynamically adapt to their environments. If your program is an editor, and the file it is about to edit is 800K, then the editor can allocate an 800K buffer to hold it.

However, a real cost is associated with dynamic memory allocation. For each allocation request, OS/2 creates an LDT descriptor, allocates a physical memory segment, moves and swaps other segments to make room for it (if necessary), edits the descriptor fields, and finally creates a selector so that the program can access the segment. Not only that, but the pure hardware overhead of loading a segment register in protected mode is as much as 8.5 times more than in real mode. Thus, the CPU architecture itself is not well-suited to interspersing references to many different segments.

All this points to an indisputable axiom: Use as much memory as necessary, but avoid frequent allocation and deallocation of small segments. In general, you should try to allocate moderately sized segments and suballocate smaller blocks within the segment, "growing" the physical segment if you need more space.

To help you in this chore, OS/2 includes a complete set of memory suballocation services, including DosSubSet (to initialize a segment for suballocation), DosSubAlloc (to allocate an element), and DosSubFree (to free an element).

The parameters for DosSubSet are as follows:

WORD	A valid segment selector
WORD	A one-word flag value, indicating if this request is to initialize or to resize a suballocated memory segment:
	0 = Increase the size suballocated segment
	1 = Prepare a segment for suballocation
WORD	A one-word value that either defines the initial size or the new size of the suballocated segment (depending on the flag value).

The parameters for DosSubAlloc are as follows:

DWRD	The selector of an initialized suballocation segment
PTR	The address of a one-word field in which OS/2 will return the offset of the memory block
WORD	The size of the requested memory block (must be a multiple of 4 bytes)

The parameters for DosSubFree are as follows:

DWRD	The selector of an initialized suballocation segment
PTR	The offset of the suballocated block that OS/2 will free
WORD	The size of the memory block (must be a multiple of 4 bytes)

For example, Figure 15-18 illustrates how a program might suballocate a memory segment. The program starts by allocating a physical segment with DosAllocSeg and initializing it for suballocation with DosSubSet. Notice that the suballocation functions use the first 8 bytes of the segment to contain control information, so you should always allocate a segment 8 bytes larger than you expect to use.

Once the segment is initialized, the program can suballocate elements with the DosSubAlloc function. In this

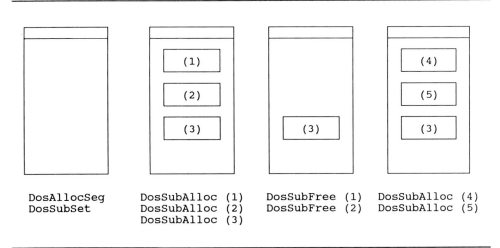

Figure 15-18. Memory suballocation

example, it has suballocated three elements (1, 2, and 3). Each element is addressed by a one-word offset into the physical segment.

You can free these suballocated segments with the DosSubFree function. In this example the program has freed elements 1 and 2. The suballocation routine has marked the area occupied by the first two elements "available," so the subsequent suballocation calls reuse it to hold elements 4 and 5.

Note that suballocated elements are *not* segments in an 80286 sense. Instead, they are small memory areas *within* a memory segment. For this reason, suballocated elements cannot be moved or swapped. Suballocation works best when the elements are the same or equivalent size because it minimizes space fragmentation within the segment.

If possible, you should try to use a different physical segment to "pool" like-sized elements. For example, if you are writing a program that allocates numerous control blocks which fall into three categories—CB1 (20 bytes long), CB2 (120 bytes long) and CB3 (20 bytes long)—you might consider creating two physical segments, one to hold CB1 and CB3 elements and one to hold CB2 elements.

Now consider the sample program named FDIR (an interactive, full-screen, directory-listing program). FDIR reads the current directory into memory and displays it a full screen at a time. This is a perfect use for suballocation, since each directory entry is exactly 36 bytes long. FDIR has the structure shown in Figure 15-19.

FDIR starts by calling the subroutine ALLOCBUF to allocate and then initialize the initial memory segment, as shown in Figure 15-20.

The size of the initial allocation is equal to an arbitrary number of entries (ENTRYC) times the size of each directory element (DIRSTR) plus 8 bytes for the suballocation segment header. Note that this segment does not (initially) have to be large enough to contain the entire directory,

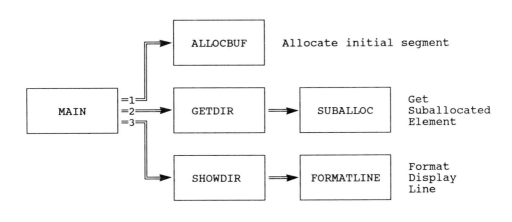

Figure 15-19. Structure of FDIR program

since it can be grown dynamically later with the DosReAllocSeg function call. The initial segment size is large enough to hold 100 entries (ENTRYC=100). The DosSubSet function prepares the allocated segment for subsequent suballocation calls. Notice that the second parameter is 1, signifying that this is an initialization request.

```
allocbuf     proc
             mov        dirsegsz,ENTRYC*DIRSTR+8 ;initialize segment size
             @DosAllocSeg dirsegsz,dirsegp,0 ;allocate segment
             @DosSubSet  dirsegp,1,dirsegsz ;prepare for suballocation
             push       dirsegp             ;put new selector
             pop        ds                  ;in DS
             ret
allocbuf     endp
```

Figure 15-20. ALLOCBUF subroutine

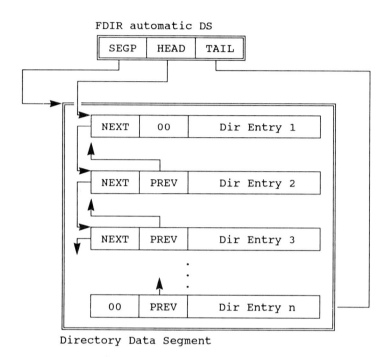

Figure 15-21. FDIR memory layout

Next, FDIR calls the GETDIR subroutine to read the current directory into memory. Before proceeding, however, look at the memory layout used by FDIR, illustrated in Figure 15-21.

The FDIR automatic data segment holds the selector of the segment which is allocated by ALLOCBUF. In this data segment, FDIR suballocates the individual directory elements. Each directory element contains a pointer to the next element, a pointer to the previous element, and the directory data. The automatic data segment also contains two pointers that locate the head and the tail of the directory element chain. Notice that the previous element pointer of the first element and the next element pointer of the last element are both set to 00 to indicate the end of the chain. This kind of double-threaded chain is common in programs that manage large numbers of data objects, and is useful for dynamically manipulating the elements (such as when sorting).

The GETDIR subprocedure, then, locates the first directory entry with the DosFindFirst function, suballocates the first element, and initializes the root pointer in the FDIR data segment and back pointer in the first element (see Figure 15-22).

Notice that GETDIR calls a subroutine named SUBALLOC to create the element. This subroutine returns the element offset in the field named DIREOFS. GETDIR then drops into a processing loop which reads the entire contents of the directory into memory (see Figure 15-23).

```
;
; Read first directory entry
;
        mov     si,offset dirdata       ;set pointer to data area
        @DosFindFirst dirall,dirhand,dirattrs,dirdata,DIRLEN,dirnum,rsv
        @jaxnz  gtd999                  ;exit if none
        mov     dircount,1              ;set initial file count
        call    suballoc                ;get initial block
        mov     di,direofs              ;get block pointer
        mov     word ptr ds:[di+2],0 ;set back pointer in first block
        mov     dirfirst,di             ;set root pointer to first block
```

Figure 15-22.   GETDIR subroutine

```
;
; Copy directory data into suballocated element
;
gtd010:         push    di                      ;save block pointer
                push    si                      ;save pointer to dirdata
                add     di,4                    ;skip fwd & back pointers
                mov     cx,DIRLEN               ;directory entry size
                push    es                      ;switch es & ds
                push    ds
                pop     es
                pop     ds
                rep     movsb                   ;move entry into block
                push    es                      ;switch es & ds
                push    ds
                pop     es
                pop     ds
                pop     si                      ;restore pointer to dirdata
                pop     di                      ;restore block pointer
;
; Read next directory entry
;
                @DosFindNext dirhand,dirdata,DIRLEN,dirnum
                @jaxnz  gtd800                  ;exit if end of directory
                inc     dircount                ;increment file count
                call    suballoc                ;get another block
                mov     bx,di                   ;save previous pointer
                mov     di,direofs              ;get new block pointer
                mov     ds:[bx+0],di            ;forward chain (in previous block)
                mov     ds:[di+2],bx            ;back chain (in new block)
                jmp     gtd010                  ;continue processing files
;
; Exit
;
gtd800:         mov     word ptr ds:[di+0],0 ;set forward pointer in last block

                        Operating System/2: From The Inside Out

                mov     dirlast,di              ;set root pointer to last block
```

Figure 15-23. Loops performed by GETDIR

GETDIR retrieves each subsequent directory entry by using the DosFindNext function, and as before, uses the SUBALLOC subroutine to suballocate a data element. GETDIR sets the previous element's forward pointer (PTR+0) to point to the new element and the new element's back pointer (PTR+2) to point to the previous element. In this way, GETDIR is creating the double-threaded chain on the fly. When it finishes processing directory

```
suballoc        proc
sal010:         @DosSubAlloc  dirsegp,direofs,DIRSTR ;suballocate block
                @jaxz       sal999              ;all OK - go exit
;
                add         dirsegsz,ENTRYC*DIRSTR ;increase segment size
                @DosReAllocSeg dirsegsz,dirsegp  ;grow segment
                @DosSubSet    dirsegp,0,dirsegsz ;re-initialize suballocation
                jmp         sal010              ;go sub-allocate block
;
sal999:         ret
suballoc        endp
```

Figure 15-24. SUBALLOC subroutine

entries, GETDIR sets the next pointer of the last element to 0 and DIRLAST to point to the last element. Thus, the data chain is complete.

Recall that the initial segment size was large enough to hold 100 directory entries. So what happens when the directory contains more than 100 files? To answer this question, you must look at the SUBALLOC subprocedure shown in Figure 15-24.

SUBALLOC starts by calling the DosSubAlloc function to carve out a new element in the directory data segment (whose selector is in DIRSEGP). If it succeeds, OS/2 places the new element offset in DIREOFS and SUBALLOC returns to its caller. However, if the segment fills up (AX<0), then SUBALLOC increases the segment size by 3,600 bytes (100 entries × 36 bytes each) and calls DosReAllocSeg to resize the physical data segment. But this is not all. Since the suballocation routines do not yet know that the segment has grown, SUBALLOC must once again call DosSubSet. However, this time the second parameter is 0, meaning that this is not an initialization request, but a resizing. If SUBALLOC had called DosSubSet with an initialization option (1), then the segment would be re-initialized and the previous directory data would be overwritten the next time it suballocated an element.

```
FDIR : Full Screen Directory Listing      <UP> Previous   <DOWN> Next <ESC> Exit
MANDEL87.OBJ    22:20:16  03/30/88   Not Archived
MANDEL87.EXE    22:20:22  03/30/88   Not Archived
ASM             13:42:01  07/03/88   Subdirectory
EDIT            13:42:20  07/03/88   Subdirectory
ARENA           13:42:22  07/03/88   Subdirectory
KEYMON.OUT      23:52:01  08/09/88   Not Archived
BEEP.OBJ        17:06:03  08/09/88   Not Archived
BEEP.MAP        17:06:06  08/09/88   Not Archived
DBG.HLP         12:37:06  05/14/88   Not Archived
FILEIO.ASM      09:27:20  08/21/88   Read-only Not Archived
DBG.EXE         14:13:28  06/22/88   Not Archived
UPCASE1.ASM     23:02:08  08/19/88   Read-only Not Archived
UPCASE2.ASM     22:54:16  08/19/88   Read-only Not Archived
CONIO.ASM       09:14:15  08/14/88   Not Archived
HEXDISP.ASM     21:50:13  08/24/88   Not Archived
UPCASE1.EXE     16:57:23  08/13/88   Not Archived
FILEIO.LST      15:46:19  08/23/88   Not Archived
UPCASE1.AB1     16:25:02  08/13/88   Not Archived
UPCASE1.AB2     16:24:26  08/13/88   Not Archived
UPCASE2.EXE     17:39:28  08/13/88   Not Archived
PROC            11:43:02  08/14/88   Not Archived
CONIO.EXE       09:15:12  08/14/88   Not Archived
SPLIT.ASM       18:02:03  08/20/88   Read-only Not Archived
HEXDISP.LST     21:51:23  08/24/88   Not Archived
```

Figure 15-25.   FDIR screen display

The remainder of FDIR interacts with the user and formats full-screen listings of the directory data contained in the suballocated elements. If you now run FDIR, you will see a display of the current directory, as shown in Figure 15-25.

Since the directory information is present in a double-threaded chain, it is not hard to imagine how FDIR could be enhanced to sort the elements (by date, size, and so forth) on the basis of user key sequences. The main display logic would remain intact, since it is independent of the element order. Similarly, other directory entries (from another directory, perhaps) could be added to the display by simply adding the elements to the chain and reinvoking the display logic.

SUMMARY

OS/2 provides significant advances over PC DOS in the area of memory management. Memory organization is the most critical aspect of a program's design. In many ways, to understand a program's data structures is to understand the program itself.

The OS/2 memory-management interfaces allow you to build programs that are based on true dynamic data structures. You can allocate, deallocate, shrink, and grow segments as needed. Programs can share these dynamically allocated segments with other processes in the system, either privately or globally.

The 80286 CPU architecture limits the size of memory segments to 64K. However, to help you deal with data objects larger than 64K, OS/2 includes a huge data object model.

Finally, with the exception of shared memory, all the OS/2 memory-management functions are part of the family API. This means that if you design your program by using the memory-management primitives, it can be bound to work on PC DOS. Naturally, in this environment the program can only access the PC DOS 640K address space. But in protected mode, it gains the advantages of OS/2 memory management.

As you move to the next chapter, remember the following points:

- How to request memory segments with DosAllocSeg
- 80286 limitations on segment size
- Program structure relationship to memory layout
- How and when to use DosMemAvail
- How to allocate and use huge memory objects
- Global and local shared-memory segments
- How and when to use memory suballocation

CHAPTER 16
PROGRAM EXECUTION CONTROL

When you write a program for OS/2, you have a number of impressive program-management facilities at your disposal. Using standard OS/2 API functions, you can create programs that start and control other (independent) processes, start and control multiple instances of execution within your program, and synchronize the activities of all these programs. This chapter reveals the true power of OS/2. With these facilities, you can construct sophisticated programs that would require a great deal of work to implement in PC DOS.

Before looking at the examples, consider several architectural principles. In OS/2, multitasking comes in several flavors. First, a process can start a second, independent, child process. The child process starts with a set of system resources (memory, files, pipes, devices, and so forth) given to it by its parent. From that point forward, it can acquire or release resources as it desires, independent of its parent. Processes are the OS/2 unit of resource management.

Secondly, any process can start multiple threads of execution within itself. Threads are highly cooperative programs that help the program perform its work. In fact, you can view them as asynchronous subroutines within a program. Each thread has equal access to all the resources acquired by, or given to, its process. For instance, one thread can open a file and a second can use the same handle to read from it. The only resource owned by a thread is its execution stack and register set. Naturally, a program that uses multiple threads must carefully coordinate its activities.

CREATING PROCESSES

This discussion begins with a look at the OS/2 facilities you use to create processes. To start a process, you use the DosExecPgm API.

The parameters for DosExecPgm are as follows:

PTR	The address of a buffer in which OS/2 will place an object that further qualifies the cause of the DosExecPgm call (for example, the name of "bad" dynamic-link library)
WORD	One word containing the length of the object buffer
WORD	The DosExec option flags used by OS/2 to process your request: 0 = Synchronous execution 1 = Asynchronous execution (discard child's result code) 2 = Asynchronous execution (save child's result code) 3 = Run program in "debug" mode 4 = Detached execution (in different session)
PTR	The address of two consecutive ASCIIZ strings. The first is the program name and the second is the "command-line" input. These are passed to the executed program in its environment segment

PTR	An ASCIIZ environment block that contains none or more ASCIIZ environment strings (in the form var-name=value), which are to be passed to the executed program in the environment segment
PTR	The address of a double-word area into which OS/2 will place process termination information. For asynchronous requests, the first word contains the PID of the terminated process. For synchronous requests, the first word contains the termination reason code: 0 = Normal exit 1 = Hard-error abort 2 = Trap 3 = DosKillProcess The second word always contains the child's (DosExit) result code.
PTR	A pointer to an ASCIIZ string that contains the name of the program to be executed

For example, the program fragment in Figure 16-1 starts the program named MYPROG.EXE as a child pro-

```
;
; Data segment
;
pgmname      db        'MYPROG.EXE',0        ;program name
pgmobj       db        10 dup(0)             ;bad exec object
pgmenv       db        'LEMONS=YELLOW',0,0   ;environment
pgmprm       db        'MYPROG.EXE',0        ;name
             db        ' 10,12',0            ;parameters
pgmpid       dw        0                     ;new process ID
             dw        0                     ;termination code area

                       .
                       .
                       .

;
; Code segment
;
             @DosExecPgm  pgmobj,10,SYNC,pgmprm,pgmenv,pgmpid,pgmname
```

Figure 16-1.   Routine to start MYPROG.EXE as child process

cess. Consider the information passed in the DOSEXEC-PGM parameter list. If the call does not succeed, the PGMOBJ area is used by OS/2 to return additional failure information. This is critical data because EXEC failures in OS/2 can be caused by seemingly distant problems (such as a failure to find a dynamic-link library). On such a failure, PGMOBJ would contain the name of the errant dynamic-link library. The second parameter (10), tells OS/2 the size of the bad object buffer.

The third parameter tells OS/2 what type of Dos-ExecPgm function you desire. OS/2 allows you to choose between five options:

1. *Synchronous execution (0).* Your program waits until the child process is finished. It "blocks" on the DosExecPgm function. This makes it equivalent to the PC DOS INT 21H 4B subfunction. You can use this type of EXEC call if the program you are running is relatively short and you have nothing else to do in the main program (such as kicking off a background print with the PRINT command).

2. *Asynchronous execution with no termination code (1).* The child process executes asynchronously and its termination code is not saved. This means that your program is free to do other things once the child process is started. In addition, you are not particularly interested in how the child program ends, so you are telling OS/2 to discard its termination code when it ends.

3. *Asynchronous execution with termination code (2).* As before, you run the child asynchronously, but this time you instruct OS/2 to keep the termination code information around so you can query it with the DosCWait API. When you use this function, OS/2 puts the child in a "zombie" state after it completes. This state is cleared when you issue DosCWait. If

you never intend to query the termination code information, you should use option 1, since it allows OS/2 to clean up immediately after the child ends.

4. *Asynchronous execution with debug capabilities (3).* This option allows you to run the program asynchronously with additional debug capabilities. Usually, one process cannot view or in any way alter the memory allocated to another process. However, this is a problem if your program is a debugger and it is executing a second program that it wants to debug. This DosExecPgm function, in conjunction with the DosPTrace API, enables a debugger to run a second process and then control its execution. You would not use this function in typical OS/2 application programs.

5. *Asynchronous execution in a null session (4).* This option starts an asynchronous child in a separate (null) session. Use this option when you wish to start a child process that will operate as a deamon (an unattended program). The child may not perform any video or keyboard I/O other than VioPopUp, since it is associated with a session that has no console I/O capabilities. Also, if your main process dies, the child will continue to execute as an orphan process.

The parameters for DosCWait are as follows:

WORD	A one-word action code that tells OS/2 for what it is to wait: 0 = Wait for process to end 1 = Wait for process and its descendants to end
WORD	A one-word wait option that tells how to wait: 0 = Synchronous (wait until process(es) end) 1 = Asynchronous (return if none have ended)
PTR	The address of a double-word area into which OS/2 will place process-termination information. The first

	word contains the termination reason code: 0 = Normal exit 1 = Hard-error abort 2 = Trap 3 = DosKillProcess The second word contains the child's (DosExit) result code
PTR	A pointer to a one-word value into which OS/2 will place the terminating PID
WORD	A one-word PID for which DosCWait is to explicitly wait. If 0, then DosCWait will wait for any process termination

As you can see, you have a great deal of flexibility when it comes to how you EXEC programs. Which technique you employ will depend on the requirements of your application.

The next two parameters in the DosExecPgm call tell OS/2 what parameter list and what environment data your program is to receive in its environment segment. Using these areas, you can "trick" a program into thinking it was run from the OS/2 command line. Notice that each is a zero-terminated string. The parameter list contains two zero-terminated strings: the first is the program name and the second is the program parameters. In the case of the environment area, it is terminated by two 0's. The first signifies the end of the last environment variable and the second signifies the end of the area itself. So in this example, the program would receive the environment segment shown in Figure 16-2. This is exactly what the program would see if it had been started from the command line.

The next double-word parameter used by OS/2 returns system and process termination-code information (for synchronous EXECs) or the PID of the child (for asynchronous EXECs).

Finally, the last parameter of the DosExecPgm call tells OS/2 the name of the EXE file that should be loaded into the child process. Notice that since this is separately specified from the program name string, you could start a

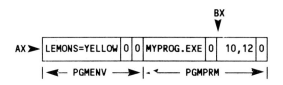

Figure 16-2.   MYPROG.EXE program environment segment

program and tell it that it has a different name. For example, if you are running different (test) versions of MYPROG, you could tell OS/2 to execute MYPROG2.EXE and still put MYPROG.EXE in the parameter area.

Note that each time you start a program with DosExecPgm, a fresh copy of the EXE file is read from disk (to initialize the automatic data areas). This is a big difference between processes and threads: when you start a process, OS/2 loads an EXE file, but when you start a thread, OS/2 runs code that is already contained in the system.

Now consider an example. Assume you have a program (RUN) that will synchronously EXEC a second program (COUNT). COUNT is simply a counting program that increments a counter from 1 to 65,535, displays the counter on the screen, and exits when it is finished (see Figure 16-3).

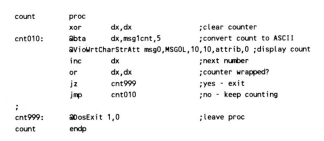

```
count      proc
           xor     dx,dx                  ;clear counter
cnt010:    @bta    dx,msg1cnt,5           ;convert count to ASCII
           @VioWrtCharStrAtt msg0,MSGOL,10,10,attrib,0 ;display count
           inc     dx                     ;next number
           or      dx,dx                  ;counter wrapped?
           jz      cnt999                 ;yes - exit
           jmp     cnt010                 ;no - keep counting
;
cnt999:    @DosExit 1,0                    ;leave proc
count      endp
```

Figure 16-3.   Simple COUNT program

```
run          proc
             @VioScrollUp 0,0,-1,-1,-1,fill,0 ;clear the screen
             @DosExecPgm  pgmobj,10,0,pgmprm,pgmenv,pgmpid,pgmname ;run COUNT
             @DosExit 1,0                ;leave proc
run          endp
```

Figure 16-4.   RUN starting COUNT and terminating when count ends

RUN starts COUNT with a synchronous DosExecPgm call and terminates when count ends, as shown in Figure 16-4. This program is not elaborate. When you start RUN, it executes COUNT and you see the following at column 10, row 10 of the screen:

Count = 22345

The number is constantly updated. Also note that when you run this program, OS/2 reads the COUNT program in from disk in response to the RUN DosExecPgm call.

However, this example is not too different from what you can do in PC DOS, since both programs are running synchronously. So now change RUN a little bit to make it run more than one copy of COUNT asynchronously. To do this, you must change COUNT to receive its screen position from RUN, so that the display counters do not overlay one another. One option you have is to pass the data to COUNT as command-line parameters, but this would involve parsing the command-line input and converting the values to binary. Instead, you can use shared memory to pass a parameter list to COUNT.

You can use a named memory segment to contain the data that COUNT will use to display its counter. But what name you could use that will uniquely identify a memory segment to an instance of COUNT is relatively simple.

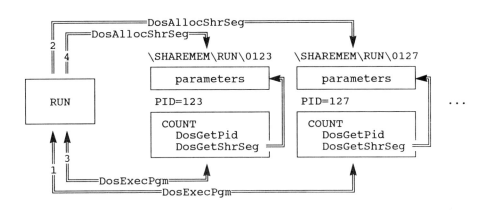

Figure 16-5. Operation of RUN and COUNT together

You can solve this dilemma when you note that each process in the system has a unique PID. The child's PID is returned to the program, which issues the EXEC call (such as RUN). Likewise, a child process (such as COUNT) can determine its own PID. Thus, RUN can execute a copy of COUNT and create a named shared-memory segment whose name is based on the child's PID. Conversely, COUNT can retrieve its PID by using the DosGetPid API function, construct a shared-memory segment name, and gain access to its parameter list. So RUN and COUNT now work as shown in Figure 16-5.

The parameters for DosGetPid are as follows:

PTR	A pointer to a three-word field in which OS/2 will place the PID information. The field has the following format:
	WORD1 The current PID WORD2 The current thread identification WORD3 The PID of the parent

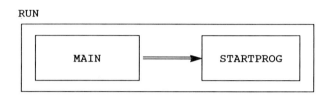

RUN

MAIN → STARTPROG

Figure 16-6. Structure of RUN program

Each instance of COUNT has a unique named shared-memory segment in which RUN can pass it parameters. The RUN program itself is structured as shown in Figure 16-6. The main routine calls the STARTPROG subroutine a number of times to start copies of COUNT (see Figure 16-7).

```
main       proc
;
           @VioScrollUp 0,0,-1,-1,-1,fill,0 ;clear the screen
           mov       cx,PCOUNT             ;program count
           lea       si,count1             ;first set of parameters
run010:    call      startprog             ;start COUNT program
           add       si,SHRSZ              ;point to next parameter area
           loop      run010                ;start next program
;
           @DosExit 1,0                     ;leave proc
main       endp
```

Figure 16-7. Main routine of RUN program

RUN starts four child processes (PCOUNT=4) and exits, thus leaving four "orphan" counting programs running in the session. Notice that the parameter data area for each version of COUNT is defined in a data structure named CDATA, as follows:

```
cdata     struc
row       dw      ?              ;Display Row
col       dw      ?              ;Display Column
attr      db      ?              ;Display Attribute
cdata     ends
```

CDATA is also used by COUNT to format the information from the shared-memory segment. RUN allocates four sets of these parameter areas with different values for each of the four COUNT programs it will eventually start:

```
count1    cdata   <4,03,1fh>     ;Count #1 initial parameters
          cdata   <4,22,2fh>     ;Count #2 initial parameters
          cdata   <4,41,4fh>     ;Count #3 initial parameters
          cdata   <4,60,6fh>     ;Count #4 initial parameters
PCOUNT    equ     4              ;program count
```

Thus, RUN is a table-driven program. To start more copies of COUNT, you simply add another table entry and increase the program count (PCOUNT).

The STARTPROG subroutine takes the parameter input from MAIN (in the SI register) and starts a COUNT program (see Figure 16-8).

Notice that after the DosExecPgm service completes, STARTPROG converts the child's PID (to ASCII), puts the value into the shared-memory segment name, allocates the shared segment, and copies the initial parameter set into it. With this simple code, RUN has created four copies of COUNT that will each run asynchronously in different portions of the screen and display their results in different colors.

```
startprog    proc
             push      cx                  ;save cx
             push      si                  ;save si
;
             @DosExecPgm  pgmobj,10,2,pgmprm,pgmenv,pgmpid,pgmname
             @bth      pgmpid,shrpid       ;convert pid to HEX (for segname)
             mov       ax,pgmpid           ;get new PID
             mov       [si].procid,ax      ;save it in parameter block
;
             @DosAllocShrSeg SHRSZ,shrname,shrsel ;allocate shared segment
             push      shrsel              ;put shared memory selector
             pop       es                  ;in ES
             xor       di,di               ;start of shared segment
             mov       cx,SHRSZ            ;data structure size
             rep       movsb               ;copy structure into shared seg
;
             pop       si                  ;restore si
             pop       cx                  ;restore cx
             ret
startprog    endp
```

Figure 16-8. STARTPROG subroutine

Now consider what COUNT does. It is structured as shown in Figure 16-9. It too has a main routine that calls a separate "worker" subroutine. In the MAIN program, COUNT gains addressability to the shared segment and runs the counter (see Figure 16-10).

Notice that since OS/2 is a preemptive dispatching sys-

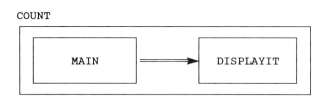

Figure 16-9. Structure of COUNT program

```
main        proc
            push        ds              ;copy ds
            pop         es              ;to es
;
            @DosGetPid piddata          ;get process ID information
            @bth        piddata.pidpid,shrpid   ;convert to hex (for sharename)
            @bth        piddata.pidpid,msg1pid   ;convert to hex (for message)
;
cnt010:     @DosGetShrSeg shrname,shrsel   ;get shared segment
            @jaxz       cnt020          ;Segment exists - go count
            @DosSleep sleepct           ;wait a little while
            jmp         cnt010          ;go try again
;
cnt020:     push        shrsel          ;put shared memory selector
            pop         ds              ;in ES
            xor         di,di           ;point to start of segment
            xor         dx,dx           ;clear counter
;
cnt030:     call        printit         ;display information
            @DosSleep sleepct           ;wait a little while
            inc         dx              ;next number
            jmp         cnt030          ;keep counting
;
main        endp
```

Figure 16-10.   Main routine of COUNT program

tem, COUNT could possibly execute *before* RUN finishes allocating the shared-memory segment. To guard against this situation, COUNT sleeps for a short period of time if the DosGetShrSeg function fails. This gives RUN the opportunity to finish allocating the segment before COUNT tries to access it again.

From this point forward, COUNT simply displays the counter information (calling PRINTIT), sleeps for a short time, increments the counter, and then repeats the entire process.

The PRINTIT subroutine shown in Figure 16-11 extracts the row (ROW), column (COL), and display attribute (ATTRIB) values from the shared-parameter area and displays a small window that contains the counter value and PID of the COUNT program. Thus, the count is displayed wherever the RUN program has requested COUNT to display it. Notice that, although this version of

```
printit     proc
            mov     al,[di].attr        ;get attribute
            mov     attrib,ax           ;put it in memory
;
            @bta    dx,msg1cnt,5        ;convert count to ASCII
            @VioWrtCharStrAtt msg0,MSG0L,[di].row,[di].col,attrib,0 ;Line 1
            mov     bx,[di].row         ;get row
            inc     bx                  ;next line
            @VioWrtCharStrAtt msg1,MSG1L,bx,[di].col,attrib,0       ;Line 2
            inc     bx                  ;next line
            @VioWrtCharStrAtt msg2,MSG2L,bx,[di].col,attrib,0       ;Line 3
            inc     bx                  ;next line
            @VioWrtCharStrAtt msg3,MSG3L,bx,[di].col,attrib,0       ;Line 4
;
            ret
printit     endp
```

Figure 16-11.   PRINTIT subroutine

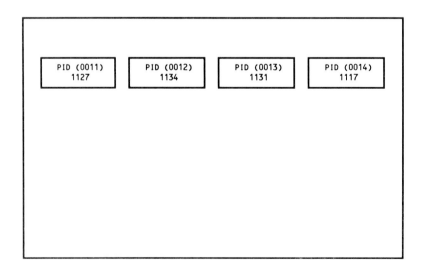

Figure 16-12.   RUN program screen display

RUN does not do it, you could dynamically move the count window by changing the coordinates in the shared-memory segment, since they are being used to position the window in each display iteration.

If you start RUN, you will see the screen illustrated in Figure 16-12.

You now have a program that creates four child processes and exits. However, notice that even when the main program terminates, OS/2 does not return the command prompt. This is because RUN did not start the processes as "detached" programs. The session remains dedicated to the four orphan processes until you press CTRL-BREAK to end them. Each COUNT program runs independently of the other, and uses the information in a shared-memory segment to display its results in a different portion of the screen. This in itself is a far cry from the capabilities of PC DOS, but is only a glimpse of what you can do with the OS/2 API functions.

MANIPULATING EXECUTION PRIORITIES

If you execute the RUN program, you notice that while the four counter values are never exactly equal, they are close to one another. This is because each COUNT program is running at the same execution priority. The OS/2 dispatcher is giving each program an equal number of CPU time slices.

However, this is not always desirable. For example, consider a point-of-sale system. In this environment you could have a process that is performing some critical work, such as looking up a price for a cash register transaction. And at the same time, the system could be running lower-priority tasks, such as generating sales reports for the home office. In this scenario, you certainly would not want the report and the price-lookup to compete for the CPU. You would want the price-lookup to run at a higher priority and temporarily displace the sales report.

Chapter 5 explained how OS/2 implements a multi-tiered priority scheme. At the top is the time-critical class. It is used to run critical programs that must be immediately dispatched when certain events occur (such as when a communications line goes down). Next is regular class where the bulk of the OS/2 programs run. Finally, idle class is used to run programs whose work is not critical and could be done with spare CPU cycles (such as a background "batch" processor).

OS/2 allows you to manipulate the priority of processes with the DosSetPrty API function.

The parameters for DosSetPrty are as follows:

WORD	The scope of the priority change: 0 = The process and all its threads 1 = The process and all its descendants 2 = A single thread within the current process
WORD	A one-word value indicating the new process/thread priority class: 0 = Do not change the current class 1 = Change to idle-priority class 2 = Change to regular-priority class 3 = Change to time-critical priority class
WORD	A one-word value indicating the delta that OS/2 should apply to the base priority level (-31 to $+31$)
WORD	The ID of the process (scope=0,1) or thread (scope=2) whose priority is to be set

DosSetPrty enables a process to change the priority class (0-2) and level (0-31) of itself or of any of its children. For example,

```
@DosSetPrty 0,0,+1,0          ;increase priority by 1
```

increases the priority level of the issuing process by 1, and leaves its priority class unchanged.

DosGetPrty, on the other hand, enables you to query yours or a child's priority class and level.

The parameters for DosGetPrty are as follows:

WORD	The scope of the query:
	0 = Return the priority of the first thread
	2 = Return the priority of the indicated thread
PTR	The address of a one-word area into which OS/2 will return the priority value
WORD	The identification of the process (scope=0) or thread (scope=2) whose priority is to be returned

For example,

```
@DosGetPrty 0,prty,CX          ;get child's priority value
```

queries the priority of a child process whose PID is in the
CX register. OS/2 returns the priority value in the field
named PRTY.

You can use these facilities in the point-of-sale example
to run the price-lookup transaction at a high priority (say,
regular class level 26) and the batch report(s) at idle class
level 31.

These functions can now be incorporated in the RUN/
COUNT programs to see the effects of the OS/2 priorities.
First, the RUN program is restructured to wait on the
keyboard instead of exiting, as shown in Figure 16-13.

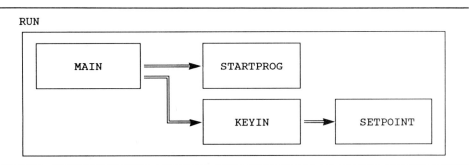

Figure 16-13. Restructured RUN program

```
keyin      proc
;
           call        setpoint              ;set pointer to active process
;
kin000:    @KbdCharIn keyd,0,0               ;read keyboard
           mov         al,keyd.charascii     ;get ASCII character
           cmp         al,0                  ;extended scan?
           jne         kin010                ;no, go check which key it was
           mov         ah,keyd.charscan      ;get scan code
;
kin010:    cmp         ax,KESC               ;escape key?
           jne         kin020                ;no - continue
           jmp         kin999                ;yes - exit
;
kin020:    cmp         ax,KLE                ;left key?
           jne         kin030                ;no - continue
           dec         curproc               ;previous process
           and         curproc,03h           ;isolate number (0-3)
           call        setpoint              ;move pointer
           jmp         kin000                ;continue
;
kin030:    cmp         ax,KRI                ;right key?
           jne         kin040                ;no - continue
           inc         curproc               ;next process
           and         curproc,03h           ;isolate number (0-3)
           call        setpoint              ;move pointer
           jmp         kin000                ;continue
;
kin040:    cmp         ax,KUP                ;up key?
           jne         kin050                ;no - continue
           @DosSetPrty 0,0,+1,[si].procid ;increase priority by 1
           jmp         kin000                ;continue
;
kin050:    cmp         ax,KDN                ;down key?
           jne         kin060                ;no - continue
           @DosSetPrty 0,0,-1,[si].procid ;decrease priority by 1
kin060:    jmp         kin000                ;continue
;
kin999:    ret
keyin      endp
```

Figure 16-14.   KEYIN subroutine of RUN program

Since RUN no longer ends after it starts the COUNT programs, it calls a new subroutine (KEYIN) to accept commands you enter from the keyboard, as shown in Figure 16-14. The ESC key ends KEYIN and causes the RUN program to end (as before). The LEFT ARROW and RIGHT ARROW keys move a pointer between the COUNT "windows." The UP ARROW and DOWN ARROW keys increase or decrease the priority of the COUNT program currently being pointed to. The SETPOINT subroutine actually displays the pointer under the correct COUNT window.

Now you see how a parent process (RUN) can use DosSetPrty to manipulate the priorities of its child processes (COUNT). By the way, you probably noticed that the CDATA structure has been expanded to save the child process identification (PROCID) in each parameter block. Thus, the UP ARROW and DOWN ARROW keys simply change the priority of the process associated with whatever parameter block is pointed to by the SI register.

But before you run this new program, make a small change to the COUNT PRINTIT subroutine so that it displays its current priority in the COUNT window:

```
;
        @DosGetPrty 0,myprty,0      ;get my current priority value
        mov         bx,myprty       ;get priority
        xor         bh,bh           ;clear priority class
        @bta        bx,msgprty,2    ;convert to displayable ASCII
;
```

So each time COUNT is about to re-display its window, it first calls DosGetPrty to determine its priority, converts the value to ASCII, and adds it to the display window. Note that in this example the parent sets the priority and the child displays it. You could also structure these programs so that RUN does not directly update the COUNT priority. Instead it might update a field in the COUNT shared segment, which COUNT would later use to update its own priority. But this method has a small disadvantage. If you rely on COUNT to update its own priority, it cannot do so until it is dispatched.

If you now run the modified RUN/COUNT programs, you will see the screen illustrated in Figure 16-15. As you press the RIGHT ARROW and LEFT ARROW keys, RUN moves the small process pointer under each COUNT win-

```
┌─────────────────────────────────────────────────────────────────┐
│                                                                   │
│                                                                   │
│   ┌────────────────┐ ┌────────────────┐ ┌────────────────┐ ┌────────────────┐ │
│   │PID(0054)   134 │ │PID(0055)   122 │ │PID(0056)   111 │ │PID(0057)   133 │ │
│   │Priority =   0  │ │Priority =   0  │ │Priority =   0  │ │Priority =   0  │ │
│   └────────────────┘ └────────────────┘ └────────────────┘ └────────────────┘ │
│            ↑                                                      │
│                                                                   │
│                                                                   │
│                    <LEFT> Previous Process                        │
│                   <RIGHT> Next Process                            │
│                      <UP> Increase Priority                       │
│                    <DOWN> Decrease Priority                       │
│                                                                   │
│                                                                   │
│                                                                   │
└─────────────────────────────────────────────────────────────────┘
```

Figure 16-15. RUN program with priority-manipulation options

dow. When you press the UP ARROW and DOWN ARROW keys, RUN changes the priority of the selected child process, which the child then reflects in its count window.

You can now play with the priority values to see the effect of the OS/2 dispatching algorithms. For example, if you set the priority values of each COUNT program to 1, 2, 3, and 4, then let the program run for two minutes, you will see the count skew illustrated in Figure 16-16.

After watching RUN execute for a while, you may ask, "If the priority of one COUNT program is greater than the other, then why is one program not getting all the CPU cycles?" The answer comes in two parts. First, the OS/2 dispatcher has a CPU starvation algorithm that gives all processes a fair shot at the CPU. Depending on the setting of the MAXWAIT= parameter in your CONFIG.SYS file,

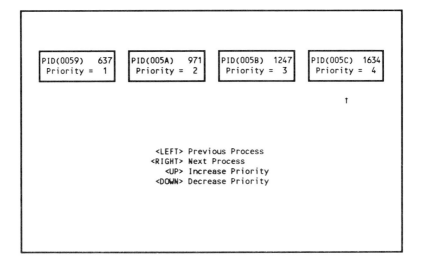

```
┌──────────────┐ ┌──────────────┐ ┌──────────────┐ ┌──────────────┐
│PID(0059)  637│ │PID(005A)  971│ │PID(005B) 1247│ │PID(005C) 1634│
│Priority =  1 │ │Priority =  2 │ │Priority =  3 │ │Priority =  4 │
└──────────────┘ └──────────────┘ └──────────────┘ └──────────────┘
                                                           ↑

               <LEFT> Previous Process
              <RIGHT> Next Process
                 <UP> Increase Priority
               <DOWN> Decrease Priority
```

Figure 16-16. RUN program with priority changes (two-minute run)

each process in the system will be guaranteed at least one CPU time slice each n seconds. The default setting is one starvation cycle per three seconds.

However, this example contains one other overriding factor. If you recall, the COUNT program has a DosSleep statement to make it sleep for a short period of time in each count cycle. Since this sleep interval is less than one time slice (30 ms), but greater than 0, each COUNT process will effectively give up the remainder of its time slice after it updates its counter. Therefore, the other lower-priority processes have ample opportunities to run. If you want to see the effect of the CPU starvation algorithm alone, set the counter sleep count to 0 and rerun the example. You will see very different results. On the other hand, if you make the sleep count much greater than a time slice (say, 400ms), then changing the priorities will not have much effect on the counter values, since each process will undoubtedly get an equal number of time slices.

This all proves one point: Manipulating the priorities of processes will give you different results, depending on the characteristics of the processes. If you have processes that are blocked most of the time while waiting for external events, then the different priorities will have little effect (since the priority change alone will not "speed up" the external events). On the other hand, if you have processes that are CPU-bound, then a higher-priority value will have a drastic effect on the distribution of CPU cycles.

MANAGING CHILD PROCESSES

You can stop any process you start with DosExecPgm by using the DosKillProcess API. DosKillProcess does just what its name implies — it kills a process with no questions asked.

The parameters of the DosKillProcess are as follows:

WORD	A one-word action code used by OS/2 to process the request: 0 = Kill the specified process and all its descendants 1 = Kill only the specified process
WORD	The one-word PID of the process to be killed

You can incorporate this function in the MAIN routine of RUN to bring it down more gracefully, without having to resort to CTRL-BREAK to bring down the child processes. So if you add the code shown in Figure 16-17 to the MAIN routine on return from KEYIN, then RUN will come down gracefully when you press the ESC key. In addition, you can make a small addition to the KEYIN routine that enables you to bring down the COUNT programs selectively with the DEL key and restart them with the INS key, as shown in Figure 16-18.

```
;
              mov       cx,PCOUNT           ;program count
              lea       si,count1           ;first set of parameters
run020:       @DosKillProcess 0,[si].procid ;Kill child process
              @DosFreeSeg [si].sel          ;Free shared memory segment
              add       si,SHRSZ            ;point to next parameter area
              loop      run020              ;loop through process list
```

Figure 16-17. Killing child processes on exit from RUN

If you press DEL, then the COUNT program associated with the pointer is killed and its PID is zeroed out in the data structure. If you press INS and the current PID is 0, then RUN calls the STARTPROG routine to restart the process.

With these small changes, you can interactively start and stop child processes from RUN. You can apply these principles in any type of multiprocess OS/2 program.

```
kin060:       cmp       ax,KINS             ;insert key?
              jne       kin070              ;no - continue
              cmp       [si].procid,0       ;process stopped?
              je        kin065              ;yes - continue
              jmp       kin000              ;no - ignore request
kin065:       call      startprog           ;start program
              jmp       kin000              ;continue
;
kin070:       cmp       ax,KDEL             ;delete key?
              jne       kin500              ;no - continue
              cmp       [si].procid,0       ;process already stopped?
              jne       kin075              ;no - continue
              jmp       kin000              ;yes - ignore request
kin075:       @DosKillProcess 0,[si].procid ;Kill child process
              @DosFreeSeg [si].sel          ;Free shared memory segment
              mov       [si].procid,0       ;mark process ID null
              jmp       kin000              ;continue
;
kin500:       jmp       kin000              ;continue
```

Figure 16-18. Modification of KEYIN subroutine

RESOURCE CLEANUP AND SYSTEM SIGNALS

You have now seen how to use the DosExecPgm API to create multiple OS/2 processes, and later use DosKillProcess to destroy them. The child processes can operate independently from their parent and perform a specific task (such as counting). This gives you a great deal of flexibility in how you structure OS/2 programs.

But what happens when a process (child or parent) is not ready to terminate? How does it "clean up" after itself? In many situations, processes must perform some type of termination processing before they exit the system.

For example, consider a communications program that processes transactions from a remote computer. Since it could be actively completing a transaction, it certainly does not want to be "killed" before it finishes, or at least before it notifies the remote program that it will never finish the transaction. Such a process could use some kind of notification to tell the remote program that it is about to end, with a little time to do some minimal shutdown processing.

This is precisely what OS/2 signals are used for. Each time OS/2 is ready to *terminate* a process, it generates a *signal*. A signal is an asynchronous event notification, much like a software interrupt in PC DOS. OS/2 generates signals for several different types of events, including process termination and CTRL-C.

To receive a signal, your process must register a signal handler by using the DosSetSigHandler API. If no signal handler is registered, OS/2 will take a default action for each type of signal. The OS/2 signals and their default actions are listed in Table 16-1. If you do not want to write your own signal handler, you can also use DosSetSigHandler to change the default actions for your process. If you do this, however, you should be careful not to create a process that cannot be killed.

Table 16-1. OS/2 Signals

Signal	Value	Default Action
CTRL-C	1	Terminate process
Terminate	3	Terminate process
CTRL-BREAK	4	Terminate process
User Flag A	5	Ignore
User Flag B	6	Ignore
User Flag C	7	Ignore

The parameters for DosSetSigHandler are as follows:

DWRD	The address (segment, offset) of a routine that OS/2 will call when the requested signal is received (can be NULL for action codes 0, 1, 3, and 4)
PTR	A pointer to a double-word area into which OS/2 will place the address of the previous signal handler routine (may be NULL)
PTR	A pointer to a one-word area into which OS/2 will place the previous action code for this signal (can be NULL)
WORD	A one-word action code that tells OS/2 how to process this request: 0 = Set the default system action 1 = Ignore the signal 2 = Give control to the specified routine 3 = Generate error if another process uses this flag 4 = Ignore the signal
WORD	The signal number (1, 3, 4, 5, 6, 7)

In the RUN/COUNT example, it would be nice if the count "windows" of dead processes were blank so you could tell which programs were running and which were not.

But to clear the windows from the RUN program defeats the purpose of running "independent" COUNT processes. Remember, the RUN program starts them and controls them, but the COUNT programs are responsible for managing their own windows. In a real-life example, the child process might have some state information that is not shared by the parent, so it would have to handle its own termination.

This is a good example of where you would use the DosSetSigHandler function. You establish a termination signal handler in COUNT by adding the code shown in Figure 16-19 to the program.

Notice that you must pass DosSetSigHandler a pointer to a double-word area containing the segment and offset of your termination procedure. When a termination signal is received by the process, OS/2 runs the signal handler using the system stack. However, other than the SS, SP, CS, and IP registers, the context of the termination routine is unchanged from what it was when the signal was received. This simply means that the contents of the other registers is unpredictable. So, the signal handler must reestablish its own addressability. In the example shown in Figure 16-20, the termination routine starts by reloading the data segment address into DS. Once it has access to the COUNT data segment, TERMPROC can check to see if the shared segment has been allocated. If it has not, it simply exits. If it has, it uses the screen coordinates in the shared segment to clear the display window and writes the string "Dead!" where the window was.

Note that even though the termination routine runs in an unpredictable register context, it is still permitted to make most API calls. The only functions that are strictly off-limits are those that will create a new process or thread (for example, DosCreateProcess).

When OS/2 starts a signal handler (any type), it places information that defines the signaling condition on the

```
         Data Segment ...

         ;
         termp        dw        offset termproc       ;termination proc
                      dw        seg termproc
         ;

         Code Segment ...

                      @DosSetSigHandler termp,NULL,NULL,2,SIGTERM ;register sig handler
```

Figure 16-19.   Registering a termination signal handler in COUNT

```
         termproc     proc
         ;
                      mov       ax,CNT_data          ;get my DS
                      mov       es,ax                ;address it
                      cmp       shrsel,0             ;shared segment in place?
                      jne       trm010               ;yes, continue processing
                      jmp       trm999               ;no - exit
         ;
         trm010:      mov       ax,shrsel            ;get shared segment
                      mov       ds,ax                ;address it
                      xor       di,di                ;point to start of segment
         ;
                      mov       bx,[di].row          ;get row number
                      add       bx,4                 ;bottom row
                      mov       dx,[di].col          ;get column number
                      push      dx                   ;save starting column
                      add       dx,MSGL              ;bottom column
                      @VioScrollUp [di].row,[di].col,bx,dx,-1,fill,0 ;clear the window
                      sub       bx,2                 ;up 2 rows
                      pop       dx                   ;restore column
                      @VioWrtCharStrAtt dead,MSGL,bx,dx,red,0 ;Dead message
         trm999:      @DosExit 0,1                   ;end process
```

Figure 16-20.   COUNT termination routine

Table 16-2.   Signal Information

Register	Function
CS	Signal handler segment
IP	Signal handler offset
Other Regs	*Indeterminate*
SS:SP	Far return address (ignore signal)
SS:SP+4	Signal number
SS:SP+6	SIGARG from DosFlagProcess (signals 5-7)

stack. Table 16-2 summarizes the signal-handler entry context.

If the signal handler performs a far return, then the process will continue to run where it was interrupted. So, the signal handler could conceivably set a flag in the data segment, exit, and tell its main process to terminate at some convenient point.

If you make these changes, execute the RUN program, and press DEL, you will see the screen depicted in Figure 16-21. Notice that, as expected, the COUNT termination procedure replaced the count window with the "Dead!" message.

CREATING MULTIPLE EXECUTION THREADS

You have now seen how to create and control "loosely coupled" OS/2 programs by creating independent processes. But that is not all there is to the OS/2 multitasking facilities. In fact, the system contains an entirely different class of "tightly coupled" multitasking facilities called *threads*. While processes are separate, autonomous in-

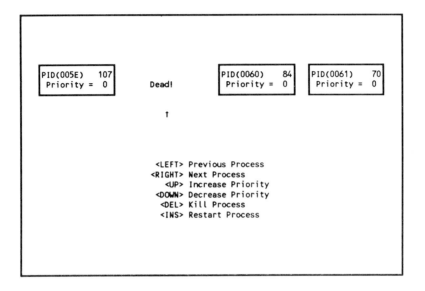

Figure 16-21. Terminated child process

stances of execution, threads are integrated, closely related portions of the same program. You can view a thread as an asynchronous subroutine within your program.

You can use threads whenever you need to do more than one thing at a time within a program, yet do not need the absolute independence of a process.

To contrast threads and processes, consider how you would build a terminal emulator program. This is a particularly good example because in a terminal emulator, you have to manage input from two asynchronous sources: the keyboard and the communications line (a COM port). In PC DOS, you would write this program with a "polling" loop, alternatively checking the status of the keyboard and the COM port. As you have already seen, however, polling is something to avoid in multitasking

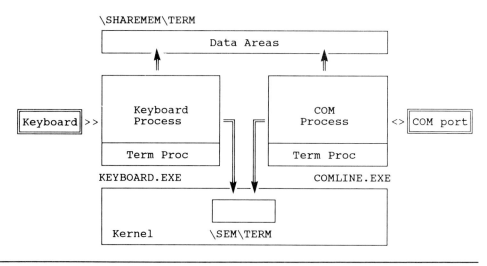

Figure 16-22. Multiprocess terminal emulator

environments. Instead, you strive to build programs that are event-driven. In OS/2 you might build this as a multiprocess program, with a structure like that shown in Figure 16-22.

But consider the cost of this proposition. If the terminal emulator were spread among multiple processes, it would have to allocate shared memory to maintain its data structures. Each time a character was entered in the "keyboard" process, it would have to be sent to the "COM" process to be sent to the COM port.

The processes would have to be tightly synchronized by using system semaphores, and each would need a termination procedure. Also, the "keyboard" and "COM" processes must be built as separate EXE files and then individually loaded when the emulator is started. This is clearly a lot of work for such a simple multitasking application.

The alternative is threads. The terminal emulator could be built as a single program with two threads of execution (depicted in Figure 16-23). The first thread

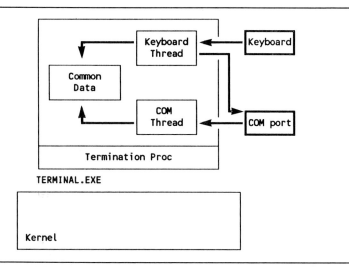

Figure 16-23. Multi-thread terminal emulator

waits on the keyboard and the second reads from the COM port. Since they are in the same process, the threads share the same address space, so they do not need to allocate shared memory.

Either thread has access to the COM device, so the keyboard thread can write directly to the COM port, without having to pass the I/O request to the COM thread. They still have to synchronize activities, but since they are in the same process, they can use the more efficient RAM semaphores. The emulator needs only one termination routine. Lastly, the code needed to run the emulator is packaged in a single EXE file. Clearly, this is a much simpler design.

Threads, then, are an effective way to build tightly coupled multitasking programs. However, they are not a substitute for multiple processes, since what they gain in efficiency they lose in isolation. Programs that are written by two different programmers (such as a transaction pro-

cessor and a transaction) must be built as separate processes, since it is unlikely that both programmers would
wish to share the same data structures and address space.

Every OS/2 process is started with one thread of execution (thread 0). Thread 0 can then create other threads
with the DosCreateThread API call.

The parameters for DosCreateThread are as follows:

PTR	A double-word pointer to the program that OS/2 will run in the thread
PTR	A pointer to a one-word field into which OS/2 will return the thread ID of the newly created thread
DWRD	A double-word value that OS/2 will use as a stack for the new thread

As OS/2 creates the threads, it gives them a thread ID
that is unique within the process. Note that the threads
are not visible outside the process. That is, a program in a
different process has no notion of how many threads you
have created within your process, much in the same way it
does not know how many subroutines you have in your
code. Threads are a tool used by a program to execute
multiple routines simultaneously, with no resource-
management implications.

In OS/2, the thread is the basic unit of dispatchability.
Each thread has its own (settable) priority class and level.
When you start a thread, it assumes the default priority of
the process, but you can change it with the DosSetPrty
call. In fact, some of the APIs presented earlier in this
chapter (DosGetPrty, DosSetPrty, DosGetPid, and so on)
work for either a process or a thread.

The code running within a thread has its own register
and stack context. If you build a multithreaded program,
you can assign different uses for each register in each
thread. You provide the stack and the starting routine
address to the DosCreateThread function. For example,
the code in Figure 16-24 first allocates a 512-byte stack
and then starts a separate thread (using the new stack)
that runs the routine named KEYBOARD. Notice that you

```
        @DosAllocSeg 512,tstack,0        ;allocate stack
        @jaxnz      mth999               ;exit if error
        mov         bx,510               ;point to last word in segment
  ;
        mov         ax,tstack            ;put stack selector
        mov         es,ax                ; in ES
        mov         di,510               ;set top of stack
        @DosCreateThread keyboard,tid,ES:DI ;start thread
```

Figure 16-24.   Using the DosCreateThread service

tell OS/2 the stack size by setting the top-of-stack as the stack offset. Since stacks grow backward (to 0), the initial stack frame offset is equal to the maximum stack size. The sample programs in the remainder of this book use a macro named @MKThread that allocates a stack and starts a thread. Like all the other macros presented thus far, it is included in the file named OS2MAC.INC.

Now it is time to have some fun. Suppose you want to create a program that draws a character-graphics "snake" on the screen. Also, you want to let the program create multiple copies of the snake and move them around simultaneously. This is a good application for a multithreaded OS/2 application. The program, called SNAKES, has the structure shown in Figure 16-25.

SNAKES

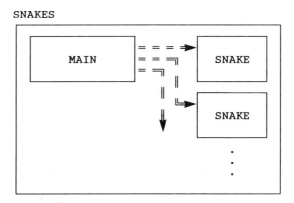

Figure 16-25.   Structure of SNAKES program

```
main       proc
           push     ds                  ;copy DS
           pop      es                  ;to ES
;
           @VioGetCurType curd,0        ;get cursor type
           mov      curd.curattr,-1     ;set 'hidden' attribute
           @VioSetCurType curd,0        ;hide cursor
;
           @VioScrollUp 0,0,-1,-1,-1,fill,0 ;clear the screen
           @VioWrtCharStrAtt msg,MSGL,24,0,msgatr,0 ;write prompt
;
           @DosGetInfoSeg gdtinfo,ldtinfo ;get system info segments
;
           @Mkthread snake,256          ;make snake thread
           mov      dx,1                ;set initial snake count
;
; Process keyboard input
;
snk000:    @KbdCharIn keyd,0,0          ;read keyboard
           xor      ax,ax               ;clear work register
           mov      al,keyd.charascii   ;get ASCII character
           cmp      al,0                ;extended scan?
           jne      snk010              ;no, go check which key it was
           mov      ah,keyd.charscan    ;get scan code
;
snk010:    cmp      ax,KESC             ;escape key?
           jne      snk020              ;no - continue
           jmp      snk999              ;yes - exit
;
snk020:    cmp      al,'+'              ;plus sign?
           jne      snk030              ;no - continue
           cmp      dx,8                ;max snakes?
           jne      snk025              ;no - go add another one
           @DosBeep 880,100             ;sound error
           jmp      snk000              ;go read next character
snk025:    @Mkthread snake,256          ;make another snake thread
           inc      dx                  ;increment snake count
snk030:    jmp      snk000              ;go read next character
;
snk999:    mov      curd.curattr,1      ;set 'normal' attribute
           @VioSetCurType curd,0        ;restore cursor
           @VioScrollUp 0,0,-1,-1,-1,fill,0 ;clear the screen
           @DosExit  1,0                ;kill all threads & exit
main       endp
```

Figure 16-26. SNAKES program

In reality, this program is quite simple, as shown in Figure 16-26. It starts by hiding the cursor, clearing the screen, and writing a prompt at the bottom of the screen.

It then issues the OS/2 DosGetInfoSeg API to retrieve the system information segments. These segments contain data relating to the overall system (GDTINFO) and the process (LDTINFO). Any OS/2 program can get (read-only) access to these segments by using the DosGetInfoSeg API. The contents of these segments are shown in Table 16-3.

Table 16-3. OS/2 InfoSeg Contents

Global	*(GDT)*	*Segment*
+00	4	Time from 1/1/70 in seconds
+04	4	Milliseconds since IPL
+08	1	Hours (TOD)
+09	1	Minutes (TOD)
+10	1	Seconds (TOD)
+11	1	Hundredths (TOD)
+12	2	Timezone (minutes from GMT)
+14	2	Timer interval (1/10000 sec)
+16	1	Day
+17	1	Month
+18	2	Year
+20	1	Day of week
+21	1	Major version number
+22	1	Minor version number
+23	1	Revision letter
+24	1	Foreground session number
+25	1	Maximum sessions
+26	1	Huge object shift count
+27	1	Protect-only indicator
+28	2	Foreground process PID
+30	1	Dynamic variation flag (1=ON)
+31	1	Max wait (seconds)
+32	2	Minimum time slice (ms)
+34	2	Maximum time slice (ms)

Table 16-3.   OS/2 InfoSeg Contents (continued)

Global	*(GDT) Segment*	
+36	2	Boot drive number
+38	32	Major trace code flags

Local	*(LDT) Segment*	
+00	2	Current Process ID
+04	2	Process ID of parent
+08	2	Priority of current thread
+10	2	Thread ID of current thread
+12	2	Current session
+14	2	Reserved
+16	2	Process is in foreground
+18	1	Process requires real mode
+19	2	AX register at startup
+21	2	BX register at startup
+23	2	CX register at startup
+25	2	DX register at startup
+27	2	SI register at startup
+29	2	DI register at startup
+31	2	DS register at startup

The parameters for DosGetInfoSeg are as follows:

PTR	A pointer to one-word field in which OS/2 will place the selector of the global information segment
PTR	A pointer to a one-word field in which OS/2 will place the selector of the local information segment

In this program, the snake-drawing thread(s) use the millisecond time stamp in GDTINFO as a pseudo-random number seed to determine the direction of the snakes. Note, in particular, that the GDTINFO selector is retrieved in the main procedure and it is later used by other threads. This is because all the threads of the process share the same address space.

In the remainder of the routine, MAIN starts an individual snake thread and then waits for keyboard input. In particular, it waits for two keys, the plus sign (+) or the ESC key. If you enter the plus sign, MAIN creates another SNAKE thread. If you press the ESC key, MAIN clears the screen, ends, and brings down all the active snake threads. Notice that the keyboard routine is running concurrently with the active snake threads. While it is waiting for keystrokes, the snakes are running.

Most of the SNAKE procedure deals with drawing a snake-like image on the screen. However, this logic is not relevant to this discussion, so it is not presented here. Refer to the complete listing in Appendix E. However, you should notice a couple of things in the start of the procedure (see Figure 16-27). First, to simplify the MAIN data segment, each SNAKE thread allocates its own work segment in which it maintains data necessary to generate the snake image. Note that it uses a stack frame to return the segment selector rather than a data area in the MAIN data segment. In this way, SNAKE does not have to worry about synchronization problems with other SNAKE threads that may be initializing simultaneously. Since each thread has its own stack, there will be no collisions.

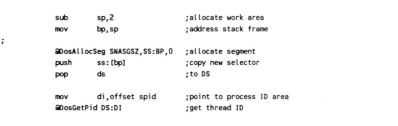

```
        sub     sp,2                    ;allocate work area
        mov     bp,sp                   ;address stack frame
;
        @DosAllocSeg SNASGSZ,SS:BP,0     ;allocate segment
        push    ss:[bp]                 ;copy new selector
        pop     ds                      ;to DS

        mov     di,offset spid          ;point to process ID area
        @DosGetPid DS:DI                 ;get thread ID
```

Figure 16-27. Beginning of the SNAKE procedure

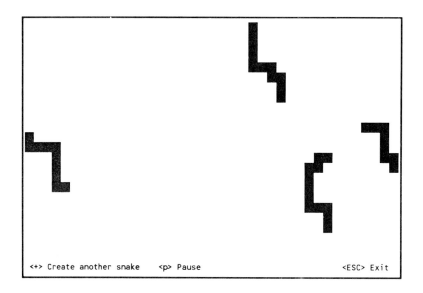

```
<+> Create another snake     <p> Pause                          <ESC> Exit
```

Figure 16-28. SNAKES with four active threads

Secondly, SNAKE uses the DosGetPid API (discussed previously in this chapter) to determine its thread identification. Since the thread is unique within a process, each SNAKE thread uses this value as a display attribute to generate a unique color of snake.

Finally, notice that SNAKE does not take any special precautions when using the CPU registers. It simply assumes that its register (and stack) context is maintained by OS/2.

If you run SNAKES, you will see a screen similar to the one depicted in Figure 16-28 with the individual snakes moving about independently.

CRITICAL SECTIONS

OS/2 threads are dispatched individually. Processes are collections of one or more individual threads. The relationship of processes to threads is not used by the OS/2 dispatcher, except in one case. An OS/2 thread may temporarily "suspend" the other threads in its process with the DosEnterCritSec API. When OS/2 receives this function call, it marks all the other threads in the process nondispatchable. They remain in that state until the thread issues the DosExitCritSec API.

Entering and exiting critical sections in this way, a thread can protect sections of code that are non-reentrant. While it is in the critical section, the thread is guaranteed that no other thread in the process will modify the memory or change the state of the devices or files. For example, if you bracket the memory allocation request in the snake thread initialization with a DosEnterCritSec and a DosExitCritSec call, all the snake threads could use the same memory area (instead of a stack frame) as a parameter to the DosAllocSeg call:

```
@DosEnterCritSec                    ;protect SEGP
@DosAllocSeg SNASGSZ,segp,0         ;allocate segment
push        segp                    ;copy new selector
pop         ds                      ;to DS
@DosExitrCritSec                    ;unprotect SEGP
```

However, this has the undesirable side effect of serializing the initialization of all the SNAKE threads. While it may be acceptable in this example, it might not be in other cases. In general, you should not write non-reentrant code, since it has the effect of nullifying the gains of overlapped program execution.

Returning to the SNAKES program, there is one reasonable application of DosEnterCritSec that demonstrates

```
;
snk030:         cmp        al,'p'              ;pause key?
                jne        snk000              ;no - continue
                @DosEnterCritSec               ;pause snake threads
                @KbdCharIn keyd,0,0            ;read keyboard
                @DosExitCritSec                ;run other threads
                jmp        snk000              ;go read next character
```

Figure 16-29. Pause function for SNAKES

how it works—as a display pause function. If you augment the MAIN keyboard processing logic as shown in Figure 16-29, you can pause the snakes by pressing the 'P' key. This key causes MAIN to issue a DosEnterCritSec API, which effectively "freezes" the snakes. When you press another key, MAIN issues DosExitCritSec and the snakes continue.

SUMMARY

OS/2 provides a number of alternatives for implementing multitasking programs. This large range of alternatives means that you can choose the type of tasking service that best matches the characteristics of your application program. You can use multiple processes to create several independent, loosely coupled programs that communicate through shared memory. Or, you can use the OS/2 thread services to create an application program with multiple tightly coupled asynchronous tasks.

   You should use the multitasking services where they make your job easier. Avoid creating overly complex programs just for the sake of using these functions. Multitasking has its price in terms of performance, memory, and complexity. When used correctly, multitasking will greatly enhance the functions and usability of your application programs.

In general, the functions you have seen in this chapter are unique to OS/2. Other than the synchronous DosExecPgn API, these calls are not part of the OS/2 family API.

Here are some points to review:

- The relationship of OS/2 resources and processes

- Using DosExecPgm to create asynchronous processes

- Parent-child process relationships

- How to change the priority of a process

- Waiting for a child process to end

- Determining the Process ID (PID)

- Killing child processes

- Processing OS/2 signals

- The difference between a process and a thread and when to use each

- Creating threads with DosCreateThread

- The thread context

- Critical sections, what they are, and when to use them

CHAPTER 17

ADVANCED MULTITASKING SERVICES

Now that you know how to build multitasking OS/2 programs, you will probably want to start on your first application. But you do not yet have all the tools necessary for this job. Thus far you have seen several multitasking programs, but in all cases the event synchronization between the program components was done with brute-force polling loops. Even when using DosSleep to space out the polls, these programs waste a lot of CPU cycles waiting for events. CPU cycles used in polling loops are wasted, since they cannot be used by other programs in the system.

The key to a good multitasking program is to what degree it is event-driven. An *event-driven program* relies on external events to trigger its actions rather than constantly "looking" for things to happen (such as peeking into memory to see if a flag has been set). This chapter discusses the OS/2 facilities that allow you to build this type of program.

First, your programs can synchronize their activities with the system clock by using OS/2 timer services. These functions allow your programs to run off a periodic system timer (asynchronously) or a "single-shot" timer (synchronously or asynchronously).

An OS/2 program can use semaphores as a signaling mechanism to notify another program that an event has occurred. Semaphores also provide a way to serialize access to a serially re-usable resource (such as a shared data structure).

Finally, a special class of OS/2 functions, called inter-process communications (IPC), combines program synchronization and data-delivery functions to form a higher-level programming service. Using IPC, your programs have access to several "standard" OS/2 data-passing protocols.

OS/2 SEMAPHORES

Recall that a semaphore is a system object shared between execution elements (threads). Programs request access to a semaphore with system calls. OS/2 guarantees that only one thread receives access to the semaphore at one time and forces all the others to block. You can use this basic mechanism to serialize access to a resource or to signal a thread.

Creating Semaphores

Before looking at the semaphore manipulation functions, consider how you would create a semaphore. OS/2 provides you with two types of semaphores: *system semaphores* and *RAM semaphores*. System semaphores are named objects that are allocated and managed by the OS/2 kernel. Whenever you request or free a system semaphore, the request is processed by the kernel. If a process dies while "holding" a system semaphore, the kernel is able to free the semaphore when it terminates the process. Thus, system semaphores are safe. Programs use the DosSem-Create API to create system semaphores. The parameters of the DosSemCreate API are as follows:

WORD	A one-word value indicating what type of semaphore OS/2 is to create: 0 = Exclusive semaphore (not shared) 1 = Nonexclusive semaphore (shared)
PTR	A pointer to a double-word field into which OS/2 will place the semaphore handle
PTR	A pointer to an ASCIIZ semaphore name that OS/2 is to associate with this semaphore (must begin with \SEM\)

In response to the DosSemCreate call, OS/2 generates a semaphore handle. This handle is then used in subsequent semaphore calls. For example, the code in Figure 17-1 creates a system semaphore named \SEM\MYSEM. Notice that semaphore names follow the OS/2 file-naming convention and must begin with the string \SEM\. The program can then use the handle returned in SEMHAND to access the semaphore.

```
Data Segment ...

semname      db      '\SEM\MYSEM',0      ;system semaphore name
semhand      dd      0                   ;system semaphore handle

Code Segment ...

             @DosCreateSem 0,semhand,semname ;create system semaphore
```

Figure 17-1. Creation of \SEM\MYSEM system semaphore

System semaphores are either *exclusive* or *nonexclusive*. If created as exclusive, a system semaphore cannot be modified by other processes. For exclusive system semaphores, OS/2 maintains a usage count. This means that if a program "requests" the semaphore multiple times, it is not "freed" until it is cleared an equal number of times. You can therefore use exclusive system semaphores in recursive routines.

Like all other OS/2 resources, system semaphores are owned by a process. All the threads in the process that created the semaphore can use the semaphore handle. Threads in a different process must use DosSemOpen to gain access to a previously created system semaphore. Like DosCreateSem, DosOpenSem accepts a system semaphore name and returns a semaphore handle. The parameters for DosOpenSem are as follows:

| PTR | A pointer to a double-word field into which OS/2 will place the semaphore handle |
| PTR | A pointer to an ASCIIZ semaphore name (must begin with \SEM \) |

When you plan to use a semaphore to signal threads *within* a process, or if you do not care about the automatic resource cleanup of system semaphores, you could instead use RAM semaphores. RAM semaphores are functionally equivalent to nonexclusive system semaphores (with no resource management). They are local to a process, and are actually allocated out of one of the data segments in the process. For example, the code shown in Figure 17-2 creates a RAM semaphore named MYSEM in the program's data segment. Notice that a RAM semaphore handle is the segment:offset (address) of the semaphore data structure. The big difference between RAM and system semaphores is that when you use a semaphore call and pass it a RAM semaphore handle, the semaphore man-

```
Data Segment ...

mysem      dd      0                   ;semaphore
semhand    dw      offset mysem        ;semaphore handle
           dw      seg    mysem
```

Figure 17-2. Allocation of a RAM semaphore (MYSEM)

agement routine runs in the context of the caller (instead of the kernel).

OS/2 performs no termination (cleanup) processing for RAM semaphores. However, this is normally not a problem, since all the threads that could possibly be holding the semaphore (as well as those waiting for the semaphore) will terminate when the process dies.

Serializing Resources with Semaphores

OS/2 programs can use the DosSemRequest and DosSemClear APIs to create *serially re-usable resources*. A serially re-usable resource is one that can be used by more than one program, but not concurrently. Two (or more) programs control access to the resource by requesting access to a semaphore before manipulating the resource.

The parameters for DosSemRequest are as follows:

DWRD	A double-word semaphore handle that is either the address of a RAM semaphore, or the handle returned from a DosOpenSem or DosCreateSem
DWRD	A double-word time-out value that defines the maximum time OS/2 will wait for this semaphore: −1 = wait indefinitely 0 = return immediately if semaphore is owned n = millisecond wait count

```
Data Segment ...

mydatarec    struc
fielda       dd       0                        ;first field
fieldb       dw       0                        ;second field
fieldc       dw       0                        ;third field
fieldd       db       0                        ;fourth field
fielde       dd       0                        ;fifth field
mydatarec    ends
```

Figure 17-3.   Shared data structure

DosSemClear accepts the following parameter:

DWRD	A double-word semaphore handle that is either the address of a RAM semaphore or the handle returned from DosOpenSem or DosCreateSem

When a program returns from the DosSemRequest call, it can assume that no other thread has the resource and no other thread will gain access to the resource until the semaphore is released with a DOSSEMCLEAR call.

For example, consider the data structure in Figure 17-3, which is shared among multiple (concurrently executing) threads. A thread that updates MYDATAREC must take special precautions to finish updating all the fields before any other thread attempts to use MYDATAREC. To understand why this is necessary, remember that OS/2 has a preemptive dispatcher. This means that a thread may be interrupted between any two instructions. Thus, if one thread updates FIELD A but its time slice expires before it can update FIELD B, then another thread could attempt to use this partially updated data structure.

A serialization semaphore solves this dilemma. If each thread that uses the data structure first requests a sema-

```
Code Segment ...

        @DosRequestSem semhand,timeout
        mov      [di].fielda,123      ;update fielda
        mov      [di].fieldb,9999     ;update fieldb
        mov      [di].fieldc,0fch     ;update fieldc
        @DosSemClear semhand
```

Figure 17-4. Serialization semaphore

phore, as shown in Figure 17-4, then only one thread at a time will ever have access to the data structure. Notice that this scheme only works if all threads that reference the data structure first request the data serialization structure semaphore.

If you build programs that expose a shared data structure, you should also provide a semaphore so that the threads using the data structure can serialize access to the data areas.

Signaling with Semaphores

You can also use semaphores (system or RAM) to *signal* events. Using a semaphore to signal events is exactly the opposite of using the semaphore to enqueue on a resource. When you use semaphores to request a resource, one thread runs (the one that sets the semaphore) and other threads wait until it is done. On the other hand, when you signal with semaphores, all the threads that are waiting for the semaphore are run. The thread that clears the semaphore gives the waiting threads a "green light."

For instance, consider the example illustrated in Figure 17-5. Here you see a system where two threads are waiting for an event by waiting on a semaphore. While the

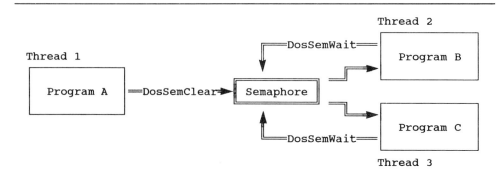

Figure 17-5. Signaling semaphores

semaphore is set, the threads are blocked. When the semaphore is cleared, the threads are run. Thus, when the
event occurs, a signaling program (which could be another
application or OS/2 itself) clears the semaphore and the
waiting threads run. Notice that the program clearing the
semaphore does not know which threads (nor even how
many threads) are waiting on the semaphore. These
details are managed by OS/2.

OS/2 has several API functions that allow you to use
semaphores to signal events. With DosSemWait, you wait
on a semaphore until someone clears it. The parameters
for DosSemWait are as follows:

DWRD	A double-word semaphore handle that is either the address of a RAM semaphore, or the handle returned from a DosOpenSem or DosCreateSem
DWRD	A double-word time-out value that defines the maximum time OS/2 will wait for this semaphore: -1 = wait indefinitely 0 = return immediately if semaphore is owned n = millisecond wait count

For example,

```
    .
    .
    .
@DosSemWait mysem,timeout
(continue processing)
    .
    .
    .
```

blocks the program on the semaphore MYSEM until it is cleared. If MYSEM is already clear when you issue DosSemWait, then the function has no effect, and the program continues running.

If you want to be sure that a semaphore is set, you can use the DosSemSet function. The parameter for this function is as follows:

DWRD	A double-word semaphore handle that is either the address of a RAM semaphore, or the handle returned from DosOpenSem or DosCreateSem

This API *unconditionally* sets a semaphore, regardless of its current state or usage. For example,

```
    .
    .
    .
@DosSemSet   mysem
@DosSemWait mysem,timeout
(continue processing)
    .
    .
    .
```

blocks the program on the semaphore, since you set the semaphore before waiting on it. However, this approach is not foolproof. It is possible that OS/2 could dispatch another program between the time you issued the DosSemSet and DosSemWait functions. If that program happened to clear the semaphore, your program would not wait. Depending on why your program was using a semaphore, this may be the desired result, or it may be a serious problem.

If you have never written programs for a preemptive system, you must learn to anticipate this type of situation. "Timing windows" will probably comprise 99% of your most serious problems in your first multitasking programs. Keep reminding yourself that a program could be interrupted at any instant, between any two instructions. OS/2 will ensure that the program's execution context is restored, but not the state of "shared" resources.

In any case, if you require that the semaphore be set before you wait on it, then use the DosSemSetWait function. The parameters for the DosSemSetWait function are as follows:

DWRD	A double-word semaphore handle that is either the address of a RAM semaphore, or the handle returned from a DosOpenSem or DosCreateSem
DWRD	A double-word time-out value that defines the maximum time OS/2 will wait for this semaphore: −1 = wait indefinitely 0 = return immediately if semaphore is owned n = millisecond wait count

This API encapsulates DosSemSet and DosSemWait into a single, atomic function. In cases where this timing window is a problem, you should use this API instead of the separate DosSemSet and DosSemWait calls.

For example,

```
       .
       .
       .
@DosSemSetWait mysem,timeout
(continue processing)
       .
       .
       .
```

performs exactly the same function as the previous example, except that the semaphore *is guaranteed* to be set at the time the wait starts.

Should you need to wait on a number of events within a single thread, you can use the DosMuxSemWait API. DosMuxSemWait is a version of DosSemWait that waits on a list of semaphores. If any semaphore on the list is cleared, OS/2 runs the program. The parameters for DosMuxSemWait are as follows:

PTR	Pointer to a one-word field into which OS/2 will place an index value corresponding to the semaphore in the semaphore list that caused the event
PTR	Pointer to a semaphore list. A semaphore list has the following format:
	DW Semaphore count
	DW 0
	DD Semaphore handle (RAM or SYS) (up to 16 allowed)
DWRD	A double-word time-out value that defines the maximum time OS/2 will wait for this semaphore. $-1 =$ wait indefinitely $0 =$ return immediately if semaphore is owned $n =$ millisecond wait count

Another important attribute of DosMuxSemWait is that it is *edge-triggered* rather than *level-triggered* (like the other OS/2 semaphore calls). This means that if any of the semaphores in the list is ever cleared, DosMuxWait will return—even if another program sets the semaphore again before your thread is redispatched.

You may have noticed that all the semaphore wait functions include a time-out parameter. This is to help you prevent deadlock situations. You can set this value to "bound" how long you wait for the semaphore. If the time-out happens before another program clears the semaphore, then your thread is run. The AX register will contain an error code signifying that a time-out occurred.

Now consider an example. In Chapter 15 you saw two programs that pass data between themselves using a shared memory segment (GIVE and TAKE). These programs used a predefined convention for signaling one another when the data was read or was ready to be read. This convention involved polling a field in a shared data structure. To make sure that this polling did not "steal" too many CPU cycles from the other programs in the system, GIVE/TAKE slept for 1/2 second between polls. But this had a serious side effect in the visible performance of the programs.

This is a perfect application for semaphores. With a pair of system semaphores, you can synchronize these two programs and eliminate the polling altogether.

So, you modify GIVE (GIVE2) as shown in Figure 17-6. The program starts by creating two system semaphores named \SEM\GIVE2 and \SEM\TAKE2. OS/2 returns the handles for these system semaphores in the fields named SEMHGIVE and SEMHTAKE. Notice that since GIVE2 and TAKE2 are two independent processes, you should use system semaphores to coordinate their actions. Also note that the first parameter in the DosCreateSem function is "1," meaning that the sema-

```
main      proc
          @DosCreateSem 1,semhgive,semgive ;create system semaphore
          @DosCreateSem 1,semhtake,semtake ;create system semaphore
          @DosAllocShrSeg ALLOCSZ,shrname,shrsel ;allocate shared segment
          push    shrsel              ;put shared memory selector
          pop     es                  ;in ES
;
giv020:   mov     di,2                ;point shared segment
          mov     cx,ALLOCSZ-2        ;point to data field
          mov     al,0                ;fill character
          rep     stosb               ;clear area
;
          mov     di,2                ;point to data field
          @DosRead  STDIN,ES:DI,ALLOCSZ-2,bytesin ;Read data into shr seg
          xor     di,di               ;point to start of buffer
          mov     ax,bytesin          ;get input byte count
          stosw                       ;write to segment
          @DosSemSet    semhtake      ;pre-set semaphore
          @DosSemClear  semhgive      ;tell TAKE data is ready
          cmp     bytesin,0           ;null input?
          je      giv999              ;yes - finished
          @DosSemWait   semhtake,noto ;wait for TAKE to remove data
          jmp     giv020              ;no - go read another string
;
giv999:   @DosFreeSeg shrsel          ;Free shared memory segment
          @DosCloseSem semhgive       ;Free the system semaphore
          @DosCloseSem semhtake       ;Free the system semaphore
          @DosExit 1,0                ;leave proc
main      endp
```

Figure 17-6. GIVE2 program

phore is to be shared with another process (nonexclusive).
If GIVE2 had created an exclusive semaphore (0), then
TAKE2 would not be permitted to modify it in any way
(including with DosSemClear).

SEMHGIVE is used by GIVE2 to signal TAKE2 that
data is in the buffer. Similarly, SEMHTAKE is used by
GIVE2 to determine when TAKE2 has finished reading
the data and the buffer can be overwritten. By alternatively clearing SEMHGIVE and waiting on SEMHTAKE,
GIVE2 paces its data transfer.

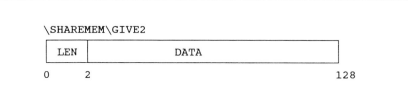

Figure 17-7.   *Layout of shared memory segment in GIVE2*

As before, GIVE2 allocates the shared segment and initializes it. However, the layout of the shared-memory segment in this program is a little different, as shown in Figure 17-7.

The flag field has been eliminated, since the semaphores are now the basis for program synchronization. As before, GIVE2 reads from STDIN, places the data and length into the buffer. But now instead of setting a flag, it clears SEMHGIVE to start the TAKE2 process. Note that GIVE2 does not use DosSemSetWait, but instead sets the semaphore with DosSemSet and then waits with DosSemWait. This is because TAKE2 could conceivably process the data and clear SEMHTAKE before GIVE2 gets around to waiting on it. Thus, if GIVE2 had used DosSemSetWait, it would miss the "return handshake" from TAKE2 and block indefinitely. Therefore, GIVE2 sets the semaphore before it clears SEMHGIVE and then simply waits. If TAKE2 clears SEMHTAKE before the wait runs, GIVE2 drops through and reads the next record.

Finally, when the data read is 0 bytes, GIVE2 drops out of the read loop, closes the semaphores, frees the shared memory, and exits.

On the other side of the shared memory, the TAKE2 program also uses the system semaphores to pace the flow of data, as shown in Figure 17-8.

However, in this case, TAKE2 uses DosSemOpen to get access to the system semaphores, since they are created by

```
main        proc
            @DosOpenSem semhgive,semgive  ;open system semaphore
            @jaxz     tak005              ;Give is present - continue
            @DosWrite stderr,msg1,msg1l,bytesout ;Write error message
            jmp       tak999              ;exit
;
tak005:     @DosOpenSem semhtake,semtake  ;open system semaphore
            @DosGetShrSeg shrname,shrsel  ;get shared segment
            @DosSemWait semhgive,noto     ;wait for initial data
;
tak010:     push      shrsel              ;put shared memory selector
            pop       es                  ;in ES
            mov       di,2                ;point to data field
;
tak020:     cmp       word ptr es:[0],0   ;null record?
            @je       tak800              ;yes - exit
            @DosWrite stdout,ES:DI,es:[0],bytesout ;Write data
            @DosSemSet    semhgive        ;pre-set semaphore
            @DosSemClear semhtake         ;tell TAKE data is done
            @DosSemWait  semhgive,noto    ;wait for more data to be present
            jmp       tak020              ;go wait for another string
;
tak800:     @DosFreeSeg shrsel            ;Free shared memory segment
            @DosCloseSem semhgive         ;Free the system semaphore
            @DosCloseSem semhtake         ;Free the system semaphore
;
tak999:     @DosExit 1,0                  ;leave proc
main        endp
```

Figure 17-8.   TAKE2 program

GIVE2. If the DosSemOpen fails, then TAKE2 knows that GIVE2 is not running, so it issues an error message and exits.

Once the semaphores are open and the shared segment is acquired, TAKE2 uses DosSemWait to wait for the data. If the data is ready, SEMHGIVE is clear and TAKE2 drops into its processing loop. If the data is not yet there (the semaphore is not clear), TAKE2 waits until it is.

Like GIVE2, TAKE2 sets one semaphore before it clears the other to ensure it does not miss a handshake. When it issues the wait, the semaphore may or may not be set, depending on whether GIVE2 had a chance to run. In any case, TAKE2 will exit the DosSemWait when the data buffer is once again full.

Now if you build these programs and rerun the piping example from Chapter 15, you will notice an immediate improvement in performance. Since GIVE2 and TAKE2 do not sleep, they run whenever data is available and thus make the optimum use of their execution times. Since they do not poll, the other programs in the system are minimally impacted. GIVE2 and TAKE2 are truly event-driven OS/2 programs.

USING OS/2
TIMER SERVICES

OS/2 has a robust set of timer services. View a *timer* as an instance of the system clock that you can use to "time" events. Timers are very useful for synchronizing the activities of multiple, asynchronous programs.

If you start multiple timers, they will run concurrently. OS/2 maintains a table of all active timers and manages which program is notified when a timer expires.

Before discussing the capabilities of these functions, you should note that the granularity of the system timer is limited to the internal OS/2 clock cycle (32 MS). So, even though you specify the timer intervals to the millisecond, the actual elapsed time is rounded to the next-highest clock interval.

Also, the timer-notification events are subject to normal execution-priority ordering. A program that expects a timer event to expire in a certain number of milliseconds may be delayed if other, higher-priority threads are running in the system when the interval expires.

Sleeping

OS/2 supports timer intervals that are either synchronous or asynchronous to your program. You have already seen the DosSleep API, which requests a synchronous timer interval. However, you should note that DosSleep is a timer service, and is therefore subject to the characteristics just discussed. Sleep intervals are rounded to the next OS/2 clock cycle, and the "sleeping" program may be delayed for some time if other (higher-priority) threads are running when the interval expires.

Asynchronous Timers

OS/2 also supports timers that run asynchronous to your program. This means that your thread can start a timer and then perform some other work. When the interval expires, the timer clears a semaphore that you can later interrogate with the semaphore API functions. The asynchronous timers come in two varieties: single time period and recurring.

The DosTimerAsync starts a "single-shot" timer. Your program regains control immediately after the call, and the timer continues to run. View DosTimerAsync as an asynchronous version of DosSleep. The parameters of DosTimerAsync are as follows:

DWRD	Double-word count of the number of milliseconds that must elapse in the timer interval
DWRD	An open system semaphore handle (returned by DosOpenSem or DosCreateSem)
PTR	Pointer to a double-word field into which OS/2 will return the timer handle

DosTimerAsync returns a timer handle, which you can use with DosTimerStop to cancel the timer before it expires (if you decide you no longer need it). The parameter for DosTimerStop is as follows:

WORD	A double-word (open) timer handle

When the timer period expires, OS/2 clears the semaphore you provided in the DosTimerAsync call. Since the only notification that you receive is this semaphore, you should make sure the semaphore is set before calling Dos-TimerAsync. Actually, you can set the semaphore at any point before the interval expires. But to be on the safe side, you probably want to set it before you start the timer. For example,

```
Data Segment ...

semhand      dd      0                 ;system semaphore handle
semname      db      '\SEM\MYSEM',0    ;system semaphore name
intervl      dd      10000             ;timer interval


Code Segment ...

             aDosCreateSem  0,semhand,semname ;create system semaphore
             aDosSemSet     semhand            ;pre-set the semaphore
             aDosTimerStart intervl,semhand    ;start timer

                          :

             (other program logic)

                          :

             aDosSemWait    semhand,timeout   ;wait for timer pop
```

starts an asynchronous timer.

Note that OS/2 timer services require you to use system semaphores in the asynchronous timer calls. So before the

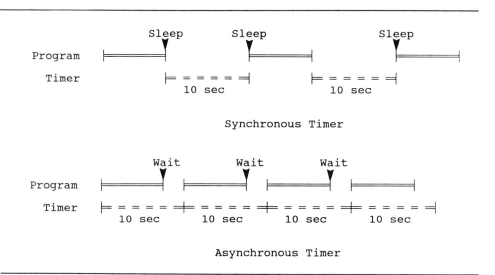

Figure 17-9. Synchronous versus asynchronous timers

program starts the timer, it creates a system semaphore. The timer is set to count down 10 seconds (10,000 milliseconds) and then clear the semaphore associated with SEMHAND.

After starting the timer, the program is free to do other work. When it finally decides to re-synchronize with the clock, it simply waits on the semaphore with the DosSemWait function.

This type of logic is useful if your program must guarantee that events are spaced out for some period of time (such as a communications-line server). This is better than using DosSleep because the preparatory work can be done in parallel with the timer.

For example, consider the difference between timers depicted in Figure 17-9. In both cases, the programs space out the events by at least 10 seconds. But in the asynchronous case, the events are much more regularly spaced, since the program work overlapped the timer interval. You could argue that in the synchronous case, you can compensate for the program work by shortening the sleep period (say, to eight seconds). But then you could not guarantee the event spacing, since the program code would run much faster on some machines versus others (6MHz 80286 versus 20MHz 80386).

The second type of asynchronous timer is a variation of the first. DosTimerStart starts an asynchronous timer that continues to run. In other words, it clears the semaphore every n milliseconds. You can use DosTimerStart to perform some activity on a regular cycle. It is effectively like restarting the single-shot timer whenever the time interval expires, except that it will be much more predictable because the thread dispatch time will not come into play. The parameters for DosTimerStart are as follows:

DWRD	Double-word count of the number of milliseconds that must elapse in the timer interval
DWRD	An open system semaphore handle (returned by DosOpenSem or DosCreateSem)
PTR	Pointer to a double-word field into which OS/2 will return the timer handle

NOTES

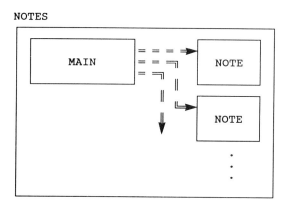

Figure 17-10.   Structure of NOTES program

As with the single-shot timer, the recurring asynchronous timer can be cancelled with the DosTimerStop API call.

Now consider an example that uses asynchronous timers. NOTES is a program that starts a series of cyclical timers, then starts a thread for each timer. Each thread is responsible for displaying and playing a musical note each time its timers expire. NOTES has the structure shown in Figure 17-10.

The MAIN routine creates a parameter table containing an entry for each NOTE thread, as shown in Figure 17-11. Each thread's parameter area includes its semaphore handle, timer handle, screen coordinates for the note, display attribute for the note, and the note frequency.

The MAIN program is very simple, as shown in Figure 17-12. It starts by clearing the screen and hiding the display cursor. It then loops through the NOTE data structures, creates a semaphore for each entry, starts an asynchronous (cyclical) timer, creates a thread, and passes to the thread the address of the data structure in SI. In this example, MAIN relies on the fact that the semaphore handle is the first field in the data structure, so DS:SI in the DosCreateSem and DosTimerStart calls points to the handle field.

```
TDATA       STRUC
shand       dd      ?                   ;Semaphore handle
thand       dw      ?                   ;Timer handle
row         dw      ?                   ;Display Row
col         dw      ?                   ;Display Column
attr        db      ?                   ;Display Attribute
freq        dw      ?                   ;Tone frequency
sname       db      '???????'           ;Semaphore name
            db      0                   ;zero termination
TDATA       ENDS
;
timerd      tdata   <0,0,14, 3,1fh, 523,'\SEM\T1'> ;Timer #1 parameters
            tdata   <0,0,13,12,2fh, 587,'\SEM\T2'> ;Timer #2 parameters
            tdata   <0,0,12,21,3fh, 660,'\SEM\T3'> ;Timer #3 parameters
            tdata   <0,0,11,30,4fh, 700,'\SEM\T4'> ;Timer #4 parameters
            tdata   <0,0,10,39,5fh, 783,'\SEM\T5'> ;Timer #5 parameters
            tdata   <0,0, 9,48,6fh, 880,'\SEM\T6'> ;Timer #6 parameters
            tdata   <0,0, 8,57,7fh, 988,'\SEM\T7'> ;Timer #7 parameters
            tdata   <0,0, 7,66,1fh,1046,'\SEM\T8'> ;Timer #8 parameters
TCOUNT      equ     8                   ;parameter area count
```

Figure 17-11. Parameter table for NOTE threads

```
;
; Clear screen & put message
;
            @HideCursor                 ;hide the cursor
            @VioScrollUp 0,0,-1,-1,-1,fill,0 ;clear the screen
            @VioWrtCharStrAtt msg,MSGL,24,0,msgatr,0 ;write prompt
            lea     si,timerd           ;timer parameter area
            mov     cx,TCOUNT           ;timer count
;
; Start timers & threads
;
tim010:     mov     di,si
            add     di,offset sname     ;semaphore name
            @DosCreateSem 1,DS:SI,DS:DI ;create shared system semaphore
            mov     di,si               ;copy pointer
            add     di,offset thand     ;timer handle
            @DosTimerStart tint,DS:SI,DS:DI ;start asynchronous timer
            @Mkthread note,256          ;make note thread
            @DosSleep sleepct           ;space out timers
            add     si,size tdata       ;next parameter area
            loop    tim010              ;go start next
```

Figure 17-12. MAIN program initialization

```
;
; Process keyboard input
;
tim020:      @KbdCharIn keyd,0,0              ;read keyboard
             xor     ax,ax                    ;clear work register
             mov     al,keyd.charascii        ;get ASCII character
             cmp     al,0                     ;extended scan?
             jne     tim030                   ;no, go check which key it was
             mov     ah,keyd.charscan         ;get scan code
;
tim030:      cmp     ax,KESC                  ;escape key?
             jne     tim040                   ;no - continue
             jmp     tim800                   ;yes - exit
;
tim040:      cmp     al,'p'                   ;pause key?
             jne     tim500                   ;no - continue
             @DosEnterCritSec                 ;pause timer threads
             @KbdCharIn keyd,0,0              ;read keyboard
             @DosExitCritSec                  ;start all the threads
tim500:      jmp     tim020                   ;go read next character
```

Figure 17-13.   MAIN keyboard input processing

You will also note that MAIN uses DosSleep to space out the loop iterations, so that the timers are started at a regular interval from one another. If MAIN did not do this, all the timers would expire at approximately the same time and the notes would all run together. OS/2 lets you use a synchronous timer in a process that has started asynchronous timers.

After the NOTE threads have been started, MAIN waits on the keyboard for a "pause" key or the ESC key (see Figure 17-13). MAIN uses the same trick that you saw in SNAKES (see Chapter 16) to pause all the other threads in the process by entering a critical section. Finally, if you press ESC, MAIN jumps to the termination routine (see Figure 17-14), which restores the screen and cursor, loops through the data structures, closes each semaphore, and stops each timer.

The code that runs in the NOTE thread is as shown in Figure 17-15. It waits for the timer interval to expire (using the semaphore handle found in its parameter block). When the timer interval expires, NOTE displays a note, sounds a tone, and erases the note. Notice that NOTE

```
;
tim800:     @ShowCursor                         ;restore the cursor
            @VioScrollUp 0,0,-1,-1,-1,fill,0 ;clear the screen
;
            lea      si,timerd                  ;timer parameter area
            mov      cx,TCOUNT                  ;timer count
tim900:     @DosCloseSem DS:SI                  ;Free the system semaphore
            @DosTimerStop [si].thand           ;Stop timer
            add      si,size tdata              ;next parameter area
            loop     tim900                     ;go stop next
;
            @DosExit 1,0                        ;kill all threads & exit
```

Figure 17-14. MAIN termination routine

uses DosSemSetWait to make sure the semaphore is set
before it waits. In this program, it really does not matter if
you miss a time period because the semaphore is constantly cleared every n milliseconds.

If you run NOTES, you will see and hear a C scale,
with each note spaced apart by approximately 200 ms.
Each time an asynchronous timer expires, a thread wakes
up and sounds its note. This simple example illustrates
how you can run multiple, concurrent, asynchronous timers.

```
note        proc
;
            lea      di,[si].attr         ;get display attribute (Color)
;
not010:     @DosSemSetWait DS:SI,noto     ;wait for semaphore 2b cleared
            @VioWrtCharStrAtt note,NOTEL,[si].row,[si].col,DS:DI,0 ;note
            @DosBeep [si].freq,100        ;sound tone
            @VioWrtNCell fill,NOTEL,[si].row,[si].col,0 ;blank out note
            jmp      not010               ;loop
;
note        endp
```

Figure 17-15. NOTE subroutine

If some other, higher-priority thread takes away the CPU, then NOTES will momentarily sound confused, but it will regain its rhythm when the other thread becomes inactive. For example, start NOTES in your foreground session, then switch to another session. For a short period of time, the OS/2 Session Manager will monopolize the CPU. Programs that run in the regular priority class (such as NOTES) lose some of their CPU cycles.

The result is a jumbled group of notes. However, once the session switch is finished, NOTES regains its rhythm. This is because the asynchronous timers are once again driving the program and it has re-established its "steady state." While the screen switch was occurring, the timers were still operating regularly. But NOTES could not be dispatched. Thus, when the CPU freed up and NOTES was dispatched, a number of semaphores were already cleared, causing a number of NOTE threads to sound their notes simultaneously.

Querying and Setting the Clock

Because you are not guaranteed to receive interval timer events exactly when you might expect them, you should never use interval timers as a means of computing time of day. Instead, use the system DosGetDateTime API. The parameter of DosGetDateTime is as follows:

PTR	Pointer to a data buffer into which OS/2 will place the Date/Time data structure

DosGetDateTime returns the current date and time values from the system clock. Its companion API, DosSetDateTime, enables you to change the system clock. The parameter of DosSetDateTime is as follows:

PTR	Pointer to a buffer that contains a Date/Time data structure

Table 17-1. Date/Time Data Structures

DosGetDateTime			*DosSetDateTime*		
+00	1	Hours	+00	1	Hours
+01	1	Minutes	+01	1	Minutes
+02	1	Seconds	+02	1	Seconds
+03	1	Hundredths	+03	1	Hundredths
+04	1	Day	+04	1	Day
+05	1	Month	+05	1	Month
+06	2	Year	+06	2	Year
+08	2	Time zone (min from GMT)	+08	2	Time zone (min from GMT)
+10	1	Day of week			

Table 17-1 lists the format of the data area used by these APIs.

The code fragment shown in Figure 17-16 retrieves and formats the system date. To improve the readability of your programs, you can use the macros @SYSDATE, @SYSTIME, and @SYSDAYOFW to format the date, time, and day of week (listed in OS2MAC.INC). For example, the program DATETIME in Figure 17-17 formats a message that contains the current system date, time, and day of week and writes it to the standard output device.

COMMUNICATING BETWEEN PROCESSES

In many cases, programs need to synchronize their executions to pass data between themselves. If passing data is your objective, you may wish to consider using OS/2 Inter Process Communications (IPC) services. IPC services com-

```
        @DosGetDateTime buffer          ;get time stamp
        lea     di,target               ;date target buffer
;
        xor     ah,ah                   ;clear high byte of work reg
        mov     al,[buffer]+5           ;get month
        aam                             ;convert to unpacked decimal
        or      ax,3030h                ;convert to ASCII
        xchg    ah,al                   ;reverse byte order
        stosw                           ;put in user buffer
;
        mov     al,'/'                  ;separator
        stosb                           ;put it in user buffer
;
        xor     ah,ah                   ;clear high byte of work reg
        mov     al,[buffer]+4           ;get day
        aam                             ;convert to unpacked decimal
        or      ax,3030h                ;convert to ASCII
        xchg    ah,al                   ;reverse byte order
        stosw                           ;put in user buffer
;
        mov     al,'/'                  ;separator
        stosb                           ;put it in user buffer
;
        mov     dx,word ptr [buffer]+6 ;get year
        sub     dx,1900                 ;drop centuries
        @bta    dx,ES:DI,2              ;convert to ASCII
```

Figure 17-16. Code to retrieve and format system date

bine data transfer and synchronization into single, high-level functions. They are standard communications protocols that are available to all programs through system APIs.

```
main    proc
        @sysdate  msg1date              ;get date
        @systime  msg1time              ;get time
        @sysday   msg1dayofw            ;get day of week
        @DosWrite STDOUT,msg1,MSG1L,bytesout ;Write data
        @DosExit 1,0                    ;leave proc
main    endp
```

Figure 17-17. DATETIME program

Semaphores and Shared Memory

The most basic form of IPC is when two programs use shared memory to pass data and semaphores in order to synchronize the data flows. This is precisely the underlying concept behind all forms of OS/2 IPC services. Semaphores and shared memory are sometimes called *private IPC* because the communicating programs use private conventions to transfer data.

You have already seen a form of private IPC in two sample programs. GIVE2 and TAKE2 implemented their IPC with a named shared segment and two flow-control (system) semaphores. This implementation is functionally equivalent to a simple "pipe."

While private IPC can be implemented by any two OS/2 programs, it has a serious disadvantage. The communicating programs must agree on a predefined set of conventions. For instance, GIVE2 and TAKE2 each agreed on the name and format of the shared segment (\SHAREMEM \GIVE2), the name of each synchronization semaphore (\SEM \GIVE2 and \SEM \TAKE2), and the semaphore usage conventions (who clears which semaphore when). Because of this, it is unlikely that a different program (written by a different programmer) could easily adapt to the conventions. Private IPC is a *nonstandard* communications protocol.

But this does not necessarily mean that private IPC is undesirable. In fact, the actual protocols are quite flexible since you define them yourself. Therefore, they could be optimized to the specific needs of your application(s).

Pipes

Recall that pipes are a form of IPC modeled after the OS/2 file system. To read from or write to a pipe, you use the DosRead and DosWrite system APIs. For example,

```
@DosRead PIPHAND,BUFFER,100,bytesin  ;Read data from pipe
```

reads 100 bytes from a pipe, and

```
@DosWrite PIPHAND,BUFFER,100,bytesout ;Write data to pipe
```

writes 100 bytes to a pipe. Programs generally cannot distinguish a pipe handle from a file handle or device handle. However, the DosQHand API does enable you to get to the information if necessary. The parameters for DosQHand-Type are as follows:

WORD	A one-word value corresponding to an open system handle
PTR	A pointer to a one-word field in which OS/2 will return the handle type: 0 = File handle 1 = Device handle 2 = Pipe handle
PTR	A pointer to a one-word field in which OS/2 will return the file attribute word if the handle is a file handle (1)

In OS/2, a pipe is created with the DosMakePipe API. When you call DosMakePipe, OS/2 allocates a memory buffer to hold the pipe data and returns a pipe read handle and a pipe write handle. You use the read handle with DosRead and the write handle with DosWrite. The parameters of DosMakePipe are as follows:

PTR	A pointer to a one-word field into which OS/2 will place the pipe read handle
PTR	A pointer to a one-word field into which OS/2 will place the pipe write handle
WORD	A one-word value corresponding to the desired pipe size (in bytes). **Note:** The maximum size is 65536

If you want to use a pipe to communicate with another program, you create the pipe and pass the other program one of the two pipe handles. Depending on which handle you passed and which one you kept, you can either read data from or send data to the other program. To communicate bidirectionally, you allocate two pipes, and pass the read handle of one and the write handle of the other. Note however that a pipe can *only* be used to communicate with a child process.

How you give a child process access to your pipe handles can be accomplished in several ways. You obviously cannot use the pipe itself, since the child must have the handle to read data. You can allocate a global shared-memory segment and place the handle(s) in predefined fields. A child that wants to communicate with you can access the memory segment, extract the handle, and use it to read/write data. For example, your program can perform the functions shown in Figure 17-18. The child can then perform the functions shown in Figure 17-19.

From this point forward, you can send data by writing to PIPE1WH and receive it by reading PIPE2RH. Conversely, the other program receives data by reading PIPE1RH (located at offset 0 in the shared-memory segment) and writing data to PIPE2WH (located at offset 2 in the shared-memory segment).

```
@DosAllocShrSeg ALLOCSZ,shrname,shrsel ;allocate shared segment
push      shrsel                   ;put shared memory selector
pop       es                       ;in ES
@DosMakePipe pipe1rh,pipe1wh,1024 ;create pipe1
@DosMakePipe pipe2rh,pipe2wh,1024 ;create pipe2
push      pipe1rh                  ;put read handle
pop       word ptr es:[0]          ;in common structure
push      pipe2wh                  ;put write handle
pop       word ptr es:[2]          ;in common structure
@DosExecPgm pgmobj,10,2,pgmprm,pgmenv,pgmpid,pgmname ;start pgm
```

Figure 17-18. Passing pipe handles in a shared segment

```
@DosGetShrSeg ALLOCSZ,shrname,shrsel ;get shared segment
push     shrsel              ;put shared memory selector
pop      es                  ;in ES
push     word ptr es:[0]     ;get read handle
pop      pipe1rh             ;
push     word ptr es:[2]     ;get write handle
pop      pipe2wh             ;
```

Figure 17-19. Program to get shared-memory segments

You can also let the child process inherit the pipe handles. The DosDupHandle API enables you to create a duplicate handle for any active handle in your process. Further, DosDupHandle enables you to define the value of the duplicate handle. The parameters for DosDupHandle are as follows:

WORD	The original file handle (word value) that OS/2 is to alias in a second handle
PTR	A pointer to a one-word field into which OS/2 is to place the new (alias) handle value. If this field is initialized to ffffh (-1), OS/2 will give you the next available handle. Otherwise, the field contains the desired handle value

So, with this capability, the child process can "assume" a particular value for the pipe read and write handles, which your parent process can establish before issuing the EXEC call. For example, the code in Figure 17-20 creates two pipes and creates alias handles numbered 3 and 4 that correspond to PIPE1RH and PIPE2WH, respectively. The child process can then read data and write data as follows:

```
@DosRead  3,BUFFER,100,bytesin  ;Read data from pipe
@DosWrite 4,BUFFER,100,bytesout ;Write data to pipe
```

```
@DosMakePipe pipe1rh,pipe1wh,1024 ;create pipe1
@DosMakePipe pipe2rh,pipe2wh,1024 ;create pipe2
mov       childin,3            ;request child in handle
@DosDupHandle pipe1rh,childin  ;set child IN to pipe1 readhand
mov       childout,4           ;request child out handle
@DosDupHandle pipe2wh,childout ;set child OUT to pipe2 writehnd
```

Figure 17-20.   Program to create two pipes and alias handles

This example has an interesting ramification. Suppose you do exactly what was outlined, except that you create duplicate pipe handles numbered 0 (STDIN) and 1 (STDOUT). Then, if the child process is a standard I/O program, it will read from what it thinks is STDIN and it will really be reading from your first pipe. When it writes to what it thinks is STDOUT, it will be writing data to your second pipe. Since the parent process owns the other end of the pipes, it can write data to the child's STDIN and read data from the child's STDOUT. Thus, you control the program as if you were running it from the command line. This is exactly how the OS/2 command interpreter (CMD.EXE) implements command-line piping. This is a useful capability. With it you can write programs that transparently "run" STDIO programs (such as OS/2 utilities).

Now consider a program named PIPE that uses this technique to run the UPCASE filter from Chapter 13. PIPE reads data from STDIN, passes the data stream to the UPCASE STDIN, reads the data written by UPCASE, and then writes the results to the screen. So, PIPE has the structure shown in Figure 17-21.

Since PIPE creates the input and output pipes, it establishes their sizes. This example uses an environment variable named PIPESIZE to tell PIPE how big the pipes

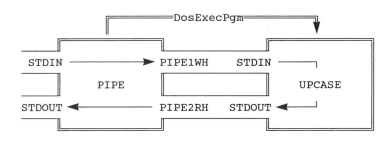

Figure 17-21.   Structure of PIPE program

should be. You set PIPESIZE with the SET PIPESIZE= command before running PIPE. The actual PIPE code is relatively straightforward (see Figure 17-22). It starts by searching for the OS/2 environment variable to determine the size of the pipe. PIPE uses the address returned by DosScanEnv to isolate the value (@STRLEN returns the ASCIIZ string length in CX) and to convert it to binary. If the conversion fails, PIPE ends with an error message. Once it has determined the pipe size, PIPE creates the pipes and sets up the handles, as shown in Figure 17-23.

```
;
; Determine pipe size
;
        @DosScanEnv varname,varptr      ;locate environment variable
        mov     dx,PIP_data             ;get data segment
        mov     ds,dx                   ;place it in DS
        @jaxnz  pip010                  ;if not found, leave default size
        les     di,varptr               ;get location in ES:DI
        @strlen ES:DI                   ;determine length of ASCIIZ
        @atb    ES:DI,cx,pipesz         ;convert number to binary
        @jaxz   pip010                  ;all OK - continue
        @DosWrite STDERR,msg1,msg1l,bytesout ;Write message
        jmp     pip999                  ;exit
```

Figure 17-22.   PIPE program environment scan routine

```
;
; Set up pipes
;
pip010:         @DosMakePipe pipe1rh,pipe1wh,pipesz ;create pipe1
                @DosMakePipe pipe2rh,pipe2wh,pipesz ;create pipe2
;
                mov        mystdin,-1           ;request new handle
                @DosDupHandle STDIN,mystdin      ;duplicate my stdin handle
                mov        mystdout,-1          ;request new handle
                @DosDupHandle STDOUT,mystdout    ;duplicate my stdout handle
;
                @DosClose    STDIN              ;close my STDIN
                @DosClose    STDOUT             ;close my STDOUT
;
                mov        childin,STDIN        ;request child stdin handle
                @DosDupHandle pipe1rh,childin   ;set child STDIN to pipe1 readhand
                mov        childout,STDOUT      ;request child stdout handle
                @DosDupHandle pipe2wh,childout  ;set child STDOUT to pipe2 writehnd
```

Figure 17-23. PIPE program main logic

Each DosMakePipe call creates a pipe and returns a read handle (PIPE—RH) and a write handle (PIPE—WH) to the pipe. The next several statements create new (duplicate) handles for STDIN and STDOUT. Notice that if you set the duplicate handle field to -1, you are telling OS/2 that you do not care what the new handle value will be, so it will assign the new handle value as the next available handle. You must create local duplicates of STDIN and STDOUT because PIPE will overlay them with duplicates of the pipe handles.

Before the pipe handles can be duplicated to 0 and 1, however, you must close the existing STDIN and STDOUT handles. This is not really a problem since PIPE already has local duplicates of these handles (MYSTDIN, MYSTDOUT). Now that 0 and 1 are available handle values, PIPE can duplicate PIPE1RH to 0 (STDIN) and PIPE2WH to 1 (STDOUT).

PIPE now starts the child process (UPCASE), with STDIN set to the PIPE1 read handle and STDOUT set to the PIPE2 write handle (see Figure 17-24). The child pro-

```
;
; Create program
;
          @DosExecPgm  pgmobj,10,2,pgmprm,pgmenv,pgmpid,pgmname
          @jaxz     pip020              ;program found - continue
          @DosWrite STDERR,msg3,msg3l,bytesout ;Write message
          jmp       pip999              ;exit
```

Figure 17-24. PIPE code to start UPCASE child process

cess *inherits* these modified standard I/O handles.

After it starts the child, PIPE begins processing data, as shown in Figure 17-25. Note that to read from standard input, PIPE uses the duplicate STDIN handle (MYSTD-IN), and to write to standard output, it uses its duplicate STDOUT handle (MYSTDOUT). To feed data to the UPCASE program, PIPE writes to the other end of the pipe that it duplicated to STDIN (PIPE1), and to read the UPCASE output it reads from the other end of the pipe it duplicated to STDOUT (PIPE2). In this way, PIPE can read data from the "real" STDIN, pass it to UPCASE to convert to uppercase, and write it to the "real" STDOUT.

```
;
; Process the data stream
;
pip020:   @DosRead  mystdin,inbuf,INBUFL,bytesin ;Read from STDIN
          cmp       bytesin,0           ;end of data?
          jne       pip030              ;no - continue
          jmp       pip999              ;yes - exit
pip030:   @DosWrite pipe1wh,inbuf,bytesin,bytesout ;write it to the child
          @DosRead  pipe2rh,inbuf,INBUFL,bytesin ;Read from child
          @DosWrite mystdout,inbuf,bytesin,bytesout ;write it to STDOUT
          jmp       pip020              ;go get next data
```

Figure 17-25. PIPE processing data after starting child

```
[C:\]PIPE
dddddddddddddddd◄CR►          ◄--- you enter
DDDDDDDDDDDDDDDD              ◄--- PIPE/UPCASE output
aaa123ABC()!#◄CR►             ◄--- you enter
AAA123ABC()!#                 ◄--- PIPE/UPCASE output
^Z◄CR►                        ◄--- you enter
[C:\]
```

Figure 17-26. Command line to run PIPE

If you now run PIPE (see Figure 17-26), you see essentially the same output that you saw in Chapter 13. While this example may not be useful (you can get the same results running UPCASE directly), it does illustrate how you can set up pipes to drive any standard I/O program.

For instance, if you replace UPCASE.EXE with MASM.EXE, then PIPE could start the assembler and then pass the parameters through the MASM STDIN, just as if you had entered them from the command line. If you then create four pipes, you could drive two assemblies in parallel. As you can see, the possibilities are endless. This programming technique allows you to perform the (CMD.EXE) command-line piping functions from an application program.

Queuing Services

The final form of standard IPC is queuing services. Recall that queues use a different data model than pipes. In queues, data is passed as discrete *packets* (queue elements). Packets are generated by a client process and they are collected in a named object called a *queue*.

Creating and destroying queues

Within a queue, the elements are stored in FIFO (first-in, first-out), LIFO (last-in, first-out), or element-priority order. The queuing order is set when you create the queue. To create the queue, you use the DosCreateQueue API. The parameters of DosCreateQueue are as follows:

PTR	A pointer to a one-word field into which OS/2 will place the queue handle
WORD	A one-word queue ordering value: 0 = FIFO 1 = LIFO 2 = Element priority
PTR	A pointer to an ASCIIZ string containing the name of the queue. **Note:** This string must start with \QUEUES\

The creator of a queue is called the *queue owner* and is the only one allowed to "dequeue" or purge elements from the queue. When you create a queue, you must give it an ASCIIZ name that starts with the character string \QUEUES\ and conforms to the OS/2 file-naming conventions. At the time you create a queue, you define the ordering rules (FIFO, LIFO, or priority) that OS/2 will use to order the individual queue elements. This ordering sequence is set for the life of the queue. For example, the code in Figure 17-27 creates a queue named \QUEUES\MYQUEUE with FIFO element ordering.

```
Data Segment ...

myhand      dw      0                       ;Queue handle
qname       db      '\QUEUES\MYQUEUE',0     ;Queue name

Code Segment ...

            @DosCreateQueue myqhand,FIFO,qname ;create input queue
```

Figure 17-27. Code to create \QUEUES\MYQUEUE queue

When you create a queue, OS/2 gives you a queue handle that you then use with other queuing APIs to remove elements from the queue. The queue exists as long as your process is active, or until you destroy it with the Dos-CloseQueue API. The parameter of DosCloseQueue is as follows:

WORD	A one-word (open) queue handle

When you close an active queue, the queue elements contained within it are purged and the queue ceases to exist. For example,

```
@DosCloseQueue myqhand        ;release queue
```

closes the queue created in a previous example.

Adding elements to a queue

Other processes gain access to the queue by issuing the DosOpenQueue API with the queue name. This API also returns a queue handle that is used to add elements to the queue. The queue owner does not have to open the queue, since it receives a handle when it creates the queue. The parameters of DosOpenQueue are as follows:

PTR	A pointer to a one-word field into which OS/2 will place the PID of the queue owner
PTR	A pointer to a one-word field into which OS/2 will place the queue handle
PTR	A pointer to an ASCIIZ string containing the name of the queue. **Note:** This string must start with \QUEUES\

Once you have a queue handle, you can use the DosWriteQueue API to add an element to the queue. The parameters of DosWriteQueue are as follows:

WORD	A one-word queue handle (returned from DosOpenQueue or DosCreateQueue)
WORD	A one-word request field that OS/2 is to pass with the queue element. This information is application-specific. OS/2 neither inspects nor modifies its contents
WORD	A one-word field that defines the size of the queue element
PTR	A pointer to the queue element that OS/2 will add to the queue
WORD	A one-word element priority value (0—15)

For example,

```
@DosOpenQueue qpid,qhand,qname         ;open queue
@jaxnz     opq999                      ;Opened error - exit
@DosWriteQueue qhand,0,32,mydata,myreq ;write to queue
```

opens a queue and then adds an element (MYDATA) whose length is 32 and priority is 0. The priority is only meaningful if the queue was created to order elements in priority sequence.

However, note that element priority is independent of process priority. It signifies the relative importance of the *data*. When using priority-based queues, the client and server processes use a pre-established convention to define what the priorities mean. For example, you could use priority 0 for normal messages and priority 1 for "expedited" messages.

MYREQ is a one-word value associated with the queue element. Like priority, the meaning of this field is prearranged. For instance, it could be a one-word element identification that tells the queue owner what kind of data is contained in the element.

Note that, unlike pipes, the queue owner does not have to be the parent of the client processes. A queue may be used to communicate between any two processes in the system.

Processing queue elements

The queue owner (server) can use several functions to manipulate the queue elements. It can "dequeue" an element by using the DosReadQueue function. The parameters for DosReadQueue are as follows:

WORD	A one-word queue handle (returned from DosOpen-Queue or DosCreateQueue)
PTR	A pointer to a double-word field in which OS/2 returns the following information:
DN	The PID of the process that created the element
DW	Application-specific data (see DosWriteQueue)
PTR	A pointer to a one-word field in which OS/2 will return the size of the "dequeued" element
PTR	A pointer to a double-word field in which OS/2 will return the address of the queue element
WORD	A one-word value that specifies the exact queue element number you want retrieved. **Note:** Elements are normally retrieved in the queue ordering sequence (FIFO, LIFO, or priority); this parameter enables you to override this ordering: 0 = Use the queue element ordering (get next element) *n* = Get *n*th element
WORD	A one-word wait indicator: 0 = Wait until an element is present (synchronous read) 1 = Post semaphore when element is present (asynchronous read)
PTR	Pointer to a one-word field in which OS/2 will return the element priority value (as set by sender).
DWRD	A double-word system semaphore handle that OS/2 will post when the element is received. **Note:** This is only valid for asynchronous requests. If the wait indicator is 0, then this parameter can be NULL

For example,

```
WAIT        equ     0                           ;WAIT value
            mov     elenum,0                    ;set element number
            @DosReadQueue qhand,elereq,elelen,eleptr,elenum,WAIT,elepri,elesemh
```

removes the next element from the queue. OS/2 places the element address in ELEPTR, the element length in ELELEN, its priority in ELEPRI, and the request data and sender PID in ELEREQ. The element code parameter (ELENUM) tells OS/2 which queue element to "dequeue." If set to 0 (as in this example), then OS/2 retrieves the next element from the top of the queue. This could be the oldest, youngest, or highest-priority element, depending on the queue element ordering sequence. If set to a nonzero value, then OS/2 retrieves a specific queue element.

Finally, the WAIT/NOWAIT indicator tells OS/2 whether or not you want to wait for the next element when the queue is empty. If you specify WAIT (0), then the thread will block until another program adds an element to the queue. If you specify NOWAIT, then DosReadQueue will return immediately and the semaphore associated with the semaphore handle in the last parameter (ELESEMH) will be cleared when an element arrives.

This semaphore handle can correspond to either a RAM semaphore or system semaphore. However, it is subject to several restrictions. If it is a RAM semaphore, the memory segment in which it is contained must be addressable by all programs that call DosWriteQueue to add an element to the queue. If it is a system semaphore, then it must be opened by all processes that call DosWriteQueue to add an element to the queue.

If you use synchronous calls, then the semaphore handle is ignored by OS/2 and can be null (0).

If you want to "look" at the contents of the queue, but do not want to "dequeue" the elements, then you can use the DosPeekQueue call. This API has exactly the same parameters and functions as DosReadQueue, except that the queue remains intact and OS/2 updates the element number field. The parameters for DosPeekQueue are as follows:

WORD	A one-word queue handle (returned from DosOpen-Queue or DosCreateQueue)
PTR	A pointer to a double-word field in which OS/2 returns the following information:
DN	The PID of the process that created the element
DW	Application-specific data (see DosWriteQueue)
PTR	A pointer to a one-word field in which OS/2 will return the size of the peeked element
PTR	A pointer to a double-word field in which OS/2 will return the address of the peeked element
PTR	A pointer to a one-word value that specifies the exact queue element number you want to peek. **Note:** Elements are normally peeked in the queue ordering sequence (FIFO, LIFO, or priority); this parameter enables you to override this ordering: 0 = Use the queue element ordering (get next element) n = Get nth element On return, OS/2 sets this field to the "next" element number in the queue
WORD	A one-word wait indicator: 0 = Wait until an element is present (synchronous peek) 1 = Post semaphore when element is present (asynchronous peek)

PTR	Pointer to a one-word field in which OS/2 will return the element priority value (as set by the sender)
DWRD	A double-word system semaphore handle that OS/2 will post when the element is received. **Note**: This is only valid for asynchronous requests. If the wait indicator is 0, this parameter can be NULL

By using DosPeekQueue, you can search the queue for a particular element, then use the element number with DosReadQueue to extract it. Each time you call DosPeekQueue, OS/2 automatically increments the element number field. If you simply call it repeatedly, you will see all the elements in the queue.

The queue owner can also purge all the elements in a queue with the DosPurgeQueue API. Be careful when you use this API, because once purged, the queue elements are lost. Also, the memory associated with each element is not freed. The parameter for DosPurgeQueue is as follows:

WORD	A one-word queue handle (returned from DosCreateQueue).

Finally, any process that has access to a queue (server and clients) can query how many elements are in the queue with the DosQueryQueue API. The parameters of DosQueryQueue are as follows:

WORD	A one-word queue handle (returned from DosCreateQueue or DosOpenQueue)
PTR	Pointer to a one-word field in which OS/2 will return a count of the number of elements currently in the queue

Allocating queue elements

You have several options for allocating queue element memory segments. First, you should realize that since queue elements are passed between processes, the memory segment containing the data must be a shared segment. This means that the actual queue elements cannot be contained in one of your application data segments. They must be in a dynamically allocated memory segment.

As you will recall from Chapter 4, shared memory can be allocated globally or privately. Queue elements can, therefore, be contained in either type of memory segment. If you do not expect to have very large or very many queue elements, you can allocate a single named shared segment and create the individual elements with the OS/2 suballocation services, as illustrated in Figure 17-28.

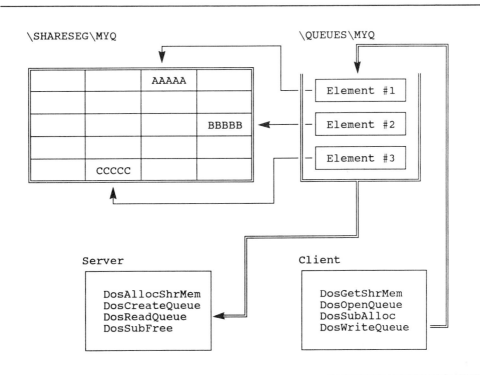

Figure 17-28. Global shared-memory queue element pool

This simple approach is probably adequate for most situations. The server process creates a named shared-memory segment to serve as a memory "pool" out of which the queue elements can be allocated. Each client process that wants to add queue element(s) to the queue must then access the named shared segment and suballocate a queue element with the DosSubAlloc function. It then uses these individual "chunks" to hold the queue element data. The server is responsible for freeing the suballocated element with DosSubFree after it reads the queue element, thus making the memory available for another client.

However, note that with this approach the total size of the outstanding queue elements cannot exceed 64K, since they must all fit in a single memory segment. If the total size of your queue elements exceeds 64K, you could use a slight variation to this approach in which the server allocates multiple named memory segments. The clients would then try to suballocate their elements out of several named segments. If the first segment is full, then it tries the second, third, and so on.

But what happens when the queue elements vary drastically in size? Recall that memory suballocation works best when the individual elements are the same (or nearly the same) size. As you increase the variation in element size, you increase the probability that the physical memory segment will become fragmented.

In this case, you may want to use the private shared-memory approach. In this approach, you allocate a data segment and then "give" it to another process with the DosGiveSeg API. So, you would allocate a separate physical segment for each queue element, give it to the server process, then use DosWriteQueue to place the element in the queue. Figure 17-29 illustrates this technique.

Notice that once you have "given" the segment to the server process, you can free it. Freeing a shared segment that is also accessed by another process does not really free the memory, rather it deletes the descriptor from your LDT. The server process will still have access to the data.

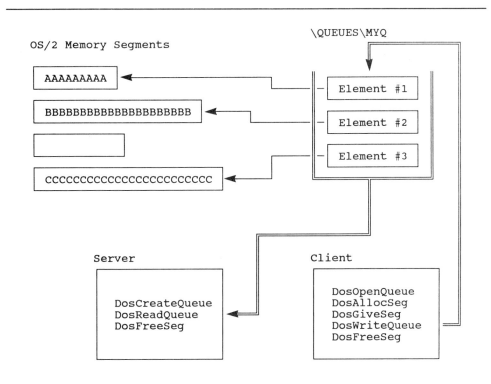

Figure 17-29. Individually allocated queue elements

In fact, in this scheme, both the server and the client must free the memory segment before the physical memory is returned to the system.

The DosOpenQueue API returns the PID of the queue owner. You use this PID in the DosGiveSeg call to pass shared-memory segments to the queue owner.

A simple queuing example

Consider two programs that use queues to pass data between themselves. MAILBOX is largely based on the RUN program from Chapter 16. It starts four child processes (QUEUE) and then waits on the keyboard. For each

```
;
; QUEUE shared memory segment layout
;
qdata       struc
row         dw       ?                          ;Display Row
col         dw       ?                          ;Display Column
myqname     db       '??????????'               ;My Queue name
            db       0                          ;zero terminated name
sendq       db       '??????????'               ;Next Queue name
            db       0                          ;zero terminated name
attr        db       ?                          ;Display Attribute
priority    dw       ?                          ;Execution priority
sel         dw       ?                          ;Shared segment selector
procid      dw       0                          ;process ID
qhand       dw       0                          ;Open queue handle
qdata       ends
SHRSZ       equ      size qdata                 ;structure size
;
; Child Process control areas
;
qparms      qdata    <1,03,'\QUEUES\Q1',,'\QUEUES\Q2',,1fh>
            qdata    <1,22,'\QUEUES\Q2',,'\QUEUES\Q3',,2fh>
            qdata    <1,41,'\QUEUES\Q3',,'\QUEUES\Q4',,4fh>
            qdata    <1,60,'\QUEUES\Q4',,'\QUEUES\Q1',,6fh>
QCOUNT      equ      4                          ;program count
```

Figure 17-30.   Queued shared-memory segment layout

child process, MAILBOX creates a shared-memory segment and initializes it to contain the child's parameter area. This parameter area contains, among other things, two queue names—one to receive elements and another to write elements (see Figure 17-30).

As each child (QUEUE) starts, it creates its queue and opens the next queue. The idea is that it will receive data from one queue and send it to the next. Because of the way the queue names are defined in the data records, a data element will be passed between the four queues forever. Thus, the structure of the MAILBOX/QUEUE system is illustrated in Figure 17-31.

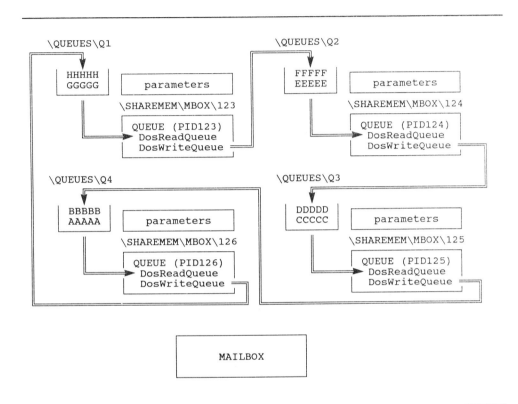

Figure 17-31.   MAILBOX/QUEUE system structure

The MAILBOX program sets up the shared-memory areas in precisely the same way RUN did. In fact, the only significant change introduced in MAILBOX is its ability to add queue elements to the QUEUE input queues. To do this, it must have write access to the queues. So, after it creates the four QUEUE processes, MAILBOX calls a new subroutine (OPENQ) to open each queue and save the child's queue handle in the process record (see Figure 17-32).

```
openq      proc
;
           mov      cx,QCOUNT              ;program count
           lea      si,qparms              ;first set of parameters
;
opq010:    lea      di,[si].myqname        ;get child queue name
           aDosOpenQueue cpid,cqhand,DS:DI ;open child's queue
           ajaxz    opq020                 ;Opened OK - go loop
           aDosSleep sleepct               ;wait a little while
           jmp      opq010                 ;go try again
;
opq020:    push     cqhand                 ;put child's Q handle
           pop      [si].qhand             ;into parameter area
           add      si,SHRSZ               ;point to next parameter area
           loop     opq010                 ;loop through process list
;
           ret
openq      endp
```

Figure 17-32.   OPENQ subroutine

Note that OPENQ must retry the DosOpenQueue calls
because it is possible that the QUEUE processes have not
yet had the opportunity to create their input queues. The
KEYIN subroutine (see Figure 17-33) is also enhanced
to look for the Plus key (+). When the user presses +,
KEYIN calls the new subroutine ADDELEMENT to
create a queue element and "insert" it into the input queue
of the current process (see Figure 17-34).

Note that MAILBOX uses the private shared-segment
technique to allocate individual queue element memory

```
kin060:    cmp      al,'+'                 ;plus key?
           jne      kin500                 ;no - continue
           call     addelement             ;add a queue element
           jmp      kin000                 ;continue
```

Figure 17-33.   Enhanced KEYIN subroutine

```
addelement    proc
;
              cmp       dx,12              ;max elements already in system?
              jb        add010             ;no, go add one
              @DosBeep  1000,100           ;sound error beep
              jmp       add999             ;exit
;
add010:       @DosAllocSeg ELESZ,segp,1    ;allocate 'shared' segment
              inc       dx                 ;bump element count
              mov       ax,dx              ;get element count
              or        al,40h             ;convert to printable ASCII
              push      segp               ;copy element pointer
              pop       es                 ;to ES
              push      di                 ;save pointer
              xor       di,di              ;start of element
              mov       cx,ELESZ           ;get element size
              rep       stosb              ;initialize it
              xor       di,di              ;point to start of segment
;
              @DosGiveSeg  segp,[si].procid,selnew ;give segment to child
              push      selnew             ;put new selector
              pop       es                 ;in ES
              @DosWriteQueue [si].qhand,0,ELESZ,ES:DI,0 ;write to child queue
              @DosFreeSeg   segp           ;free the element
;
              pop       di                 ;restore pointer
;
add999:       ret
addelement    endp
```

Figure 17-34. ADDELEMENT subroutine

segments. Thus, to create an element, ADDELEMENT allocates a "shareable" segment with DosAllocSeg and initializes it with uppercase letters corresponding to the element number (1=A, 2=B, and so forth). It then uses DosGiveSeg to give the queue owner addressability to the segment.

Note that when it makes the DosWriteQueue call, ADDELEMENT uses the selector returned to DosGiveSeg to pass the data. This is because this new selector is what the queue owner must use to address the buffer (not the "local" selector). After the data is added to the queue of the child process, ADDELEMENT frees the segment, making the child process the only owner of the segment.

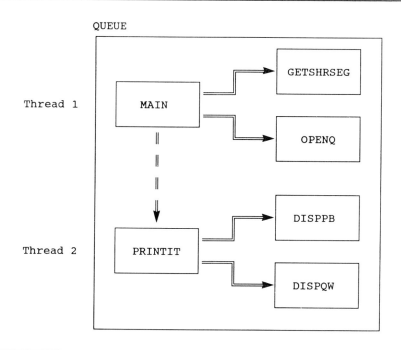

QUEUE

Thread 1 — MAIN → GETSHRSEG, OPENQ

Thread 2 — PRINTIT → DISPPB, DISPQW

Figure 17-35.   QUEUE program structure

Now consider the QUEUE program, which has the structure shown in Figure 17-35. The MAIN thread calls two subroutines—GETSHRSEG to get addressability to the named shared segment and OPENQ to establish the queue linkages.

Before it drops into its main processing loop, MAIN creates a separate thread, PRINTIT, to display the queue information on the screen. You use a separate thread in this situation so that PRINITIT can set itself to run at a high priority and display the queue buildups that may occur in its lower-priority "worker" thread (MAIN).

The GETSHRSEG procedure is identical to the logic found in COUNT (see Chapter 16). OPENQ, on the other hand, is new to this program, as shown in Figure 17-36. It

```
openq        proc
             lea      si,[di].myqname          ;get my queue name from shrseg
opq000:      @DosCreateQueue myqhand,FIFO,DS:SI ;create my input queue
;            db       0cch
             @jaxz    opq010                   ;Opened OK - exit
             @DosSleep count1                  ;wait a little while
             jmp      opq000                   ;go try again
;
opq010:      lea      si,[di].nxqname          ;get next queue nam from shrseg
             @DosOpenQueue nxqpid,nxqhand,DS:SI ;open next queue
             @jaxz    opq999                   ;Opened OK - exit
             @DosSleep count1                  ;wait a little while
             jmp      opq010                   ;go try again
;
opq999:      ret
openq        endp
```

Figure 17-36. Enhanced OPENQ subroutine

creates its process input queue using the name it finds in the field MYQNAME and opens the output queue whose name is in NXQNAME. If either call fails, it waits a short period of time and retries. This is because at the time QUEUE is starting up, the other processes may not yet have initialized. The short sleep periods help synchronize the initialization processes. When the DosOpenQueue call successfully completes, the PID of the process that owns the "next" queue is in the field NXQPID. This PID will be used in the MAIN routine to pass ownership of the queue element segments to the next process.

The remainder of the MAIN routine does all the work required to read and write the queue elements, as shown in Figure 17-37. It first reads the queue element by using a synchronous DosReadQueue call. When it receives an element, it immediately gives the segment to the next queue owner process (NXQPID). Note that since Intel CPUs store double-word values in reverse order, the queue element selector is in the second word of the pointer field (ELEPTR+2). On return from DosGiveSeg, the field NXSEL

```
que010:     @DosReadQueue  myqhand,elereq,elelen,eleptr,0,0,elepri,NULL
            @DosGiveSeg eleptr+2,nxqpid,nxsel ;give segment to next proc
            push      nxsel              ;put next recipient's selector
            pop       ds                 ;in DS
            @DosWriteQueue nxqhand,0,elelen,DS:DI,elepri ;write to next queue
            @DosFreeSeg mysel             ;free the element
            @VioScrollUp qwtop,qwleft,qwbot,qwright,1,fill,0 ;erase element
            @DosSemClear semhand          ;re-display queue list
            jmp       que010             ;go read the next element
```

Figure 17-37. Remainder of MAIN routine

contains a selector that can be used by the next process to address the queue element segment. So, in the DosWrite-Queue call, MAIN uses NXSEL as the selector portion of the element address. Each QUEUE program is simply "passing along" ownership of the queue elements to the next process in the chain.

After putting the element in the next queue, MAIN deletes the segment descriptor from its LDT by calling DosFreeSeg with its local selector. Thus, the queue element is now in the next queue, and the segment that contains the queue element data is addressable by the process associated with the next queue.

Once it has passed the data element to the next process, MAIN clears a semaphore to "wake up" the display thread to update the queue display.

While this is all going on, the other thread in QUEUE is displaying the queue information. Recall that before it dropped into the processing loop, MAIN created the PRINTIT thread. The only role of PRINTIT is to continuously display the process information and the queue contents (see Figure 17-38).

The first thing PRINTIT does is increase its priority to time-critical level 0. At this level, PRINTIT is guaranteed to run before the other thread it is monitoring, since the other thread runs in the regular priority class.

```
printit     proc
            xor     di,di                   ;address parameter block
            @DosGetPid  piddata             ;Get my thread ID
            @DosSetPrty 2,3,0,piddata.pidtid ;boost myself to Time Critical 0
;
prt010:     mov     al,[di].attr            ;get attribute
            mov     attrib,ax               ;put it in memory
;
            @DosQueryQueue myqhand,elecnt    ;get current element count
            @bta    elecnt,msgcnt,2         ;convert element count to ASCII
;
            @DosGetPrty 0,myprty,0          ;get thread 0 priority data
            mov     bx,myprty               ;move it to register
            xor     bh,bh                   ;clear priority class
            @bta    bx,msgprty,2            ;convert to displayable ASCII
;
            call    disppb                  ;display process 'box'
            call    dispqw                  ;display queue elements
;
            @DosSemSetWait semhand,count1   ;wait a little while
            jmp     prt010                  ;go refresh
printit     endp
```

Figure 17-38. PRINTIT subroutine

Now PRINTIT starts a processing loop. First it determines the number of elements in the input queue, then it retrieves the current priority level of the other (worker) thread. It calls subroutines named DISPPB and DISPQW to display the "process box" and "queue window," sleeps for a short period of time, and then repeats the entire process.

DISPPB simply displays the process box, as shown in Figure 17-39, at the coordinates specified in the QUEUE shared-memory parameter area. The DISPQW routine shown in Figure 17-40 is a little more interesting. It computes the coordinates of the queue element window and places it immediately below the process box. It then reads the individual queue elements by using DosPeekQueue and displays their contents on the display (in the queue element window). As it displays each element, it moves the

```
disppb      proc
            @VioWrtCharStrAtt msg0,MSGL,[di].row,[di].col,attrib,0 ;Line 1
            mov     bx,[di].row        ;get row
            inc     bx                 ;next line
            @VioWrtCharStrAtt msg1,MSGL,bx,[di].col,attrib,0       ;Line 2
            inc     bx                 ;next line
            @VioWrtCharStrAtt msg2,MSGL,bx,[di].col,attrib,0       ;Line 3
            inc     bx                 ;next line
            @VioWrtCharStrAtt msg3,MSGL,bx,[di].col,attrib,0       ;Line 4
            ret
disppb      endp
```

Figure 17-39. DISPPB routine

```
dispqw      proc
            mov     bx,[di].row        ;get row number
            add     bx,4               ;top q window row
            mov     qwtop,bx           ;save coordinate
            add     bx,12              ;bot q window row
            mov     qwbot,bx           ;save coordinate
;
            mov     bx,[di].col        ;get col number
            add     bx,2               ;center queue
            mov     qwleft,bx          ;save coordinate
            add     bx,MSGL            ;right q window col
            mov     qwright,bx         ;save coordinate
;
            mov     peekel,0           ;initialize element number
            push    qwtop              ;put top row
            pop     trow               ;into work buffer
            push    ds                 ;save share mem pointer
dsq030:     @DosPeekQueue myqhand,peekreq,peeklen,peekptr,peekel,0,peekpri,NULL
            @jaxnz  dsq050             ;exit if queue is empty
            lds     si,peekptr         ;put element address in DS:SI
            @VioWrtCharStrAtt DS:SI,peeklen,trow,qwleft,attrib,0 ;write elemt
            inc     trow               ;next line
            jmp     dsq030             ;display next element
dsq050:     pop     ds                 ;restore share mem pointer
;
            @VioScrollUp trow,qwleft,qwbot,qwright,-1,fill,0 ;clear Q window
;
            ret
dispqw      endp
```

Figure 17-40. DISPQW routine

top of the window down one line. When it finishes displaying the queue elements, it clears the remaining lines in the
window. Thus, DISPQW displays the current contents of
the queue immediately below the process box.

Note that the DosSemSetWait ensures that PRINTIT
will not spin indefinitely displaying the queue. Since
PRINTIT runs at a high priority, it must use CPU cycles
judiciously. In conjunction with the wait, you use a time-
out value (200 ms) to force the thread to "sleep" for a short
period of time. In fact, this semaphore wait with a time-
out performs exactly the same function as a DosSleep,
with one important exception. The MAIN thread can clear
the semaphore to "wake up" the PRINTIT thread before

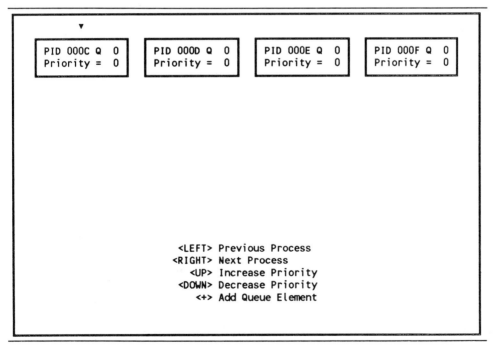

Figure 17-41. MAILBOX display (dormant state)

the timeout. Thus, MAIN can force it to come alive to re-display the queue each time an element is "removed" from the queue.

This example illustrates an important concept about OS/2 queues. More than one thread in a process can access the same queue. Furthermore, while one thread is waiting on the queue with a DosReadQueue, a second thread can be peeking the same queue. If both threads were using asynchronous DosReadQueue/DosPeekQueue calls, then they would both have to use the same semaphore.

Now run MAILBOX to see what happens. If you start the program, you will see the display illustrated in Figure 17-41. Since you have not added any queue elements, the four QUEUE programs are dormant.

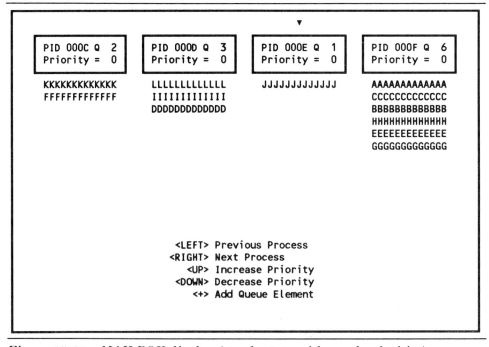

Figure 17-42. MAILBOX display (steady state with equal priorities)

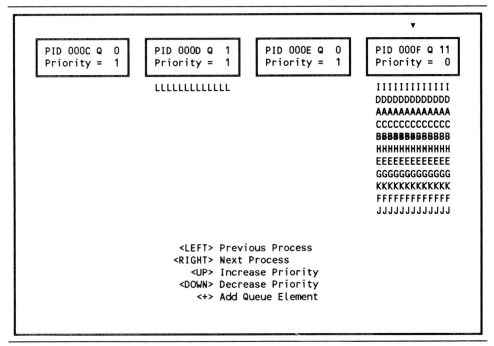

Figure 17-43. MAILBOX display (steady state with unequal priorities)

However, as soon as you press the plus (+) key, the display immediately starts flashing a queue element as it is passed between the four processes. If you press the plus key 11 more times, MAILBOX creates the maximum number of queue elements. As you will notice, the queues temporarily build up in one process, then another (see Figure 17-42).

If you increase the priority of three of the four processes, then the queue will quickly build up in the lower-priority process. This is because all the other processes run before the fourth process, and can therefore "dump" the queue elements faster than the low-priority process can read them. This is illustrated in Figure 17-43.

SUMMARY

You now have a number of important tools in your repertoire. With the functions you have seen in this chapter, you can coordinate the activities of multiple processes and threads.

Semaphores enable you to create serially reuseable resources and provide an effective mechanism for signaling events between threads (processes).

Timer services range from asynchronous program timers (cyclical or single-shot) to a synchronous sleep function. These facilities enable you to synchronize program activities with the system clock.

Finally, OS/2 includes a wide range of IPC functions that combine data passing with program synchronization into single, high-level, services. In addition to semaphores and shared memory, the OS/2 IPC models include pipes (serial character streams) and queues (discrete data elements).

These functions are all important. You will use most of them in OS/2 multitasking programs. Before proceeding to the next chapter, review the following topics:

- What are semaphores and why you need them

- RAM semaphores versus system semaphores

- Creating a system semaphore

- Allocating a RAM semaphore

- Using a semaphore to create a serially reuseable resource

- Using a semaphore to signal a thread

- Waiting on multiple semaphores with DosMuxSem-Wait

- Synchronous timers (DosSleep)
- Asynchronous timers
- When to use asynchronous timers
- Setting and retrieving the system clock
- What pipes are and how to use them
- Running a standard I/O program
- What queues are and how to use them
- Allocating queue data elements

CHAPTER 18
DEVICE MONITORS

Because it is a multitasking system, OS/2 imposes more formal controls on the system I/O than its predecessor, PC DOS. However, this does not imply that OS/2 applications are slow and lethargic. Quite to the contrary, the OS/2 I/O subsystems are among the fastest in the industry.

But more than one facet contributes to the great popularity PC DOS enjoys among application developers. Certainly, one facet is performance, or rather, the ability to write highly responsive applications. PC DOS is seldom in your way. If you need to manipulate the hardware, you do it (directly). These I/O performance issues are more than adequately addressed by the OS/2 I/O subsystems.

Another facet is flexibility. If a PC DOS application program needs to see the raw keystrokes, it simply "hooks" the hardware interrupt and filters the data before sending it up to the system. But to do this in OS/2 (where the application programs are not in the interrupt-management business) involves a special facility called device monitor. A *device monitor* is a structured task-time extension of the

OS/2 character device drivers. Device monitors provide the ability to inspect, modify, generate, or consume character device I/O from an application. Thus, you do not have to sacrifice the flexibility of PC DOS.

This chapter explains how to use the device monitor services. With them you will be able to build application programs that are tightly coupled to the device character streams, but not the device-interrupt management.

MONITOR ARCHITECTURE

Consider a brief review of the underlying architecture of device monitors. A monitor is an application program (or subsystem) that has notified OS/2 that it is interested in viewing the data stream of a particular character device.

As explained in previous chapters, OS/2 only allows device driver interrupt service routines to handle interrupts. Interrupt management in a multitasking system with overlapped I/O is tricky business and much more complex than in PC DOS. But monitors are not interrupt-management routines. They receive the raw data long after the interrupt has been dismissed by the device driver. However, they do see the data before the device driver passes it to the kernel (and the application). You can view a device monitor as a task-time exit routine that is called by the device driver(s) (see Figure 18-1).

However, this does not mean that you should write a monitor any less carefully than you would write a device driver. Since the actual device data traverses the monitor chain, the device monitors are an integral part of the overall system data flows. As compared to an application (which is the ultimate destination of an input character) a monitor is an intermediate step. If a monitor "forgets" to pass a character along, it could cause an application program to hang or, in the extreme case, a system to hang.

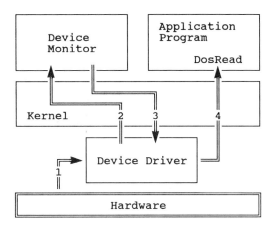

Figure 18-1. Device monitor data flows

Since monitors play such a critical role in the overall system, they must always be available to process characters. Because of this, OS/2 implements a more complex buffering scheme in monitors than in simple application I/O.

For example, consider Figure 18-2. The device driver has two monitors associated with it. As each character is received, the device driver encapsulates it in a packet and sends it up the monitor chain. Since the monitor may not be immediately dispatchable when the interrupt is received, it provides an input buffer that can temporarily hold one (or more) device monitor packets. The device monitor router (a kernel component) moves packets into the monitor input buffer until the monitor can be dispatched.

When the actual monitor thread gains control, it reads each individual packet into an internal work buffer. From there it does whatever work is necessary and writes the packet out to an output buffer. Once again, the monitor

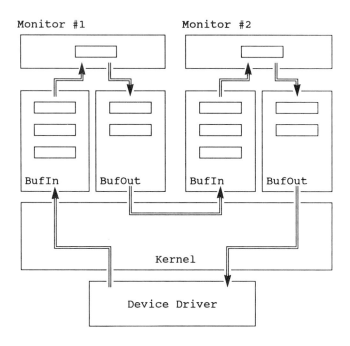

Figure 18-2. Device monitor buffers

router moves the packet to the input buffer of the next monitor. This process repeats until the packet winds up back in the device driver.

These intermediate buffers are crucial since they must buffer the data between the time the interrupt happens and the time the monitor runs. In effect, the sum total of the monitor buffers becomes the device "pipeline." For example, if you install a keyboard monitor with input and output buffers large enough to hold 100 keystrokes, the effective size of the keyboard type-ahead buffer is increased by about 50 characters.

The OS/2 device monitor mechanism is a *generic transport facility*. This means that the specific characteristics of the data packets and data flows vary from device to device. The next section discusses how each OS/2 character device supports monitors. Although the technique is not discussed in this book, you can add monitor support to any character device driver you write by using the monitor DevHlp services.

The monitors run in a task context. This is important because it means that monitor threads are free to issue any OS/2 system call. However, keep in mind that the monitor is in the system data path. So, the thread that is doing the actual monitoring should refrain from doing things that will unnecessarily slow down the data (such as reading or writing to a disk). Instead, monitor applications should have at least two threads of execution—one to monitor the data stream and another to perform application I/O.

Finally, a monitor application has the capability to monitor all character I/O going to or coming from a particular device. A monitor application is not bound by a particular process. For example, if you monitor the printer output, you will see all the characters being sent to the printer device. If you monitor the keyboard input, you will see all the input destined for the session. With this facility, you can create the equivalent of a PC DOS "popup" application.

DEVICES SUPPORTED

Before an application can monitor a device, the device driver must be written so that it supports monitoring. Furthermore, you can only use the OS/2 monitor support with character device drivers. Block device drivers (such as a disk) do not process data as a serial character stream. Hence, the monitor model is not valid.

Table 18-1. Device Buffer Sizes

Name	Device	Buffer Size
KBD$	Keyboard	14
MOUSE	Mouse (pointer)	12
LPT1-3	Printer(s)	5

The monitor input and output buffers must be as large as the internal device driver buffer plus 20 bytes. This buffer size varies from device to device, as shown in Table 18-1. Make sure that your monitor program provides buffers that are larger than this or else the program will not be able to register itself to the device.

When you "read" data from a monitor input buffer, OS/2 gives you a monitor packet. All monitor packets start with a monitor flag word. This information is broken up into a monitor-specific byte and a device-dependent byte, as shown in Figure 18-3.

A monitor may receive packets that only contain a monitor flag word. OS/2 device drivers generate special packets whenever a process opens, closes, or flushes the device. You must make sure that your monitor passes these requests along, or else the system might hang. The remainder of the monitor packet is device-specific.

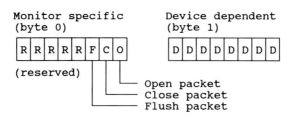

Figure 18-3. Contents of a monitor packet

OS/2 supports monitors in three devices: the keyboard, the mouse, and the printer.

Keyboard Device

Probably the most useful type of monitor is a keyboard monitor. With it you can "see" each type of keystroke interrupt much in the same way you see data by hooking INT 9 under PC DOS. For each key, the hardware generates a "make" interrupt when the key is pressed and a "break" interrupt when it is released. The keyboard device driver, in turn, generates a monitor packet for each. Figure 18-4 illustrates the keyboard monitor packet layout.

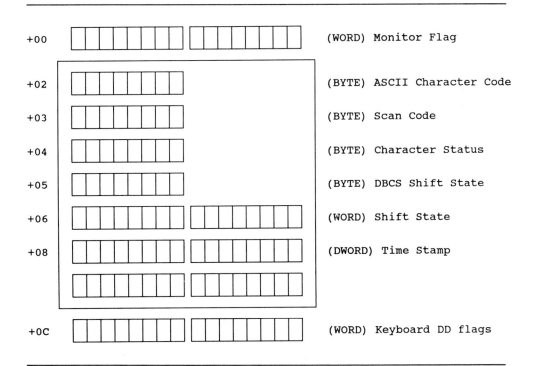

Figure 18-4. Keyboard monitor data packet

The first word in each keyboard monitor packet is the monitor flag word. In keyboard monitor packets, the device-specific byte of this word contains the original scan code, as presented by the hardware. If you generate a keyboard monitor packet, you should initialize this entire word to 0.

The actual keystroke data is encapsulated in a KBD character data structure. This is the same data structure discussed in Chapter 14 and is used in conjunction with the KbdCharIn API. All the keystroke information (including the ASCII translation) that will ultimately be sent to the application program is contained in the KBD data structure.

The keyboard monitor packet also contains a keyboard device driver (DD) flag word. This is internal state information that is used by the device driver, but will never be seen by the application. It is included in the keyboard monitor packet because a keyboard monitor needs it to understand the contents of the keyboard monitor packet. The keyboard DD flag word contains the information shown in Figure 18-5, where the following is true:

A (Available bits)	You can use these bits to communicate between monitors. OS/2 will not alter nor use this information
R (Reserved)	Do not modify these bits in any way. If you generate a monitor packet, initialize them to 0
C (Accented indicator)	The key was translated using the previous keyboard monitor packet, which was an accent key. This is used in National Language Standard (NLS) keyboards that have accent keys
M (Multimake)	Indicates that the character is a "typematic" repeat of a toggle key

S (Scan code)	The scan code in the keyboard monitor packet that preceded this one was a secondary key prefix
B (Key break)	This bit is not set if the monitor packet resulted from pressing the key (make), and it is set if the monitor packet resulted from releasing the key (break)
R (Reserved)	Used by the keyboard DD to determine if it must take special action(s) when the monitor packet is returned from the monitor chain. If you generate a packet, you must set this field to 0

You can generate keystrokes from a monitor by inserting packets into the monitor chain. However, remember that you must create a make and break key for each keystroke you send to the device driver, exactly as it would have been received from the hardware.

The keyboard device driver acts on certain keystrokes before it generates the monitor packets (if at all). In other cases, it does not take actions until the packet is returned from the monitor chain. Table 18-2 lists the pre- and post-monitor keyboard actions.

Figure 18-5. Keyboard DD flag

Table 18-2.   Keyboard Device Driver Actions

Pre-Monitor(s)		Post-Monitor(s)	
CTRL-ALT-DEL	Boot System	CTRL-BREAK	End program
CTRL-ALT-NUMLOCK	Dump System	CTRL-C	End program
PAUSE	Pause System	SHIFT-PRTSC	Print screen
CTRL-S	Pause System	CTRL-PRTSC	Toggle print
		CTRL-P	Toggle print
Wake up (any key)	Resume	CTRL-ALT-PRTSC	Flush printer

You must register keyboard monitors by session identification. A single process can monitor the keystrokes being generated in all the sessions, but to do so it must dedicate a thread per session.

Mouse Device

Like the keyboard device driver, the mouse device driver also generates a monitor packet for each mouse "event." With a mouse monitor, your program can intercept the mouse movements before they are read by the application with the MOU calls. A mouse monitor can filter, modify, delete, or insert monitor packets. Figure 18-6 illustrates the mouse monitor packet layout.

Note that the first word in each mouse monitor packet is the monitor flag word. The device-specific byte of this word is not used. If you generate mouse monitor packets, then you should initialize the entire monitor flag word to 0.

The next information in the packet is the mouse event mask, followed by a double-word (millisecond) time stamp, the absolute row position, and the absolute column position.

Like the keyboard monitors, mouse monitors are registered on a per-session basis. A single process can monitor the mouse events generated in all the sessions, but to do so it must dedicate a thread per session.

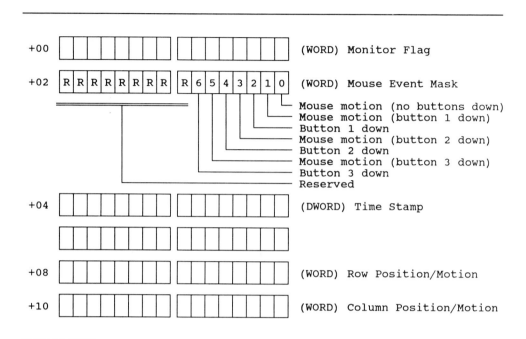

Figure 18-6.   Mouse monitor data packet

Printer Device

The OS/2 printer device driver also generates monitor packets for each character it is about to print. Rather than monitoring an input data stream (as with the keyboard and mouse), printer monitors process output data streams. This is conceptually similar to input monitoring, except that the monitor packet is generated immediately before the character is sent to the hardware (instead of the kernel).

Printer monitors are analogous to intercepting INT17H under PC DOS. Every character printed by OS/2 or the OS/2 application programs (including in the DOS-compatibility session) is funneled through the monitor chain. In fact, the OS/2 spooler uses printer monitor packets to spool data, and later generates monitor packets

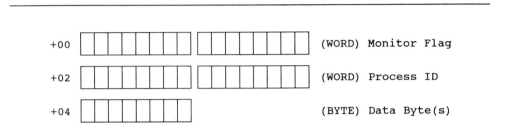

Figure 18-7.   Printer monitor data packet

to print it. Figure 18-7 shows the printer monitor packet layout.

The first word in the packet is the monitor flag word. The device-dependent data field is unused. As always, you should zero out this entire word if you insert a monitor packet into the monitor chain. The rest of the data consists of the PID of the program that is printing the data, and one or more data bytes.

The OS/2 printer device driver supports two monitor chains—one for data and the other for printer controls. You may register a monitor that will intercept either. If you wish to monitor both, you must create a separate thread to process each chain.

USING A MONITOR

This section examines the OS/2 API functions you use to create a device monitor program. In building a device monitor, you will use much of what you have already learned about OS/2.

Registering a Device

Before you can read device data from a monitor, you must do several things. First, your program must gain access to the device you intend to monitor. Previous chapters discussed how to access a device by using the OS/2 DosOpen API. To access a device for monitoring, you use a similar function called DosMonOpen. The parameters for DosMonOpen are as follows:

PTR	Pointer to an ASCIIZ device name
PTR	Pointer to a one-word field in which OS/2 will place the monitor device handle

DosMonOpen accepts an ASCIIZ device name and returns a device handle. For example, the code shown in Figure 18-8 opens the keyboard device for monitoring. Notice that this does not actually start the monitoring, but rather identifies your program to the device driver. To run a monitor, you must also register an input and an output

```
Data Segment ...

devname      db       'KBD$',0           ;device name
monhand      dw       0                  ;monitor handle

Code Segment ...

             @DosMonOpen devname,monhand  ;Open Monitor interface
             @jaxnz      error            ;jump if error
```

Figure 18-8. Code to open a keyboard device for monitoring

buffer with the monitor data router by using the DosMonReg API. Parameters for DosMonReg are as follows:

WORD	A device monitor handle (returned by DosMonOpen)
PTR	A pointer to a data buffer that OS/2 will use as the monitor input buffer. The first word in the buffer must contain the buffer length (including the word-length field)
PTR	A pointer to a data buffer that OS/2 will use as the monitor output buffer. The first word in the buffer must contain the buffer length (including the word-length field)
WORD	A one-word positional preference indicator: 0 = no preference 1 = put monitor at the head of the monitor chain 2 = put monitor at the end of the monitor chain
WORD	A one-word index value (device-dependent)

This call actually inserts your buffers in the monitor buffer chain and begins routing the monitor data through them. For example,

```
mov       mposp,1              ;head of chain
mov       mindex,0             ;my session
@DosMonReg  monhand,bin,bout,mposp,mindex ;monitor kbd
```

registers the input and output buffers (named BIN and BOUT) to the keyboard monitor chain. You use the device monitor handle returned in the previous example to identify the device you want to monitor. The BIN and BOUT size is stored as the first word in each buffer. Remember, the buffer sizes must be at least 20 bytes larger than the internal data buffer of the device you are monitoring.

At the time you register your buffers, you give OS/2 two other parameters. The positional preference (MPOSP) tells OS/2 where in the monitor chain you prefer to be placed (relative to other, existing monitors). You may request that your monitor be placed at the head of the monitor chain (1), at the end of the monitor chain (2), or that you have no preference (0). This is not guaranteed over time, since other monitor programs could be started that supersede your request. But this request does give you a way to initially insert a monitor in a particular position of an existing chain.

For instance, if you wanted to see the print data before it reaches the system spooler, you would start your monitor program after you start at the spooler and request the head-of-chain position. If you wanted to monitor the print output as it comes out of the spooler, you would again start the monitor program after the spooler, but in this case, request the end-of-chain position.

The INDEX parameter (MINDEX), tells OS/2 which monitor chain in the target device you want to monitor. Index chains are device-dependent data that the device driver uses to identify the monitor chains. In the keyboard and mouse, this index corresponds to session identification (each session has its own monitor chain). In the printer, the index corresponds to the data (1) or control (2) monitor chain.

You should be aware that once registered, a program must be prepared to immediately start processing monitor packets. Until it does, the device data stream is blocked. To finish processing data, a monitor can use the DosMonClose API.

The parameter for DosMonClose is as follows:

| WORD | A device monitor handle (returned by DosMonOpen) |

This call deregisters the monitor input and output buffers

and closes the device handle. For example:

```
@DosMonClose monhand              ;finish monitoring
```

would close the keyboard monitor you created in the previous example.

Reading and Writing Character Data

Once you have opened a device for monitoring and have registered your monitor buffers, you can begin processing the monitor packets. To retrieve a packet from your input buffer, you use the DosMonRead call. The parameters for DosMonRead are as follows:

PTR	Pointer to the monitor input buffer (registered with DosMonReg)
WORD	A one-word BLOCK/RUN indicator: 0 = Wait until data is present 1 = Do not wait if data is not present
PTR	Pointer to a data buffer in which OS/2 will place the monitor input record
PTR	Pointer to a one-word field in which OS/2 will return the number of bytes in the data record. On input, you must set this field to the input buffer size

For example,

```
mov       paklen,32             ;buffer size
@DosMonRead bin,BLOCK,pakbuf,paklen ;read packet
@jaxnz    error                 ;exit if error code is set
```

will read a single keyboard packet into the user buffer named PAKBUF. You must also give DosMonRead the address of the monitor input buffer that you registered with DosMonReg. In effect, DosMonRead shields you from the format of the input buffer by removing the monitor data packet from the input buffer and placing the results in your application buffer.

When you make the DosMonRead call you should make sure the input buffer length is set correctly. On return from DosMonRead, OS/2 will change this length field to reflect the size of the data returned in the input buffer. So, if your monitor program calls this function repeatedly to read multiple packets, you should reset the value before each call.

DosMonRead also enables you to specify if you want to wait for the next packet to arrive, or to simply return if the input buffer is empty. With the NOWAIT option, you can drive several monitor chains from a single thread. But you should be careful with this option because if you "poll" the input buffers too often the thread will waste CPU time. If you "sleep" too long between polls, then you risk congesting the device driver data flow. The best approach is to use multiple threads that issue synchronous (BLOCK) monitor read requests.

Note that you use DosMonRead in the thread context at task time (versus interrupt time). This means a program that reads from the monitor buffer can issue other OS/2 calls. But again, you could get in trouble here if you call OS/2 functions that could wind up blocking on input from an external device. This includes all forms of device and file I/O, memory allocation (remember, OS/2 might have to swap segments out), or any kind of semaphore wait. You should consider dedicating the monitor thread for reading the monitor packets. A different thread could perform the I/O operations on behalf of the monitor thread.

Once you have received a monitor packet and have done whatever you want with the data, you can re-insert the packet into the monitor chain with the DosMonWrite API.

The parameters of DosMonWrite are as follows:

PTR	Pointer to the monitor output buffer (registered with DosMonReg)
PTR	Pointer to a data buffer from which OS/2 will read the monitor output record
WORD	A one-word value indicating the total length of the data record in the output buffer

This function writes the data back to the device driver. For example,

```
@DosMonWrite bout,pakout,paklen ;write packet
@jaxnz     error                ;exit if error code is set
```

writes the data packet contained in PAKOUT to the monitor chain. As with DosMonRead, you must tell OS/2 the size of the packet data and give it a pointer to the monitor output buffer that you registered with DosMonReg. View DosMonWrite as a subroutine that moves a data packet into the output monitor buffer from an internal buffer.

In order to create monitor packets (keystrokes, mouse motion, and so forth), you format the information in the user buffer and insert it in the monitor chain with DosMonWrite. For example, you could translate a single keystroke into a series of keystrokes with a keyboard monitor that looks for a particular key sequence, discards it, and then generates a series of (different) keys. In PC DOS, this type of program (called a keyboard extender or keyboard macro program) is implemented by hooking the keyboard interrupt (INT 9).

A Simple Monitor Example

Consider how you could use a keyboard monitor to implement a simple "popup" program. This program (KEY-MON) is a new twist on a previous example. Chapter 15 showed an OS/2 filter program that converted standard input to uppercase (UPCASE). While this program is a useful utility from the command line, it is of no value with programs that do not use the standard I/O facilities (such as a full-screen editor implemented with VIO/KBD services). To translate nonstandard I/O to uppercase, you must perform the conversion at a lower level. A keyboard monitor provides just such a capability.

It would also be nice to be able to turn the translation on and off so you could switch back to lowercase as the need arises. To do this, KEYMON has a small user interface in the form of a popup window. To bring up the popup, KEYMON looks for a hot key (ALT-DEL), which signals it to force itself to the foreground and receive commands from the keyboard.

Thus, KEYMON has the structure shown in Figure 18-9. Notice that KEYMON uses two threads. One thread processes the popup and the other manages the monitor I/O. The MAIN program is listed in Figure 18-10.

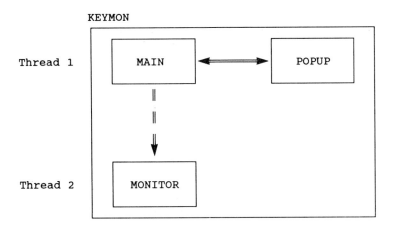

Figure 18-9. Structure of KEYMON

```
main        proc
;
            @MKThread monitor,1024        ;Make monitor thread
;
kbm010:     @DosSemSetWait semhand,noto   ;wait for hot-key
            call       popup              ;process pop-up
            @jaxnz     kbm999             ;exit on error
            jmp        kbm010             ;go wait again
;
kbm999:     @DosMonClose monhand          ;flush monitor
            @DosExit  1,0                 ;leave (just my thread)
main        endp
```

Figure 18-10.   KEYMON MAIN routine

The program starts a thread that runs the subprocedure named MONITOR and then waits on a RAM semaphore (SEMHAND). This semaphore is used by the monitor thread to "wake up" the main thread if it receives a hot key. When SEMHAND is cleared, MAIN calls the subroutine named POPUP to put up the popup and process the user command(s). On return from POPUP, MAIN will either go back to wait for the next hot key, or it will close the keyboard monitor and exit, depending on the return code (in the AX register). Most of the time, MAIN lies dormant. It is only running while the KEYMON popup window is on the screen.

Now, consider the POPUP routine shown in Figure 18-11. This routine calls VioPopUp to place itself in the foreground. The POPOPT field is initialized to 03H, so OS/2 creates a "transparent" popup and waits if the popup cannot be immediately generated. As discussed in Chapter 13, OS/2 allows only one background process at a time to generate a popup. So, if another one (like a hard-error popup) is active, OS/2 will block this procedure until the user clears it. When it has successfully acquired the foreground session, POPUP continues by hiding the cursor and writing a small popup "menu" in the center of the screen. Since it uses a transparent popup, the remainder of the screen is left intact.

```
popup       proc
;
            @VioPopUp popopt,0              ;put myself in foreground
            @HideCursor                    ;hide cursor
            @DosBeep  2000,200             ;sound beep
;
            lea     si,msg0                ;window line #1
            mov     cx,MSGLC               ;line count
            mov     dx,5                   ;pop-up on line 5
pop000:     @VioWrtCharStrAtt DS:SI,MSGL,dx,24,red,0 ;Put line
            inc     dx                     ;next row
            add     si,MSGL                ;next line
            @loop   pop000                 ;go put it out
;
pop005:     @KbdCharIn kbdbuf,0,0          ;get character
            mov     al,kbdbuf.charascii    ;get ASCII character
            cmp     al,0                   ;extended scan?
            jne     pop010                 ;no, go check which key it was
            mov     ah,kbdbuf.charscan     ;get scan code
;
pop010:     cmp     ax,KESC                ;escape key?
            @jne    pop020                 ;no - continue
            mov     ax,0ffh                ;set error code
            jmp     pop999                 ;exit
;
pop020:     xor     al,'a'-'A'             ;convert ASCII key to upper case
            cmp     al,'X'                 ;translate key?
            @jne    pop030                 ;no - continue
            mov     xflag,ON               ;set translate flag on
            xor     ax,ax                  ;clear RC
            jmp     pop999                 ;exit
;
pop030:     cmp     al,'N'                 ;no xlate key?
            @jne    pop005                 ;no - go wait for next keystroke
            mov     xflag,OFF              ;set translate flag off
            xor     ax,ax                  ;clear RC
;
pop999:     push    ax                     ;save RC
            @ShowCursor                    ;restore cursor
            @VioEndPopUp 0                 ;return to background
            pop     ax                     ;restore RC
            ret
popup       endp
```

Figure 18-11. POPUP subroutine

Now POPUP uses KbdCharIn to wait for the user response. Remember, when you use VioPopUp to make yourself the foreground session, you receive the input focus for the mouse and the keyboard. If POPUP had tried to use KbdCharIn before it called VioPopUp, it might block indefinitely, since it could be reading the keyboard from a session not in the foreground.

The keyboard handling routine looks much like the others you have seen before. It uses KbdCharIn (synchronous) to read a character from the keyboard, then it tests to see if it was "x," "n," or ESC. If it was either of the first two, it changes the translate flag (XFLAG), clears the return code (AX), and returns to MAIN. If it was the ESC key, it sets the return code to a nonzero value and then returns to MAIN. MAIN uses this return code to either continue processing (AX=0) or to terminate the monitor program (AX<>0).

If you enter any other key, POPUP goes back to read the next character. Thus, from the user's perspective, POPUP works like this: When you press the KEYMON hot key, you see a small popup window in the middle of your screen. If you press X or N (in uppercase or lowercase), the window disappears and the monitor continues to run. If you press ESC, the window disappears and the hot key is no longer active. Thus, you have the OS/2 equivalent of a PC DOS popup program, with none of the hassles.

Unfortunately, so far the KEYMON application still does nothing, other than clear and set an internal flag. To see what makes it really work, you must examine the MONITOR subroutine. You will remember that the first thing that MAIN did was to start MONITOR as a separate thread.

So, MONITOR looks like Figure 18-12. The first thing MONITOR does is to set its priority to time-critical level 0. It is extremely important that all programs monitoring device character streams run at a priority level high enough to "stay out of the fray." Since a monitor is processing data at a low level, it must be able to run when it needs to. If it could not run, then it would congest the device data flow.

MONITOR uses DosMonOpen to open the device (DEVNAME='KBD$'), and then uses the returned handle (MONHAND) to register its input and output buffers. The

```
monitor     proc
            @DosSetPrty 2,3,0,0              ;thread to TC 0
            @DosMonOpen devname,monhand     ;Open Monitor interface
            @DosMonReg  monhand,monibuf,monobuf,1,0 ;monitor FG session
;
mon010:     mov     buflen,MONDBUFL         ;initialize buffer size
            @DosMonRead monibuf,BLOCK,mondbuf,buflen ;read packet
            @jaxnz  mon999                  ;exit if error code is set
            mov     ah,monkeybuf.charscan   ;get scan code
            mov     al,monkeybuf.charascii  ;get ASCII value
;
            cmp     ax,KDEL                 ;DEL key?
            @jne    mon050                  ;no - skip popup
            test    monkeybuf.charshift,CHARALT ;Alt key down?
            @je     mon050                  ;no - skip popup
            test    monkbdflg,040h          ;'Break' packet?
            @jne    mon010                  ;no - 'eat' the 'make' packet
            @DosSemClear semhand            ;start pop-up thread
            jmp     mon010                  ;loop (skip hot key)
;
mon050:     cmp     xflag,OFF               ;translation off?
            @je     mon060                  ;no - go write packet
            cmp     al,'a'                  ;less than a ?
            jb      mon060                  ;yes - skip byte
            cmp     al,'z'                  ;greater than z ?
            ja      mon060                  ;yes - skip byte
            sub     al,'a'-'A'              ;make upper case
            mov     monkeybuf.charascii,al  ;put it back in the packet
;
mon060:     @DosMonWrite monobuf,mondbuf,buflen ;write packet
            @jaxnz  mon999                  ;exit if error code is set
            jmp     mon010                  ;go read next packet
;
mon999:     @DosMonClose monhand            ;flush monitor
            @DosExit  1,0                    ;leave (kill all threads)
monitor     endp
```

Figure 18-12. MONITOR subroutine

input and output buffers are defined in the MONITOR data segment, as shown in Figure 18-13.

Although the data buffer length is 2K, the length field (the first word in the structure) includes the 18-byte reserved data area and the length field itself (2 bytes). Once the buffers have been registered, OS/2 begins placing the device data stream in the input buffer.

```
monbuf      struc
monblen     dw      2068                    ;total length
monrsv0     db      18    dup(0)            ;reserved
mondata     db      2048 dup(0)             ;data
monbuf      ends
;
monibuf     monbuf      <>                  ;monitor input buffer
monobuf     monbuf      <>                  ;monitor output buffer
```

Figure 18-13. Definition of input and output buffers

KEYMON then begins draining the input buffer and filling the output buffer. It uses a simple processing loop that calls DosMonRead to bring a monitor packet into its internal work buffer (MONDBUF) and then calls DosMonWrite to copy it to the output buffer. MONITOR processes the individual keystrokes.

Before examining this logic, note two things about DosMonRead. Each time MONITOR calls DosMonRead, it first re-initializes the user-buffer length field. This is because DosMonRead resets the field to the length of the monitor packet. Thus, if MONITOR did not re-initialize it, the read operation would fail in the next call after a small data packet was read. Remember, not all data packets are the same size. For example, a flush packet only contains the monitor flag word and is only two bytes long.

Secondly, the data structure MONDBUF is defined as follows:

```
monbuf      struc
monblen     dw      2068                    ;total length
monrsv0     db      18    dup(0)            ;reserved
mondata     db      2048 dup(0)             ;data
monbuf      ends
;
monibuf     monbuf      <>                  ;monitor input buffer
monobuf     monbuf      <>                  ;monitor output buffer
```

It includes the monitor flag word (MONDBUF), the KBD character data structure (MONKEYBUF), and the keyboard device driver flag word (MONKBFLG). The total length of the buffer area is computed in the MONDBUFL constant.

After calling DosMonRead, MONITOR tests to see if the user pressed the KEYMON hot key (ALT-DEL). To do this, MONITOR looks for three conditions:

1. That the actual key contained in the key data structure is the DEL key.

2. That, at the time the DEL key was pressed, the ALT SHIFT state is on.

3. That this is the key-break packet. (**Note:** This means that the popup will not occur until the user releases the hot key.)

The last condition is important because it is unique to monitors. If you read a character with the KbdCharIn function call, you will never see the make/break key sequences. They are masked by the keyboard device driver. However, in a keyboard monitor, you see both events. This example uses the key-break sequence as the hot key. So, if the packet passes the first two tests but not the third, MONITOR "eats" the keystroke and goes on to read the next packet.

When it encounters the ALT-DEL key break, MONITOR signals the MAIN thread by clearing the RAM semaphore and then "eats" the key. So, while KEYMON is active, other applications will never see the ALT-DEL key sequence. Note that, by using a semaphore, MONITOR has actually relegated the popup to the lower priority MAIN thread.

If the keystroke is not a hot key and the translation flag (XFLAG) is not off, then MONITOR converts the key to uppercase by using the algorithm used in UPCASE, and writes the packet to the monitor output buffer. Notice that

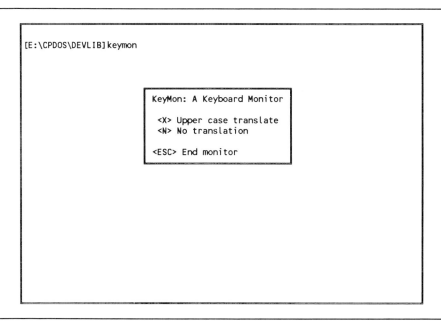

Figure 18-14. KEYMON popup menu

DosMonWrite uses the BUFLEN field as it was returned from DosMonRead because it always reflects the correct packet size.

If you now start KEYMON from the command line and press ALT-DEL, you will see the screen in Figure 18-14. The popup functions all seem to work, but what about the translation? This is difficult to gauge because no program in the current session is reading from the keyboard and displaying the results. In fact, started in this way, KEYMON is somewhat useless. Other than putting up and taking down a popup window, it does absolutely nothing.

You can easily fix this problem if you use the OS/2 DETACH command to start KEYMON in an invisible background session. If you enter

[C:\]DETACH KEYMON

The Process Identification Number is 128

[C:\]

and then press ALT-DEL, you will see absolutely nothing. What happened to KEYMON? It was obviously started, since the "Process ID" message appeared on the screen. So why does it not respond to the hot key? Although a bit perplexing, the answer is simple. When you start a program with the DETACH command, CMD.EXE executes it into a "null" session. Since KEYMON monitors the keystrokes from its current session, it will never see the hot key (nor any other keys, for that matter).

You can circumvent this problem with a small observation: KEYMON does not have to monitor its own session. In fact, by setting the INDEX field in the DosMonReg call, KEYMON could monitor an entirely different session. Now the only question is, what session should it monitor? The information provided by DosInfoSeg solves this dilemma.

One of the fields in the global information segment is the session identification of the current foreground session. So, with a small modification (see Figure 18-15), the MONITOR subroutine extracts the current foregound session identification from the GDT information segment and uses this value to register to the "correct" session identification.

```
@DosGetInfoSeg gdtsel,ldtsel
push      gdtsel
pop       es
xor       dx,dx              ;clear work register
mov       dl,es:[gdtsesfg]   ;get foreground session number
@DosMonReg monhand,monibuf,monobuf,1,DX ;monitor FG session
```

Figure 18-15. Modification to MONITOR subroutine

```
The Process Identification Number is 14.

[E:\OS2\DEVLIB]DIR

Volume in drive E has no label.
 Directory of E:\OS2\DEV┌──────────────────────────────────┐
                         │   KeyMon: A Keyboard Monitor        │
 .             <DIR>      │                                     │
 ..            <DIR>      │   <X> Upper case translate          │
STOP     COM    258    1  │   <N> No translation                │
CPMASM   BAT    135       │                                     │
BEEP     ASM   1656       │   <ESC> End monitor                 │
LATENCY  EXE   4608       └──────────────────────────────────┘
LATENCY  MAP   2415      6-23-87   11:50a
SYSBTH   ASM   1249      7-14-86   10:46p
TEMP     ASM   3406      7-14-86   10:31p
MULTI    EXE   2365      6-19-87    8:16a
MULTI    MAP   2553      6-19-87    8:16a
MULTI    ASM   9524      2-21-87    3:04p
OS2MAC   INC  31147      9-18-87    2:20p
PE2      PRO   1508      7-12-86   10:22a
MULTVIO  EXE   2954      7-11-86   12:18p
MULTVIO  ASM   5645      7-11-86   11:49a
LATENCY  ASM   4864      2-21-87    2:03p
VIOTEST  ASM   3964      7-10-86    1:10p
```

Figure 18-16.   Detached KEYMON popup menu

Now if you DETACH the updated version of KEYMON, the hot key will work in your foreground session. If you press ALT-DEL at any time, regardless of what the session is doing, the KEYMON popup will appear (see Figure 18-16). You can therefore turn the uppercase translation (which, by the way, you can now see) on or off at any time. When on, all the input characters are converted to uppercase, even those destined for VIO/KBD-style full-screen programs.

PERFORMANCE CONSIDERATIONS

Unlike most OS/2 applications, a monitor can potentially harm the overall system performance. If a monitor has a serious error, it could even hang the entire system. In many ways, monitors are a task-time extension of a device driver. They actually reside in the device data path. You must carefully design monitor programs.

Consider some of the lessons you have learned in this chapter. First, consider the input and output buffer sizes. The sum of the monitor buffers comprises a data "pipeline." Each monitor program is responsible for moving the data through this pipeline with the DosMonRead and DosMonWrite API calls. But how big should you make these buffers? You already know that the minimum size is the size of the internal device driver buffers, and the maximum is half of one segment (32K). An "optimum" size is somewhere in between.

Unfortunately, this optimum is not a single magic number. It is dependent on a number of factors, such as the interarrival rate of monitor packets, the system load, and the processing time of all the monitors in the chain. Generally, the larger the buffer, the lower the likelihood that the monitor chain will "hang" while one of the monitors crunches data. On the other hand, the larger the buffer, the longer the monitor(s) will "shuffle" data between buffers. If the monitors are all running at a high priority, and the device being monitored has a high interrupt rate, then the device data will not get back to the device driver until the entire pipeline fills, or until the device pauses long enough to give the monitors a chance to catch up.

You might have seen this phenomenon in the KEYMON example. If you detach enough copies of KEYMON (around 5), then press a key until it generates keys at a "typematic" rate, you will see a considerable lag until the pipeline (4K) fills. After that, the characters appear at the "keymatic" rate. You can control this by reducing the size of the buffers.

Another significant factor you should keep in mind while designing a monitor program is the priority of the monitor thread(s). You will generally want to run them at a low time-critical priority because the monitors must process the device data stream(s) before the other, normal priority threads are dispatched.

Avoid using high-priority time-critical threads. Although the monitors are important, they are not more critical than programs that manage external hardware devices. For example, if KEYMON does not get enough CPU cycles, then the keyboard responsiveness will lag. If a communications subsystem loses CPU cycles, then it might not be able to keep a communications line active. Clearly, a slow keyboard is preferable to a lost communications line. Make sure that your monitor programs set their priorities below this type of program.

Monitors are one of the few examples where you can justify using time-critical priorities in an application. But with this power comes responsibility. A monitor, or any other thread in the time-critical priority class, must do as little work as possible at that level. It must relegate non-critical activities to other, lower-priority threads.

In this example, the MONITOR subroutine does little work other than inspect the monitor packets for the session hot key and translate characters to uppercase. This is the minimum it can do, since the actual translations must be performed in line. However, when it comes to putting up the popup, MONITOR passes the request along to the MAIN routine, which runs at a normal priority.

SPECIAL CONSIDERATIONS

When you build your first monitor program, you will find that it is a bit more complicated to debug than a "normal" application program. For instance, when you debug KEYMON, you will discover that you cannot use Code-View. This is because CodeView runs the program being debugged in its own session. Thus, the keystrokes for the "foreground" session (CodeView) are, in fact, being trapped by the program being debugged. If you try to single-step through the monitor code, then both sessions will immediately hang. CodeView hangs because it can no longer receive keyboard input and KEYMON hangs because it is being single-stepped by CodeView.

This problem is not easy to overcome, since what you really need is a debugger that does not use OS/2 I/O services. Such debuggers exist, but they are usually hardware-based and relatively expensive. You could use the API trace capabilities of the function call macros to "see" the logic flows. This technique is not as convenient as a debugger, but effective nonetheless.

Another problem you should look out for is that the monitor must pass on the keyboard flush packets. If you do not do this, the session will lock up and you may have to restart the system.

As you see, writing monitors is not as easy as writing a "normal" OS/2 application. The more time you can invest thinking about how it will work, the better off you will be when it comes to debugging your program.

SUMMARY

Device monitors are the last major piece in the OS/2 application-development puzzle. With monitors, you can do many of the things commonly done in PC DOS by "taking over" interrupt vectors. The OS/2 monitor facilities are conceptually similar to this, but they are better structured and architecturally sound.

Using a keyboard monitor, you can build an application that responds to a user hot key and creates a popup window over the current session. With a mouse monitor, you can do the same thing, except that the hot key is a combination of mouse buttons. Finally, printer monitors can be used to intercept (and translate) a data stream destined for the printer. You will undoubtedly find numerous other uses for this powerful facility.

You should also remember that monitors (more than any other type of OS/2 user program) can affect the overall system performance and operation. You should carefully design monitor applications. Monitors are a powerful tool when used correctly.

This chapter completes your tour of the OS/2 services. There are, of course, countless other OS/2 functions you have not yet seen. However, file I/O services, subsystem I/O, memory management, basic and advanced multitasking, and device monitors provide a sound foundation on which you can base many OS/2 programs. If you wish to explore some of the other capabilities of the system, read Appendix A, which summarizes all the OS/2 APIs.

Appendix A:

OS/2 Function Calls

DosAllocHuge	
WORD	A one word value indicating the number of 65535 byte (whole) segments which OS/2 is to allocate.
WORD	The length of the last segment.
PTR	The address of a one word data area which is to receive the initial segment selector.
WORD	The maximum number of 65535 byte segments to which OS/2 will allow you to grow this huge segment group (with the DosReallocSeg call).
WORD	A one word sharing indicator: RRRRRRRR RRRRRDEI Shareable with DosGiveSeg Shareable with DosGetSeg Segment is Discardable Reserved (must be 0)

Description:

Allocate a huge memory object.

Notes:

1. The memory segment(s) are addressed through the calling process' LDT.

2. The allocated memory is moveable and swappable.

3. The share indicator must be set if you intend to use DosGiveSeg to pass the huge memory object to another process.

DosAllocSeg	
WORD	One word containing the number of bytes to be allocated (maximum 65536).
PTR	Pointer to a one word value which on return will contain the selector of the allocated segment.
WORD	A one word sharing indicator: RRRRRRRR RRRRRDEI Shareable with DosGiveSeg Shareable with DosGetSeg Segment is Discardable Reserved (must be 0)

Description:

Allocate a memory segment.

Notes:

1. The memory segment is addressed through the calling process' LDT.

2. The allocated memory is moveable and swappable.

3. The share indicator must be set if you intend to use DosGiveSeg to pass the segment to another process.

DosAllocShrSeg	
WORD	A one word value which tells OS/2 the size of the new segment.
PTR	A pointer to an ASCIIZ string which OS/2 will use to locate the 'named' memory segment.
PTR	A pointer to a one word memory area in which OS/2 will place the segment selector.

Description:

Allocate a named shared memory segment.

Notes:

1. The memory segment is addressed through the calling process' LDT.

2. The allocated memory is moveable and swappable.

3. The name is used by other processes with the DosGetShrSeg API to gain addressability to the memory segment.

4. The maximum number of named shared segments which can be allocated by any process is 30.

DosBeep	
WORD	A one word sound frequency value (in Hz) in the range 25 to 32K.
WORD	A one word duration value (in milliseconds).

Description:

Sound a beep from the system speaker.

Notes:

1. DosBeep operates synchronous to the calling thread (the thread waits until the beep ends).

2. Only one DosBeep at a time will be sounded. If more than one thread issued DosBeep, then they are serialized.

3. DosBeep can be interrupted by a signal.

DosCaseMap	
WORD	One word length of the string which OS/2 will case map.
PTR	Pointer to an input data structure: DW Country Code DW Code Page ID
PTR	Pointer to an input binary string.

Description:

Case maps a binary input string according to an OS/2 country code.

Notes:

1. Country code field is set to the country code which OS/2 is to use to perform the case mapping. If set to 0, then OS/2 uses the default country code. On return from DosCaseMap, the country code field will be set to the actual country code which was used in the case mapping.

2. The case map information comes from the OS/2 country information file.

3. Code page ID is set to the code page which OS/2 is to use to perform the case mapping. If set to 0, then OS/2 uses the active code page.

4. The input character string is mapped in place. The new (mapped) output string is placed in the same input string buffer.

DosChDir	
PTR	Pointer to an ASCIIZ directory name (max 64 bytes).
DWRD	Reserved (must be 0).

Description:

Change the current directory.

Notes:

1. DosChDir will fail if any element in the path is invalid.

2. The current directory is only changed for the calling process.

DosChgFilePtr	
WORD	Open file handle
DWRD	A doubleword value indicating the distance the file pointer will be moved
WORD	A one word value indicating the method OS/2 must use to move the file pointer: 0 = Relative to the start of the file 1 = Relative to current location in the file 0 = Relative to the end of the file
PTR	The address of a double word field in which OS/2 will place the new file pointer value.

Description:

Change the logical file pointer.

Notes:

1. DosChgFilePtr will only accept file handles. If you call this API with a pipe or device handle, the request will fail. You can use DosQHandType to determine the handle type.

DosCLIAccess

Description:

Request permission to disable interrupts (with CLI/STI instructions).

Notes:

1. Ring 2 (I OPS) segments must issue this call to receive permission to disable interrupts with the CLI instruction.

2. Permission must be requested only once. Subsequent to this call, the program may disable/enable interrupts freely.

3. This call does not (necessarily) grant I/O access (see DosPortsAccess).

DosClose	
WORD	File/device handle which is to be closed

Description:

Close an open I/O handle.

Notes:

1. You use DosClose to close open file, device or pipe handles.

2. If you close a file handle, OS/2 updates the file directory and flushes any sector buffers associated with the file.

3. If you close a pipe handle, OS/2 breaks your connection to the pipe and decrements the use count. When both pipe handles (read & write) are closed, the pipe ceases to exist and the memory is returned to the system.

4. When you close a device handle, OS/2 breaks your connection to the device.

5. You can only close handles which were created by your process with the DosOpen or DosCreatePipe calls. Or those which you inherited from your parent process.

DosCloseQueue	
WORD	A one word (open) queue handle.

Description:

Close an open queue handle.

Notes:

1. If you are the queue owner, then OS/2 purges all outstanding queue elements and deletes the queue. Other processes with active queue handles will receive a *queue does not exist* error the next time they attempt to write to the queue.

2. If you are not the queue owner, OS/2 disables your link to it, but it does not affect the queue contents. If the queue contains active queue elements which originated from your process, they are not purged.

DosCloseSem	
DWRD	A double-word system semaphore handle returned from DosOpenSem DosCreateSem.

Description:

Close a system semaphore.

Notes:

1. A system semaphore is deleted when all processes which have opened (or created) it issue the DosCloseSem call.

2. If a process dies while it is holding a system semaphore, OS/2 automatically closes the semaphore and wakes all processes which are waiting for it with the *semaphore owner ended* error code. Note: this code indicates that the owner ended, but not that the termination was necessarily abnormal.

DosCreateCSAlias	
WORD	A one word data selector.
PTR	Pointer to a one word field in which OS/2 will return a code (executable) selector which maps the same segment as the data selector.

Description:

Create an executable alias for a data segment.

Notes:

1. After the alias is created, the data selector is still valid.

2. When you create an alias selector with this call, OS/2 increments the segment use count by 1. Thus, if you call DosFreeSeg with either the data selector or the alias selector, the other selector is still valid. To de-allocate an aliased data segment, you must free *both* the original data selector and the executable alias.

3. You cannot use DosCreateCSAlias with shareable segments, including those which you allocated with the non-sharing option, named shared memory segments or dynamically linked global data segments.

4. Likewise, DosCreateCSAlias is not supported for segments which are part of huge memory objects (created with DosAllocHuge).

DosCreateQueue	
PTR	A pointer to a one word field into which OS/2 will place the queue handle.
WORD	A one word queue ordering value: 0 = FIFO 1 = LIFO 2 = Element priority
PTR	A pointer to an ASCIIZ string containing the name of the queue. Note: this string must start with '\QUEUES\'.

Description:

Create an input queue.

Notes:

1. A queue must be created before another process can open it (with DosOpenQueue).

2. The process which creates a queue with DosCreateQueue is called the queue 'owner'.

3. The queue owner does not have to open the queue, it uses the handle returned by DosCreateQueue to access the queue with the other queue management APIs.

4. Only the queue owner can read, peek or purge the queue.

DosCreateSem	
WORD	A one word value indicating what type of semaphore OS/2 is to create: 0 = Exclusive semaphore (not shared) 1 = Non-exclusive semaphore (shared)
PTR	A pointer to a double-word field into which OS/2 will place the semaphore handle.
PTR	A pointer to an ASCIIZ semaphore name which OS/2 is to associate with this semaphore (must begin with '\SEM\').

Description:

Create a system semaphore.

Notes:

1. A system semaphore must be created before other processes can open it (with DosOpenSem).

2. The process which creates a system with DosCreateSem is called the semaphore 'creator'. The semaphore 'owner' is the process which successfully aquires it with the DosSemRequest API.

3. The semaphore creator does not have to open the semaphore, it uses the handle returned by DosCreateSem to access the semaphore with the other semaphore APIs.

4. The Non-exclusive option creates a system semaphore which can be modified by other threads other than the creator (including with DosSemSet).

5. An Exclusive system semaphore includes a use count which keeps track of the number of times it was requested with DosSemRequest. It must be cleared an equal number of times before it is actually freed.

DosCreateThread	
PTR	A double-word pointer to the program which OS/2 will run in the thread.
PTR	A pointer to a one word field into which OS/2 will return the thread ID of the newly created thread.
DWRD	A double-word value which OS/2 will use as a stack for the new thread.

Description:

Create a new thread of execution.

Notes:

1. A thread is started with a far call to the entry point specified in this call.

2. The new thread 'inherits' the caller's registers except CS, IP, SS and SP. Once started, its register context is maintained by OS/2.

3. The initial execution priority of the new thread is identical to the priority of the thread which created it. Once started, it can change its priority with the DosSetPrty API.

4. The new thread can access all of the process resources (pipes, files, devices, queues, etc.).

DosCWait	
WORD	A one word action code which tells OS/2 what it is to wait for: 0 = Wait for process to end 1 = Wait for process & its descendants to end
WORD	A one word wait option which tells how to wait: 0 = Synchronous (wait until process(es) end) 1 = Asynchronous (return if none have ended)
PTR	The address of a doubleword area into which OS/2 will place process termination information. The first word contains the termination reason code: 0 = Normal exit 1 = Hard error abort 2 = Trap 3 = DosKillProcess The second word contains the child's (DosExit) result code.
PTR	A pointer to a one word value into which OS/2 will place the terminating process' ID (PID).
WORD	A one word process ID which DosCWait is to explicitly wait for. If zero, then DosCWait will wait for any process termination.

Description:

Wait/check for the termination of one or more child process(es).

Notes:

1. If no child process(es) exist, then DosCWait returns an error.

2. You may call DosCwait more than once if you started multiple child processes, or if the child process(es) started grandchildren.

DosDevIOCtl	
PTR	Pointer to IOCTL data area
PTR	Pointer to IOCTL parameter area
WORD	Device sub-function code
WORD	Device category
WORD	Open device handle

Description:

Pass a device specific I/O Control (IOCTL) packet to a device driver.

Notes:

1. The information contained in the IOCTL packet is device specific. Refer to Appendix C for a summary of the IOCTL functions which are supported by the OS/2 system device drivers.

2. If AX contains a value in the range FE00H to FEFFH, then the error originated in the device driver (rather than the DosDevIOCtl call).

3. Error values FF00H to FFFFH are reserved for user error codes (for custom device drivers).

DosDupHandle	
WORD	The original file handle (word value), which OS/2 is to alias in a second handle.
PTR	A pointer to a one word field into which OS/2 is to place the new (alias) handle value. If this field is initialized to ffffh (-1), then OS/2 will give you the next available handle. Otherwise the field contains the desired handle value.

Description:

Duplicate a file/pipe/device handle.

Notes:

1. When a handle is duplicated with this function, so are all the handle-specific characteristics. For example, if you duplicate a file handle, then move the file pointer (with DosRead, DosWrite or DosChgFilePtr) using one handle, then the file pointer is updated for both handles.

2. If you close one of the two handles, the other remains valid. Thus, to close a duplicated handle, you must issue DosClose with *both* the original and the duplicate handle.

DosEnterCritSec

Description:

Stop dispatching the other threads in the process.

Notes:

1. To resume dispatching the other threads in the process, use the DosExitCritSec API.

2. DosEnterCritSec/DosExitCritSec increment and decrement a critical section use count. The critical section does not end until the use count becomes zero. Thus, you can use critical sections in recursive routines.

3. If a signal is received while the process is in a critical section, then OS/2 will run thread 1 (as always). Thread 1 will process the signal even though another thread may be holding the critical section.

DosErrClass	
WORD	A one word error number.
PTR	Pointer to a one word field in which OS/2 will return the error classification associated with the input error number.
PTR	Pointer to a one word field in which OS/2 will return a recommended error recovery action for the input error number.
PTR	Pointer to a one word field in which OS/2 will return the error locus of the input error number.

Description:

Classify an OS/2 error code.

Notes:

1. Wherever possible, base your program recovery on the 'generic' error classifications, rather than specific error numbers. This makes the program more upwardly compatible with future OS/2 releases.

DosError	
WORD	A one word action flag: 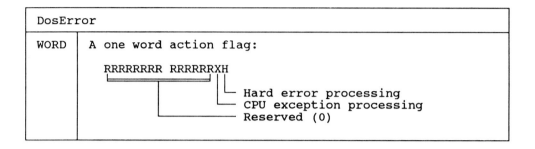

Description:

Enable or disable system hard error processing.

Notes:

1. The Hard Error bit enables/disables automatic system hard error processing (pop-up). When HE processing is disabled, then OS/2 will automatically FAIL the operation and return the hard error to the application as an error code (in AX). Use this option if you want to recover from hard errors in your program (without user intervention).

2. The CPU exception bit enables/disables automatic user notification when a program generates a CPU or Co-Processor exception (pop-up). When exception processing is disabled, then OS/2 not create the pop-up window, but will still terminate the faulting program.

DosExecPgm	
PTR	The address of a buffer in which OS/2 will place an object which further qualifies the cause of a DosExecPgm failure (eg - name of a 'bad' dynamic link library)
WORD	One word containing the length of the object buffer.
WORD	The DosExec option flags. Used by OS/2 to process your request: 0 = Synchronous execution 1 = Asynchronous execution (discard child's result code) 2 = Asynchronous execution (save child's result code) 3 = Run program in 'debug' mode 4 = Detached execution (in different session)
PTR	The address of two consecutive ASCIIZ strings. The first is the program name, and the second is the 'command line' input. These are passed to the EXEC'ed program in its environment segment.
PTR	An ASCIIZ environment block, containing none or more ASCIIZ environment strings (in the form varname=value) which are to be passed to the EXEC'ed program in the environment segment.
PTR	The address of a doubleword area into which OS/2 will place process termination information. For asynchronous requests the first word contains the process ID of the terminated process. For synchronous requests, the first word contains the termination reason code: 0 = Normal exit 1 = Hard error abort 2 = Trap 3 = DosKillProcess The second word always contains the child's (DosExit) result code.
PTR	A pointer to an ASCIIZ string which contains the name of the program which is to be EXEC'ed.

Description:

Start an OS/2 program as a child process.

Notes:

1. OS/2 creates a new LDT for the child process.

2. The child process inherits all pipes/files and devices which were opened (or created) by the parent process with inheritance enabled (See DosOpen).

DosExit	
WORD	A one word action code which tells OS/2 how much of your program it should terminate: 0000h = Terminate the current thread (only) 0001h = Terminate all the threads
WORD	A one word termination code which OS/2 will pass to your parent process (if the parent requests it)

Description:

End execution of a thread (or a process).

Notes:

1. OS/2 takes the process down if either, the request indicates that all threads are to be ended, or, the request is issued by the last thread in the process.

2. If the DosExit causes the process to end, the termination code is returned to the parent via the DosCWait API (asynchronous EXEC) or the DosExec API (synchronous exec).

3. If you want to take down the process, always set action code = 1, even though you think that all other application threads have ended. This is because in some situations (eg - Async I/O, Monitors) the system may have created additional threads 'under the covers'.

DosExitCritSec

Description:

Resume dispatching the other threads in the process.

Notes:

1. DosExitCritSec reverses the effect of DosEnterCritSec by resuming
   execution of the other threads in the process.

2. DosEnterCritSec/DosExitCritSec increment and decrement a critical section
   use count. The critical section does not end until the use count becomes
   zero. Thus, you can use critical sections in recursive routines.

DosExitList	
WORD	A one word action code: 1 = Add the routine to the termination list 2 = Remove the routine from the termination list 3 = Done - transfer to next routine
DWRD	A doubleword pointer to a routine which OS/2 will add to the termination list (action=1) or remove from the termination list (action=2). Can be set to any value when action=3.

Description:

Adds or removes a routine to the process termination list.

Notes:

1. You use this function if you need to run a cleanup routine when a process terminates. It is typically used by programs which provide dynamic link services to client processes. The ExitList routine gives you an opportunity to free your resources when the client process terminates.

2. More than one routine can register itself to the DosExitList. OS/2 calls each routine in the list before it takes the process down. An ExitList notifies OS/2 that it is done by calling this API with function code = 3.

3. ExitList routines should be as short as possible. Until they issue function code = 3, OS/2 cannot take the process down.

4. OS/2 transfers control to the ExitList routine with a JMP instruction, so it must not execute a RET instruction. Instead, the routine must call DosExitList with function code = 3.

5. An ExitList routine cannot call OS/2 API functions which create a new process or thread.

6. When the ExitList routine starts, OS/2 places the process termination code at SS:[SP + 4] (see DosCwait).

DosFileLocks	
WORD	An open file handle
PTR	A pointer to a pair of doubleword values. The first doubleword contains the starting offset in the file where the data is to be unlocked. The second doubleword is the length of the unlocked area. A null pointer signifies that no data is to be unlocked.
PTR	A pointer to a pair of doubleword values. The first doubleword contains the starting offset in the file where the data is to be locked. The second doubleword is the length of the locked area. A null pointer signifies that no data is to be locked.

Description:

Set or reset a byte lock range in an open file.

Notes:

1. Use this function with files which were opened with DENY_READ or DENY_NONE sharing modes.

2. If you Lock beyond the end-of-file, OS/2 will not generate an error.

3. If you specify both a lock and an unlock range, then DosFileLocks will unlock first and lock second.

4. You cannot lock a range which contains other locked sub-ranges.

5. If you create a duplicate file handle with DosDupHandle, then the duplicate handle will inherit the lock ranges. Subsequent lock/unlock operations performed to one handle are reflected in the other. However, you cannot inherit lock ranges from your parent process.

6. If you close a file with locked ranges (or your process dies while you have locked ranges), then OS/2 will free the locks.

DosFindClose	
WORD	A one word directory search handle.

Description:

Close an active directory search handle.

Notes:

1. Use this function to invalidate an active search handle.

2. If you attempt to use a closed search handle (with DosFindNext), the search function will fail. However, you can re-use the handle if you call DosFindFirst to restart the search.

DosFindFirst	
PTR	Pointer to an ASCIIZ string which defines the search criteria.
PTR	Pointer to a one word value where OS/2 will place the directory handle. If this field contains 0FFFFH, then OS/2 creates a new handle. Else, the value in this field is used as the handle. 0001h is always available as a directory handle.
WORD	An attribute byte which tells OS/2 what type of files should be included in the search: 　00h = Only search for normal files 　02h = Include hidden files 　04h = Include system files 　10h = Include subdirectory entries
PTR	Pointer to the result buffer. The buffer may be large enough to receive more then one directory entry.
WORD	The length of the result buffer
PTR	Pointer to a one word result count. On entry, this word contains the number of entries which you want OS/2 to put in the result buffer. On return, this field is updated by OS/2 to indicate how many entries were found (valid). The result buffer must be big enough to accept the data.
DWRD	Reserved (must be 0)

Description:

Find the first file in a directory which matches the search pattern.

Notes:

1. The search attribute is inclusive. That is, if you specify that the search must include directory entries, DosFindFirst/DosFindNext will retrieve directories <u>and</u> normal files.

2. You may use wild cards in the search specification.

DosFindNext	
WORD	A valid directory search handle
PTR	Pointer to the result buffer. The buffer may be large enough to receive more then one directory entry.
WORD	The length of the result buffer
PTR	Pointer to a one word result count. On entry, this word contains the number of entries which you want OS/2 to put in the result buffer. On return, this fields is updated by OS/2 to indicate how many entries were found (valid). The result buffer must be big enough to accept the data.

Description:

Get the next file from a particular search (identified by handle).

Notes:

1. You can have more than one active directory search. The search handle identifies which search you want DosFindNext to use.

2. OS/2 uses the search criteria established in DosFindFirst to continue the search.

3. When no more files match the search criteria, DosFindNext will return an error code and set the returned count to zero.

DosFlagProcess	
WORD	A one word value corresponding to the process ID you want to flag.
WORD	A one word action flag: 0 = Flag the process and all its descendants 1 = Flag the process
WORD	A one word flag value: 0 = Flag 'A' 1 = Flag 'B' 2 = Flag 'C'
WORD	A one word flag argument which is to be placed in the stack of the 'flagged' process.

Description:

Flag a particular process (and descendants).

Notes:

1. By definition, a 'flag' is another name for an application generated signal.

2. To receive a flag, the 'flagged' process must have established a signal handler to process the specific flag type (A, B or C). If the signal handler does not exist, OS/2 throws away the flag event. See DosSetSigHandler for details about setting up a signal handler.

DosFreeModule	
WORD	A one word module handle.

Description:

Free a dynamic link module reference.

Notes:

1. This API is used to delete the reference to a particular dynamic link module library. If this call deletes the last reference to the library, then OS/2 deletes the library from memory.

2. You can only use this API to 'free' module libraries which you previously 'loaded' with DosLoadModule. If you try to free a module library which was not previously loaded, then the function fails with an error.

3. If this function succeeds, then the module handle associated with the dynamic link library is no longer valid.

4. Also, the individual entry points associated with the dynamic link routines are invalidated. If you attempt to call one of these entry points after you free the module, then the processor will generate a GP fault, and your program will be terminated.

DosFreeSeg	
WORD	The one word selector of the memory segment which is to be released

Description:

De-allocate a memory segment.

Notes:

1. You can use DosFreeSeg to de-allocate segments which were allocated with DosAllocSeg (shared or private), segments which were passed to your process with DosGiveSeg, executable alias selectors created by DosCreateCSAlias, and huge memory objects allocated by DosAllocHuge.

2. To de-allocate a complete huge data object, you simply free the first (base) segment. OS/2 will free the remaining segments on your behalf.

3. When you free a shared memory segment, DosFreeSeg decrements the segment use count. The segment memory is not released until the use count reaches zero.

4. If this function succeeds, then the selector value is invalidated. If you attempt to load a 'freed' selector, then the CPU will generate a GP fault, and your program will be terminated.

DosGetCollate	
WORD	A one word value representing the length of the buffer you are providing OS/2 to copy the collate table. A collate table is typically 256 bytes long. If the buffer is smaller than this, the table is truncated. If the buffer is larger, the extra bytes are zeroed out.

PTR	Pointer to a data request structure:
	
	    DW Country Code (set to 0 for default country)
	    DW Code Page ID (set to 0 for current CP)

PTR	Pointer to a memory buffer which into which OS/2 will place the collate table (per the previous parameter).
PTR	Pointer to a one word field in which OS/2 will return the actual length of the collate table.

Description:

Retrieve a collating sequence table to be used for sorting data in a national language environment.

Notes:

1. If you set the request structure to (0,0) then OS/2 will return the collate table for the default country ID and current code page.

DosGetCP	
WORD	A one word value representing the length of the buffer to receive the code page list. If the buffer is too small to receive the entire list, the data is truncated. If the buffer is too large, the extra bytes are zeroed out.

PTR	Pointer to a code page list data area (filled in by OS/2):
	
	    DW Current process code page
	    DW Alternate code page #1
	          .
	          .
	          .
	    DW Alternate code page #n

PTR	Pointer to a one word field in which OS/2 will return the actual length of the code page list.

Description:

Retrieve the process code page information.

Notes:

1. You must provide a data area which is at least 2 bytes, or else DosGetCP will fail.

2. The data area length should be an even-byte multiple.

3. OS/2 1.0 will always return a primary and secondary code page ID (4 bytes).

DosGetCtryInfo	
WORD	A one word value representing the length of the buffer you are providing OS/2 to copy the country information table. In OS/2 1.0, this table is 38 bytes long. If the buffer which smaller than this, the table is truncated. If the buffer is larger, the extra bytes are zeroed out.

PTR	Pointer to a data request structure:
	
	    DW Country Code (set to 0 for default country)
	    DW Code Page ID (set to 0 for current CP)

PTR	Pointer to a memory buffer which into which OS/2 will place the country information table (per previous size parameter).
PTR	Pointer to a one word field in which OS/2 will return the actual length of the country information table.

Description:

Retrieve the system country information table.

Notes:

1. If you set the request structure to (0,0) then OS/2 will return the country information table for the default country ID and current code page.

DosGetDateTime	
PTR	Pointer to a data buffer into which OS/2 will place the Date/Time data structure.

Description:

Retrieve the current date and time information.

Notes:

1. The day of week value is based on Sunday being equal to 0.

2. The time zone field equals the number of minutes from GMT. If the current time zone is earlier than GMT, then the value is positive. If later than GMT, then the value is negative.

3. Alternatively, you can use the global information segment (see DosGetInfoSeg) to query the date/time. This segment contains a continuously updated date/time data structure. However, you should use DosGetDateTime in FAMAPI programs, because in the PC/DOS environment, the info segment is not dynamically updated.

DosGetDBCSEv	
WORD	A one word value representing the length of the buffer to receive the DBCS vector. If the buffer is too small to receive the entire vector, the data is truncated. If the buffer is too large, the extra bytes are zeroed out.
PTR	Pointer to a data request structure: DW Country Code (set to 0 for default country) DW Code Page ID (set to 0 for current CP)
PTR	Pointer to a DBCS vector data area (filled in by OS/2): DW Start Value for range #1 DW End Value for range #1 DW Start Value for range #2 DW End Value for range #2 . . . DW Start Value for range #n DW End Value for range #n

Description:

Retrieve the DBCS environmental vector.

Notes:

1. This function is only meaningful in DBCS-enabled OS/2 systems.

2. If you set the request structure to (0,0) then OS/2 will return the DBCS vector for the default country ID and current code page.

DosGetEnv	
PTR	Pointer to a one word field in which OS/2 will return the environment segment selector.
PTR	Pointer to a one word field in which OS/2 will return the offset of the command line parameters within the environment segment.

Description:

Get the process environment segment.

Notes:

1. This function can be used by dynamic link programs to retrieve the environment information which was passed to its client (caller).

DosGetHugeShift	
DWRD	The address of a one word area which is to receive the Huge shift count

Description:

Retrieve the OS/2 huge segment object selector shift count.

Notes:

1. The returned number is the shift count of the selector increment. To use it, you must shift the number 1 by the number of bits returned from this call. The resulting number is the selector increment, which you add to the base selector to address the next segment in the object.

DosGetInfoSeg	
PTR	A pointer to a one word field in which OS/2 will place the selector of the global information segment.
PTR	A pointer to a one word field in which OS/2 will place the selector of the local information segment.

Description:

Retrieve the OS/2 global and local information segments.

Notes:

1. The selectors returned by this API correspond to 'read-only' data segments. If you attempt to modify these segments, the CPU will generate a GP fault and the program will be terminated.

2. The DATE/TIME information in the GDT segment is continuously updated. You can use this information in place of DosGetDateTime.

DosGetMachineMode	
PTR	Pointer to a one word field in which OS/2 will return a CPU mode indicator: 0 = Real Mode (&pc. or DOS environment) 1 = Protected Mode

Description:

Retrieve the current CPU processor mode.

Notes:

1. The program's CPU mode will not change over time. In other words, you only have to determine the CPU mode once, it will remain unchanged for the life of the program.

2. This API lets you bracket 'environment-dependent' logic in FAMAPI programs. You should use the DosGetMachineMode rather than DosGetVersion, because the OS/2 version number is identical in the DOS environment and in a protected-mode session.

DosGetMessage	
PTR	Pointer to a variable insertion data table. Each table entry is a double-word pointer to an ASCIIZ text string (up to nine entries).
WORD	A one word count defining how many variable pointers are included in the variable insertion table. The maximum count is nine. If zero, then the previous parameter is ignored.
PTR	Pointer to a buffer into which OS/2 will place the message text.
WORD	One word length of the message buffer. If the buffer is too small to receive the requested message, then the text is truncated to fit.
WORD	A one word message number which OS/2 will retrieve from the message file (or segment).
PTR	A pointer to a fully qualified (ASCIIZ) message file name from which OS/2 will retrieve the message text. If the messages are bound to the EXE file, then only the message file 'name' is required.
PTR	Pointer to a one word field in which OS/2 will return the actual message length.

Description:

Retrieve a message from a message file/segment (with variable substitution).

Notes:

1. DosGetMessage inserts the data from the variable insertion table into the place holders (%1 - %9) in the message text.

2. If the insertion count is greater than nine, then DosGetMessage will fail.

3. For 'warning' or 'error' messages, OS/2 creates a message number and includes it in the message text.

4. This API reads message files which were previously created with MKMSGF, or message segments which were bound to the EXE file with MSGBIND.

5. If the message text retrieval fails, OS/2 places a 'default' message in the user buffer (eg - 'Message file not found').

DosGetModHandle	
PTR	Pointer to a field which contains the ASCIIZ module name.
PTR	Pointer to a one word field in which OS/2 will return the module handle.

Description:

Retrieve handle of a (loaded) dynamic link module.

Notes:

1. You must use the (max 8 character) module name, not the name of the dynamic link library file.

2. Use this call if you want to verify that a module is already loaded.

DosGetModName	
WORD	A one word module handle whose file name is to be returned.
WORD	A one word buffer length.
PTR	Pointer to the data buffer in which OS/2 will return the fully qualified (ASCIIZ) file name.

Description:

Retrieve the file name of a previously loaded dynamic link module.

Notes:

1. This call returns the file name associated with the module handle. This is not necessarily the 'module name' which you use with the DosGetModHandle API.

2. The buffer must be large enough to hold the fully qualified file name. If it is not big enough to hold the entire path/name, then the call will fail.

DosGetPid	
PTR	A pointer to a three-word field in which OS/2 will place the process ID information. The field has the following format: DW The current process ID DW The current thread ID DW The process ID of the parent

Description:

Retrieve the process id information associated with the requesting process.

Notes:

1. You can also get this information directly from the local InfoSeg (see DosGetInfoSeg).

DosGetProcAddr	
WORD	A one word module handle associated with the dynamic link module which contains the desired procedure.
PTR	Pointer to a field which contains the ASCIIZ procedure name which you want to access.
PTR	Pointer to a double-word field in which OS/2 will return the procedure address.

Description:

Retrieve a dynamic link module entry point.

Notes:

1. Use this function to get addressability to an entry point contained in a dynamic link module which was 'loaded' with DosLoadModule. Load-time dynamic link entry points are automatically resolved by the OS/2 loader, so you do not need to make this call.

2. The routine address is returned as a 32-bit value.

DosGetPrty	
WORD	The scope of the query: 0 = Return the priority of the first thread 2 = Return the priority of the indicated thread
PTR	The address of a one word area into which OS/2 will return the priority value.
WORD	The ID of the process (scope=0) or thread (scope=2) whose priority is to be returned.

Description:

Retrieve the thread/process priority value.

Notes:

1. If you request the priority of the process, then OS/2 returns the priority data of thread 0. If thread 0 no longer exists, then the function call will fail.

DosGetShrSeg	
PTR	A pointer to an ASCIIZ string which OS/2 will use to locate the 'named' memory segment.
PTR	A pointer to a one word memory area in which OS/2 will place the segment selector.

Description:

Get addressability to a named shared memory segment.

Notes:

1. The selector returned by this call is identical in every process which gets access to the segment, including the process which created it with the DosCreateShrSeg API.

2. When you get access to a shared segment, OS/2 increments an internal use count.

3. To release the shared segment you use the DosFreeSeg API. This call will also decrement the segment use count. The segment is not actually freed until the use count reaches zero (all processes freed it).

DosGetVersion	
PTR	Pointer to a one word field in which OS/2 will return its major and minor version numbers.

Description:

Get the OS/2 major and minor version numbers.

Notes:

1. The version word contains the minor version number in the high byte and the major version number in the low byte.

2. The OS/2 major version numbers begin at 10. So, the OS/2 1.0 major version number is returned as 10.

3. You can also get the version numbers from the global information segment (see DosGetInfoSeg).

DosGiveSeg	
WORD	The selector of the segment which is to be 'given' to another process.
WORD	The process id (PID) of the process which is to be given access to the segment.
PTR	A pointer to a one word area which, on return, will contain the selector a selector which the 'target' process can use to access the memory segment.

Description:

Make a dynamically allocated segment addressable by another process.

Notes:

1. The selector returned by this call can only be used by the target process. You must pass this selector to the target process using some other form of inter process communications (eg - pipe, queue, named shared memory).

2. When you call DosGiveSeg, OS/2 makes an entry in the target process' LDT and increments the segment use count. Each process has equal access to the shared segment.

3. You may use DosGiveSeg to pass along a segment which was 'given' to you by another process.

4. You may mark a shared segment 'discardable' with the DosUnlockSeg API. However, when you do, it is discardable for all processes which may be sharing it.

5. To release the shared segment you use the DosFreeSeg API. This call will also decrement the segment use count. The segment is not actually freed until the use count reaches zero (all processes freed it).

6. If you use DosGiveSeg with a huge memory object, you must pass it the first selector in the object. The receiving process can use the huge memory shift count to access the remaining segments.

DosHoldSignal	
WORD	A one word signal processing indicator: 0 = Signal processing is enabled 1 = Signal processing is disabled

Description:

Temporarily disable or re-enable signal processing in the current process.

Notes:

1. DosHoldSignal has no effect on the numeric co-processor (NPX) signals. All other signals are postponed until the process re-enables signal processing.

2. OS/2 maintains a DosHoldSignal use count which is incremented each time signals are held and decremented when they are re-enabled. The signal processing is not activated until the count reaches zero. Therefore, you can call DosHoldSignal in a recursive routine.

3. You should avoid disabling signal processing for extended periods of time. DosHoldSignal disables 'software' interrupts, much in the same way the CLI/STI instructions disable 'external' interrupts. Use the same guidelines for this API which you would use in device driver interrupt routines for disabling interrupts.

4. You would use DosHoldSignal in dynamic link routines or sybsystems while locking a critical resource. By disabling signals, you prevent the un-expected termination of the 'client' process.

DosInsMessage	
PTR	Pointer to a variable insertion data table. Each table entry is a double-word pointer to an ASCIIZ text string (up to nine entries).
WORD	A one word count defining how many variable pointers are included in the variable insertion table. The maximum count is nine. If zero, then the previous parameter is ignored.
PTR	Pointer to a buffer which contains the message text.
WORD	One word length of the input message buffer.
PTR	Pointer to an output buffer in which OS/2 will return the expanded message text.
WORD	One word length of the output message buffer. If the buffer is too small to receive the expanded message, then the text is truncated to fit.
PTR	Pointer to a one word field in which OS/2 will return the actual message length.

Description:

Insert message variable data into a message contained in a memory buffer.

Notes:

1. This API is the variable substitution function of the DosGetMessage API without the actual message retrieval. You would use DosInsMessage to insert variable substitution text in a message which is already contained in an application buffer.

2. The substitution variable count must be less than 10, or else the call will fail. If it fails, OS/2 will place a 'default' message in the output buffer.

3. The variable text can contain blanks.

DosKillProcess	

WORD	A one word action code used by OS/2 to process the request:
	
	   0 = Kill the specified process & all its descendants
	   1 = Kill only the specified process

WORD	The one word process ID (PID) of the process which is to be killed.

Description:

Terminate a process and its descendants (optionally).

Notes:

1. DosKillProcess does not actually terminate the target process(es), rather it generates a process termination signal (SIGTERM). In the default case, this signal terminates the process(es), however a process can override SIGTERM with DosSetSigHandler.

2. DosKill process causes the process(es) to terminate as if they had each issued the DosExit function. During termination processing, OS/2 reclaims process resources (files, pipes, devices, semaphores, etc.), flushes the file buffers, and frees the process memory.

DosLoadModule	
PTR	The address of a buffer in which OS/2 will place an object which further qualifies the cause of a DosLoadModule failure (eg - name of missing 'nested' dynamic link library).
WORD	One word containing the length of the object buffer.
PTR	A pointer to field which contains an ASCIIZ module name (1-8 character).
PTR	A pointer to a one word field in which OS/2 will return the module handle.

Description:

Load a dynamic link module.

Notes:

1. The module name must be a one to eight character dynamic link name. DosLoadModule assumes that the file specification is this module name with a '.DLL' extension (eg - modname.DLL).

2. The dynamic link library must be contained in one of the directories named in the CONFIG.SYS LIBPATH= statement.

3. The handle returned by DosLoadModule is used with DosGetProcAddr to retrieve individual entry points within the library, and with DosFreeModule to delete the library.

DosLockSeg	
WORD	A one word selector associated with the segment which is to be locked.

Description:

Lock a discardable data segment.

Notes:

1. Discardable data segments are special types of dynamically allocated memory segments which can be discarded instead of swapped. A discardable segment must have been allocated with the 'discardable' option of the DosAllocSeg API.

2. You use these segments as temporary storage for data which can be re-created if discarded.

3. An unlocked discardable segment may be thrown away by OS/2 if the system is in a low memory condition. In this case, the next DosLockSeg call will fail - you must re-allocate a fresh copy of the segment and re-initialize its contents.

4. A locked discardable segment will not be discarded, but it may be moved or swapped.

5. When you allocate a discardable segment, OS/2 sets it to 'locked' state. You are not required call DosLockSeg for newly allocated segments.

6. DosLockSeg increments a lock count and DosUnlockSeg decrements it. The segment is not unlocked until the count reaches zero. You can therefore use these calls in recursive routines.

DosMakePipe	
PTR	A pointer to a one word field into which OS/2 will place the pipe read handle.
PTR	A pointer to a one word field into which OS/2 will place the pipe write handle.
WORD	A one word value corresponding to the desired pipe size (in bytes). Note: The maximum size is 65536.

Description:

Create a pipe.

Notes:

1. The pipe is not deleted until both the read and the write handles are closed with DosClose.

2. If the process reading the pipe ends (or closes the handle), the next write to the pipe will fail with the 'broken pipe' error code.

DosMemAvail	
PTR	The address of a doubleword field in which OS/2 will return the size of the largest (un-allocated) memory segment in the system.

Description:

Determine the size of the largest block of free memory.

Notes:

1. The returned value is a 'snapshot' in time. It will change dynamically as other system processes allocate and deallocate memory.

DosMKDir	
PTR	Pointer to a field which contains an ASCIIZ directory name.
WORD	Reserved (must be 0).

Description:

Create a new directory.

Notes:

1. All the directories in the path preceeding the new directory name must exist. If any are not present, the call fill fail with an error.

2. If the path name does not start with '\' (root directory), then the path is relative to the drive current directory.

DosMonClose	
WORD	A device monitor handle (returned by DosMonOpen).

Description:

Ends device monitoring for a particular device.

Notes:

1. In response to a DosMonClose, OS/2 will flush all the monitor buffers associated with the calling process.

2. You can create more than one monitor thread (different index) using the same device monitor handle. However, when you close the handle, all the monitor threads are terminated.

3. After you issue DosMonClose, you can no longer use DosMonRead or DosMonWrite to read or write monitor packets from/to the device.

DosMonOpen	
PTR	Pointer to an ASCIIZ device name.
PTR	Pointer to a one word field in which OS/2 will place the monitor device handle.

Description:

Opens an OS/2 character device for monitoring.

Notes:

1. You must use the handle returned by DosMonOpen to create data monitor threads (with DosMonRegister). The same device handle can be used to start multiple monitor threads (using different device indices).

2. You may only issue one DosMonOpen per device.

DosMonRead	
PTR	Pointer to the monitor input buffer (registered with DosMonReg).
WORD	A one word BLOCK/RUN indicator: 0 = Wait until data is present 1 = Do not wait if data is not present
PTR	Pointer to a data buffer in which OS/2 will place the monitor input record.
PTR	Pointer to a one word field in which OS/2 will return the number of bytes in the data record. On input, you must set this field to the input buffer size.

Description:

Read a data packet from a monitor chain.

Notes:

1. Each call to DosMonRead returns a single, complete monitor packet. You will never receive multiple or partial packets.

2. OS/2 will set the data record length field to the length of the received data packet. Since these packets may vary in length, you should make sure that you reset the value before re-issuing DosMonRead.

3. You may only call DosMonRead using an input buffer which was previously registered (with DosMonReg) to a device opened with DosMonOpen. The DosMonOpen, DosMonReg and DosMonRead calls must all be issued by the same process. You may not read data packets from a data buffer which was registered by a different process.

4. If the DosMonReg function has not successfuly completed, the DosMonRead call will fail.

5. If you close the monitor (with DosMonClose) then all subsequent DosMonRead calls to the device will fail.

6. This function actually de-blocks a monitor packet from the monitor input buffer and places into the application buffer.

DosMonReg	
WORD	A device monitor handle (returned by DosMonOpen).
PTR	A pointer to a data buffer which OS/2 will use as the monitor input buffer. The first word in the buffer must contain the buffer length (including the word length field).
PTR	A pointer to a data buffer which OS/2 will use as the monitor output buffer. The first word in the buffer must contain the buffer length (including the word length field).
WORD	A one word positional preference indicator: 0 = no preference 1 = put monitor at the head of the monitor chain 2 = put monitor at the end of the monitor chain
WORD	A one word index value (device dependent).

Description:

Register input/output data buffers and begin monitoring an OS/2 device.

Notes:

1. Before you register input and output buffers to a device, you must first open the device for monitoring with the DosMonOpen API.

2. The DosMonReg function inserts the device input and output buffers in the monitor chain and causes OS/2 to begin routing data packets into the input buffer.

3. The monitor input and output data buffers must be in the same memory segment.

4. The first word of each buffer must be initialized to the total buffer length (including the length field itself).

5. You cannot issue DosMonRead or DosMonWrite API calls until the DosMonReg call completes successfully.

DosMonWrite	
PTR	Pointer to the monitor output buffer (registered with DosMonReg).
PTR	Pointer to a data buffer from which OS/2 will read the monitor output record.
WORD	A one word value indicating the total length of the data record in the output buffer.

Description:

Write a data packet to a monitor chain.

Notes:

1. Each call to DosMonWrite writes a single, complete monitor packet. You cannot write multiple or partial packets.

2. You may only call DosMonWrite using an output buffer which was previously registered (with DosMonReg) to a device opened with DosMonOpen. The DosMonOpen, DosMonReg and DosMonWrite calls must all be issued by the same process. You may not write data packets to a data buffer which was registered by a different process.

3. If the DosMonReg function has not successfuly completed, the DosMonWrite call will fail.

4. If you close the monitor (with DosMonClose) then all subsequent DosMonWrite calls to the device will fail.

5. This function actually inserts the monitor packet contained in the application buffer into the monitor output buffer.

DosMove	
PTR	Pointer to an ASCIIZ string which contains the old path/file name.
PTR	Pointer to an ASCIIZ string which contains the new path/file name.
DWRD	Reserved (must be zero)

Description:

Rename or move a file.

Notes:

1. If you specify a drive letter in the new path name, it must be identical to the drive specified in the old path name (or implied by the current drive).

2. If the source and target directory path names are not the same, OS/2 will move the file between directories.

3. You may not use wild card characters in the path/file names.

DosMuxSemWait	
PTR	Pointer to a one word field into which OS/2 will place an index value corresponding to the semaphore in the semaphore list which caused the event.
PTR	Pointer to a semaphore list. Semaphore list has the following format: DW Semaphore count DW 0 ⌐ Up to 16 DD Semaphore handle (RAM or SYS) ⌐ of these
DWRD	A double-word timeout value, defining the maximum time OS/2 will wait for this semaphore: -1 = wait indefinitely 0 = return immediately if semaphore is owned n = millisecond wait count

Description:

Wait for one or more semaphores to be cleared.

Notes:

1. This function returns immediately if any of the semaphores in the list is clear, otherwise it will block.

2. DosMuxSemWait differs from the other semaphore wait functions in that it is 'edge' triggered. This means that even if a semaphore is cleared and immediately reset (before the thread issuing DosMuxSemWait can be dispatched) the caller will still be 'awakened'.

DosNewSize	
WORD	An open file handle.
DWRD	A double-word value containing the new file size.

Description:

Change the size of a file.

Notes:

1. The handle you provide to DosNewSize must correspond to an open file. The call will fail if you use any other type of handle (pipe, device).

2. You cannot change the size of a file which is marked READ_ONLY. You must first reset the file attribute (with DosSetFileMode), then reset the size.

3. The data bytes in the extended portion of the file are not initialized.

4. The file system always attempts to allocate the new data in contiguous disk sectors.

DosOpen	
PTR	The address of an ASCIIZ name string
PTR	Address of a word field in which OS/2 will place the device/file handle
PTR	Address of a one word field in which OS/2 returns an action code: 0001H = Device/file existed 0002H = File was created 0003H = File was replaced
DWRD	Address of a word field which OS/2 uses to establish the initial file size (only valid when file is OPENED or CREATED)
WORD	A one word file attribute

WORD	An open flag, used by OS/2 to process your request:
	
	If file does not exist,
	     0000 xxxx Fail
	     0001 xxxx Create it
	If the file exists,
	     xxxx 0000 Fail
	     xxxx 0001 Open it
	     xxxx 0010 Create it

WORD	The open mode, used by OS/2 to process your request:
	
	DWFRRRRRISSSRAAA
	
	    Access Mode
	    Reserved
	    Sharing Mode
	    Inheritance characteristics
	    Reserved
	    Fail Errors
	    Unbuffered I/O flag
	    DASD open

DWRD	Reserved (must be 0).

Description:

Open a device/file for application I/O.

Notes:

1. When you open a file, OS/2 sets the file pointer to the first byte in the file.

2. The DosOpen function does not automatically use the data path (DPATH) environment variable to search for the file. If you need this capability, you can use the DosSearchPath function to first locate the file in the DPATH, then DosOpen to open the file.

3. The file size parameter is only used by OS/2 when a file is created or replaced. Otherwise, the parameter is ignored.

4. The DASD open bit lets you open the entire logical volume (disk partition) as a block device. Your program can then read or write individual disk sectors without passing through the file system. If you access a disk in this way, you must first lock the volume with a category 8 sub-function 0 IOCTL. This prevents other programs from manipulating the disk while you are reading individual sectors.

5. DosOpen will open any file whose name matches the input name, including system and hidden files.

6. The file system always attempts to allocate a file in contiguous disk sectors.

7. DosOpen cannot be used to open volume labels. If you set the file attribute to 'volume label', the call will fail.

8. If you pass the file handle to a child process, the child inherets the file sharing and access restrictions.

DosOpenQueue	
PTR	A pointer to a one word field into which OS/2 will place the process ID (PID) of the queue owner.
PTR	A pointer to a one word field into which OS/2 will place the queue handle.
PTR	A pointer to an ASCIIZ string containing the name of the queue. Note: this string must start with '\QUEUES\'.

Description:

Get access to a named queue.

Notes:

1. The DosOpenQueue function will not work until the queue has been successfully created with DosCreateQueue.

2. You must open the queue before you write a queue element (with DosWriteQueue).

3. The process which created the queue (the server) does not have to use this call since DosCreateQueue opens the queue and returns a valid queue handle.

4. The queue handle returned by DosOpenQueue can only be used by the process which issued the call.

DosOpenSem	
PTR	A pointer to a double-word field into which OS/2 will place the semaphore handle.
PTR	A pointer to an ASCIIZ semaphore name (must begin with '\SEM\').

Description:

Get access to a system semaphore.

Notes:

1. The DosOpenSem function will not work until the system semaphore has been successfully created with DosCreateSem.

2. You must open the system semaphore before you use it in a semaphore function (eg - DosSemWait, DosSemSetWait).

3. When you create a child process, it will inherit the parents' open semaphore handles. However, if the parent owns the semaphore at the time it creates the child, the child will not inherit the semaphore ownership.

4. A system semaphore only exists while there are active processes which have open semaphore handles. When all the processes terminate (or close the semaphore), OS/2 deletes the semaphore.

DosPeekQueue	
WORD	A one word queue handle (returned from DosOpenQueue or DosCreateQueue).
PTR	A pointer to a double-word field in which OS/2 returns the following information: DW PID of process which wrote the element DW Application-specific data
PTR	A pointer to a one word field in which OS/2 will return the size of the peeked element.
PTR	A pointer to a double-word field in which OS/2 will return the address of the peeked element.
PTR	A pointer to a one word value which specifies the exact queue element number you want to peek. Note: normally elements are peeked in the queue ordering sequence (FIFO, LIFO or priority), this parameter lets you override this ordering: 0 = Use the queue element ordering (get next element) n = Get nth element On return, OS/2 sets this field to the 'next' element number in the queue.
WORD	A one word wait indicator: 0 = Wait until element present (synchronous peek) 1 = Clear Sem when element present (async peek)
PTR	Pointer to a one word field in which OS/2 will return the element priority value (as set by the sender).
DWRD	A double-word system semaphore handle which OS/2 will post when the element is received. Note: this is only valid for asynchronous requests, if the wait indicator is 0, then this parameter can be NULL.

Description:

Retrieve a queue element without removing it from the queue.

Notes:

1. DosPeekQueue returns a queue element without removing it from the queue.

2. If the queue is empty and you specified 'WAIT', then DosPeekQueue will block until a queue element is added to the queue.

3. If the queue is empty and you specified 'NOWAIT', then DosPeekQueue returns immediately with an error code indicating that no elements are available.

4. The element number tells DosPeekQueue the last element you have retrieved. So, the call returns the element *following* the element number. For example, if you set the element number field to '2', then OS/2 returns element number '3' (if it exists).

5. On return from DosPeekQueue, OS/2 sets the element number field equal to the element number which was retrieved.

6. If you set the element number field to zero, then OS/2 will return the first element in the queue (if any exists).

7. Only the queue *owner* (which created the queue) can use DosPeekQueue.

DosPhysicalDisk	
WORD	A one word request type: 1 = Query number of partitionable disks 2 = Get IOCTL handle 3 = Release IOCTL handle
PTR	Pointer to a data buffer which is to receive the requested data.
WORD	One word data buffer length. Varies by request type as follows: Type 1 = 2 bytes Type 2 = 2 bytes Type 3 = 0 bytes (pointer must be 0)
PTR	Pointer to a user parameter area. Contents of parameter area varies by request type as follows: Type 1 = null (pointer must be 0) Type 2 = ASCIIZ partition identification Type 3 = Partition handle to be released (one word)
WORD	A one word parameter area length.

Description:

Get disk partition information or access disk.

Notes:

1. The format of the ASCIIZ file name must be as follows:

   num ':' 0

   Where num is the disk number (1=first disk, 2=second disk, etc.). The colon (':') is required and the string must be null terminated.

2. This function gives you access to the entire physical disk, rather than a logical partition. Use the DosOpen API (DASD open) to get a logical disk handle.

3. The disk handle can only be used with category 9 IOCTL packets. It is not valid with other file system API functions (eg - DosRead, DosWrite), or logical disk I/O (category 8) IOCTL packets.

DosPortAccess	
WORD	Reserved (must be 0).
WORD	One word access request type: 0 = Request access to port(s) 1 = Release access to port(s)
WORD	First port you want to access.
WORD	Last port you want to access.

Description:

Request/release access to I/O ports.

Notes:

1. This function is used in I/O Privileged Segments (IOPS) to request access to a range of I/O ports. This is necessary to insure that OS/2 programs do not interfere with one another while doing direct hardware I/O.

2. Once you have been granted access to the port(s), you may issue IN and OUT instructions. When you release the port(s), you should stop issuing I/O instructions.

3. You request (or release) ports in a contiguous range which starts with 'first port' and ends with 'last port'. If you only wish to access a single port, you must set both parameters to the same port number.

4. When you have device I/O access, you automatically get interrupt disable privilege (CLI/STI). You do not have to call DosCLIAccess.

5. If a program *calls* a dynamic link package which does direct I/O operations, it does not have to request I/O access. Only the program which issues the actual I/O operations is required to make this call.

DosPurgeQueue	
WORD	A one word queue handle (returned from DosCreateQueue).

Description:

Purge all the elements out of a queue.

Notes:

1. This call can only be made by threads in the process which created the queue (with DosCreateQueue).

2. Note: If you purge the elements from a queue, you are responsible for freeing the actual data elements. The purge function clears the queue elements, but it does nothing to the memory which holds the elements.

DosPutMessage	
WORD	A one word output handle
WORD	The total length of the output message.
PTR	Pointer to a field which contains the message text which you want to write.

Description:

Write a message.

Notes:

1. Unlike the other forms of OS/2 I/O, DosPutMessage is sensitive to the output data stream. It writes the message to the output handle and insures that a word will never wrap across lines.

2. DosPutMessage assumes that the output line length is 80 characters.

3. If the output data stream contains double byte characters (eg - Kanji), then DosPutMessage will also insure that the final character on the line is not split.

DosQCurDir	
WORD	The drive number which you want to query. Note: this must be a numeric value, defined as follows: 0 = Default drive 1 = A: drive 2 = B: drive etc.
PTR	Pointer to a memory buffer in which OS/2 will place the current directory path.
PTR	Pointer to a none word field in which OS/2 will place the path length.

Description:

Determine the current directory of a logical drive.

Notes:

1. The path information is returned without the drive letter or leading backslash ('\') and is terminated by a null character (00h).

2. The current directory is process-specific information. DosQCurDir returns the information for the requesting process.

DosQCurDisk	
PTR	Pointer to a one word field in which OS/2 will **return** the current drive number. Note: this must be a numeric value (A=1, B=2, etc.).
PTR	Pointer to a double-word field in which OS/2 will return a logical drive bit map which identifies the logical drives defined to the system. Each bit (0-25) corresponds to an individual logical drive (A:-Z:). If the bit is turned on, then the corresponding logical drive exists.

Description:

Determine the default drive.

Notes:

1. The default drive is process-specific information. DosQCurDisk returns the information for the requesting process.

DosQFHandState	
WORD	A one word (open) file handle.
PTR	Pointer to a one word field in which OS/2 will return the file handle state. This word has the same format as the 'open mode' word which was used to open the file.

Description:

Query a file handle's current 'open mode'.

Notes:

1. This API is used to retrieve the current settings of the 'open mode' options associated with a file handle. Note: these options are set when the file is created (with DosOpen) and can be changed with DosSetFHandState.

DosQFileInfo	
WORD	An open file handle
WORD	A one word value corresponding to the file information data level. Level 1 is the only valid level for OS/2 1.0.
PTR	Pointer to a buffer into which OS/2 will place the file information data.
WORD	The length of the data buffer.

Description:

Retrieve a file information record.

Notes:

1. The type 1 file information record is equivalent to the file directory data returned by DosFindFirst/DosFindNext. The time and date fields use the same bit encoding as the corresponding directory fields.

DosQFileMode	
PTR	Pointer to a field which contains an ASCIIZ file name. The name may be fully or partially qualified.
PTR	Pointer to a one word field in which OS/2 will return the file attribute.
DWRD	Reserved (must be 0).

Description:

Get a file's attribute byte.

Notes:

1. The returned value is the file attribute byte which was set when the file was created (with DosOpen) or modified with DosSetFileMode.

2. You do not have to open the target file to use this API.

3. The information returned by this call can also be retrieved from its directory entry (see DosFindFirst/DosFindNext) or with the DosQFileInfo function.

4. You may not use this function to retrieve the attribute byte of an disk volume label. To retrieve volume label information, you should use DosQFSInfo.

DosQFSInfo	
WORD	A one word value representing the drive number whose file system information is to be retrieved (0=current drive).
WORD	The file system information level: 1 = File system statistics (always exists) 2 = Volume label information (may not exist)
PTR	A pointer to a data buffer in which OS/2 will place the requested file system information.
WORD	The data buffer length.

Description:

Retrieve file system information data.

Notes:

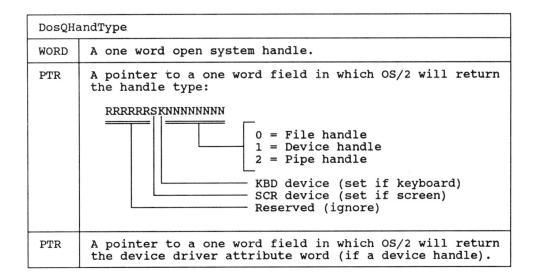

DosQHandType	
WORD	A one word open system handle.
PTR	A pointer to a one word field in which OS/2 will return the handle type:
PTR	A pointer to a one word field in which OS/2 will return the device driver attribute word (if a device handle).

Description:

Determine handle type.

Notes:

1. The S and K bits are only valid when the handle is a device handle (n = 1). Otherwise, they are undefined.

DosQueryQueue	
WORD	A one word queue handle (returned from DosCreateQueue or DosOpenQueue).
PTR	Pointer to a one word field in which OS/2 will return a count of the number or elements currently in the queue.

Description:

Query number of elements in a queue.

Notes:

1. Any process which has access to a queue can use this function to determine how many elements it contains.

DosQVerify	
PTR	Pointer to a one word field in which OS/2 will return the current verify setting: 0 = Verify mode is off 1 = Verify mode is on

Description:

Determine the verify mode.

Notes:

1. The verify mode is process-specific. This function returns the current verify mode for the process which issued the request.

DosRead	
WORD	An open device/file handle.
PTR	Pointer to a user input buffer.
WORD	Length of the input buffer.
PTR	Address of a word field which OS/2 will update with the number of bytes it transferred.

Description:

Read characters from a device/pipe/file.

Notes:

1. The bytes read could be less than the requested read length. If bytes read is zero, then you have read past the end of file or character stream.

2. If you are reading from a file, OS/2 will automatically re-position the file pointer to the next byte following the input data.

DosReadAsync	
WORD	An open device/file handle.
DWRD	A RAM semaphore handle.
PTR	Pointer to a one word field in which OS/2 will place the I/O return code.
PTR	Pointer to a user input buffer.
WORD	Length of the input buffer.
PTR	Address of a word field which OS/2 will update with the number of bytes it transferred.

Description:

Read characters from a device/pipe/file (asynchronously).

Notes:

1. The bytes read could be less than the requested read length. If bytes read is zero, then you have read past the end of file or character stream.

2. If you are reading from a file, OS/2 will automatically re-position the file pointer to the next byte following the input data.

3. The request semaphore must be set before you start the asynchronous I/O operation. This is because in certain conditions, the I/O could complete before your program is re-dispatched. You should therefore use the following general sequence of API calls:

   DosSemSet   iosem
   DosReadAsync iosem, ...
   DosSemWait iosem

4. Until the semaphore is clear, the contents of the return code, bytes read and data buffer fields is undefined.

DosReadQueue	
WORD	A one word queue handle (returned from DosOpenQueue or DosCreateQueue).

PTR	A pointer to a double-word field in which OS/2 returns the following information:
	
	    DW PID of process which created element
	    DW Application-specific data

PTR	A pointer to a one word field in which OS/2 will return the size of the de-queued element.
PTR	A pointer to a double-word field in which OS/2 will return the address of the queue element.

WORD	A one word value which specifies the exact queue element number you want retrieved. Note: normally elements are retrieved in the queue ordering sequence (FIFO, LIFO or priority), this parameter lets you override this ordering:
	
	    0 = Use the queue element ordering (get next element)
	    n = Get nth element

WORD	A one word wait indicator:
	
	    0 = Wait until element present (synchronous read)
	    1 = Clear sem when element present (async read)

PTR	Pointer to a one word field in which OS/2 will return the element priority value (as set by sender).
DWRD	A double-word system semaphore handle which OS/2 will post when the element is received. Note: this is only valid for asynchronous requests, if the wait indicator is 0, then this parameter can be NULL.

Description:

Retrieve a queue element from a queue.

Notes:

1. DosReadQueue returns a queue element from a queue.

2. If the queue is empty and you specified 'WAIT', then DosReadQueue will block until a queue element is added to the queue.

3. If the queue is empty and you specified 'NOWAIT', then DosReadQueue returns immediately with an error code indicating that no elements are available.

4. If you set the element number to zero, then DosReadQueue will return the next element from the top of the queue (FIFO, LIFO or highest priority). If you set the element number to a non-zero value, then OS/2 will return that specific element - bypassing the normal queue sequencing.

5. Only the queue *owner* (which created the queue) can use DosReadQueue.

DosReallocHuge	
WORD	The number of 65535 segments which will exist after the re-allocation.
WORD	The size of the last (non-65535) byte segment after the re-allocation.

Description:

Change the size of a huge memory object.

Notes:

1. You cannot grow a huge memory object beyond the max size specified in the original DosAllocHuge call. New segments are allocated, as needed, to satisfy the re-allocation request.

2. The contents of the re-allocated segment(s) is unmodified. If you grow the object, then the new memory area is un-initialized. If you shrink the object, then data is truncated.

DosReallocSeg	
WORD	A one word value defining the new size of the memory segment.
WORD	A valid segment selector.

Description:

Change the size of memory segment.

Notes:

1. The contents of the re-allocated segment is unmodified. If you grow the segment, then the new memory area is un-initialized. If you shrink the segment, then data is truncated.

2. You can use DosReallocSeg with shared or un-shared segments, however shared segments can be increased but not decreased in size.

DosResumeThread	
WORD	A one word thread identification number.

Description:

Resume execution of a suspended thread.

Notes:

1. This call can only be made from a thread in the process which contains the suspended thread.

DosRmDir	
PTR	Pointer to a field containing an ASCIIZ directory name (max 64 bytes).
DWRD	Reserved (must be 0).

Description:

Delete a subdirectory.

Notes:

1. The last entry in the path is the subdirectory which will be deleted.

2. This call will only work if the target subdirectory does not contain other files or subdirectories (except for the system subdirectories - "." and "..").

3. You cannot delete the root directory or the system directories.

4. DosRmDir will also fail if the subdirectory is the "current directory" of another system process.

DosScanEnv	
PTR	Pointer to an ASCIIZ environment variable name which is to be located in the environment
PTR	Pointer to a double-word field in which OS/2 returns a pointer to the requested environment variable's data area

Description:

Search environment string for a specific environment variable.

Notes:

1. If the environment variable exists, then the returned pointer will point to the first byte in the environment variable data area. The data is null terminated.

DosSearchPath	

WORD	A one word function control vector:
	
	RRRRRRRRRRRRRRPI
	                              └─ Implied current indicator
	                            ── Path source indicator
	                      ── Reserved (0)

PTR	Pointer to a field which contains a path string. If the path source indicator is off (0), then this field contains an ASCIIZ path. If the path source indicator is on (1), then this field contains the ASCIIZ name of an environment variable (eg - DPATH) which contains the search path.
PTR	Pointer to a field which contains the ASCIIZ file name for which you are searching.
PTR	Pointer to a user buffer in which OS/2 will return the actual file path (if found).
WORD	A one word user buffer length.

Description:

Locate a file in an arbitrary path list.

Notes:

1. The DosOpen function does not use the OS/2 search path to locate files. In OS/2, the application programs are responsible for implementing the DPATH support. This function is a generalized path searching function which an application can use to locate the desired file. The returned path can then be used with DosOpen to gain access to the file.

2. See the DPATH and APPEND commands for the search path format.

3. DosSearchPath uses either an arbitrary character string (generated by the application) or the contents of an environment variable name (eg - "DPATH") as the search path.

DosSelectDisk	
WORD	A one word value corresponding to the new default drive. Note: this must be a numeric value (A=1, B=2, etc.).

Description:

Change the current disk.

Notes:

1. The default drive is process-specific information. DosSelectDisk changes the default drive for the requesting process.

DosSelectSession	
WORD	A one word value corresponding to the session ID which is to be switched to the foreground. If this is set to 0, then OS/2 will switch your parent session to the foreground.
DWRD	Reserved (must be 0).

Description:

Move a child session to the foreground.

Notes:

1. This function may only used by a 'parent' session to put itself or one of its child sessions to the foreground.

2. A 'child' session is a session which was started with the relation option = 1 (see DosStartSession).

3. DosSelectSession will only work when the parent or one of its other child sessions is already the foreground session. In other words, DosSelectSession cannot be used to 'preempt' an arbitrary (unrelated) session. If you need to do this, you must use the VioPopUp function.

4. DosSelectSession may not be used to select a grandchild session.

DosSemClear	
DWRD	A double-word semaphore handle which is either the address of a RAM semaphore, or the handle returned from a DosOpenSem or DosCreateSem.

Description:

Clear a System or RAM semaphore.

Notes:

1. Clearing a semaphore causes OS/2 to 'wake up' any threads which are currently waiting on the semaphore.

2. DosSemClear can be used to reset RAM or System semaphores, however it cannot clear an exclusive system semaphore which was created by another process. Exclusive system semaphores may only be modified by the process which created them.

DosSemRequest	
DWRD	A double-word semaphore handle which is either the address of a RAM semaphore, or the handle returned from DosOpenSem or DosCreateSem.
DWRD	A double-word timeout value, defining the maximum time OS/2 should wait for this semaphore: -1 = wait indefinitely 0 = return immediately if semaphore is owned n = millisecond wait count

Description:

Obtain a resource serialization semaphore.

Notes:

1. DosSemRequest is typically used to serialize the use of a shared resource (eg - the display) among multiple execution threads.

2. Only one thread at a time will get 'ownership' of the semaphore. All other requesting threads will be blocked.

3. DosSemRequest can be used to request RAM or System semaphores.

4. For exclusive system semaphores, OS/2 maintains an owner request count. This count is incremented each time the semaphore is requested and decremented each time it is cleared. The semaphore is not released until the request count reaches zero. This means that you can request/clear system semaphores in recursive programs.

5. When a semaphore is clear it is not owned. When you allocate a RAM semaphore (initialized to 0) or create a System semaphore (with DosCreateSem), its initial setting is 'not owned'. You can set the initial semaphore state as 'owned' with the DosSemSet function.

6. If a thread dies while it owns a system semaphore, the next thread which gets the semaphore via the DosSemRequest function will receive the 'semaphore owner died' error code.

DosSemSet	
DWRD	A double-word semaphore handle which is either the address of a RAM semaphore, or the handle returned from DosOpenSem or DosCreateSem.

Description:

Unconditionally set a semaphore.

Notes:

1. This function is typically used in conjunction with DosSemWait and DosSemClear to signal events between threads.

2. DosSemSet can be used to set RAM or System semaphores, however it cannot set an exclusive system semaphore which was created by another process. Exclusive system semaphores may only be modified by the process which created them.

DosSemSetWait	
DWRD	A double-word semaphore handle which is either the address of a RAM semaphore, or the handle returned from a DosOpenSem or DosCreateSem.
DWRD	A double-word timeout value, defining the maximum time OS/2 will wait for this semaphore: -1 = wait indefinitely 0 = return immediately if semaphore is owned n = millisecond wait count

Description:

Set a semaphore then wait until it is cleared.

Notes:

1. DosSemSetWait sets then waits for a semaphore in a single atomic operation. No system thread will execute between the time the semaphore is set and the time the wait starts.

2. This function is typically used in conjunction with DosSemClear to signal events between threads.

3. DosSemSetWait can be used with RAM or System semaphores, however it will not work with an exclusive system semaphore which was created by another process. Exclusive system semaphores may only be modified by the process which created them.

4. This function will not return to the caller unless the semaphore is still clear when the calling thread is re-dispatched. For example, if another (higher priority) thread is dispatched and it sets the semaphore before your thread can run, then the DosSemSetWait function will continue to wait.

DosSemWait	
DWRD	A double-word semaphore handle which is either the address of a RAM semaphore, or the handle returned from a DosOpenSem or DosCreateSem.
DWRD	A double-word timeout value, defining the maximum time OS/2 will wait for this semaphore: -1 = wait indefinitely 0 = return immediately if semaphore is owned n = millisecond wait count

Description:

Wait until a semaphore is cleared.

Notes:

1. This function is typically used in conjunction with DosSemSet and DosSemClear to signal events between threads.

2. DosSemWait can be used with RAM or System semaphores.

3. This function will not return to the caller unless the semaphore is still clear when the calling thread is re-dispatched. For example, if another (higher priority) thread is dispatched and it sets the semaphore before your thread can run, then the DosSemWait function will continue to wait.

DosSendSignal	
WORD	A one word process ID (PID) value identifying the command subtree which is to receive the signal. A command subtree starts with the specified process and includes all its descendants.
WORD	A one word signal number. It may only be one of the following: 1 - Ctrl-C Signal (SIGINTR) 4 - Ctrl-Break Signal (SIGBREAK)

Description:

Send a Ctrl-C or Ctrl-Break signal to a command subtree.

Notes:

1. The signal is sent to the lowest level descendant in the specified PID's command subtree which has a Ctrl-C or Ctrl-Break signal handler.

2. The specified process ID must be a direct child of the of the caller.
   Note: the process does not have to still be alive.

DosSetCP	
WORD	A one word code page identification. In OS/2 1.0, it must be one of the following: 437 IBM PC (US) code page 850 Multilingual code page 860 Portuguese code page 863 Canadian-French code page 865 Nordic code page
WORD	Reserved (must be set to 0).

Description:

Set the process (default) code page.

Notes:

1. This API sets the default code page for the calling process. The initial keyboard, video and printer code pages are set with this function.

2. You may independently change the keyboard and video code pages with the KbdSetCp and VioSetCp functions, respectively.

3. Printer output is tagged with the current process code page before it is sent to the printer. However, you should note that this function is only available when the OS/2 spooler has been loaded.

DosSetDateTime	
PTR	Pointer to a buffer which contains a Date/Time data structure.

Description:

Set the system clock.

Notes:

1. This function has global scope. Meaning that if you change the clock setting in one process, it will change all the system processes.

2. The day of week value is based on Sunday being equal to 0.

3. The time zone field equals the number of minutes from GMT. If the current time zone is earlier than GMT, then the value is positive. If later than GMT, then the value is negative.

DosSetFHandState	
WORD	An open file handle.

WORD	A one word value corresponding to the new file handle state. This word has the same format as the 'open mode' word which was used to open the file. However, you may only change the following fields with this call:
	
	    Inheritance flag
	    Write-through flag
	    Fail-errors flag
	
	The DASD Open, Sharing Mode, and Access Mode fields must be set to zero. All reserved bits must be set as they were returned by DosQFHandState.

Description:

Change the state of a file (handle).

Notes:

1. DosSetFHandState can only be used with a file handle. Any other type of handle will cause the request to fail.

2. This API is used to change the setting of the 'open mode' options associated with a file handle. Note: These options are first set when the file was created (with DosOpen).

3. If you opened a file with system error processing disabled, and you encounter an error which you cannot handle from the application, you can use DosSetFHandState to re-enable system error processing and re-issue the failing I/O operation. The system hard error handler will then process the next failure.

DosSetFileInfo	
WORD	An open file handle
WORD	The file information level which you want to set. Level 1 is the only valid level for OS/2 1.0.

PTR	Pointer to a buffer which contains the new file information data:
	
	    DW Creation date
	    DW Creation time
	    DW Last access date
	    DW Last access time
	    DW Last write date
	    DW Last write time

WORD	The length of the data buffer.

Description:

Change a file's directory information.

Notes:

1. Level 1 information (file date & time) is the only data which can be changed in OS/2 release 1.0.

2. This function will only work if the file was opened with WRITE access.

3. If both the date and time associated with a particular field (eg - the creation date/time) are zero, then the field is not changed. If either date or time is non-zero, then the field is changed.

DosSetFileMode	
PTR	Pointer to a field which contains an ASCIIZ file name. The name may be fully or partially qualified.
WORD	The new file attribute.
DWRD	Reserved (must be 0).

Description:

Change a file's attribute.

Notes:

1. This function may not be used to change the attribute of a volume label (08h) or a subdirectory (10h). Likewise, this call cannot be used to change an existing file to a volume label or directory.

DosSetFSInfo	
WORD	A one word value representing the drive number whose file system information is to be changed (0=current drive).
WORD	The file system information level: 2 = Volume label information (only supported level)
PTR	A pointer to a data buffer which contains the new ASCIIZ volume label.
WORD	The data buffer length.

Description:

Change the file system information (volume label) for a particular drive.

Notes:

1. The volume label may only be changed after you have opened the disk in a mode that allows WRITE access.

DosSetMaxFH	
WORD	A one word value corresponding to the new maximum handle count (for the current process).

Description:

Change the maximum number of file handles for the current process.

Notes:

1. Any pre-existing file handles are not affected by this function.

DosSetPrty	
WORD	The scope of the priority change: 0 = The process & all its threads 1 = The process & all its descendants 2 = A single thread within the current process
WORD	A one word value indicating the new process/thread priority class: 0 = Do not change the current class 1 = Change to idle priority class 2 = Change to regular priority class 3 = Change to time-critical priority class
WORD	A one word value indicating the delta which OS/2 should apply to the base priority level (-31 to +31).
WORD	The ID of the process (scope=0,1) or thread (scope=2) whose priority is to be set.

Description:

Change the priority of a thread or process.

Notes:

1. If the priority class is unchanged (0), the priority delta field represents a signed value which is added to the current priority level.

2. If the priority class is changed (non-0), then the priority level is set to 0 and the priority delta field is relative to this new base priority level (0).

3. The resulting priority level value is restricted to the legal priority range (between -31 and +31).

4. If you use this call to change the priority of one of your descendants, you can only change the priority level (not the class).

5. When a new process is created (with the DosExecPgm function), it inherits the priority class and level of the parent process.

DosSetSession	
WORD	A one word value corresponding to the child session ID whose status is to be changed.

PTR	Pointer to a session status data record:
	
	DW Structure length (6)
	DW Session selectability indicator:
	    0 = Leave setting as is
	    1 = Make session selectable
	    2 = Make session non-selectable
	DW Bond indicator:
	    0 = Leave setting as is
	    1 = Bond child session to parent
	    2 = Break parent/child session bond

Description:

Change the status of a child session.

Notes:

1. Only direct child sessions may be changed with this call.

2. Either the bonding or the selectability session attribute may be changed without affecting the other.

3. These attributes affect the sessions which are selected by the user from the session manager shell, but they do not affect session selections made by the parent session using the DosSelectSession API. When a parent session selects itself, it is brought to the foreground even when it has bonded a child session to itself. Likewise, when the parent session selects a child session, the child is brought to the foreground, even if it had been set 'non-selectable'.

4. DosSetSession may only be used by the parent session to manipulate the status of child sessions it started with the related attribute = 1.

DosSetSigHandler	
DWRD	The address (segment, offset) of a routine which OS/2 will call when the requested signal is received (can be NULL for action codes 0, 1, 3, and 4).
PTR	A pointer to a double word area into which OS/2 will place the address of the previous signal handler routine (may be NULL).
PTR	A pointer to a one word area into which OS/2 will place the previous action code for this signal will be placed (can be NULL).
WORD	A one word action code, telling OS/2 how to process this request: 0 = Set the default system action 1 = Ignore the signal 2 = Give control to the specified routine 3 = Generate error if another process uses this Flag 4 = Ignore the signal
WORD	The signal number (1, 3, 4, 5, 6, 7).

Description:

Establish a signal handler.

Notes:

1. The signals are always handled by the first thread of the process.

2. The signal handler routine is responsible for removing the signal number and signal argument from the stack before returning to its caller. In assembly language, this means that the signal handler must issue a 'RET 4' instruction. Most high level languages will automatically take care of this for you.

3. This call is invalid once thread one has terminated.

4. If thread one terminates and other threads are still active, then the system will re-instate the default actions for all the signals.

DosSetVec	
WORD	A one word value corresponding to the exception vector which you want to process. The valid exception numbers are: 00 (Divide overflow) 04 (Overflow) 05 (Bound) 06 (Invalid opcode) 07 (Processor extension not available) 16 (Processor extension exception)
DWRD	The address (segment, offset) of a routine which OS/2 will call when the indicated exception occurs.
PTR	Pointer to a double-word field in which OS/2 returns the address of the previous exception handler.

Description:

Establish an exception vector handler.

Notes:

1. This function allows a process to handle recoverable machine exceptions. It is analogous to placing an address in the interrupt vector table in real mode.

2. If an exception ocurrs which corresponds to a registered handler, then OS/2 calls the routine as if it had been directly chained to the interrupt vector.

3. If a process registers an exception handler for VecNum 7 (NPX not available), then OS/2 sets the machine status word (MSW) for that process to indicate that there is no NPX in the machine. The emulate bit is set and the monitor processor bit is reset. This means that a process can emulate the NPX even if one is present in the machine.

4. When the process de-registers a VecNum 7 handler, then OS/2 updates the MSW accordingly.

5. When a real NPX exception is processed, OS/2 pushes the 80287/80387 status word on the stack prior to calling the handler. The exception handler is responsible for removing this word prior to terminating with the IRET instruction.

DosSetVerify	
WORD	A one word value corresponding to the new verify setting: 0 = Turn verify mode off 1 = Turn verify mode on

Description:

Set/Reset the verify mode.

Notes:

1. When verify mode is set, OS/2 will verify each disk write operation.

DosSleep	
DWRD	A double-word value containing the number of Milliseconds OS/2 is to suspend the calling thread.

Description:

Suspend the calling thread for a period of time.

Notes:

1. If the sleep period is 0, then the thread will forego the remainder of its time slice. Note: If no other (higher priority) threads are ready to run, OS/2 will immediately return to the calling thread.

2. If the time period is greater than 0, then OS/2 rounds the value up to the next clock interval.

DosStartSession	

PTR	Pointer to a session start data record:
	
	DW Structure length (24)
	DW Relationship:
	     0 = New session is independent
	     1 = New session is child
	DW Foreground/Background status:
	     0 = Start new session in foreground
	     1 = Start new session in background
	DW Session trace status:
	     0 = New session is not traceable
	     1 = New session is traceable
	DD Ptr to ASCIIZ session title (none if null)
	DD Ptr to ASCIIZ pgm name to be run in session
	DD Ptr to ASCIIZ parameter list (passed to pgm)
	DD Ptr to ASCIIZ termination queue name (none if null)

PTR	Pointer to a word field in which OS/2 will return the new session ID. This value is only returned when the relationship field is set to 1.
PTR	Pointer to a word field in which OS/2 will return the Process ID of the program running in the new session. This value is only returned when the relationship field is set to 1.

Description:

Start a new session.

Notes:

1. This API can only be used when the caller's session or one of the caller's descendant sessions is currently in the foreground.

2. If the program name is a null ASCIIZ string, OS/2 will start a copy of the default command processor in the new session (as specified in the PROTSHELL CONFIG.SYS statement). This is normally CMD.EXE.

3. This API can only be used to start protected mode sessions.

4. When a child session running in the foreground terminates, the parent session becomes the new foreground session.

5. When the parent session ends, all child sessions which were started with the related=1 option are also terminated.

6. If an independent session ends (one which was started with related = 0), then the session manager shell choses the next foreground session.

7. The program name and program parameter fields may not (together) exceed 384 bytes.

8. The parent session may only have one termination queue. The queue must be created before any sessions are started. Termination queue element ID values 0-99 are reserved for session manager queue elements. The remaining ID values are available for application use.

DosStopSession	
WORD	A one word termination option: 0 = Terminate specified session 1 = Terminate session and all descendants
WORD	The session ID of the session which is to be terminated. Note: This must be a related (child) session.
DWRD	Reserved (must be 0)

Description:

Stop a session.

Notes:

1. DosStopSession may only be used by a parent session to stop one of its related child sessions. The parent session may not use this function to terminate itself nor grandchild sessions. If the stopped child session has descendant sessions, then OS/2 will stop them when it terminates the child session.

2. Independent sessions may not be stopped with this API. The target child session must have been started with the related = 1 operand.

3. The parent session may issue the DosStopSession call while it is either in the foreground or in the background.

4. The process running in the target session may refuse to terminate. The only way to insure that the session has really ended is to wait on the termination queue.

DosSubAlloc	
DWRD	The selector of an initialized suballocation segment.
PTR	The address of a one word field in which OS/2 will return the offset of the memory block.
WORD	The size of the requested memory block (must be a multiple of 4 bytes.

Description:

Suballocate an element out of a memory segment.

Notes:

1. To use this function, you must first initialize the target memory segment with DosSubSet function.

2. The allocation size should be a multiple of four bytes. If it is not, OS/2 will round the allocation request to the next largest four byte multiple.

3. The maximum element size is the total segment size minus eight bytes.

DosSubFree	
DWRD	The selector of an initialized suballocation segment.
PTR	The offset of the suballocated block which OS/2 will free.
WORD	The size of the memory block (must be a multiple of 4 bytes).

Description:

Free a suballocated element.

Notes:

1. Use this function to free a memory element which was allocated with DosSubAlloc.

2. If the element overlaps unallocated memory, the call will fail with an error.

3. The element size should be a multiple of four bytes. If it is not, OS/2 will round the free request to the next largest four byte multiple.

DosSubSet	
WORD	A valid segment selector.
WORD	A one word flag value, indicating if this request is to initialize or to re-size a suballocated memory segment: 0 = Increase the size suballocated segment 1 = Prepare a segment for suballocation
WORD	A one word value which either defines the initial size or the new size of the suballocated segment (depending on the flag value).

Description:

Initialize/reinitialize a memory segment for suballocation.

Notes:

1. Use this function to prepare a previously allocated (with DosAllocSeg or DosAllocShrSeg) memory segment for suballocation. Function code = 1 initializes the segment.

2. To increase the size of a previously initialized suballocated segment, use DosReallocSeg to increase the size of the segment and DosSubSet (function code = 0) to reset the suballocation information. If you use this function, the contents of the previously allocated elements is unchanged.

DosSuspendThread	
WORD	The one word thread ID of the thread which is to be terminated.

Description:

Temporarily suspend the execution of a thread.

Notes:

1. You may only suspend other threads within your process.

2. Any thread in a process may suspend the execution of any other thread in the process.

DosTimerAsync	
DWRD	Double-word count of the number of milliseconds which must elapse in the timer interval.
DWRD	An open system semaphore handle (returned by DosOpenSem or DosCreateSem).
PTR	Pointer to a double-word field into which OS/2 will return the timer handle.

Description:

Run a single asynchronous timer.

Notes:

1. This API is the asynchronous analog of the DosSleep function.

2. An asynchronous timer may be cancelled (before it expires) with the DosTimerStop API.

3. To insure reliable detection of the timer expiration, you should set the semaphore immediately before you start the timer. You should then use DosSemWait to detect the timer expiration.

DosTimerStart	
DWRD	Double-word count of the number of milliseconds which must elapse in the timer interval.
DWRD	An open system semaphore handle (returned by DosOpenSem or DosCreateSem).
PTR	Pointer to a double-word field into which OS/2 will return the timer handle.

Description:

Run a cyclical asynchronous timer.

Notes:

1. The timer interval will continue to expire indefinitely.

2. An asynchronous cyclical timer may be cancelled with the DosTimerStop API.

DosTimerStop	
WORD	A double-word (open) timer handle.

Description:

Stop an asynchronous timer.

Notes:

1. This API can be used to stop single shot (DosTimerAsync) or cyclical (DosTimerStart) asynchronous timers.

2. The state of the semaphore after the timer has been cancelled is indeterminate.

3. The timer handle (returned by DosTimerAsync or DosTimerStart) is used to identify the timer.

DosUnlockSeg	
WORD	The selector of a discardable data segment which you wish to unlock.

Description:

Unlock a discardable segment.

Notes:

1. DosUnlockSeg can only be used to unlock segments which were allocated with the allocation flags bit 2 set (0004h).

DosWrite	
WORD	An open device/file handle
PTR	Address of a user output buffer
WORD	Length of the user buffer
PTR	Address of a word field which OS/2 will update with the number of bytes it transferred.

Description:

Write characters to a device/pipe/file.

Notes:

1. The bytes written could be less than output data length. If this happens, it usually indicates that there is insufficient space on the disk for the data.

2. If you are writing to a file, OS/2 will automatically reposition the file pointer to the next byte following the output data.

3. An output length of zero will not generate an error.

4. If the file is marked READ_ONLY, or if the device/file was opened in a read only mode, then DosWrite will fail.

DosWriteAsync	
WORD	An open device/file handle.
DWRD	A RAM semaphore handle.
PTR	Pointer to a one word field in which OS/2 will place the I/O return code.
PTR	Pointer to a user output buffer.
WORD	Length of the output buffer.
PTR	Address of a word field which OS/2 will update with the number of bytes it transferred.

Description:

Write characters to a device/pipe/file (asynchronously).

Notes:

1. The bytes written could be less than output data length. If this happens, it usually indicates that there insufficient space on the disk for the data.

2. If you are writing to a file, OS/2 will automatically reposition the file pointer to the next byte following the output data.

3. An output length of zero will not generate an error.

4. If the file is marked READ ONLY, or if the device/file was opened in a read only mode, then DosWriteAsync will fail.

5. The request semaphore must be set before you start the asynchronous I/O operation. This is because in certain conditions, the I/O could complete before your program is re-dispatched. You should therefore use the following general sequence of API calls:

    DosSemSet   iosem
    DosReadAsync iosem, ...
    DosSemWait iosem

6. Until the semaphore is clear, the contents of the return code and bytes read fields are undefined and the contents of the buffer should not be modified.

DosWriteQueue	
WORD	A one word queue handle (returned from DosOpenQueue or DosCreateQueue).
WORD	A one word request field which OS/2 is to pass with the queue element. This information is application-specific, OS/2 neither inspects nor modifies its contents.
WORD	A one word field which defines the size of the queue element.
PTR	A pointer to the queue element which OS/2 will add to the queue.
WORD	A one word element priority value (0-15).

Description:

Add an element to a queue.

Notes:

1. If the queue owner terminates (or closes the queue) before this request is issued, then the API will fail with an 'invalid queue handle' error code.

2. If the queue owner uses a system semaphore to retrieve elements from the queue asynchronously, then the process which issues the DosWriteQueue call must have gained access to the semaphore (using DosOpenSem).

3. Likewise, if the queue owner uses a RAM semaphore to retrieve elements from the queue asynchronously, then the process which issues the DosWriteQueue call must have addressability to the memory segment which contains the semaphore data structure.

KbdCharIn	
PTR	A pointer to a character input data structure: DB ASCII character code DB Scan code DB Character status DB NLS shift status DW Shift state DD Time stamp
WORD	A one word value which tells OS/2 if it is to wait for the character: 0 = Wait for character 1 = Do not wait
WORD	A one word KBD handle.

Description:

Read a character data record from the keyboard.

Notes:

1. Extended ASCII codes are represented by a 00h or 0Eh value in the ASCII field and an extended code in the scan code field. The 0Eh values are generated by the enhanced keyboard (not the original AT keyboard).

2. The secondary enter key on the enhanced keyboard is returned as a Carriage Return (0Dh) in the ASCII field and a 0Eh value in the scan code field.

3. Double byte (DBCS) characters require two KbdCharIn function calls to retrieve the entire character.

4. This function call will complete when the specified keyboard handle has the physical keyboard focus.

5. The ASCII character and scan code fields are set to zero when the character buffer is a shift state (change) report.

6. Bit six of the status byte is set when the character buffer contains a character.

7. The ASCII character and scan code fields are set to zero when the character buffer is a shift state (change) report.

8. This function will block if the keyboard handle does not have the keyboard focus. It will un-block when the keyboard handle is given the focus. Note: the default keyboard handle (0) 'owns' the physical keyboard when no other handle has input focus.

KbdClose	
WORD	A one word KBD handle

Description:

Close a logical keyboard.

Notes:

1. This function call causes OS/2 to flush the logical keyboard (KbdFlushBuffer) and free the physical keyboard focus (KbdFreeFocus) for the logical keyboard associated with the handle.

2. Using KbdClose with a zero (default) handle, has no effect on the default keyboard.

KbdDeRegister

Description:

De-register a replacement keyboard subsystem.

Notes:

1. Only the process which issued KbdRegister (for the session) may call KbdDeRegister.

2. Once the subsystem is released, any other process in the session can take over the keyboard subsystem functions by issuing KbdRegister.

KbdFlushBuffer	
WORD	A one word KBD handle.

Description:

Flush the current keyboard buffer.

Notes:

KbdFreeFocus	
WORD	A one word KBD handle

Description:

Free the logical keyboard focus.

Notes:

1. This call gives the physical keyboard to another thread in the session (if one is waiting) or it will make the keyboard revert to the default keyboard (handle 0).

2. KbdFreeFocus can be replaced with KbdRegister, however, unlike other KBD functions, the replaced routine is only called when there is an outstanding focus request.

KbdGetCP	
DWRD	Reserved (must be 0).
PTR	Pointer to a one word field in which OS/2 will return the active keyboard code page (see KbdSetCP).
WORD	A one word KBD handle.

Description:

Query the active keyboard code page.

Notes:

1. The keyboard code page is maintained on a per-handle basis.

2. This function will block if the keyboard handle does not have the keyboard focus. It will un-block when the keyboard handle is given the focus. Note: the default keyboard handle (0) 'owns' the physical keyboard when no other handle has input focus.

KbdGetFocus	
WORD	A one word options indicator: 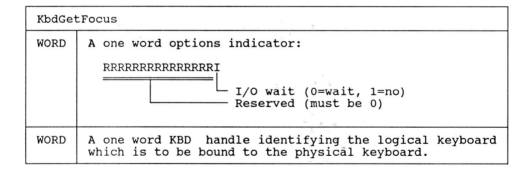
WORD	A one word KBD handle identifying the logical keyboard which is to be bound to the physical keyboard.

Description:

Bind a logical keyboard handle to the physical keyboard.

Notes:

1. The scope of this call is the session of the calling thread.

2. If the physical keyboard is not bound to another logical (or the default) keyboard, then the call completes immediately and the logical keyboard associated with the handle receives all subsequent keystrokes (for this session).

3. If the physical keyboard is already bound to another logical keyboard (in the session), then the call blocks until the previous bond is ended.

KbdGetStatus	
PTR	Pointer to a keyboard status data structure in which OS/2 will return the current status.
WORD	A one word KBD handle.

Description:

Query the current keyboard state.

Notes:

1. The keyboard state is maintained on a per-handle basis.

2. This function will block if the keyboard handle does not have the keyboard focus. It will un-block when the keyboard handle is given the focus. Note: the default keyboard handle (0) 'owns' the physical keyboard when no other handle has input focus.

KbdOpen	
PTR	Pointer to a one word field in which OS/2 will return the new logical keyboard handle.

Description:

Create a new logical keyboard.

Notes:

1. KbdOpen returns a new keyboard handle which is used by a thread (in the session) to access the logical keyboard.

2. Before the handle can be used with the KBD calls, it must be bound to the physical keyboard with the KbdGetFocus function.

3. The new logical keyboard code page is initialized to the system (default) code page.

KbdPeek	
PTR	A pointer to a character input data structure (see KbdCharIn).
WORD	A one word KBD handle.

Description:

Peek a character data record from the keyboard.

Notes:

1. This function is similar to KbdCharIn, except that the key is not removed from the keyboard buffer.

2. Extended ASCII codes are represented by a 00h or 0Eh value in the ASCII field and an extended code in the scan code field. The 0Eh values are generated by the enhanced keyboard (not the original AT keyboard).

3. The secondary enter key on the enhanced keyboard is returned as a Carriage Return (0Dh) in the ASCII field and a 0Eh value in the scan code field.

4. This function call will complete when the specified keyboard handle has the physical keyboard focus.

5. The ASCII character and scan code fields are set to zero when the character buffer is a shift state (change) report.

6. Bit six of the status byte is set when the character buffer contains a character.

7. The ASCII character and scan code fields are set to zero when the character buffer is a shift state (change) report.

KbdRegister	
PTR	Pointer to an ASCIIZ module name which contains the dynamic link replacement routine(s).
PTR	Pointer to an ASCIIZ entry point name within the dynamic link module which is to gain control when the KBD function(s) are called by an application program.
DWRD	A double-word function mask indicating which KBD functions are being replaced by this KbdRegister call.

Description:

Register a replacement keyboard subsystem for the current session.

Notes:

1. There can only be one active replacement subsystem per session. If you attempt to register a second subsystem while another process has an active replacement, then the KbdRegister call will fail.

2. The keyboard subsystem is released with the KbdDeRegister call. KbdDeRegister may be called by any thread in the process which called KbdRegister.

KbdSetCP	
WORD	Reserved (must be 0).
WORD	A one word code page number which OS/2 will set as the active keyboard code page: 000 Resident code page 437 IBM PC US 850 Multi-lingual 860 Portuguese 863 French-Canadian 865 Nordic Note: the selected value must have been configured using the CONFIG.SYS CODEPAGE statement.
WORD	A one word KBD handle.

Description:

Set the keyboard code page.

Notes:

1. The keyboard code page is maintained on a per-handle basis.

2. The code page value must be either 0 (default code page) or one of the two code pages which were specified in the CODEPAGE CONFIG.SYS statement.

3. When you reset the keyboard code page, OS/2 flushes the keyboard input queue associated with the logical keyboard.

4. This function will block if the keyboard handle does not have the keyboard focus. It will un-block when the keyboard handle is given the focus. Note: the default keyboard handle (0) 'owns' the physical keyboard when no other handle has input focus.

KbdSetCustXT	
PTR	Pointer to a translate table.
WORD	A one word KBD handle.

Description:

Set a custom translation table.

Notes:

1. The keyboard translation table is maintained on a per-handle basis.

2. The actual translation table must be maintained in a user buffer. KbdSetCustXt does not copy the table, so you must never free the segment which contains the table.

3. The KbdSetCP function resets the custom translation table to an OS/2 code page table.

4. When you reset the translation table, OS/2 flushes the keyboard input queue associated with the logical keyboard.

5. This function will block if the keyboard handle does not have the keyboard focus. It will un-block when the keyboard handle is given the focus. Note: the default keyboard handle (0) 'owns' the physical keyboard when no other handle has input focus.

KbdSetStatus	
PTR	Pointer to a keyboard status data structure which OS/2 will use to set the keyboard status.
WORD	A one word KBD handle.

Description:

Change the current keyboard state.

Notes:

1. The keyboard state is maintained on a per-handle basis.

2. Shift report is not valid in ASCII mode.

3. This function will block if the keyboard handle does not have the keyboard focus. It will un-block when the keyboard handle is given the focus. Note: the default keyboard handle (0) 'owns' the physical keyboard when no other handle has input focus.

KbdStringIn	
PTR	Pointer to an input character buffer. Note: this buffer must be large enough to hold the string whose length is in the buffer length parameter.
PTR	Pointer to a two word buffer length data structure: DW Input buffer length DW Returned data length
WORD	A one word WAIT/NOWAIT indicator: 0 = Wait until the buffer is full (or CR pressed) 1 = Return immediately with whatever is in buffer
WORD	A one word KBD handle (0 for default keyboard).

Description:

Read a character string from the keyboard.

Notes:

1. The keystrokes are echoed to the display if the keyboard ECHO mode is set (see KbdSetStatus).

2. Double byte (DBCS) character codes are returned in final form.

3. The received input length field is used to define how much of the input area will participate in the OS/2 line edit functions.

4. This function will block if the keyboard handle does not have the keyboard focus. It will un-block when the keyboard handle is given the focus. Note: the default keyboard handle (0) 'owns' the physical keyboard when no other handle has input focus.

5. The maximum input string length is 255 bytes.

KbdXlate	
PTR	Pointer to a translate data record.
WORD	A one word KBD handle.

Description:

Translate a scan code to final ASCII form.

Notes:

1. KbdXlate uses the current keyboard translation table (and code page) to translate the input scan code to a final form ASCII character.

2. You must set the desired character shift state in the character buffer before calling KbdXlate.

3. Due to accent key combinations, you may have to call KbdXlate several times to complete the translation of a scan code.

4. This function will block if the keyboard handle does not have the keyboard focus. It will un-block when the keyboard handle is given the focus. Note: the default keyboard handle (0) 'owns' the physical keyboard when no other handle has input focus.

MouClose	
WORD	A one word MOU handle

Description:

Close the mouse device for the current display session.

Notes:

1. The MOU handle is removed from the list of valid handles.

MouDeRegister

Description:

De-register the replacement mouse subsystem.

Notes:

1. Only the process which issued MouRegister (for the session) may call MouDeRegister.

2. Once the subsystem is released, any other process in the session can take over the mouse subsystem functions by issuing MouRegister.

MouDrawPtr	
WORD	A one word MOU handle

Description:

Releases the mouse collision area.

Notes:

1. A collision area is defined by the MouRemovePtr or MouOpen functions. This area is a portion of the screen which is exclusively reserved for application use. If the user drags the mouse into a collision area, the mouse subsystem hides the pointer.

2. If there is no active collision area when MouDrawPtr is called, the function is ignored.

MouFlushQue	
WORD	A one word MOU handle

Description:

Flushes the mouse event queue.

Notes:

1. The mouse events associated with the session of the caller are flushed.

MouGetDevStatus	
PTR	Pointer to a one word field in which OS/2 will return the mouse device status word. 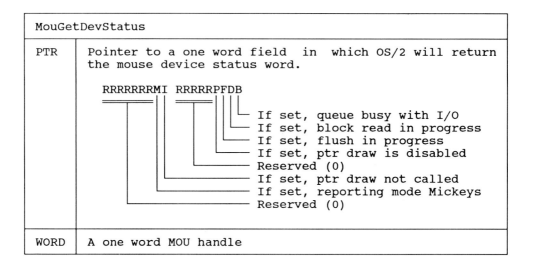
WORD	A one word MOU handle

Description:

Retrieves the mouse status flags for the current session.

Notes:

1. The status flags are associated with the session of the caller.

MouGetEventMask	
PTR	A one word field in which OS/2 will return the current mouse event mask: 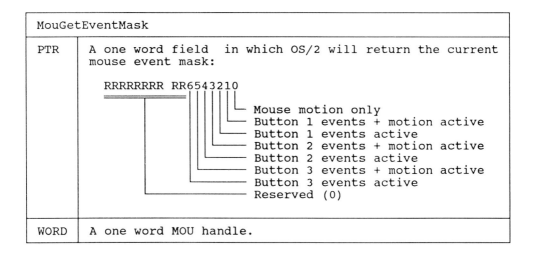
WORD	A one word MOU handle.

Description:

Retrieves the mouse event mask for the current session.

Notes:

1. The mouse event mask is associated with the session of the caller.

2. The mouse buttons are logically numbered from left to right.

MouGetNumButtons	
PTR	A pointer to a one word field in which OS/2 will return the number of buttons on the mouse.
WORD	A one word MOU handle.

Description:

Retrieves the number of buttons on the mouse.

Notes:

MouGetNumMickeys	
PTR	A pointer to a one word field in which OS/2 will return the number of Mickeys per centimeter.
WORD	A one word MOU handle.

Description:

Retrieves the number of mickeys per centimiter.

Notes:

1. The returned value is associated with the session of the caller.

MouGetNumQueEl	
PTR	A pointer to a double word field in which OS/2 will return a mouse event queue status data record: DW The current number of mouse queue elements DW The maximum mouse queue elements (configured)
WORD	A one word MOU handle.

Description:

Retrieves the mouse events queue element count.

Notes:

1. The mouse event queue is associated with the session of the caller.

2. The naximum size of the mouse event queue is determined when the mouse device driver is installed.

MouGetPtrPos	
PTR	A pointer to a double word field in which OS/2 will return the current mouse pointer coordinates: DW The pointer row coordinate DW The pointer column coordinate
WORD	A one word MOU handle.

Description:

Retrieves the current mouse pointer coordinates.

Notes:

1. The mouse coordinates are associated with the session of the caller.

MouGetPtrShape	
PTR	Pointer to a buffer in which OS/2 will return the pointer bit image.
PTR	A pointer to a field in which OS/2 will return the current pointer shape data record: DW Total length of the pointer buffer DW Pixel width of ptr shape (1 in text modes) DW Pixel height of ptr shape (1 in text modes) DW Col offset to tracking pointer (0 in text modes) DW Row offset to tracking pointer (0 in text modes)
WORD	A one word MOU handle.

Description:

Retrieves the current mouse pointer shape.

Notes:

1. The pointer shape is associated with the session of the caller.

2. The pointer shape may be set with the MouSetPtrShape function.

3. If the user pointer buffer is not large enough to contain the entire pointer image, the call will fail and the buffer size field is set to the size required to contain the pointer image.

MouGetScaleFact	
PTR	A pointer to a one word field in which OS/2 will return the mouse scaling factors: DW Row scale DW Column scale
WORD	A one word MOU handle.

Description:

Retrieves the mouse scale factor.

Notes:

1. The scale factors are associated with the session of the caller.

2. The units of the scale factors depend on the mode of the display in the session of the caller.

3. If the display is in text mode, the scale factors are relative to single character cells.

4. If the display is in graphics mode, the scale factors are relative to pixels.

MouOpen	
PTR	The address of an ASCIIZ name string corresponding to the pointer draw device name.
PTR	Address of a word field in which OS/2 will place the MOU handle

Description:

Opens the mouse device for the current session.

Notes:

1. The mouse handle is associated with the session of the caller.

2. The pointer draw device must correspond to a device driver which was installed with a DEVICE statement in the CONFIG.SYS file.

3. The returned handle must be used in subsequent MOU calls.

4. When the mouse device is opened, the mouse subsystem marks the entire display device as a mouse collision area. To begin displaying the mouse pointer, use the MouDrawPtr function call.

MouReadEventQue	
PTR	A pointer to a field in which OS/2 will return the mouse event record: 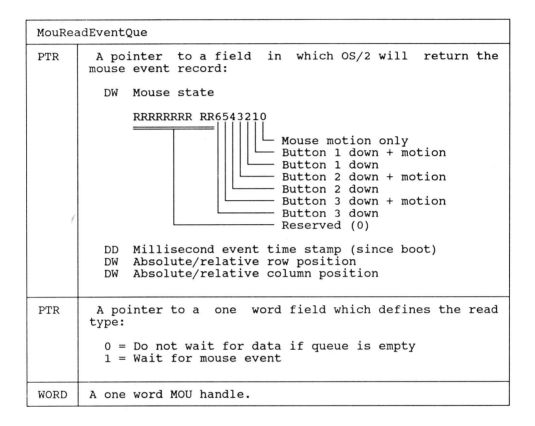
PTR	A pointer to a one word field which defines the read type: 0 = Do not wait for data if queue is empty 1 = Wait for mouse event
WORD	A one word MOU handle.

Description:

Read from the mouse event queue.

Notes:

1. The event queue is associated with the session of the caller.

2. What type of events are placed in the mouse event queue is determined by the current setting of the mouse event mask. The MouGetEventMask and MouSetEventMask API functions query and set the value of the mouse event mask, respectively.

3. To recognize mouse transitions, examine the mouse state word in the returned data element.

MouRegister	
PTR	Pointer to an ASCIIZ module name which contains the dynamic link replacement routine(s).
PTR	Pointer to an ASCIIZ entry point name within the dynamic link module which is to gain control when the MOU function(s) are called by an application program.
DWRD	A double-word function mask indicating which MOU functions are being replaced by this MouRegister call.

Description:

Register a replacement mouse subsystem for the current session.

Notes:

1. There can only be one active replacement subsystem per session. If you attempt to register a second subsystem while another process has an active replacement, then the MouRegister call will fail.

2. The mouse subsystem is released with the MouDeRegister call. MouDeRegister may be called by any thread in the process which called MouRegister.

MouRemovePtr	
PTR	A pointer to a data structure which defines an application-exclusive area of the screen: DW Upper left column DW Upper left row DW Lower right column DW Lower right row
WORD	A one word MOU handle.

Description:

Establishes the mouse collision area.

Notes:

1. A collision area is a portion of the screen which is exclusively reserved for application use. If the user drags the mouse into a collision area, the mouse subsystem hides the pointer.

2. The collision area is associated with the session of the caller.

3. Any process in the session may call MouRemovePtr to establish the mouse collision area. However, there can only be one collision area per session. Each time this function is called, it will 'reset' the collison area to the new coordinates.

4. The MouDrawPtr function cancels the MouRemovePtr function and allows the mouse pointer to appear anywhere on the screen.

MouSetDevStatus	
PTR	Pointer to a one word field which OS/2 will use to set the mouse device status word (see MouGetDevStatus for bit definitions).
WORD	A one word MOU handle

Description:

Change the mouse status word.

Notes:

1. The mouse status is associated with the session of the caller.

2. The relative/absolute reporting bit can be set to request the device driver to report the mouse position in relative (mickeys) rather than absolute screen coordinates.

3. The pointer draw bit can be set to disable the OS/2 pointer draw routine. Once disabled, the application assumes the responsibility of drawing its own pointer.

MouSetEventMask	
PTR	Pointer to a one word field which OS/2 will use to set the mouse event mask (see MouGetEventMask for bit definitions).
WORD	A one word MOU handle

Description:

Set the mouse event mask.

Notes:

1. The mouse event mask is associated with the session of the caller.

2. Setting a bit in the event mask means that the corresponding event will be reported through the mouse event queue. You can set more than one bit in the mask.

MouSetPtrPos	

PTR	A pointer to a double word field which defines the new mouse pointer coordinates:
	
	    DW The pointer row coordinate
	    DW The pointer column coordinate

WORD	A one word MOU handle.

Description:

Changes the current mouse pointer coordinates.

Notes:

1. The mouse coordinates are associated with the session of the caller.

2. You are responsible for insuring that the requested coordinates conform to the display mode of the session.

3. The coordinates are expressed in pixels when the display is in a graphics mode and in characters when the display is in a text mode.

4. If you place the pointer in the mouse collision area, the pointer will not be drawn until the user moves it out of the area, or you delete the collision area with MouDrawPtr.

MouSetPtrShape	
PTR	Pointer to a pointer shape buffer which contains the pixel configuration of a new mouse pointer shape.
PTR	Pointer to pointer shape data structure (see MouGetPtrShape for definition).
WORD	A one word MOU handle

Description:

Set the mouse pointer shape.

Notes:

1. The mouse pointer shape is associated with the session of the caller.

2. The OS/2 pointer draw routine only supports display modes 0-7.

3. In text modes, the pointer is an entire character cell.

MouSetScaleFact	

PTR	A pointer to a two word structure which contains the new mouse scaling factors:
	
	    DW Row scale
	    DW Column scale

WORD	A one word MOU handle.

Description:

Change the mouse scaling factor.

Notes:

1. The scaling factor is associated with the session of the caller.

2. This function sets the mickey to pixel ratio for mouse motion.

3. The row and column scale ratios specify the number of mickeys per eight pixels. The defaults are eight mickeys to eight pixels for the row and 16 mickeys to eight pixels for the column.

4. The scaling factor defines the sensitivity for the mouse. This sensitivity determines how fast the mouse moves on the screen (relative to the real mouse motion).

VioDeRegister

Description:

De-register the replacement video subsystem.

Notes:

1. Only the process which issued VioRegister (for the session) may call VioDeRegister.

2. Once the subsystem is released, any other process in the session can take over the video subsystem functions by issuing VioRegister.

VioEndPopUp	
WORD	The VIO handle (must be 0)

Description:

End an error pop-up operation.

Notes:

1. VioEndPopUp must be issued by a thread in the same process which called VioPopUp.

2. After this call, the process returns to the (foreground/background) state it was in before it issued VioPopUp.

3. On completion of the pop-up, OS/2 will honor any other (pending) VioPopUp requests.

VioGetANSI	
PTR	Pointer to a one word field in which OS/2 will return the current ANSI state: 0 = Off 1 = On
WORD	A one word VIO handle (0).

Description:

Query the current ANSI state.

Notes:

1. The ANSI state is maintained on a session per session basis. This call will return the ANSI state associated with the caller's session.

VioGetBuf	
PTR	Pointer to a double-word area into which OS/2 will place a far pointer to the logical video buffer (LVB).
PTR	Pointer to a one word field into which OS/2 will place the LVB size (in bytes).
WORD	A one word VIO handle (0).

Description:

Return the address of the session Logical Video Buffer (LVB).

Notes:

1. The LVB is maintained on a session per session basis. This call will return a pointer to the LVB associated with the caller's session.

2. After updating the LVB, you must issue VioShowBuf to reflect the changes to the physical display.

3. If the application is in the foreground session VioShowBuf will directly update the display.

4. If the application is in the background, then VioShowBuf does not affect the physical display. Instead, the LVB changes will appear when the user switches the session to the foreground.

5. Once you have issued VioGetBuf, all VIO character write calls (VioWrtxxxx) made while the session is in the foreground update both the LVB and the physical display.

6. VioGetBuf cannot be used when the display is in a graphics mode (see VioGetPhysBuf).

7. The LVB size is based on the physical screen geometry (rows, cols). Use VioGetMode to determine these values for your display session.

VioGetConfig	

PTR	Pointer to a configuration data area:
	
	DW Structure length (includes length field)
	DW Adaptor type
	     0 = Monochrome/printer
	     1 = CGA
	     2 = EGA
	     3 = VGA
	     7 = 8514A
	DW Display type
	     0 = Monochrome
	     1 = Color
	     2 = Enhanced color
	     3 = IBM PS/2 8503 (monochrome)
	     4 = IBM PS/2 8512/8513 (color)
	     9 = IBM PS/2 8514 (color)
	DD Adaptor memory size

WORD	A one word VIO handle (0).

Description:

Determine the video hardware configuration.

Notes:

1. The reported configuration is the best determination of the video subsystem. Note that certain conditions, such as a display adaptor with no attached display or invalid configuration switch settings, cannot be detected by software. In these situations, VioGetConfig will report the video configuration it assumes is present.

VioGetCP	
WORD	Reserved (must be 0).
PTR	Pointer to a one word field in which OS/2 will return the active video code page (see VioSetCP).
WORD	A one word VIO handle (must be 0).

Description:

Query the current video code page.

Notes:

1. The video code page is maintained on a session per session basis. This call will return the active code page in the caller's session.

2. The code page 000 indicates that the session is currently using the (default) ROM code page. This is the only value returned in systems with a display device that does not support downloaded fonts (such as CGA).

3. The code page number will always be one of the two code pages loaded by the CODEPAGE CONFIG.SYS statement (or 0).

VioGetCursorPos	
PTR	Pointer to a one word field in which OS/2 will return the current cursor row number.
PTR	Pointer to a one word field in which OS/2 will return the current cursor row.
WORD	A one word VIO handle (0).

Description:

Query the current cursor position.

Notes:

1. The cursor position is maintained on a session per session basis. This call will return the cursor position in the caller's session.

VioGetCurType	

PTR	Pointer to a cursor type data area:
	
	    DW Cursor start line
	    DW Cursor end line
	    DW Cursor width
	    DW Cursor attribute (-1=hidden)

WORD	The VIO handle (must be 0)

Description:

Query the cursor size.

Notes:

1. The cursor size is maintained on a session per session basis. This call will return the cursor size in the caller's session.

VioGetFont	

PTR	Pointer to a request block, in one of two formats:
	
	    Type 0 - Return RAM font (EGA, VGA)
	    Type 1 - Return ROM font (CGA, EGA, VGA)

WORD	A one word VIO handle (0).

Description:

Retrieve the active display font.

Notes:

1. The display font is maintained on a session per session basis. This call will retrieve the current display font in the caller's session.

2. If you use request type 1 (get ROM font), then the character cell size must be supported by the display adaptor (see Chapter 14).

3. If you use request type 1, then OS/2 will return a pointer to the ROM font.

VioGetMode	

PTR	A pointer to a video mode data structure:
	
	    DW Structure length (Including this field)
	    DB Mode characteristics
	         -------0 Monochrome/printer adaptor
	         -------1 Other adaptor
	         ------0- Text Mode
	         ------1- Graphics Mode
	         -----0-- Enable color burst
	         -----1-- Disable color burst (B/W)
	    DB Number of colors supported by display
	         1 = 2 colors
	         2 = 4 colors
	         4 = 16 colors
	    DW Number of text columns
	    DW Number of text rows
	    DW Horizontal Resolution (pels)
	    DW Vertical Resolution (pels)
	    DD Reserved
	
	Note: OS/2 returns only the data which will fit in the buffer. Minimum buffer length 3 bytes, maximum buffer length 12 bytes (fields cannot be split).

WORD	A one word VIO handle (0).

Description:

Query the current video mode.

Notes:

1. The video mode is maintained on a session per session basis. This call returns the video mode of the caller's session.

VioGetPhysBuf	

PTR	Pointer to a physical display buffer data structure:
	
	    DD Buffer start address (32-bit physical address)
	    DD Buffer length
	    DW (n) Selector list
	
	Note: you must allocate enough space in this structure
	to hold n selectors, where n=(display memory/64KB)+1.

WORD	A one word VIO handle (0).

Description:

Gain addressability to the physical display buffer.

Notes:

1. The selector(s) returned by this call are only valid when the session is in the foreground.

2. To write into the physical buffer, you must first lock the display with the VioScrLock API.

3. Before making this call, you must initialize the physical (32-bit) display address and buffer length fields. The display address must be in the range A0000H-BFFFFH.

4. The VioGetPhysBuf call will fail if it is not issued from the foreground session.

VioGetState	
PTR	Pointer to a video state data structure, in one of several formats: Type 0: Values of palette regs (EGA, VGA) Type 1: Border color (CGA, VGA) Type 2: Blink/bgnd intensity state (CGA, EGA, VGA)
WORD	A one word VIO handle (0).

Description:

Query the video state.

Notes:

1. The video state is maintained on a session per session basis. This call will return the video state of the caller's session.

VioModeUndo	
WORD	A one word ownership indicator: 0 = Process reserves ownership of ModeWait 1 = Process can give up ownership
WORD	A one word 'kill' indicator. 0 = Do not kill ModeWait thread 1 = Kill ModeWait thread
WORD	A one word VIO handle (0).

Description:

Undo a previous ModeWait thread

Notes:

1. The VioModeUndo function may only be issued by one of the threads in the process which currently owns the VioModeWait function.

VioModeWait	
WORD	A one word request type. Must be set to 0.
PTR	Pointer to a one word field in which OS/2 will place a type code. The only code supported in OS/2 1.0 is 0 (restore mode).
WORD	A one word VIO handle (0).

Description:

Establish a ModeWait thread.

Notes:

1. This function registers a VioModeWait thread for the caller's session.

2. VioModeWait returns to its caller whenever the session display mode needs to be reestablished. Normally this is after an application or a system hard error pop-up.

3. The VioModeWait function is used by application programs which set the display device in an application-specific state by directly writing to the display hardware I/O ports. Otherwise, the OS/2 video subsystem will automatically restore the physical display buffer, video state and mode at the end of the pop-up.

4. There may be only one active VioModeWait thread per session.

5. The VioModeWait thread must reset the video mode and registers and immediately re-issue the VioModeWait call.

6. Warning: the VioModeWait function should never do anything which might result in a hard error. This is because, on return from a hard error pop-up, the VioModeWait code (which generated the hard error to begin with) will be called to restore the video mode. In general, you should make no dynamic link calls in the VioModeWait routine.

VioPopUp	

PTR	Pointer to a one word option flags field:
	
	RRRRRRRR RRRRRRXW
	
	R = Reserved
	
	X = Transparency indicator
	    0 - Non-transparent
	    1 - Transparent (text modes only)
	
	W = Wait flag
	    0 - return with error if popup n/a
	    1 - wait for popup

WORD	The VIO handle (must be 0)

Description:

Temporarily request the foreground session.

Notes:

1. An application must wait until VioPopUp completes before writing information to the display. If it does not wait, the output might instead be directed to the normal application LVB.

2. When a program 'holds' a VioPopUp, it receives the input focus for the mouse and keyboard.

3. During the pop-up, the application may only write to the screen using the VIO character write functions (VioWrtxxxx).

4. There may only be one VioPopUp at a time. If two threads issue VioPopUp simultaneously, only one of the requests will be honored. The other request will return with an error or block, depending on the VioPopUp options it set.

5. You may not call DosExecPgm nor any session management API functions during a pop-up.

6. While the pop-up is active, all threads in other sessions will continue to run.

7. The pop-up gives temporary foreground status to all the threads in the process which issued VioPopUp. Other processes in the session will continue to run, but they will block if they issue any VIO call.

8. The session manager does not allow the user to switch to a different session until the pop-up ends.

9. The pop-up ends when you issue the VioEndPopUp call.

VioReadCellStr	
PTR	Pointer to a buffer into which OS/2 will place the cell string.
PTR	Pointer to a one word field which on entry tells OS/2 the length of the cell buffer (in bytes), and on return, contains the number of bytes actually read. Note: each cell is 2 bytes, so the number of cells read is equal to one half of this buffer length.
WORD	A one word value indicating the row where the read is to start.
WORD	A one word value indicating the column where the read is to start.
WORD	A one word VIO handle (0).

Description:

Read a display cell string.

Notes:

1. The data is read from the caller's LVB.

2. If the read goes beyond the end of a line, the read continues at the start of the next line.

3. If the read goes beyond the end of a screen, the read ends and the buffer length is set to the number of bytes transferred.

4. This is a cell read, so the number of bytes transferred is 2x the number of screen character positions which were read.

VioReadCharStr	
PTR	Pointer to a buffer into which OS/2 will place the character string.
PTR	Pointer to a one word field which on entry tells OS/2 how many characters are to be read, and on return, contains the number of characters actually read.
WORD	A one word value indicating the row where the read is to start.
WORD	A one word value indicating the column where the read is to start.
WORD	A one word VIO handle (0).

Description:

Read a display character string.

Notes:

1. The data is read from the caller's LVB.

2. If the read goes beyond the end of a line, the read continues at the start of the next line.

3. If the read goes beyond the end of a screen, the read ends and the buffer length is set to the number of bytes transferred.

VioRegister	
PTR	Pointer to an ASCIIZ module name which contains the dynamic link replacement routine(s).
PTR	Pointer to an ASCIIZ entry point name within the dynamic link module which is to gain control when the VIO function(s) are called by an application program.
DWRD	A double-word function mask indicating which VIO functions are being replaced by this VioRegister call (1 of 2).
DWRD	A double-word function mask indicating which VIO functions are being replaced by this VioRegister call (2 of 2).

Description:

Register a replacement video subsystem for the current session.

Notes:

1. There can only be one active replacement subsystem per session. If you attempt to register a second subsystem while another process has an active replacement, then the VioRegister call will fail.

2. The video subsystem is released with the VioDeRegister call. VioDeRegister may be called by any thread in the process which called VioRegister.

VioSaveRedrawUndo	
WORD	A one word SavRedrawWait ownership indicator: 0 = Process reserves ownership 1 = Process can give up ownership
WORD	A one word 'kill' indicator: 0 = Do not kill SaveRedrawWait thread 1 = Kill SaveRedrawWait thread
WORD	A one word VIO handle (0).

Description:

Undo a previous SavRedrawWait thread

Notes:

1. The VioSavRedrawUndo function may only be issued by one of the threads in the process which currently owns the VioSavRedrawWait function.

VioSaveRedrawWait	
WORD	A one word request type: 0 = Notify on save or redraw 1 = Notify on redraw only
PTR	Pointer to a one word field in which OS/2 will place a notification type code: 0 = save the screen image 1 = restore the screen image
WORD	A one word VIO handle (0).

Description:

Establish a SavRedrawWait thread.

Notes:

1. This function registers a VioSavRedrawWait thread for the caller's session.

2. VioSavRedrawWait returns to its caller whenever the physical display buffer needs to be saved or restored. Normally this is before or after a session switch.

3. The VioSavRedrawWait function is used by application programs that write directly to the physical display buffer (see VioGetPhysBuf). Otherwise, the OS/2 video subsystem will automatically save and restore the physical display buffer before and after session switches.

4. There may be only one active VioSavRedrawWait thread per session.

5. The VioSavRedrawWait thread must save/restore the physical buffer and immediately re-issue the VioSavRedrawWait call.

6. The physical display selectors (aquired using VioGetPhysBuf) are valid when the SavRedrawWait thread is started. This thread does not need to lock/unlock the display while it saves or restores its contents.

7. As with ModeWait, the SavRedrawWait thread should do the minimum work required. An error in this routine could cause a recursive system hang condition.

VioScrLock	

WORD	A one word wait flag:
	
	    0 = Return if screen is not available (NOWAIT)
	    1 = Wait until screen is available

PTR	Pointer to a one word field in which OS/2 will place the lock success code (if NOWAIT option is used):
	
	    0 = Lock successful
	    1 = Lock unsuccessful

WORD	A one word VIO handle (0).

Description:

Serialize access to the physical screen.

Notes:

1. The VioScrLock function is used by application programs that write directly to the physical display buffer (see VioGetPhysBuf). This API is used to request (exclusive) access to the display.

2. OS/2 will insure that the session manager does not preempt the display while an application is holding the screen lock.

3. If a user requests a screen switch while an application is holding a screen lock, and the screen is not voluntarily relinquished in a specified period of time, then OS/2 will freeze the application which holds the lock and place it in the background.

4. If a program issues the VioScrLock call while it is in a background session, then VioScrLock will either return an error or block until the session returns to the foreground (depending on the wait flag).

5. The same thread which issues VioScrLock must issue VioScrUnLock.

VioScrollDn	
WORD	A one word value defining the top row of the scroll area.
WORD	A one word value defining the left column of the scroll area.
WORD	A one word value defining the bottom row of the scroll area.
WORD	A one word value defining the right column of the scroll area.
WORD	A one word value defining the number of rows which OS/2 is to scroll. Note: -1 causes OS/2 to 'clear' the area.
PTR	A pointer to a two byte cell (attr,char) which OS/2 will use to fill the scrolled area.
WORD	The VIO handle (must be 0)

Description:

Scroll a portion of the screen (down).

Notes:

1. The display is updated if the caller's session is in the foreground. If the session is in the background, then the caller's LVB is updated.

2. If you enter a value greater than the maximum for any of the coordinates or the line count, then OS/2 will use the maximum value for that parameter.

3. If the scroll value is 65535 (-1), then the entire window is filled with the specified cell.

VioScrollLe	
WORD	A one word value defining the top row of the scroll area.
WORD	A one word value defining the left column of the scroll area.
WORD	A one word value defining the bottom row of the scroll area.
WORD	A one word value defining the right column of the scroll area.
WORD	A one word value defining the number of columns which OS/2 is to scroll. Note: -1 causes OS/2 to 'clear' the area.
PTR	A pointer to a two byte cell (attr,char) which OS/2 will use to fill the scrolled area.
WORD	The VIO handle (must be 0)

Description:

Scroll a portion of the screen (left).

Notes:

1. The display is updated if the caller's session is in the foreground. If the session is in the background, then the caller's LVB is updated.

2. If you enter a value greater than the maximum for any of the coordinates or the line count, then OS/2 will use the maximum value for that parameter.

3. If the scroll value is 65535 (-1), then the entire window is filled with the specified cell.

VioScrollRi	
WORD	A one word value defining the top row of the scroll area.
WORD	A one word value defining the left column of the scroll area.
WORD	A one word value defining the bottom row of the scroll area.
WORD	A one word value defining the right column of the scroll area.
WORD	A one word value defining the number of columns which OS/2 is to scroll. Note: -1 causes OS/2 to 'clear' the area.
PTR	A pointer to a two byte cell (attr,char) which OS/2 will use to fill the scrolled area.
WORD	The VIO handle (must be 0)

Description:

Scroll a portion of the screen (right).

Notes:

1. The display is updated if the caller's session is in the foreground. If the session is in the background, then the caller's LVB is updated.

2. If you enter a value greater than the maximum for any of the coordinates or the line count, then OS/2 will use the maximum value for that parameter.

3. If the scroll value is 65535 (-1), then the entire window is filled with the specified cell.

VioScrollUp	
WORD	A one word value defining the top row of the scroll area.
WORD	A one word value defining the left column of the scroll area.
WORD	A one word value defining the bottom row of the scroll area.
WORD	A one word value defining the right column of the scroll area.
WORD	A one word value defining the number of rows which OS/2 is to scroll. Note: -1 causes OS/2 to 'clear' the area.
PTR	A pointer to a two byte cell (attr,char) which OS/2 will use to fill the scrolled area.
WORD	The VIO handle (must be 0)

Description:

Scroll a portion of the screen (up).

Notes:

1. The display is updated if the caller's session is in the foreground. If the session is in the background, then the caller's LVB is updated.

2. If you enter a value greater than the maximum for any of the coordinates or the line count, then OS/2 will use the maximum value for that parameter.

3. If the scroll value is 65535 (-1), then the entire window is filled with the specified cell.

VioScrUnLock	
WORD	A one word VIO handle (0).

Description:

Release the physical screen lock.

Notes:

1. The VioUnScrLock function is used by application programs that write directly to the physical display buffer (see VioGetPhysBuf). This API is used to release the exclusive access to the display.

2. The same thread which issued VioScrLock must issue VioScrUnLock.

VioSetANSI	
PTR	A one word value word value indicating how ANSI processing is to be set: state: 0 = Off 1 = On
WORD	A one word VIO handle (0).

Description:

Set the ANSI state.

Notes:

1. The ANSI state is maintained on a session per session basis. This call sets the ANSI state of the caller's session.

VioSetCP	
WORD	Reserved (must be 0).
WORD	A one word code page number which OS/2 will set as the active video code page: 000 Resident code page 437 IBM PC US 850 Multi-lingual 860 Portugese 863 French-Canadian 865 Nordic Note: the selected value must have been configured using the CONFIG.SYS CODEPAGE= statement.
WORD	A one word VIO handle (must be 0).

Description:

Set the video code page.

Notes:

1. The video code page is maintained on a session per session basis. This call will change the active code page in the caller's session.

2. Code page 000 indicates that the session is should use the (default) ROM code page. This is the only value that can be set in systems with a display device that does not support downloaded fonts (such as CGA).

3. The code page number must be one of the two code pages loaded by the CODEPAGE CONFIG.SYS statement (or 0).

VioSetCursorPos	
WORD	Cursor row number.
PTR	Cursor column number.
WORD	A one word VIO handle (0).

Description:

Set the cursor position.

Notes:

1. The cursor position is maintained on a session per session basis. This call will change the cursor position in the caller's session.

VioSetCurType	
PTR	Pointer to a cursor type data area: DW Cursor start line DW Cursor end line DW Cursor width DW Cursor attribute (-1=hidden)
WORD	The VIO handle (must be 0)

Description:

Set the cursor size.

Notes:

1. The cursor size is maintained on a session per session basis. This call will change the cursor size in the caller's session.

VioSetFont	
PTR	Pointer to a request block containing the information OS/2 needs to set the display font.
WORD	A one word VIO handle (0).

Description:

Set the display font.

Notes:

1. The display font is maintained on a session per session basis. This call will change the current display font in the caller's session.

2. When you change the display font, the current code page information is reset.

3. VioSetFont may only be used in conjunction with an EGA, VGA or 8514A display adaptor.

VioSetMode	
PTR	A pointer to a video mode data structure (see VioGetMode). Note: You can specify a partial video mode buffer. Minimum buffer length 3 bytes, maximum buffer length 12 bytes (fields cannot be split). The remaining fields are set to default values.
WORD	A one word VIO handle (0).

Description:

Set the video mode.

Notes:

1. The video mode is maintained on a session per session basis. This call changes the video mode of the caller's session.

2. VioSetMode always re-initializes the cursor position and size to their default values.

3. The 'disable color burst' bit in the mode data structure is only valid on a CGA display adaptor.

VioSetState	
PTR	Pointer to a video state data structure, in one of several formats: Type 0: Values of palette regs (EGA, VGA) Type 1: Border color (CGA, VGA) Type 2: Blink/bgnd intensity state (CGA, EGA, VGA)
WORD	A one word VIO handle (0).

Description:

Set the video state.

Notes:

1. The video state is maintained on a session per session basis. This call will change the video state of the caller's session.

VioShowBuf	
WORD	Offset into the LVB where OS/2 is to begin refreshing the physical screen.
WORD	Length of the refreshed area.
WORD	A one word VIO handle (0).

Description:

Refresh the physical display with a portion of the LVB.

Notes:

1. VioShowBuf will fail if the caller's session is set to a graphics display mode.

2. VioShowBuf is ignored unless the session is running in the foreground and at least one process in the session has gained addressability to the LVB (using VioGetBuf).

VioWrtCellStr	
PTR	A pointer to the cell (attr,char) string which OS/2 will write on the screen.
WORD	A one word value containing the character string length.
WORD	A one word value defining the row where the string is to be written.
WORD	A one word value defining the column where the string is to be written.
WORD	The VIO handle (must be 0)

Description:

Write a cell string.

Notes:

1. The data is written to the display if the caller's session is in the foreground or into the LVB if the session is in the background.

2. If the write goes beyond the end of a line, it continues at the start of the next line.

3. The write terminates at the end of the screen.

VioWrtCharStr	
PTR	A pointer to the character string which OS/2 will write on the screen.
WORD	A one word value containing the character string length.
WORD	A one word value defining the row where the string is to be written.
WORD	A one word value defining the column where the string is to be written.
WORD	The VIO handle (must be 0)

Description:

Write a character string (leave existing attributes).

Notes:

1. The data is written to the display if the caller's session is in the foreground or into the LVB if the session is in the background.

2. If the write goes beyond the end of a line, it continues at the start of the next line.

3. The write terminates at the end of the screen.

VioWrtCharStrAtt	
PTR	A pointer to the character string which OS/2 will write on the screen.
WORD	A one word value containing the character string length.
WORD	A one word value defining the row where the string is to be written.
WORD	A one word value defining the column where the string is to be written.
PTR	A pointer to a one byte display attribute which OS/2 will associate with each character in the string.
WORD	The VIO handle (must be 0)

Description:

Write a character string with a constant attribute.

Notes:

1. The data is written to the display if the caller's session is in the foreground or into the LVB if the session is in the background.

2. If the write goes beyond the end of a line, it continues at the start of the next line.

3. The write terminates at the end of the screen.

VioWrtNAttr	
PTR	A pointer to a display attribute which OS/2 will replicate on the screen.
WORD	A one word value containing the replication count.
WORD	A one word value defining the row where the attribute(s) are to be written.
WORD	A one word value defining the column where the attribute(s) are to be written.
WORD	The VIO handle (must be 0)

Description:

Replicate an attribute byte (leave characters unchanged).

Notes:

1. The data is written to the display if the caller's session is in the foreground or into the LVB if the session is in the background.

2. If the write goes beyond the end of a line, it continues at the start of the next line.

3. The write terminates at the end of the screen.

VioWrtNCell	
PTR	A pointer to a cell (attr,char) which OS/2 will replicate on the screen.
WORD	A one word value containing the replication count.
WORD	A one word value defining the row where the cell(s) are to be written.
WORD	A one word value defining the column where the cell(s) are to be written.
WORD	The VIO handle (must be 0)

Description:

Replicate a cell.

Notes:

1. The data is written to the display if the caller's session is in the foreground or into the LVB if the session is in the background.

2. If the write goes beyond the end of a line, it continues at the start of the next line.

3. The write terminates at the end of the screen.

VioWrtNChar	
PTR	A pointer to a character which OS/2 will replicate on the screen.
WORD	A one word value containing the replication count.
WORD	A one word value defining the row where the character(s) are to be written.
WORD	A one word value defining the column where the character(s) are to be written.
WORD	The VIO handle (must be 0)

Description:

Replicate a character (leave attributes unchanged).

Notes:

1. The data is written to the display if the caller's session is in the foreground or into the LVB if the session is in the background.

2. If the write goes beyond the end of a line, it continues at the start of the next line.

3. The write terminates at the end of the screen.

VioWrtTTY	
PTR	A pointer to a character string which OS/2 will write on the screen.
WORD	A one word value containing the string length.
WORD	The VIO handle (must be 0)

Description:

Write a cell string.

Notes:

1. The data is written to the display if the caller's session is in the foreground or into the LVB if the session is in the background.

2. If the write goes beyond the end of a line, it continues at the start of the next line.

3. The write terminates at the end of the screen.

4. The special TTY characters (CR, LF, BACKSPACE, TAB, BELL) are treated as display commands rather than data. Tabs are expanded to eight byte tab stops.

5. ANSI escape sequences are supported.

Appendix B:
The Family API

FAPI Call	Restriction(s)
DosAllocHuge	1) Allocation size: The value will be rounded up to the next paragraph size. The memory request is satisfied out of (and is constrained by) the PC DOS 640K address space. 2) Selector: A real mode segment address is returned (instead of a selector).
DosAllocSeg	1) Allocation size: The value will be rounded up to the next paragraph size. The memory request is satisfied out of (and is constrained by) the PC DOS 640K address space. 2) Selector: A real mode segment address is returned (instead of a selector). 3) Share indicator: If this field is set to 1 (shared segment), then the call will fail with an 'invalid function' error.
DosBeep	No restrictions
DosBufReset	No restrictions
DosCaseMap	1) Assumes that the COUNTRY.SYS file is in the root directory of the current drive.
DosChDir	No restrictions
DosChgFilePtr	No restrictions
DosClose	No restrictions
DosCreateCSAlias	1) Selector: A real mode segment address is returned (instead of a selector). 2) If you free the aliased segment, then the memory is released. This is different than protected mode where both the original and the alias selectors must be freed before the memory is released.
DosDelete	No restrictions
DosDevConfig	No restrictions

FAPI Call	Restriction(s)

DosDevIOCTL	1) The function call can be used to send an IOCTL packet to a device driver subject to the following restrictions:
	
	Category 1: The following are supported
	  41H (Set Baud rate)
	  42H (Set line control)
	
	Category 2: Not supported
	
	Category 3: Not supported
	
	Category 4: Not supported
	
	Category 5: The following are supported
	  42H (Set frame control)
	  44H (Set infinite retry)
	  46H (Initialize printer)
	  62H (Get frame control)
	  64H (Get infinite retry)
	  66H (Get printer status)
	
	Category 6: Not supported
	
	Category 7: Not supported
	
	Category 8: The following are supported
	  00H (Lock drive) DOS 3.2 Rqd
	  01H (Unlock drive) DOS 3.2 Rqd
	  02H (Redetermine media) DOS 3.2 Rqd
	  03H (Set logical map) DOS 3.2 Rqd
	  20H (Block removeable media) DOS 3.2 Rqd
	  21H (Get logical map) DOS 3.2 Rqd
	
	Category 9: Not supported
	
	Category A: Not supported
	
	Category B: Not supported

DosDupHandle	No restrictions
DosErrClass	No restrictions

FAPI Call	Restriction(s)
DosError	1) Action flags: Setting this flag to zero causes all subsequent INT 24h functions to be 'failed'. This allows the program handle hard errors in inline code. Setting this flag to '1', allows the (previous) INT 24h handler to process the hard errors. 2) This function has no effect in the OS/2 DOS environment, because the system does not generate INT 24H events.
DosExecPgm	1) Option Flags: Only the synchronous (0) EXEC function is supported. 2) Object Buffer: Always filled with blanks. 3) Termination Codes: Supported in the same two word format. The first word contains one of the following: 0 = Normal exit (INT 21H AH=31H) 1 = Hard error abort 3 = Ctrl-Break termination The second word contains the value passed to DosExit (or INT 21H AH=4CH)
DosExit	1) Action Code: Ignored
DosFileLocks	No restrictions
DosFindClose	1) The directory search handle must be 1. 2) If you call this function, then the next DosFindNext call will always fail (unless you start the search over by calling DosFindFirst).
DosFindFirst	1) Search handle: This parameter must be set to either 1 or 0ffffh the first time that DosFindFirst is called. 2) Subsequent calls to DosFindFirst must only use the search handle 1, unless the first search is ended with a call to DosFindClose (then 1 or 0ffffh could once again be used). Note: This means that the FAPI version of the directory search functions do not support multiple, concurrent directory searches.

FAPI Call	Restriction(s)
DosFindNext	1) Search handle: This parameter must always be 1 (see DosFindFirst).
DosFreeSeg	1) If you free a segment which you previously aliased with DosCSAlias. then the memory is released. This is different than protected mode where both the original and the alias selectors must be freed before the memory is released.
DosGetCollate	1) Assumes that the COUNTRY.SYS file is in the root directory of the current drive.
DosGetCtryInfo	1) Assumes that the COUNTRY.SYS file is in the root directory of the current drive.
DosGetDBCSEV	1) Assumes that the COUNTRY.SYS file is in the root directory of the current drive.
DosGetDateTime	No restrictions
DosGetEnv	No restrictions
DosGetHugeShift	No restrictions
DosGetMachineMode	No restrictions
DosGetMessage	1) Assumes that the message file is in the root directory of the current drive.
DosGetVersion	No restrictions
DosHoldSignal	1) The only signals which may be turned off in the PC DOS environment are SIGINTR (Ctrl-C) and SIGBREAK (Ctrl-Break). 2) The SIGHDERR signal is also generated, but it must be handled by the hard error handler.
DosIOAccess	No restrictions
DosInsMessage	1) Assumes that the message file is in the root directory of the current drive.

FAPI Call	Restriction(s)
DosMkDir	No restrictions
DosMove	No restrictions
DosNewSize	No restrictions
DosOpen	1) If you call DosOpen with the 'DASD bit' (in open mode) set, then the returned handle can only be used with the DosDevIOCTL call. DosRead/DosWrite of a disk volume is not supported. 2) The open mode inheritance bit is not supported when the FAPI program runs in a PC DOS 2.X system. 3) The open mode 'write through' flag must be set to zero. 4) The open mode 'fail errors' flag must be set to zero. All PC DOS hard errors are processed by the hard error handler. 5) The open mode 'sharing mode' options are valid if the FAPI program is run in a PC DOS 3.X system with SHARE loaded. Otherwise, this parameter is ignored. 6) The open mode 'access' options are valid if the FAPI program is run in a PC DOS 3.X system with SHARE loaded. Otherwise, this parameter is ignored. 7) The file access mode is only valid if the FAPI program is run in a PC DOS 3.X system with SHARE loaded. Otherwise, this parameter is ignored.
DosPutMessage	1) Assumes that the message file is in the root directory of the current drive.
DosQCurDir	No restrictions
DosQCurDisk	No restrictions
DosQFHandState	No restrictions

FAPI Call	Restriction(s)
DosQFSInfo	No restrictions
DosQFileInfo	No restrictions
DosQFileMode	No restrictions
DosQVerify	No restrictions
DosReAllocHuge	1) Allocation size: The value will be rounded up to the next paragraph size. The memory request is satisfied out of (and is constrained by) the PC DOS 640K address space.
DosReAllocSeg	1) Allocation size: The value will be rounded up to the next paragraph size. The memory request is satisfied out of (and is constrained by) the PC DOS 640K address space.
DosRead	1) If you call DosRead to read data from the 'CON:' device (or STDIO 1), then the read is ultimately processed by the KbdStringIn function. However, FAPI does not buffer this call (it used the user buffer passed to DosRead), so its operational characteristics are a little different than in protected mode: - In protected mode, the user can enter many more characters than the program allowed for in the input buffer. The extra characters are held in the system and can be retrieved by subsequent DosRead calls. - In real mode, the user can only enter as many characters as the program has allowed for in the input buffer. If more are entered, the system will beep and the extra characters are discarded.
DosRmDir	No restrictions
DosSelectDisk	No restrictions
DosSetCtryCode	1) The country data code table does not support YES_INPUT and NO_INPUT values.

FAPI Call	Restriction(s)
DosSetDateTime	No restrictions
DosSetFHandState	1) File handle: this value is not checked to insure that it is a valid (open) file handle.
	2) The handle 'inheritance' bit is not supported when the FAPI program runs in a PC DOS 2.X system.
	3) The handle 'write through' flag must be set to zero.
	4) The handle 'fail errors' flag must be set to zero. All PC DOS hard errors are processed by the hard error handler.
DosSetFSInfo	No restrictions
DosSetFileInfo	No restrictions
DosSetFileMode	No restrictions
DosSetSigHandler	1) Action: All action codes are supported except for 3. If you specify 3, then the call will fail with an 'invalid signal number' error.
	2) Signal Number: Only SIGBREAK (Ctrl-Break) and SIGINTR (Ctrl-C) may be coded. Any other signal number will cause the call to fail with an 'invalid signal number' error.
	3) If you specify SIGINTR, then SIGINTR and SIGBREAK are transferred to the SIGINTR handler. If you specify SIGBREAK, then the request is ignored. Thus, to insure compatability in both OS/2 and PC DOS, you should always register SIGINTR and be prepared to handle both.
DosSetVec	1) Vector number 7 (NPX) is not supported. The NPX does not raise this interrupt in 8086/8088 machines.
DosSetVerify	No restrictions

FAPI Call	Restriction(s)
DosSleep	No restrictions
DosSubAlloc	No restrictions
DosSubFree	No restrictions
DosSubSet	No restrictions
DosWrite	No restrictions
KbdCharIn	1) The millisecond time stamp in the returned character data structure is set to 0. 2) The API does not provide interim character support. 3) The keyboard handle is ignored.
KbdFlushBuffer	1) The keyboard handle is ignored.
KbdGetStatus	1) The turnaround character is not supported. 2) There is no interim character support. 3) The NLS shift state will always be null. 4) The keyboard handle is ignored.
KbdPeek	1) The millisecond time stamp in the returned character data structure is set to 0. 2) The keyboard status field can be 0 or 1. 3) The API does not provide interim character support. 4) The keyboard handle is ignored.
KbdSetStatus	1) The turnaround character is not supported. 2) There is no interim character support. 3) You cannot set a BINARY input mode with ECHO on. If you attempt to do so, the call will fail. 4) The keyboard handle is ignored.

FAPI Call	Restriction(s)
KbdStringIn	1) The keyboard handle is ignored.
VioGetBuf	No restrictions
VioGetCurPos	No restrictions
VioGetCurType	No restrictions
VioGetMode	No restrictions
VioGetPhysBuf	No restrictions
VioReadCellStr	No restrictions
VioReadCharStr	No restrictions
VioScrLock	1) The lock will always succeed.
VioScrUnLock	No restrictions
VioScrollDn	No restrictions
VioScrollLe	No restrictions
VioScrollRi	No restrictions
VioScrollUp	No restrictions
VioSetCurPos	No restrictions
VioSetCurType	No restrictions
VioSetMode	No restrictions
VioShowBuf	No restrictions
VioWrtCellStr	No restrictions
VioWrtCharStr	No restrictions
VioWrtCharStrAtt	No restrictions
VioWrtNAttr	No restrictions
VioWrtNCell	No restrictions
VioWrtNChar	No restrictions
VioWrtTTY	No restrictions

FAPI Call	Restriction(s)
BadDynLink	1) This function is internally generated by the BIND utility to resolve OS/2 API calls which are not included in FAMAPI. 2) A FAMAPI application could be built to conditionally execute some application code in real mode and different code in protected mode (see DosGetMachMode). 3) If called in real mode, this function will terminate the application with an 'Invalid function' completion code.

Appendix C:
OS/2 Error Codes

Num	Description
1	Invalid function code
2	File not found
3	Path not found
4	Too many open files
5	Access denied
6	Invalid handle
7	Arena (memory data structure) was corrupted
8	Not enough memory
9	Bad block
10	Bad environment
11	Bad format
12	Invalid access
13	Invalid data
15	Invalid drive
16	Error in the current directory
17	Not the same device
18	No more files
19	Write protection error
20	Bad unit number
21	Drive not ready
22	Bad command
23	CRC error
24	Bad length
25	Seek error
26	Not an OS/2 (or DOS) disk
27	Sector was not found
28	Out of paper
29	Write fault
30	Read Fault
31	General Failure
32	Sharing Violation
33	File lock violation
34	Wrong disk
35	FCB is unavailable
36	Sharing buffer was exceeded
50	Not supported
65	Network access was denied
80	File already exists
81	Duplicate FCB encountered
82	Cannot make
83	INT 24H fail action
84	Out of data structures (internal error)
85	Already assigned
86	Invalid password
87	Invalid parameter
88	Network write error
89	No process slots available
90	Process is not frozen
91	Timer service table overflow
92	Timer service table duplicate
93	No items to work on

Num	Description
95	Interrupted system call
100	Open semaphore limit has been exceeded
101	Exclusive system semaphore is already owned
102	SemClose found that the semaphore was already set
103	Too many outstanding requests for an exclusive system semaphore
104	Operation is invalid at interrupt time
105	Semaphore owner died (while holding system semaphore)
106	Total semaphore limit has been exceeded
107	Disk A needs to be changed (single diskette system)
108	The drive cannot be accessed, it is locked by another process
109	The process reading the pipe had died (broken pipe)
110	The open/create function failed due to an explicit fail command
111	The buffer passed to the system call is too small
112	There is not enough space on the disk
113	Search handle limit has been exceeded
114	The target handle (in DosDupHandle) is invalid
115	Invalid memory address passed by user
116	Internal VIO failure
117	The requested IOCTL category is undefined
118	Invalid value for verify switch
119	Invalid driver level
120	Internal error
121	Time out occurred while waiting for a semaphore
122	The data buffer is too small
123	Invalid character or file name format
124	Invalid request packet level
125	No volume label found on specified disk
126	Specified module was not found
127	Specified entry point (proc) was not found
128	No child process(es)
129	No child process(es) have died (DosCWait)
130	The requested handle operation is invalid for a disk
131	The requested file pointer resulted in a negative file offset
132	Cannot use DosChgFilePtr with a device or pipe handle
133	Invalid operation for joined disk
134	The disk is joined
135	The directory is substituted
136	The disk is not joined
137	The directory is not substituted
138	Cannot join a joined disk
139	Cannot substitute a substituted directory
140	Cannot join to a substituted directory
141	Cannot substitute a joined disk
142	The specified drive is busy
143	The same drive was specified
144	The requested operation requires the root directory
145	The directory is not empty
146	Substituted directory path error
147	Joined drive path error
148	Path is busy
149	Cannot use substituted directory as target

Num	Description
150	System trace error
151	An error was encountered in the DosMuxSemWait count field
152	DosMuxSemWait limit has been exceeded
153	Invalid list format
154	The specified volume label is too long
155	Cannot create another thread control block
156	The signal was refused
157	The segment was discarded
158	The segment was not locked
159	Bad thread ID address (internal error)
160	Invalid environment pointer
161	Invalid path name
162	A signal is already pending
163	Uncertain disk media detected
164	Maximum thread count exceeded
165	Monitors are not supported
180	Invalid segment number (internal error)
181	Invalid call gate (internal error)
182	Invalid ordinal (internal error/EXE file error)
183	Shared segment already exists
184	There are no child processes to wait for
185	There is a live child, but NoWait was specified
186	Invalid flag number
187	The system semaphore does not exist
188	Invalid starting code segment (EXE file error)
189	Invalid stack segment (EXE file error)
190	Invalid module type (EXE file error)
191	Invalid EXE file signature (EXE file error)
192	The EXE file is marked invalid (EXE file error)
193	Invalid EXE format (EXE file error)
194	Iterated data exceeds 64K (EXE file error)
195	Invalid minimum allocation size (EXE file error)
196	Dynamic link from invalid ring (EXE file error)
197	IOPL is not enabled
198	Segment DPL is not 3 (EXE file error)
199	Automatic data segment > 64K (EXE file error)
200	Ring 2 segment must be moveable (EXE file error)
201	Relocation chain exceeds limit (EXE file error)
202	Infinite loop in relocation chain (EXE file error)
203	Environment variable was not found
204	Not current country
205	No signal was sent
206	File name exceeded range
207	Ring 2 stack is in use
208	Meta expansion is too long
209	Invalid signal number
303	Invalid process ID
304	Invalid priority delta
305	The target process is not a descendant
306	The requestor is not the session manager
307	Invalid priority class

Num	Description
308	Invalid scope
309	Invalid thread ID
310	Cannot shrink a suballocated segment
311	Out of room in the suballocated segment
312	Invalid element overlap in DosSubFree
313	Bad element size parameter
314	Bad flag parameter
315	Invalid segment selector
316	Message is too long for buffer
317	The requested message ID cannot be found
318	Unable to access the requested message file
319	The message file format is invalid
320	Invalid insertion variable count
321	Unable to perform function (DosGetMsg)
322	Unable to wake up
323	Invalid system semaphore
324	No timers available
326	Invalid timer handle
327	Date or time is invalid
328	Internal system error
329	Current queue name does not exist
330	The current process does not own queue
331	The current process owns the queue
332	The specified queue name already exists
333	The specified element does not exist
334	Insufficient memory
335	The specified queue name is invalid
336	Invalid queue element priority value
337	Invalid queue handle
338	Queue link not found (internal error)
339	Queue memory error (internal error)
340	The previous element was at the end of the queue
341	The process does not have access to the queue
342	The queue is empty
343	The specified queue name does not exist
344	The queue is not initialized
345	Unable to access queue
346	Unable to add new queue (internal error)
347	Unable to initialize queue (internal error)
349	Invalid VIO function mask
350	Invalid pointer to parameter area
355	Unsupported display mode
356	Invalid cursor width value
358	Invalid row value
359	Invalid column value
366	Invalid wait flag setting
367	The screen was not previously locked
369	Invalid session ID
370	Session limit has been reached
371	the requested session was not found
372	The title cannot be changed

Num	Description
373	Invalid parameter to KBD call
375	Invalid I/O wait flag value
376	Invalid length
377	Invalid echo mask
378	Invalid input mode mask
379	Invalid parameters to DosMonxxxx
380	Invalid device name string
381	Invalid device handle
382	The supplied buffer is too small
383	Buffer is empty
384	The data is too large
386	The mouse device is closed - the handle is invalid
389	The specified parameters are invalid for current display mode
391	The module entry point is not valid
392	The function mask is invalid
394	The mouse pointer was drawn (no error)
395	Invalid beep frequency
396	Cannot locate country.sys
397	Cannot open country.sys
398	The country code (or code page) was not found
399	The NLS table was truncated - the buffer is too small
400	NLS error
401	NLS error
402	This VIO function is only valid from the session manager
403	Invalid VIO ASCIIZ length
404	VioDeRegister is not allowed
405	The pop-up was not allocated
406	A pop-up is already on the screen (no wait error code)
407	This KBD function is only valid from the session manager
408	Invalid VIO ASCIIZ length
409	Invalid VIO subsystem replacement mask
410	KbdRegister is not allowed
411	KbdDeRegister is not allowed
412	This MOU function is only valid from the session manager
413	Invalid MOU ASCIIZ length
414	Invalid MOU subsystem replacement mask
415	MouRegister is not allowed
416	MouDeRegister is not allowed
417	Invalid session manager action specified
418	Initialization called more than once (SM)
419	New session number not found
420	The caller must be the shell
421	Invalid VIO parameters
422	The SavRestoreWait thread is already owned
423	SavRestoreWait thread was freed by another thread in the process
425	The caller is not session manager
426	VioRegister is disallowed
427	No ModeWait thread in the session
428	No SavRestoreWait thread in the session
429	The physical display selector reqd while in the bgnd (error)
430	Illegal function call during pop-up

Num	Description
431	The caller is not the base system shell
432	Invalid status was requested
433	The nowait parameter is out of bounds
434	A screen lock failure occurred (nowait option)
435	Invalid parameters for MOU I/O wait
436	Invalid VIO handle
438	Invalid VIO length
439	Invalid KBD handle
440	Out of keyboard handles
441	Internal keyboard error
442	Unsuccessful code page load
443	Invalid code page ID
444	No code page support
445	Keyboard focus required
446	Caller already has the keyboard focus
447	The keyboard is busy
448	Invalid code page
449	Attempt to get keyboard focus failed
450	The session is not selectable
451	The function failed because you/child are not in fgnd
452	Not the parent of the specified child
453	Invalid session start mode
454	Invalid session start related option
455	Invalid session bond option
456	Invalid session select option
457	The session was started in the background
458	Invalid session stop option
459	The reserved parameters are not zero
460	The session parent process already exists
461	Invalid data length
462	The parent was not bound
463	Retry the request block allocation
464	KBD call disallowed for detached process
465	VIO call disallowed for detached process
466	MOU call disallowed for detached process
467	There is no font available to support mode
468	A user font is active
469	Invalid code page was specified
470	The system display does not support the code page
471	The current display does not support the code page
472	Invalid code page
473	The code page list is too small
474	The code page was not moved
475	Mode switch initialization error
476	The code page was not found
477	Internal error
478	Invalid start session trace indicator
479	VIO internal resource error
480	VIO shell initialization error
481	No session manager hard errors
482	DosSetCP unable to set KBD/VIO CP

Num	Description
483	Error during VioPopUp
484	Critical section overflow
485	Critical section underflow
486	Reserved VIO parameter is not zero

Appendix D:

The Linker Control Statements

This Appendix summarizes the control statements which you can include in LINK module definition (DEF) files. A definition file gives the linker additional information about your program which it then uses to build the EXE file. Certain EXE characteristics (such as individual segment attributes) can only be specified with this file. In most cases, you will not need to create DEF files, since all the information the linker needs is usually contained in the LIB files.

<u>*CODE STATEMENT*</u>

Description:

Defines the default attribute(s) for the program code segment(s).

Syntax:

```
CODE [load] [xonly] [iopl]
```

Where: **LOAD** is an optional keyword which defines when the code segment is to be physically loaded. The following values are permitted:

PRELOAD - The segments are loaded when the EXE program is started.

LOADONCALL - An entry is made in the LDT, but the segment(s) are not brought into memory until the program references them (faults). This is the default attribute.

XONLY is an optional keyword which defines the access rights of the segments. The following values are permitted:

EXECUTEONLY - Indicates that the code segments can be executed but not read. If a program attempts to read an EXECUTEONLY code segment it will cause a CPU fault.

EXECUTEREAD - Marks the code segment access rights so that the segment(s) are both executable and readable. This is the default attribute.

IOPL is an optional keyword which specifies that the code segments(s) have I/O privilege. If this keyword is not included, then the program code segments will not be permitted to issue I/O (IN, OUT, CLI and STI) instructions.

Example:

```
CODE  EXECUTEONLY PRELOAD IOPL
```

Notes:

1. If the file does not contain a CODE statement, the default code segment attributes are LOADONCALL EXECUTEREAD (no IOPL).

2. All OS/2 code segments are shareable, moveable and discardable.

DATA STATEMENT

Description:

Defines the default attribute(s) for the program data segment(s).

Syntax:

```
DATA [load] [read] [instance] [iopl] [shared]
```

Where: **LOAD** is an optional keyword which defines when the data segment is to be physically loaded. The following values are permitted:

PRELOAD - The segments are loaded when the EXE program is started.

LOADONCALL - An entry is made in the LDT, but the segment(s) are not brought into memory until the program references them (faults). This is the default attribute.

READ is an optional keyword which defines the access rights of the segments. The following values are permitted:

READONLY - Indicates that the data segments can be read but not written. If a program attempts to write into a READONLY data segment it will cause a CPU fault.

READWRITE - Marks the data segment access rights so that the segment(s) are both readable and writable. This is the default attribute.

INSTANCE is an optional keyword which defines how the automatic data segment is to be shared. An automatic data segment is the physical segment defined by the group named 'DGROUP'. The following values are permitted:

NONE - Indicates that there is no automatic data segment.

SINGLE - Indicates that the automatic data segment is to be shared by all instances of the module. Note: this is only valid for dynamic link modules. This is the default value for dynamic link programs.

MULTIPLE - A new automatic data segment is created for each instance of the module. This is the default value for normal programs.

IOPL is an optional keyword which specifies that the data segments(s) can be accessed by I/O privilege routines.

SHARED is an optional keyword which specifies that a unique copy of the READWRITE data segments should be loaded for each process which is using a dynamic link module. The following values are permitted:

SHARED - A single copy of each data segment is loaded. This copy is shared by all the processes which use the dynamic link module. This is the default value for dynamic link modules.

NONSHARED - Causes OS/2 to load a unique copy of each READWRITE data segment for each process which uses the dynamic link module. This is the default value for normal (program) modules.

Example:

```
DATA   SHARED IOPL NONE READWRITE PRELOAD
```

Notes:

1. If the file does not contain a DATA statement, the default data segment attributes are PRELOAD, READWRITE, MULTIPLE, NONSHARED, (no IOPL). for programs, and data segment attributes are PRELOAD, READWRITE, SINGLE, SHARED, (no IOPL) for dynamic link modules.

DESCRIPTION STATEMENT

Description:

Adds an text ASCII string to the EXE file. You can use this to include copyright information in the file.

Syntax:

```
DESCRIPTION 'text'
```

Where: **TEXT** is an ASCII string, delimited by quotation marks.

Example:

```
DESCRIPTION 'My Program, Version 1.07 driver 3.77'
```

Notes:

EXPORTS STATEMENT

Description:

Defines the names and the attributes of routines which can be called from outside your program (exports). This statement is used to define dynamic link library entry points.

Syntax:

```
EXPORTS   xname [ord] [res] [parmc]
```

Where: **XNAME** is the required export (routine) name. It can have the following form:

xname[=iname]

XNAME - Is the external name which is used by other programs to call your code segment (required).

INAME - Is an optional parameter that defines the internal name of the entry point. This name must be a PUBLIC routine name in one of the OBJ files which is being linked to form the module. If you do not specify INAME, the export name (XNAME) is used.

ORD is an optional keyword which specifies the function's ordinal position within the module's entry table. If this keyword is included, then the entry point may be invoked by either ordinal number or name. The ordinal has the following format:

@ordinal-number

Where ordinal-number is an integer which defines the function's ordinal value within the module.

RES is the keyword RESIDENTNAME. If included in the EXPORT statement, this keyword specifies that the function's entry point name string should be kept in memory. This option is only applicable to entry points which are exported by ordinal number. This option improves the performance of dynamic linking.

PARMC is an optional numeric value which must be specified for exported IOPL entry points. Routines which execute with IOPL run in a different privilege level (2). OS/2 allocates a 512 byte ring 2 stack for these programs. The PARMC value defines the number of parameters (words) which must be copied from the caller's stack to the routine stack.

Example:

```
EXPORTS myserv
EXPORTS myserv2=aau090a
EXPORTS myserv3=aau090a ord @4 myserv3
EXPORTS myserv4 ord @4
EXPORTS adms010 8
```

Notes:

1. EXPORTS is normally used to build dynamic link libraries. However, it must also used to build a programs which have IOPL code segments. In this case, the valid arguments are the export name and the IOPL parameter count.

HEAPSIZE STATEMENT

Description:

Defines the number of bytes which are needed by the program for its local heap.

Syntax:

```
HEAPSIZE   number
```

Where: **NUMBER** is an integer value that defines the heap size, in bytes.

Example:

```
HEAPSIZE 4096
```

Notes:

IMPORTS STATEMENT

Description:

Defines the names of dynamic link routines which are used by the program.

Syntax:

```
IMPORTS   [iname=]modname[.entry]
```

Where: **INAME** is an optional ASCII string which defines a name by which the program calls the function.

MODNAME is the name of the dynamic link module (DLL) which contains the function.

ENTRY describes which function within the DLL is to be imported. It has the following form:

.name = is the name of the function
.ord = is ordinal number of the function

Example:

```
IMPORTS   VIOCALLS.VioWrtTTY
IMPORTS   VIOCALLS.27
IMPORTS   MyRead=DOSCALLS.1
```

Notes:

1. External references to dynamic link routines are normally resolved by the .LIB file provided with the dynamic link library. This statement gives you an alternate way to do the same thing.

2. OS/2 functions in the DOSCALLS module may only be imported by ordinal.

LIBRARY STATEMENT

Description:

Identifies a module as a dynamic link library. This statement also tells OS/2 how the dynamic link library is to be initialized.

Syntax:

```
LIBRARY   [modname] [init]
```

Where: **MODNAME** is an optional module name. This is the name by which OS/2 knows the library. MODNAME is not normally specified. The linker defaults to the name of the EXE file (less the extension). MODNAME may be up to eight characters long, and may only be comprised of those valid ASCII characters which are permitted in file names.

INIT is an optional keyword which defines what type of initialization is required. If the DLL has no initialization routine, then this keyword is ignored. INIT must be one of the following:

INITGLOBAL - The initialization routine is only called when the DLL is first loaded. This is the default value. INITINSTANCE - The initialization routine is called each time a new process is started which calls the DLL function(s).

Example:

```
LIBRARY   mylib INITINSTANCE
```

Notes:

1. The NAME statement is mutually exclusive with the LIBRARY statement.

2. If included in the file, it must appear as the first statement in the the DEF file.

NAME STATEMENT

Description:

Adds the program module name to an OS/2 executable file.

Syntax:

```
NAME   [modname]
```

Where: **MODNAME** is an optional module name. This is the name by which
             the program is known in OS/2. MODNAME is not normally
             specified. The linker defaults to the name of the EXE file
             (less the extension). MODNAME may be up to eight
             characters long, and may only be comprised of those
             valid ASCII characters which are permitted in file names.

Example:

```
NAME   myprog
```

Notes:

1. The NAME statement is mutually exclusive with the LIBRARY statement.

2. If included in the file, it must appear as the first statement in the the DEF file.

OLD STATEMENT

Description:

Directs the linker to use export ordinals from a specific dynamic link module (DLL). The exported names in this module matching names in the old module are assigned the ordinal values from the old module unless,

1. The name in the old module did not have an assigned ordinal

2. An ordinal was explicitly assigned to the name in this module.

Syntax:

```
OLD   'filename'
```

Where: **FILENAME** is an ASCII (DLL) file name, delimited by quotation marks.

Example:

```
OLD   'mylib.dll'
```

Notes:

1. The OLD statement can be used to preserve export ordinals across successive versions of a dynamic link module.

2. If the named file is not found in the current disk/directory, then the LINK program will search the PATH string.

PROTMODE STATEMENT

Description:

Directs the linker to mark the EXE file as a module which will only run in protected mode.

Syntax:

```
PROTMODE
```

Example:

```
PROTMODE
```

Notes:

1. Do not use this option if you intend to convert the EXE file to FAPI format.

SEGMENTS STATEMENT

Description:

Defines the attribute of program code and data segment(s).

Syntax:

```
SEGMENTS segname [class] [load] [xonly] [iopl]
                 [read] [instance] [shared]
```

SEGNAME identifies the code or data segment whose attributes are described by this statement. The segment name can (optionally) be enclosed in single quotes. However, if the segment is named 'CODE' or 'DATA', then the quotes are required to differentiate the segment name from the class.

> **CLASS** an optional keyword which specifies the segment class. This statement has the following format:
>
>> CLASS 'classname'
>
> If you do not specify a class name, then the segment will default to 'CODE' class.
>
> **READ** is an optional keyword which defines the read/write access rights of the segment. The following values are permitted:
>
>> READONLY - Indicates that the segment can be read but not written. If a program attempts to write into a READONLY segment it will cause a CPU fault.
>>
>> READWRITE - Marks the segment access rights so that the segment is both readable and writable. This is the default attribute.

SHARED is an optional keyword which specifies that a unique copy of the READWRITE data segment should be loaded for each process which is using a dynamic link module. The following values are permitted:

SHARED - A single copy of the segment is loaded. This copy is shared by all the processes which use the dynamic link module. This is the default value for dynamic link modules.

NONSHARED - Causes OS/2 to load a unique copy of the READWRITE segment for each process which uses the dynamic link module. This is the default value for normal (program) modules.

Where: **LOAD** is an optional keyword which defines when the segment is to be physically loaded. The following values are permitted:

PRELOAD - The segment is loaded when the EXE program is started.

LOADONCALL - An entry is made in the LDT, but the segment is not brought into memory until referenced (faults). This is the default attribute.

XONLY is an optional keyword which defines the access rights of a code segment. The following values are permitted:

EXECUTEONLY - Indicates that the code segment can be executed but not read. If a program attempts to read an EXECUTEONLY code segment it will cause a CPU fault.

EXECUTEREAD - Marks the code segment access rights so that the segment is both executable and readable. This is the default attribute.

IOPL is an optional keyword which specifies that the code segments has I/O privilege. If this keyword is not included, then the code segment will not be permitted to issue I/O (IN, OUT, CLI and STI) instructions.

Example:

```
SEGMENTS
      MYCS1   LOADONCALL
      MYCS2   PRELOAD IOPL
      MYCS3   EXECUTEONLY CLASS 'HICODE'
      MYDAT   READONLY CLASS 'READDATA'
```

Notes:

STACKSIZE STATEMENT

Description:

Defines the number of bytes which are needed by the program for its execution stack.

Syntax:

```
STACKSIZE   number
```

Where: **NUMBER** is an integer value that defines the stack size, in
          bytes.

Example:

```
STACKSIZE 256
```

Notes:

STUB STATEMENT

Description:

Adds a PC DOS program to the OS/2 EXE file which will run if the program is loaded in a PC DOS system.

Syntax:

```
STUB  'filename'
```

Where: **FILENAME** is an ASCII (EXE) file name, delimited by quotation marks.

Example:

```
OLD  'mylib.dll'
```

Notes:

1. The named file must be a PC DOS 2.X or 3.X executable file.

2. If the named file is not found in the current disk/directory, then the LINK program will search the PATH string.

Appendix E:

Sample Programs

Chapter 13 (continued)

UPDATE	Update FILEIO data files

```
DosChgFilePtr
DosClose
DosExit
DosFileLocks
DosOpen
DosRead
DosWrite
```

MOVE	Move file between directories

```
DosExit
DosMove
DosRead
DosWrite
```

LISTDIR	List directory hierarchy

```
DosChDir
DosExit
DosFindFirst
DosFindNext
DosWrite
```

INFO	Display File information

```
DosClose
DosExit
DosOpen
DosQFileInfo
DosQFsInfo
DosWrite
```

Chapter 15

ALLOCMEM	Allocate memory segments

```
DosAllocSeg
DosExit
DosFreeSeg
DosMemAvail
DosSleep
VioScrollUp
VioWrtCharStrAtt
```

Chapter 15 (continued)

```
HEXDISP        Display file in hexadecimal

               DosAllocHuge
               DosBeep
               DosChgFilePtr
               DosClose
               DosExit
               DosGetHugeShift
               DosOpen
               DosRead
               DosWrite
               KbdCharIn
               VioScrollUp
               VioWrtCharStr
               VioWrtCharStrAtt


FDIR           Full screen directory display

               DosAllocSeg
               DosExit
               DosFindFirst
               DosFindNext
               DosReAllocSeg
               DosSubAlloc
               DosSubSet
               KbdCharIn
               VioScrollDn
               VioScrollUp
               VioWrtCharStr
               VioWrtCharStrAtt


GIVE           Copy STDIN to shared memory segment

               DosAllocShrSeg
               DosExit
               DosFreeSeg
               DosRead
               DosSleep


TAKE           Copy shared memory to STDOUT

               DosExit
               DosFreeSeg
               DosGetShrSeg
               DosSleep
               DosWrite
```

Chapter 16

RUN	Create multiple child processes	

```
DosAllocShrSeg
DosExecPgm
DosExit
DosFreeSeg
DosKillProcess
DosSetPrty
KbdCharIn
VioScrollUp
VioWrtCellStr
VioWrtCharStrAtt
```

COUNT   Display counter on screen (RUN child process)

```
DosExit
DosGetPid
DosGetPrty
DosGetShrSeg
DosSetSigHandler
DosSleep
VioScrollUp
VioWrtCharStrAtt
```

SNAKES   Run multiple asynchronous threads

```
DosAllocSeg
DosBeep
DosEnterCritSec
DosExit
DosExitCritSec
DosGetInfoSeg
DosGetPid
DosSemClear
DosSemRequest
KbdCharIn
VioGetCurType
VioReadCharStr
VioScrollUp
VioSetCurType
VioWrtCellStr
VioWrtCharStrAtt
```

Chapter 17

DATETIME   Display OS/2 Date and Time stamps

```
DosExit
(DosGetDateTime)
DosWrite
```

Chapter 17 (continued)

NOTES	Run multiple asynchronous timers

```
DosBeep
DosCloseSem
DosCreateSem
DosEnterCritSec
DosExit
DosExitCritSec
DosSemSetWait
DosSleep
DosTimerStart
DosTimerStop
KbdCharIn
VioScrollUp
VioWrtCharStrAtt
VioWrtNCell
```

TAKE2	Copy shared memory to STDOUT, with synchronization

```
DosCloseSem
DosExit
DosFreeSeg
DosGetShrSeg
DosOpenSem
DosSemClear
DosSemSet
DosSemWait
DosWrite
```

GIVE2	Copy STDIN to shared memory, with synchronization

```
DosAllocShrSeg
DosCloseSem
DosCreateSem
DosExit
DosFreeSeg
DosRead
DosSemClear
DosSemSet
DosSemWait
```

PIPE	Run an OS/2 Pipe

```
DosClose
DosDupHandle
DosExecPgm
DosExit
DosKillProcess
DosMakePipe
DosRead
DosScanEnv
DosWrite
```

Chapter 17 (continued)

```
            MAILBOX       Run multiple QUEUE programs

                          DosAllocSeg
                          DosAllocShrSeg
                          DosBeep
                          DosExecPgm
                          DosExit
                          DosFreeSeg
                          DosGiveSeg
                          DosKillProcess
                          DosOpenQueue
                          DosSetPrty
                          DosSleep
                          DosWriteQueue
                          KbdCharIn
                          VioScrollUp
                          VioWrtCellStr
                          VioWrtCharStrAtt


            QUEUE         Pass data packets between OS/2 queues

                          DosCloseQueue
                          DosCreateQueue
                          DosExit
                          DosFreeSeg
                          DosGetPid
                          DosGetPrty
                          DosGetShrSeg
                          DosGiveSeg
                          DosOpenQueue
                          DosPeekQueue
                          DosQueryQueue
                          DosReadQueue
                          DosSetPrty
                          DosSetSigHandler
                          DosSleep
                          DosWriteQueue
                          VioScrollUp
                          VioWrtCharStrAtt
```

Chapter 18

KEYMON   An OS/2 keyboard monitor program

                DosBeep
                DosExit
                DosGetInfoSeg
                DosMonClose
                DosMonOpen
                DosMonRead
                DosMonReg
                DosMonWrite
                DosSemClear
                DosSemSetWait
                DosSetPrty
                KbdCharIn
                VioEndPopUp
                VioPopUp
                VioWrtCharStrAtt

Miscellaneous Service Routines & Macros

OS2MAC.INC   An OS/2 Macro Library

                Structures

                DIRENTRY   Directory structure
                FINFO   Query file information structure
                FSINFO1   File system data (record type 1)
                FSINFO2   File system data (record type 2)
                PID   DosGetPid output structure
                CUR   Cursor data structure
                CHARBUF   Key input data structure
                MODEDATA   Video mode data structure
                VS1   Video state information (record type 1)
                VS2   Video state information (record type 2)
                VS3   Video state information (record type 3)
                GDT   Global info seg data structure
                LDT   Local info seg data structure

Miscellaneous Service Routines & Macros (continued)

```
                    Macros

                    @MOVS       Move string
                    @STRLEN     Compute ASCIIZ string length
                    @ATB        ASCII to binary conversion
                    @BTA        Binary to ASCII conversion
                    @DATE       Convert file system date word to ASCII
                    @SYSDATE    Convert system date to ASCII
                    @TIME       Convert file system time word to ASCII
                    @SYSTIME    Convert system time to ASCII
                    @SYSDAY     Get Day-Of-Week (ASCII)
                    @GETPARMS   Parse parameter input into application segment
                    @BTHS       Convert binary string to HEX ASCII
                    @BTH        Convert binary word to HEX ASCII
                    @LOOP       Loop macro (target > 128 bytes)
                    @JE         Jump Equal macro (target > 128 bytes)
                    @JZ         Jump Zero macro (target > 128 bytes)
                    @JNE        Jump Not Equal macro (target > 128 bytes)
                    @JNZ        Jump Not Zero macro (target > 128 bytes)
                    @JAXZ       Jump on AX Zero (no error)
                    @JAXNZ      Jump on AX Not Zero (error)
                    @MKTHREAD   Create a thread & allocate a stack


OS2PROCS.ASM        OS/2 Subroutines - called by macros

                    OS2ATB      ASCII to binary
                    OS2BTA      Binary to ASCII
                    OS2DATE     File system date conversion
                    OS2TIME     File system time conversion
                    OS2PARMS    Input parse
                    OS2BTHS     Binary to hex (string)
                    OS2BTH      Binary to hex (word)
                    OS2MKTH     Make thread
                    OS2SDATE    System date conversion
                    OS2STIME    System time conversion
                    OS2SDAY     Day-of-week formatting


BUILD.CMD           Command file to assemble & link sample programs


BUILDF.CMD          Command file to assemble/link/bind family programs
```

API Cross-Reference

OS/2 API	Sample Program(s)
DosAllocHuge	HEXDISP
DosAllocSeg	MAILBOX ALLOCMEM SNAKES FDIR
DosAllocShrSeg	MAILBOX GIVE2 RUN GIVE
DosBeep	HEXDISP MAILBOX NOTES KEYMON SNAKES

API Cross-Reference (continued)

OS/2 API	Sample Program(s)
DosChDir	LISTDIR
DosChgFilePtr	UPDATE HEXDISP
DosClose	PIPE INFO SPLIT HEXDISP FILEIO UPDATE SET9600
DosCloseQueue	QUEUE
DosCloseSem	GIVE2 NOTES TAKE2
DosCreateQueue	QUEUE
DosCreateSem	GIVE2 NOTES
DosDevIOCTL	SET9600
DosDupHandle	PIPE
DosEnterCritSec	SNAKES NOTES
DosExecPgm	PIPE RUN MAILBOX
DosExit	FILEIO SNAKES HEXDISP KEYMON FDIR TAKE RUN MAILBOX SET9600 COUNT INFO UPCASE NOTES MOVE LISTDIR GIVE2 TAKE2 GIVE SPLIT UPDATE DATETIME QUEUE ALLOCMEM PIPE
DosExitCritSec	NOTES SNAKES
DosFileLocks	UPDATE
DosFindFirst	LISTDIR FDIR
DosFindNext	LISTDIR FDIR
DosFreeSeg	TAKE RUN ALLOCMEM TAKE2 GIVE QUEUE MAILBOX GIVE2
DosGetDateTime	DATETIME
DosGetHugeShift	HEXDISP
DosGetInfoSeg	SNAKES KEYMON
DosGetPid	QUEUE COUNT SNAKES
DosGetPrty	COUNT QUEUE
DosGetShrSeg	QUEUE TAKE2 COUNT TAKE
DosGiveSeg	QUEUE MAILBOX
DosKillProcess	PIPE RUN MAILBOX
DosMakePipe	PIPE
DosMemAvail	ALLOCMEM
DosMonClose	KEYMON
DosMonOpen	KEYMON

API Cross-Reference (continued)

OS/2 API	Sample Program(s)
DosMonRead	KEYMON
DosMonReg	KEYMON
DosMonWrite	KEYMON
DosMove	MOVE
DosOpen	SET9600 UPDATE INFO FILEIO SPLIT HEXDISP
DosOpenQueue	MAILBOX QUEUE
DosOpenSem	TAKE2
DosPeekQueue	QUEUE
DosQFileInfo	INFO
DosQFsInfo	INFO
DosQueryQueue	QUEUE
DosReAllocSeg	FDIR
DosRead	GIVE UPCASE GIVE2 MOVE SPLIT FILEIO PIPE UPDATE HEXDISP
DosReadQueue	QUEUE
DosScanEnv	PIPE
DosSemClear	TAKE2 SNAKES KEYMON GIVE2
DosSemRequest	SNAKES
DosSemSet	TAKE2 GIVE2
DosSemSetWait	KEYMON NOTES
DosSemWait	TAKE2 GIVE2
DosSetPrty	MAILBOX QUEUE RUN KEYMON
DosSetSigHandler	COUNT QUEUE
DosSleep	QUEUE ALLOCMEM COUNT GIVE MAILBOX TAKE NOTES
DosSubAlloc	FDIR
DosSubSet	FDIR
DosTimerStart	NOTES
DosTimerStop	NOTES
DosWrite	FILEIO HEXDISP UPCASE SPLIT INFO UPDATE MOVE LISTDIR TAKE2 PIPE DATETIME TAKE

API Cross-Reference (continued)

OS/2 API	Sample Program(s)
DosWriteQueue	MAILBOX QUEUE
KbdCharIn	FDIR KEYMON HEXDISP RUN MAILBOX NOTES SNAKES
VioEndPopUp	KEYMON
VioGetCurType	SNAKES
VioPopUp	KEYMON
VioReadCharStr	SNAKES
VioScrollDn	FDIR
VioScrollUp	QUEUE HEXDISP SNAKES ALLOCMEM NOTES MAILBOX FDIR COUNT RUN
VioSetCurType	SNAKES
VioWrtCellStr	MAILBOX RUN SNAKES
VioWrtCharStr	HEXDISP FDIR
VioWrtCharStrAtt	KEYMON MAILBOX NOTES RUN QUEUE SNAKES FDIR ALLOCMEM COUNT HEXDISP
VioWrtNCell	NOTES

UPCASE.ASM

```
                    PAGE    ,132
                    TITLE   OS/2 sample filter
;-----------------------------------------------------------------
;   NAME: UPCASE
;
;   DESC: Translate standard input to upper case
;
;  INPUT: Character stream
;
; OUTPUT: Upper case character stream
;
;  PROCS: none
;
;   AUTH: E. E. Iacobucci
;
;   DATE: 10/15/87
;
;-----------------------------------------------------------------
                .286c
                .xlist
                include    os2mac.inc
                .list

dgroup   group    UPC_data                  ;defines automatic data segment

;
;=======================================
;
; UPC stack
;
;=======================================
UPC_stack    segment para stack
;
                dw    256 dup('s')
;
UPC_stack    ends
;
;=======================================
;
; UPC data segment
;
;=======================================
UPC_data     segment para public 'auto'
;
in_buffer    db        256 dup(0)         ;input data buffer
in_leng      dw        $-offset(in_buffer) ;input data buffer length
bytesxfer    dw        0                   ;bytes transfered
;
UPC_data     ends
```

```
;
;=====================================
;
; UPC code segment
;
;=====================================
UPC_code     segment para public 'code'
             assume  cs:UPC_code,ds:UPC_data,es:UPC_data,ss:UPC_stack
;
main         proc
             pusha                            ;Save registers
;
; Address Data Segment
;
             mov      ax,UPC_data
             push     ax                      ;put data segment selector
             pop      ds                      ;in DS
;.pa
;
; Read character
;
upc010:      @DosRead stdin,in_buffer,in_leng,bytesxfer
             cmp      bytesxfer,0             ;done?
             je       upc999                  ;yes - leave
;
; Translate to upper case
;
             mov      cx,bytesxfer            ;set loop count
             mov      di,offset(in_buffer)    ;set pointer to buffer
;
upc020:      cmp      byte ptr [di],'a'       ;less than a ?
             jb       upc030                  ;yes - skip byte
             cmp      byte ptr [di],'z'       ;greater than z ?
             ja       upc030                  ;yes - skip byte
             sub      byte ptr [di],'a'-'A'   ;make upper case
upc030:      inc      di                      ;point to next byte
             loop     upc020                  ;continue processing
;
; Write character
;
upc040:      @DosWrite stdout,in_buffer,bytesxfer,bytesxfer
             jmp      upc010                  ;go read next character
;
; Termination processing
;
upc999:      popa                             ;Restore saved registers
             @DosExit 1,0                     ;leave proc
main         endp
;
             include  os2procs.asm            ;miscellaneous procedures
;
UPC_code     ends
             end      main
```

SPLIT.ASM

```
                PAGE    ,132
                TITLE  OS/2 console I/O program
;-----------------------------------------------------------------
;   NAME: SPLIT
;
;   DESC: Splits the input data stream and writes to it
;         to STDOUT and a user specified device
;
;  INPUT: Character stream
;         Device name as parameter
;
; OUTPUT: Character stream
;
;  PROCS: none
;
;   AUTH: E. E. Iacobucci
;
;   DATE: 10/15/87
;
;-----------------------------------------------------------------
                .286c
                .xlist
                include   os2mac.inc
                .list

dgroup  group   SPL_data                ;defines automatic data segment

;
;========================================
;
; SPL stack
;
;========================================
SPL_stack       segment para stack
;
                dw    256 dup('s')
;
SPL_stack       ends
;
;========================================
;
; SPL data segment
;
;========================================
SPL_data        segment para public 'auto'
;
msg0            db          'Invalid device',CR,LF
MSG0L           equ         $ - offset msg0
```

```
;
msg_temp      db        4   dup(0)              ;message work area
in_buffer     db        256 dup(0)              ;input data buffer
in_leng       dw        $-offset in_buffer      ;input data buffer length
bytesin       dw        0                       ;bytes read
bytesout      dw        0                       ;bytes written
nulldev       db        'NUL',0                 ;null device name
;
; Open parameters
;
dev_name      db        64 dup(0)               ;device/file name
dev_hand      dw        0
dev_act       dw        0
dev_size      dd        0
dev_attr      dw        0
dev_flag      dw        0                       ;open flags
dev_mode      dw        0                       ;open mode
dev_rsv       dd        0                       ;reserved
;
SPL_data      ends
;
;=======================================
;
; SPL code segment
;
;=======================================
SPL_code      segment para public 'code'
              assume  cs:SPL_code,ds:SPL_data,es:SPL_data,ss:SPL_stack
;
main          proc
              pusha                             ;Save registers
;
; Address Data Segment
;
              push      ds                      ;put data segment selector
              pop       es                      ;in ES
;
; Parse input device name
;
              mov       es,ax                   ;environment selector
              mov       di,bx                   ;command line offset
              mov       cx,63                   ;maximum name length
              push      cx                      ;save count
;
              mov       ax,0                    ;end of command name delimiter
              repne     scasb                   ;search for end of command name
              mov       ax,' '                  ;blank
              repe      scasb                   ;skip leading blanks
              dec       di                      ;back up to first character
```

```
;
                push    es                      ;switch
                push    ds                      ;      ES
                pop     es                      ;              &
                pop     ds                      ;                DI (for MOVSB)
                mov     si,di                   ;set string source
                mov     di,offset dev_name      ;point to dev_name field (target)
                pop     cx                      ;restore count
;
spl010:         cmp     byte ptr [si],':'       ;end of device name?
                je      spl020                  ;yes - exit
                cmp     byte ptr [si],0         ;end of parameters?
                je      spl020                  ;yes - exit
                movsb                           ;copy byte
                loop    spl010                  ;continue copying
;
spl020:         push    es                      ;copy SPL DS ...
                pop     ds                      ;    ... to DS reg
                cmp     byte ptr dev_name,0     ;device name entered?
                jne     spl025                  ;yes - go process
                @movs   dev_name,nulldev,4      ;move NUL device name to dev_name
;
; Open output device
;
spl025:         mov     dev_flag,00000001b              ;open if it exists
                                ;eeeennnn
                mov     dev_mode,0000000011000001b ;open mode
                                ;dwfrrrrrisssraaa
                @DosOpen dev_name,dev_hand,dev_act,dev_size,dev_attr,dev_flag,dev_mode,dev_rsv
                @jaxz    spl030                  ;opened OK, continue
                @DosWrite stderr,msg0,msg0l,bytesout  ;Write error message
                jmp      spl999                 ;exit
;
; Read character string
;
spl030:         @DosRead  stdin,in_buffer,in_leng,bytesin ;read string
                cmp     bytesin,0               ;done?
                jne     spl040                  ;no - continue
                jmp     spl999                  ;yes - leave
;
;
; Write character string
;
spl040:         @DosWrite dev_hand,in_buffer,bytesin,bytesout ;to device
                @DosWrite stdout,in_buffer,bytesin,bytesout    ;to stdout
                jmp     spl030                  ;go read next character(s)
;
; Termination processing
;
spl999:         @DosClose dev_hand              ;Close the device
                popa                            ;Restore saved registers
                @DosExit 1,0                    ;leave proc
main            endp
;
                include  os2procs.asm           ;miscellaneous procedures
;
SPL_code        ends
                end     main
```

SET9600.ASM

```
                    PAGE    ,132
                    TITLE   OS/2 IOCTL program
;----------------------------------------------------------------
;   NAME: SET9600
;
;   DESC: Sets com1: to 9600 baud, 8 data bits, no parity
;         and 1 stopbit.
;
;  INPUT: none
;
; OUTPUT: COM1: characteristics are changed
;
;  PROCS: none
;
;   AUTH: E. E. Iacobucci
;
;   DATE: 10/15/87
;
;----------------------------------------------------------------
                    .286c
                    .xlist
                    include os2mac.inc
                    .list

dgroup  group  S96_data                         ;defines automatic data segment

;-----------------------------------------
;
; S96 stack
;
;-----------------------------------------
S96_stack        segment para stack
                 db    256 dup('s')
S96_stack        ends
;-----------------------------------------
;
; S96 data segment
;
;-----------------------------------------
S96_data         segment para public 'DATA'
;
; Open parameters
;
s96_name         db        'COM1',0             ;port name
s96_hand         dw        0
s96_act          dw        0
s96_size         dd        0
s96_attr         dw        0
s96_flag         dw        0                     ;open flags
s96_mode         dw        0                     ;open mode
s96_rsv          dd        0                     ;reserved
;
; IOCTL parameters
;
s96_speed        dw        0                     ;Line Speed
```

```
;
S96_data      ends
;
;---------------------------------------
;
; S96 code segment
;
;---------------------------------------
S96_code      segment para public 'code'
              assume  cs:S96_code,ds:S96_data,es:S96_data,ss:S96_stack
;
main          proc
;
; Open COM1:  & set line speed
;
              mov       s96_flag,00000001b    ;open if it exists
              mov       s96_mode,0000000010010010b ;open mode
              @DosOpen  s96_name,s96_hand,s96_act,s96_size,s96_attr,s96_flag,s96_mode,s96_rsv
              @jaxnz    s96999                ;exit if error
;
              mov       s96_speed,9600        ;set line speed
              @DosDevIOCTL NULL,s96_speed,041h,01h,s96_hand ;set line speed
;
              @DosClose s96_hand              ;close device handle
s96999:       @DosExit  1,0                   ;end program
main          endp
;
              include os2procs.asm            ;miscellaneous procedures
;
S96_code      ends
              end      main
```

FILEIO.ASM

```
                    PAGE    ,132
                    TITLE   OS/2 File I/O program
;----------------------------------------------------------------
;   NAME: FILEIO
;
;   DESC: Write data records to a file
;
;  INPUT: File name
;
; OUTPUT: Data records
;
;  PROCS: GETFN     (get data file name)
;         OPENF     (Open data file)
;         GETINPUT  (Get data record from console)
;         PUTREC    (Write data record)
;         CLOSEF    (Close file)
;         BTA       (convert binary to ASCII)
;
;   AUTH: E. E. Iacobucci
;
;   DATE: 10/15/87
;
;----------------------------------------------------------------
                    .286c
                    .xlist
                    include   os2mac.inc
                    .list

dgroup  group   FIO_data                  ;defines automatic data segment

;
;=======================================
;
; FIO stack
;
;=======================================
FIO_stack    segment para stack
;
                    dw    256 dup('s')
;
FIO_stack    ends
;
;=======================================
;
; FIO data segment
;
;=======================================
FIO_data     segment para public 'auto'
```

```
;
msg0            db         'OS/2 File I/O program',CR,LF
nl              db         CR,LF
MSG0L           equ        $ - offset msg0
;
msg1            db         'Enter File Name: '
MSG1L           equ        $ - offset msg1
;
msg2            db         CR,LF
                db         'File is now OPEN, enter data or null record to End'
                db         CR,LF
MSG2L           equ        $ - offset msg2
;
msg3            db         'File Open Error',CR,LF
MSG3L           equ        $ - offset msg3
;
msg4            db         'Record '
msg4rec         db         '00'
                db         ' ==> '
MSG4L           equ        $ - offset msg4
;
;
msg5            db         'File Open Error',CR,LF
MSG5L           equ        $ - offset msg5
;
msg_temp        db         4    dup(0)              ;message work area
;
in_data         dw         0
in_buffer       db         62   dup(' ')            ;input data buffer
in_leng         dw         $-offset in_buffer       ;input data buffer length
;
bytesin         dw         0                        ;bytes read
bytesout        dw         0                        ;bytes written
recno           dw         1                        ;record number
;
; File parameters
;
dev_name        db         64 dup(0)                ;device/file name
dev_hand        dw         0
dev_act         dw         0
dev_size        dd         0
dev_attr        dw         0
dev_flag        dw         0                        ;open flags
dev_mode        dw         0                        ;open mode
dev_rsv         dd         0                        ;reserved
;
FIO_data        ends
;
;========================================
;
; FIO code segment
;
;========================================
FIO_code        segment para public 'code'
                assume  cs:FIO_code,ds:FIO_data,es:FIO_data,ss:FIO_stack
```

```
;
main            proc
                pusha                                   ;Save registers
;
; Address Data Segment
;
                push    ds                      ;put data segment selector
                pop     es                      ;in ES
;
; Program Banner
;
                @DosWrite stdout,msg0,MSG0L,bytesout   ;message #0
;
; Main processing
;
                call    getfn                   ;get filename
                call    openf                   ;open the file
                @jaxnz  fio999                  ;open error, exit
;
fio010:         call    getinput                ;get record from user
                @jaxnz  fio030                  ;done, go exit
                call    putrec                  ;put data record in file
                jmp     fio010                  ;go get next record
;
fio030:         call    closef                  ;close the file
;
; Termination processing
;
fio999:         popa                            ;Restore saved registers
                @DosExit 1,0                     ;leave proc
main            endp
;
;
;        NAME: GETFN
; DESCRIPTION: Prompt user for file name
;       INPUT: none
;      OUTPUT: File name in dev_name
;
getfn           proc
                @DosWrite stdout,msg1,msg1l,bytesout ;Prompt for file name
                @DosRead  stdin,dev_name,63,bytesin  ;Read device name
                mov     si,offset dev_name      ;get address of input buffer
                add     si,bytesin              ;point to last byte
                sub     si,2                    ;back up before CR & LF
                mov     byte ptr [si],0         ;zero terminate the string
                ret
getfn           endp
```

```
;
;
;          NAME: OPENF
; DESCRIPTION: Open file & create control record (if necessary)
;        INPUT: File name in dev_name
;       OUTPUT: File handle in dev_hand
;
openf        proc
             mov       dev_flag,00010010b             ;open flags
                            ;eeeennnn
             mov       dev_mode,0000000010010010b    ;open mode
                            ;dwfrrrrrisssraaa
             @DosOpen  dev_name,dev_hand,dev_act,dev_size,dev_attr,dev_flag,dev_mode,dev_rsv
             @jaxz     ope010                   ;opened OK - continue
;
             @DosWrite stderr,msg3,msg3l,bytesout  ;Write error message
             mov       ax,0ffh                  ;set error code
             jmp       ope999                   ;exit
;
ope010:      @DosWrite stdout,msg2,msg2l,bytesout  ;Write file OPEN message
             xor       ax,ax                    ;clear error code
ope999:      ret
openf        endp
;
;
;          NAME: GETINPUT
; DESCRIPTION: Get data record from user
;        INPUT: none
;       OUTPUT: Data record in dev_name
;
getinput     proc
             @BTA      recno,msg4rec,2          ;convert to ASCII
             @DosWrite stdout,msg4,msg4l,bytesout  ;Write prompt
;
             @DosRead  stdin,in_buffer,in_leng,bytesin ;Read data
             mov       bx,bytesin               ;get byte count
             add       bx,offset in_buffer - 2 ;address last two bytes
             mov       word ptr [bx],'  '       ;strip CR & LF
;
             xor       ax,ax                    ;set return code
             cmp       bytesin,2                ;done?
             jne       gti999                   ;no - continue
             mov       ax,0ffh                  ;set return code
gti999:      ret
getinput     endp
```

```
;
;
;         NAME: PUTREC
; DESCRIPTION: Put data record
;       INPUT: Record in in_bufer
;              Record length in bytesin
;      OUTPUT: Data record to file
;
putrec          proc
                @DosWrite dev_hand,in_buffer,in_leng,bytesout ;write data record
                inc     recno                   ;bump record number
                ret
putrec          endp
;
;
;         NAME: CLOSEF
; DESCRIPTION: Close file
;       INPUT: File handle in dev_hand
;      OUTPUT: Data file is closed
;
closef          proc
                @DosClose dev_hand              ;close data file
                ret
closef          endp
;
                include os2procs.asm            ;miscellaneous procedures
;
FIO_code        ends
                end     main
```

UPDATE.ASM

```
                    PAGE    ,132
                    TITLE  OS/2 File record update program
;-------------------------------------------------------------------
;   NAME: UPDATE
;
;   DESC: Update records in a file
;
;  INPUT: File name
;
; OUTPUT: Data records
;
;  PROCS: GETFN    (get data file name)
;         OPENF    (Open data file)
;         GETINPUT (Get data record from console)
;         PUTREC   (Write data record)
;         CLOSEF   (Close file)
;         ATB      (convert ASCII to binary)
;
;   AUTH: E. E. Iacobucci
;
;   DATE: 10/15/87
;
;-------------------------------------------------------------------
            .286c
            .xlist
            include   os2mac.inc
            .list

dgroup      group     UPD_data                ;defines automatic data segment

;
;=======================================
;
; UPD stack
;
;=======================================
UPD_stack   segment para stack
;
            dw    256 dup('s')
;
UPD_stack   ends
;
;=======================================
;
; UPD data segment
;
;=======================================
UPD_data    segment para public 'auto'
```

```
;
; Messages
;
msg0        db          'OS/2 File update program',CR,LF
nl          db          CR,LF
MSG0L       equ         $ - offset msg0
;
msg1        db          'Enter File Name: '
MSG1L       equ         $ - offset msg1
;
msg2        db          CR,LF
            db          'File is now Open, enter record # or NULL to end'
            db          CR,LF
MSG2L       equ         $ - offset msg2
;
msg3        db          'File Open Error',CR,LF
MSG3L       equ         $ - offset msg3
;
msg4        db          'Can''t go past end of file',CR,LF
MSG4L       equ         $ - offset msg4
;
msg5        db          'File Open Error',CR,LF
MSG5L       equ         $ - offset msg5
;
;
msg6        db          CR,LF,'Record Number: '
MSG6L       equ         $ - offset msg6
;
msg7        db          'Invalid record number',CR,LF
MSG7L       equ         $ - offset msg7
;
msg8        db          '               ==> '
MSG8L       equ         $ - offset msg8
;
msg9        db          '        Update ==> '
MSG9L       equ         $ - offset msg9
;
msg10       db          'Sorry, that record is already in use - try again later'
            db          CR,LF
MSG10L      equ         $ - offset msg10
;
; Data areas
;
in_data     dw          0
in_buffer   db          62  dup(' ')            ;input data buffer
in_leng     dw          $-offset in_buffer      ;input data buffer length
;
bytesin     dw          0                       ;bytes read
bytesout    dw          0                       ;bytes written
recno       dw          1                       ;record number
```

```
;
; File parameters
;
dev_name        db      64 dup(0)               ;device/file name
dev_hand        dw      0
dev_act         dw      0
dev_size        dd      0
dev_attr        dw      0
dev_flag        dw      0                       ;open flags
dev_mode        dw      0                       ;open mode
dev_rsv         dd      0                       ;reserved
dev_ofs         dd      0                       ;file offset
new_ofs         dd      0                       ;new file offset
;
dev_lock_ptr    dd      0                       ;record lock pointer
dev_lock_len    dd      0                       ;record lock length
dev_unlock_ptr dd       0                       ;record unlock pointer
dev_unlock_len dd       0                       ;record unlock length
;
NULL            equ     0
;
UPD_data        ends
;
;=========================================
;
; UPD code segment
;
;=========================================
UPD_code        segment para public 'code'
                assume  cs:UPD_code,ds:UPD_data,es:UPD_data,ss:UPD_stack
;
main            proc
;
; Address data segment
;
                push    ds                      ;put DS ...
                pop     es                      ;in ES
;
; Program Banner
;
                @DosWrite stdout,msg0,MSGOL,bytesout   ;message #0
;
; Main processing
;
                call    getfn                   ;get filename
                call    openf                   ;open the file
                @jaxnz  upd999                  ;open error - go exit
```

```
;
upd010:     call      getrecno              ;get record # from user
            cmp       recno,0               ;null record?
            je        upd030                ;yes - exit
            call      getrec                ;get record from file
            @jaxnz    upd010                ;error - go re-prompt
            call      getinput              ;get record data from user
            @jaxnz    upd010                ;no update - go re-prompt
            call      putrec                ;put data record in file
            jmp       upd010                ;go get next record
;
upd030:     call      closef                ;close the file
;
; Termination processing
;
upd999:     @DosExit 1,0                    ;leave proc
main        endp
;
;
;      NAME: GETFN
; DESCRIPTION: Prompt user for file name
;      INPUT: none
;     OUTPUT: File name in dev_name
;
getfn       proc
            @DosWrite stdout,msg1,msg1l,bytesout ;Prompt for file name
            @DosRead  stdin,dev_name,63,bytesin  ;Read device name
            mov       si,offset dev_name    ;get address of input buffer
            add       si,bytesin            ;point to last byte
            sub       si,2                  ;back up before CR & LF
            mov       byte ptr [si],0       ;zero terminate the string
            ret
getfn       endp
;
;
;      NAME: OPENF
; DESCRIPTION: Open file & create control record (if necessary)
;      INPUT: File name in dev_name
;     OUTPUT: File handle in dev_hand
;
openf       proc
            mov       dev_flag,00000001b              ;open flags
                      ;eeeennnn
            mov       dev_mode,0000000011000010b      ;open mode
                      ;dwfrrrrrisssraaa
            @DosOpen  dev_name,dev_hand,dev_act,dev_size,dev_attr,dev_flag,dev_mode,dev_rsv
            @jaxz     ope010                ;opened OK - continue
            @DosWrite stderr,msg3,msg3l,bytesout  ;Write error message
            mov       ax,0ffh               ;set error code
            jmp       ope999
;
ope010:     @DosWrite stdout,msg2,msg2l,bytesout  ;Write file OPEN message
            xor       ax,ax                 ;clear error code
ope999:     ret
openf       endp
```

```
;
;
;          NAME: GETRECNO
; DESCRIPTION: Get record number from user
;        INPUT: none
;       OUTPUT: Record number in RECNO
;
getrecno     proc
gtn010:      @DosWrite stdout,msg6,msg6l,bytesout  ;Write prompt
             @DosRead  stdin,in_buffer,in_leng,bytesin ;Read data
             mov       si,offset in_buffer  ;data area
             mov       cx,bytesin           ;data area length
             sub       cx,2                 ;less CR & LF
             @atb      DS:SI,cx             ;convert to binary
             @jaxz     gtn999               ;valid number - finished
             @DosWrite stdout,msg7,msg7l,bytesout  ;Write error message
             jmp       gtn010               ;go prompt again
gtn999:      mov       recno,bx             ;record number
             ret
getrecno     endp
;
;          NAME: GETREC
; DESCRIPTION: Get data record
;       INPUT: Record number in recno
;      OUTPUT: Data record in in_buf
;
getrec       proc
;
; Determine file size
;
             mov       word ptr dev_ofs,0   ;no bytes past end-of-file
             @DosChgFilePtr dev_hand,dev_ofs,2,new_ofs ;move file ptr to eof
;
; Compute file offset
;
             mov       bx,recno             ;get record number
             dec       bx                   ;adjust (record zero base)
             mov       ax,in_leng           ;get buffer length
             mul       bx                   ;compute file offset
             cmp       ax,word ptr new_ofs  ;past end-of-file?
             jae       gtr005               ;yes - go write error
             jmp       gtr010               ;no - go set file pointer
gtr005:      @DosWrite stdout,msg4,msg4l,bytesout ;write error message
             jmp       gtr800               ;exit with error
;
;
;
; Move file pointer
;
gtr010:      mov       word ptr dev_ofs,ax  ;set offset (low order word)
             @DosChgFilePtr dev_hand,dev_ofs,0,new_ofs ;move file pointer
             @jaxz     gtr020               ;not invalid offset, continue
             @DosWrite stdout,msg7,msg7l,bytesout ;Write error message
             jmp       gtr800               ;exit with error
```

```
;
; Lock record
;
gtr020:         push        word ptr dev_ofs           ;put record start offset
                pop         word ptr dev_lock_ptr      ;in record lock field
                push        in_leng                    ;put record length
                pop         word ptr dev_lock_len      ;in length field
                @DosFileLocks dev_hand,NULL,dev_lock_ptr ;request lock
                @jaxz       gtr030                     ;worked - continue
                @DosWrite stdout,msg10,msg10l,bytesout ;Write error message
                jmp         gtr800                     ;exit with error
;
; Read record
;
gtr030:         @DosRead dev_hand,in_buffer,in_leng,bytesin ;read data record
                jmp         gtr999                     ;exit

gtr800:         mov         al,0ffh                    ;set error code
gtr999:         ret
getrec          endp
;
;
;       NAME: GETINPUT
; DESCRIPTION: Get data input from user
;      INPUT: none
;     OUTPUT: Data record in in_buffer
;
getinput        proc
;
; put out prompt
;
                @DosWrite stdout,msg8,msg8l,bytesout            ;Write prompt (1)
                @DosWrite stdout,in_buffer,bytesin,bytesout ;Write record
                @DosWrite stdout,nl,2,bytesout                  ;New Line
                @DosWrite stdout,msg9,msg9l,bytesout            ;Write prompt (2)
;
; get user input
;
                @DosRead  stdin,in_buffer,in_leng,bytesin ;Read data
;
; blank out remainder of data buffer
;
                mov         cx,in_leng                 ;get buffer size
                sub         cx,bytesin                 ;less what was entered
                add         cx,2                       ;compensate for CR & LF
                mov         di,bytesin                 ;get byte count
                add         di,offset in_buffer-2 ;address end of data (skip CR & LF)
                mov         al,' '                     ;fill character
                rep         stosb                      ;blank remainder of buffer
;
                xor         ax,ax                      ;set return code
                cmp         bytesin,2                  ;done? (only CR & LF)
                @jne        gti999                     ;no - continue
```

```
;
;
; Unlock record
;
            push        word ptr dev_ofs            ;put record start offset
            pop         word ptr dev_unlock_ptr     ;in record lock field
            push        in_leng                     ;put record length
            pop         word ptr dev_unlock_len     ;in length field
            @DosFileLocks dev_hand,dev_unlock_ptr,NULL ;unlock record
            mov         ax,0ffh                     ;set return code
;
gti999:     ret
getinput    endp
;
;
;       NAME: PUTREC
; DESCRIPTION: Put data record
;       INPUT: Record in in_bufer
;      OUTPUT: Data record to file
;
putrec      proc
;
; Write record
;
            @DosChgFilePtr dev_hand,dev_ofs,0,new_ofs ;reset file pointer
            @DosWrite dev_hand,in_buffer,in_leng,bytesout ;write data record
;
; Unlock record
;
            push        word ptr dev_ofs            ;put record start offset
            pop         word ptr dev_unlock_ptr     ;in record lock field
            push        in_leng                     ;put record length
            pop         word ptr dev_unlock_len     ;in length field
            @DosFileLocks dev_hand,dev_unlock_ptr,NULL ;unlock record
            ret
putrec      endp
;
;
;       NAME: CLOSEF
; DESCRIPTION: Close file
;       INPUT: File handle in dev_hand
;      OUTPUT: Data file is closed
;
closef      proc
            @DosClose dev_hand                      ;close data file
            ret
closef      endp
;
include     os2procs.asm                            ;miscellaneous procedures
;
UPD_code    ends
            end         main
```

MOVE.ASM

```
                    PAGE    ,132
                    TITLE   OS/2 move file program
;-------------------------------------------------------------------
;   NAME: MOVE
;
;   DESC: Move a file between directories
;
;  INPUT: File name
;
; OUTPUT: File moved to different directory
;
;  PROCS: none
;
;   AUTH: E. E. Iacobucci
;
;   DATE: 10/15/87
;
;-------------------------------------------------------------------
            .286c
            .xlist
            include    os2mac.inc
            .list

dgroup  group   MOV_data                ;defines automatic data segment

;
;=======================================
;
; MOV stack
;
;=======================================
MOV_stack       segment para stack
;
                dw    256 dup('s')
;
MOV_stack       ends
;
;=======================================
;
; MOV data segment
;
;=======================================
MOV_data        segment para public 'auto'
;
; Messages
;
msg0            db        CR,LF
                db        'Enter Source File Name: '
MSGOL           equ       $ - offset msg0
;
msg1            db        CR,LF
                db        'Enter Target Subdirectory\filename: '
MSG1L           equ       $ - offset msg1
```

```
;
msg2            db          CR,LF
                db          'File Move Error'
                db          CR,LF
MSG2L           equ         $ - offset msg2
;
bytesout        dw          0                        ;bytes written
bytesin         dw          0                        ;bytes read
source_file     db          63 dup(0)                ;source file name
                db          0                        ;zero terminate byte
target_file     db          63 dup(0)                ;target file name
                db          0                        ;zero terminate byte
rsv             dd          0                        ;reserved double word
;
MOV_data        ends
;
;=========================================
;
; MOV code segment
;
;=========================================
MOV_code        segment para public 'code'
                assume  cs:MOV_code,ds:MOV_data,es:MOV_data,ss:MOV_stack
;
main            proc
;
; Read source file name
;
                @DosWrite stdout,msg0,MSG0L,bytesout    ;prompt
                @DosRead  stdin,source_file,63,bytesin ;Read device name
                mov       si,offset source_file ;get address of input buffer
                add       si,bytesin             ;point to last byte
                sub       si,2                   ;back up before CR & LF
                mov       byte ptr [si],0        ;zero terminate the string
;
; Read target file name
;
                @DosWrite stdout,msg1,MSG1L,bytesout    ;prompt
                @DosRead  stdin,target_file,63,bytesin ;Read device name
                mov       si,offset target_file ;get address of input buffer
                add       si,bytesin             ;point to last byte
                sub       si,2                   ;back up before CR & LF
                mov       byte ptr [si],0        ;zero terminate the string
;
; Move it
;
                @DosMove  source_file,target_file,rsv ;Move file
                @jaxz     mov999                     ;finished
                @DosWrite stderr,msg2,MSG2L,bytesout  ;error message
;
;
; Termination processing
;
mov999:         @DosExit 1,0                         ;leave proc
main            endp
;
MOV_code        ends
                end         main
```

LISTDIR.ASM

```
                PAGE    80,132
                TITLE   OS/2 directory list program
;-------------------------------------------------------------------
;   NAME: LISTDIR
;
;   DESC: Display disk directory structure
;
;  INPUT: none
;
; OUTPUT: directories listed
;
;  PROCS: none
;
;   AUTH: E. E. Iacobucci
;
;   DATE: 10/15/87
;
;-------------------------------------------------------------------
                .286c
                .xlist
                include   os2mac.inc
                .list

dgroup  group   LDI_data                    ;defines automatic data segment

;========================================
;
; LDI stack
;
;========================================
LDI_stack       segment para stack
;
                dw      256 dup('s')
;
LDI_stack       ends
;========================================
;
; LDI data segment
;
;========================================
LDI_data        segment para public 'auto'
;
; Messages
;
NAMLEN          equ         15
msg1            db          '('
msg1lvl         db          'X) '
msg1name        db          NAMLEN dup (' ')
                db          'Created: '
msg1wt          db          'HH:MM:SS '
msg1wd          db          'MM/DD/YY ',CR,LF
MSG1L           equ         $ - offset msg1
```

```
;
; Data
;
dirdata       direntry    <>                         ;directory data
dirdatal      dw          $-offset dirdata           ;directory data length
dirhand       dw          0ffffh                     ;directory handle
dirattrs      dw          10h                        ;search attribute
dirnum        dw          1                          ;number of directory entries
dirprev       db          '..',0                     ;previous directory
dirall        db          '*.*',0                    ;global search
indent        db          12 dup ('.')               ;indent characters
lastdir       db          11 dup (' ')               ;name of last directory processed
bytesout      dw          0                          ;bytes written
bytesin       dw          0                          ;bytes read
drive         dw          0                          ;drive number
rsv           dd          0                          ;reserved double word
;
LDI_data      ends
;
;=======================================
;
; LDI code segment
;
;=======================================
LDI_code      segment para public 'code'
              assume  cs:LDI_code,ds:LDI_data,es:LDI_data,ss:LDI_stack
main          proc
              push    ds                             ;copy data segment selector
              pop     es                             ;to ES
;
; Display directory data
;
              xor     cx,cx                          ;set nesting level (0)
              call    dispdir                        ;display current directory
;
; Termination processing
;
              @DosExit 1,0                            ;leave proc
main          endp
;
;       NAME: DISPDIR
; DESCRIPTION: Display all subdirectories in current directory
;      INPUT: Directory level in CX
;             Name pointer in DI
;     OUTPUT: subdirectory list
;
dispdir       proc
              push    ax                             ;save registers
              push    bx
              push    cx
              push    dx
```

```
;
; Read first directory entry
;
                mov       dirhand,0ffffh        ;set dir initial handle
                @DosFindFirst dirall,dirhand,dirattrs,dirdata,dirdatal,dirnum,rsv
                @jaxnz    dcd999                ;exit if none
;
; Process valid directory entries (loop)
;
dcd010:         cmp       dirdata.dirattr,10h   ;directory entry?
                je        dcd015                ;yes - continue
                inc       bx                    ;bump file count
                jmp       dcd020                ;read next file
;
dcd015:         cmp       byte ptr dirdata.dirname,'.' ;system directory?
                je        dcd020                ;yes - skip it
                call      printit               ;print data
                @DosChDir dirdata.dirname,rsv   ;go down one directory level
                inc       cx                    ;increment level
                push      dirhand               ;save directory handle
                call      dispdir               ;call self for next level
                pop       dirhand               ;restore directory handle
                dec       cx                    ;retore level
                @DosChDir dirprev,rsv           ;return to prev (..) dir level
;
dcd020:         @DosFindNext dirhand,dirdata,dirdatal,dirnum
                @jaxnz    dcd999                ;exit if end of directory
                jmp       dcd010                ;else continue processing files
;
; Termination
;
dcd999:         mov       dirnum,1              ;reset 1 record (reset by EOD)
                pop       dx                    ;restore registers
                pop       cx
                pop       bx
                pop       ax
                ret
dispdir         endp
;
;
;       NAME: PRINTIT
; DESCRIPTION: Display subdirectory record
;      INPUT: level in CX
;             current name pointer in DI
;     OUTPUT: display line
;
printit         proc
```

```
;
                mov       al,' '                    ;blank
                lea       di,msg1name               ;get name buffer address
                push      cx                        ;save level
                push      di                        ;save pointer
                mov       cx,NAMLEN                 ;buffer length
                rep       stosb                     ;erase it
                pop       di                        ;restore pointer
                pop       cx
;
                push      cx
                lea       si,indent                 ;source
                rep       movsb                     ;indent data
                pop       cx
;
                push      cx
                mov       cl,dirdata.dirnlen        ;get directory name length
                lea       si,dirdata.dirname        ;set pointer to directory name
                rep       movsb                     ;copy it to name buffer
                pop       cx                        ;restore level
;
                @date     dirdata.dirwd,msg1wd      ;convert creation date
                @time     dirdata.dirwt,msg1wt      ;convert creation time
                @bta      cx,msg1lvl,1              ;convert directory level
                @DosWrite stdout,msg1,msg1l,bytesout ;write message
;
                ret
;
printit         endp
;
                include   os2procs.asm              ;general purpose procedures
;
LDI_code        ends
                end       main
```

INFO.ASM

```
                    PAGE    ,132
                    TITLE  OS/2 file information program
;-------------------------------------------------------------
;   NAME: INFO
;
;   DESC: Display File Information
;
;  INPUT: File name
;
; OUTPUT: File info written to STDOUT
;
;  PROCS: GETDRIVE  (Parse drive number)
;
;   AUTH: E. E. Iacobucci
;
;   DATE: 10/15/87
;
;-------------------------------------------------------------
              .286c
              .xlist
              include   os2mac.inc
              .list

dgroup  group   INF_data                  ;defines automatic data segment

;=======================================
;
; INF stack
;
;=======================================
INF_stack     segment para stack
;
              dw    256 dup('s')
;
INF_stack     ends
;
;=======================================
;
; INF data segment
;
;=======================================
INF_data      segment para public 'auto'
;
; Messages
;
msg0          db         CR,LF
              db         'File does not exist ',CR,LF,CR,LF
MSGOL         equ        $ - offset msg0
```

```
;
msg4        db       CR,LF                              ;file information
            db       '                File Name: '
msg4fn      db       63 dup(' '),CR,LF,CR,LF
            db       '                  Created: '
msg4dc      db       'MM/DD/YY  '
msg4tc      db       'HH:MM:SS  ',CR,LF
            db       '              Last Update: '
msg4dw      db       'MM/DD/YY  '
msg4tw      db       'HH:MM:SS  ',CR,LF
            db       '                 Last Use: '
msg4da      db       'MM/DD/YY  '
msg4ta      db       'HH:MM:SS  ',CR,LF
            db       '                File Size: '
msg4eh      db       'HHHH'
msg4el      db       'HHHH',CR,LF
            db       '                   In Use: '
msg4ah      db       'HHHH'
msg4al      db       'HHHH',CR,LF,CR,LF
MSG4L       equ      $ - offset msg4
;
msg5        db       CR,LF,'          File System ID: '   ;file system data
msg5fsid    db       'XXXXXXXX',CR,LF
            db       'Sectors per Allocation unit: '
msg5spa     db       'XXXXXXXX',CR,LF
            db       ' Number of allocation units: '
msg5nal     db       'XXXXXXXX',CR,LF
            db       ' Available Allocation units: '
msg5aal     db       'XXXXXXXX',CR,LF
            db       '            Bytes per sector: '
msg5bps     db       'XXXX',CR,LF
MSG5L       equ      $ - offset msg5
;
msg6        db       '                Volume ID: '
msg6vid     db       11 dup(' '),CR,LF
            db       '                  Created: '
msg6vda     db       'MM/DD/YY  '
msg6vti     db       'HH:MM:SS  ',CR,LF
MSG6L       equ      $ - offset msg6
;
bytesout    dw       0                         ;bytes written
bytesin     dw       0                         ;bytes read
drive       dw       0                         ;drive number
rsv         dd       0                         ;reserved double word
```

```
;
fname       db         64 dup(0)            ;file name
fnlen       dw         0                    ;file name length
fhand       dw         0                    ;file handle
fact        dw         0
fsize       dd         0
fattr       dw         0
fflag       dw         00000001b            ;open flags
                       ;nnnneeee
fmode       dw         0000000011000000b    ;open mode
                       ;dwfrrrrrisssraaa
frsv        dd         0                    ;reserved
;
fidata      finfo      <>                   ;file info buffer
fisize      dw         $ - fidata           ;file info buffer size
filvl       dw         1                    ;file info level
;
fsdata1     fsinfo1    <>                   ;file system information #1
fssiz1      dw         $ - fsdata1          ;file system info buffer size
fslvl1      dw         1                    ;file system info level
;
fsdata2     fsinfo2    <>                   ;file system information #2
fssiz2      dw         $ - fsdata2          ;file system info buffer size
fslvl2      dw         2                    ;file system info level
;
INF_data    ends
;
;=========================================
;
; INF code segment
;
;=========================================
INF_code    segment para public 'code'
            assume  cs:INF_code,ds:INF_data,es:INF_data,ss:INF_stack
;
main        proc
            push       ds                   ;copy data segment selector
            pop        es                   ;to ES
;
;
; Parse input data & open file (if entered)
;
            @getparms fname,63              ;get command parameters
            @jaxz      inf050               ;jump if no data entered
;
            mov        cx,ax                ;get data length
            mov        di,offset fname      ;address buffer
            mov        al,' '               ;blank
            repne      scasb                ;scan for blank
            jcxz       inf010               ;skip adjustment if end of string
            dec        di                   ;point to blank
inf010:     mov        byte ptr [di],0      ;make name zero terminated
            sub        di,offset fname      ;compute name length
            mov        fnlen,di             ;save it
```

```
;
            call      getdrive              ;get drive number in input
            mov       drive,ax              ;save drive value
;
            @DosOpen  fname,fhand,fact,fsize,fattr,fflag,fmode,rsv
            @jaxz     inf030                ;go print data if file opened OK
            @DosWrite stderr,msg0,msg0l,bytesout ;Write invalid file name msg
            jmp       inf050                ;go print data
;
; Print file data
;
inf030:     @DosQFileInfo fhand,filvl,fidata,fisize   ;get file information
            @movs     fname,msg4fn,fnlen          ;file name
            @date     fidata.ficd,msg4dc           ;creation date
            @time     fidata.fict,msg4tc           ;creation time
            @date     fidata.fiad,msg4da           ;last access date
            @time     fidata.fiat,msg4ta           ;last access time
            @date     fidata.fiwd,msg4dw           ;last write date
            @time     fidata.fiwt,msg4tw           ;last write time
            @bth      fidata.fieh,msg4eh           ;file end to hex
            @bth      fidata.fiel,msg4el           ;file end to hex
            @bth      fidata.fiah,msg4ah           ;file end to hex
            @bth      fidata.fial,msg4al           ;file end to hex
            @DosWrite stdout,msg4,msg4l,bytesout   ;write file data
;
; Print file system info
;
inf050:     @DosQFsInfo drive,fslvl2,fsdata2,fssiz2 ;get file system data 2
            @jaxnz    inf060                ;no volume data - skip display
            xor       dx,dx                 ;clear ax
            mov       dl,fsdata2.vlen       ;move length to AX
            @movs     fsdata2.volid,msg6vid,dx ;file sys ID (char)
            @date     fsdata2.vdate,msg6vda ;Volume date
            @time     fsdata2.vtime,msg6vti ;Volume time
            @DosWrite stdout,msg6,msg6l,bytesout ;write file system data
;
inf060:     @DosQFsInfo drive,fslvl1,fsdata1,fssiz1 ;get file system data 1
            @bths     fsdata1.fsid,msg5fsid,4 ;file system ID
            @bth      <word ptr fsdata1.spa+2>,msg5spa ;sect/alloc unit   (high)
            @bth      <word ptr fsdata1.spa>,msg5spa+4 ;sect/alloc unit   (low)
            @bth      <word ptr fsdata1.nal+2>,msg5nal ;# alloc units     (high)
            @bth      <word ptr fsdata1.nal>,msg5nal+4 ;# alloc units     (low)
            @bth      <word ptr fsdata1.aal+2>,msg5aal ;avail alloc units (high)
            @bth      <word ptr fsdata1.aal>,msg5aal+4 ;avail alloc units (low)
            @bth      fsdata1.bps,msg5bps   ;bytes per sector
            @DosWrite stdout,msg5,msg5l,bytesout ;write file system data
```

```
;
; Close file
;
              @DosClose fhand
;
; Termination processing
;
inf999:       @DosExit 1,0                    ;leave proc
main          endp
;
;
;      NAME: GETDRIVE
; DESCRIPTION: Determine drive ID in file name
;      INPUT: file name in fname
;     OUTPUT: drive # in AX (zero if none)
;
getdrive      proc
              xor       ax,ax                 ;clear drive id
              cmp       byte ptr fname+1,':'  ;drive specified?
              jne       gtd999                ;no
              mov       al,fname              ;get drive value
              and       al,0fh                ;isolate drive # (a=1, b=2, ...)
gtd999:       ret
getdrive      endp
;
              include   os2procs.asm          ;general purpose procedures
;
INF_code      ends
              end       main
```

ALLOCMEM.ASM

```
                PAGE    80,132
                TITLE   OS/2 memory allocation program
;-----------------------------------------------------------------
;   NAME: ALLOCMEM
;
;   DESC: Allocate & deallocate data segments
;
;  INPUT: none
;
; OUTPUT: none
;
;  PROCS: none
;
;   AUTH: E. E. Iacobucci
;
;   DATE: 10/15/87
;
;-----------------------------------------------------------------
                .286c
                .xlist
                include    os2mac.inc
                .list

dgroup  group    ALO_data                ;defines automatic data segment
;=========================================
;
; ALO stack
;
;=========================================
ALO_stack       segment para stack
;
                dw     256 dup('s')
;
ALO_stack       ends
;=========================================
;
; ALO data segment
;
;=========================================
ALO_data        segment para public 'auto'
;
msg1            db          'Segment Number '
msg1no         db          'xx '
msg1type       db          'Allocated      (Size '
msg1sz         db          'xxxxx, Selector '
msg1sel        db          'xxxx)'
MSG1L          equ         $ - offset msg1
;
msg2           db          'Available Memory: '
msg2as         db          'HHHHHHHH'
MSG2L          equ         $ - offset msg2
```

```
;
segsz        dw       4000h               ;physical segment size
segp         dw       0                   ;physical segment selector
alloc        db       'Allocated   '      ;message string
dealloc      db       'De-Allocated'      ;message string
bytesout     dw       0                   ;bytes output
sleepcount   dd       200                 ;pause 200 MS
;
availsizel   dw       0                   ;available memory (low)
availsizeh   dw       0                   ;available memory (high)
attrib       dw       0                   ;attribute (for display)
fill         db       ' ',07h             ;fill cell (for scroll)
GREEN        equ      02Fh                ;green attribute
YELLOW       equ      06Fh                ;Yellow attribute
RED          equ      0cFh                ;red (flashing) attribute
COUNT        equ      64                  ;inner loop count
ALO_data     ends
;
;=======================================
;
; ALO code segment
;
;=======================================
ALO_code     segment para public 'code'
             assume  cs:ALO_code,es:nothing,ds:ALO_data,ss:ALO_stack
;
main         proc
             @VioScrollUp 0,0,-1,-1,-1,fill,0 ;clear the screen
             xor     dx,dx               ;segment count
             mov     cx,4                ;outer loop
alo010:      push    cx                  ;save outer loop count
;
             mov     cx,COUNT            ;inner loop count
             @movs   alloc,msg1type,12   ;type of operation (allocate)
alo020:      @DosAllocSeg  segsz,segp,0  ;allocate segment
             push    segp                ;save value
             push    segsz               ;save size
             inc     dx                  ;increment segment count
             call    displaymsg          ;display message
             cmp     attrib,RED          ;over committed?
             je      alo025              ;yes - skip remaining allocations
             add     segsz,100h          ;increase segment size
             loop    alo020              ;continue
;
alo025:      mov     cx,dx               ;set segment count
             @movs   dealloc,msg1type,12 ;type of operation (deallocate)
alo030:      pop     segsz               ;restore segment size
             pop     segp                ;restore segment pointer
             @DosFreeSeg segp            ;de-allocate segment
             call    displaymsg          ;display message
             dec     dx                  ;decrement segment count
             loop    alo030              ;continue
```

```
;
                pop        cx                      ;restore outer loop
                dec        cx                      ;decrement loop count
                jcxz       alo999                  ;done
                jmp        alo010                  ;loop
;
alo999:         @DosExit 1,0                        ;leave proc
main            endp
;
;       NAME: DISPLAYMSG
; DESCRIPTION: Display message
;       INPUT: segment number in DX
;              segment size in segsz
;              segment selector in segp
;      OUTPUT: Data is displayed in a message
;
displaymsg      proc
                mov        attrib,GREEN            ;normal attribute
                @bta       segsz,msg1sz,5          ;convert segment size
                @bta       dx,msg1no,2             ;convert segment number
                @bth       segp,msg1sel            ;convert selector value
                @VioWrtCharStrAtt msg1,MSG1L,10,4,attrib,0 ;write message
                @DosSleep sleepcount               ;pause for a while
;
                @DosMemAvail availsizel             ;get available memory
                @bth       availsizeh,msg2as       ;available memory (high)
                @bth       availsizel,msg2as+4     ;available memory (low)
                cmp        availsizeh,0            ;less than 64KB?
                jbe        dis010                  ;yes - warning
                jmp        dis030                  ;go display
dis010:         cmp        availsizel,4096         ;less than 4KB?
                jbe        dis020                  ;yes - warning
                mov        attrib,YELLOW           ;attribute
                jmp        dis030                  ;go display
dis020:         mov        attrib,RED              ;attribute
dis030:         @VioWrtCharStrAtt msg2,MSG2L,12,20,attrib,0 ;write number
                ret
displaymsg      endp
;
                include    os2procs.asm             ;general purpose procedures
;
ALO_code        ends
                end        main
```

HEXDISP.ASM

```
                PAGE   80,132
                TITLE  OS/2 hex browse program
;-------------------------------------------------------------
;   NAME: HEXDISP
;
;   DESC: Display file in hexadecimal
;
;  INPUT: none
;
; OUTPUT: full screen display of file
;          ESC  - Ends HEXDISP
;          PGUP - Pages up one screen
;          PGDN - Pages down one screen
;
;  PROCS: none
;
;   AUTH: E. E. Iacobucci
;
;   DATE: 10/15/87
;-------------------------------------------------------------
                .286c
                .xlist
                include   os2mac.inc
                .list

dgroup  group   HEX_data                  ;defines automatic data segment

;========================================
;
; HEX stack
;
;========================================
HEX_stack       segment para stack
;
                dw    256 dup('s')
;
HEX_stack       ends
;
;========================================
;
; HEX data segment
;
;========================================
HEX_data        segment para public 'auto'
```

```
;
; Display data
;
dline      db            '    '
dofsh      db            'HHHH'
dofsl      db            'HHHH   '
dhex1      db            'HHHHHHHH '
dhex2      db            'HHHHHHHH   '
dhex3      db            'HHHHHHHH '
dhex4      db            'HHHHHHHH       * '
ddata      db            'dddddddddddddddd* '
           db            5   dup (' ')
;
topmsg     db            'HEXDISP: '
topfn      db            33 dup (' ')
           db            '<PgUp> <PgDn> <ESC>   Page '
topcur     db            'xxxx of '
toptot     db            'xxxx '
;
; Messages
;
msg1       db            'You must enter a file name',CR,LF
MSG1L      equ           $ - offset msg1
;
msg2       db            'Open error',CR,LF
MSG2L      equ           $ - offset msg2
;
; Data
;
keydata    charbuf       <>                      ;charin data structure
XX         equ           01bh                    ;escape character
UP         equ           4900h                   ;PgUp key
DN         equ           5100h                   ;PgDown key
;
hexsegsz   dw            0                        ;physical segment size
hexsegp    dw            0                        ;physical segment selector
hexseg     dw            0                        ;current segment in data
hexofs     dw            0                        ;current offset in data
hexlaspar  dw            0                        ;last paragraph
hexlasbyt  dw            0                        ;last byte
shift      dw            0                        ;selector shift value
;
green      db            2Fh                      ;green attribute
fill       db            ' ',1Fh                  ;fill cell (for scroll)
bytesin    dw            0                        ;input bytes
bytesout   dw            0                        ;output bytes
temp       dw            0                        ;temporary binary page number
;
; File parameters
;
```

```
fname         db        64 dup(0)           ;file name
fnamel        dw        0                   ;file name length
fhand         dw        0
fact          dw        0
fsize         dd        0
fattr         dw        0
fflag         dw        00000001b           ;open flags
                        ;nnnneeee
fmode         dw        0000000011000000b   ;open mode
                        ;dwfrrrrrisssraaa
frsv          dd        0                   ;reserved
fofsl         dw        0                   ;file offset (low)
fofsh         dw        0                   ;file offset (high)
nofs          dd        0                   ;file offset
;
HEX_data      ends
;
;========================================
;
; HEX code segment
;
;========================================
HEX_code      segment para public 'code'
              assume   cs:HEX_code,ds:nothing,es:HEX_data,ss:HEX_stack
;
main          proc
              push      ds                  ;copy data segment
              pop       es                  ;to ES
;
              call      openf               ;open file
              @jaxnz    hex999              ;error
              call      getfile             ;read file in memory
              @jaxnz    hex999              ;error
              call      showfile            ;show data file
;
hex999:       @DosExit 1,0                  ;leave proc
main          endp
;
;
;       NAME: OPENF
; DESCRIPTION: Parse input & open file
;      INPUT: BX points to environment segment
;             AX is command_line offset
;     OUTPUT: open handle in fhandle
;             file name in fname
;             file name length in fnamel
;
openf         proc
              @getparms fname,63            ;get command parameters
              @jaxnz    opf010              ;jump if data was entered
              @DosWrite stderr,msg1,MSG1L,bytesout ;Write error message
              mov       ax,0ffh             ;set error code
              jmp       opf999              ;exit with error
```

```
;
opf010:     mov     cx,ax                   ;get data length
            mov     di,offset fname         ;address buffer
            mov     al,' '                  ;blank
            repne   scasb                   ;scan for blank
            jcxz    opf020                  ;skip adjustment if end of string
            dec     di                      ;point to blank
opf020:     mov     byte ptr [di],0         ;make name zero terminated
            sub     di,offset fname         ;compute name length
            mov     fnamel,di               ;save it
;
            @DosOpen  fname,fhand,fact,fsize,fattr,fflag,fmode,frsv
            @jaxz     opf999                ;go exit if file opened OK
            @DosWrite stderr,msg2,msg2l,bytesout ;Write invalid file name msg
            mov     ax,0ffh                 ;set error code
opf999:     ret
openf       endp
;
;
;         NAME: GETFILE
;  DESCRIPTION: Read file into memory
;        INPUT: none
;       OUTPUT: segment allocated & file read in
;
;
getfile     proc
;
; Determine file size
;
            mov     fofsl,0                 ;no bytes past end-of-file
            @DosChgFilePtr fhand,fofsl,2,fofsl ;move file ptr to end of file
            mov     word ptr nofs,0         ;file offset
            @DosChgFilePtr fhand,nofs,0,nofs ;move file ptr to start of file
;
; Allocate buffer
;
get010:     mov     dx,fofsl                ;get low file size word
            add     dx,16                   ;add pad bytes
            mov     hexsegsz,dx             ;save segment (file) size
            @DosAllocHuge  fofsh,dx,hexsegp,0,0  ;allocate segment
            mov     ax,0ffh                 ;set error code
            jmp     get999                  ;exit
;
get015:     push    hexsegp                 ;put new selector
            pop     ds                      ;in DS
            @DosGetHugeShift shift          ;get shift count
            mov     di,1                    ;set increment base
            mov     cx,shift                ;get huge shift value
            shl     di,cl                   ;compute segment shift count
            mov     shift,di                ;save it for later use
```

```
;
;
;
; Read it into memory
;
                push    ds                      ;save initial selector
                xor     si,si                   ;set data area offset
                mov     cx,fofsh                ;get segment count
                jcxz    get030                  ;jump if no additional segments
;
get020:         @DosRead fhand,DS:SI,-1,bytesin ;read complete segment(s)
                push    cx
                mov     ax,ds                   ;get selector
                add     ax,shift                ;compute next segment
                mov     ds,ax                   ;set segment register
                pop     cx
                loop    get020                  ;get all complete segments
;
get030:         @DosRead fhand,DS:SI,hexsegsz,bytesin ;read remainder of file
                @DosClose fhand                 ;close data file
                xor     ax,ax                   ;clear return code
                pop     ds
;
get999:         ret
getfile         endp
;
;       NAME: SHOWFILE
; DESCRIPTION: Display file in hex
;      INPUT: none
;     OUTPUT: Formatted data listed on display
;
;
showfile        proc
;
; Display first screen
;
                push    ds                      ;save data pointer
                push    es                      ;copy my data segment
                pop     ds                      ;to ds
                lea     si,fname                ;get file name offset
                lea     di,topfn                ;get file display field
                mov     cx,fnamel               ;get file name length
                cmp     cx,33                   ;will it fit in display area?
                jle     shf010                  ;yes, go move it in
                mov     cx,33                   ;no, get first 33 characters
shf010:         rep     movsb                   ;move it in
                pop     ds                      ;restore data pointer
;
                mov     dx,fofsh                ;get high word of file size
                mov     ax,fofsl                ;get low word of file size
                mov     bx,16*24                ;divisor
                div     bx                      ;compute total page count
                mov     temp,ax                 ;binary page number
                @bta    temp,toptot,4           ;set total page count
```

```
;
                @VioScrollUp 0,0,-1,-1,-1,fill,0 ;clear the screen
                @VioWrtCharStrAtt topmsg,80,0,0,green,0 ;write banner
                mov       hexofs,0              ;set file offset
                mov       hexseg,0              ;set segment
                mov       dx,fofsh              ;set file segment count
                mov       bx,fofsl              ;get file size
                call      showscreen            ;display first screen
;
;
; Process keyboard commands
;
shf020:         @KbdCharIn keydata,0,0          ;read keyboard
                cmp       keydata.charascii,XX  ;escape character?
                jne       shf030                ;no - continue
                jmp       shf999                ;yes - exit
;
shf030:         cmp       word ptr keydata.charascii,UP ;up key?
                jne       shf040                ;no - continue
                cmp       hexofs,0              ;already at top?
                jne       shf035                ;no, go display
                cmp       hexseg,0              ;already at top?
                jne       shf035                ;no, go display
                @DosBeep 1000,200               ;beep
                jmp       shf020                ;get next key
shf035:         mov       di,hexofs             ;save offset value
                sub       hexofs,16*24          ;one page less
                cmp       hexofs,di             ;backed into previous segment?
                jb        shf037                ;no, go display
                mov       ax,ds                 ;get data segment selector
                sub       ax,shift              ;compute previous selector value
                mov       ds,ax                 ;set segment register
                dec       hexseg                ;previous segment
;
shf037:         push      hexseg                ;save hex segment
                push      ds                    ;save segment
                call      showscreen            ;display screen
                pop       ds                    ;restore segment
                pop       hexseg                ;restore hex segment
                jmp       shf020                ;read next character
;
shf040:         cmp       word ptr keydata.charascii,DN ;down key?
                jne       shf050                ;no - continue
                add       hexofs,16*24          ;one page more
;
shf043:         cmp       dx,hexseg             ;at last segment?
                jne       shf045                ;no - continue
                cmp       bx,hexofs             ;past end of file?
                jae       shf045                ;no, go display
                @DosBeep 1000,200               ;beep
                sub       hexofs,16*24          ;back up
                jmp       shf020                ;get next key
shf045:         call      showscreen            ;display screen
                jmp       shf020                ;read next character
```

```
;
shf050:        jmp        shf020              ;read next character
shf999:        ret
showfile       endp
;
;        NAME: SHOWSCREEN
; DESCRIPTION: Display one screen of data
;       INPUT: data offset in hexofs
;      OUTPUT: 24 lines of data displayed on screen
;
;
showscreen     proc
               push       hexofs              ;save displacement
;
               push       dx                  ;save registers
               push       bx                  ;
               mov        dx,hexseg           ;get high word of file size
               mov        ax,hexofs           ;get low word of file size
               mov        bx,16*24            ;divisor
               div        bx                  ;compute current page #
               mov        temp,ax             ;binary page number
               @bta       temp,topcur,4       ;set current page #
               @VioWrtCharStrAtt topmsg,80,0,0,green,0 ;write banner
               pop        bx                  ;
               pop        dx                  ;
;
               mov        cx,24               ;set loop count
               mov        si,1                ;starting line number
shs010:        call       formatline          ;get data in dline
               @VioWrtCharStr dline,80,si,1,0 ;write d line
               add        hexofs,16           ;next 16 bytes
               cmp        hexofs,0            ;new segment?
               jne        shs020              ;no - continue
;
               mov        ax,ds               ;get selector
               add        ax,shift            ;compute next selector value
               mov        ds,ax               ;set segment register
               inc        hexseg              ;next segment
;
shs020:        inc        si                  ;next display line
               loop       shs010              ;continue
               ;
               pop        hexofs              ;restore displacement
               ret
showscreen     endp
```

```
;
;           NAME: FORMATLINE
; DESCRIPTION: Format 16 bytes of file data
;          INPUT: entry pointer in BX
;         OUTPUT: Formatted directory in dline data structure
;
;
formatline   proc

             push      cx                    ;save registers
             push      si                    ;
;
             cmp       dx,hexseg             ;at last segment?
             jne       fmt010                ;no, continue
             cmp       bx,hexofs             ;at end of file?
             jae       fmt010                ;no, go format line
;
             mov       cx,40                 ;line length
             mov       ax,' '                ;blank characters
             lea       di,dline              ;display line offset
             rep       stosw                 ;blank it out
             jmp       fmt999                ;exit
;
fmt010:      mov       cx,16                 ;length
             mov       si,hexofs             ;file offset
             lea       di,ddata-1            ;destination
             mov       al,'*'                ;divider
             stosb                           ;put divider
             rep       movsb                 ;move the raw data
             stosb                           ;put divider
;
             @bth      hexofs,dofsl,4        ;convert offset
             @bth      hexseg,dofsh,4        ;convert segment value
             @bths     ddata+00,dhex1,4      ;convert 1st chunk
             @bths     ddata+04,dhex2,4      ;convert 2nd chunk
             @bths     ddata+08,dhex3,4      ;convert 3rd chunk
             @bths     ddata+12,dhex4,4      ;convert 4th chunk
;
fmt999:      pop       si                    ;restore registers
             pop       cx                    ;
             ret
formatline   endp
;
             include   os2procs.asm          ;general purpose procedures
;
HEX_code     ends
             end       main
```

FDIR.ASM

```
                PAGE    80,132
                TITLE   OS/2 full screen directory
;-------------------------------------------------------------
;   NAME: FDIR
;
;   DESC: Display directory
;
;  INPUT: none
;
; OUTPUT: full screen display of directory
;         ESC  - Ends FDIR
;         PGUP - Pages up one screen
;         PGDN - Pages down one screen
;
;  PROCS: none
;
;   AUTH: E. E. Iacobucci
;
;   DATE: 10/15/87
;
;-------------------------------------------------------------
                .286c
                .xlist
                include   os2mac.inc
                .list

dgroup  group   FDR_data                ;defines automatic data segment

;========================================
;
; FDR stack
;
;========================================
FDR_stack       segment para stack
;
                dw      256 dup('s')
;
FDR_stack       ends
;
;========================================
;
; FDR data segment
;
;========================================
FDR_data        segment para public 'auto'
```

```
;
; Display data
;
dline       db          ' '
dname       db          12 dup (' ')
DNAMELEN    equ         $ - offset dname
            db          4  dup (' ')
dtime       db          'HH:MM:SS '
ddate       db          'MM/DD/YY '
dattr       db          44  dup (' ')
;
topmsg      db          'FDIR : Full Screen Directory Listing    '
            db          ' <UP> Previous  <DOWN> Next  <ESC> Exit'
;
strro       db          'Read-only '
STRROL      equ         $-offset strro
;
strhi       db          'Hidden '
STRHIL      equ         $-offset strhi
;
strsy       db          'System File '
STRSYL      equ         $-offset strsy
;
strvo       db          'Volume Label '
STRVOL      equ         $-offset strvo
;
strsu       db          'Subdirectory '
STRSUL      equ         $-offset strsu
;
strar       db          'Not Archived '
STRARL      equ         $-offset strar
;
; Data
;
keydata     charbuf     <>                      ;charin data structure
XX          equ         01bh                    ;escape character
UP          equ         4800h                   ;up key
DN          equ         5000h                   ;down key
;
dirdata     direntry    <>                      ;directory data
DIRLEN      equ         $-offset dirdata         ;directory data length
DIRSTR      equ         DIRLEN+4                ;total block size
ENTRYC      equ         10                      ;entry count per re-allocation
;
dircount    dw          0                       ;total entry count
dirattrs    dw          16h                     ;search attribute (all files)
dirnum      dw          1                       ;number of directory entries
dirall      db          '*.*',0                 ;global search
dirhand     dw          1                       ;directory handle
direofs     dw          0                       ;directory block pointer
dirsegsz    dw          0                       ;physical segment size
dirsegp     dw          0                       ;physical segment selector
dirfirst    dw          0                       ;head of dir element chain
dirlast     dw          0                       ;tail of dir element chain
```

```
;
green           db      2Fh                     ;green attribute
fill            db      ' ',1Fh                 ;fill cell (for scroll)
;
rsv             dd      0                       ;reserved double word
;
FDR_data        ends
;
;=========================================
;
; FDR code segment
;
;=========================================
FDR_code        segment para public 'code'
                assume  cs:FDR_code,ds:nothing,es:FDR_data,ss:FDR_stack
;
main            proc
                push    ds                      ;put data segment
                pop     es                      ;in ES
;
                call    allocbuf                ;allocate buffer (initial)
                call    getdir                  ;read directory
                call    showdir                 ;show directory
;
                @DosExit 1,0                     ;leave proc
main            endp
;
;
;       NAME: ALLOCBUF
; DESCRIPTION: Allocate initial data segment
;      INPUT: none
;     OUTPUT: segment pointer set
;             header initialized
;
allocbuf        proc
                mov             dirsegsz,ENTRYC*DIRSTR+8 ;initialize segment size
                @DosAllocSeg    dirsegsz,dirsegp,0 ;allocate segment
                @DosSubSet      dirsegp,1,dirsegsz ;prepare for suballocation
                push    dirsegp                 ;put new selector
                pop     ds                      ;in DS
                ret
allocbuf        endp
;
;
;       NAME: GETDIR
; DESCRIPTION: Read directory information into memory
;      INPUT: none
;     OUTPUT: segment records allocated
;
;
getdir          proc
```

```
;
; Read first directory entry
;
                mov       si,offset dirdata       ;set pointer to data area
                @DosFindFirst dirall,dirhand,dirattrs,dirdata,DIRLEN,dirnum,rsv
                @jaxnz    gtd999                  ;exit if none
                mov       dircount,1              ;set initial file count
                call      suballoc                ;get initial block
                mov       di,direofs              ;get block pointer
                mov       word ptr ds:[di+2],0 ;set back pointer in first block
                mov       dirfirst,di             ;set root pointer to first block
;
; Process valid directory entries (loop)
;
;
gtd010:         push      di                      ;save block pointer
                push      si                      ;save pointer to dirdata
                add       di,4                    ;skip fwd & back pointers
                mov       cx,DIRLEN               ;directory entry size
                push      es                      ;switch es & ds
                push      ds
                pop       es
                pop       ds
                rep       movsb                   ;move entry into block
                push      es                      ;switch es & ds
                push      ds
                pop       es
                pop       ds
                pop       si                      ;restore pointer to dirdata
                pop       di                      ;restore block pointer
;
                @DosFindNext dirhand,dirdata,DIRLEN,dirnum
                @jaxnz    gtd800                  ;exit if end of directory
                inc       dircount                ;increment file count
                call      suballoc                ;get another block
                mov       bx,di                   ;save previous pointer
                mov       di,direofs              ;get new block pointer
                mov       ds:[bx+0],di            ;forward chain (in previous block)
                mov       ds:[di+2],bx            ;back chain (in new block)
                jmp       gtd010                  ;continue processing files
;
; Exit
;
gtd800:         mov       word ptr ds:[di+0],0 ;set forward pointer in last block
                mov       dirlast,di              ;set root pointer to last block
gtd999:         ret
getdir          endp
```

```
;
;          NAME: SUBALLOC
; DESCRIPTION: Sub-allocate memory segment & grow physical
;              segment (if needed).
;        INPUT: current physical segment size in DIRSEGSZ
;       OUTPUT: Sub-allocated element address in DIREOFS
;
suballoc      proc
sal010:       @DosSubAlloc  dirsegp,direofs,DIRSTR ;suballocate block
              @jaxz      sal999                ;all OK - go exit
;
              add        dirsegsz,ENTRYC*DIRSTR ;increase segment size
              @DosReAllocSeg dirsegsz,dirsegp  ;grow segment
              @DosSubSet   dirsegp,0,dirsegsz  ;re-initialize suballocation
              jmp        sal010                ;go sub-allocate block
;
sal999:       ret
suballoc      endp
;
;          NAME: SHOWDIR
; DESCRIPTION: Display directory information
;        INPUT: none
;       OUTPUT: Formatted directory data listed on display
;
;
showdir       proc
;
; Display first screen
;
              @VioScrollUp 0,0,-1,-1,-1,fill,0 ;clear the screen
              @VioWrtCharStrAtt topmsg,80,0,0,green,0 ;write banner
;
              mov        cx,24                 ;set loop count
              mov        bx,dirfirst           ;get top entry
              add        bx,4                  ;point to data
              mov        si,bx                 ;display start
              mov        dx,1                  ;initial display line
;
sdr010:       call       formatline           ;get data in dline
              @VioWrtCharStr dline,80,dx,1,0  ;write d line
              inc        dx                    ;next line
              cmp        word ptr [bx-4],0     ;end of directory?
              je         sdr015                ;yes, exit
              mov        bx, [bx-4]            ;get next entry
              add        bx,4                  ;point to data (skip pointers)
              loop       sdr010                ;continue
sdr015:       mov        di,bx                 ;save end of display
```

```
;
; Process keyboard commands
;
sdr020:         @KbdCharIn keydata,0,0          ;read keyboard
                cmp        keydata.charascii,XX ;escape character?
                jne        sdr030               ;no - continue
                jmp        sdr999               ;yes - exit
;
sdr030:         cmp        word ptr keydata.charascii,UP ;up key?
                jne        sdr040               ;no - continue
                cmp        word ptr [si-2],0    ;end of data?
                je         sdr020               ;yes - exit routine
                mov        si,[si-2]            ;point to prev record  (top)
                mov        di,[di-2]            ;point to prev record  (bottom)
                add        si,4                 ;point to data (skip pointers)
                add        di,4                 ;point to data (skip pointers)
                mov        bx,si                ;set record to be displayed
                call       formatline           ;do it
                @VioScrollDn 1,0,24,79,1,fill,0 ;scroll down 1 line
                @VioWrtCharStr dline,80,1,1,0   ;write top line
                jmp        sdr020               ;read next character
;
sdr040:         cmp        word ptr keydata.charascii,DN ;down key?
                jne        sdr050               ;no - continue
                cmp        word ptr [di-4],0    ;end of data?
                jne        sdr025               ;no - continue
                jmp        sdr020               ;yes - exit routine
sdr025:         mov        si,[si-4]            ;point to next record  (top)
                mov        di,[di-4]            ;point to next record  (bottom)
                add        si,4                 ;point to data (skip pointers)
                add        di,4                 ;point to data (skip pointers)
                mov        bx,di                ;set record to be displayed
                call       formatline           ;do it
                @VioScrollUp 1,0,24,79,1,fill,0 ;scroll up line
                @VioWrtCharStr dline,80,24,1,0  ;write bottom line
                jmp        sdr020               ;read next character
;
sdr050:         jmp        sdr020               ;read next character
sdr999:         ret
showdir         endp
;
;       NAME: FORMATLINE
; DESCRIPTION: Format directory information
;      INPUT: entry pointer in BX
;     OUTPUT: Formatted directory in dline data structure
;
;
formatline      proc

                push       si                   ;save registers
                push       di                   ;
                push       cx
```

```
;
            mov         di,offset dline         ;display line name field
            push        di
            mov         cx,40                   ;length
            mov         ax,' '                  ;blanks
            rep         stosw                   ;clear it
            pop         di
            mov         si,offset dirname       ;directory structure name
            add         si,bx                   ;block offset
            mov         cl,[bx].dirnlen         ;get name length
            rep         movsb                   ;move to display line
            @date       [bx].dirwd,ddate        ;last write date
            @time       [bx].dirwt,dtime        ;last write time
;
; Display attribute(s)
;
            mov         di,offset dattr         ;address attribute area
            mov         ax,[bx].fiattr          ;get attribute byte
            push        ds                      ;save block segment
            push        es                      ;get FDIR data segment
            pop         ds                      ;
;
            push        ax                      ;save it
            and         ax,0001h                ;isolate Read only attribute
            @jaxz       fmt010                  ;check next
            mov         si,offset strro         ;'read only' string
            mov         cx,STRROL               ;get length
            rep         movsb                   ;move it into display
;
fmt010:     pop         ax                      ;restore attribute
            push        ax                      ;save attribute
            and         ax,0002h                ;isolate Hidden attribute
            @jaxz       fmt020                  ;check next
            mov         si,offset strhi         ;'hidden' string
            mov         cx,STRHIL               ;get length
            rep         movsb                   ;move it into display
;
fmt020:     pop         ax                      ;restore attribute
            push        ax                      ;save attribute
            and         ax,0004h                ;isolate System attribute
            @jaxz       fmt030                  ;check next
            mov         si,offset strsy         ;'System' string
            mov         cx,STRSYL               ;get length
            rep         movsb                   ;move it into display
;
fmt030:     pop         ax                      ;restore attribute
            push        ax                      ;save attribute
            and         ax,0008h                ;isolate Volume attribute
            @jaxz       fmt040                  ;check next
            mov         si,offset strvo         ;'Volume' string
            mov         cx,STRVOL               ;get length
            rep         movsb                   ;move it into display
```

```
;
fmt040:         pop       ax                    ;restore attribute
                push      ax                    ;save attribute
                and       ax,0010h              ;isolate Subdirectory attribute
                ajaxz     fmt050                ;check next
                mov       si,offset strsu       ;'Subdirectory' string
                mov       cx,STRSUL             ;get length
                rep       movsb                 ;move it into display
;
fmt050:         pop       ax                    ;restore attribute
                and       ax,0020h              ;isolate Archive attribute
                ajaxz     fmt999                ;exit
                mov       si,offset strar       ;'Archive' string
                mov       cx,STRARL             ;get length
                rep       movsb                 ;move it innto display
;
fmt999:         pop       ds                    ;restore block selector
                pop       cx                    ;restore registers
                pop       di                    ;
                pop       si                    ;
                ret
formatline      endp
;
                include   os2procs.asm          ;general purpose procedures
;
FDR_code        ends
                end       main
```

GIVE.ASM

```
                    PAGE    80,132
                    TITLE   OS/2 shared memory sample program
;----------------------------------------------------------------
;   NAME: GIVE
;
;   DESC: Write data into shared memory
;
;  INPUT: none
;
; OUTPUT: none
;
;  PROCS: none
;
;   AUTH: E. E. Iacobucci
;
;   DATE: 10/15/87
;
;----------------------------------------------------------------
                    .286c
                    .xlist
                    include    os2mac.inc
                    .list

dgroup  group   GIV_data                ;defines automatic data segment

;
;========================================
;
; GIV stack
;
;========================================
GIV_stack       segment para stack
;
                dw    256 dup('s')
;
GIV_stack       ends
;
;========================================
;
; GIV data segment
;
;========================================
GIV_data        segment para public 'auto'
;
msg1            db          'You can only start one copy of GIVE at a time!',CR,LF
MSG1L           equ         $ - offset msg1
;
msg2            db          'Shared Memory Allocated',CR,LF,CR,LF
MSG2L           equ         $ - offset msg2
```

```
;
msg3            db              'Enter Text: '
MSG3L           equ             $ - offset msg3
;
shrname         db              '\SHAREMEM\GIVE',0      ;shared segment name
shrsel          dw              0                      ;shared segment selector
bytesin         dw              0                      ;bytes read
bytesout        dw              0                      ;bytes written
sleepct         dd              500                    ;500 millisecond sleep count
ALLOCSZ         equ             128                    ;shared segment size
;
GIV_data        ends
;
;=========================================
;
; GIV code segment
;
;=========================================
GIV_code        segment para public 'code'
                assume  cs:GIV_code,es:nothing,ds:GIV_data,ss:GIV_stack
;
main            proc
;
                @DosAllocShrSeg ALLOCSZ,shrname,shrsel ;allocate shared segment
                push            shrsel                 ;put shared memory selector
                pop             es                     ;in ES
;
giv020:         mov             di,4                   ;point shared segment
                mov             cx,ALLOCSZ-4           ;point to data field
                mov             al,0                   ;fill character
                rep             stosb                  ;clear area
;
                mov             di,4                   ;point to data field
                @DosRead        STDIN,ES:DI,ALLOCSZ-4,bytesin ;Read data into shr seg
                xor             di,di                  ;point to start of buffer
                mov             ax,bytesin             ;get input byte count
                stosw                                  ;write to segment
                mov             word ptr es:[2],1      ;indicate data is present
                cmp             bytesin,0              ;null input?
                je              giv999                 ;yes - finished
;
giv030:         @DosSleep sleepct                      ;wait a little while
                cmp             word ptr es:[2],1      ;data still present?
                je              giv030                 ;yes - continue waiting
                jmp             giv020                 ;no - go read another string
;
giv999:         @DosFreeSeg shrsel                     ;Free shared memory segment
                @DosExit 1,0                           ;leave proc
main            endp
;
                include         os2procs.asm           ;general purpose procedures
;
GIV_code        ends
                end             main
```

TAKE.ASM

```
                PAGE    80,132
                TITLE   OS/2 shared memory sample program
;---------------------------------------------------------------
;   NAME: TAKE
;
;   DESC: Read data from shared memory
;
;  INPUT: Data record in \SHAREMEM\GIVE
;
; OUTPUT: Record is written to STDOUT
;
;  PROCS: none
;
;   AUTH: E. E. Iacobucci
;
;   DATE: 10/15/87
;
;---------------------------------------------------------------
                .286c
                .xlist
                include    os2mac.inc
                .list

dgroup   group    TAK_data              ;defines automatic data segment

;
;=======================================
;
; TAK stack
;
;=======================================
TAK_stack    segment para stack
;
              dw    256 dup('s')
;
TAK_stack    ends
;
;=======================================
;
; TAK data segment
;
;=======================================
TAK_data       segment para public 'auto'
;
msg1          db        'GIVE is not running!',CR,LF
MSG1L         equ       $ - offset msg1
;
msg2          db        'Shared Memory Acquired',CR,LF,CR,LF
MSG2L         equ       $ - offset msg2
```

```
;
shrname         db              '\SHAREMEM\GIVE',0      ;shared segment name
shrsel          dw              0                       ;shared segment selector
bytesin         dw              0                       ;bytes read
bytesout        dw              0                       ;bytes written
sleepct         dd              500                     ;500 millisecond sleep count
ALLOCSZ         equ             128                     ;shared segment size
;
TAK_data        ends
;
;=======================================
;
; TAK code segment
;
;=======================================
TAK_code        segment para public 'code'
                assume  cs:TAK_code,es:nothing,ds:TAK_data,ss:TAK_stack
;
main            proc
;
                @DosGetShrSeg shrname,shrsel    ;get shared segment
                @jaxz       tak010              ;Segment acquired OK - continue
                @DosWrite stderr,msg1,msg1l,bytesout ;Write error message
                jmp         tak999              ;exit
;
tak010:         push        shrsel              ;put shared memory selector
                pop         es                  ;in ES
                mov         di,4                ;point to data field
                jmp         tak030              ;go check for string


;
tak020:         @DosSleep sleepct               ;wait a little while
tak030:         cmp         word ptr es:[2],1   ;data exists?
                jne         tak020              ;no - continue waiting
                cmp         word ptr es:[0],0   ;null record?
                je          tak999              ;yes - exit
                @DosWrite stdout,ES:DI,es:[0],bytesout ;Write data
                mov         word ptr es:[2],0   ;indicate data has been read
                jmp         tak030              ;go check for another string
;
tak999:         @DosFreeSeg shrsel              ;Free shared memory segment
                @DosExit 0,1                    ;leave proc
main            endp
;
                include     os2procs.asm        ;general purpose procedures
;
TAK_code        ends
                end         main
```

RUN.ASM

```
                PAGE    80,132
                TITLE   OS/2 counting program
;--------------------------------------------------------------
;
;   NAME: RUN
;
;   DESC: Run multiple copies of COUNT
;
;  INPUT: Screen position for numeric counter (ROW,COL)
;
; OUTPUT: Data is written on the screen
;
;  PROCS: none
;
;   AUTH: E. E. Iacobucci
;
;   DATE: 10/15/87
;
;--------------------------------------------------------------
                .286c
                .xlist
                include   os2mac.inc
                .list

dgroup  group   RUN_data                ;defines automatic data segment


;
;=======================================
;
; RUN stack
;
;=======================================
RUN_stack       segment para stack
;
                dw      256 dup('s')
;
RUN_stack       ends
;
;=======================================
;
; RUN data segment
;
;=======================================
RUN_data        segment para public 'auto'
;
msg             db          ' <LEFT> Previous Process  '
MSGL            equ         $ - offset msg
                db          ' <RIGHT> Next Process     '
                db          '    <UP> Increase Priority '
                db          '  <DOWN> Decrease Priority '
                db          '   <DEL> Kill Process     '
                db          '   <INS> Restart Process  '
MSGLINES        equ         6
```

```
;
cdata           struc
row             dw      ?                       ;Display Row
col             dw      ?                       ;Display Column
attr            db      ?                       ;Display Attribute
priority        dw      ?                       ;Execution priority
sel             dw      ?                       ;Shared segment selector
procid          dw      ?                       ;process ID
cdata           ends
SHRSZ           equ     size cdata              ;structure size
;
count1          cdata   <4,03,1fh,31,0>         ;Count #1 initial parameters
                cdata   <4,22,2fh,31,0>         ;Count #2 initial parameters
                cdata   <4,41,4fh,31,0>         ;Count #3 initial parameters
                cdata   <4,60,6fh,31,0>         ;Count #4 initial parameters
PCOUNT          equ     4                       ;program count
;
pgmname         db      'COUNT.EXE',0           ;program name
pgmobj          db      10 dup(0)               ;bad exec object
pgmenv          db      0,0                     ;environment
pgmprm          db      0,0                     ;parameters
pgmpid          dw      0                       ;new process ID
                dw      0                       ;termination code area
;
shrname         db      '\SHAREMEM\RUN\'        ;shared segment name
shrpid          db      'HHHH',0                ;process ID
shrsel          dw      0                       ;shared segment selector
;
curproc         dw      0                       ;current (selected) process
prow            dw      0                       ;previous pointer row
pcol            dw      0                       ;previous pointer column
fill            db      ' ',07h                 ;fill cell (for scroll)
highlight       db      0Fh                     ;intensified white/black bgnd
point           db      '↑'                     ;process pointer
yellow          db      0Eh                     ;yellow/black bgnd
;
keyd            charbuf <>                      ;charin data structure
;
curd            cur     <>                      ;cursor data structure
;
RUN_data        ends
;
;=======================================
;
; RUN code segment
;
;=======================================
RUN_code        segment para public 'code'
                assume  cs:RUN_code,es:nothing,ds:RUN_data,ss:RUN_stack
;
main            proc
```

```
;
                @HideCursor                             ;blank out cursor
                @VioScrollUp 0,0,-1,-1,-1,fill,0 ;clear the screen
                mov       cx,MSGLINES              ;display line count
                mov       dx,14                    ;first line number
                lea       si,msg                   ;first message string
run000:         @VioWrtCharStrAtt DS:SI,MSGL,dx,26,highlight,0 ;prompt line
                inc       dx                       ;next display line
                add       si,MSGL                  ;next message
                loop      run000                   ;write all messages
;
                mov       cx,PCOUNT                ;program count
                lea       si,count1                ;first set of parameters
run010:         call      startprog                ;start COUNT program
                add       si,SHRSZ                 ;point to next parameter area
                loop      run010                   ;loop through process list
;
                call      keyin                    ;process keyboard input
;
                mov       cx,PCOUNT                ;program count
                lea       si,count1                ;first set of parameters
run020:         @DosKillProcess 0,[si].procid     ;Kill child process
                @DosFreeSeg [si].sel               ;Free shared memory segment
                add       si,SHRSZ                 ;point to next parameter area
                loop      run020                   ;loop through process list
;
                @ShowCursor                        ;Restore cursor
                @DosExit 1,0                        ;leave proc
main            endp
;
;       NAME: STARTPROG
; DESCRIPTION: Start a copy of COUNT
;      INPUT: Parameter block in SI
;     OUTPUT: none
;
startprog       proc
                push      cx                       ;save cx
                push      si                       ;save si
;
                @DosExecPgm  pgmobj,10,2,pgmprm,pgmenv,pgmpid,pgmname
                @bth      pgmpid,shrpid            ;convert pid to HEX (for segname)
                mov       ax,pgmpid                ;get new PID
                mov       [si].procid,ax           ;save it in parameter block
;
                @DosAllocShrSeg SHRSZ,shrname,shrsel ;allocate shared segment
                push      shrsel                   ;put shared memory selector
                pop       es                       ;in ES
                xor       di,di                    ;start of shared segment
                mov       cx,SHRSZ                 ;data structure size
                rep       movsb                    ;copy structure into shared seg
;
                pop       si                       ;restore si
                pop       cx                       ;restore cx
                ret
startprog       endp
```

```
;
;          NAME: KEYIN
; DESCRIPTION: Process keyboard commands
;        INPUT: none
;       OUTPUT: none
;
keyin          proc
;
               call      setpoint              ;set pointer to active process
;
kin000:        @KbdCharIn keyd,0,0              ;read keyboard
               mov       al,keyd.charascii     ;get ASCII character
               cmp       al,0                  ;extended scan?
               jne       kin010                ;no, go check which key it was
               mov       ah,keyd.charscan      ;get scan code
;
kin010:        cmp       ax,KESC               ;escape key?
               jne       kin020                ;no - continue
               jmp       kin999                ;yes - exit
;
kin020:        cmp       ax,KLE                ;left key?
               jne       kin030                ;no - continue
               dec       curproc               ;previous process
               and       curproc,03h           ;isolate number (0-3)
               call      setpoint              ;move pointer
               jmp       kin000                ;continue
;
kin030:        cmp       ax,KRI                ;right key?
               jne       kin040                ;no - continue
               inc       curproc               ;next process
               and       curproc,03h           ;isolate number (0-3)
               call      setpoint              ;move pointer
               jmp       kin000                ;continue
;
kin040:        cmp       ax,KUP                ;up key?
               jne       kin050                ;no - continue
               @DosSetPrty 0,0,+1,[si].procid  ;increase priority by 1
               jmp       kin000                ;continue
;
kin050:        cmp       ax,KDN                ;down key?
               jne       kin060                ;no - continue
               @DosSetPrty 0,0,-1,[si].procid  ;decrease priority by 1
               jmp       kin000                ;continue
;
kin060:        cmp       ax,KINS               ;insert key?
               jne       kin070                ;no - continue
               cmp       [si].procid,0         ;process stopped?
               je        kin065                ;yes - continue
               jmp       kin000                ;no - ignore request
kin065:        call      startprog             ;start program
               jmp       kin000                ;continue
```

```
;
kin070:         cmp      ax,KDEL                ;delete key?
                jne      kin500                 ;no - continue
                cmp      [si].procid,0          ;process already stopped?
                jne      kin075                 ;no - continue
                jmp      kin000                 ;yes - ignore request
kin075:         @DosKillProcess 0,[si].procid   ;Kill child process
                @DosFreeSeg [si].sel            ;Free shared memory segment
                mov      [si].procid,0          ;mark process ID null
                jmp      kin000                 ;continue
;
kin500:         jmp      kin000                 ;continue
;
kin999:         ret
keyin           endp
;
;       NAME: SETPOINT
; DESCRIPTION: Display current process pointer
;       INPUT: current process value in CURPOINT
;      OUTPUT: pointer displayed on screen
;
setpoint        proc
;
                @VioWrtCellStr fill,2,prow,pcol,0 ;clear previous pointer
;
                mov      ax,curproc             ;get pointer value
                mov      ah,SHRSZ               ;get structure size
                mul      ah                     ;compute offset
                lea      si,count1              ;data structure base address
                add      si,ax                  ;compute structure pointer
;
                mov      bx,[si].row            ;get row
                add      bx,5                   ;five lines down
                mov      dx,[si].col            ;get column
                add      dx,8                   ;eight columns over
                @VioWrtCharStrAtt point,1,bx,dx,yellow,0 ;write new pointer
                mov      prow,bx                ;save previous row
                mov      pcol,dx                ;save previous column
;
                ret
setpoint        endp
;
                include  os2procs.asm           ;general purpose procedures
;
RUN_code        ends
                end      main
```

COUNT.ASM

```
                        PAGE    80,132
                        TITLE  OS/2 counting program
;----------------------------------------------------------------
;   NAME: COUNT
;
;   DESC: Loop through a counter & display results on screen
;
;  INPUT: Data structure in shared memory segment
;
; OUTPUT: Data is written on the screen
;
;  PROCS: none
;
;   AUTH: E. E. Iacobucci
;
;   DATE: 10/15/87
;
;----------------------------------------------------------------
                .286c
                .xlist
                include    os2mac.inc
                .list

dgroup  group   CNT_data                ;defines automatic data segment

;
;=======================================
;
; CNT stack
;
;=======================================
CNT_stack       segment para stack
;
                dw    256 dup('s')
;
CNT_stack       ends
;
;=======================================
;
; CNT data segment
;
;=======================================
CNT_data        segment para public 'auto'
;
cdata           struc
row             dw        ?             ;Display Row
col             dw        ?             ;Display Column
attr            db        ?             ;Display Attribute
priority        dw        ?             ;Execution priority
sel             dw        ?             ;Shared segment selector
cdata           ends
```

```
;
;
msg0         db          '┌──────────────┐'
MSGL         equ         $ - offset msg0
;
msg1         db          '│PID('
msgpid       db          '....) '
msgcnt       db          '.....│'
;
msg2         db          '│ Priority = '
msgprty      db          '.. │'
;
msg3         db          '└──────────────┘'
;
dead         db          '     Dead!     '   ;dead process message
;
shrname      db          '\SHAREMEM\RUN\'     ;shared segment name
shrpid       db          'HHHH',0            ;process ID
shrsel       dw          0                   ;shared segment selector
;
piddata      pid         <>                  ;process ID information
;
attrib       dw          0                   ;local attribute variable
red          db          04h                 ;red attribute
fill         db          ' ',07h             ;fill cell (for scroll)
;
termp        dw          offset termproc     ;termination proc
             dw          seg termproc
;
myprty       dw          0                   ;GetPriority work area
sleepct      dd          30                  ;30 millisecond sleep count
;
CNT_data     ends
;
;=======================================
;
; CNT code segment
;
;=======================================
CNT_code     segment para public 'code'
             assume  cs:CNT_code,ds:nothing,es:CNT_data,ss:CNT_stack
;
main         proc
             push        ds                  ;copy ds
             pop         es                  ;to es
;
             @DosSetSigHandler termp,NULL,NULL,2,SIGTERM ;register sig handler
;
             @DosGetPid piddata              ;get process ID information
             @bth        piddata.pidpid,shrpid  ;convert to hex (for sharename)
             @bth        piddata.pidpid,msgpid  ;convert to hex (for message)
```

```
;
cnt010:      @DosGetShrSeg shrname,shrsel    ;get shared segment
             @jaxz     cnt020                ;Segment exists - go count
             @DosSleep sleepct               ;wait a little while
             jmp       cnt010                ;go try again
;
cnt020:      push      shrsel                ;put shared memory selector
             pop       ds                    ; in ES
             xor       di,di                 ;point to start of segment
             xor       dx,dx                 ;clear counter
;
cnt030:      call      printit               ;display information
             @DosSleep sleepct               ;wait a little while
             inc       dx                    ;next number
             jmp       cnt030                ;keep counting
;
cnt999:      @DosExit 1,0                     ;end process
main         endp
;
;      NAME: PRINTIT
; DESCRIPTION: Display counter on screen
;      INPUT: count in DX
;               shared segment in ES:DI
;     OUTPUT: none
;
printit      proc
             mov       al,[di].attr          ;get attribute
             mov       attrib,ax             ;put it in memory
             @bta      dx,msgcnt,5           ;convert count to ASCII
;
             @DosGetPrty 0,myprty,0          ;get my current priority value
             mov       bx,myprty             ;get priority
             xor       bh,bh                 ;clear priority class
             @bta      bx,msgprty,2          ;convert to displayable ASCII
;
             @VioWrtCharStrAtt msg0,MSGL,[di].row,[di].col,attrib,0 ;Line 1
             mov       bx,[di].row           ;get row
             inc       bx                    ;next line
             @VioWrtCharStrAtt msg1,MSGL,bx,[di].col,attrib,0        ;Line 2
             inc       bx                    ;next line
             @VioWrtCharStrAtt msg2,MSGL,bx,[di].col,attrib,0        ;Line 3
             inc       bx                    ;next line
             @VioWrtCharStrAtt msg3,MSGL,bx,[di].col,attrib,0        ;Line 4
;
             ret
printit      endp
;
;      NAME: TERMPROC
; DESCRIPTION: Handle termination signal
;      INPUT: Shared segment in ES:DI
;     OUTPUT: Display is cleared
;
termproc     proc
```

```
;
                mov     ax,CNT_data             ;get my DS
                mov     es,ax                   ;address it
                cmp     shrsel,0                ;shared segment in place?
                jne     trm010                  ;yes, continue processing
                jmp     trm999                  ;no - exit
;
trm010:         mov     ax,shrsel               ;get shared segment
                mov     ds,ax                   ;address it
                xor     di,di                   ;point to start of segment
;
                mov     bx,[di].row             ;get row number
                add     bx,4                    ;bottom row
                mov     dx,[di].col             ;get column number
                push    dx                      ;save starting column
                add     dx,MSGL                 ;bottom column
                @VioScrollUp [di].row,[di].col,bx,dx,-1,fill,0 ;clear the window
                sub     bx,2                    ;up 2 rows
                pop     dx                      ;restore column
                @VioWrtCharStrAtt dead,MSGL,bx,dx,red,0 ;Dead message
trm999:         @DosExit 0,1                    ;end process
termproc        endp
;
                include os2procs.asm            ;general purpose procedures
;
CNT_code        ends
                end     main
```

SNAKES.ASM

```
                 PAGE   80,132
                 TITLE  OS/2 thread demonstration
;------------------------------------------------------------------
;   NAME: SNAKE
;
;   DESC: A sample program which uses threads to draw
;         different figures on the screen.
;
;  INPUT: none
;
; OUTPUT: Data is written on the screen
;
;  PROCS: none
;
;   AUTH: E. E. Iacobucci
;
;   DATE: 10/15/87
;
;------------------------------------------------------------------
                 .286c
                 .xlist
                 include   os2mac.inc
                 .list

dgroup  group   SNA_data                 ;defines automatic data segment

public  snake


;
;========================================
;
; SNA stack
;
;========================================
SNA_stack       segment para stack
;
                dw    256 dup('s')
;
SNA_stack       ends
;
;========================================
;
; SNA data segment
;
;========================================
SNA_data        segment para public 'auto'
;
msg             db        ' <+> Create another snake    <p> Pause
                db        '                     <ESC> Exit '
MSGL            equ       $ - offset msg
```

```
;
dirtab          db          0,1                             ;up
                db          2,0                             ;right
                db          0,0ffh                          ;down
                db          0feh,0                          ;left
;
keyd            charbuf     <>                              ;charin data structure
curd            cur         <>                              ;cursor data structure
;
blok            db          '█'                             ;character (for snake)
fill            db          ' ',07h,' ',07h                 ;fill cells
msgatr          db          0eh                             ;message attribute (yellow)
;
gdtinfo         dw          0                               ;gdt info selector
ldtinfo         dw          0                               ;ldt info selector
screensem       dd          0                               ;screen semaphore
semhand         dw          offset screensem                ;screen semaphore handle
                dw          seg     screensem
noto            dd          -1                              ;no time out value (for semaphore)
;
SNA_data        ends
;
;=======================================
;
; SNA code segment
;
;=======================================
SNA_code        segment para public 'code'
                assume  cs:SNA_code,es:nothing,es:SNA_data,ss:SNA_stack
;
main            proc
                push        ds                              ;copy DS
                pop         es                              ;to ES
;
                @VioGetCurType curd,0                       ;get cursor type
                mov         curd.curattr,-1                 ;set 'hidden' attribute
                @VioSetCurType curd,0                       ;hide cursor
;
                @VioScrollUp 0,0,-1,-1,-1,fill,0 ;clear the screen
                @VioWrtCharStrAtt msg,MSGL,24,0,msgatr,0 ;write prompt
;
                @DosGetInfoSeg gdtinfo,ldtinfo ;get system info segments
;
                @Mkthread snake,256                         ;make snake thread
                mov         dx,1                            ;set initial snake count
;
; Process keyboard input
;
snk000:         @KbdCharIn keyd,0,0                         ;read keyboard
                xor         ax,ax                           ;clear work register
                mov         al,keyd.charascii               ;get ASCII character
                cmp         al,0                            ;extended scan?
                jne         snk010                          ;no, go check which key it was
                mov         ah,keyd.charscan                ;get scan code
```

```
;
snk010:        cmp       ax,KESC                    ;escape key?
               jne       snk020                     ;no - continue
               jmp       snk999                     ;yes - exit
;
snk020:        cmp       al,'+'                     ;plus sign?
               jne       snk030                     ;no - continue
               cmp       dx,8                       ;max snakes?
               jne       snk025                     ;no - go add another one
               @DosBeep  880,100                    ;sound error
               jmp       snk000                     ;go read next character
snk025:        @Mkthread snake,256                  ;make another snake thread
               inc       dx                         ;increment snake count
               jmp       snk000                     ;go read next character
;
snk030:        cmp       al,'p'                     ;pause key?
               jne       snk000                     ;no - continue
               @DosEnterCritSec                     ;pause snake threads
               @KbdCharIn keyd,0,0                  ;read keyboard
               @DosExitCritSec                      ;run other threads
               jmp       snk000                     ;go read next character
;
snk999:        mov       curd.curattr,1             ;set 'normal' attribute
               @VioSetCurType curd,0                ;restore cursor
               @VioScrollUp 0,0,-1,-1,-1,fill,0 ;clear the screen
               @DosExit  1,0                        ;kill all threads & exit
main           endp
;
;       NAME: SNAKE
; DESCRIPTION: Write character string to screen
;       INPUT: none
;      OUTPUT: figures written on screen
;
snake          proc
;
snaseg         struc
head           dw        ?                          ;current head of snake
circbuf        dw        16 dup(?)                  ;circular buffer
readchar       db        ?                          ;read character
readcharl      dw        ?                          ;character length
spid           dw        ?                          ;process ID
stid           dw        ?                          ;thread ID
sppid          dw        ?                          ;parent process ID
snaseg         ends
SNASGSZ        equ       size snaseg
;
               sub       sp,2                       ;allocate work area
               mov       bp,sp                      ;address stack frame
```

```
;
            @DosAllocSeg SNASGSZ,SS:BP,0    ;allocate segment
            push     ss:[bp]               ;copy new selector
            pop      ds                    ;to DS

            mov      di,offset spid        ;point to process ID area
            @DosGetPid DS:DI               ;get thread ID
            xor      di,di                 ;point to structure
            mov      [di].head,0c28h       ;initial snake coordinate (12,40)
            mov      [di].readcharl,1      ;buffer read length
            xor      bx,bx                 ;set circular buffer pointer
;
; Get new coordinates
;
sna000:     push     bx                    ;save circular buffer index
sna010:     push     ds                    ;dave ds
            push     gdtinfo               ;copy info seg
            pop      ds                    ;to ds
            mov      bx,ds:[4]             ;get TOD value (milliseconds)
            mov      ax,ds:[4]             ;get TOD value (milliseconds)
            mul      bx                    ;hash numbers
            mov      bx,dx                 ;get 'random' value
            pop      ds                    ;restore ds
;
            and      bx,06h                ;determine 'direction'
            lea      si,dirtab             ;direction table
            mov      bx,es:[bx+si]         ;direction
            mov      cx,[di].head          ;get head
            add      ch,bh                 ;new row
            add      cl,bl                 ;new column
            cmp      ch,22                 ;past bottom of screen?
            jg       sna010                ;yes - go try again
            cmp      ch,0                  ;above top line?
            jl       sna010                ;yes - go try again
            cmp      cl,79                 ;past right edge?
            jg       sna010                ;yes - go try again
            cmp      cl,0                  ;past left edge?
            jl       sna010                ;yes - go try again
            pop      bx                    ;restore circular buffer index
;
; Blank previous tail
;
sna015:     @DosSemRequest semhand,noto    ;request screen (no timeout)
            push     bx                    ;save element number
            shl      bx,1                  ;convert to table offset
            push     cx                    ;save new coordinates
            mov      dx,word ptr [di+bx].circbuf ;get tail
            mov      cx,dx                 ;copy it to cx
            xor      dh,dh                 ;clear row
            xchg     ch,cl                 ;get row in low byte
            xor      ch,ch                 ;clear col
            @VioWrtCellStr fill,4,cx,dx,0  ;blank it out
            pop      cx                    ;restore new coordinates
```

```
;
; Check for existing character in 'new' head coordinates
;
                push    cx                      ;save new coordinates
                push    di                      ;save segment offset
                mov     dx,cx                   ;copy coordinate
                xor     dh,dh                   ;clear row
                xchg    ch,cl                   ;get row in low byte
                xor     ch,ch                   ;clear col
                lea     si,[di].readchar        ;character buffer
                lea     di,[di].readcharl       ;character buffer length
                @VioReadCharStr DS:SI,DS:DI,cx,dx,0 ;read character
                pop     di                      ;restore segment offset
                pop     cx                      ;restore new coordinates
                cmp     byte ptr [di].readchar,' ' ;blank?
                je      sna020                  ;yes - go process
                mov     cx,[di].head            ;stay put
;
; Write new head
;
sna020:         mov     word ptr [di+bx].circbuf,cx ;put it in circular buffer
                mov     dx,word ptr [di+bx].circbuf ;get head
                mov     [di].head,dx            ;save it for later use
                mov     cx,dx                   ;copy it to cx
                xor     dh,dh                   ;clear row
                xchg    ch,cl                   ;get row in low byte
                xor     ch,ch                   ;clear col
                mov     si,offset stid          ;get thread ID (color attribute)
                @VioWrtCharStrAtt blok,2,cx,dx,DS:SI,0 ;write character
                @DosSemClear semhand            ;release screen
;
; Move buffer pointer
;
                pop     bx                      ;restore element number
                inc     bx                      ;next position
                and     bx,0fh                  ;make it 0-15 (circular buffer)
                jmp     sna000                  ;go do it all again
snake           endp
;
                include os2procs.asm            ;general purpose procedures
;
SNA_code        ends
                end     main
```

DATETIME.ASM

```
                PAGE    80,132
                TITLE   OS/2 DATE/TIME sample program
;-------------------------------------------------------------------
;   NAME: DATETIME
;
;   DESC: Query System Date/Time and write it to STDOUT
;
;  INPUT: none
;
; OUTPUT: Data is written to STDOUT
;
;  PROCS: none
;
;   AUTH: E. E. Iacobucci
;
;   DATE: 10/15/87
;
;-------------------------------------------------------------------
                .286c
                .xlist
                include   os2mac.inc
                .list

dgroup  group   DTI_data                    ;defines automatic data segment

;
;=========================================
;
; DTI stack
;
;=========================================
DTI_stack       segment para stack
;
                dw    256 dup('s')
;
DTI_stack       ends
;
;=========================================
;
; DTI data segment
;
;=========================================
DTI_data        segment para public 'auto'
;
msg1            db          ' '
msg1dayofw      db          'dddddddd '
msg1date        db          'mm/dd/yy '
msg1time        db          'hh:mm:ss ',CR,LF
MSG1L           equ         $ - offset msg1
```

```
;
bytesout        dw          0
;
DTI_data        ends
;
;=======================================
;
; DTI code segment
;
;=======================================
DTI_code        segment para public 'code'
                assume  cs:DTI_code,es:nothing,ds:DTI_data,ss:DTI_stack
;
main            proc
;
                @sysdate  msg1date                ;get date
                @systime  msg1time                ;get time
                @sysday   msg1dayofw              ;get day of week
                @DosWrite stdout,msg1,MSG1L,bytesout ;Write data
                @DosExit 1,0                       ;leave proc
;
main            endp
;
                include   os2procs.asm            ;general purpose procedures
;
DTI_code        ends
                end       main
```

NOTES.ASM

```
                PAGE   80,132
                TITLE  OS/2 Asynchronous timers
;----------------------------------------------------------------
;   NAME: TIMERS
;
;   DESC: Use asynchronous timers to sound multiple alarms
;
;  INPUT: none
;
; OUTPUT: Multiple tones are sounded
;
;  PROCS: none
;
;   AUTH: E. E. Iacobucci
;
;   DATE: 10/15/87
;
;----------------------------------------------------------------
                .286c
                .xlist
                include    os2mac.inc
                .list

dgroup  group   TIM_data                ;defines automatic data segment


;
;======================================
;
; TIM stack
;
;======================================
TIM_stack       segment para stack
;
                dw     256 dup('s')
;
TIM_stack       ends
;
;======================================
;
; TIM data segment
;
;======================================
TIM_data        segment para public 'auto'
;
msg             db        ' TIMERS: Asynchronous timers are running
                db        '                  <ESC> Exit '
MSGL            equ       $ - offset msg
;
notec           db        CR                        ;note character
NOTEL           equ       $ - offset notec
```

```
;
TDATA           STRUC
shand           dd        ?                                   ;Semaphore handle
thand           dw        ?                                   ;Timer handle
row             dw        ?                                   ;Display Row
col             dw        ?                                   ;Display Column
attr            db        ?                                   ;Display Attribute
freq            dw        ?                                   ;Tone frequency
sname           db        '???????'                           ;Semaphore name
                db        0                                   ;zero termination
TDATA           ENDS
;
timerd          tdata     <0,0,14, 3,08h, 523,'\SEM\T1'> ;Timer #1 parameters
                tdata     <0,0,13,12,09h, 587,'\SEM\T2'> ;Timer #2 parameters
                tdata     <0,0,12,21,0ah, 660,'\SEM\T3'> ;Timer #3 parameters
                tdata     <0,0,11,30,0bh, 700,'\SEM\T4'> ;Timer #4 parameters
                tdata     <0,0,10,39,0ch, 783,'\SEM\T5'> ;Timer #5 parameters
                tdata     <0,0, 9,48,0dh, 880,'\SEM\T6'> ;Timer #6 parameters
                tdata     <0,0, 8,57,0eh, 988,'\SEM\T7'> ;Timer #7 parameters
                tdata     <0,0, 7,66,0fh,1046,'\SEM\T8'> ;Timer #8 parameters
TCOUNT          equ       8                                   ;parameter area count
;
keyd            charbuf   <>                                  ;charin data structure
curd            cur       <>                                  ;cursor data structure
;
msgatr          db        0eh                                 ;message attribute (yellow)
fill            db        ' ',07h                             ;fill cell (for screen clearing)
noto            dd        -1                                  ;no time out value (for semaphore)
tint            dd        INTERVAL                            ;timer interval field
sleepct         dd        INTERVAL/(TCOUNT+1)                 ;timer spacing
INTERVAL        equ       TCOUNT*200                          ;200 MS per timer
;
TIM_data        ends
;
;========================================
;
; TIM code segment
;
;========================================
TIM_code        segment para public 'code'
                assume  cs:TIM_code,es:nothing,ds:TIM_data,ss:TIM_stack
;
main            proc
;
;   Clear screen & put message
;
                @HideCursor                         ;hide the cursor
                @VioScrollUp 0,0,-1,-1,-1,fill,0 ;clear the screen
                @VioWrtCharStrAtt msg,MSGL,24,0,msgatr,0 ;write prompt
                lea     si,timerd                   ;timer parameter area
                mov     cx,TCOUNT                   ;timer count
```

```
;
;   Start timers & threads
;
tim010:         mov     di,si
                add     di,offset sname         ;semaphore name
                @DosCreateSem 1,DS:SI,DS:DI     ;create shared system semaphore
                mov     di,si                   ;copy pointer
                add     di,offset thand         ;timer handle
                @DosTimerStart tint,DS:SI,DS:DI ;start asynchronous timer
                @Mkthread note,256              ;make NOTE thread
                @DosSleep sleepct               ;space out timers
                add     si,size tdata           ;next parameter area
                loop    tim010                  ;go start next
;
; Process keyboard input
;
tim020:         @KbdCharIn keyd,0,0             ;read keyboard
                @DosExitCritSec                 ;start all the threads
                xor     ax,ax                   ;clear work register
                mov     al,keyd.charascii       ;get ASCII character
                cmp     al,0                    ;extended scan?
                jne     tim030                  ;no, go check which key it was
                mov     ah,keyd.charscan        ;get scan code
;
tim030:         cmp     ax,KESC                 ;escape key?
                jne     tim040                  ;no - continue
                jmp     tim800                  ;yes - exit
;
tim040:         cmp     al,'p'                  ;pause key?
                jne     tim500                  ;no - continue
                @DosEnterCritSec                ;pause timer threads
tim500:         jmp     tim020                  ;go read next character
;
tim800:         @ShowCursor                     ;restore the cursor
                @VioScrollUp 0,0,-1,-1,fill,0   ;clear the screen
;
                lea     si,timerd               ;timer parameter area
                mov     cx,TCOUNT               ;timer count
tim900:         @DosCloseSem  DS:SI             ;Free the system semaphore
                @DosTimerStop [si].thand        ;Stop timer
                add     si,size tdata           ;next parameter area
                loop    tim900                  ;go stop next
;
                @DosExit  1,0                   ;kill all threads & exit
main            endp
;
;       NAME: NOTE
; DESCRIPTION: Sound a note on timer expiration
;       INPUT: DS:SI points to parameter block
;      OUTPUT: Short beep
;              Note is flashed on the screen
;
note            proc
```

```
;
              lea       di,[si].attr            ;get display attribute (Color)
;
not010:       @DosSemSetWait  DS:SI,noto        ;wait for semaphore 2b cleared
              @VioWrtCharStrAtt notec,NOTEL,[si].row,[si].col,DS:DI,0 ;note
              @DosBeep  [si].freq,100           ;sound tone
              @VioWrtNCell fill,NOTEL,[si].row,[si].col,0 ;blank out note
              jmp       not010                  ;loop
;
note          endp
;
              include   os2procs.asm            ;general purpose procedures
;
TIM_code      ends
              end       main
```

TAKE2.ASM

```
                        PAGE    80,132
                        TITLE   OS/2 shared memory sample program
;-----------------------------------------------------------------
;   NAME: TAKE
;
;   DESC: Read data from shared memory
;
;  INPUT: Data record in \SHAREMEM\GIVE
;
; OUTPUT: Record is written to STDOUT
;
;  PROCS: none
;
;   AUTH: E. E. Iacobucci
;
;   DATE: 10/15/87
;
;-----------------------------------------------------------------
                        .286c
                        .xlist
                        include   os2mac.inc
                        .list

dgroup  group   TAK_data                     ;defines automatic data segment

;
;=======================================
;
; TAK stack
;
;=======================================
TAK_stack     segment para stack
;
              dw     256 dup('s')
;
TAK_stack     ends
;
;=======================================
;
; TAK data segment
;
;=======================================
TAK_data      segment para public 'auto'
;
msg1          db            'GIVE is not running!',CR,LF
MSG1L         equ           $ - offset msg1
```

```
;
semgive      db          '\SEM\GIVE2',0       ;system semaphore name
semtake      db          '\SEM\TAKE2',0       ;system semaphore name
semhtake     dd          0                    ;system semaphore handle
semhgive     dd          0                    ;system semaphore handle
noto         dd          -1                   ;no timeout
shrname      db          '\SHAREMEM\GIVE2',0  ;shared segment name
shrsel       dw          0                    ;shared segment selector
bytesin      dw          0                    ;bytes read
bytesout     dw          0                    ;bytes written
sleepct      dd          500                  ;500 millisecond sleep count
ALLOCSZ      equ         128                  ;shared segment size
;
TAK_data     ends
;
;=======================================
;
; TAK code segment
;
;=======================================
TAK_code     segment para public 'code'
             assume  cs:TAK_code,es:nothing,ds:TAK_data,ss:TAK_stack
;
main         proc
;
             @DosOpenSem semhgive,semgive     ;open system semaphore
             @jaxz      tak005                 ;Give is present - continue
             @DosWrite stderr,msg1,msg1l,bytesout ;Write error message
             jmp        tak999                 ;exit
;
tak005:      @DosOpenSem semhtake,semtake     ;open system semaphore
             @DosGetShrSeg shrname,shrsel     ;get shared segment
             @DosSemWait semhgive,noto        ;wait for initial data
;
tak010:      push       shrsel                 ;put shared memory selector
             pop        es                     ;in ES
             mov        di,2                   ;point to data field
;
tak020:      cmp        word ptr es:[0],0     ;null record?
             @je        tak800                 ;yes - exit
             @DosWrite stdout,ES:DI,es:[0],bytesout ;Write data
             @DosSemSet    semhgive            ;pre-set semaphore
             @DosSemClear semhtake             ;tell TAKE data is done
             @DosSemWait  semhgive,noto        ;wait for more data to be present
             jmp        tak020                 ;go wait for another string
;
tak800:      @DosFreeSeg shrsel               ;Free shared memory segment
             @DosCloseSem semhgive            ;Free the system semaphore
             @DosCloseSem semhtake            ;Free the system semaphore
;
tak999:      @DosExit 1,0                      ;leave proc
main         endp
;
             include    os2procs.asm          ;general purpose procedures
;
TAK_code     ends
             end        main
```

GIVE2.ASM

```
                PAGE    80,132
                TITLE   OS/2 shared memory sample program
;-----------------------------------------------------------------
;   NAME: GIVE
;
;   DESC: Write STDIN data stream into shared memory segment.
;
;  INPUT: none
;
; OUTPUT: none
;
;  PROCS: none
;
;   AUTH: E. E. Iacobucci
;
;   DATE: 10/15/87
;
;-----------------------------------------------------------------
                .286c
                .xlist
                include    os2mac.inc
                .list

dgroup  group   GIV_data                ;defines automatic data segment


;
;=======================================
;
; GIV stack
;
;=======================================
GIV_stack       segment para stack
;
                dw    256 dup('s')
;
GIV_stack       ends
;
;=======================================
;
; GIV data segment
;
;=======================================
GIV_data        segment para public 'auto'
;
msg1            db         'You can only start one copy of GIVE at a time!',CR,LF
MSG1L          equ        $ - offset msg1
```

```
;
semgive      db          '\SEM\GIVE2',0        ;system semaphore name
semtake      db          '\SEM\TAKE2',0        ;system semaphore name
semhtake     dd          0                     ;system semaphore handle
semhgive     dd          0                     ;system semaphore handle
noto         dd          -1                    ;no timeout
shrname      db          '\SHAREMEM\GIVE2',0   ;shared segment name
shrsel       dw          0                     ;shared segment selector
bytesin      dw          0                     ;bytes read
bytesout     dw          0                     ;bytes written
sleepct      dd          500                   ;500 millisecond sleep count
ALLOCSZ      equ         128                   ;shared segment size
;
GIV_data     ends
;
;========================================
;
; GIV code segment
;
;========================================
GIV_code     segment para public 'code'
             assume  cs:GIV_code,es:nothing,ds:GIV_data,ss:GIV_stack
;
main         proc
;
             @DosCreateSem 1,semhgive,semgive ;create system semaphore
             @DosCreateSem 1,semhtake,semtake ;create system semaphore
             @DosAllocShrSeg ALLOCSZ,shrname,shrsel ;allocate shared segment
             push        shrsel                ;put shared memory selector
             pop         es                    ;in ES
;
giv020:      mov         di,2                  ;point shared segment
             mov         cx,ALLOCSZ-2          ;point to data field
             mov         al,0                  ;fill character
             rep         stosb                 ;clear area
;
             mov         di,2                  ;point to data field
             @DosRead    STDIN,ES:DI,ALLOCSZ-2,bytesin ;Read data into shr seg
             xor         di,di                 ;point to start of buffer
             mov         ax,bytesin            ;get input byte count
             stosw                             ;write to segment
             @DosSemSet    semhtake            ;pre-set semaphore
             @DosSemClear semhgive             ;tell TAKE data is ready
             cmp         bytesin,0             ;null input?
             je          giv999                ;yes - finished
             @DosSemWait semhtake,noto         ;wait for TAKE to remove data
             jmp         giv020                ;no - go read another string
```

```
;
giv999:         @DosFreeSeg shrsel              ;Free shared memory segment
                @DosCloseSem semhgive           ;Free the system semaphore
                @DosCloseSem semhtake           ;Free the system semaphore
                @DosExit 1,0                    ;leave proc
main            endp
;
                include    os2procs.asm         ;general purpose procedures
;
GIV_code        ends
                end        main
```

PIPE.ASM

```
                PAGE   80,132
                TITLE  OS/2 pipe program
;------------------------------------------------------------------
;   NAME: PIPE
;
;   DESC: Creates 2 pipes, execs an OS/2 filter (UPCASE), and
;         sets up the child's STDIN and STDOUT to the other
;         ends of the pipes. Once connected in this way, PIPE
;         reads from STDIN, writes to the output pipe, reads
;         from the input pipe and writes on the screen. The size
;         of the pipe is determined from an environment variable
;         named PIPESIZE.
;
;  INPUT: STDIN character stream
;
; OUTPUT: Upper case version of STDIN chatacter stream
;
;  PROCS: none
;
;   AUTH: E. E. Iacobucci
;
;   DATE: 10/15/87
;
;------------------------------------------------------------------
                .286c
                .xlist
                include    os2mac.inc
                .list

dgroup  group   PIP_data                    ;defines automatic data segment

;
;=======================================
;
; PIP stack
;
;=======================================
PIP_stack       segment para stack
;
                dw    256 dup('s')
;
PIP_stack       ends
;
;=======================================
;
; PIP data segment
;
;=======================================
PIP_data        segment para public 'auto'
;
msg1            db          'Invalid pipe size',CR,LF
MSG1L          equ         $ - offset msg1
```

```
;
msg3        db          'Program not found'
            db          CR,LF
MSG3L       equ         $ - offset msg3
;
pgmname     db          'UPCASE.EXE',0          ;program name
pgmobj      db          10 dup(0)               ;bad exec object
pgmenv      db          0,0                     ;environment
pgmprm      db          0,0                     ;parameters
pgmpid      dw          0                       ;new process ID
            dw          0                       ;termination code area
pgmrc       dd          0                       ;return code area (for DosCWait)
;
varname     db          'PIPESIZE',0            ;environment variable name
varptr      dd          0                       ;pointer to variable
;
bytesin     dw          0                       ;bytes read
bytesout    dw          0                       ;bytes written
;
inbuf       db          128 dup (' ')           ;input buffer
INBUFL      equ         $ - offset inbuf        ;input buffer length
;
pipesz      dw          512                     ;default pipe size
pipe1rh     dw          0                       ;pipe 1 read handle
pipe1wh     dw          0                       ;pipe 1 write handle
pipe2rh     dw          0                       ;pipe 2 read handle
pipe2wh     dw          0                       ;pipe 2 write handle
mystdin     dw          0                       ;local copy of the STDIN handle
mystdout    dw          0                       ;local copy of the STDOUT handle
childin     dw          0                       ;Child process STDIN handle
childout    dw          0                       ;Child process STDOUT handle
;
PIP_data    ends
;
;========================================
;
; PIP code segment
;
;========================================
PIP_code    segment para public 'code'
            assume  cs:PIP_code,ds:PIP_data,es:nothing,ss:PIP_stack
;
main        proc
;
; Determine pipe size
;
            @DosScanEnv varname,varptr     ;locate environment variable
            mov         dx,PIP_data        ;OS/2 BUG BUG
            mov         ds,dx              ;OS/2 BUG BUG
            @jaxnz      pip010             ;if not found, leave default size
            les         di,varptr          ;get location in ES:DI
            @strlen     ES:DI              ;determine length of ASCIIZ
            @atb        ES:DI,cx,pipesz    ;convert number to binary
            @jaxz       pip010             ;all OK - continue
            @DosWrite STDERR,msg1,msg1l,bytesout ;Write message
            jmp         pip999             ;exit
```

```
;
; Set up pipes
;
pip010:        @DosMakePipe pipe1rh,pipe1wh,pipesz ;create pipe1
               @DosMakePipe pipe2rh,pipe2wh,pipesz ;create pipe2
;
               mov      mystdin,-1              ;request new handle
               @DosDupHandle STDIN,mystdin      ;duplicate my stdin handle
               mov      mystdout,-1             ;request new handle
               @DosDupHandle STDOUT,mystdout    ;duplicate my stdout handle
;
               @DosClose    STDIN               ;close my STDIN
               @DosClose    STDOUT              ;close my STDOUT
;
               mov      childin,STDIN           ;request child stdin handle
               @DosDupHandle pipe1rh,childin    ;set child STDIN to pipe1 readhand
               mov      childout,STDOUT         ;request child stdout handle
               @DosDupHandle pipe2wh,childout   ;set child STDOUT to pipe2 writehnd
;
; Create program
;
               @DosExecPgm  pgmobj,10,2,pgmprm,pgmenv,pgmpid,pgmname
               @jaxz        pip020              ;program found - continue
               @DosWrite STDERR,msg3,msg3l,bytesout ;Write message
               jmp          pip999              ;exit
;
; Process the data stream
;
pip020:        @DosRead   mystdin,inbuf,INBUFL,bytesin ;Read from STDIN
               cmp        bytesin,0            ;end of data?
               jne        pip030               ;no - continue
               jmp        pip999               ;yes - exit
pip030:        @DosWrite pipe1wh,inbuf,bytesin,bytesout ;write it to the child
               @DosRead  pipe2rh,inbuf,INBUFL,bytesin ;Read from child
               @DosWrite mystdout,inbuf,bytesin,bytesout ;write it to STDOUT
               jmp        pip020               ;go get next data
;
; Cleanup & end
;
pip999:        @DosKillProcess 0,pgmpid         ;kill child process
               @DosClose pipe1wh                ;close pipe1
               @DosClose pipe2rh                ;close pipe2
               @DosExit 1,0                     ;leave proc
;
main           endp
;
               include   os2procs.asm          ;general purpose procedures
;
PIP_code       ends
               end       main
```

MAILBOX.ASM

```
                       PAGE   80,132
                       TITLE  OS/2 queueing program
;----------------------------------------------------------------
;   NAME: MAILBOX
;
;   DESC: Run multiple copies of QUEUE
;
;  INPUT: none
;
; OUTPUT: Starts QUEUE programs and adds data elements to the
;         queues.
;
;  PROCS: none
;
;   AUTH: E. E. Iacobucci
;
;   DATE: 10/15/87
;
;----------------------------------------------------------------
               .286c
               .xlist
               include   os2mac.inc
               .list

dgroup  group   MBX_data                    ;defines automatic data segment


;
;=======================================
;
; MBX stack
;
;=======================================
MBX_stack      segment para stack
;
               dw    256 dup('s')
;
MBX_stack      ends
;
;=======================================
;
; MBX data segment
;
;=======================================
MBX_data       segment para public 'auto'
;
msg            db        ' <LEFT> Previous Process  '
MSGL           equ       $ - offset msg
               db        ' <RIGHT> Next Process     '
               db        '   <UP> Increase Priority '
               db        ' <DOWN> Decrease Priority '
               db        '    <+> Add Queue Element  '
MSGLINES       equ       5
```

```
;
; QUEUE shared memory segment layout
;
qdata           struc
row             dw          ?                           ;Display Row
col             dw          ?                           ;Display Column
myqname         db          '??????????'                ;My Queue name
                db          0                           ;zero terminated name
nxqname         db          '??????????'                ;Next Queue name
                db          0                           ;zero terminated name
attr            db          ?                           ;Display Attribute
priority        dw          ?                           ;Execution priority
sel             dw          ?                           ;Shared segment selector
procid          dw          0                           ;process ID
qhand           dw          0                           ;Open queue handle
qdata           ends
SHRSZ           equ         size qdata                  ;structure size
;
; Child Process control areas
;
qparms          qdata       <1,03,'\QUEUES\Q1',,'\QUEUES\Q2',,1fh>
                qdata       <1,22,'\QUEUES\Q2',,'\QUEUES\Q3',,2fh>
                qdata       <1,41,'\QUEUES\Q3',,'\QUEUES\Q4',,4fh>
                qdata       <1,60,'\QUEUES\Q4',,'\QUEUES\Q1',,6fh>
QCOUNT          equ         4                           ;program count
;
pgmname         db          'QUEUE.EXE',0               ;program name
pgmobj          db          10 dup(0)                   ;bad exec object
pgmenv          db          0,0                         ;environment
pgmprm          db          0,0                         ;parameters
pgmpid          dw          0                           ;new process ID
                dw          0                           ;termination code area
;
shrname         db          '\SHAREMEM\MBOX\'           ;shared segment name
shrpid          db          'HHHH',0                    ;process ID
shrsel          dw          0                           ;shared segment selector
;
curproc         dw          0                           ;current (selected) process
prow            dw          0                           ;previous pointer row
pcol            dw          0                           ;previous pointer column
fill            db          ' ',07h                     ;fill cell (for scroll)
highlight       db          0Fh                         ;intensified white/black bgnd
point           db          'v'                         ;process pointer
yellow          db          0Eh                         ;yellow/black bgnd
;
cqhand          dw          0                           ;child's queue handle
cpid            dw          0                           ;child's PID
segp            dw          0                           ;element selector
selnew          dw          0                           ;new selector
sleepct         dd          100                         ;sleep count
ELESZ           equ         13                          ;queue element size
;
keyd            charbuf     <>                          ;charin data structure
```

```
;
curd            cur         <>                      ;cursor data structure
;
MBX_data        ends
;
;=======================================
;
; MBX code segment
;
;=======================================
MBX_code        segment para public 'code'
                assume  cs:MBX_code,es:nothing,ds:MBX_data,ss:MBX_stack
;
main            proc
                @VioScrollUp 0,0,-1,-1,-1,fill,0 ;clear the screen
                @HideCursor                     ;Hide the cursor
                call        putprompt           ;write prompt
;
                mov         cx,QCOUNT           ;program count
                lea         si,qparms           ;first set of parameters
run010:         call        startprog           ;start COUNT program
                add         si,SHRSZ            ;point to next parameter area
                loop        run010              ;loop through process list
;
                call        openq               ;open queues
                call        keyin               ;process keyboard input
;
                mov         cx,QCOUNT           ;program count
                lea         si,qparms           ;first set of parameters
run020:         @DosKillProcess 0,[si].procid   ;Kill child process
                @DosFreeSeg [si].sel            ;Free shared memory segment
                add         si,SHRSZ            ;point to next parameter area
                @loop       run020              ;loop through process list
;
                @VioScrollUp 0,0,-1,-1,-1,fill,0 ;clear the screen
                @ShowCursor                     ;restore the cursor
                @DosExit 1,0                    ;leave proc
;
main            endp
;
;       NAME: STARTPROG
; DESCRIPTION: Start a copy of QUEUE
;       INPUT: Parameter block in SI
;      OUTPUT: none
;
startprog       proc
                push        cx                  ;save cx
                push        si                  ;save si
;
                @DosExecPgm  pgmobj,10,2,pgmprm,pgmenv,pgmpid,pgmname
                @bth        pgmpid,shrpid       ;convert pid to HEX (for segname)
                mov         ax,pgmpid           ;get new PID
                mov         [si].procid,ax      ;save it in parameter block
```

```
;
                @DosAllocShrSeg SHRSZ,shrname,shrsel ;allocate shared segment
                push      shrsel                ;put shared memory selector
                pop       es                    ;in ES
                xor       di,di                 ;start of shared segment
                mov       cx,SHRSZ              ;data structure size
                rep       movsb                 ;copy structure into shared seg
;
                pop       si                    ;restore si
                pop       cx                    ;restore cx
                ret
startprog       endp
;
;       NAME: KEYIN
; DESCRIPTION: Process keyboard commands
;       INPUT: none
;      OUTPUT: none
;
keyin           proc
;
                xor       dx,dx                 ;initialize element count
                call      setpoint              ;set pointer to active process
;
kin000:         @KbdCharIn keyd,0,0             ;read keyboard
                mov       al,keyd.charascii      ;get ASCII character
                cmp       al,0                  ;extended scan?
                jne       kin010                ;no, go check which key it was
                mov       ah,keyd.charscan      ;get scan code
;
kin010:         cmp       ax,KESC               ;escape key?
                jne       kin020                ;no - continue
                jmp       kin999                ;yes - exit
;
kin020:         cmp       ax,KLE                ;left key?
                jne       kin030                ;no - continue
                dec       curproc               ;previous process
                and       curproc,03h           ;isolate number (0-3)
                call      setpoint              ;move pointer
                jmp       kin000                ;continue
;
kin030:         cmp       ax,KRI                ;right key?
                jne       kin040                ;no - continue
                inc       curproc               ;next process
                and       curproc,03h           ;isolate number (0-3)
                call      setpoint              ;move pointer
                jmp       kin000                ;continue
;
kin040:         cmp       ax,KUP                ;up key?
                @jne      kin050                ;no - continue
                @DosSetPrty 0,0,+1,[si].procid  ;increase priority by 1
                jmp       kin000                ;continue
```

```
;
kin050:     cmp       ax,KDN                   ;down key?
            @jne      kin060                   ;no - continue
            @DosSetPrty 0,0,-1,[si].procid     ;decrease priority by 1
            jmp       kin000                   ;continue

;
kin060:     cmp       al,'+'                   ;plus key?
            jne       kin500                   ;no - continue
            call      addelement               ;add a queue element
            jmp       kin000                   ;continue

;
kin500:     jmp       kin000                   ;continue

;
kin999:     ret
keyin       endp
;
;       NAME: OPENQ
; DESCRIPTION: Open child input queues
;      INPUT: none
;     OUTPUT: none
;
openq       proc
;
            mov       cx,QCOUNT                ;program count
            lea       si,qparms                ;first set of parameters

;
opq010:     lea       di,[si].myqname          ;get child queue name
            @DosOpenQueue cpid,cqhand,DS:DI     ;open child's queue
            @jaxz     opq020                   ;Opened OK - go loop
            @DosSleep sleepct                  ;wait a little while
            jmp       opq010                   ;go try again

;
opq020:     push      cqhand                   ;put child's Q handle
            pop       [si].qhand               ;into parameter area
            add       si,SHRSZ                 ;point to next parameter area
            @loop     opq010                   ;loop through process list

;
            ret
openq       endp
;
;       NAME: ADDELEMENT
; DESCRIPTION: Add a queue element to the current child
;              process' input queue.
;      INPUT: SI points to current process work area
;             DX contains current element number
;     OUTPUT: element allocated & written to queue
;
addelement  proc
;
            cmp       dx,12                    ;max elements already in system?
            @jne      add010                   ;no, go add one
            @DosBeep  1000,100                 ;sound error beep
            jmp       add999                   ;exit
```

```
;
add010:       @DosAllocSeg ELESZ,segp,1      ;allocate 'shared' segment
              inc      dx                    ;bump element count
              mov      ax,dx                 ;get element count
              or       al,40h                ;convert to printable ASCII
              push     segp                  ;copy element pointer
              pop      es                    ;to ES
              push     di                    ;save pointer
              xor      di,di                 ;start of element
              mov      cx,ELESZ              ;get element size
              rep      stosb                 ;initialize it
              xor      di,di                 ;point to start of segment
;
              @DosGiveSeg    segp,[si].procid,selnew ;give segment to child
              push     selnew                ;put new selector
              pop      es                    ;in ES
              @DosWriteQueue [si].qhand,0,ELESZ,ES:DI,0 ;write to child queue
              @DosFreeSeg    segp            ;free the element
;
              pop      di                    ;restore pointer
;
add999:       ret
addelement    endp
;
;      NAME: PUTPROMPT
; DESCRIPTION: Write prompt on screen
;      INPUT: none
;     OUTPUT: none
;
putprompt     proc
;
              mov      cx,MSGLINES           ;display line count
              mov      dx,18                 ;first line number
              lea      si,msg                ;first message string
ppt000:       @VioWrtCharStrAtt DS:SI,MSGL,dx,26,highlight,0 ;prompt line
              inc      dx                    ;next display line
              add      si,MSGL               ;next message
              @loop    ppt000                ;write all messages
;
              ret
putprompt     endp
;
;      NAME: SETPOINT
; DESCRIPTION: Display current process pointer
;      INPUT: current process value in CURPOINT
;     OUTPUT: pointer displayed on screen
;
setpoint      proc
;
              push     dx
              @VioWrtCellStr fill,2,prow,pcol,0 ;clear previous pointer
```

```
;
          mov      ax,curproc            ;get pointer value
          mov      ah,SHRSZ              ;get structure size
          mul      ah                    ;compute offset
          lea      si,qparms             ;data structure base address
          add      si,ax                 ;compute structure pointer
;
          mov      bx,[si].row           ;get row
          sub      bx,1                  ;one line up
          mov      dx,[si].col           ;get column
          add      dx,8                  ;eight columns over
          @VioWrtCharStrAtt point,1,bx,dx,yellow,0 ;write new pointer
          mov      prow,bx               ;save previous row
          mov      pcol,dx               ;save previous column
;
          pop      dx
          ret
setpoint  endp
;
          include  os2procs.asm          ;general purpose procedures
;
MBX_code  ends
          end      main
```

QUEUE.ASM

```
                        PAGE    80,132
                        TITLE   OS/2 Queue processor
;----------------------------------------------------------------
;   NAME: QUEUE
;
;   DESC: Retrieves shared memory segment, extracts queue name
;         and creates it. Then, as it receives queue elements from
;         other processes it writes them to the 'next' queue.
;
;  INPUT: Data structure in shared memory segment
;
; OUTPUT: Data is written on the screen
;
;  PROCS: none
;
;   AUTH: E. E. Iacobucci
;
;   DATE: 10/15/87
;
;----------------------------------------------------------------
                .286c
                .xlist
                include    os2mac.inc
                .list

dgroup  group   QUE_data                ;defines automatic data segment

;
;=======================================
;
; QUE stack
;
;=======================================
QUE_stack    segment para stack
;
                dw     512 dup('s')
;
QUE_stack    ends
;
;=======================================
;
; QUE data segment
;
;=======================================
QUE_data     segment para public 'auto'
;
; Shared memory segment data structure
```

```
;
qdata           struc
row             dw      ?                       ;Display Row
col             dw      ?                       ;Display Column
myqname         db      '??????????'            ;My Queue name
z1              db      0                       ;zero terminated name
nxqname         db      '??????????'            ;Next Queue name
z2              db      0                       ;zero terminated name
attr            db      ?                       ;Display Attribute
priority        dw      ?                       ;Execution priority
sel             dw      ?                       ;Shared segment selector
procid          dw      ?                       ;process ID
qdata           ends
;
; Messages
;
msg0            db      '┌────────────┐'
MSGL            equ     $ - offset msg0
;
msg1            db      '│ PID '
msgpid          db      '.... Q '
msgcnt          db      '.. │'
;
msg2            db      '│ Priority = '
msgprty         db      '.. │'
;
msg3            db      '└────────────┘'
;
dead            db      '      Dead!      '      ;dead process message
;
; Local QUEUE data
;
shrname         db      '\SHAREMEM\MBOX\'        ;shared segment name
shrpid          db      'HHHH',0                 ;process ID
shrsel          dw      0                       ;shared segment selector
piddata         pid     <>                      ;process ID information
attrib          dw      0                       ;local attribute variable
red             db      04h                     ;red attribute
fill            db      ' ',07h                  ;fill cell (for scroll)
shortct         dd      SLEEPCT                 ;display sleep count
longct          dd      SLEEPCT*2               ;read queue sleep count
SLEEPCT         equ     200                     ;200 millisecond base sleep count
;
myprty          dw      0                       ;GetPriority work area
myqhand         dw      0                       ;My queue handle
mysel           dw      0                       ;my element selector
;
nxqpid          dw      0                       ;Next queue owner process ID
nxqhand         dw      0                       ;Next queue handle
nxsel           dw      0                       ;Next queue owner element selector
```

```
;
elereq          dd      0                       ;Element request data
elelen          dw      0                       ;Element Length
eleptr          dw      0                       ;Element selector
eleofs          dw      0                       ;Element offset
elepri          dw      0                       ;Element priority
elecnt          dw      0                       ;Element count (in queue)
;
peekreq         dd      0                       ;Element request data (for qpeek)
peeklen         dw      0                       ;Element Length      (for qpeek)
peekptr         dd      0                       ;Element address     (for qpeek)
peekpri         dw      0                       ;Element priority    (for qpeek)
peekel          dw      0                       ;Element to be peeked (for qpeek)
;
trow            dw      0                       ;top row (temporary work buffer)
qwtop           dw      0                       ;top row of qwindow
qwbot           dw      0                       ;bottom row of qwindow
qwleft          dw      0                       ;left column of qwindow
qwright         dw      0                       ;right column of qwindow
;
termp           dw      offset termproc         ;termination proc
                dw      seg termproc
;
QUE_data        ends
;
;=======================================
;
; QUE code segment
;
;=======================================
QUE_code        segment para public 'code'
                assume  cs:QUE_code,ds:nothing,es:QUE_data,ss:QUE_stack
;
main            proc
                push    ds                      ;copy ds
                pop     es                      ;to es
;
                @DosSetSigHandler termp,NULL,NULL,2,SIGTERM ;register sig handler
;
                call    getshrseg               ;find shared segment
                call    openq                   ;open input & output queues
                @MKthread printit,1024          ;start high priority display thread
;
que010:         @DosReadQueue myqhand,elereq,elelen,eleptr,0,0,elepri,NULL ;BUGBUG
                @DosGiveSeg eleptr+2,nxqpid,nxsel ;give segment to next proc
                push    nxsel                   ;put next recipient's selector
                pop     ds                      ;in DS
                @DosWriteQueue nxqhand,0,elelen,DS:DI,elepri ;write to next queue
                @DosFreeSeg mysel                ;free the element
                @VioScrollUp qwtop,qwleft,qwbot,qwright,1,fill,0 ;erase element
                @DosSleep longct                ;slow down display
                jmp     que010                  ;go read the next element
```

```
;
main          endp
;
;        NAME: PRINTIT
; DESCRIPTION: Display data on screen
;       INPUT: shared segment in DS:DI
;      OUTPUT: none
;
printit       proc
              xor       di,di                     ;address parameter block
              @DosGetPid piddata                  ;Get my thread ID
              @DosSetPrty 2,3,0,piddata.pidtid ;boost myself to Time Critical 0
;
prt010:       mov       al,[di].attr             ;get attribute
              mov       attrib,ax                ;put it in memory
;
              @DosQueryQueue myqhand,elecnt       ;get current element count
              @bta      elecnt,msgcnt,2          ;convert element count to ASCII
;
              @DosGetPrty 0,myprty,0             ;get thread 0 priority data
              mov       bx,myprty                ;move it to register
              xor       bh,bh                    ;clear priority class
              @bta      bx,msgprty,2             ;convert to displayable ASCII
;
              call      disppb                   ;display process 'box'
              call      dispqw                   ;display queue elements
;
              @DosSleep shortct                  ;sleep for a little while
              jmp       prt010                   ;go refresh
printit       endp
;
;        NAME: DISPPB
; DESCRIPTION: Display process box
;       INPUT: Common data area in DS:DI
;              Display data is in MSG0-3
;      OUTPUT: Process box is displayed on the screen
;
disppb        proc
              @VioWrtCharStrAtt msg0,MSGL,[di].row,[di].col,attrib,0 ;Line 1
              mov       bx,[di].row              ;get row
              inc       bx                       ;next line
              @VioWrtCharStrAtt msg1,MSGL,bx,[di].col,attrib,0        ;Line 2
              inc       bx                       ;next line
              @VioWrtCharStrAtt msg2,MSGL,bx,[di].col,attrib,0        ;Line 3
              inc       bx                       ;next line
              @VioWrtCharStrAtt msg3,MSGL,bx,[di].col,attrib,0        ;Line 4
              ret
disppb        endp
```

```
;
;           NAME: DISPQW
;    DESCRIPTION: Display element queue window
;          INPUT: Element count in ELECNT
;                 Valid queue handle in MYQHAND
;                 Common data area in DS:DI
;         OUTPUT: Queue elements displayed under process 'box'
;
dispqw        proc
;
              mov       bx,[di].row           ;get row number
              add       bx,4                  ;top q window row
              mov       qwtop,bx              ;save coordinate
              add       bx,12                 ;bot q window row
              mov       qwbot,bx              ;save coordinate
;
              mov       bx,[di].col           ;get col number
              add       bx,2                  ;center queue
              mov       qwleft,bx             ;save coordinate
              add       bx,MSGL               ;right q window col
              mov       qwright,bx            ;save coordinate
;
dsq020:       mov       peekel,0              ;initialize element number
              push      qwtop                 ;put top row
              pop       trow                  ;into work buffer
              push      ds                    ;save share mem pointer
dsq030:       @DosPeekQueue myqhand,peekreq,peeklen,peekptr,peekel,0,peekpri,NULL
              @jaxnz    dsq050                ;exit if queue is empty
              lds       si,peekptr            ;put element address in DS:SI
              @VioWrtCharStrAtt DS:SI,peeklen,trow,qwleft,attrib,0 ;write elemt
              inc       trow                  ;next line
              jmp       dsq030                ;display next element
dsq050:       pop       ds                    ;restore share mem pointer
;
              @VioScrollUp trow,qwleft,qwbot,qwright,-1,fill,0 ;clear Q window
;
              ret
dispqw        endp
;
;          NAME: GETSHRSEG
;   DESCRIPTION: Get access to shared memory segment
;         INPUT: none
;        OUTPUT: Shared segment in ES:DI
;
getshrseg     proc
;
              @DosGetPid piddata                ;get process ID information
              @bth      piddata.pidpid,shrpid ;convert to hex (for sharename)
              @bth      piddata.pidpid,msgpid ;convert to hex (for message)
;
gss010:       @DosGetShrSeg shrname,shrsel      ;get shared segment
              @jaxz     gss020                  ;Segment exists - go exit
              @DosSleep shortct                 ;wait a little while
              jmp       gss010                  ;go try again
```

```
;
gss020:         push      shrsel               ;put shared memory selector
                pop       ds                   ;in ES
                xor       di,di                ;point to start of segment
;
                ret
getshrseg       endp
;
;        NAME: OPENQ
; DESCRIPTION: Open input & output queues
;       INPUT: none
;      OUTPUT: Shared segment in DS:DI
;
openq           proc
;
                lea       si,[di].myqname            ;get my queue name from shrseg
opq000:         @DosCreateQueue myqhand,FIFO,DS:SI ;create my input queue
                @jaxz     opq010               ;Opened OK - exit      bug
                @DosSleep shortct              ;wait a little while   bug
                jmp       opq000               ;go try again          bug
;
opq010:         lea       si,[di].nxqname            ;get next queue name from shrseg
                @DosOpenQueue nxqpid,nxqhand,DS:SI ;open next queue
                @jaxz     opq999               ;Opened OK - exit
                @DosSleep shortct              ;wait a little while
                jmp       opq010               ;go try again
;
opq999:         ret
openq           endp
;
;        NAME: TERMPROC
; DESCRIPTION: Handle termination signal
;       INPUT: none
;      OUTPUT: Display is cleared
;
termproc        proc
;
                mov       ax,QUE_data          ;get my DS
                mov       es,ax                ;address it
                cmp       shrsel,0             ;shared segment in place?
                jne       trm010               ;yes, continue processing
                jmp       trm999               ;no - exit
;
trm010:         mov       ax,shrsel            ;get shared segment
                mov       ds,ax                ;address it
                xor       di,di                ;point to start of segment
;
                @DosCloseQueue myqhand         ;release queue
```

```
;
              mov       bx,[di].row            ;get row number
              add       bx,4                   ;bottom row
              mov       dx,[di].col            ;get column number
              push      dx                     ;save starting column
              add       dx,MSGL                ;bottom column
              @VioScrollUp [di].row,[di].col,bx,dx,-1,fill,0 ;clear the window
              sub       bx,2                   ;up 2 rows
              pop       dx                     ;restore column
              @VioWrtCharStrAtt dead,MSGL,bx,dx,red,0 ;Dead message
trm999:       @DosExit 1,0                     ;end process
termproc      endp
;
              include   os2procs.asm           ;general purpose procedures
;
QUE_code      ends
              end       main
```

KEYMON.ASM

```
                PAGE    ,132
                TITLE   OS/2 keyboard monitor sample
;ugflag         equ 1
;-----------------------------------------------------------------
;   NAME: KEYMON
;
;   DESC: Monitor the OS/2 keyboard & convert keystrokes to
;         upper case
;
;  INPUT: Keystrokes
;
; OUTPUT: Upper-case keystrokes
;
;  PROCS: MONITOR (monitor keyboard)
;         POPUP   (create pop-up screen)
;
;   AUTH: E. E. Iacobucci
;
;   DATE: 9/02/87
;
;-----------------------------------------------------------------
                .286c
                .xlist
                include    os2mac.inc
                .list

dgroup   group    KBM_data                ;defines automatic data segment


;
;=======================================
;
; KBM stack
;
;=======================================
KBM_stack       segment para stack
;
                db     512 dup('s')
;
KBM_stack       ends
;
;=======================================
;
; KBM data segment
;
;=======================================
KBM_data        segment para public 'auto'
```

```
;
msg0            db          '                                         '
                db          '  ┌─────────────────────────────────┐  '
                db          '  │  KeyMon: A Keyboard Monitor     │  '
                db          '  │                                 │  '
                db          '  │   <X> Upper case translate      │  '
                db          '  │   <N> No translation            │  '
                db          '  │                                 │  '
                db          '  │  <ESC> End monitor              │  '
msg             db          '  └─────────────────────────────────┘  '
MSGL            equ         $ - offset msg
MSGLC           equ         8
;
popopt          dw          03h                 ;pop-up options
devname         db          'KBD$',0            ;device name
monhand         dw          0                   ;monitor handle
ldtsel          dw          0                   ;LDT InfoSeg selector
gdtsel          dw          0                   ;GDT InfoSeg selector
red             dw          04Fh                ;red attribute (for window)
xflag           db          0                   ;translate active flag
;
kbdbuf          charbuf     <>                  ;keyboard input buffer
;
monbuf          struc                           ;monitor buffer structure
mlen            dw          128                 ;total buffer length
mrsv            db          18  dup (0)          ;reserved area (must be 0)
mdta            db          108 dup (0)          ;data area
monbuf          ends
;
monibuf         monbuf      <>                  ;monitor input buffer
monobuf         monbuf      <>                  ;monitor output buffer
;
mondbuf         dw          0                   ;monitor flag word
monkeybuf       charbuf     <>                  ;keyboard data structure
monkbdflg       dw          0                   ;keyboard DD flag word
MONDBUFL        equ         $ - offset mondbuf   ;buffer length
buflen          dw          0                   ;buffer size returned from MonRead
;
sempopup        dd          0                   ;RAM semaphore
semhand         dw          offset sempopup      ;screen semaphore handle
                dw          seg     sempopup
noto            dd          -1                  ;no time out value (for semaphore)
;
KBM_data        ends
;
;=========================================
;
; KBM code segment
;
;=========================================
KBM_code        segment para public 'code'
                assume  cs:KBM_code,ds:KBM_data,es:nothing,ss:KBM_stack
;
main            proc
```

```
;
                @MKThread monitor,1024          ;Make monitor thread
;
kbm010:         @DosSemSetWait semhand,noto     ;wait for hot-key
                call      popup                 ;process pop-up
                @jaxnz    kbm999                ;exit on error
                jmp       kbm010                ;go wait again
;
kbm999:         @DosMonClose monhand            ;flush monitor
                @DosExit  1,0                   ;leave (just my thread)
main            endp
;
;       NAME: POPUP
; DESCRIPTION: Create Pop-up and process user input
;
;       INPUT: Keystokes
;               ESC - terminate keymon
;               U - turn on XFLAG
;               L - turn off XFLAG
;
;
;       OUTPUT: XFLAG set/reset
;
popup           proc
;
                @VioPopUp popopt,0              ;put myself in foreground
                @HideCursor                    ;hide cursor
                @DosBeep  2000,200             ;sound beep
;
                lea       si,msg0               ;window line #1
                mov       cx,MSGLC              ;line count
                mov       dx,5                  ;pop-up on line 5
pop000:         @VioWrtCharStrAtt DS:SI,MSGL,dx,24,red,0 ;Put line
                inc       dx                    ;next row
                add       si,MSGL               ;next line
                @loop     pop000                ;go put it out
;
pop005:         @KbdCharIn kbdbuf,0,0           ;get character
                mov       al,kbdbuf.charascii   ;get ASCII character
                cmp       al,0                  ;extended scan?
                jne       pop010                ;no, go check which key it was
                mov       ah,kbdbuf.charscan    ;get scan code
;
pop010:         cmp       ax,KESC               ;escape key?
                @jne      pop020                ;no - continue
                mov       ax,0ffh               ;set error code
                jmp       pop999                ;exit
;
pop020:         xor       al,'a'-'A'            ;convert ASCII key to upper case
                cmp       al,'X'                ;translate key?
                @jne      pop030                ;no - continue
                mov       xflag,ON              ;set translate flag on
                xor       ax,ax                 ;clear RC
                jmp       pop999                ;exit
```

```
;
pop030:         cmp     al,'N'                      ;no xlate key?
                @jne    pop005                      ;no - go wait for next keystoke
                mov     xflag,OFF                   ;set translate flag off
                xor     ax,ax                       ;clear RC
;
pop999:         push    ax                          ;save RC
                @ShowCursor                         ;restore cursor
                @VioEndPopUp 0                      ;return to background
                pop     ax                          ;restore RC
                ret
popup           endp
;
;       NAME: MONITOR
; DESCRIPTION: Filter keystoke data stream
;       INPUT: XFLAG setting (1 or 0)
;      OUTPUT: characters converted to upper case
;
monitor         proc
;
                @DosGetInfoSeg gdtsel,ldtsel
                push    gdtsel
                pop     es
;
                @DosSetPrty 2,3,0,0                 ;thread to TC 0
                @DosMonOpen devname,monhand         ;Open Monitor interface
                xor     dx,dx                       ;clear work register
                mov     dl,es:[gdtsesfg]            ;get foreground session number
                @DosMonReg  monhand,monibuf,monobuf,1,DX ;monitor FG session
;
mon010:         mov     buflen,MONDBUFL             ;initialize buffer size
                @DosMonRead monibuf,BLOCK,mondbuf,buflen ;read packet
                @jaxnz  mon999                      ;exit if error code is set
                mov     ah,monkeybuf.charscan       ;get scan code
                mov     al,monkeybuf.charascii      ;get ASCII value
;
                cmp     ax,KDEL                     ;DEL key?
                @jne    mon050                      ;no - skip popup
                test    monkeybuf.charshift,CHARALT ;Alt key down?
                @je     mon050                      ;no - skip popup
                test    monkbdflg,040h              ;'Break' packet?
                @jne    mon050                      ;no - skip popup
                @DosSemClear semhand                ;start pop-up thread
                jmp     mon010                      ;loop (skip hot key)
;
mon050:         cmp     xflag,OFF                   ;translation off?
                @je     mon060                      ;no - go write packet
                cmp     al,'a'                      ;less than a ?
                jb      mon060                      ;yes - skip byte
                cmp     al,'z'                      ;greater than z ?
                ja      mon060                      ;yes - skip byte
                sub     al,'a'-'A'                  ;make upper case
                mov     monkeybuf.charascii,al      ;put it back in the packet
```

```
;
mon060:        @DosMonWrite monobuf,mondbuf,buflen ;write packet
               @jaxnz      mon999                  ;exit if error code is set
               jmp         mon010                  ;go read next packet
;
mon999:        @DosMonClose monhand                ;flush monitor
               @DosExit  1,0                        ;leave (kill all threads)
monitor        endp
;
               include os2procs.asm
;
KBM_code       ends
               end       main
```

OS2MAC.INC

```
;----------------------------------------------------------------
;   NAME: OS2MAC.INC
;
;   DESC: This library includes all the macros used in the
;         OS/2 Programmer's guide. Note: This library requires
;         that the file named OS2PROCS.ASM be included in the
;         code segment.
;
;  INPUT: none
;
; OUTPUT: none
;
;  PROCS: none
;
;   AUTH: E. E. Iacobucci
;
;   DATE: 10/15/87
;
;----------------------------------------------------------------
;==========================================
;
; Global system equates
;
;==========================================
;
CR          equ      0dh
LF          equ      0ah
CRLF        equ      0d0ah
;
FIFO        equ      0                       ;FIFO queue organization
LIFO        equ      1                       ;LIFO queue organization
PRTY        equ      2                       ;Priority queue organization
;
BLOCK       equ      0
RUN         equ      1
;
ON          equ      1
OFF         equ      0
;
STDIN       equ      0                       ;Standard intput handle
STDOUT      equ      1                       ;Standard output handle
STDERR      equ      2                       ;Standard error handle
;
SIGINTR     equ      1                       ;Ctrl-C signal
SIGTERM     equ      3                       ;Program termination signal
SIGBREAK    equ      4                       ;Ctrl-Break signal
SIGFLAGA    equ      5                       ;Process flag A
SIGFLAGB    equ      6                       ;Process flag B
SIGFLAGC    equ      7                       ;Process flag C
```

```
;
; Key scan codes
;
KESC        equ         01Bh                    ;Escape key
KUP         equ         4800h                   ;Up key
KDN         equ         5000h                   ;Down key
KLE         equ         4B00h                   ;Left key
KRI         equ         4D00h                   ;Right key
KPGUP       equ         4900h                   ;Page Up Key
KPGDN       equ         5100h                   ;Page Down Key
KINS        equ         5200h                   ;Insert Key
KDEL        equ         5300h                   ;Delete Key
KF1         equ         5400h                   ;F1
KF2         equ         5500h                   ;F2
KF3         equ         5600h                   ;F3
KF4         equ         5700h                   ;F4
KF5         equ         5800h                   ;F5
KF6         equ         5900h                   ;F6
KF7         equ         5A00h                   ;F7
KF8         equ         5B00h                   ;F8
KF9         equ         5C00h                   ;F9
KF0         equ         5D00h                   ;F10
;
;=========================================
;
; OS/2 Data Structures
;
;=========================================
;
;
; OS/2 Directory structure
;
;       Used by: DosFindFirst
;                DosFindNext
;
direntry    struc
dircd       dw          ?                       ;creation date
dirct       dw          ?                       ;creation time
dirad       dw          ?                       ;last access date
dirat       dw          ?                       ;last access time
dirwd       dw          ?                       ;last write date
dirwt       dw          ?                       ;last write time
direl       dw          ?                       ;end of data (low)
direh       dw          ?                       ;end of data (high)
diral       dw          ?                       ;file allocation (low)
dirah       dw          ?                       ;file allocation (high)
dirattr     dw          ?                       ;file attribute
dirnlen     db          ?                       ;name length
dirname     db          13 dup(?)               ;ASCIIZ name (variable length)
direntry    ends
```

```
;
;
; OS/2 File Data structure
;
;       Used by: DosQFileInfo
;
finfo      struc
ficd       dw        ?                       ;creation date
fict       dw        ?                       ;creation time
fiad       dw        ?                       ;last access date
fiat       dw        ?                       ;last access time
fiwd       dw        ?                       ;last write date
fiwt       dw        ?                       ;last write time
fiel       dw        ?                       ;end of data (low)
fieh       dw        ?                       ;end of data (high)
fial       dw        ?                       ;file allocation (low)
fiah       dw        ?                       ;file allocation (high)
fiattr     dw        ?                       ;file attribute
finfo      ends
;
;
; DosQFSInfo data structures
;
;
fsinfo1    struc                             ;record type=1
fsid       db        4 dup(?)                ;file system ID
spa        dd        ?                       ;sectors per allocation unit
nal        dd        ?                       ;number of allocation units
aal        dd        ?                       ;available allocation units
bps        dw        ?                       ;bytes per sector
fsinfo1    ends
;
fsinfo2    struc                             ;record type=2
vdate      dw        ?                       ;volume creation date
vtime      dw        ?                       ;volume creation time
vlen       db        ?                       ;volume label length
volid      db        11 dup(?)               ;volume label (variable length)
fsinfo2    ends
;
;
; DosGetPID output structure
;
;
pid        struc
pidpid     dw        ?                       ;Current process ID
pidtid     dw        ?                       ;Current thread ID
pidppid    dw        ?                       ;Parent process ID
pid        ends
```

```
;
;
; DosGet/SetCurType data structure
;
;
cur           struc
cursline      dw          ?                 ;cursor start line
cureline      dw          ?                 ;cursor end line
curwidth      dw          ?                 ;cursor width
curattr       dw          ?                 ;cursor attribute
cur           ends
;
;
; KBD character input structure
;
;
charbuf       struc
charascii     db          ?                 ;ASCII character code
charscan      db          ?                 ;scan code
charstat      db          ?                 ;status
charDBCSs     db          ?                 ;DBCS shift state
charshift     dw          ?                 ;shift state
chartimehi    dw          ?                 ;time stamp hi
chartimelo    dw          ?                 ;time stamp lo
charbuf       ends
;
CHARSYSREQ    equ         8000h             ;SysReq Key down
CHARCAPSLOK   equ         4000h             ;Caps Lock Key down
CHARNUMLOK    equ         2000h             ;Num Lock Key down
CHARSCRLOK    equ         1000h             ;Scroll Lock Key down
CHARRALT      equ         0800h             ;Right Alt Key down
CHARRCTRL     equ         0400h             ;Right Ctrl Key down
CHARLALT      equ         0200h             ;Left Alt Key down
CHARLCTRL     equ         0100h             ;Left Ctrl Key down
CHARSINS      equ         0080h             ;Insert state on
CHARSCAPSL    equ         0040h             ;Caps lock state on
CHARSNUMLOK   equ         0020h             ;Num lock state on
CHARSSCRLOK   equ         0010h             ;Scroll lock state on
CHARALT       equ         0008h             ;Either Alt key down
CHARCTRL      equ         0004h             ;Either Ctrl key down
CHARLSHIFT    equ         0002h             ;Left Shift key down
CHARRSHIFT    equ         0001h             ;Right Shift key down
;
CHARNO        equ         0                 ;no character available
CHARYES       equ         1                 ;character available
CHARINT       equ         2                 ;Interim character
CHARFIN       equ         3                 ;Final character
```

```
;
;
; Video mode data buffer
;
;
modedata        struc
modelen         dw      12                      ;buffer length
modetype        db      ?                       ;mode characteristics
modecolor       db      ?                       ;color
modecol         dw      ?                       ;Columns
moderow         dw      ?                       ;Rows
modehor         dw      ?                       ;Horizontal resolution
modever         dw      ?                       ;Vertical resolution
modedata        ends
;
;
; Video state data structures
;
;
vs1             struc
                dw      38                      ;buffer length
                dw      0                       ;get palette registers
                dw      0                       ;first palette register to return
vs1reg0         dw      ?                       ;palette register # 0
vs1reg1         dw      ?                       ;palette register # 1
vs1reg2         dw      ?                       ;palette register # 2
vs1reg3         dw      ?                       ;palette register # 3
vs1reg4         dw      ?                       ;palette register # 4
vs1reg5         dw      ?                       ;palette register # 5
vs1reg6         dw      ?                       ;palette register # 6
vs1reg7         dw      ?                       ;palette register # 7
vs1reg8         dw      ?                       ;palette register # 8
vs1reg9         dw      ?                       ;palette register # 9
vs1reg10        dw      ?                       ;palette register # 10
vs1reg11        dw      ?                       ;palette register # 11
vs1reg12        dw      ?                       ;palette register # 12
vs1reg13        dw      ?                       ;palette register # 13
vs1reg14        dw      ?                       ;palette register # 14
vs1reg15        dw      ?                       ;palette register # 15
vs1             ends
;
vs2             struc
                dw      6                       ;buffer length
                dw      1                       ;get overscan (border) color
vs2color        dw      ?                       ;border color
vs2             ends
;
vs3             struc
                dw      6                       ;buffer length
                dw      2                       ;get blink/bgnd intensity state
vs3bbgdi        dw      ?                       ;blink/bgnd intensity state
vs3             ends
```

```
;
;
;
; DosGetInfoSeg Data Structures
;
;
;
; Global InfoSeg
;
gdt        struc
gdtstime   dd      ?                        ;Time from db/db/70 in seconds
gdtms      dd      ?                        ;Milliseconds since IPL
gdthr      db      ?                        ;Hours (TOD)
gdtmin     db      ?                        ;Minutes (TOD)
gdtsec     db      ?                        ;Seconds (TOD)
gdthdth    db      ?                        ;Hundreths (TOD)
gdttz      dw      ?                        ;Timezone (minutes from GMT)
gdtti      dw      ?                        ;Timer interval (db/db0000 sec)
gdtday     db      ?                        ;Day
gdtmo      db      ?                        ;Month
gdtyr      dw      ?                        ;Year
gdtdow     db      ?                        ;Day of week
gdtmav     db      ?                        ;Major Version number
gdtmiv     db      ?                        ;Minor Version number
gdtrv      db      ?                        ;Revison letter
gdtsesfg   db      ?                        ;Foreground session number
gdtsesmx   db      ?                        ;Maximum sessions
gdthsc     db      ?                        ;Huge object shift count
gdtpoi     db      ?                        ;Protect-only Indicator
gdtfgpid   dw      ?                        ;Foreground process PID
gdtdvf     db      ?                        ;Dynamic variation flag (db=ON)
gdtmw      db      ?                        ;Max wait (seconds)
gdtmits    dw      ?                        ;Minimum time slice (millisec)
gdtmats    dw      ?                        ;Maximum time slice (millisec)
gdtbd      dw      ?                        ;Boot drive number
gdttrac    db      32 dup(?)                ;Major trace code flags
gdt        ends
;
; Local InfoSeg
;
ldt        struc
ldtpid     dw      ?                        ;Current process ID
ldtppid    dw      ?                        ;Process ID of parent
ldtprty    dw      ?                        ;Priority of current thread
ldttid     dw      ?                        ;Thread ID of current thread
ldtses     dw      ?                        ;Current session
ldtrsv     dw      ?                        ;Reserved
ldtfgi     dw      ?                        ;Process is in foreground (Ind)
ldtrmi     db      ?                        ;Process requires real mode (Ind)
ldtax      dw      ?                        ;AX register at startup
ldtbx      dw      ?                        ;BX register at startup
ldtcx      dw      ?                        ;CX register at startup
ldtdx      dw      ?                        ;DX register at startup
ldtsi      dw      ?                        ;SI register at startup
ldtdi      dw      ?                        ;DI register at startup
ldtds      dw      ?                        ;DS register at startup
ldt        ends
```

```
;.pa
;
;==========================================
;
; Service Routine Macros
;
;==========================================
;.sk 2
;
; MACRO: MOVS
;
;  DESC: Move character string
;
; INPUT: Name of dest string
;        Name of target string
;        Length to be moved
;
@MOVS        MACRO        FROM,TO,LEN
             .errb        <to>
             .errb        <from>
             .errb        <len>
             push         cx
             push         es
             push         ds
             mov          si,offset FROM
             mov          ax,seg FROM
             push         ax
             pop          es
             mov          di,offset TO
             mov          ax,seg TO
             push         ax
             pop          ds
             mov          cx,LEN
             rep          movsb
             pop          ds
             pop          es
             pop          cx
             ENDM
```

```
;.pa
;
; MACRO: STRLEN
;
;  DESC: Compute length of ASCIIZ string
;
; INPUT: String name
;        Output length (optional)
;
@STRLEN      MACRO     STR,TO
             .ERRB     <STR>
             IFNB      <TO>
               push    cx
             ENDIF
             push      ax
             push      es
             push      di
             IFIDN     < ES:DI >,< STR >
             ELSE
             IFIDN     < DS:SI >,< STR >
               push    ds
               pop     es
               mov     di,si
             ELSE
               mov     di,offset STR
               mov     cx,seg STR
               push    ax
               pop     es
             ENDIF
             ENDIF
             push      di
             mov       cx,-1
             xor       al,al
             repne     scasb
             mov       cx,di
             pop       di
             sub       cx,di
             dec       cx
             pop       di
             pop       es
             pop       ax
             IFNB      <TO>
               mov     TO,cx
               pop     cx
             ENDIF
             ENDM
```

```
;.pa
; MACRO: ATB
;
;  DESC: ASCII to binary
;
; INPUT: Name of source buffer
;        Buffer length
;        Destination word (optional)
;
@ATB        MACRO      FROM,LEN,TO
            .ERRB      <FROM>
            .ERRB      <LEN>
            IFNB       <TO>
              push       bx
            ENDIF
            push       cx
            push       ds
            push       si
            IFIDN      < DS:SI >,< FROM >
            ELSE
            IFIDN      < ES:DI >,< FROM >
              push       es
              pop        ds
              mov        si,di
            ELSE
              mov        cx,seg FROM
              push       cx
              pop        ds
              mov        si,offset FROM
            ENDIF
            ENDIF
            mov        cx,LEN
            call       os2atb
            pop        si
            pop        ds
            pop        cx
            IFNB       <TO>
              mov        TO,bx
              pop        bx
            ENDIF
            ENDM
```

```
;.pa
;
;
; MACRO: BTA
;
;  DESC: Binary to ASCII
;
; INPUT: Name of dest buffer
;        buffer length
;        source (binary)
;        leading zero strip indicator
;
@BTA        MACRO       FROM,TO,LEN
            .ERRB       <FROM>
            .ERRB       <LEN>
            .ERRB       <TO>
            push        cx
            push        es
            push        di
            push        ax

            IFIDN       < ES:DI >,< TO >
            ELSE

            IFIDN       < DS:SI >,< TO >
              push        ds
              pop         es
              mov         di,si
            ELSE

            IFIDN       < SS:BP >,< TO >
              push        ss
              pop         es
              mov         di,bp
            ELSE
              mov         ax,seg TO
              push        ax
              pop         es
              mov         di,offset TO
            ENDIF
            ENDIF
            ENDIF
            mov         ax,FROM
            mov         cx,LEN
            call        os2bta
            pop         ax
            pop         di
            pop         es
            pop         cx
            ENDM
```

```
;.pa
;
; MACRO: DATE
;
;  DESC: Convert binary value to date string
;
; INPUT: Name of dest buffer (must be 8 bytes)
;        source (binary OS/2 date format)
;
@DATE          MACRO        FROM,TO
               .ERRB        <FROM>
               .ERRB        <TO>
               push         es
               push         di
               push         ax
               mov          di,offset TO
               mov          ax,seg TO
               push         ax
               pop          es
               mov          ax,word ptr FROM
               call         os2date
               pop          ax
               pop          di
               pop          es
               ENDM
;.pa
;
; MACRO: SYSDATE
;
;  DESC: Generate system date
;
; INPUT: Name of dest buffer (must be 8 bytes)
;        Name of date/time data structure
;
@SYSDATE       MACRO        TO
               .ERRB        <TO>
               push         es
               push         di
               push         ax
               mov          di,offset TO
               mov          ax,seg TO
               push         ax
               pop          es
               call         os2sdate
               pop          ax
               pop          di
               pop          es
               ENDM
```

```
;.pa
;
; MACRO: TIME
;
;  DESC: Convert binary value to time string
;
; INPUT: Name of dest buffer (must be 8 bytes)
;        source (binary OS/2 time format)
;
@TIME           MACRO       FROM,TO
                .ERRB       <FROM>
                .ERRB       <TO>
                push        es
                push        di
                push        ax
                mov         di,offset TO
                mov         ax,seg TO
                push        ax
                pop         es
                mov         ax,word ptr FROM
                call        os2time
                pop         ax
                pop         di
                pop         es
                ENDM
;.pa
;
; MACRO: SYSTIME
;
;  DESC: Format system time
;
; INPUT: Name of dest buffer (must be 8 bytes)
;
;
@SYSTIME        MACRO       TO
                .ERRB       <TO>
                push        es
                push        di
                push        ax
                mov         di,offset TO
                mov         ax,seg TO
                push        ax
                pop         es
                call        os2stime
                pop         ax
                pop         di
                pop         es
                ENDM
```

```
;.pa
;
; MACRO: SYSDAY
;
;   DESC: Generate day of week
;
; INPUT: Name of dest buffer (must be 8 bytes)
;
;
@SYSDAY        MACRO        TO
               .ERRB        <TO>
               push         es
               push         di
               push         ax
               mov          di,offset TO
               mov          ax,seg TO
               push         ax
               pop          es
               call         os2sday
               pop          ax
               pop          di
               pop          es
               ENDM
;.pa
;
; MACRO: GETPARMS
;
;   DESC: Copy command line input into user buffer
;
; INPUT: Name of dest buffer
;        Length of dest buffer
;
@GETPARMS      MACRO        TO,LEN
               .ERRB        <TO>
               .ERRB        <LEN>
               push         es
               push         di
               push         cx
               mov          cx,seg TO
               push         cx
               pop          es
               mov          cx,LEN
               mov          di,offset TO
               call         os2parms
               pop          cx
               pop          di
               pop          es
               ENDM
```

```
;.pa
;
; MACRO: BTHS
;
;  DESC: Binary (string) to ASCII Hexadecimal
;
; INPUT: Source buffer
;        Source buffer length
;        Target buffer (length must be 2x source)
;
@BTHS       MACRO     FROM,TO,LEN
            .ERRB     <FROM>
            .ERRB     <LEN>
            .ERRB     <TO>
            push      cx
            push      es
            push      di
            push      ds
            push      si
            mov       cx,seg FROM
            push      cx
            pop       ds
            mov       si,offset FROM
            mov       cx,seg TO
            push      cx
            pop       es
            mov       di,offset TO
            mov       cx,LEN
            call      os2bths
            pop       si
            pop       ds
            pop       di
            pop       es
            pop       cx
            ENDM
```

```
;.pa
;
; MACRO: BTH
;
;  DESC: Binary (word) to ASCII Hexadecimal
;
; INPUT: Source word
;        Target buffer (length must be 4 bytes)
;
@BTH            MACRO       FROM,TO
                .ERRB       <FROM>
                .ERRB       <TO>
                push        ax
                push        es
                push        di
                mov         di,offset TO
                mov         ax,seg TO
                push        ax
                pop         es
                mov         ax,FROM
                call        os2bth
                pop         di
                pop         es
                pop         ax
                ENDM
;.pa
;
; MACRO: LOOP
;
;  DESC: Loop on target
;
;        Note: this macro does the same thing as the
;              LOOP instruction, except that it works
;              with far targets ( > +-128 bytes)
;
; INPUT: loop label
;
@LOOP           MACRO       TARGET
                .ERRB       <TARGET>
                dec         cx
                jcxz        $+5
                jmp         TARGET
                nop                                 ;in case jump is short
                ENDM
```

```
;.pa
;
; MACRO: JE/JZ
;
;  DESC: Jump if equal
;
;        Note: this macro does the same thing as the
;              JE instruction, except that it works
;              with far targets ( > +-128 bytes)
;
; INPUT: target for far jump
;
@JE         MACRO      TARGET
            .ERRB      <TARGET>
            jnz        $+5
            jmp        TARGET
            nop                             ;in case jump is short
            ENDM

@JZ         MACRO      TARGET              ;alias
            @je        TARGET
            ENDM
;.pa
;
; MACRO: JNE/JNZ
;
;  DESC: Jump if not equal
;
;        Note: this macro does the same thing as the
;              JNE instruction, except that it works
;              with far targets ( > +-128 bytes)
;
; INPUT: target for far jump
;
@JNE        MACRO      TARGET
            .ERRB      <TARGET>
            jz         $+5
            jmp        TARGET
            nop                             ;in case jump is short
            ENDM

@JNZ        MACRO      TARGET              ;alias
            @jne       TARGET
            ENDM
```

```
;.pa
;
; MACRO: JAXZ
;
;  DESC: Jump if AX is zero
;
; INPUT: target for far jump
;
@JAXZ       MACRO      TARGET
            .ERRB      <TARGET>
            or         ax,ax
            jnz        $+5
            jmp        TARGET
            nop                              ;in case jump is short
            ENDM
;.pa
;
; MACRO: JAXNZ
;
;  DESC: Jump if AX is not zero
;
; INPUT: target for far jump
;
@JAXNZ      MACRO      TARGET
            .ERRB      <TARGET>
            or         ax,ax
            jz         $+5
            jmp        TARGET
            nop                              ;in case jump is short
            ENDM
;.pa
;
; MACRO: HIDECURSOR
;
;  DESC: Hide cursor - retaining its size characteristics
;
; INPUT: none
;
@HIDECURSOR MACRO
            push       bp                    ;save BP
            sub        sp,size CUR           ;allocate work area
            mov        bp,sp                 ;address stack frame
            @VioGetCurType SS:BP,0           ;get current cursor type
            mov        word ptr ss:[bp].curattr,-1 ;set 'hidden' attribute
            @VioSetCurType SS:BP,0           ;set it
            add        sp,size CUR           ;de-allocate buffer
            pop        bp                    ;restore BP
            ENDM
```

```
;.pa
;
; MACRO: SHOWCURSOR
;
;  DESC: Restore cursor - retaining its size characteristics
;
; INPUT: none
;
@SHOWCURSOR    MACRO
               push        bp                      ;save BP
               sub         sp,size CUR             ;allocate work area
               mov         bp,sp                   ;address stack frame
               @VioGetCurType SS:BP,0              ;get current cursor type
               mov         word ptr ss:[bp].curattr,0 ;set 'normal' attribute
               @VioSetCurType SS:BP,0              ;set it
               add         sp,size CUR             ;de-allocate buffer
               pop         bp                      ;restore BP
               ENDM
;.pa
;
;  MACRO: MKTHREAD
;
;   DESC: allocate stack, create thread &
;         return to caller.
;
;   INPUT: name of procedure
;          stack size
;          word to hold thread ID (optional)
;
@MKTHREAD      MACRO       PROG,STACKSZ,TID
               .ERRB       <PROG>
               .ERRB       <STACKSZ>
               IFNB        <TID>
               push        bx
               ENDIF
               push        cx
               push        di
               mov         cx,seg PROG
               mov         di,offset PROG
               mov         bx,STACKSZ
               call        os2mkth
               pop         di
               pop         cx
               IFNB        <TID>
               mov         TID,bx
               pop         bx
               ENDIF
               ENDM
```

```
;.pa
;
;=============================================
;
; OS/2 System Calls
;
;    Note: each system call has an associated
;    macro. All system call macros are comprised
;    of the function name with a leading '@'
;    character.
;
;    Indirect reference parameters (PTR type)
;    also support the following arguments:
;
;     NULL = double-word of 0 pushed on the stack
;    ES:DI = Parameter is addressed by DI into ES
;    ES:SI = Parameter is addressed by SI into ES
;    DS:DI = Parameter is addressed by DI into DS
;    DS:SI = Parameter is addressed by SI into DS
;    SS:BP = Parameter is addressed by BP into SS
;
;    If the following statement is included in the
;    source file, the system call macros generate
;    an entry/exit execution trace:
;
;    bugflag    equ      1
;
;    The trace output is directed to STDOUT.
;
;=============================================


;
;
; Push word
;
@dw             macro    p0
                mov      ax,p0
                push     ax
                endm
```

```
;
; Push pointer
;
@do        macro      p0
           .errb      <p0>

           IFIDN      < SS:BP >,< p0 >
           push       ss
           push       bp
           ELSE

           IFIDN      < ES:DI >,< p0 >
           push       es
           push       di
           ELSE

           IFIDN      < ES:SI >,< p0 >
           push       es
           push       si
           ELSE

           IFIDN      < DS:DI >,< p0 >
           push       ds
           push       di
           ELSE

           IFIDN      < DS:SI >,< p0 >
           push       ds
           push       si
           ELSE

           IFIDN      < NULL >,< p0 >
           xor        ax,ax
           push       ax
           push       ax
           ELSE

           mov        ax,SEG p0
           push       ax
           lea        ax,p0
           push       ax
           ENDIF
           ENDIF
           ENDIF
           ENDIF
           ENDIF
           ENDIF
           endm
```

```
;
; Push doubleword
;
@dd         MACRO       p0
            .ERRB       <p0>

            IFIDN       < SS:BP >,< p0 >
            push        ss:[bp]
            push        ss:[bp+2]

            ELSE
            IFIDN       < ES:DI >,< p0 >
            push        es:[di]
            push        es:[di+2]

            ELSE
            IFIDN       < ES:SI >,< p0 >
            push        es:[si]
            push        es:[si+2]

            ELSE
            IFIDN       < DS:DI >,< p0 >
            push        ds:[di]
            push        ds:[di+2]

            ELSE
            IFIDN       < DS:SI >,< p0 >
            push        ds:[si+2]
            push        ds:[si]

            ELSE
            IFIDN       < NULL >,< p0 >
            xor         ax,ax
            push        ax
            push        ax

            ELSE
            push        ds                  ;save data segment
            push        bx                  ;save current bx value
            mov         ax, SEG p0          ;load ds with seg loc of 32 bit value
            mov         ds,ax
            mov         bx, OFFSET p0       ;load bx with offset value
            push        word ptr [bx]       ;push low-order of 32 bit val stack
            mov         ax,[bx+2]           ;put high order 32-bit value in ax
            push        bp                  ;save bp
            push        sp
            pop         bp
            xchg        [bp+6],ax           ;
            pop         bp                  ;restore
            mov         ds,ax               ;restore ds to saved value.
            pop         ax                  ;pop off low order 32 bit val
            pop         bx                  ;restore bx to saved value.
            push        ax                  ;put low order 32 bit value on stack
            ENDIF
```

```
                         ENDIF
                         ENDIF
                         ENDIF
                         ENDIF
                         ENDIF
                         ENDM
;
; Define external entry point
;
@define       MACRO       NAME
              IFNDEF      NAME
              extrn       NAME:far
              %OUT        Function NAME Defined
              ENDIF
              ENDM

;
; Call routine macro
;
@callproc     MACRO        PROC
              .ERRB        <PROC>
              @define      PROC
              @dbugentry   PROC
              call far ptr PROC
              @dbugexit    PROC
              ENDM

;
; Debug entry point macro
;
@dbugentry    MACRO       PROC
              local       DOIT1,MSG1,MSG1L
              IFDEF       bugflag
              jmp         DOIT1
MSG1          db          ' Call --> &PROC',CR,LF
MSG1L         equ         $-offset MSG1
              @define     DosWrite
DOIT1:        push        bp                       ;save BP
              sub         sp,2                     ;allocate buffer
              mov         bp,sp                    ;address stack frame
              @dw         2                        ;stderr
              @do         MSG1
              @dw         MSG1L
              @do         SS:BP
              call        far ptr DosWrite         ;write 'call' message
              add         sp,2                     ;de-allocate buffer
              pop         bp                       ;restore BP
              IFIDN       < %BUGFLAG >,< 2 >
              db          0cch                     ;stop
              ENDIF
              ENDIF
              ENDM
```

```
;
; Debug exit point macro
;
@dbugexit       MACRO       PROC
                LOCAL       DOIT2,MSG2,MSG2L,NL
                IFDEF       bugflag
                jmp         DOIT2
MSG2            db          'Return --> &PROC'
                db          30 - ($ - offset MSG2) dup (' ') ;align AX=
                db          'AX='
MSG2L           equ         $-offset MSG2
NL              db          CR,LF
DOIT2:          push        ax
                push        dx
                push        bp                  ;save BP
                sub         sp,7                ;allocate buffer
                mov         bp,sp               ;address stack frame
                mov         dx,ax               ;get return code
                @dw         2                   ;stderr
                @do         MSG2
                @dw         MSG2L
                push        ss
                mov         ax,bp
                add         ax,5
                push        ax
                call        far ptr DosWrite    ;write 'return' message
                @bta        dx,SS:BP,5
                @dw         2                   ;stderr
                @do         SS:BP
                @dw         5
                push        ss
                mov         ax,bp
                add         ax,5
                push        ax
                call        far ptr DosWrite    ;write AX contents
                @dw         2                   ;stderr
                @do         NL
                @dw         2
                push        ss
                mov         ax,bp
                add         ax,5
                push        ax
                call        far ptr DosWrite    ;write CR/LF
                add         sp,7                ;de-allocate buffer
                pop         bp                  ;restore BP
                pop         dx
                pop         ax
                ENDIF
                ENDM
```

```
;
; System calls
;
@DosAllocHuge          MACRO      p0,p1,p2,p3,p4
                       @DW        p0
                       @DW        p1
                       @DO        p2
                       @DW        p3
                       @DW        p4
                       @CALLPROC  DosAllocHuge
                       ENDM

@DosAllocSeg           MACRO      p0,p1,p2
                       @DW        p0
                       @DO        p1
                       @DW        p2
                       @CALLPROC  DosAllocSeg
                       ENDM

@DosAllocShrSeg        MACRO      p0,p1,p2
                       @DW        p0
                       @DO        p1
                       @DO        p2
                       @CALLPROC  DosAllocShrSeg
                       ENDM

@DosBeep               MACRO      p0,p1
                       @DW        p0
                       @DW        p1
                       @CALLPROC  DosBeep
                       ENDM

@DosCaseMap            MACRO      p0,p1,p2
                       @DW        p0
                       @DO        p1
                       @DO        p2
                       @CALLPROC  DosCaseMap
                       ENDM

@DosChgDir             MACRO      p0,p1
                       @DO        p0
                       @DD        p1
                       @CALLPROC  DosChgDir
                       ENDM

@DosChgFilePtr         MACRO      p0,p1,p2,p3
                       @DW        p0
                       @DD        p1
                       @DW        p2
                       @DO        p3
                       @CALLPROC  DosChgFilePtr
                       ENDM
```

```
@DosCLIAccess          MACRO
                       @CALLPROC DosCLIAccess
                       ENDM

@DosClose              MACRO       p0
                       @DW         p0
                       @CALLPROC DosClose
                       ENDM

@DosCloseQueue         MACRO       p0
                       @DW         p0
                       @CALLPROC DosCloseQueue
                       ENDM

@DosCloseSem           MACRO       p0
                       @DD         p0
                       @CALLPROC DosCloseSem
                       ENDM

@DosCreateCSAlias               MACRO       p0,p1
                       @DW         p0
                       @DO         p1
                       @CALLPROC DosCreateCSAlias
                       ENDM

@DosCreateQueue        MACRO       p0,p1,p2
                       @DO         p0
                       @DW         p1
                       @DO         p2
                       @CALLPROC DosCreateQueue
                       ENDM

@DosCreateSem          MACRO       p0,p1,p2
                       @DW         p0
                       @DO         p1
                       @DO         p2
                       @CALLPROC DosCreateSem
                       ENDM

@DosCreateThread       MACRO       p0,p1,p2
                       @DO         p0
                       @DO         p1
                       @DD         p2
                       @CALLPROC DosCreateThread
                       ENDM

@DosCWait              MACRO       p0,p1,p2,p3,p4
                       @DW         p0
                       @DW         p1
                       @DO         p2
                       @DO         p3
                       @DW         p4
                       @CALLPROC DosCWait
                       ENDM
```

```
@DosDevIOCtl        MACRO       p0,p1,p2,p3,p4
                    @DO         p0
                    @DO         p1
                    @DW         p2
                    @DW         p3
                    @DW         p4
                    @CALLPROC DosDevIOCtl
                    ENDM

@DosDupHandle       MACRO       p0,p1
                    @DW         p0
                    @DO         p1
                    @CALLPROC DosDupHandle
                    ENDM

@DosEnterCritSec    MACRO
                    @CALLPROC DosEnterCritSec
                    ENDM

@DosErrClass        MACRO       p0,p1,p2,p3
                    @DW         p0
                    @DO         p1
                    @DO         p2
                    @DO         p3
                    @CALLPROC DosErrClass
                    ENDM

@DosError           MACRO       p0
                    @DW         p0
                    @CALLPROC DosError
                    ENDM

@DosExecPgm         MACRO       p0,p1,p2,p3,p4,p5,p6
                    @DO         p0
                    @DW         p1
                    @DW         p2
                    @DO         p3
                    @DO         p4
                    @DO         p5
                    @DO         p6
                    @CALLPROC DosExecPgm
                    ENDM

@DosExit            MACRO       p0,p1
                    @DW         p0
                    @DW         p1
                    @CALLPROC DosExit
                    ENDM

@DosExitCritSec     MACRO
                    @CALLPROC DosExitCritSec
                    ENDM
```

```
@DosExitList     MACRO     p0,p1
                 @DW       p0
                 @DD       p1
                 @CALLPROC DosExitList
                 ENDM

@DosFileLocks    MACRO     p0,p1,p2
                 @DW       p0
                 @DO       p1
                 @DO       p2
                 @CALLPROC DosFileLocks
                 ENDM

@DosFindClose    MACRO     p0
                 @DW       p0
                 @CALLPROC DosFindClose
                 ENDM

@DosFindFirst    MACRO     p0,p1,p2,p3,p4,p5,p6
                 @DO       p0
                 @DO       p1
                 @DW       p2
                 @DO       p3
                 @DW       p4
                 @DO       p5
                 @DD       p6
                 @CALLPROC DosFindFirst
                 ENDM

@DosFindNext     MACRO     p0,p1,p2,p3
                 @DW       p0
                 @DO       p1
                 @DW       p2
                 @DO       p3
                 @CALLPROC DosFindNext
                 ENDM

@DosFlagProcess  MACRO     p0,p1,p2,p3
                 @DW       p0
                 @DW       p1
                 @DW       p2
                 @DW       p3
                 @CALLPROC DosFlagProcess
                 ENDM

@DosFreeModule   MACRO     p0
                 @DW       p0
                 @CALLPROC DosFreeModule
                 ENDM

@DosFreeSeg      MACRO     p0
                 @DW       p0
                 @CALLPROC DosFreeSeg
                 ENDM
```

```
@DosGetCollate          MACRO     p0,p1,p2,p3
                        @DW       p0
                        @DO       p1
                        @DO       p2
                        @DO       p3
                        @CALLPROC DosGetCollate
                        ENDM

@DosGetCP               MACRO     p0,p1,p2
                        @DW       p0
                        @DO       p1
                        @DO       p2
                        @CALLPROC DosGetCP
                        ENDM

@DosGetCtryInfo         MACRO     p0,p1,p2,p3
                        @DW       p0
                        @DO       p1
                        @DO       p2
                        @DO       p3
                        @CALLPROC DosGetCtryInfo
                        ENDM

@DosGetDateTime         MACRO     p0
                        @DO       p0
                        @CALLPROC DosGetDateTime
                        ENDM

@DosGetDBCSEv           MACRO     p0,p1,p2
                        @DW       p0
                        @DO       p1
                        @DO       p2
                        @CALLPROC DosGetDBCSEv
                        ENDM

@DosGetHugeShift        MACRO     p0
                        @DD       p0
                        @CALLPROC DosGetHugeShift
                        ENDM

@DosGetInfoSeg          MACRO     p0,p1
                        @DO       p0
                        @DO       p1
                        @CALLPROC DosGetInfoSeg
                        ENDM

@DosGetMachineMode              MACRO     p0
                        @DO       p0
                        @CALLPROC DosGetMachineMode
                        ENDM
```

```
@DosGetMessage        MACRO      p0,p1,p2,p3,p4,p5,p6
                      @DO        p0
                      @DW        p1
                      @DO        p2
                      @DW        p3
                      @DW        p4
                      @DO        p5
                      @DO        p6
                      @CALLPROC  DosGetMessage
                      ENDM

@DosGetModHandle      MACRO      p0,p1
                      @DO        p0
                      @DO        p1
                      @CALLPROC  DosGetModHandle
                      ENDM

@DosGetModName        MACRO      p0,p1,p2
                      @DW        p0
                      @DW        p1
                      @DO        p2
                      @CALLPROC  DosGetModName
                      ENDM

@DosGetPid            MACRO      p0
                      @DO        p0
                      @CALLPROC  DosGetPid
                      ENDM

@DosGetProcAddr       MACRO      p0,p1,p2
                      @DW        p0
                      @DO        p1
                      @DO        p2
                      @CALLPROC  DosGetProcAddr
                      ENDM

@DosGetPrty           MACRO      p0,p1,p2
                      @DW        p0
                      @DO        p1
                      @DW        p2
                      @CALLPROC  DosGetPrty
                      ENDM

@DosGetShrSeg         MACRO      p0,p1
                      @DO        p0
                      @DO        p1
                      @CALLPROC  DosGetShrSeg
                      ENDM

@DosGetVersion        MACRO      p0
                      @DO        p0
                      @CALLPROC  DosGetVersion
                      ENDM
```

```
@DosGiveSeg        MACRO    p0,p1,p2
                   @DW      p0
                   @DW      p1
                   @DO      p2
                   @CALLPROC DosGiveSeg
                   ENDM

@DosHoldSignal     MACRO    p0
                   @DW      p0
                   @CALLPROC DosHoldSignal
                   ENDM

@DosInsMessage     MACRO    p0,p1,p2,p3,p4,p5,p6
                   @DO      p0
                   @DW      p1
                   @DO      p2
                   @DW      p3
                   @DO      p4
                   @DW      p5
                   @DO      p6
                   @CALLPROC DosInsMessage
                   ENDM

@DosKillProcess    MACRO    p0,p1
                   @DW      p0
                   @DW      p1
                   @CALLPROC DosKillProcess
                   ENDM

@DosLoadModule     MACRO    p0,p1,p2,p3
                   @DO      p0
                   @DW      p1
                   @DO      p2
                   @DO      p3
                   @CALLPROC DosLoadModule
                   ENDM

@DosLockSeg        MACRO    p0
                   @DW      p0
                   @CALLPROC DosLockSeg
                   ENDM

@DosMakePipe       MACRO    p0,p1,p2
                   @DO      p0
                   @DO      p1
                   @DW      p2
                   @CALLPROC DosMakePipe
                   ENDM

@DosMemAvail       MACRO    p0
                   @DO      p0
                   @CALLPROC DcsMemAvail
                   ENDM
```

```
@DosMKDir            MACRO      p0,p1
                     @DO        p0
                     @DW        p1
                     @CALLPROC  DosMKDir
                     ENDM

@DosMonClose         MACRO      p0
                     @DW        p0
                     @CALLPROC  DosMonClose
                     ENDM

@DosMonOpen          MACRO      p0,p1
                     @DO        p0
                     @DO        p1
                     @CALLPROC  DosMonOpen
                     ENDM

@DosMonRead          MACRO      p0,p1,p2,p3
                     @DO        p0
                     @DW        p1
                     @DO        p2
                     @DO        p3
                     @CALLPROC  DosMonRead
                     ENDM

@DosMonReg           MACRO      p0,p1,p2,p3,p4
                     @DW        p0
                     @DO        p1
                     @DO        p2
                     @DW        p3
                     @DW        p4
                     @CALLPROC  DosMonReg
                     ENDM

@DosMonWrite         MACRO      p0,p1,p2
                     @DO        p0
                     @DO        p1
                     @DW        p2
                     @CALLPROC  DosMonWrite
                     ENDM

@DosMove             MACRO      p0,p1,p2
                     @DO        p0
                     @DO        p1
                     @DD        p2
                     @CALLPROC  DosMove
                     ENDM

@DosMuxSemWait       MACRO      p0,p1,p2
                     @DO        p0
                     @DO        p1
                     @DD        p2
                     @CALLPROC  DosMuxSemWait
                     ENDM
```

```
@DosNewSize       MACRO     p0,p1
                  @DW       p0
                  @DD       p1
                  @CALLPROC DosNewSize
                  ENDM

@DosOpen          MACRO     p0,p1,p2,p3,p4,p5,p6,p7
                  @DO       p0
                  @DO       p1
                  @DO       p2
                  @DD       p3
                  @DW       p4
                  @DW       p5
                  @DW       p6
                  @DD       p7
                  @CALLPROC DosOpen
                  ENDM

@DosOpenQueue     MACRO     p0,p1,p2
                  @DO       p0
                  @DO       p1
                  @DO       p2
                  @CALLPROC DosOpenQueue
                  ENDM

@DosOpenSem       MACRO     p0,p1
                  @DO       p0
                  @DO       p1
                  @CALLPROC DosOpenSem
                  ENDM

@DosPeekQueue     MACRO     p0,p1,p2,p3,p4,p5,p6,p7
                  @DW       p0
                  @DO       p1
                  @DO       p2
                  @DO       p3
                  @DO       p4
                  @DW       p5
                  @DO       p6
                  @DD       p7
                  @CALLPROC DosPeekQueue
                  ENDM

@DosPhysicalDisk  MACRO     p0,p1,p2,p3,p4
                  @DW       p0
                  @DO       p1
                  @DW       p2
                  @DO       p3
                  @DW       p4
                  @CALLPROC DosPhysicalDisk
                  ENDM
```

```
@DosPortAccess      MACRO       p0,p1,p2,p3
                    @DW         p0
                    @DW         p1
                    @DW         p2
                    @DW         p3
                    @CALLPROC DosPortAccess
                    ENDM

@DosPurgeQueue      MACRO       p0
                    @DW         p0
                    @CALLPROC DosPurgeQueue
                    ENDM

@DosPutMessage      MACRO       p0,p1,p2
                    @DW         p0
                    @DW         p1
                    @DO         p2
                    @CALLPROC DosPutMessage
                    ENDM

@DosChDir           MACRO       p0,p1
                    @DO         p0
                    @DD         p1
                    @CALLPROC DosChDir
                    ENDM

@DosQCurDisk        MACRO       p0,p1
                    @DO         p0
                    @DO         p1
                    @CALLPROC DosQCurDisk
                    ENDM

@DosQFHandState     MACRO       p0,p1
                    @DW         p0
                    @DO         p1
                    @CALLPROC DosQFHandState
                    ENDM

@DosQFileInfo       MACRO       p0,p1,p2,p3
                    @DW         p0
                    @DW         p1
                    @DO         p2
                    @DW         p3
                    @CALLPROC DosQFileInfo
                    ENDM

@DosQFileMode       MACRO       p0,p1,p2
                    @DO         p0
                    @DO         p1
                    @DD         p2
                    @CALLPROC DosQFileMode
                    ENDM
```

```
@DosQFSInfo          MACRO     p0,p1,p2,p3
                     @DW       p0
                     @DW       p1
                     @DO       p2
                     @DW       p3
                     @CALLPROC DosQFSInfo
                     ENDM

@DosQHandType        MACRO     p0,p1,p2
                     @DW       p0
                     @DO       p1
                     @DO       p2
                     @CALLPROC DosQHandType
                     ENDM

@DosQueryQueue       MACRO     p0,p1
                     @DW       p0
                     @DO       p1
                     @CALLPROC DosQueryQueue
                     ENDM

@DosQVerify          MACRO     p0
                     @DO       p0
                     @CALLPROC DosQVerify
                     ENDM

@DosRead             MACRO     p0,p1,p2,p3
                     @DW       p0
                     @DO       p1
                     @DW       p2
                     @DO       p3
                     @CALLPROC DosRead
                     ENDM

@DosReadAsync        MACRO     p0,p1,p2,p3,p4,p5
                     @DW       p0
                     @DD       p1
                     @DO       p2
                     @DO       p3
                     @DW       p4
                     @DO       p5
                     @CALLPROC DosReadAsync
                     ENDM

@DosReadQueue        MACRO     p0,p1,p2,p3,p4,p5,p6,p7
                     @DW       p0
                     @DO       p1
                     @DO       p2
                     @DO       p3
                     @DW       p4
                     @DW       p5
                     @DO       p6
                     @DD       p7
                     @CALLPROC DosReadQueue
                     ENDM
```

```
@DosReallocHuge        MACRO      p0,p1
                       @DW        p0
                       @DW        p1
                       @CALLPROC  DosReallocHuge
                       ENDM

@DosReallocSeg         MACRO      p0,p1
                       @DW        p0
                       @DW        p1
                       @CALLPROC  DosReallocSeg
                       ENDM

@DosResumeThread       MACRO      p0
                       @DW        p0
                       @CALLPROC  DosResumeThread
                       ENDM

@DosRmDir              MACRO      p0,p1
                       @DO        p0
                       @DD        p1
                       @CALLPROC  DosRmDir
                       ENDM

@DosScanEnv            MACRO      p0,p1
                       @DO        p0
                       @DO        p1
                       @CALLPROC  DosScanEnv
                       ENDM

@DosSearchPath         MACRO      p0,p1,p2,p3,p4
                       @DW        p0
                       @DO        p1
                       @DO        p2
                       @DO        p3
                       @DW        p4
                       @CALLPROC  DosSearchPath
                       ENDM

@DosSelectDisk         MACRO      p0
                       @DW        p0
                       @CALLPROC  DosSelectDisk
                       ENDM

@DosSelectSession      MACRO      p0,p1
                       @DW        p0
                       @DD        p1
                       @CALLPROC  DosSelectSession
                       ENDM

@DosSemClear           MACRO      p0
                       @DD        p0
                       @CALLPROC  DosSemClear
                       ENDM
```

```
@DosSemRequest        MACRO      p0,p1
                      @DD        p0
                      @DD        p1
                      @CALLPROC DosSemRequest
                      ENDM

@DosSemSet            MACRO      p0
                      @DD        p0
                      @CALLPROC DosSemSet
                      ENDM

@DosSemSetWait        MACRO      p0,p1
                      @DD        p0
                      @DD        p1
                      @CALLPROC DosSemSetWait
                      ENDM

@DosSemWait           MACRO      p0,p1
                      @DD        p0
                      @DD        p1
                      @CALLPROC DosSemWait
                      ENDM

@DosSendSignal        MACRO      p0,p1
                      @DW        p0
                      @DW        p1
                      @CALLPROC DosSendSignal
                      ENDM

@DosSetCP             MACRO      p0,p1
                      @DW        p0
                      @DW        p1
                      @CALLPROC DosSetCP
                      ENDM

@DosSetDateTime       MACRO      p0
                      @DO        p0
                      @CALLPROC DosSetDateTime
                      ENDM

@DosSetFHandState     MACRO      p0,p1
                      @DW        p0
                      @DW        p1
                      @CALLPROC DosSetFHandState
                      ENDM

@DosSetFileInfo       MACRO      p0,p1,p2,p3
                      @DW        p0
                      @DW        p1
                      @DO        p2
                      @DW        p3
                      @CALLPROC DosSetFileInfo
                      ENDM
```

```
@DosSetFileInfo        MACRO     p0,p1,p2,p3
                       @DW       p0
                       @DW       p1
                       @DO       p2
                       @DW       p3
                       @CALLPROC DosSetFileInfo
                       ENDM

@DosSetFileMode        MACRO     p0,p1,p2
                       @DO       p0
                       @DW       p1
                       @DD       p2
                       @CALLPROC DosSetFileMode
                       ENDM

@DosSetMaxFH           MACRO     p0
                       @DW       p0
                       @CALLPROC DosSetMaxFH
                       ENDM

@DosSetPrty            MACRO     p0,p1,p2,p3
                       @DW       p0
                       @DW       p1
                       @DW       p2
                       @DW       p3
                       @CALLPROC DosSetPrty
                       ENDM

@DosSetSession         MACRO     p0,p1
                       @DW       p0
                       @DO       p1
                       @CALLPROC DosSetSession
                       ENDM

@DosSetSigHandler      MACRO     p0,p1,p2,p3,p4
                       @DD       p0
                       @DO       p1
                       @DO       p2
                       @DW       p3
                       @DW       p4
                       @CALLPROC DosSetSigHandler
                       ENDM

@DosSetVec             MACRO     p0,p1,p2
                       @DW       p0
                       @DD       p1
                       @DO       p2
                       @CALLPROC DosSetVec
                       ENDM

@DosSetVerify          MACRO     p0
                       @DW       p0
                       @CALLPROC DosSetVerify
                       ENDM
```

```
@DosSleep              MACRO     p0
                       @DD       p0
                       @CALLPROC DosSleep
                       ENDM

@DosStartSession       MACRO     p0,p1,p2
                       @DO       p0
                       @DO       p1
                       @DO       p2
                       @CALLPROC DosStartSession
                       ENDM

@DosStopSession        MACRO     p0,p1,p2
                       @DW       p0
                       @DW       p1
                       @DD       p2
                       @CALLPROC DosStopSession
                       ENDM

@DosSubAlloc           MACRO     p0,p1,p2
                       @DD       p0
                       @DO       p1
                       @DW       p2
                       @CALLPROC DosSubAlloc
                       ENDM

@DosSubFree            MACRO     p0,p1,p2
                       @DD       p0
                       @DO       p1
                       @DW       p2
                       @CALLPROC DosSubFree
                       ENDM

@DosSubSet             MACRO     p0,p1,p2
                       @DW       p0
                       @DW       p1
                       @DW       p2
                       @CALLPROC DosSubSet
                       ENDM

@DosSuspendThread      MACRO     p0
                       @DW       p0
                       @CALLPROC DosSuspendThread
                       ENDM

@DosTimerAsync         MACRO     p0,p1,p2
                       @DD       p0
                       @DD       p1
                       @DO       p2
                       @CALLPROC DosTimerAsync
                       ENDM
```

```
@DosTimerStart      MACRO     p0,p1,p2
                    @DD       p0
                    @DD       p1
                    @DO       p2
                    @CALLPROC DosTimerStart
                    ENDM

@DosTimerStop       MACRO     p0
                    @DW       p0
                    @CALLPROC DosTimerStop
                    ENDM

@DosUnlockSeg       MACRO     p0,p1
                    @DO       p0
                    @DW       p1
                    @CALLPROC DosUnlockSeg
                    ENDM

@DosWrite           MACRO     p0,p1,p2,p3
                    @DW       p0
                    @DO       p1
                    @DW       p2
                    @DO       p3
                    @CALLPROC DosWrite
                    ENDM

@DosWriteAsync      MACRO     p0,p1,p2,p3,p4,p5
                    @DW       p0
                    @DD       p1
                    @DO       p2
                    @DO       p3
                    @DW       p4
                    @DO       p5
                    @CALLPROC DosWriteAsync
                    ENDM

@DosWriteQueue      MACRO     p0,p1,p2,p3,p4
                    @DW       p0
                    @DW       p1
                    @DW       p2
                    @DO       p3
                    @DW       p4
                    @CALLPROC DosWriteQueue
                    ENDM

@KbdCharIn          MACRO     p0,p1,p2
                    @DO       p0
                    @DW       p1
                    @DW       p2
                    @CALLPROC KbdCharIn
                    ENDM
```

```
@KbdClose          MACRO      p0
                   @DW        p0
                   @CALLPROC  KbdClose
                   ENDM

@KbdDeRegister     MACRO
                   @CALLPROC  KbdDeRegister
                   ENDM

@KbdFlushBuffer    MACRO      p0
                   @DW        p0
                   @CALLPROC  KbdFlushBuffer
                   ENDM

@KbdFreeFocus      MACRO      p0
                   @DW        p0
                   @CALLPROC  KbdFreeFocus
                   ENDM

@KbdGetCP          MACRO      p0,p1,p2
                   @DD        p0
                   @DO        p1
                   @DW        p2
                   @CALLPROC  KbdGetCP
                   ENDM

@KbdGetFocus       MACRO      p0,p1
                   @DW        p0
                   @DW        p1
                   @CALLPROC  KbdGetFocus
                   ENDM

@KbdGetStatus      MACRO      p0,p1
                   @DO        p0
                   @DW        p1
                   @CALLPROC  KbdGetStatus
                   ENDM

@KbdOpen           MACRO      p0
                   @DO        p0
                   @CALLPROC  KbdOpen
                   ENDM

@KbdPeek           MACRO      p0,p1
                   @DO        p0
                   @DW        p1
                   @CALLPROC  KbdPeek
                   ENDM

@KbdRegister       MACRO      p0,p1,p2
                   @DO        p0
                   @DO        p1
                   @DD        p2
                   @CALLPROC  KbdRegister
                   ENDM
```

```
@KbdSetCP              MACRO      p0,p1,p2
                       @DW        p0
                       @DW        p1
                       @DW        p2
                       @CALLPROC  KbdSetCP
                       ENDM

@KbdSetCustXT          MACRO      p0,p1
                       @DO        p0
                       @DW        p1
                       @CALLPROC  KbdSetCustXT
                       ENDM

@KbdSetStatus          MACRO      p0,p1
                       @DO        p0
                       @DW        p1
                       @CALLPROC  KbdSetStatus
                       ENDM

@KbdStringIn           MACRO      p0,p1,p2,p3
                       @DO        p0
                       @DO        p1
                       @DW        p2
                       @DW        p3
                       @CALLPROC  KbdStringIn
                       ENDM

@KbdXlate              MACRO      p0,p1
                       @DO        p0
                       @DW        p1
                       @CALLPROC  KbdXlate
                       ENDM

@MouClose              MACRO      p0
                       @DW        p0
                       @CALLPROC  MouClose
                       ENDM

@MouDeRegister         MACRO
                       @CALLPROC  MouDeRegister
                       ENDM

@MouDrawPtr            MACRO      p0
                       @DW        p0
                       @CALLPROC  MouDrawPtr
                       ENDM

@MouFlushQue           MACRO      p0
                       @DW        p0
                       @CALLPROC  MouFlushQue
                       ENDM
```

```
@MouGetDevStatus      MACRO     p0,p1
                      @DO       p0
                      @DW       p1
                      @CALLPROC MouGetDevStatus
                      ENDM

@MouGetEventMask      MACRO     p0,p1
                      @DO       p0
                      @DW       p1
                      @CALLPROC MouGetEventMask
                      ENDM

@MouGetHotKey         MACRO     p0,p1
                      @DO       p0
                      @DW       p1
                      @CALLPROC MouGetHotKey
                      ENDM

@MouGetNumButtons     MACRO     p0,p1
                      @DO       p0
                      @DW       p1
                      @CALLPROC MouGetNumButtons
                      ENDM

@MouGetNumMickeys     MACRO     p0,p1
                      @DO       p0
                      @DW       p1
                      @CALLPROC MouGetNumMickeys
                      ENDM

@MouGetNumQueEl       MACRO     p0,p1
                      @DO       p0
                      @DW       p1
                      @CALLPROC MouGetNumQueEl
                      ENDM

@MouGetPtrPos         MACRO     p0,p1
                      @DO       p0
                      @DW       p1
                      @CALLPROC MouGetPtrPos
                      ENDM

@MouGetPtrShape       MACRO     p0,p1,p2
                      @DO       p0
                      @DO       p1
                      @DW       p2
                      @CALLPROC MouGetPtrShape
                      ENDM

@MouGetScaleFact      MACRO     p0,p1
                      @DO       p0
                      @DW       p1
                      @CALLPROC MouGetScaleFact
                      ENDM
```

```
@MouOpen                MACRO     p0,p1
                        @DO       p0
                        @DO       p1
                        @CALLPROC MouOpen
                        ENDM

@MouReadEventQue        MACRO     p0,p1,p2
                        @DO       p0
                        @DO       p1
                        @DW       p2
                        @CALLPROC MouReadEventQue
                        ENDM

@MouRegister            MACRO     p0,p1,p2
                        @DO       p0
                        @DO       p1
                        @DD       p2
                        @CALLPROC MouRegister
                        ENDM

@MouRemovePtr           MACRO     p0,p1
                        @DO       p0
                        @DW       p1
                        @CALLPROC MouRemovePtr
                        ENDM

@MouSetDevStatus        MACRO     p0,p1
                        @DO       p0
                        @DW       p1
                        @CALLPROC MouSetDevStatus
                        ENDM

@MouSetEventMask        MACRO     p0,p1
                        @DO       p0
                        @DW       p1
                        @CALLPROC MouSetEventMask
                        ENDM

@McuSetHotKey           MACRO     p0,p1
                        @DO       p0
                        @DW       p1
                        @CALLPROC MouSetHotKey
                        ENDM

@MouSetPtrPos           MACRO     p0,p1
                        @DO       p0
                        @DW       p1
                        @CALLPROC MouSetPtrPos
                        ENDM

@MouSetPtrShape         MACRO     p0,p1,p2
                        @DO       p0
                        @DO       p1
                        @DW       p2
                        @CALLPROC MouSetPtrShape
                        ENDM
```

```
@MouSetScaleFact        MACRO       p0,p1
                        @DO         p0
                        @DW         p1
                        @CALLPROC MouSetScaleFact
                        ENDM

@VioDeRegister          MACRO
                        @CALLPROC VioDeRegister
                        ENDM

@VioEndPopUp            MACRO       p0
                        @DW         p0
                        @CALLPROC VioEndPopUp
                        ENDM

@VioGetANSI             MACRO       p0,p1
                        @DO         p0
                        @DW         p1
                        @CALLPROC VioGetANSI
                        ENDM

@VioGetBuf              MACRO       p0,p1,p2
                        @DO         p0
                        @DO         p1
                        @DW         p2
                        @CALLPROC VioGetBuf
                        ENDM

@VioGetConfig           MACRO       p0,p1
                        @DO         p0
                        @DW         p1
                        @CALLPROC VioGetConfig
                        ENDM

@VioGetCP               MACRO       p0,p1,p2
                        @DW         p0
                        @DO         p1
                        @DW         p2
                        @CALLPROC VioGetCP
                        ENDM

@VioGetCursorPos        MACRO       p0,p1,p2
                        @DO         p0
                        @DO         p1
                        @DW         p2
                        @CALLPROC VioGetCursorPos
                        ENDM

@VioGetCurType          MACRO       p0,p1
                        @DO         p0
                        @DW         p1
                        @CALLPROC VioGetCurType
                        ENDM
```

```
@VioGetFont          MACRO      p0,p1
                     @DO        p0
                     @DW        p1
                     @CALLPROC  VioGetFont
                     ENDM

@VioGetMode          MACRO      p0,p1
                     @DO        p0
                     @DW        p1
                     @CALLPROC  VioGetMode
                     ENDM

@VioGetPhysBuf       MACRO      p0,p1
                     @DO        p0
                     @DW        p1
                     @CALLPROC  VioGetPhysBuf
                     ENDM

@VioGetState         MACRO      p0,p1
                     @DO        p0
                     @DW        p1
                     @CALLPROC  VioGetState
                     ENDM

@VioModeUndo         MACRO      p0,p1,p2
                     @DW        p0
                     @DW        p1
                     @DW        p2
                     @CALLPROC  VioModeUndo
                     ENDM

@VioModeWait         MACRO      p0,p1,p2
                     @DW        p0
                     @DO        p1
                     @DW        p2
                     @CALLPROC  VioModeWait
                     ENDM

@VioPopUp            MACRO      p0,p1
                     @DO        p0
                     @DW        p1
                     @CALLPROC  VioPopUp
                     ENDM

@VioReadCellStr      MACRO      p0,p1,p2,p3,p4
                     @DO        p0
                     @DO        p1
                     @DW        p2
                     @DW        p3
                     @DW        p4
                     @CALLPROC  VioReadCellStr
                     ENDM
```

```
@VioReadCharStr    MACRO       p0,p1,p2,p3,p4
                   @DO         p0
                   @DO         p1
                   @DW         p2
                   @DW         p3
                   @DW         p4
                   @CALLPROC VioReadCharStr
                   ENDM

@VioRegister       MACRO       p0,p1,p2,p3
                   @DO         p0
                   @DO         p1
                   @DD         p2
                   @DD         p3
                   @CALLPROC VioRegister
                   ENDM

@VioSaveRedrawUndo MACRO       p0,p1,p2
                   @DW         p0
                   @DW         p1
                   @DW         p2
                   @CALLPROC VioSaveRedrawUndo
                   ENDM

@VioSaveRedrawWait MACRO       p0,p1,p2
                   @DW         p0
                   @DO         p1
                   @DW         p2
                   @CALLPROC VioSaveRedrawWait
                   ENDM

@VioScrLock        MACRO       p0,p1,p2
                   @DW         p0
                   @DO         p1
                   @DW         p2
                   @CALLPROC VioScrLock
                   ENDM

@VioScrollDn       MACRO       p0,p1,p2,p3,p4,p5,p6
                   @DW         p0
                   @DW         p1
                   @DW         p2
                   @DW         p3
                   @DW         p4
                   @DO         p5
                   @DW         p6
                   @CALLPROC VioScrollDn
                   ENDM
```

```
@VioScrollRi        MACRO     p0,p1,p2,p3,p4,p5,p6
                    @DW       p0
                    @DW       p1
                    @DW       p2
                    @DW       p3
                    @DW       p4
                    @DO       p5
                    @DW       p6
                    @CALLPROC VioScrollRi
                    ENDM

@VioScrollRi        MACRO     p0,p1,p2,p3,p4,p5,p6
                    @DW       p0
                    @DW       p1
                    @DW       p2
                    @DW       p3
                    @DW       p4
                    @DO       p5
                    @DW       p6
                    @CALLPROC VioScrollRi
                    ENDM

@VioScrollUp        MACRO     p0,p1,p2,p3,p4,p5,p6
                    @DW       p0
                    @DW       p1
                    @DW       p2
                    @DW       p3
                    @DW       p4
                    @DO       p5
                    @DW       p6
                    @CALLPROC VioScrollUp
                    ENDM

@VioScrUnLock       MACRO     p0
                    @DW       p0
                    @CALLPROC VioScrUnLock
                    ENDM

@VioSetANSI         MACRO     p0,p1
                    @DO       p0
                    @DW       p1
                    @CALLPROC VioSetANSI
                    ENDM

@VioSetCP           MACRO     p0,p1,p2
                    @DW       p0
                    @DW       p1
                    @DW       p2
                    @CALLPROC VioSetCP
                    ENDM
```

```
@VioSetCursorPos      MACRO     p0,p1,p2
                      @DW       p0
                      @DO       p1
                      @DW       p2
                      @CALLPROC VioSetCursorPos
                      ENDM

@VioSetCurType        MACRO     p0,p1
                      @DO       p0
                      @DW       p1
                      @CALLPROC VioSetCurType
                      ENDM

@VioSetFont           MACRO     p0,p1
                      @DO       p0
                      @DW       p1
                      @CALLPROC VioSetFont
                      ENDM

@VioSetMode           MACRO     p0,p1
                      @DO       p0
                      @DW       p1
                      @CALLPROC VioSetMode
                      ENDM

@VioSetState          MACRO     p0,p1
                      @DO       p0
                      @DW       p1
                      @CALLPROC VioSetState
                      ENDM

@VioShowBuf           MACRO     p0,p1,p2
                      @DW       p0
                      @DW       p1
                      @DW       p2
                      @CALLPROC VioShowBuf
                      ENDM

@VioWrtCellStr        MACRO     p0,p1,p2,p3,p4
                      @DO       p0
                      @DW       p1
                      @DW       p2
                      @DW       p3
                      @DW       p4
                      @CALLPROC VioWrtCellStr
                      ENDM

@VioWrtCharStr        MACRO     p0,p1,p2,p3,p4
                      @DO       p0
                      @DW       p1
                      @DW       p2
                      @DW       p3
                      @DW       p4
                      @CALLPROC VioWrtCharStr
                      ENDM
```

```
@VioWrtCharStrAtt      MACRO     p0,p1,p2,p3,p4,p5
                       @DO       p0
                       @DW       p1
                       @DW       p2
                       @DW       p3
                       @DO       p4
                       @DW       p5
                       @CALLPROC VioWrtCharStrAtt
                       ENDM

@VioWrtNAttr           MACRO     p0,p1,p2,p3,p4
                       @DO       p0
                       @DW       p1
                       @DW       p2
                       @DW       p3
                       @DW       p4
                       @CALLPROC VioWrtNAttr
                       ENDM

@VioWrtNCell           MACRO     p0,p1,p2,p3,p4
                       @DO       p0
                       @DW       p1
                       @DW       p2
                       @DW       p3
                       @DW       p4
                       @CALLPROC VioWrtNCell
                       ENDM

@VioWrtNChar           MACRO     p0,p1,p2,p3,p4
                       @DO       p0
                       @DW       p1
                       @DW       p2
                       @DW       p3
                       @DW       p4
                       @CALLPROC VioWrtNChar
                       ENDM

@VioWrtTTY             MACRO     p0,p1,p2
                       @DO       p0
                       @DW       p1
                       @DW       p2
                       @CALLPROC VioWrtTTY
                       ENDM
```

OS2PROCS.ASM

```
;============================================================
;
; OS2PROCS  A subroutine library containing the
;           procedures which are called by the
;           macros in OS2MAC. Must be included in
;           the code segment.
;
;============================================================
                .xlist
;
;
;           NAME: OS2ATB
; DESCRIPTION: Convert ASCII value to binary
;       INPUT: Source buffer length in CX
;              Source buffer in DS:SI
;      OUTPUT: Number in BX
;              Return code in AX
;
os2atb          proc
public          os2atb
;
                push    si                  ;save registers
                push    di
                push    cx
                push    dx
;
                cmp     cx,6                ;input too big?
                jge     atb800              ;yes - go to error processing
                cmp     cx,0                ;null string entered?
                jg      atb010              ;no - continue processing
                xor     bx,bx               ;zero value
                xor     ax,ax               ;zero return code
                jmp     atb999              ;exit normally
;
; Convert character string to number
;
atb010:         add     si,cx               ;point to last byte of number
                dec     si                  ;adjust for displacement
                mov     bx,1                ;set initial multiplier
                xor     di,di               ;zero accumulator
atb030:         xor     ax,ax               ;clear work register
                mov     al,[si]             ;get digit
;
                cmp     al,'0'              ;compare to low digit
                jae     atb040              ;above 0 - continue
                jmp     atb800              ;terminate with error
atb040:         cmp     al,'9'              ;compare to high digit
                jbe     atb050              ;below 9 - continue
                jmp     atb800              ;terminate with error
```

```
;
atb050:        and      al,0fh                 ;mask high order nibble
               mul      bx                     ;multiply by power of ten
               add      di,ax                  ;add to accumulator
               mov      ax,10                  ;move ten multiplier
               mul      bx                     ;next multiplier
               xchg     ax,bx                  ;move multiplier to bx register
               dec      si                     ;point to next digit
               loop     atb030                 ;loop through number
               mov      bx,di                  ;set data for caller
               xor      ax,ax                  ;clear return code
               jmp      atb999                 ;exit
;
; Error processing
;
atb800:        mov      al,0ffh                ;indicate error return code
               xor      dx,dx                  ;zero data area
;
; Termination
;
atb999:        pop      dx                     ;restore registers
               pop      cx
               pop      di
               pop      si
               ret                             ;return to caller
os2atb         endp
;
;
;       NAME: OS2BTA
; DESCRIPTION: Convert binary value to printable number
;       INPUT: Number in AX
;              Target buffer length in CX
;              Target buffer in ES:DI
;      OUTPUT: ASCII number in user buffer
;
os2bta         proc
public         os2bta
WBLEN          equ      5
;
               push     bp                     ;save BP
               sub      sp,WBLEN               ;allocate buffer
               mov      bp,sp                  ;address stack frame
;
               push     ax                     ;Save registers
               push     bx
               push     cx
               push     di
               push     dx
               xor      dx,dx                  ;clear high order word
```

```
;
; clear user buffer
;
                push    cx                      ;save count
                push    di                      ;save length
                push    ax                      ;save number
                mov     al,' '                  ;blank byte
                rep     stosb                   ;clear it
                pop     ax                      ;restore number
                pop     di                      ;restore length
                pop     cx                      ;restore count
;
; convert number to printable ASCII
;
                push    cx                      ;save buffer size
                mov     cx,WBLEN                ;set loop count (buffer size)
                mov     bx,10000                ;Move initial divisor into BX
                push    bp                      ;save buffer pointer
;
bta010:         div     bx                      ;Divide by multiple of ten
                aam                             ;Cnvrt AX to 2 dig unpacked decimal
                or      ax,'00'                 ;Convert to ASCII
                mov     ss:[bp],al              ;Move ASCII digit to temp buffer
                inc     bp
                push    dx                      ;Save remainder
                mov     ax,bx                   ;Move tens divisor to accumulator
                xor     dx,dx                   ;Zero out extension
                mov     bx,10                   ;Move divisor
                div     bx                      ;Reduce tens operator
                mov     bx,ax                   ;Set up new divisor
                pop     ax                      ;Restore remainder
                loop    bta010                  ;Loop through remaining digits
                pop     bp                      ;restore buffer pointer
;
; Strip leading zeroes
;
                mov     cx,WBLEN-1              ;at least one 0 to remain
bta015:         cmp     byte ptr ss:[bp],'0'    ;leading zero?
                jne     bta020                  ;no, done
                mov     byte ptr ss:[bp],' '    ;blank it out
                inc     bp                      ;next character
                loop    bta015                  ;continue
bta020:         mov     ax,cx                   ;save character count
;
                pop     cx                      ;get buffer size
                cmp     ax,cx                   ;Buffer big enough?
                jl      bta030                  ;Yes - go copy
;
; User buffer too small
;
                mov     al,'*'                  ;Fill character
                rep     stosb                   ;fill area with '*'
                jmp     bta999                  ;Done
```

```
;
; Copy ASCII number from stack frame to user buffer
;
bta030:        inc      ax                   ;pick up last character
               add      di,cx                ;point to last character
               sub      di,ax                ;start of number
               mov      cx,ax                ;loop count
bta035:        mov      al,ss:[bp]           ;get character from buffer
               stosb                         ;put in user buffer
               inc      bp                   ;next digit
               loop     bta035               ;continue
;
; Termination
;
bta999:        pop      dx                   ;Restore registers
               pop      di                   ;
               pop      cx                   ;
               pop      bx                   ;
               pop      ax                   ;
;
               add      sp,WBLEN             ;de-allocate buffer
               pop      bp                   ;restore BP
               ret
os2bta         endp
;
;
;          NAME: OS2DATE
; DESCRIPTION: Convert binary date value to printable ASCII
;         INPUT: Binary date in AX
;                Target buffer in ES:DI
;        OUTPUT: ASCII date in user buffer
;
os2date        proc
public         os2date
;
datemap        record   YY:7,MM:4,DAY:5
               push     cx                   ;save register
;
               push     ax                   ;save date
               and      ax,mask MM           ;isolate month
               mov      cl,MM                ;get shift count
               shr      ax,cl                ;right justify month
               aam                           ;convert ax to 2 digit unpacked decimal
               or       ax,'00'              ;convert to ascii
               xchg     ah,al                ;flip characters for store
               stosw                         ;move ascii month value into buffer
               mov      al,'/'               ;date separator
               stosb                         ;move character
               pop      ax                   ;restore date
```

```
;
            push    ax                      ;save date
            and     ax,mask DAY             ;isolate day
            mov     cl,DAY                  ;get shift count
            shr     ax,cl                   ;right justify day
            aam                             ;convert ax to 2 digit unpacked decimal
            or      ax,'00'                 ;convert to ascii
            xchg    ah,al                   ;flip characters for store
            stosw                           ;move ascii day value into buffer
            mov     al,'/'                  ;date separator
            stosb                           ;move character
            pop     ax                      ;restore date
;
            and     ax,mask YY              ;isolate year
            mov     cl,YY                   ;get shift count
            shr     ax,cl                   ;right justify year
            aam                             ;convert ax to 2 digit unpacked decimal
            or      ax,'80'                 ;convert to ascii
            xchg    ah,al                   ;flip characters for store
            stosw                           ;move ascii year value into buffer
;
; Termination
;
dat999:     pop     cx                      ;Restore registers
            ret
os2date     endp
;
;
;       NAME: OS2TIME
; DESCRIPTION: Convert binary date value to printable ASCII
;      INPUT: Binary time in AX
;             Target buffer in ES:DI
;     OUTPUT: ASCII time in user buffer
;
os2time     proc
public      os2time
;
timemap     record  HH:5,MIN:6,SEC:5
            push    cx                      ;save register
;
            push    ax                      ;save time
            and     ax,mask HH              ;isolate hours
            mov     cl,HH                   ;get shift count
            shr     ax,cl                   ;right justify hours
            aam                             ;convert ax to 2 digit unpacked dec
            or      ax,'00'                 ;convert to ascii
            xchg    ah,al                   ;flip characters for store
            stosw                           ;move ascii hour value into buffer
            mov     al,':'                  ;time separator
            stosb                           ;move character
            pop     ax                      ;restore time
```

```
;
                push    ax                      ;save time
                and     ax,mask MIN             ;isolate minutes
                mov     cl,MIN                  ;get shift count
                shr     ax,cl                   ;right justify minutes
                aam                             ;convert ax to 2 digit unpacked dec
                or      ax,'00'                 ;convert to ascii
                xchg    ah,al                   ;flip characters for store
                stosw                           ;move ascii minutes val into buffer
                mov     al,':'                  ;time separator
                stosb                           ;move character
                pop     ax                      ;restore time
;
                and     ax,mask SEC             ;isolate seconds
                mov     cl,SEC                  ;get shift count
                shr     ax,cl                   ;right justify seconds
                aam                             ;convert ax to 2 digit unpacked dec
                or      ax,'00'                 ;convert to ascii
                xchg    ah,al                   ;flip characters for store
                stosw                           ;move ascii seconds val into buffer
;
; Termination
;
tim999:         pop     cx                      ;Restore registers
                ret
os2time         endp
;
;
;        NAME: OS2PARMS
; DESCRIPTION: Copy command line input into user buffer
;       INPUT: Environment selector in AX
;              Command offset in BX
;              Target buffer in ES:DI
;              Buffer length in CX
;      OUTPUT: Command string in user buffer
;              Command line length in AX
;
os2parms        proc
public          os2parms
;
                push    si                      ;save user registers
                push    ds                      ;
```

```
;
                push   cx                    ;save count
                push   di                    ;save buffer offset
                push   es                    ;save buffer segment
                push   ax                    ;save command selector
                mov    cx,64                 ;maximum name length
                mov    es,ax                 ;environment selector
                mov    di,bx                 ;command line offset
                mov    ax,0                  ;end of command name delimiter
                repne  scasb                 ;search for end of command name
                mov    ax,' '                ;blank
                repe   scasb                 ;skip leading blanks
                dec    di                    ;back up to first character
                pop    ds                    ;restore command selector
                pop    es                    ;restore buffer selector
                mov    si,di                 ;save command pointer
                pop    di                    ;restore buffer offset
                pop    cx                    ;restore count
;
                xor    ax,ax                 ;clear count
par010:         cmp    byte ptr [si],0       ;end of device parms?
                je     par999                ;yes - exit
                movsb                        ;copy byte
                inc    ax                    ;transfer count
                loop   par010                ;continue copying
;
; Termination
;
par999:         pop    ds                    ;Restore registers
                pop    si                    ;
                ret
os2parms        endp
;
;
;           NAME: OS2BTHS
;
; DESCRIPTION: Convert input binary string into output HEX string
;
;       INPUT: Source buffer in DS:SI
;              Buffer length in CX
;              Target buffer in ES:DI (target buffer MUST be 2x source)
;
;      OUTPUT: ASCII hex values in target buffer
;
os2bths         proc
public          os2bths
;
                push   bx                    ;save register
                push   ax                    ;
;
                xor    ax,ax                 ;clear accumulator
                mov    bx,offset hextab      ;get table offset
```

```
;
bhs010:     lodsb                               ;get character
            push    cx                          ;save loop count
            push    ax                          ;save character
            and     al,0f0h                     ;first character
            mov     cl,4                        ;set shift count
            shr     al,cl                       ;shift number
            push    bx                          ;save table pointer
            add     bx,ax                       ;compute pointer
            mov     al,byte ptr cs:[bx]         ;get character
            pop     bx                          ;restore table pointer
            stosb                               ;put in target
;
            pop     ax                          ;restore value
            and     al,0fh                      ;isolate number
            push    bx                          ;save table pointer
            add     bx,ax                       ;compute pointer
            mov     al,byte ptr cs:[bx]         ;get character
            pop     bx                          ;restore table pointer
            stosb                               ;put in target
            pop     cx                          ;restore loop count
            loop    bhs010                      ;continue
;
; Termination
;
bhs999:     pop     ax                          ;Restore registers
            pop     bx                          ;Restore registers
            ret
hextab      db      '0123456789ABCDEF'
os2bths     endp
;
;
;       NAME: OS2BTH
;
; DESCRIPTION: Convert input binary word into output HEX string
;
;       INPUT: Source AX
;              Target buffer in ES:DI (target buffer MUST be 4 bytes)
;
;      OUTPUT: ASCII hex values in target buffer
;
os2bth      proc
public      os2bth
;
            push    bx                          ;save registers
            push    cx                          ;
            push    si                          ;
;
            mov     si,offset hextab            ;get table offset
```

```
;
        push    ax                      ;save character
        and     ax,0f000h               ;first character
        mov     cl,12                   ;set shift count
        shr     ax,cl                   ;shift number
        mov     bx,ax                   ;set index
        mov     al,byte ptr cs:[bx+si]  ;get character
        stosb                           ;put in target
;
        pop     ax                      ;restore value
        push    ax                      ;save character
        and     ax,0f00h                ;second character
        mov     cl,8                    ;set shift count
        shr     ax,cl                   ;shift number
        mov     bx,ax                   ;set index
        mov     al,byte ptr cs:[bx+si]  ;get character
        stosb                           ;put in target
;
        pop     ax                      ;restore value
        push    ax                      ;save character
        and     ax,0f0h                 ;second character
        mov     cl,4                    ;set shift count
        shr     ax,cl                   ;shift number
        mov     bx,ax                   ;set index
        mov     al,byte ptr cs:[bx+si]  ;get character
        stosb                           ;put in target
;
        pop     ax                      ;restore value
        and     ax,0fh                  ;second character
        mov     bx,ax                   ;set index
        mov     al,byte ptr cs:[bx+si]  ;get character
        stosb                           ;put in target
;
; Termination
;
bth999: pop     si                      ;Restore registers
        pop     cx                      ;
        pop     bx                      ;
        ret
os2bth  endp
;
;
;       NAME: OS2MKTH
;
; DESCRIPTION: Make Thread
;
;       INPUT: Program address in CX:DI
;              Stack size in BX
;
;      OUTPUT: Thread ID in BX
;
os2mkth proc
public  os2mkth
```

```
;
                IFNDEF      DosCreateThread
                extrn       DosCreateThread:far
                ENDIF
;
                push        bp
                sub         sp,2                    ;move frame pointer
                mov         bp,sp                   ;save stack frame
;
                @DosAllocSeg bx,SS:BP,0             ;allocate stack
                @jaxnz      mth999                  ;exit if error
                sub         bx,2                    ;point to last word in segment
;
                push        cx                      ;procedure segment
                push        di                      ;procedure offset
                push        ss                      ;thread ID selector
                push        bp                      ;thread ID offset
                push        ss:[bp]                 ;stack selector
                sub         bx,2                    ;start of stack
                push        bx                      ;stack offset
                call        far ptr DosCreateThread ;create the thread
                mov         bx,ss:[bp]              ;get ThreadID
;
mth999:         add         sp,2                    ;restore frame
                pop         bp
                ret
os2mkth         endp
;
;
;       NAME: OS2SDATE
;
; DESCRIPTION: Generate system date
;
;       INPUT: Output buffer in ES:DI
;
;      OUTPUT: Buffer filled in with date
;
os2sdate        proc
public          os2sdate
;
                push        dx
                push        bp
                sub         sp,11                   ;move frame pointer
                mov         bp,sp                   ;save stack frame
;
                @DosGetDateTime SS:BP               ;get time stamp
;
                xor         ah,ah                   ;clear high byte of work reg
                mov         al,ss:[bp+5]            ;get month
                aam                                 ;convert to unpacked decimal
                or          ax,3030h                ;convert to ASCII
                xchg        ah,al                   ;reverse byte order
                stosw                               ;put in user buffer
```

```
;
                mov        al,'/'                ;separator
                stosb                            ;put it in user buffer
;
                xor        ah,ah                 ;clear high byte of work reg
                mov        al,ss:[bp+4]          ;get day
                aam                              ;convert to unpacked decimal
                or         ax,3030h              ;convert to ASCII
                xchg       ah,al                 ;reverse byte order
                stosw                            ;put in user buffer
;
                mov        al,'/'                ;separator
                stosb                            ;put it in user buffer
;
                mov        dx,ss:[bp+6]          ;get year
                sub        dx,1900               ;drop centuries
                @bta       dx,ES:DI,2            ;convert to ASCII
;
                add        sp,11                 ;restore frame
                pop        bp
                pop        dx
                ret
os2sdate        endp
;
;
;       NAME: OS2STIME
;
; DESCRIPTION: Generate system time
;
;      INPUT: Output buffer in ES:DI
;
;     OUTPUT: Buffer filled in with time
;
os2stime        proc
public          os2stime
;
                push       dx
                push       bp
                sub        sp,11                 ;move frame pointer
                mov        bp,sp                 ;save stack frame
;
                @DosGetDateTime SS:BP            ;get time stamp
;
                xor        ah,ah                 ;clear high byte of work reg
                mov        al,ss:[bp+0]          ;get hours
                aam                              ;convert to unpacked decimal
                or         ax,3030h              ;convert to ASCII
                xchg       ah,al                 ;reverse byte order
                stosw                            ;put in user buffer
;
                mov        al,':'                ;separator
                stosb                            ;put it in user buffer
```

```
;
            xor         ah,ah               ;clear high byte of work reg
            mov         al,ss:[bp+1]        ;get minutes
            aam                             ;convert to unpacked decimal
            or          ax,3030h            ;convert to ASCII
            xchg        ah,al               ;reverse byte order
            stosw                           ;put in user buffer
;
            mov         al,':'              ;separator
            stosb                           ;put it in user buffer
;
            xor         ah,ah               ;clear high byte of work reg
            mov         al,ss:[bp+2]        ;get seconds
            aam                             ;convert to unpacked decimal
            or          ax,3030h            ;convert to ASCII
            xchg        ah,al               ;reverse byte order
            stosw                           ;put in user buffer
;
            add         sp,11               ;restore frame
            pop         bp
            pop         dx
            ret
os2stime    endp
;
;
;       NAME: OS2SDAY
;
; DESCRIPTION: Generate day of week
;
;      INPUT: Output buffer in ES:DI
;
;     OUTPUT: Buffer filled in with day
;
os2sday     proc
public      os2sday
;
            push        ds
            push        si
            push        cx
            push        bx
            push        bp
            sub         sp,11               ;move frame pointer
            mov         bp,sp               ;save stack frame
;
            @DosGetDateTime SS:BP           ;get time stamp
            xor         bh,bh               ;clear 1st byte of work reg
;
            mov         bl,ss:[bp+10]       ;get day number
            mov         cl,3                ;shift count
            shl         bx,cl               ;compute index
            lea         si,daynames         ;get name table base
            add         si,bx               ;point to name
            push        cs                  ;copy CS
            pop         ds                  ;to DS
            mov         cx,8                ;name length
            rep         movsb               ;move it to user buffer
```

```
        ;
                        add     sp,11               ;restore frame
                        pop     bp
                        pop     bx
                        pop     cx
                        pop     si
                        pop     ds
                        ret
        daynames        db      'Sunday  '
                        db      'Monday  '
                        db      'Tuesday '
                        db      'Wednesday'
                        db      'Thursday '
                        db      'Friday  '
                        db      'Saturday'
        os2sday         endp
        ;
                        .list
```

BUILD.CMD

```
@echo %echo%
:
:           NAME: BUILD.CMD
:
: DESCRIPTION: Assemble and link an OS/2 program.
:
:          INPUT: File name (extension not required)
:
:                 Environment Variables:
:
:                 If ECHO=ON   CMD file statements are displayed
:                 If PRINT=ON  Listing is printed
:
:        OUTPUT: EXE file on current disk/directory
:                LST file on current disk/directory
:                LST file printed            (if PRINT=ON)
:                ERR file displayed on screen    (if error)
:
:           AUTH: E. E. Iacobucci
:
:           DATE: 10/15/87
setlocal
if not exist %1.asm goto end3
:
: Assemble File
:
ECHO **** Program %1 being assembled
masm %1.asm,%1.obj,%1.lst; > %1.err
if errorlevel 1 goto end2
if %print%. == on. print %1.lst >nul:
erase %1.err >nul:
:
: Link File
:
ECHO **** Program %1 being linked
link %1,%1,%1,doscalls;        >%1.err
if errorlevel 1 goto end1
erase %1.err >nul:
goto endit
:
: Link Error
:
:end1
erase %1.obj >nul:
echo **** Link Failed
type %1.err | more
goto endit
:
: Assembly Error
:
:end2
```

```
erase %1.obj >nul:
echo **** Assembly Failed
type %1.err | more
goto endit
:
: Parameter Error
:
:end3
echo **** Invalid Program Name
:endit
endlocal
```

BUILDF.CMD

```
@echo %echo%
:
:          NAME: BUILDF.CMD
:
: DESCRIPTION: Assemble, link and bind an OS/2 program.
:
:         INPUT: File name (extension not required)
:
:                Environment Variables:
:
:                If ECHO=ON   CMD file statements are displayed
:                If PRINT=ON  Listing is printed
:
:        OUTPUT: EXE file on current disk/directory
:                COM file (family version of EXE file)
:                LST file on current disk/directory
:                LST file printed                (if PRINT=ON)
:                ERR file displayed on screen     (if error)
:
:          AUTH: E. E. Iacobucci
:
:          DATE: 10/15/87
:
setlocal
if not exist %1.asm goto end3
:
: Assemble File
:
ECHO **** Program %1 being assembled
masm %1.asm,%1.obj,%1.lst; > %1.err
if errorlevel 1 goto end2
if %print%. == on. print %1.lst >nul:
erase %1.err >nul:
:
: Link File
:
ECHO **** Program %1 being linked
link %1,%1,%1,doscalls;        >%1.err
if errorlevel 1 goto end1
erase %1.err >nul:
:
: Bind EXE file
:
ECHO **** Program %1 being bound
bind %1.exe doscalls.lib api.lib -o %1.com >%1.err
if errorlevel 1 goto end0
erase %1.err >nul:
goto endit
```

```
:
: Bind Error
:
:end0
echo **** Bind Failed
erase %1.obj >nul:
type %1.err | more
goto endit
:
: Link Error
:
:end1
echo **** Link Failed
erase %1.obj >nul:
type %1.err | more
goto endit
:
: Assembly Error
:
:end2
echo **** Assembly Failed
type %1.err | more
goto endit
:
: Parameter Error
:
:end3
echo **** Invalid Program Name
:endit
endlocal
```

TRADEMARKS

CodeView®	Microsoft Corporation
DESQ™	Quarterdeck Office Systems
IBM PC®	International Business Machines Corporation
Microsoft®	Microsoft Corporation
MASM™	Microsoft Corporation
MS DOS®	Microsoft Corporation
MS OS/2®	Microsoft Corporation
MS Windows™	Microsoft Corporation
OS/2®	International Business Machines Corporation
PC Convertible®	International Business Machines Corporation
PC/AT®	International Business Machines Corporation
PS/2®	International Business Machines Corporation
PC/XT® 286	International Business Machines Corporation
PCjr®	International Business Machines Corporation
PC DOS®	International Business Machines Corporation
TopView™	International Business Machines Corporation

INDEX

The manuscript for this book was prepared and
submitted to Osborne/McGraw-Hill in electronic form.
The acquisitions editor for this project was Cynthia Hudson.
The technical reviewer was Kris Jamsa.
Text design by Judy Wohlfrom, using Century Expanded
for text body and Eurostyle for display.
Cover art by Bay Graphics Design Associates.
Cover supplier, Phoenix Color Corporation.
Book printed and bound by R. R. Donnelley & Sons
Company, Crawfordsville, Indiana.

DOS USER'S GROUP
P.O. Box 26601
Las Vegas, Nevada 89126
(702) 363-3419

U.S. Members $25.00 annual fee
Canada, Mexico, and Europe $35.00 annual fee

Quarterly newsletter which includes:

DOS Command Tutorials
— Basic overview
— Tips, tricks, and traps
— Source code for implementation

DOS Customization Hints
— Thorough examination of CONFIG.SYS entries
— Tips, tricks, and traps

Question and Answer Forum
— Large user base of experience

Third Party Software Reviews and Discounts
— Indepth reviews of major software packages
— Discounts to user group members

Turbo Pascal Secrets
— Low level DOS programming techniques from Turbo Pascal

Programming Hints
— Linker and Librarian commands
— Tips, tricks, and traps

MS Windows
— User perspective
— Programmer prospective

OS/2
— General overview
— Programmer information
— Advanced concepts

Batch Processing
— DOS batch commands
— Tips, tricks, and traps

The DOS User's Group is an international user group consisting of members who are:

Novice Users, Programmers, Buyers, Manufacturers, Developers, Authors, MIS Directors

each of whom want to maximize their knowledge of DOS, MS Windows, and OS/2.

$25.00 Annual Membership Fee (U.S.)
$35.00 Annual Membership Fee (Canada - Europe)

☐ Money Order
☐ Personal Check

Name_____

Address_____

City_____ State_____ Zip_____

Other related Osborne/McGraw-Hill titles include:

1-2-3® Made Easy
by Mary Campbell

Osborne's famous "Made Easy" format, which has helped hundreds of thousands of WordStar® users master word processing, is now available to Lotus® 1-2-3® beginners. *1-2-3® Made Easy* starts with the basics and goes step by step through the process of building a worksheet so you can use Lotus' spreadsheet with skill and confidence. Each chapter provides a complete 1-2-3 lesson followed by practical "hands-on" exercises that help you apply 1-2-3 immediately to the job. When you've got worksheets down, you'll learn to create and print graphs, manipulate 1-2-3's data management features, use advanced file features ... even design keyboard macros. As the author of *1-2-3®: The Complete Reference*, and a columnist for IBM® PC UPDATE, ABSOLUTE REFERENCE, and CPA JOURNAL, Mary Campbell has plenty of experience with 1-2-3. With her know-how, you'll soon be handling 1-2-3 like a pro.

$18.95 p
0-07-881293-3, 400 pp., 7³/₈ x 9¹/₄

dBASE III PLUS™ Made Easy
by Miriam Liskin

Liskin's *Advanced dBASE III PLUS™* and Jones' *Using dBASE III PLUS™* have been so successful that we're filling in the gap for beginners with *dBASE III PLUS™ Made Easy*. Learning dBASE III PLUS™ couldn't be simpler. You'll install and run the program, enter and edit data. Discover all the features of using dBASE III PLUS at the dot prompt. Each concept is clearly explained and followed by examples and exercises that you can complete at your own speed. Liskin discusses sorting and indexing, performing calculations, and printing reports and labels. Multiple databases are emphasized, and Liskin presents strategies for working with them. You'll also find chapters on customizing the working environment and exchanging data with other software. If you're curious about higher-level use, Liskin's final chapter shows how to combine the commands you've learned into batch programs so you can begin to automate your applications. (Includes two command cards for quick reference.)

$18.95 p
0-07-881294-1, 350 pp., 7³/₈ x 9¹/₄

WordStar® 4.0 Made Easy
by Walter A. Ettlin

WordStar® Made Easy, the original "Made Easy" guide with 350,000 copies sold worldwide, has been so successful that Osborne has published a companion volume on the new WordStar® version 4.0. All 4.0 commands and features are thoroughly described and illustrated in practical exercises so you can put WordStar to immediate use, even if you've never used a computer before. Walter Ettlin, who has written four books and taught high school for 23 years, guides you from the fundamentals of creating a memo or report to using WordStar's calculator mode, macro commands, and Word Finder™. You'll also learn to use WordStar's latest spelling checker. *WordStar® 4.0 Made Easy* puts you in control of your software with the acclaimed "Made Easy" format now found in 11 Osborne titles. (Includes a handy pull-out command card.)

$16.95 p
0-07-881011-6, 300 pp., 7³/₈ x 9¹/₄

DisplayWrite 4™ Made Easy
by Gail Todd

Upgrading from DisplayWrite 3™ to DisplayWrite 4™? Here's the book that provides a thorough introduction to IBM's word processing software. Handle new menus, screens, and options with ease as Todd leads you from basic steps to more sophisticated procedures. The famous "Made Easy" format offers hands-on exercises and plenty of examples so you can quickly learn to produce letters and reports. All of DisplayWrite 4's new features are covered, including printing interfaces; the voice add-on; Paper Clip, the cursor control that lets you take up where you left off; and Notepad, a convenience that enables you to insert notes into documents. Todd, the author of numerous user guides and manuals, has the know-how to get you up and running fast.

$19.95 p
0-07-881270-4, 420 pp., 7³/₈ x 9¹/₄

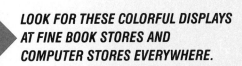

MAXIT™ increases your DOS addressable conventional memory beyond 640K for only $195.

- Add up to 256K above 640K for programs like FOXBASE+ and PC/FOCUS.

- Short card works in the IBM PC, XT, AT, and compatibles.

- Top off a 512 IBM AT's memory to 640K and add another 128K beyond that.

- Run resident programs like Sidekick above 640K.

- Add up to 96K above 640K to all programs, including PARADOX and 1-2-3.

- Compatible with EGA, Network, and other memory cards.

Break through the 640 barrier.
MAXIT increases your PC's available memory by making use of the vacant unused address space between 640K and 1 megabyte. (See illustrations)

Big gain—no pain.
Extend the productive life of your, IBM PC, XT, AT or compatible. Build more complex spreadsheets and databases without upgrading your present software.

Installation is a snap.
The MAXIT 256K memory card and software works automatically. You don't have to learn a single new command.

If you have questions, our customer support people will answer them, fast. MAXIT is backed by a one-year warranty and a 30-day money-back guarantee.

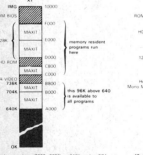

XT class machine (8088, 8086) w/640K and a CGA Color Monitor or a Compaq Type Dual Mode Display

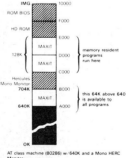

AT class machine (80286) w/640K and a Mono HERC Monitor

Order toll free 1-800-227-0900. MAXIT is just $195 plus $4 shipping, and applicable state sales tax. Buy MAXIT today and solve your PC's memory crisis. Call Toll free 1-800-227-0900 (In California 800-772-2531). Outside the U.S.A. call 1-415-548-2805. We accept VISA, MC.